EXCELLENCE IN EDUCATING
Gifted & Talented Learners
Third Edition

Joyce VanTassel-Baska
College of William and Mary

With chapters by:

Camilla Persson Benbow
Iowa State University

John F. Feldhusen
Purdue University

Kenneth Seeley
Colorado Foundation, Denver, Colorado

Linda Kreger Silverman
Gifted Development Center, Denver, Colorado

LOVE PUBLISHING COMPANY©
Denver • London • Sydney

~

To Inez

~

Cover Design: Jo Culbertson Design, Denver, Colorado

Published by Love Publishing Company
Denver, Colorado 80222

The first edition was titled, *Toward Excellence in Gifted Education*, copyright © 1985. The second edition was titled, *Excellence in Educating the Gifted*, copyright © 1989. Both the 1985 and 1989 editions were edited by John F. Feldhusen.

Library of Congress Catalog Card Number 97-74578

Copyright © 1998 Love Publishing Company
Printed in the U.S.A.
ISBN 0-89108-255-7

Contents

12 Programs and Services at the Elementary Level

211

John F. Feldhusen

13 Programs and Services at the Secondary Level

225

John F. Feldhusen

14 Key Issues and Problems in Secondary Programming

241

Joyce VanTassel-Baska

15 Grouping Intellectually Advanced Students for Instruction

261

Camilla Persson Benbow

16 Acceleration as a Method for Meeting the Academic Needs of Intellectually Talented Children   **279**

Camilla Persson Benbow

17 Evaluating Programs for the Gifted   **295**

Ken Seeley

18 A Comprehensive Model of Program Development   **309**

Joyce VanTassel-Baska

~ Introduction to Part Three   **335** Providing Effective Curriculum and Instruction for Gifted and Talented Learners

22 Thinking Skills for the Gifted 399

John F. Feldhusen

23 Mathematics and Science for Talented Learners 419

Joyce VanTassel-Baska

24 Social Studies and Language Arts for Talented Learners 441

Joyce VanTassel-Baska

25 Arts and Humanities for Talented Learners 463

Joyce VanTassel-Baska

Preface ⁓

This book offers a comprehensive introduction to major topics and issues in gifted and talented education. Eight chapters focus on the general nature of giftedness; some of these focus on specific gifted subpopulations, such as underachievers, gifted girls, the disadvantaged, and the disabled. Ten chapters deal with aspects of developing programs for the gifted in response to their characteristics and needs. Seven chapters are devoted to the organization of curriculum and instruction for the gifted. Finally, three chapters emphasize the role of facilitators (teachers, counselors, mentors) and their training, counseling the gifted, and a general philosophical position on helping the gifted achieve excellence. Overall, the goal of the book is to provide a strong overview of key issues and ideas in educating the gifted and talented.

This third edition of the text contains eight new chapters, representing a diverse collection of ideas and perspectives on several aspects of the field of gifted education deemed important to include in a comprehensive text. Some of these new chapters contribute to our understanding of giftedness and talent in students as exemplified by the Feldhusen chapter on conceptions of giftedness and the Silverman chapters on personality and developmental stages. Other new chapters enhance a deeper appreciation of program development by focusing on acceleration, grouping, and secondary programming, such as those by Benbow and VanTassel-Baska. New chapters in the curriculum section provide insight into strategies and models that support the talent development enterprise. The introductory and closing chapter have also been reshaped to provide a sharp emphasis on the past and future of the field as seen through a focus on excellence. Moreover, all of the remaining chapters have been updated and revised to reflect current ideas, research, and practice in schools. The questions for further reflection and study presented at the end of each chapter have been developed with an eye to current problems in the field.

Excellence in Educating Gifted and Talented Learners grew out of the continued collaboration of the Keystone Consortium, a group of educators in the field of gifted education who, although all engaged in talent development work and a common interest in high-functioning individuals, nonetheless represent very different perspectives and expertise. This group has been together for 16 years and produced two editions of a curriculum text, one of a counseling text, and this third edition of a comprehensive text in gifted education. The group also has conducted numerous workshops and conferences based on our writings.

It may be important for readers to know what perspectives are represented in this volume, so a short review of the Keystone group as individuals follows.

John Feldhusen, the Robert Kane distinguished professor of education at Purdue University, brings a broad and deep perspective to this work based on almost 40 years of studying gifted learners as an educational psychologist in a research context both at Purdue and earlier at the University of Wisconsin. In later years, John's involvement in the field increased considerably with direct service programs for students and families as well as through an internationally recognized teacher preparation program at masters and doctoral levels. John's work bridges theory, research, and practice in the field.

Dr. Linda Silverman, a practicing clinical psychologist and Director of The Gifted Development Center in Denver, Colorado, brings more than 30 years of experience at every level of the educational continuum to her understanding of giftedness. From teaching elementary students to graduate students to testing and counseling children and families, Linda's up-close and personal view of gifted individuals is exceptional.

Dr. Camilla Benbow, trained as a psychologist and now the Dean of the College of Education at Iowa State University, brings to this text a rich background from the world of research on individual differences with highly gifted populations. Her ongoing longitudinal research on mathematically precocious youth (SMPY), coupled with a newer emphasis on career dispositions, has made a significant contribution to our understanding of gifted students at various stages of development.

Dr. Ken Seeley, currently director of The Colorado Foundation, brings many years of school administration and broader policy expertise to the group. Ken's work on behalf of children and families exemplifies the collaboration model so revered in these times; he has shown himself to be an individual who can work as effectively with social service agency personnel as with universities and schools. His perspectives on advocacy, program development, and facilitation are profound.

The perspective I, Joyce VanTassel-Baska, bring to this endeavor comes out of more than 30 years of working as a teacher and administrator at all levels in the educational enterprise and having directed a multitude of special projects in each of those roles. It is a fused one, grounded in the reality of schools, yet optimistic about the future of education as the best hope we have for a better world.

The Keystone Consortium continues to believe that through the serious work of talent development, students of promise may develop to optimal levels of performance. This text was written to provide schools and parents the essential guidance to help realize that end.

Acknowledgments ∼

This edition was a team effort. I have worked with the contributing authors over many years creating, developing, articulating, and critiquing the ideas presented in this book. Special thanks must go to their collective efforts.

Although I am the lead author and editor of this volume, it is appropriate to acknowledge the work of John Feldhusen, who performed the task so well in the first and second editions.

Appreciation is expressed to Catherine Little and Linda Avery, my graduate students, for their work on this volume.

Joyce VanTassel-Baska
Williamsburg, Virginia

Introduction to
Part One

Conceptions of Talented Learners:
Focus on Individual and Group Differences

The initial section of this book explores the varied facets of giftedness, its origins, and its development. As such, the section represents the different faces of giftedness and talent that one may encounter—faces that change based on the conception of intelligence employed; the personality and learning style of individuals; their defining characteristics of being young, disabled, minority, disadvantaged, highly gifted, or female; and the stage of development at which they may be. All of these faces are important to discern as we seek to better understand the nature of gifted and talented individuals.

Feldhusen's chapter on intelligence (Chapter 2) focuses on differing conceptions that have shaped our understanding and use of the construct of giftedness. Intelligence is used to describe the ability to think, to learn, to solve problems, and to create new ideas. The work of Spearman, Thurstone, Cattell, and Horn are reviewed to provide a foundation for understanding how intelligence has been studied in the past. Feldhusen also describes more recent theoretical models by Gardner (1983) and Sternberg (1991) and discusses the work of John Carroll (1993). Gardner has posited seven different autonomous intelligences that are reflected in learning accomplishment: the linguistic, the logical/mathematical, the musical, the kinesthetic, the spatial, the interpersonal, and the intrapersonal. Sternberg's theory relates intelligence to information processing with metacomponents, performance components, and knowledge-acquisition components. These components function together to enable an individual to pursue goals in adapting to, shaping, or selecting an environment. Carroll (1993) reanalyzed factor analytic data from 461 previous studies to confirm the existence of a *g* factor supported by eight specific factors—general memory and learning, broad auditory perception, broad visual perception, broad cognitive processing, reaction time or speed, broad retrieval ability, and both fluid and crystallized intelligence represented by sequential reasoning and language development.

Since Terman (1925) undertook his landmark study of gifted children, the measurement of intelligence has been a central issue in gifted education. Although there is general agreement on an empirical validity to the notion of a *g* factor, there is less consensus that such a factor is helpful in the design and implementation of specific educational services. In addition, the tools used to measure various aspects of intelligence are often the source of criticism, a key issue explored effectively by Feldhusen in his chapter.

The Silverman chapter on personality and learning styles (Chapter 3) examines the question of whether gifted students have different profiles in temperament from their nongifted peers. The degree to which such differences emerge appears to be related to the theoretical construct and measurement scale being used. Some approaches show sizable variations across both groups; the Seattle Project and the Fullerton Longitudinal Study, however, revealed no significant differences between groups based on the nine categories of temperament that were assessed.

Silverman explores three major ways of defining personality style in the gifted, focusing on the Dabrowski model of overexcitability, the Myers-Briggs Type Indicator, and various learning style inventories. Through the use of instruments that discern individual differences in personality and learning style, educators may better learn to provide more effective instruction to gifted learners.

Silverman cites the major findings regarding distinctive aspects of gifted learners on these measures. Dabrowski's theory of positive disintegration (TPD) recognizes five areas of overexcitability (OE), innate strengths or stable characteristics that are variables of temperament. These categories are psychomotor, imaginational, intellectual, emotional, and sensual and reflect an expression of high levels of stimulation. Using a scale to measure self-report on these categories, gifted students tend to show higher levels of imaginational, emotional, and intellectual OE than nongifted groups.

The Myers-Briggs Type Indicator, based on the theory of Carl Jung, creates a typology from the intersection of four different scales: extroversion (E) and introversion (I); sensing (S) and intuition (N); thinking (T) and feeling (F); and judging (J) and perceiving (P). The instrument has been studied with numerous gifted populations, who have been shown to represent all 16 types. Clear group preferences have been seen for introversion, intuition, and perceiving, whereas the populations seem to be more evenly split on the thinking/feeling continuum.

Psychometric assessment has enabled the identification of two key learning style groups: visual-spatial learners and auditory-sequential learners. Although many gifted children score very well on both styles, some subpopulations show great levels of dispersion on the two scores, which might even suggest a learning disability. For these children, specific changes in the learning environment that support their style of learning are critical in maximizing their educational experiences.

Seeley's chapter on early childhood (Chapter 4) stresses that gifted children experience rapid and uneven development from birth through age 8 and that giftedness during this time must therefore be understood as multidimensional. Characteristics such as attention, alertness, and preference toward novelty in the environment as well as social-emotional maturity may be discerned in young gifted children, but surprisingly little correlation has been observed between advanced scores on developmental scales, such as the Bayley's, and later intellectual development. Other social characteristics descriptive of young gifted children include being competitive, independent, and task-motivated.

Seeley also notes that there are a number of myths about parents of gifted children, but the truth is that they may be the most well-informed sources of information about their children and can be very helpful in identifying gifted behaviors. Seeley advises that data obtained from parents be amplified with information from standardized tests and observations in natural settings. The guiding purpose of all such assessments is to promote the development of the child through a match with appropriate resources and programs.

Seeley also contends that quality early childhood education is characterized by being child-centered, family-friendly, individualized, experiential, developmentally appropriate, and attending to the holistic needs of the student. The environments are warm and nurturing, and the curricula tend to be theme-based. When this context is combined with an awareness of the needs of the gifted for accelerated pacing and advanced content, Seeley notes, an optimum model emerges for serving the gifted child. An example is the general model designed under the High Scope program in Michigan, a model that is teacher-facilitated and child-directed and uses a plan-do-review instructional process to address growth across an appropriate range of learning objectives. Seeley also describes the adaptation of this model for use with disadvantaged gifted youngsters.

In Chapter 5, Seeley discusses both the underachieving and the disabled gifted student, a grouping based on issues common to both. Although the term gifted underachiever is ambiguous, it calls attention to the disparity between performance and ability that is evidenced in many at-risk and disabled students. Identification procedures can be tailored to be more sensitive to such characteristics but should culminate in individual testing when appropriate. Strategies that hold promise for impacting this population are alternative schools, community service options, individualized learning plans, focusing on interests, involvement of family, and mentorships. Disabled gifted students may have some advantages with the resources available from federal and state funding, but unless additional services are targeted to their strength areas, the focus of intervention will be remedial rather than accelerative.

Chapter 6 on the educationally disadvantaged learner with talent, written by VanTassel-Baska, explores various approaches to the definition and identification of such students and to means of effective intervention, including a discussion of recent literature on promising practices for identification and programming. It highlights the need for value-added options for this group of learners, especially in the delivery of personalized services. Major emphasis is placed on issues related to ensuring representation of these students in programs for the gifted and ensuring that their education is at the highest level.

Silverman's chapter on the highly gifted (Chapter 7) provides guidelines for identifying, assessing, and serving such students. Just as the special education field recognizes the distinctions among mild, moderate, and profound, giftedness can be similarly categorized. Highly gifted children demonstrate precocity early in life with remarkable language development and complexity of thought. Silverman stresses that interventions should be tied to the child's level of giftedness. The more advanced the intellectual ability, the more differentiated the model needs to be. The author mentions that the highly gifted are best served in self-contained classrooms through acceleration options or by homeschooling.

Chapter 8 on girls of promise, written by VanTassel-Baska, uses a similar organizing framework, that of examining who the population is, how to identify the population, and how to provide appropriate services. In this updated chapter, a strong emphasis is placed on the barriers experienced by girls and women in traversing the talent development continuum and the uneven path that it takes. Particularly strong in recent literature on gifted and talented females is the refrain of insufficient role models of women who balance home and family responsibilities with career responsibilities. There appears still to be a paucity of successful examples of such a balancing act (Arnold, Noble, & Subotnik, 1996), and evidence from several spheres points to role models as being central to assuring the next generation of gifted women a better future for becoming eminent than has been the case in either the past or the present.

The Silverman chapter on developmental stages (Chapter 9) addresses the inherent differences in development from birth through maturity between gifted individuals and others. Clear signs of exceptionality may emerge by 18 months of age, and the phenomenon continues throughout the lifespan with such behaviors as abstract reasoning ability, rapid learning, curiosity, marked need for stimulation, and extensive vocabulary as well as other characteristics maintained throughout the senior citizen years.

According to Silverman, the three most frequent indicators of giftedness in infants and toddlers appear to be early attention, memory, and advanced language development. Their need for constant stimulation and little sleep can deplete the energies of even the best intentioned parents. Early identification at this stage can allow for parent education programs that help parents cope with the immediate concerns of raising a gifted child.

Silverman notes that the preschool and primary years tend to emphasize social connections, which may lead to confusion and frustration for the gifted child as he or she interacts with age-mates but not intellectual peers. Young gifted boys are more likely to showcase their knowledge; gifted girls at this stage already show signs of trying to blend in.

At the preadolescent stage, Silverman notes, gifted learners experience different stressors. Development becomes difficult for the gifted preadolescent girl who is told by the culture that her abilities are unattractive. For gifted boys, feelings of hopelessness appear to peak during junior high school. Silverman credits the talent searches and regional summer programs in helping gifted students find appropriate peer groups.

Adolescence for gifted students is a period of transition, with many of them coping with the psychological dimensions earlier than their nongifted peers. Silverman advises parents to be strict but loving and to strike a delicate balance between security and freedom. Such support is necessary, she asserts, to usher the child into adulthood, where he or she will continue to face unique social, emotional, moral, and spiritual issues.

References ⌇

Arnold, K., Noble, K., & Subotnik, R. (Eds.) (1996). *Remarkable women: Perspectives on female talent development.* Cresskill, NJ: Hampton Press.

Carroll, J. B. (1993). *Human cognitive abilities.* New York: Cambridge University Press.

Gardner, H. (1983). *Frames of mind: The theory of multiple intelligences.* New York: Basic Books.

Sternberg, R. J. (1991). Giftedness according to the triarchic theory of human intelligence. In N. Colangelo & G. A. Davis (Eds.), *Handbook of gifted education* (pp. 45–54). Boston: Allyn & Bacon.

Terman, L. M. (1925). *Genetic studies of genius (Vol. 1).* Stanford, CA: Stanford University Press.

1

Introduction

Joyce VanTassel-Baska

Introducing this text on gifted education, I find myself engaged in Janusian thinking, holding, simultaneously, both a retrospective view of the past and a prospective view for the future. There is much to reflect on in the rich 108-year history of gifted education and much to look forward to in the next century. Will the landmark work of Terman and Hollingworth continue to be seen as foundational to our understanding of giftedness? Will the trends of the past few decades continue? Will the current issues be resolved? Will the field prosper and grow in a planful way, or will it continue to experience the ebb and flow of popularity associated with its history? Although this text cannot answer all of those questions, a useful place to begin in understanding the field of gifted education is with its history and its current complexion. Through such views, we may better understand both the unique psychology of gifted individuals and their place in our society.

The Historical Background of Gifted Education

The movement to find and nurture the gifted has waxed and waned for many decades. The work of Lewis Terman and his colleagues over a period of approximately 40 years (Terman & Oden, 1959) laid the groundwork for the scientific understanding of giftedness and paved the way for practical efforts to identify and nurture the gifted in schools. In 1921, Terman and his colleagues began a longitudinal study of 1,528 gifted youth with IQs greater than 140 who were approximately 12 years old. Terman died in 1959, but the study will continue until 2020, by which time the subjects still alive today probably will have died. Results of the study have, so far, debunked myths about the social and emotional abnormalities of gifted youth, showed that a large number went on to high-level achievements, found that only one had achieved international eminence, and suggested that for those who were highly successful, a motivational or persistence factor and a capacity to get organized to accomplish tasks were present in youth.

Excellent research on the gifted was conducted by a number of other researchers in this same period, notably by Havighurst, Stivers, and DeHaan (1955), Hollingworth (1926, 1942), Passow, Goldberg, Tannenbaum, and French (1955), and Witty (1951). Their work extended our insights about the highly gifted, gave us a broader conception of giftedness, and led to trial efforts in educating the gifted.

Thus, the United States was ready to react in 1959 when the Soviet Union successfully launched *Sputnik*. That event was perceived by many as a huge educational failure on our part in the United States and especially as a failure to find and nurture scientific, engineering, and mathematical talent. Substantial research and development efforts were therefore launched in the early 1960s to improve educational services for the gifted and talented with major support from the National Education Association (Bish, 1961). A flurry of publications from the association offered guidance to teachers on how to teach or counsel the gifted and talented. This thrust from the National Education Association and related research and development efforts in the 1960s led to sporadic programming for the gifted, but there was still no uniform service in all American schools. As the decade of the 1960s wore on, interest in the gifted was eclipsed by major legislation and funding to serve the handicapped and the disadvantaged.

But interest in the gifted continued, and in 1969 the Congress of the United States authorized the Commissioner of Education, Sidney Marland, to conduct a study of the status of educational services for the gifted in our schools. The report, completed in 1972, came to be known as the Marland Report. Its impact was immediate, and it set in motion events that continue to this day.

The report suggested that gifted youth were left to languish or were unserved in American schools and that one might even find school personnel who were antagonistic to the gifted. The report had a monumental effect in establishing a new definition of the gifted. According to the report:

> Gifted and talented children are those identified by professionally qualified persons who by virtue of outstanding abilities are capable of high performance. These are children who require differentiated educational programs and services beyond those normally provided by the regular school program in order to realize their contribution to self and society.
>
> Children capable of high performance include those with demonstrated achievement and/or potential ability in any of the following areas:
>
> 1. General intellectual ability
> 2. Specific academic aptitude
> 3. Creative or productive thinking
> 4. Leadership ability
> 5. Visual and performing arts
> 6. Psychomotor ability. (p. 2)

Thus, the older monolithic view of giftedness as simply high intelligence began to be displaced in favor of a multifaceted view of talents and abilities. That view would later be extended and modified in many ways. Figure 1.1 shows the broadening conception of giftedness that marks the evolution of the field.

In 1974, with small appropriations from the U.S. Congress, an office was established in the U.S. Office of Education to support the development of programs for the gifted in American schools. The office established two leadership training institutes, one in Reston, Virginia, and the other in Los Angeles, to work with state education agencies and with school districts and to develop systematic plans for programs to serve the gifted and talented. The institutes, consolidated into one center in Los Angeles in 1977, were extremely influential in bringing about an awareness of the educational needs of gifted and talented youth and in establishing sound guidelines for program services.

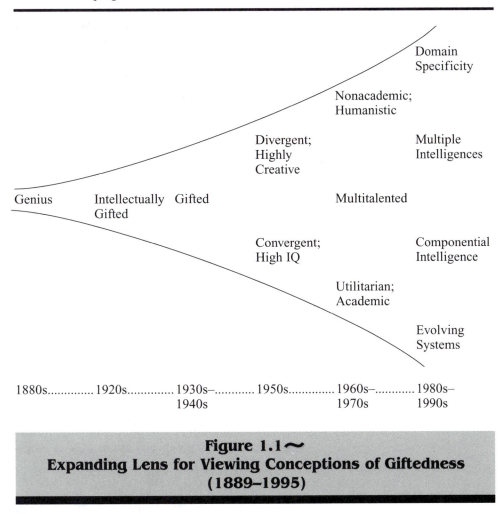

Figure 1.1 ~
Expanding Lens for Viewing Conceptions of Giftedness
(1889–1995)

Throughout the remainder of the 1970s and during the 1980s, despite the closing of the Federal Office for the Gifted in 1981, programs for the gifted grew and prospered, supported increasingly by state educational funding. Every state in the United States established some kind of leadership effort in this realm, with at least a part-time consultant or coordinator guiding the effort. In some states, the support was so strong that an extensive staff was employed and budgets reached as high as $80 million annually. In the 1990s, a new wave of federal support has been available through the U.S. Office of Education, especially for promising projects to serve educationally disadvantaged gifted students. In addition, the department established the National Research Center on the Gifted and Talented in 1990, which allowed a consortium of universities to address research needs in the field, and has funded major curriculum projects. At the state level, progress has been more uneven during the 1990s. For the majority of states, funding has remained steady or increased, but a minority have reduced allocations during this period. In an age of restructuring, many personnel who had worked with gifted programs have been shifted to other areas of responsibility at state and local levels. Local-level programming in the 1990s might be characterized as embattled, dealing with reduced staff and funding as well as reduced philosophical support for special programs.

Figure 1.2 presents a chronology of dates highlighting landmark events in the field over the past 108 years.

Current Trends and Issues in Gifted Education ~

At the same time that knowledge of the history of the field of gifted education is important to understanding our roots, an examination of future directions can provide us with the vision necessary to sustain current efforts. What are the dominant trends and issues in the field that are significant indicators of the future of the field? Several are highlighted here.

In education, a trend typically represents a change in course or direction brought about by external forces, needs, and problems. Thus, a trend carries with it the connotation of a solution, even a panacea, for a perceived problem in education. A trend also must show evidence of a knowledge base in the literature. It must be widely accepted within a field as judged by its use in practice over a period of years.

An issue speaks to a topic that is highly debatable within a field, one that has clear lines of demarcation in respect to perspectives shared. Issues by their very nature are controversial, based on real-world occurrences, and require the articulation of at least opposing viewpoints if not multiple perspectives. In gifted education, several timely topics may be considered trends and others may be better termed issues.

1889   Galton's *Heredity Genius* published
1905   Binet's *Intelligence Scale* published
1925   Terman's *Genetic Studies of Genius* published
1936   Thurstone's factorial study of primary mental abilities
1942   Hollingworth's *Children Above 180 IQ* published
1950   Guilford's Presidential Address to the American Psychological Association, considering 120 aspects of intelligence
1957   Launching of *Sputnik*
1962   Project TALENT
1963   Torrance's work on creativity begun
1971   Cattell's work on fluid and crystallized intelligence; elaborated by Horn in 1976
1972   *Marland Report* published—first national study of gifted and talented commissioned by Congress
1974   First national legislation on gifted and talented; federal definition developed recognizing intellectual, academic, creative, visual and performing arts, leadership, and psychomotor abilities
1975   First World Conference on Gifted Children held in Israel; talent search model and Study of Mathematically Precocious Youth begun
1977   Stanley's *Mathematical Talent* published, demonstrating a national system for identifying and serving precocious talent
1983   Gardner's *Frames of Mind* published, introducing a multiple intelligences view
1985   Sternberg's *Beyond IQ* published, introducing a componential theory of giftedness
1989   Ploman's work on population genetics published, arguing for the substantial heritability of both intelligence and personality variables
1993   John Carroll's *Human Cognitive Abilities* published, introducing the three stratum theory based on massive reanalyses of earlier studies on intelligence
1994   *National Excellence* report published—second national study commissioned by the U.S. Department of Education

Figure 1.2 ∼
Historical Overview of Gifted Education Landmarks

The Trend Toward Talent Development as the Central Metaphor for the Work of the Field

The trend toward an emphasis on talent development as the central metaphor for gifted education might be traced to two central events. One of them was the publication of *Frames of Mind* (Gardner, 1983), a work that excited the imaginations of many educators and stimulated their thinking about applying Gardner's ideas on multiple intelligences to classroom contexts and curricula. The other precipitating event was the publication of the *National Excellence* report (USDOE, 1994), in which the term "talent development" was used as the backdrop to describe problems in current schooling practices that inhibit the development of America's talented youth as well as the context within which the report recommendations were generated. These two events in education have spawned many editorials, articles, and reactions from general educators who see the trend in highly positive ways.

Yet it is clear that the trend toward thinking about the field as a talent development enterprise did not originate with Gardner or the *National Excellence* report. The work of Julian Stanley and his colleagues in the 1970s placed a major emphasis on precocious talent in specific academic areas (Stanley, Keating, & Fox, 1974). The work of A. Harry Passow in the 1960s with Project TALENT also focused the field on domain-specific abilities to be found through looking for emergent talent. Calvin Taylor in the 1960s and 1970s developed the "multiple talent totem poles," providing a theoretical base for the popular program Talents Unlimited, which is recommended for use with most learners.

The case could be made that all of education is about talent development, a view of schooling at its best. And, as has been cited, talent development has dominated the work of the field for decades. More recent development in this area merely substantiates it as an enduring trend.

The trend also has seen considerable action in the arena of practice. Whole schools have been founded and many schools reorganized around the talent development concept, especially as it applies to all learners. The more particularized talent search model for finding precocious talent identifies and serves over 200,000 students per year through four national searches. Talent development efforts in the arts, especially through private lessons and tutorials continue to thrive. And parents as the engineers of their own children's talent development process are becoming ever more discerning about appropriate opportunities at given stages of development.

The Trend Toward Identification and Programming for Underrepresented Groups

Considerable evidence has been amassed that giftedness and talent may be found in all segments of our population—including minority students and the disabled. Yet talent-find mechanisms have not systematically tried to find promising learners in less than promising circumstances. Newer approaches to identification of such learners coupled with value-added programming and learning contexts augur well for a larger percentage of these students gracing the ranks of the gifted and talented in schools. This trend also has deep roots in the field. Work carried out in urban center programs for the gifted since the early 1970s has focused attention on service to the disadvantaged gifted, a large percentage of whom have been minority students. Chicago, San Diego, and New York all provided multiple delivery system options to such learners at all stages of development, beginning with full-day kindergartens and extending to the International Baccalaureate program and specialized schools. The emphasis in identification was on lowered cutoff scores for program participation rather than alternative assessment measures and in programming on rigorous academic experiences inside subject matter areas rather than the alternatives of general enrichment. Other early projects stressed the need for an interdisciplinary curriculum, counseling, and work with families (VanTassel, 1976). In the 1980s, foundations funded several efforts to learn more about the disadvantaged gifted as a population (Olszewski-Kubilius & Scott, 1992; VanTassel-Baska & Chepko-Sade, 1986). In the 1990s, a major national emphasis was given to this area through a priority assignment in the Javits program and an emerging recommendation in the *National Excellence* report.

The Trend Toward Alternative Models for Talented Students

Over the past 20 years, there have been major efforts to expand opportunities for gifted and talented learners outside the walls of traditional schooling. These efforts have focused on several types of experiences:

- *University-Based Programs.* More than 500 universities nationwide offer some form of summer or Saturday program experiences for gifted learners at varying stages of development. Many of these program efforts were spawned by the widespread popularity of the talent search for middle-school students instituted at The Johns Hopkins University, and at Duke, Northwestern, and Denver Universities in the 1980s. Over 300 institutions also offer courses on the education of the gifted for teachers and parents in the field; and 25 university centers provide multipurpose services to gifted learners and their families (Parker & Karnes, 1991).

- *Specialized Schools.* Since 1980, over a dozen residential public high schools for the gifted have been developed in selected states (Kolloff, 1991). Moreover, Governor's schools have remained a popular option, particularly in southern states, for academic year as well as summer opportunities. Other specialized day schools, public and private, have emerged in response to the needs of these learners and the doctrine of parental choice.

- *Homeschooling.* An interesting development in the past several years has been an emphasis on homeschooling among the parents of gifted children. In my area of Williamsburg, Virginia, for example, there are over 100 homeschooling families. Where the gifted student is an atypical learner or is highly gifted, or where families have strong concerns about local schooling, such an intervention may be very appropriate. Just as tutorials over the years have served the Edisons and Einsteins well, so too the focused attention provided in a homeschooling context may today be the most appropriate placement for some children's learning.

- *Technology-Based Options.* Another current alternative to traditional programs is the employment of technology as a delivery system of high-powered curriculum. The Stanford mathematics program, featured in Chapter 23 of this book, is a prime example. Administered by both parents in the home and selected schools, it offers advanced learners opportunity for self-paced learning with on-line tutorial assistance. Other similar innovative uses of technology for gifted programming are probably only a few years away.

The Issue of Differentiation

The issue of differentiation for the gifted has been perceived by educators within and outside the field in very different ways. One common misunderstanding of the term implies that gifted students receive a totally "different" program from other students. Under this misconception, it is believed that average students take subject matter courses and gifted students learn higher order skills, with the strong implication that the gifted do not need content and that the average do not need higher level skills. Obviously, this is a fallacious assumption about what would constitute differentiation. Yet there continues to be a disparity in the field about this issue. For some researchers, the heart of differentiated practice rests with students engaging in independent project work (Renzulli, 1996). For others, differentiation is best satisfied through individualized approaches in the general education classroom (Treffinger, 1995). For still others, differentiation requires an integrative and comprehensive set of experiences, conducted in a conducive setting of intellectual peers (VanTassel-Baska, 1995). Another view often espoused is that differentiation is related to the response of the learner, not the stimulus provided through the teaching-learning process; thus, a high-level stimulus provided to all learners will yield self-differentiated responses (Passow & Rudnitski, 1994).

Obviously, there is a level at which all of these points of view converge, and that is where full-time learning experiences have been developed for gifted learners, primarily in specialized settings and schools. Only in those contexts has a comprehensive approach to differentiation been possible. Based on current evidence available, general classrooms are probably the least differentiated settings for gifted students (Westberg, Archambault, Dobyns, & Salvin, 1993).

What is the source of such varying interpretations of the term *differentiation*? One source lies in the characteristics of the gifted on which we focus when determining appropriate programs and services. If we respond primarily to precocity, then advanced content is the logical form of differentiation, with other approaches deemed inappropriate. However, if we pay attention to complexity of thought as a characteristic, then a differentiated set of experiences that provides real-world problems to solve becomes the differentiated response.

Another source of disagreement on this issue relates to the level of analysis at which differentiation should occur. For some educators, the focus is on the individual child level, with the programs always responding to the interests and abilities evidenced at a given point in time. For other educators, differentiation occurs through a manipulation of curriculum goals and outcomes for groups of learners. For still other educators, it emerges through the offerings of general provisions such as mentorships or chess clubs. Perhaps "differentiation" is best understood in the context of appropriateness for a given member of a population as well as that population as a whole, a fusion of perspectives yet to occur in the field.

The Issue of Inclusion Classrooms

The term *inclusion* has come to be a metaphor for equity in education. We speak of inclusion schools, typically managed according to effective schools research; inclusion classrooms, usually referring to all students learning in the same classroom setting; and even inclusion curricula, which speaks to the implementation of the curriculum reform agenda. What does inclusion really imply, however, in the world of practice? It clearly implies that all students will learn best in the same general education classroom, that higher standards for all learners can best be effected in this setting, and that teachers are prepared to make learning meaningful for the full range of student abilities. What's so wrong with this idea?

Based on the research in gifted and talented education and research in special education, there are reasons to be skeptical about how well inclusion will work with students exhibiting significant individual differences from the classroom norm. Limited studies in gifted and talented education have found some disturbing trends. General classroom service provided to gifted students in schools with formal gifted programs is generally similar to that provided in schools without formal gifted programs; only minor modifications in the curriculum for gifted students have occurred (Archambault et al., 1993). The research has shown that little differentiation in instructional and curricular practices has been provided for gifted and talented students in general classrooms. Indeed, one study found that the students observed received no instructional or curricular differentiation in 84% of the instructional activities in which they participated (Westberg et al., 1993).

In another study (Delcourt & McIntire, 1993), students in within-class programs reported less frequently than those in pullout programs that their classwork presented them with new content or challenging work and were less satisfied with peer relationships. Parents with children in within-class programs were less likely to view the program as beneficial than parents of children in other models. In the same study, however, teachers and administrators did not report any differences in their perceptions of the level of challenge offered or appropriateness as a program delivery model across four program types, including heterogeneous.

Moreover, special educators and their research on collaboration also raise important questions to consider about implementing inclusionary classrooms. Teacher collegiality research has found higher personal achievement, higher self-esteem, and more positive work relationships for teachers involved in ongoing collaborative teaching tasks than for those in inclusive settings (Johnson, Pugach, & Delvin, 1990). Friend, Reisling, and Cook (1993) found that although teachers were better able to ask each other for help and talk over problems with one another in collaborative settings, teacher follow-through on use of strategies and an intervention plan was only 40%. Moreover, studies of learning disabled students in inclusive settings suggest that instruction is insufficiently intensive to meet their needs (Zigmond, 1995).

The fundamental issue to be considered is how to keep in place appropriate flexibility when placing gifted students in a program. Figure 1.3 reflects a continuum of placement settings and services for gifted students, necessary for flexible planning

Placement Settings		Services
• Special residential/day schools (state or interdistrict)	⟷	• Teachers advanced in subject matter knowledge provide specialized curriculum and extracurricular experiences in a cross-district model
• Special district-wide centers and schools (district pupil/teacher ratios)	⟷	• Gifted/talented trained staff deliver a totally integrated and differentiated program
• Special class(es) (20–35 students)	⟷	• Gifted/talented trained teachers work in differentiated curricula and instruction in school subject matter and/or special topics
• Pullout resource room (15–25 gifted students)	⟷	• Resource specialist for the gifted delivers appropriate instruction
• Cluster grouping in classroom (3–8 gifted students)	⟷	• Resource specialist for the gifted works as a coteacher *or* Trained classroom teacher delivers differentiated services
• Random assignment to general classroom (1–5 gifted students)	⟷	• Individualized instruction by general classroom teacher

Figure 1.3～
Continuum of Placement Settings and Services for Gifted Students

of a student program. The movement toward inclusion would severely reduce such placement options to only one, potentially a limiting influence on the optimal development of talent.

The past and the present of gifted education represent major efforts to define the field through research, program development, and state and national advocacy. The future of gifted education will depend on the continued efforts of educators in all three arenas of activity. Regardless of the vacillation of public attitudes, support, and funding for the gifted as a population or the field as an educational enterprise, gifted and talented students do not go away. Their educational needs are real and pervasive. Our response to those needs must be forceful and clear if we want to have a more intelligent and thoughtful universe.

References ⁓

Archambault, F. X., Westberg, K. L., Brown, S., Hallmark, B., Emmons, C., & Zhang, W. (1993). Classroom practices used with gifted third and fourth grade students. *Journal for the Education of the Gifted, 16*(2), 103–119.

Bish, C. E. (1961). The academically talented. *National Education Association Journal, 50*(2), 33–37.

Delcourt, M., & McIntire, J. (1993). An investigation of student learning outcomes: Results of a program satisfaction survey. *National Research Center on the Gifted and Talented Newsletter*, pp. 6–7. Storrs, CT: NRCGT.

Friend, M., Reisling, M., & Cook, L. (1993). Co-teaching: An overview of the past, a glimpse at the present, and considerations for the future. *Preventing School Failure, 37*(4), 6–10.

Gardner, H. (1983). *Frames of mind: The theory of multiple intelligences*. London: Paladin.

Havighurst, R. J., Stivers, E., & DeHaan, R. F. (1955). *A survey of education of gifted children*. Chicago: University of Chicago Press.

Hollingworth, L. S. (1926). *Gifted children: Their nature and nurture*. New York: Macmillan.

Hollingworth, L. S. (1942). *Children above 180 IQ*. New York: World Book.

Johnson, L. J., Pugach, M. C., & Delvin, S. (1990). Professional collaboration. *Teaching Exceptional Children, 22*(2), 9–11.

Kolloff, P. B. (1991). Special residential high schools. In N. Colangelo & G. Davis (Eds.), *Handbook of gifted education* (pp. 209–215). Boston: Allyn & Bacon.

Olszewski-Kubilius, P. M., & Scott, J. M. (1992). An investigation of the college and career counseling needs of economically disadvantaged minority gifted students. *Roeper Review, 14*(3), 141–148.

Parker, J. P., & Karnes, F. A. (1991). Graduate degree programs and resource centers in gifted education: An update and analysis. *Gifted Child Quarterly, 35*(1), 43–48.

Passow, A. H., Goldberg, M. L., Tannenbaum, A. J., & French, W. (1955). *Planning for talented youth*. New York: Teachers College Press.

Passow, A. H., & Rudnitski, R. A. (1994). Transforming policy to enhance educational services for the gifted. *Roeper Review, 16*(4), 271–275.

Renzulli, J. S. (1996). Schools for talent development: A practical plan for total school improvement. *School Administrator, 53*(1), 20–22.

Stanley, J., Keating, D., & Fox, L. (1974). *Mathematical talent: Discovery, description, and development*. Baltimore, MD: Johns Hopkins University Press.

Terman, L. M., & Oden, M. H. (1959). *The gifted group at mid-life*. Stanford, CA: Stanford University Press.

Treffinger, D. J. (1995). School improvement, talent, development, and creativity. *Roeper Review, 18*(2), 93–97.

United States Department of Education Office of Educational Research and Improvement. (1994). *National excellence: A case for developing America's talent*. Washington, DC: Author.

VanTassel, J. (1976). *The Phoenix Project, a program for disadvantaged gifted students*. Toledo, OH: Toledo Public Schools.

VanTassel-Baska, J. (1995). The development of talent through curriculum. *Roeper Review, 18*(2), 98–102.

VanTassel-Baska, J., & Chepko-Sade, S. (1986). *An incidence study of disadvantaged gifted students in the Midwest*. Evanston, IL: Northwestern University, Center for Talent Development.

Westberg, K. L., Archambault, F., Dobyns, S., & Salvin, T. (1993). The classroom practices observation study. *Journal for the Education of the Gifted, 16*(2), 120–146.

Witty, P. (1951). *The gifted child*. Boston: Heath.

Zigmond, N. (1995). An exploration of the meaning and practice of special education in the context of full inclusion of students with learning disabilities. *Journal of Special Education, 29*(2), 109–115.

2

Conceptions of Intelligence

John F. Feldhusen

Intelligence is the ability to think, to learn, to solve problems, and to create new ideas. Levels and types of intelligence vary widely from student to student. Consider David, a fifth grader, who took calculus and earned straight A's on all tests. Many high-school students who were enrolled in the same calculus class called him at home at night for help with problems. David obviously has high-level mathematical intelligence, or aptitude as we might alternatively call it. Mathematical aptitude is one factor of intelligence.

We might choose to avoid altogether any conceptions of intelligence or aptitude and simply say that David is mathematically precocious. However, to do so might really be a case of avoiding the cause and defining by result. Some productivity or facilitating condition in David may instead be the underlying cause and that cause may be what we hypothesize as intelligence.

Of course, other causes may also be invoked. For instance, David's father is a mathematically talented psychologist with a Ph.D. who has tutored David a great deal. Or David is a highly motivated and energetic child who may simply be a high-powered goal-setter and successful achiever.

The selection of alternatives can be resolved by asserting that there is an intelligence or there are intelligences that are cognitive, neural conditions of individuals, probably partly genetically determined or inherited (Bouchard, 1984; Plomin, DeFries, & McClearn, 1990; Wachs, 1992), which grow in individuals as a result of interactions between genetic potentials and environmental stimulations. Despite the controversy in psychology and education as well as the popular press about the heritability of intelligence and the viability of the concept of intelligence, a study by Snyderman and Rothman (1990) showed that psychologists find the conception of intelligence to be a useful construct in understanding human behavior and learning.

19

General Intelligences ～

general, pervasive human ability "g"

In 1904 Charles Spearman proposed that there is a <u>general, pervasive human ability,</u> which he labeled *g*, that is a major factor measured by most intelligence tests. In addition to *g*, intelligence tests typically measure other abilities. This central ability *g* is probably the basic, genetically determined or influenced ability that we call "general intelligence." The concept of general intelligence was built into the many tests of intelligence developed in the United States including and following the publication of the Stanford-Binet Intelligence Scale by Terman in 1916. Tests of the general *g* are still widely used as assessment tools, particularly in the assessment of retardation and other exceptionalities. They are also widely used in the identification of gifted youth for special school programs.

Although there have been numerous attacks on intelligence tests from a theoretical point of view (Gould, 1981) and from critics who see racial bias in the tests, Snyderman and Rothman's (1990) extensive study of the judgments of leading psychologists revealed that among these experts there is consensus that intelligence tests yield valuable diagnostic information for assessment and therapeutic purposes.

Well known as a measure of general intelligence throughout the world is the nonverbal Raven's Progressive Matrices (1947), a test that yields a *g* score for general intelligence and that is widely used to avoid verbal biases in test content. This test involves examinees in an analysis of visual patterns and sequences of increasing complexity. Numerous studies attest to the predictive and concurrent validity of the test as well as to its high reliability.

Charles Spearman and the Birth of Factor Analysis ～

general factors

Early measures of mental ability or intelligence consisted of a series of short tasks involving such skills as recall of information, recognition of correct and incorrect details, perceptual ability, and attention span. Building on conceptions first advanced by Francis Galton (1869), Spearman (1904) <u>advanced the notion that there is a gen</u><u>eral condition or capacity of mind that he called *general intelligence* and that later,</u> <u>as an outgrowth of the new statistical method he developed, *factor analysis*, he</u> <u>would denote with the symbol "g."</u> That symbol is now firmly entrenched in psychological and educational practice as our way of contrasting <u>the general condition</u> <u>or measure of intelligence</u> with specific factors currently advanced by the arguments of Gardner (1983), Sternberg (1981), and others. Credit for viewing intelligence as consisting of specific factors, however, can be traced to Thurstone (1938).

For educators and clinicians in gifted education, the concept and measure of general intelligence provides valuable insights into the nature, nurture, and educational needs of precocious youth. The global score and subscores from intelligence tests afford insights about the overall levels of ability that characterize individual children and about their specific strengths or aptitudes. Children with general IQs above 180 (Hollingworth, 1942) present challenges to teachers, counselors, and parents far different from children with IQs in the 125–140 range. Yet both may be classified as *gifted*.

Spearman brought to us the conception of g, but he also alerted us to the fact that in addition to g, a test may also reflect other specific mental abilities not subsumed in g. This other portion was later shown by Cattell (1940) to reflect *learned* capacities or abilities.

L. L. Thurstone and Primary Mental Abilities

The earliest and most theoretically sound model of human intelligences or abilities was proposed by L. L. Thurstone (1938). In his primary mental abilities theory, Thurstone posited that there are seven primary intelligence factors or abilities. The conception grew out of the statistical model he had developed, based on the work of Spearman (1927) and others, called factor analysis. Using item correlations and later matrix algebra, these statisticians were able to analyze the results of intelligence tests given to large numbers of examinees and determine if the tests were measuring one large, general, comprehensive construct called intelligence or, in different subgroups of items, were actually measuring several different factors, constructs, aptitudes, or abilities. Put another way, the statistical analysis addressed the question, "Is the test a measure of one homogeneous trait, or is it actually a measure of several traits?"

Thurstone's seven factors, described in the following list, remain viable conceptions of the specific aptitudes or components of intelligence to this day:

- *Word fluency* is the ability to think of a lot of words, given a specific stimulus. For example, think of all the words you can that begin with "or" or that contain the letters *e, a, s,* and *t*. Later, in the evaluation of factor analytic studies of human abilities, Guilford and Hoepfner (1971) identified this factor as one of their divergent cognitive abilities.
- *Verbal comprehension* is the ability to derive meaning from words. This ability could be what we call understanding and could refer to both single words and strings of words in phrases and sentences.
- *Number*, or numerical ability, is involved in all arithmetic tasks. Thus, when children add, subtract, multiply, divide, reduce fractions, calculate percentages, or solve problems, they are using number intelligence.
- *Memory* essentially refers to simple or rote memory of new material, both in verbal and in pictorial form. The ability of memory is often denigrated as inconsequential by school-based professionals, but it was seen as a fundamental aspect of intelligence by Thurstone and his followers.
- *Induction* is the ability to examine verbal, numerical, or pictorial material and derive from it a generalization, rule, concept, or principle. One form of induction, often assessed in intelligence tests, is the analogy in which examinees are

expected to see the relationship between A and B in order to find the extension from C, as in this equation: A is to B as C is to _?_. Thus, bird is to sky as fish is to _?_.

- *Spatial perception* is the ability to see objects in space and to visualize varying arrangements of those objects.
- *Perceptual speed* is the final factor or aptitude. It is the ability to discern minute aspects or elements of pictures, letters, words, and so forth, as rapidly as possible. Later researchers, including Jensen (1980) and Eysenck (1979), suggested that this ability is really at the heart of intelligence, especially as measured by very precise reaction time.

Thurstone went on to develop tests of the primary mental abilities that were widely used in schools. Close examination of the list of seven primary mental abilities reveals some parallels to the currently popular multiple intelligences of Gardner (1983) which include linguistic, musical, logical-mathematical, spatial, bodily kinesthetic, interpersonal, and intrapersonal. Although this model enjoys wide acceptance by practitioners, the theory lacks the empirical support necessary to employ it in a broad-based way. Thurstone's greatest long-range impact on test theory and development, however, derived mainly from his advances in the statistical procedures of factor analysis, which, although greatly extended and improved beyond his models, are still used.

Cattell's Fluid and Crystallized Intelligence

R. B. Cattell (1943) developed through factor analysis the concepts of fluid and crystallized intelligence. Fluid intelligence is the basic and general ability measured by intelligence tests that reflects the ability to reason well, deductively and inductively. It is, in the Cattell conception, very much genetically determined or inherited. Crystallized intelligence is the intelligence students use on a daily basis to solve problems and cope with daily tasks in school and within the realities of the cultural context in which they live.

Through extensive and repeated factor analyses, Cattell (1971) and his principal disciple, John Horn (Horn, 1988; Horn & Cattell, 1966), elaborated the model through a long series of factor analytic studies and identified the following basic components of intelligences:

1. *Fluid reasoning:* ability in inductive, deductive, conjunctive, and disjunctive reasoning, understanding relationships, drawing inferences
2. *Acculturation knowledge:* skill or ability in using the knowledge base of one's culture to think, reason, and solve problems
3. *Visual processing:* ability to visualize objects in space, rotated, and from different perspectives
4. *Auditory processing:* perception of sound patterns

5. *Processing speed:* the rapidity of responding, a basic characteristic of all intelligent behavior
6. *Correct decision speed:* ability to solve problems quickly
7. *Short-term memory:* ability to recall information after immediate stimulation
8. *Long-term memory:* ability to retrieve information from storage
9. *Visual sensory detection:* awareness of or scanning ability with large amounts of information
10. *Auditory sensory detection:* ability to respond to large amounts of auditory stimulation with short-term exposure

In our efforts as educators to understand the intelligent behavior of gifted or talented students, we are probably most concerned with the advanced levels of intelligent behavior in the areas of fluid reasoning, acculturation knowledge, visual and auditory processing, speed of processing, and long- and short-term memory. Gifted and talented students will differ from individual to individual but are likely to manifest superior intelligence in reasoning, memory functions, and speed of processing. Their mental prowess is an interactive product of innate, inherited abilities and culturally determined experiences.

R. S. Sternberg's Information Processing Model

In this day and age of the computer, artificial intelligence, and modeling of human intelligence, it is natural that an information processing model of human intelligence should emerge. The work of Sternberg is recognized as the major information processing model of human intelligence dominating the worlds of psychology and education. Although the conceptual framework of the model is pervasive in these professional worlds, practical applications are limited because no good measure has been developed as a method of implementing the conception. Until such a measure is developed, there is no way to test the effectiveness of the model in providing more useful information than existing approaches.

The Sternberg model (1991) proposes a triarchic structure of intelligence and three fundamental information processing abilities: metacomponents, performance components, and knowledge-acquisition components.

Metacomponents are much like the processes of metacognition. They consist of planning, monitoring, and evaluative functions. These subfunctions include (1) recognizing the existence of problems, (2) clarifying the nature of problems, (3) planning to solve problems, (4) choosing a solution strategy, (5) representing the solution process mentally, (6) mustering mental resources for action, (7) monitoring the solving process, and (8) judging success at the end of a problem-solving sequence.

Performance components are mental processes that carry out the metacomponential activities. These are skills or abilities that may be unique to different domains of knowledge. They are considered lower order mental operations, possibly more automatic in nature than the highly cognitive metacomponents.

The *knowledge-acquisition components* are selective encoding, selective combination, and selective comparison. *Selective encoding* is the ability to identify crucial information and take it into long-term memory and to reject noncrucial information. *Selective combination* is a process of combining information into schemas, gestalts, conceptions, ideas, and so forth. (Long-term memory is more accessible and useful when information is well organized into chunks of related material.) *Selective comparison* is the ability to see connections between present and past information and to see the relevance of information to current problems.

Sternberg argued that intelligent thought is directed to three behavioral goals: adaptation to an environment, shaping or changing an environment, and selection of an environment. *Adaptation to an environment* with reference to intelligence means that a child's manifestation of intelligence might differ substantially from home to school to neighborhood. *Shaping* means that youth may use their intelligence to create environments that function best for them. The youth gang is a good example of such shaping. Finally, one may *select an environment* in which one can function intelligently. School choice may afford youth such opportunities of choice.

Sternberg wisely stressed that intelligent behavior is context-bound. That is, we may function best in environments to which we can adapt, environments that we can change to suit us, or environments that we can select as best for us. Thus, the nature and conditions established in a school, in a particular classroom, in the curriculum, by a particular teacher and group of children may not be the optimum environment for some gifted and talented youth. A teacher may teach no science, much to the disappointment of several scientifically talented youth. Another classroom and school may be characterized by negative peer pressure on identified gifted students. Can highly gifted students function intelligently in such environments? Sternberg's theory would argue that they cannot. Sternberg has taught us that there are many subaspects to intelligences and that they are dependent upon the context in which children find themselves from day to day.

Carroll's Factor Analyses ⁓

As a summary to our examination of the different conceptions of intelligence and its measurement, I turn to the massive factor analyses of intelligence test data carried out by John B. Carroll (1993). Carroll amassed 461 data sets from previous factor analytic studies such as those reviewed earlier in this chapter, dating back to 1925 and carried out in 19 different countries. The majority, 349, were conducted in the United States.

The major broad factors or areas of intelligence or cognitive ability that emerged from Carroll's refactoring of all these available data sets are as follows:

1. General intelligence, or *g*
2. Fluid intelligence
3. Crystallized intelligence

4. General memory and learning
5. Broad visual perception, including spatial relations and visualization
6. Broad auditory perception
7. Broad cognitive speediness
8. Broad retrieval ability

Each of these broad factors corresponds to factors previously described in this chapter, and each has a number of subfactors. Carroll went on to explain the absence of a quantitative factor as resulting from its being an inexact combination of many higher and lower order factors. However, it can fairly safely be specified as a ninth factor, mathematical ability. Carroll concluded that in our present state of knowledge we can safely refer to both general intelligence and its many factor components in our efforts to assess, understand, and use the construct of intelligence in teaching and counseling.

#9

Emotional Intelligence

academic ↔ moti v, emot
rational must work w/ emot

As an extension, elaboration, and validation of Gardner's intrapersonal and interpersonal intelligences (Gardner, 1983), Goldman's theory of emotional intelligence (Goldman, 1995) is heralded as the linkage between the traditional intellectual or academic intelligence and the motivational and emotional processes in human thought. Goldman argued that our emotions function as an integral system with our cognitive processes and often enhance our understanding or control of thinking and success at solving problems and achieving our goals. He wrote, "Intellect cannot work at its best without emotional intelligence" (p. 28). He contended that the rational and the emotional must work together at all times and in all places in our lives, an idea not different from what was suggested by studies of neurological impairment (Da Masio, 1994).

Goldman went on to show how much more effective we can be as teachers of gifted and talented youth if we can help them achieve that depth of self-understanding and empathy with the feeling-emotional states of other people that manifests itself in the "flow" experience (Csikszentmihalyi, 1990). This is the achievement of a talented student who learns and performs at a level of excellence, is motivated to work hard, loves the learning experience, and is utterly absorbed in it. Teachers set the stage for "flow" in talented youngsters when they help them master tasks or new learnings and provide for the kinds of self-awareness and positive evaluation that help students understand and enjoy such experiences.

Group Versus Individual Tests

Intelligence tests may be designed to be administered to groups or individuals. Individual tests are a costly process because they require a highly trained professional to give and score them and to interpret the test results, whereas group tests, otherwise called pencil-and-paper tests, are administered to a number of examinees at one time, are more easily scored (often automatically by machine), and are more easily interpreted. Thus, a less highly trained examiner is required.

The major individual tests are the Wechsler Intelligence Scales and the Stanford-Binet Revision. The Wechsler Intelligence Scale for Children—Third Edition uses verbal tasks (information, comprehension, arithmetic, similarities, vocabulary, and digit span) and performance tasks (picture completion, picture arrangement, block design, puzzle assembly, coding, and mazes) to assess children's intelligence. Three scores (verbal, performance, and full scale) are reported. The Stanford-Binet Intelligence Scale, Fourth Edition, assesses verbal reasoning (vocabulary, comprehension, absurdities, and verbal relations), abstract-visual reasoning (pattern analysis, copying, matrices, paper folding, paper cutting), quantitative reasoning (quantitative, number series, equation building), and short-term memory (bead memory, memory for sentences, memory for digits, memory for objects).

In assessing students for gifted education, it is preferable to have individual intelligence test scores for all nominees, because scores from these tests are much more reliable and valid than are group test scores, and the individually administered tests give us much more diagnostic information to use in planning programs and services for gifted and talented children. Often, however, time and money obviate the use of such measures.

Summary ~

High intelligence, either as general intelligence (*g*) or as factor components, is central to all gifted and talented functioning. Giftedness and talent are, first and foremost, cognitive conceptions related to the ability to think well. Much more is, of course, involved in the development of giftedness (Feldhusen, 1986), but giftedness is dependent on high intelligence. The level of intelligence required for high-level, creative functioning varies from field to field. It also seems likely that to a limited extent intelligence can be evoked, raised, or improved somewhat when children are exposed to cognitively stimulating environments at home and school (Sternberg, 1986). In any event, knowing students' general mental ability as well as factors or components of their intelligence can help us to better understand and educate them.

References ~

Bouchard, T. J. (1984). Twins reared together and apart: What they tell us about human diversity. In S. W. Fox (Ed.), *Individuality and determination* (pp. 147–184). New York: Plenum.

Carroll, J. B. (1993). *Human cognitive abilities.* New York: Cambridge University Press.

Cattell, R. B. (1940). A culture-free intelligence test. *Journal of Educational Psychology, 31,* 161–179.

Cattell, R. B. (1943). The measurement of adult intelligence. *Psychological Bulletin, 40,* 153–193.

Cattell, R. B. (1971). *Abilities: Their structure, growth and action.* Boston: Houghton Mifflin.

Csikszentmihalyi, M. (1990). *Flow: The psychology of optimal experience.* New York: Harper & Row.

Da Masio, A. (1994). *Descartes' error, emotion, reason, and the human brain.* New York: Putnam.

Eysenck, H. J. (1979). *The structure and measurement of intelligence.* Berlin, Germany: Springer-Verlag.

Feldhusen, J. F. (1986). A conception of giftedness. In R. S. Sternberg & J. E. Davidson (Eds.), *Conceptions of giftedness* (pp. 112–127). New York: Cambridge University Press.

Galton, F. (1869). *Hereditary genius*. London: Julian Friedman.

Gardner, H. (1983). *Frames of mind: The theory of multiple intelligences*. New York: Basic Books.

Goldman, D. (1995). *Emotional intelligence*. New York: Bantam.

Gould, S. J. (1981). *The mismeasure of man*. New York: Norton.

Guilford, J. P., & Hoepfner, R. (1971). *The analysis of intelligence*. New York: McGraw-Hill.

Hollingworth, L. S. (1942). *Children above 180 IQ*. New York: World Book.

Horn, J. L. (1988). Thinking about human abilities. In J. R. Nesselrode & R. B. Cattell (Eds.), *Handbook of multivariate experimental psychology* (pp. 645–685). New York: Plenum.

Horn, J., & Cattell, R. B. (1966). Refinement of the theory of fluid and crystallized general intelligences. *Journal of Educational Psychology, 57*, 253–270.

Jensen, A. R. (1980). *Bias in mental testing*. New York: Free Press.

Plomin, R., DeFries, J. C., & McClearn, G. E. (1990). *Behavioral genetics: A primer* (2nd ed.). New York: Freeman.

Raven, J. (1947). *Raven's progressive matrices*. Los Angeles: Western Psychological Services.

Snyderman, M., & Rothman, S. (1990). *The IQ controversy, the media and public library*. New Brunswick, NJ: Transaction Publishers.

Spearman, C. (1904). General intelligence, objectively determined and measured. *American Journal of Psychology, 15*, 201–293.

Spearman, C. (1927). *The abilities of man*. New York: Macmillan.

Sternberg, R. J. (1981). A componential theory of intellectual giftedness. *Gifted Child Quarterly, 25*, 86–93.

Sternberg, R. J. (1986). *Conceptions of giftedness*. New York: Cambridge University Press.

Sternberg, R. J. (1991). Giftedness according to the triarchic theory of human intelligence. In N. Colangelo & G. Davis (Eds.), *Handbook of gifted education* (pp. 45–54). Boston: Allyn & Bacon.

Terman, L. M. (1916). *Measurement of intelligence: An explanation of and a complete guide for the use of the Stanford revision and extension of the Binet-Simon intelligence scale*. Boston: Houghton Mifflin.

Thurstone, L. L. (1938). *Primary mental abilities*. Chicago: University of Chicago Press.

Wachs, T. D. (1992). *The nature of nurture*. Newbury Park, CA: Sage.

Study Questions ~

1. What is the relationship between intelligence and giftedness?
2. What is the difference between the concept of a *g* factor and the specific components of intelligence that have been identified by various theorists?
3. Identify at least three key theorists. What were their contributions to our understanding of intellectual ability?
4. How would you describe the relationship between Carroll's research-based model of intelligence and Gardner's and Sternberg's models?
5. What are the advantages and disadvantages of using individually administered intelligence tests to identify gifted students?
6. What are the implications of the concepts of intelligence described in this chapter for gifted programming? How might these theories be translated into educational practice?
7. How might the adoption of a specific theory of intelligence affect who might be served in a gifted program?

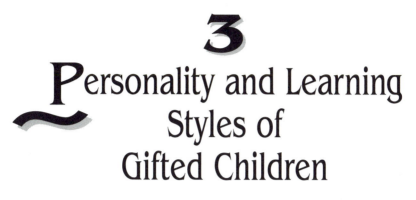

3
Personality and Learning Styles of Gifted Children

Linda Kreger Silverman

At 2 years, 1 month, M's favorite gift was a Mickey Mouse calculator. He'd sit for an hour or more pressing the buttons, adding and subtracting by one. By 2½, he was counting to 100 forwards and from 100 to 0 backwards. Then he started counting by 10s. "Clocks and gears entered our life around this time. He got clocks for gifts, and we'd sit on the bed watching them. He wanted to know about gears and had to see the engine of the car. We'd be riding and he'd be listening for the gears operating. The summer when he was 2½ we'd go to the amusement park, and the kids loved the rides but I was a nervous wreck. He would lean way over to see how the ride operated. On the merry-go-round his head was always up watching the poles to see how they operated or else he was leaning into the center of the ride to see the gears. On one of the little car rides, he started crawling under one of the cars. We ran with the attendant, and when we got there he looked up and asked, 'What makes this thing run, anyway?' "

One toddler can sit and listen to books being read for hours on end: "B was very interested in books even as an infant. We noted rapt attention to his favorite book at 2½ months old." Yet another is in constant motion, exploring every facet of his environment: "He literally consumed his world with eagerness, wanting to learn, see, feel and touch everything, all at once" (Rogers & Silverman, 1988, p. 5). A third child demonstrates vivid imagination: "She talks to 'people' that aren't there—conducts elaborate 'sessions' with pretend playmates." A fourth is captivated by puzzles: "H is remarkable at putting puzzles together. She could do puzzles with 25 pieces before she was 2 years old." And a fifth is obsessed with gadgetry: "E had a total preoccupation with electrical and mechanical apparatus. As a tot he would follow exposed wiring and cords to find plugs and hookups." Why are young children—even gifted ones—so different from each other in personality, talents, interests, and learning styles? One answer comes from the study of temperament.

Differences in temperament have been a source of fascination throughout recorded history. Hippocrates suggested that individuals could be categorized into four basic temperaments: sanguine (hopeful), melancholic (depressed), choleric (hot-tempered), and phlegmatic (lethargic). These four types corresponded to Empedocles' four basic elements: air, water, fire, and earth (Hall & Lindzey, 1970). Today, we are still dividing people into types or styles in order to enhance our understanding of each other, to work together more effectively, to guide parents in raising their children, and to improve our instructional methods with children. Classification systems of personality and learning styles abound, and though limited empirical support exists for many of these systems, the concept of temperament rests on a solid foundation of research.

Studies of Temperament ⌒

Inherent differences in behavioral style have been documented from the earliest moments of life. Thomas, Chess, and Birch (1968), leaders in the study of temperament, devised a model of temperament that was used in the New York Longitudinal Study and the Fullerton Longitudinal Study (Gottfried, Gottfried, Bathurst, & Guerin, 1994). Their nine categories of temperament include:

1. *Activity level:* the level, tempo, and frequency of the motor component of behavior.
2. *Rhythmicity:* the degree of regularity of biological functions (e.g., sleeping and waking, feeding).
3. *Approach or withdrawal:* the nature of the initial response to a new stimulus.
4. *Adaptability:* the successive course of the child's responses to new stimuli (i.e., slow vs. fast).
5. *Intensity of reaction:* the energy level of response.
6. *Threshold of responsiveness:* the level of extrinsic stimulation necessary to evoke a noticeable response.
7. *Quality of mood:* the amount of pleasant, joyful, friendly behavior versus unpleasant, crying, unfriendly behavior.
8. *Distractibility:* the effectiveness of extraneous environmental stimuli in interfering with or altering the course of an ongoing behavior.
9. *Attention span and persistence:* the length of time a particular activity is pursued (attention span) and the continuation of an activity in spite of obstacles to continuation (persistence). (Gottfried et al., 1994, pp. 21–22)

Using this model no significant differences were found in temperament between groups of gifted and nongifted children in the Seattle Project (Roedell, Jackson, & Robinson, 1980) or the Fullerton Longitudinal Study (Gottfried et al., 1994); however, Roedell et al. reported that the children in the Seattle Project varied widely in terms of temperament. Some of the variables of temperament are echoed in Dabrowski's (1937) "overexcitabilities" as well as in the literature on personality type (e.g., Jung, 1923/1938). Differences in temperament within the population of gifted children give rise to differentiated learning as well as behavioral and personality styles. These differences, combined with considerable variation in talents, interests, motivation, family backgrounds, and environmental support, render the gifted quite a diverse group, indeed. In fact, some writers have suggested that highly gifted children vary from one another to a greater degree than average children (Lewis, 1984; Tolan, 1995). (See Chapter 7 on the highly gifted.)

In this chapter, three classification systems are discussed in depth that offer insights into the personality development and learning styles of the gifted: Dabrowski's overexcitabilities, the Jungian classification of types embedded in the Myers-Briggs Type Indicator (Myers, 1962), and sequential versus spatial learning styles. These models were selected because (1) they all rest on solid theoretical foundations; (2) they have been applied extensively to the gifted; (3) all three used gifted populations as the basis for norming the instruments used in assessment; (4) although they all have much wider applicability, study of the gifted was critical to their conceptualization; (5) the small number of factors in each paradigm (5, 4, and 2, respectively) enable powerful, in-depth analyses of personality and learning styles of the gifted as well as facilitate relatively easy translation to classroom practice; and (6) of the various models available, these seemed to offer three distinct views with relatively little overlap in constructs, which permits them to be applied and studied in conjunction with one another.

Dabrowski's Theory ~

Dabrowski's theory of positive disintegration (TPD) is a theory of human development particularly suited to the gifted. Dabrowski based his theory on extensive clinical experience with intellectually and creatively gifted children, adolescents, and adults (Piechowski, 1992) as well as on analyses of the biographies of eminent personalities (Dabrowski, with Kawczak & Piechowski, 1970). A gifted and creative man himself, with both an M.D. in psychiatry and a Ph.D. in psychology, Kazimierz Dabrowski authored 400 articles and books in six languages, wrote poetry and plays, and played the violin and piano (Nelson, 1992). At the age of 12, he witnessed the devastation of World War I. During World War II, at the risk of his life, he provided refuge for Polish Jews escaping the Nazis and was eventually sent to a concentration camp. He miraculously survived, had a brief respite after the war, and then was imprisoned under the Communist regime because his ideas about human development conflicted with Socialist policies (Nelson, 1992). His theory of human development grew out of his own confrontations with death, suffering, and injustice and his desire to understand the meaning of human existence. As described by Nelson (1992),

TPD accounts for the development of affective characteristics associated with the gift-ed: emotional intensity; unusual sensitivity to the feelings of others; heightened self-awareness; feelings of being different; idealism and sense of justice; early development of inner locus of control; high expectations; perfectionism; strong need for consisten-cy between abstract values and personal actions; advanced levels of moral judgment; early concern about death; high energy; aesthetic sensitivity. (p. 362–364)

The theory describes five levels of adult development and five indicators of developmental potential—the overexcitabilities (OEs)—that appear in young chil-dren. Development is conceptualized along a continuum from primitive, instinctive, self-centered behavior to the heights of universal compassion and altruism. The five levels are not related to age; it takes great personal courage and effort to attain "mul-tilevel development," the rich inner territory of the highest three levels. Dabrowski's lowest level of development is rigidly self-serving, focused on power, status, wealth, conquest, or self-preservation, with a notable lack of concern for others. Level II is marked by ambivalence and strong influence of environmental forces. At the gate-way to multilevel development, Level III, the individual enters into a life of self-examination and painful awareness of his or her moral shortcomings. Those excep-tional people who reach Level IV live their lives in concert with higher order values: authenticity, autonomy, self-control, responsibility, empathy, and conscious self-direction toward a personality ideal. Beyond Level IV lies the pinnacle of develop-ment, Level V, where the personality ideal is attained. The rare soul who evolves to Level V becomes a moral inspiration, exemplifying inner peace and harmony, altru-ism, all-embracing love, and devotion to service. One level usually dominates the psyche, but that level often coexists with vestiges of a lower level and precursors to a higher level of development. This coexistence creates intense friction between opposing world views, and the beliefs of the lower level must disintegrate in order for the values of the higher levels to gain strength; this is where the theory of posi-tive disintegration derives its name.

Of particular interest is Dabrowski's (1937) concept of overexcitabilities, since the five OEs greatly influence learning and personality style. The term "overex-citability" is a translation of the Polish term *"nadpobudliwosc,"* which literally means "superstimulatability" (Falk, Piechowski, & Lind, 1994). The five overex-citabilities, like Gardner's (1983) seven intelligences, are innate strengths. They have been considered variables of temperament (Nixon, 1996) and relate most closely to activity level, intensity of reaction, and threshold of responsiveness. Dabrowski observed that schoolchildren had characteristic ways of releasing tension and responding to stimulation: Some squirmed in their seats, some escaped into fantasy, some were emotionally tense, some became more mentally alert, and some chewed on their pencils. He categorized these reactions as psychomotoric, imaginational, emotional, intellectual, and sensual overexcitability. In *Social-Educational Child Psychiatry*, published in Poland in 1959 and revised in 1964, Dabrowski provided his fullest treatment of the five forms of psychic overexcitability, discussing the clinical and educational implications of the OEs "as well as the challenges they pose in rais-ing a child prone to high levels of stimulation" (Piechowski, 1995, p. 3):

> Dabrowski emphasized the disequilibrating, disorganizing, and disintegrating action of overexcitability on various areas of psychological functioning.... Overexcitability was defined by the following characteristics: (1) a reaction that exceeds the stimulus, (2) a reaction that lasts much longer than average, (3) the reaction often not being related to the stimulus (e.g., a fantasy image in response to an intellectual stimulus), and (4) a ready relaying of emotional experience to the sympathetic nervous system (fast beating of the heart, flushing, perspiring, headaches). (Piechowski, 1995, p. 3)

Only when excitation is beyond the norm does it contribute to developmental potential and qualify as overexcitability (Piechowski, 1979):

> Each form of overexcitability can be viewed as a mode of being in the world, or as a *dimension of mental functioning*.... These are modes of personal experience and personal action. Each mode can be viewed as a channel through which flows information.... They determine to what occurrences and in what way one is capable of responding.... These "channels" can be wide open, narrow or operating at bare minimum. They are assumed to be part of a person's constitution and to be more or less independent of each other. If more than one of these channels, or all five, have wide apertures, then the abundance and diversity of feeling, thought, imagery, and sensation will inevitably lead to dissonance, conflict and tension, but at the same time it enriches, expands, and intensifies the individual's mental development. (pp. 28–29)

Dabrowski's forms and expressions of overexcitability are summarized in Table 3.1.

Psychomotor OE is a surplus of energy or the expression of emotional tension "through general hyperactivity" (Dabrowski, with Kawczak & Piechowski, 1970, p. 31). Manifestations include rapid speech, compulsive talking and chattering, nervous habits, workaholism, impulsive actions, marked competitiveness, love of fast games, and pressure for action (Piechowski, 1979). The actor and comedian Robin Williams exhibits strong psychomotor OE.

Sensual OE is enhanced sensory and aesthetic pleasure and the sensual expression of emotional tension (Falk et al., 1994). Heightened experiences of sight, hearing, smell, taste, touch, and sexuality, greater discernment of the senses, delight in beautiful objects, overeating, buying sprees, and wanting to be in the limelight are all facets of sensual OE. Linus's love affair with his blanket, in the Charles Schulz cartoons, and Sandra Boynton's hippopotamus who never met a dessert she did not like both illustrate sensual OE.

Imaginational OE involves frequent play of the imagination, capacity for living in a world of fantasy, spontaneous imagery as an expression of emotional tension, and low tolerance for boredom (Falk et al., 1994). "Imaginational hyperexcitability can provide a basis for the development of prospection and retrospection, that is to say, the ability to use one's past experience in the planning of the future" (Dabrowski, with Kawczak & Piechowski, 1970, p. 31). Inventiveness, poetic and dramatic capabilities, frequent use of image and metaphor, the ability to visualize in detail, elaborate dreams, imaginary companions, and mixing of truth and fiction are all aspects of imaginational OE. Calvin, of Bill Watterson's Calvin and Hobbes, is the quintessential example of a child high in imaginational OE.

Table 3.1 ~
Forms and Expressions of Psychic Overexcitability

Psychomotor
> Surplus of energy
> Psychomotor expression of emotional tension

Sensual
> Enhanced sensory and aesthetic pleasure
> Sensual expression of emotional tension

Intellectual
> Intensified activity of the mind
> Penchant for probing questions and problem solving
> Reflective thought

Imaginational
> Free play of the imagination
> Capacity for living in a world of fantasy
> Spontaneous imagery as an expression of emotional tension
> Low tolerance of boredom

Emotional
> Feelings and emotions intensified
> Strong somatic expressions
> Strong affective expressions
> Capacity for strong attachments, deep relationships
> Well-differentiated feelings toward self

Note: Adapted from *Criteria for Rating the Intensity of Overexcitabilities* by R. F. Falk, M. Piechowski, & S. Lind, 1994, unpublished manuscript, University of Akron, Department of Sociology, and from "Developmental Potential" by M. M. Piechowski, in *New Voices in Counseling the Gifted* (pp. 25–57), edited by N. Colangelo & R. T. Zaffran, 1979, Dubuque, IA: Kendall/Hunt.

Intellectual OE encompasses intensified activity of the mind, a penchant for probing questions and problem solving, and reflective thought (Falk et al., 1994). These qualities, so often noted in the gifted, are expressed as curiosity, keen observation, avid reading, capacity for intense concentration, detailed visual recall, love of theory and analysis, tenacity in problem solving, forming of new concepts, introspection, moral thinking, and searching for truth. Sherlock Holmes (Doyle, 1892/1930) stands out as an excellent model of intellectual OE.

The last overexcitability, *emotional OE*, is the most important of the five in terms of its contribution to developmental potential (Piechowski, 1979; Rankel, 1994). Intense feelings and emotions, capacity for strong attachments and deep relationships, well-differentiated feelings toward self, and strong somatic and affective expressions are the main qualities of emotional OE. They are manifested as extremes of emotion; complex emotions and feelings; awareness of a large range of feelings; strong emotional ties to people, animals, and places; difficulty adjusting to new environments; compassion; responsiveness to others; sensitivity in relationships; loneliness; self-judgment; somatic expressions, such as blushing, flushing, sweaty palms, pounding heart; ecstasy; pride; fears and anxieties; feelings of guilt and shame; concern with death; depressive and suicidal moods; and inhibition (shyness) (Falk et al., 1994). The cartoon character Cathy is a prototype of emotional OE, with some sensual OE thrown in for good measure: "Only love can thrill a heart...but chocolate can come close" (Guisewite, 1994).

In 1979, Piechowski called for a broadened conceptualization of giftedness, beyond that which can be gleaned from standardized testing, and introduced to gifted education the five OEs as a means of assessing creative potential. He suggested that the OEs, or "original equipment," are basic components of giftedness shared by many types of gifted individuals. "The overexcitabilities," he noted, "may be regarded as the *actual psychological* potential of the creative person" (p. 49). He went on to say, "The assessment of the strength and richness of these forms should allow a reliable qualitative assessment of creative giftedness" (p. 54). Since the time Piechowski's article was published, a considerable number of studies have been conducted assessing overexcitabilities in the gifted. A brief synopsis of these studies follows.

Based on Piechowski's hypothesis that the strength of the OEs can be used as a measure of the person's giftedness (Piechowski & Colangelo, 1984), master's and doctoral theses in the United States and Canada have explored the use of OEs in the identification of gifted and creative individuals from different national, ethnic, and socioeconomic backgrounds (e.g., Ackerman, 1993, in press; Breard, 1994; Buerschen, 1995; Calic, 1994; Domroese, 1993; Ely, 1995; Falk, Manzanero, & Miller, in press; Gallagher, 1985; Manzanero, 1985; Rogers, 1986; Schiever, 1985). The instrument employed in these studies was the Overexcitabilities Questionnaire (OEQ), devised by Lysy and Piechowski (1983). The OEQ consists of 21 open-ended questions, such as "What kinds of things get your mind going?" and "When you ask yourself 'Who am I?' what is the answer?" The narrative responses are coded using content analysis techniques. Two trained raters independently score the OEs on a scale from 0 to 3 according to specific criteria outlined in the coding manual, *Criteria for Rating the Intensity of Overexcitabilities* (Falk et al., 1994). Raters attempt to reach consensus through discussion of differences or the ratings are averaged. To obtain information about the reliability of the instrument, interrater reliabilities were calculated for all OEs in 10 studies conducted between 1985 and 1996 (N = 427). Interrater reliability prior to consensus ranged from .66 to .86. Test-retest reliability for OEQs completed 3 to 6 weeks apart by a group of 60 adults was .65 (Ammirato, 1987). Further information about reliability and validity of the OEQ is reported in Falk et al. (in press), Miller, Silverman, and Falk (1994), and Piechowski and Miller (1995).

Psychomotor OE differentiated better than the other four OEs between a group of identified gifted high-school students and an unselected group in Calgary

(Ackerman, 1993). No other study unveiled significant differences between gifted and control groups in psychomotor OE. Although clinicians report high levels of sensual OE in this population (e.g., Meckstroth, 1991), only one study of gifted adults yielded statistically significant differences in sensual OE between the gifted and control groups (Silverman & Ellsworth, 1980). Gifted adolescents have been found to be consistently higher in imaginational OE than their average peers (Gallagher, 1985; Schiever, 1985) and even higher than a group of graduate students (Piechowski & Colangelo, 1984). Artists surpassed the intellectually gifted in imaginational OE and emotional OE and equaled them in intellectual OE (Piechowski, Silverman, & Falk, 1985). All gifted samples studied scored high in intellectual OE and exhibited high levels of emotional OE (Gallagher, 1985; Piechowski & Colangelo, 1984; Piechowski & Cunningham, 1985; Schiever, 1985; Silverman, 1983; Silverman & Ellsworth, 1980).

It appears from OE studies that many teachers who choose to specialize in working with gifted children are gifted themselves. A study of 14 graduate students in gifted education (Silverman, 1982) matched closely the overexcitability profiles of 37 gifted adults (Silverman & Ellsworth, 1980), with both groups showing significantly elevated imaginational, intellectual, and emotional OE scores compared to a group of graduate students in different disciplines (Lysy & Piechowski, 1983). The primarily female gifted education majors also scored significantly higher than primarily male chemical engineering graduate students on imaginational and emotional OE (Felder, 1982). They also scored significantly higher than an unselected group of women at midlife on intellectual and imaginational OE, but the two groups scored very similarly in emotional OE (Sorell & Silverman, 1983).

Piechowski and Colangelo (1984) compared several groups of gifted and creative individuals, varying in age from 9 through adulthood, from different parts of the country, and reported constancy of OE scores across the age span. "The youngest gifted groups (age 9 and 11 in the Denver sample)," they noted, "have each the same OE profile of T [Intellectual], M [Imaginational], and E [Emotional] as the gifted adults. This constancy supports the idea of developmental potential as original equipment" (p. 87).

Gifted children can display one or all of the overexcitabilities, and the relative strength of each OE significantly affects the child's interests and attentiveness in different subjects and with different teaching strategies. For example, Alex has strong psychomotor OE and relatively weaker intellectual OE. His favorite subject is physical education, and he is involved in a number of after-school competitive sports. Alex becomes restless and unmotivated in classes requiring passive absorption of material, but he gets excited in courses allowing movement, manipulatives, or hands-on exploration. Alex needs action and physical activity. He is a doer: He takes the lead in class projects and group activities. When he is interested in a subject, he takes constant notes because he has learned that he can concentrate only when he is physically engaged in an activity. He is a hardworking, well-organized student with leadership ability, and the other children look up to him. However, when he is asked to sit still and listen for too long, he is likely to act out, be the class clown, and compete with the teacher for the attention of his classmates. Action-oriented students like Alex need frequent outlets for their excess physical energy.

Bonnie's greatest strength is her sensual OE. She is an excellent dancer who adores performing and being the center of attention. Bonnie is fussy about nearly everything. She likes the feel of only certain clothes and she has to have all the labels cut out because they "scratch" her. She loves to eat, but she is a picky eater, avoiding certain textures, colors, and smells. Her favorite subject is art, not because she is particularly artistic but because she loves the feel of clay, the smell of paints, and the opportunity to create. Bonnie has an enormous appreciation of beauty. She writes poetry and prose with lovely, flowing words and she takes great pains to make her homework neat. Children like Bonnie blossom with teachers who experience the beauty of mathematics, the eloquence of words, or the splendor of scientific creation. They need opportunities for creative expression in all subject areas.

Charles is a dreamer with a faraway look in his eyes. High in imaginational OE, Charles spends most of his time in class doodling or daydreaming. He is good at math concepts, science, computers, and art. He is poor at computation, spelling, handwriting, and the mechanics of language, such as capitalization, punctuation, and paragraphing. Charles reads science fantasy books endlessly and is the dungeon master for his Dungeons and Dragons group. He learns best through visualization. Instructions such as "picture in your mind..." help him to use his gift of imagination to learn subjects he finds difficult to master. Children like Charles are more successful when they are taught visually and allowed to use a computer for written assignments.

Dana has several overexcitabilities, but she is most outstanding in intellectual OE. She began reading at age 3, and books have become her best friends. She is curious about everything and asks a lot of questions in class. Analytical and argumentative, she will often correct her teachers and friends if the information they are sharing is not exactly accurate. Dana is extremely concerned with fairness, and she can appear self-righteous to her classmates. She is happiest when she is given a difficult problem to solve. Dana is an eager learner in all subject areas as long as she is challenged. If the pace is too slow or the teacher is reviewing material she has already mastered, she finds school insufferable. Students like Dana need to be allowed to progress as far as they can go as fast as they can learn. They are perfect candidates for acceleration, thriving on advanced coursework.

Edmund is a shy, sensitive boy who is keenly aware of other people's feelings. His strong emotional OE makes him vulnerable to teasing by the boys at his school. Edmund is disconsolate because his best friend moved away before school started. Although he is a kind and caring boy, Edmund does not find it easy to make friends. He does not like the rough and tumble games the other boys play, he becomes terrified in scary movies that the other boys enjoy, and he often feels like an outsider. He is not a good competitor in games, because instead of experiencing the thrill of winning, he has great empathy with those who were defeated and feels guilt at causing them pain. Edmund should not receive messages to "toughen up"; instead, teachers need to intervene to stop the teasing. He can learn to hide his feelings on the playground as long as there is a haven at home and at school where it is safe to be sensitive. Many gifted boys like Edmund are at risk of being scapegoated because they do not fit the macho mold. They flourish in gifted classes with other sensitive children who also feel like outsiders. Above all, gifted programs provide psychological safety for children who think, feel, and experience life differently.

Piechowski and Colangelo (1984) emphasized that the OEs are not specific domains of talent or prodigious achievement. "Rather," they stated, "they represent the kind of endowment that feeds, nourishes, enriches, empowers and amplifies talent" (p. 87). Dabrowski's model "promises to uncover for every individual child its principal mode of responding to the world" (Piechowski, 1974, p. 91). The various permutations and strengths of the OEs at least partially account for the wide range of individual differences within the gifted population. As Piechowski (1974) summarized,

> One highly psychomotor combined with intellectual, and another highly imaginative combined with emotional, have little in common in their experience of the world; i.e., in their mode of being and acting. While the first will strive for logic, precision, strict reliance on data, great volume and pace of work, achievement and accomplishment, and will oppose any intuitive conceptions, the other will strive for the expression of feelings, for unique relationships, for the legitimacy of dreams, daydreams and poetry, and will grasp things intuitively rather than analytically; external success and achievement may mean little to him. The two will oppose each other but never will they be able to comprehend and reconcile their differences. (p. 92)

Similar to the variables in temperament observed in infants, the overexcitabilities appear to be stable characteristics that differentiate the interests, motivation, and behavior of children with different kinds of gifts.

The Myers-Briggs Type Indicator ～

The conception of "differing gifts" also applies to the work of Isabel Briggs Myers (1962), who created the Myers-Briggs Type Indicator (MBTI). The history of the development of the MBTI offers a fascinating excursion into the dynamics of a gifted family. Katharine Cook Briggs, Isabel's mother, developed a typology of personality during World War I, based, like Dabrowski's, on the study of biography. When she discovered that Jung's (1923/1938) system was quite similar to her own and more detailed, she began to explore and elaborate on Jungian typology. Isabel, Katharine's only child, received most of her education at home, during which time Jung's psychological types played an important part in her education. Isabel proved to be a highly gifted student. Admitted to Swarthmore College at age 16, she married Clarence Myers in her junior year and graduated first in her class in 1919 (Black, 1980). Like Dabrowski, Isabel Briggs Myers was deeply affected by World War II:

> The suffering and tragedies of the war stirred Myers's desire to do something that might help peoples understand each other and avoid destructive conflicts. Having long since absorbed her mother's admiration of Jungian typology, she determined to devise a

method of making the theory of practical use. Thus was born the idea of a "type indicator." (Black, 1980, p. x)

In the summer of 1942, after waiting a long time for someone else to devise an instrument based on Jung's types, Isabel Myers and Katharine Briggs decided to create such a tool themselves. Thus, the Myers-Briggs Type Indicator bears the name of mother and daughter. It took Myers two decades of dedicated, unsupported work to create, validate, and refine her item pool of attitudes, feelings, perceptions, and behaviors representing the different psychological types. MacKinnon (1962) was one of the first to accept the new scale and use it in assessing creative architects, writers, mathematicians, and scientists. The book that synthesized Myers' life's work, *Gifts Differing*, was written with the help of her son, Peter. She corrected the proofs at the age of 82, in a very weak state, but did not live to see the book published.

The MBTI is the mother of most modern assessments of personality type and learning style. It contains four sets of preferences: extraversion and introversion; sensing and intuition; thinking and feeling; and judging and perceiving. The various combinations of these four sets generate 16 personality types that influence interests, values, needs, traits, and habitual ways of understanding and functioning in the world (Myers with Myers, 1980). An objective self-report questionnaire, the MBTI consists of 50 to 166 forced-choice items, depending on the form. The results of a considerable number of studies of the instrument's reliability and validity, particularly concurrent studies, are reported in the manual (Myers & McCaulley, 1985). Internal consistency reliabilities for adult populations range from .75 to .85, which is considered adequate. Test-retest reliabilities show consistency over time. Reliabilities tend to be somewhat lower for teenage respondents but stabilize for groups over age 20.

A description of the different types follows. *Extraversion* (E) is being oriented toward the outer world, becoming energized through interaction with people and things, and being directed toward action. *Introversion* (I) is being oriented toward the subjective world of thoughts and concepts, gaining energy from within oneself, and being inclined toward reflection. The *sensing* (S) function describes a preference for facts and verifiable information acquired from the five senses, whereas the *intuitive* (N) function describes indirect perception by way of the unconscious—an affinity with possibilities, metaphoric meanings, and abstraction. The *thinking* (T) function determines that decisions will be made in an unbiased manner, on the basis of logic, analysis, objectivity, justice, and fairness. The *feeling* (F) function determines that decisions will be made with consideration for harmony, subjective values, and an appreciation of human needs, which vary in different situations. *Judging* (J) describes a preference for decision making (through the T or F functions), while *perceiving* (P) describes a preference for acquiring information (through the S or N functions) and delaying decisions. J personality types plan, decide, organize, emphasize production, like closure, and attempt to lead settled, orderly lives. P personality types are curious, spontaneous, flexible, adaptable, focus on process rather than product, avoid closure, and like to keep their options open.

According to Jung (1923/1938), the types are randomly distributed among individuals in various social classes, ethnic groups, and nationalities. Introverted and extraverted children can be found in the same family, and these natural dispositions become apparent in early childhood. The preferred mode is constantly practiced from early childhood on and becomes trustworthy, while the other modes are relatively underdeveloped. According to Myers, "The child who prefers feeling becomes more adult in the handling of human relationships. The child who prefers thinking grows more adept in the organization of facts and ideas" (Myers with Myers, 1980, p. 4). Attempts to coerce a child into a "falsification of type" are "exceedingly harmful to the physiological well-being [of the child]" (Jung, 1923/1938, pp. 415–416), often leading the child to an acute state of exhaustion and the likelihood of neurosis. Numerous books have been written describing these types and the interpretation and practical uses of the MBTI (e.g., Farris, 1991; Keirsey & Bates, 1978; Lawrence, 1982; Myers with Myers, 1980). The remainder of this discussion concentrates on applications of the MBTI to the gifted.

Both MBTI manuals (Myers, 1962; Myers & McCaulley, 1985) report the findings of numerous studies of the use of the instrument with gifted populations. The instrument was published and used extensively by the Educational Testing Service with college-bound populations, National Merit finalists, and students enrolled in Ivy League colleges. In addition, the MBTI was employed by the Institute for Personality Assessment and Research in research with creative men and women (e.g., Helson, 1965; MacKinnon, 1962). Several studies of MBTI profiles in gifted students have been conducted in the past decade, all of which substantiate the findings reported in the manuals (e.g., Delbridge-Parker, 1988; Gallagher, 1990; Jackson, 1995; Piirto, 1992).

Gifted individuals come in all 16 types, but they are not equally distributed among the various types. The distribution of junior-high gifted students reported in the MBTI manual is typical of the distributions found in other studies:

> Certain preferences are conspicuously more frequent in the gifted sample as compared to the very good pre-academic sample. Seventy-nine percent of male gifted students were intuitive types, compared to 28% of pre-academic males (p <.001). The frequency of introverts in the male gifted sample is 50% compared to 32%, and the relationship of perceptives is 62% compared to 51%. The proportions for female gifted compared to pre-academic students are similar: 88% intuitives compared to 30%, 42% introverts compared to 25%, and 65% perceptives compared to 53%. (Myers & McCaulley, 1985, p. 100)

In addition, the distribution of thinkers and feelers was nearly identical in the gifted and pre-academic groups. Fifty-six percent of the boys in both groups were Ts, and 44% were Fs; 42% of the gifted girls were Ts and 58% were Fs (41% of the pre-academic girls were Ts and 59% were Fs). These percentages on the thinking-feeling dimension are typical of gender differences found in adult samples (Lawrence, 1982).

The data from the manual and other studies of the gifted reveal that gifted children are often introverted, intuitive perceivers (Delbridge-Parker & Robinson, 1989;

Hoehn & Bireley, 1988; Maker, 1975). More males are thinkers and more females are feelers. Preliminary studies of highly gifted children at the Gifted Development Center suggest that T might also be a function of IQ, with moderately gifted children more likely to be Fs and highly gifted more likely to be Ts. Whereas the primary type found among gifted elementary-aged children is INFP, the dominant profile of talented male teens is INTP (Delbridge-Parker, 1988; Gallagher, 1990; Hoehn & Bireley, 1988).

The strongest correlation with giftedness is in the dimension of intuition. The majority of gifted and creative populations studied were highly intuitive: 83% of the sample of National Merit finalists; 97.4% of creative men (MacKinnon, 1965); 96% of creative women (Helson, 1965); and over 75% of 1,725 talented high-school students (Gallagher, 1990). Lysy and Piechowski (1983) found that the intuitive function of the MBTI was the third strongest predictor of higher level development (Levels III, IV, and V), after emotional and intellectual OE.

The adjustment of intuitives is complicated by the fact that 75% of the American population and 61% of elementary teachers are sensing types (Lawrence, 1982; Myers, 1962). Children who prefer sensing need practical, hands-on experiences; factual, detailed information; concrete skills; didactic approaches moving from concrete to abstract concepts; step-by-step presentations; demonstrations; more time for tests; test-taking strategies; a limited amount of reading; and assistance in gaining the main points and abstract concepts in various subjects. Intuitives need exposure to abstract concepts, symbolic reasoning, problem-finding and problem-solving activities, inductive (discovery-oriented) strategies, complex material with multiple layers of meaning, more independence and less structure, opportunities to envision possibilities, futuristic studies, and creative outlets. These learning differences are easier to accommodate when highly intuitive, gifted children are congregated for instruction.

Introverts represent about 25 percent of the general population (Bradway, 1964; Myers, 1962) and at least 50 percent of the gifted population (Delbridge-Parker & Robinson, 1989; Gallagher, 1990; Hoehn & Bireley, 1988; Rogers, 1986). Much higher proportions of introverts have been found among the highly gifted (Silverman, 1986), particularly those who have extremely advanced verbal abilities (Dauber & Benbow, 1990). High achievers are often introverted intuitives (INs) (Myers, 1962). This combination of personality variables is associated with scholastic potential, as measured by the Scholastic Aptitude Test (SAT), IQ scores on Terman's Concept Mastery Test, and higher grade-point averages at prestigious colleges (Myers & McCaulley, 1985). The proportion of introverts increases with educational level. Extraversion and introversion relate most closely to the temperamental variables of approach or withdrawal and adaptability. Extraverts approach new situations with greater ease and adapt more quickly than introverts. Essential differences between extraverts and introverts are listed in Table 3.2.

Introverts need time to think and reflect. In analyzing taped classroom discussions, Rowe (1974) discovered that teachers tend to wait less than 1 second for students to reply to their questions. It is a good idea to initiate "think time" (longer

Table 3.2 ~
Extraversion and Introversion

Extraverts	Introverts
Gain energy from interaction with others	Gain energy in solitude; need alone time
Focus on people and things around them	Focus on inner thoughts and feelings
Are outgoing	Are reserved
Think out loud	Mentally rehearse before speaking
Are similar in public and private	May appear different at home and in public
Like attention	Avoid attention
Learn by doing	Learn by observing
Adapt quickly in new situations	Are uncomfortable with changes
Make lots of friends easily	Are loyal to a few close friends
Tend to be impulsive	Tend to be reflective
Can focus on many ideas at once	Like to concentrate on one activity at a time
Are risk-takers in groups	Fear humiliation; are quiet in large groups

pauses) after questions to students. A private corner of the room set aside to allow students to get away from the group and think enables introverts to maintain higher energy levels in the classroom. Cooperative learning groups are useful for extraverts who value consensus decision-making, but introverts should be allowed to do individual projects. Extraverts love to talk because in doing so they sharpen their thought processes. They profit from class discussions and any opportunities for interaction. They enjoy action-oriented activities, new situations, sharing personal experiences and opinions, teaching other students, taking on leadership roles, and multitasking—doing several things at once. They are better with short-term than long-term projects.

Systems can be devised to give quieter students more of an opportunity to participate in rapid-fire class discussions. One method is for a student to use a hand signal when he or she has something to contribute but does not want to interrupt a classmate. The teacher acknowledges the signal with a nod and keeps track of whose turn it is to speak. Creativity exercises are more fun for introverts when time is provided to write down answers before sharing them verbally. Introverts also appreciate it when teachers intersperse whole-class discussion with time for dyadic or small-group discussions. In a class in which the students learned about their personality types, one child was overheard excitedly saying to his introverted classmate, "We need your input on this. Think about it and get back to us." More than anything, introverts need respect for their introversion. *Discover the Power of Introversion* (Card, 1994) is recommended reading for more information on this topic.

Thinking and feeling are both strong functions in gifted populations; however, their polarization in this model, as well as gender and age issues, make the T-F dimension of the MBTI difficult to interpret. Silver and Hanson (1980), using their Learning Preference Inventory (Silver & Hanson, 1978), found that gifted boys and girls at the elementary level preferred feeling but that 60% to 70% of all groups (gifted and average, male and female) preferred thinking in adolescence. Hoehn and Bireley (1988) found similar results: 67.5% of their gifted sample preferred feeling, but there were substantial differences between elementary and secondary students. Combining N with T or F, and categorizing the results by gender and age, the patterns shown in Table 3.3 emerged.

It appears that gifted boys in elementary school are three times more likely to be feeling types than are gifted boys in secondary school. A substantial number of gifted girls also seem to prefer thinking to feeling as they mature. Bireley (1991) interpreted these results as follows:

> The adolescent movement toward the more logical, objective style of the thinker (apparent in both males and females, but to a greater degree in males) may reflect a movement from the egocentrism of the younger child, an adaptation to societal gender expectations, a response to curricular demands, or a maturation of the ability to think more objectively and logically. (p. 196)

Another possibility is that intellectual development, particularly in gifted males, is supported at the expense of emotional development (Miller et al., 1994).

The combination of intuition and thinking (NT) creates a propensity to argue and an intense desire to win. A class of college freshmen was divided into four groups based upon their MBTI profiles: NFs, NTs, SFs, and STs. The groups were asked to discuss the question, "How do you learn best?" The first answer that the NTs wrote on the sheet of butcher paper they were given was **"ARGUE"**—in large block letters! With an unbeatable combination of incisive logic and highly developed intuition, NTs are excellent on debate teams, can easily argue opposing points of view, and will often play devil's advocate in conversations, simply to hear the other person's rationale—which they will likely advocate later in another discussion (Silverman, 1993b). However, the world is not composed entirely of NTs, and these individuals can be intimidating to every other personality type.

Table 3.3 ～
Changes in Personality Style from Childhood to Adolescence in Gifted Males and Females

	NT	NF
Elementary gifted males	18.3%	48.5%
Secondary gifted males	41.9%	16.3%
Elementary gifted females	12.6%	41.2%
Secondary gifted females	35.5%	35.5%

Note: Data from "Mental Processing Preferences of Gifted Children" by L. Hoehn and M. K. Bireley, 1988, *Illinois Council for the Gifted Journal, 7,* p. 29.

For many highly gifted students, arguing is a form of mental exercise, engaged in for pure pleasure and as a method of learning. Recognizing this tendency in children above 170 IQ, Hollingworth (1939) provided them with special training in "disputation" so that they would learn how to argue fairly. One of Hollingworth's students, Herbert Carroll, designed a training program for gifted students including how to argue with oneself, the etiquette of polite disagreement with others, rules for public argumentation, and the art of persuasion of crowds. By teaching students about different personality types, teachers and counselors can help NTs temper their sharp intellectual fencing skills with understanding of other people's feelings and reactions to their argumentativeness. Another characteristic of NTs, particularly highly gifted ones, is devotion to honesty, often at the expense of tact. They do not protect people from "the truth" as they see it. Hollingworth (1939) recommended that gifted students be taught to withhold absolute honesty when it is likely to do more harm than good.

To reach the thinking types in a classroom, teachers need to impartially enforce all rules that they set up at the beginning of the class. A structured classroom and a well-ordered curriculum with clear goals and expectations assure the comfort of the Ts. Clarity of presentation is essential to their learning. Activities requiring analysis, persistence, and mastery of skills appeal to their need for intellectual achievement. Feeling types perform better with teachers who like, respect, and encourage them. Their efforts need to be acknowledged. Teachers who deeply appreciate the subjects they are teaching or who appreciate their students and the learning process are ideal for Fs. Cooperative learning experiences are particularly appropriate for EFs. They enjoy group projects and team learning (Lawrence, 1982). Whereas NTs can enjoy the challenge of learning abstract theories, principles, and concepts, for NFs learning must have relevance and applicability—they need to see how the information they are learning will help someone. Fs who are highly empathic require assigned reading material without violent content (which may be hard to find).

Studies of talented teens have found that they generally have stronger preferences for perceiving than for judging. Both Gallagher (1990) and Delbridge-Parker (1988) reported that approximately 60% of their samples were Ps. In MacKinnon's (1965) sample of creative men, 55% favored P over J. And in Piirto's (1990, 1992) studies, the predominant pattern for creative artists of all ages was NP. In one group of 50 creative adolescents from 30 cities in Ohio, 95% were intuitive perceptive types, as were all of the faculty in the summer gifted program (Piirto, 1990).

Not only are the most creative individuals Ps, so are most, if not all, underachievers. Because between 60% and 70% of teachers at all levels prefer judging to perceiving (Lawrence, 1982), there is a basic clash in perspectives between task-committed teachers and task-avoidant underachievers. Most gifted underachievers brought to the Gifted Development Center have a parent who is a high J (Silverman, 1993a). Js are organized, goal oriented, and enjoy planning and completing tasks. They pay attention to deadlines and are punctual, so they are usually not thrilled to have offspring who are Ps. P can be said to stand for play and procrastinate—but definitely not for plan. Ps are spontaneous, playful, interested in many things, and like to take in a great deal of information before they pull it all together. They are likely to go overboard on the research aspects of a project but do not begin the writing until the night before the project is due and then stay up all night. Perceivers who are chronic underachievers take in all the information but are unable to synthesize it and put it down on paper. They would probably perform well on an oral test because they do gain a considerable amount of knowledge. Teachers who were among the "organizationally impaired" at some point in their lives tend to be effective in teaching organizational skills to underachievers.

In contrast to Js, who are comfortable with structure, guidelines, and predictability, Ps learn more when they are presented with variety, novelty, and freedom (Lawrence, 1982). Js need many of the same strategies as Ts, and TJs adjust well in classrooms in which the roles, rules, and routines are clear and consistent. Gifted perceivers, particularly NPs, learn for the love of learning itself. They are less interested than Js in mastery, accomplishment, achievement, and the rewards of high grades. Once a teacher stimulates their curiosity, they will go into high gear in absorbing knowledge. However, they may never turn in a project that synthesizes that knowledge or they will turn in a project late that is three times the length of any of the other students'. Ps have a difficult time adapting to time schedules. Sympathetic teachers will grade "work in progress" and allow extra time for lengthy productions. Ps need assistance in carving out a small enough part of the territory they are curious about so that they can be graded on their understanding of that one part of a much larger, more complex picture. Teachers need to help them limit the scope of their projects and the resources they will bring to bear on them. In addition, it is necessary to carefully monitor their progress. The work style of Ps is frustratingly erratic to Js, but it is far easier to teach Ps effective ways to cram for tests and how to submit work in progress than it is to teach them how to use their time in the same manner as Js. Provost's (1988) 10-page guide entitled *Procrastination* is recommended for students of all types who contend with this issue.

It is possible that many gifted Ps, even underachievers, become more J-like in adult life in order to juggle multiple responsibilities. They learn some of the time-management skills of Js, almost as a second language, just as introverts learn the behaviors of extraverts. In the J/P realm more than the others, a little moderation goes a long way: Js would profit from some of the flexibility of Ps, and Ps could use some of the planning abilities of Js.

How can teachers modify their programs to take all of these diverse profiles into account? Myers and McCaulley (1985) answered this question in the following manner:

> Good teachers who learn about type report that in one sense they are learning what they already know: that some children do better with a step-by-step, hands-on approach (S), whereas others learn best from books that challenge their imaginations (N). Good teachers recognize that there are children for whom appreciation is essential to learning (F), and others for whom appreciation means little, but for whom clarity of presentation is everything (T). Teachers know there are children actively attuned to changes around them (E), and other quieter children who occasionally astonish them with their depth of

understanding (I). And teachers know there are children who thrive on structure and clear guidelines (J) and other children who are free spirits, imprisoned by the same structure that gives security to their classmates (P). Teachers report that a knowledge of type differences makes teaching at once more complex, and more simple. (p. 133)

Gifted students are excited to learn about their personality types. The MBTI can be given to children with a sixth-grade reading level, and second- through fifth-grade students can take the Murphy-Meisgeier Type Indicator for Children (Meisgeier & Murphy, 1987). Administration of these instruments usually takes 30 to 45 minutes, but there are several short forms, including a self-scoring abbreviated version, that can be completed in 10 to 20 minutes. Assessment of type permits students to be grouped by type for instruction and peer tutoring (Runions, 1988).

The strong likelihood that a class of gifted children will be populated with Ns and, to a lesser degree, Is, Fs, and Ps suggests that teachers of the gifted will be most effective if they share some of the personality traits and learning characteristics of their students. Maker (1975) found that gifted children were likely to be INFPs and that effective teachers of the gifted tended to be ENFPs. A study using the MBTI was conducted with 61 graduate students in gifted education to determine which personality types were attracted to this field of study (Silverman, 1985). One-third of the group were found to be extraverts (34%) and two-thirds introverts (66%). Only 15% were sensing types, while 85% were intuitives. About one-fourth (26%) were thinking types and three-fourths (74%) were feeling types. The group was fairly evenly split between judgers (48%) and perceivers (52%). The predominant personality profile was introverted, intuitive, feeling perceivers. Over twice as many INFPs than any other type were enrolled in gifted education courses: 28% of the sample. ENFPs made up another 13%. Js were strongly represented—11% were ENFJs, 11% were INFJs, 10% were INTJs, and 7% were ISFJs—and a number of Js went on to become program administrators. The preponderance of INFPs matches the typical profile of gifted children and, as with the overexcitability profiles, suggests that gifted adults gravitate toward this field of study.

Learning Styles Inventories

Personality types and learning styles overlap to a great extent, and some authors use the terms synonymously (Bireley, 1991). Rita Dunn (1983) defined learning style as "the way individuals concentrate on, absorb, and retain new or difficult information or skills" (p. 496). Excellent inventories of learning styles and learning preferences were developed for children and adults during the late 1970s and early 1980s. Unfortunately, several of these instruments by different authors bear the same name—Learning Style Inventory (Dunn, Dunn, & Price, 1979; Kolb, 1976; Renzulli & Smith, 1978)—or a very similar title—Learning Style Inventory: Primary Version (Perrin, 1982), Learning Style Profile (Keefe & Monk, 1986), and the Learning Preference Inventory (Silver & Hanson, 1978).

One of the most popular of these inventories was constructed by Rita and Kenneth Dunn and their associates (Dunn & Dunn, 1975; Dunn, Dunn, & Price, 1979) through content and factor analysis. Designed for students in grades 3 through

12, the Learning Style Inventory takes 30 to 40 minutes to complete and is easy to administer. In the Dunn's model, learning style comprises a complex matrix of 24 environmental, sociological, physical, and psychological elements, of which at least six strongly influence a person's abilities to receive, store, and use knowledge (see Table 3.4).

Table 3.4 ~
Elements of Learning Style
Rita and Kenneth Dunn

Environmental
Silence versus sound
Bright versus low light
Warm versus cool temperatures
Formal versus informal design of space

Emotional
Motivation
Persistence
Responsibility
Structure versus options

Sociological
Thinking and working with peers
Thinking and working alone
Thinking and working in pairs
Thinking and working in teams
Thinking and working with adults
Thinking and working in several ways

Physical
Perceptual strengths:
    Auditory
    Visual
    Tactile/kinesthetic
With or without intake of food or drink
Time of day or night
Mobility versus passivity

Psychological
Global versus analytic
Hemispheric preference
Impulsivity versus reflectivity

This inventory has been used on several occasions in research with gifted children. Dunn (1983), for example, analyzed seven studies of the learning styles of gifted students in grades 4 through 12 using the Learning Styles Inventory and a variety of other measures and concluded that the gifted are independent, internally controlled, nonconforming, self-motivated, persistent, and perceptually strong. They prefer (1) independent study and learning alone; (2) discussions rather than lectures; (3) time to complete tasks; (4) teaching games; (5) peer teaching; and (6) having options. They dislike drill, lectures, and recitations. She also reviewed another ten studies, all of which demonstrated that identifying preferences and matching students' learning styles with appropriate instructional materials, teaching strategies, or teachers with complementary styles significantly increased academic achievement, improved attitudes toward school, and reduced discipline problems. "If we are to respond appropriately to gifted students," Dunn and her coworkers concluded, "their learning styles should be diagnosed at the elementary level and during the transition into junior high school and then matched to complementary teaching strategies" (Price, Dunn, Dunn, & Griggs, 1981, p. 38).

The Learning Styles Inventory developed by Renzulli and Smith (1978) was designed to assess which specific instructional strategies are preferred by gifted students. The 66 items in the questionnaire focus on nine areas: lecture, discussion, drill and recitation, independent study, projects, teaching games, programmed instruction, peer teaching, and simulations. Stewart (1981) employed the instrument with gifted students and reported that they favored independent study and discussions rather than lectures.

Another model developed by two veterans of gifted education is the Swassing-Barbe Modality Index (SBMI) (Barbe, Swassing, & Milone, 1979a). Barbe and Swassing defined a modality as "any of the sensory channels through which an individual receives and retains information" (Barbe & Swassing, with Milone, 1979b, p. 1). Modalities, according to this model, comprise of three elements—sensation, perception, and memory. The researchers defined the educationally relevant modalities as "the visual, auditory, and kinesthetic" (p. 71), with the kinesthetic modality consisting of large muscle, small muscle, and tactile abilities. A modality strength is the most efficient or dominant mode through which an individual processes information. Visual learners learn by seeing and watching demonstrations; auditory learners through hearing verbal instructions from others or through self-talk; and kinesthetic learners by doing and direct involvement.

Although no data have been reported on modality strengths in the gifted, at the Gifted Development Center it has been observed that some gifted children tend to be stronger in processing auditory information, others excel with visual information, many are proficient with both modalities, and a few who suffer from visual and auditory deficiencies are more likely to be kinesthetic learners. Assessments of over 2,000 children reveal that vision and audition are the two major modalities used by gifted children, and these are usually coupled with capabilities in sequential or spatial reasoning (Silverman, 1989a, 1989b). A model has emerged from these data that can simplify to a great extent the task of adapting for gifted students with different learning styles. The model involves visual-spatial and auditory-sequential learning. The theoretical basis of the model stems primarily from the fields of neurophysiology and neuropsychology, with philosophical underpinnings dating back to ancient Greece.

Two Ways of Knowing

Socrates, the founder of the inductive method (Watson, 1978), was a master at analytical reasoning. Plato, his student, believed in the reality of abstract "Forms" perceivable only through "the mind's eye" and imperfectly represented in everyday life (Plato's Republic, Jowett trans., 1871/1944, p. 258). Aristotle, Plato's student, denied the Platonic Forms and turned to biological classification in his search for truth. Like Plato, Aristotle believed that imagery was important, but he added the element of sequentiality: "We recall these images by ordering them in sequence, associating them with one another according to the principles of similarity, contrast, and contiguity" (cited in Wittrock, 1978, p. 61). These opposing threads of analytical, sequential reasoning and of nonsequential, geometric visions of reality create a fascinating dialectic of differing world views throughout the history of psychology. Consider Locke's associationism, Pavlov's classical conditioning, Watson's behaviorism, Skinner's operant conditioning, and Bloom's taxonomy and contrast them to Kant's *a priori Anschauungen*—"the spatial arrangement of objects given in perception" (Boring, 1950, p. 248); the Gestalt psychologists—Wertheimer, Kohler, and Koffka; Piaget's assessment of formal operational thought; and Guilford's structure of intellect model. Some of the greatest minds in psychology conveyed their ideas in analytical sequences, while others tried to communicate images and geometrical relationships. Is it possible that the clashes in conceptualization can be traced to differences in the cerebral processing modes of the theorists?

In an attempt to answer that question, let us turn to the field of neurophysiology. Well before the turn of the 20th century, John Hughlings Jackson, a pioneer in brain research, hypothesized that the processing of visual information, perception, and visual imagery are all the province of the right cerebral hemisphere, whereas the processing of auditory information, verbal expression, and propositional thinking are the domain of the left hemisphere (Taylor, 1932/1958). (It is interesting to note that Hughlings Jackson's formulation of a hierarchy of levels in the evolution of the nervous system, from simple to complex and from automatic to voluntary, was also pivotal in the development of Dabrowski's theory.) Bogen (1969) asserted that the duality of the hemispheres is the basis for many other dualities throughout history—the yin and yang of human experience. He summarized the ways in which the two hemispheres have been described since the mid-19th century: the "major" hemisphere characterized as expressive, linguistic, executive, symbolic, verbal, discrete, logical, analytic, and propositional, and the "minor" hemisphere described as visual, visuospatial, kinesthetic, imaginative, perceptual, synthetic, preverbal, nonverbal, diffuse, and appositional.

The deduction that the right and left hemispheres specialize in different functions has been fairly well accepted in the past three decades. Statements like the following fill the literature: "The left cortical hemisphere...specializes somewhat in a propositional, analytic-sequential, time-oriented serial organization well adapted to learning and remembering verbal information" (Wittrock, 1978, p. 65), whereas "the processing of visual images, spatial relationships, face and pattern recognition, gesture, and proportion are seen to be specialized in the right hemisphere" (West, 1991, p. 14). Levy (1980) concluded the following from her research:

> A converging body of evidence from unilaterally brain-damaged patients, from investigatings of normal people, and from split-brain research points to the conclusion that the left hemisphere is vastly superior and dominant to the right in linguistic processing, that it thinks logically, deductively, analytically, and sequentially, that its superiority derives from fundamental differences in the way it processes, decodes, encodes, and arranges information. The right hemisphere is superior and dominant to the left in visuospatial construction, in recording the literal properties of the physical world, in visualizing the relationships of objects in space, and probably, in reaching accurate conclusions in the absence of logical justification. (p. 253)

Benbow and her associates have found evidence that intellectually gifted students have enhanced right hemispheric functioning (Benbow, 1986, 1992; O'Boyle & Benbow, 1990). Referring to the work of Geschwind and Behan (1982), in which left-handedness and immune disorders were correlated with enhanced right-hemispheric development, Benbow (1986) found that "80% of mathematically and/or verbally extremely precocious students were left-handed, myopic, and/or had allergies" (p. 724). Summarizing two decades of research, Benbow (1992) reported:

> For the chimeric face task, the right hemisphere was markedly more active than the left, especially at the temporal lobe, while for the average ability students the left hemisphere was somewhat more active. For the verbal task (noun/verb determination), the right hemisphere of the extremely precocious was somewhat more active with the opposite pattern found for the average ability subjects. These electrophysiological data corroborated the behavioral findings of O'Boyle and Benbow [1990], and support their hypothesis of enhanced right hemisphere processing involvement being a correlate of intellectual precocity....
>
> In this context, it is interesting to note that some of the characteristics that long have been found to describe intellectually talented students...are also thought to characterize the cognitive functions or contributions of the right hemisphere to problem-solving (e.g., see things holistically, deep comprehension, advanced moral reasoning, and humor).... The right hemisphere is thought to be better at dealing with novelty than the left hemisphere.
>
> In summary, evidence is beginning to emerge indicating that the organization of cognitive functions within the left and right hemispheres in the intellectually precocious differs from that found for individuals with more average abilities. The intellectually precocious exhibit enhanced right hemispheric functioning. (p. 104)

However, not all researchers are in complete agreement with the localization of brain functions. For example, Gazzaniga (1985) contended that the left hemisphere, the seat of language processes for the majority of the population, controls general cognitive functioning. He proposed a modular view of brain organization, similar to Howard Gardner's (1983):

> Clearly what is important is not so much where things are located, but that specific brain systems handle specific tasks. We begin to see that the brain has a modular nature, a point that comes out of all of the data.... That is, it is not important that the left brain does this or the right brain does that. But it is highly interesting that by studying patients with their cerebral hemispheres separated certain mental skills can be observed in isolation. It is a hugely significant point. (Gazzaniga, 1985, pp. 58–59)

It must be kept in mind that there is a complex interaction between the two hemispheres, particularly for higher level thought processes. Wittrock (1978) reminded us that "no dichotomy of function does justice to the sophistication and complexity of the human brain" (p. 66).

Alexander Luria (1973), a leading neuropsychologist, also questioned the localization of verbal functions in the left hemisphere and perceptual or nonverbal functions in the right hemisphere. Like Gazzaniga, he attributed greater cognitive power to the left hemisphere, perceiving it as the source of volitional control of behavior, with the right hemisphere responsible for subconscious, automatic processes not under volitional control. Luria distinguished between simultaneous (all-at-once) and successive (sequential) processing, but he placed successive processing in the frontal-temporal regions of the brain and simultaneous processing in the occipital-parietal region. Simultaneous processing is essential to the discovery of relationships between components and the integration of many stimuli at once, often with spatial overtones (Kaufman, 1984); successive processing enables the serial ordering of information.

Das, Kirby, and Jarman (1979) developed a successive-simultaneous battery based on Luria's theory and validated the model with several studies of children. Several years later, the simultaneous/sequential distinction became the basis of one of the leading assessments of children's intelligence: the Kaufman Assessment Battery for Children (K–ABC) (Kaufman & Kaufman, 1983). A study of gifted young children (ages 4–6) conducted with the K–ABC (Hafenstein, 1986) found intellectual giftedness to be more strongly correlated with simultaneous than sequential processing, and highly gifted children were found to be strong in both types of processing. Sequential processing was related to reading recognition, and simultaneous processing was related to reading comprehension.

From a completely different perspective, Raymond Cattell (1963) proposed a two-factor theory of intelligence—fluid and crystallized abilities—based on factor analytic evidence of the structure among primary mental abilities. Fluid intelligence, according to Cattell, is general reasoning ability, particularly the process of perceiving relations in figural and spatial material, whereas crystallized intelligence is the product of acculturation—education, training, and practice—and comprises such abilities as verbal and quantitative reasoning, sequential memory, vocabulary, and reading comprehension. The latter type of intelligence "uses verbal mediation, sound inference, and sequential steps of logic in problem solving" (Harvey & Seeley, 1984, p. 76). Cattell (1963) proposed that fluid intelligence is physiologically determined, but his collaborator, Horn (1976), and many other researchers who accept the basic theory (e.g., Snow, 1981; Thorndike, 1963) have rejected the implication that fluid abilities are innate. Cattell's theory of fluid and crystallized abilities strongly influenced Sternberg's (1985) triarchic theory of intelligence and became the basis of another major intelligence test: the Stanford-Binet Intelligence Scale, Fourth Edition (Thorndike, Hagen, & Sattler, 1986).

Harvey and Seeley (1984) used Cattell's theory in their analysis of the abilities of youth in a juvenile detention center. Fifteen percent of the youth scored in the top third percentile on selected subtests of the Wechsler Intelligence Scale for Children (WISC) and the Wechsler Adult Intelligence Scale (WAIS), and the gifted offenders demonstrated higher fluid than crystallized abilities. They concluded,

> This pronounced elevation of the nonverbal areas of ability is evidenced among the gifted students in this study.... The fluid ability of these students had the greatest contribution to the gifted classification.... The traditional classroom situation appeared to have suppressed these students' high fluid abilities in the process of their learning of academic skills. (p. 77)

Fluid intelligence sounds very much like Luria's simultaneous factor and the visual-spatial abilities attributed to the right hemisphere. Crystallized intelligence seems to incorporate Luria's successive factor and the linguistic competencies attributed to the left hemisphere. Regardless of their location in the brain, there appear to be two factors—two basic ways of knowing—that need to be taken into account in educating gifted children: spatial or fluid abilities and sequential or crystallized abilities. Hughlings Jackson (in Taylor, 1932/1958) proposed that the left hemispheric abilities are related to audition and the right hemispheric abilities are related to vision. Indeed, spatial and visual abilities are often combined as a single factor: "spatial-visualization ability" (Lohman, 1989). Further, the connection between sequencing and audition has been established in studies of impaired auditory processing (Northern & Downs, 1994) and studies of the development of reading skills (Jackson, in press). The eye is considered a "synthetic organ," since it mixes different wavelengths of light so that we perceive a single color, while the ear is considered an "analytical organ," since it analyzes different frequencies of sound waves so that we can detect the individual components (Carlson, 1995, pp. 171–172). Temporal (time-sequenced) information is processed auditorily and spatial information is processed visually.

Visual-Spatial and Auditory-Sequential Learners ~

Two basic learning styles—visual-spatial and auditory-sequential—have been found in gifted children through psychometric assessment (Silverman, 1989a, 1989b). Highly gifted children have been found to excel at both types of learning. In 1980, a pattern of visual-spatial strengths was observed in children whose scores on the Stanford-Binet Intelligence Scale (Form L-M) (Terman & Merrill, 1973) fell beyond the norms in the test manual. Item analyses revealed that it was exceptional performance on visual-spatial items that enabled some children to attain extremely high IQ scores. A second group of children was identified in 1981 who had very high visual-spatial abilities coupled with significantly lower auditory-sequential abilities. They could perform well beyond their age level on memory for abstract designs, spatial orientation, visualization, and mathematical induction, but they could not repeat five random digits, repeat sentences accurately, or name the days of the week in order. The majority of children in the second group were underachieving in school, with marked weaknesses in spelling, computation, and writing skills. In addition, a correlation was found between this second pattern and chronic otitis media (ear infections) within the first 3 years of life (Silverman, 1989a). The sequential weaknesses observed were often tied to weak auditory processing abilities, confirmed in later audiological evaluations.

Over time, the term *visual-spatial learner* has become synonymous with children who are strong on visual-spatial items and weak on auditory-sequential items. From the descriptors of sequential and spatial learners listed in Table 3.5, it becomes apparent why the educational system works more effectively for sequential learners than for spatial learners and why sequential learners are more often selected for gifted programs than spatial learners (Dixon, 1983; Silverman, 1989a).

Contrary to the suppositions that gifted visual-spatial learners are less able in verbal reasoning (e.g., Dixon, 1983; Gardner, 1983; West, 1991), they usually obtain higher scores on verbal than on nonverbal measures (Silverman, in press). They excel in the verbal comprehension factor (Vocabulary, Similarities, Information, and Comprehension) of the Wechsler Intelligence Scales and in verbally loaded intelligence tests, such as the Stanford-Binet Intelligence Scale (Form L–M). Their primary weakness tends to be in sequential processing, as indicated by significantly lower scores on subtests with high sequential loadings (e.g., Digit Span, Coding, and Arithmetic). Lohman (1994), in an article aptly entitled "Spatially Gifted, Verbally Inconvenienced," made a similar argument about the verbal/spatial dichotomy:

> The problem is erroneously labeled a discrepancy between verbal and spatial abilities, which it is not. The key is not verbal ability, but fluency in retrieving words, particularly on the basis of their sound patterns, or fluidity in assembling novel utterances. On the spatial side, it is the ability to generate and manipulate gestalten or whole patterns, usually of a fairly concrete sort, but in a fluid and flexible way. (p. 252)

Visual-spatial learners describe their learning process as "thinking in images," while auditory-sequential learners appear to think in words. Spatial learning is all-at-once, whereas sequential learning is step-by-step. At times, gifted spatial students have been referred to as "inverted learners" or "upside-down learners" because they learn difficult, abstract material easily but find the easy, sequential skills difficult to master (West, 1991). Areas of strength for visual-spatial learners often include building things with construction toys (e.g., LEGOs), completing puzzles and mazes,

Table 3.5 ~
Sequential and Spatial Learners

Sequential Learner	Spatial Learner
Step-by-step learner	Whole-part learner
Learns by trial-and-error	Learns concepts all at once
Analytic thinker	Systems thinker—sees complex relationships
Learns sequentially from easy to difficult material	Learns complex systems easily; struggles with easy work
Can show work easily	Arrives at correct answers without taking steps
Good at computation	Good at mathematical reasoning
Good at decoding words	Better at reading comprehension than at decoding
Good at biology and foreign languages	Good at geometry and physics
Learns from models	Prefers to develop own methods of problem solving
May need repetition to reinforce learning	Learning usually permanent; turned off by repetition
Well organized	May be disorganized
Follows oral directions well	May be inattentive in class
Learns phonics easily	May be poor at phonics
Good at spelling	May be poor at spelling
Good at rote memorization	May be poor at rote memorization; prefers abstraction
Good at timed tests	May be poor at timed tests
Good handwriting; neat	May have poor handwriting
Academically talented	Creatively, technologically, or emotionally gifted
Early bloomer	Late bloomer

chess, mathematical reasoning, map reading, geometry, topology, science, computer programming, metaphoric thinking, and interdisciplinary studies. Some gifted spatial learners excel in the fine arts or in mechanical abilities rather than mathematics, science, and technology. Still others with highly developed empathy or intuition demonstrate unusual emotional, moral, or spiritual sensitivity. Areas of weakness may include phonics, spelling, handwriting, foreign languages, rote memorization, timed situations, verbal fluency under pressure, and attention when information is presented verbally without visual aids.

Auditory-sequential learners are good listeners, are comfortable with step-by-step approaches to instruction, tend to be rapid processors of verbal information, and are generally able to express themselves well verbally. Schools are tailored to this kind of learning style. In contrast, visual-spatial learners are astute observers, think holistically in images, may arrive at conclusions without going through a series of steps (which makes it difficult for them to show their work), and may take longer than auditory-sequential learners to express their imaged perceptions in words. They often feel out of step in traditional educational settings. Gifted auditory-sequential learners are more likely to be high achievers in academic subjects, to be selected for gifted programs, to be recognized by their teachers as having high potential, and to be considered leaders. Gifted visual-spatial learners are more often counted among underachieving and disenfranchised groups, "twice exceptional" children (giftedness combined with learning disabilities), dyslexics, children with attention deficit disorders, and creative children from minority groups.

Auditory-sequential learners can often be recognized by scholastic success. Visual-spatial learners usually need diagnostic testing to determine if the degree of disparity between their strengths and weaknesses is severe enough to indicate a learning disability. Students who score 16 or above on the Block Design subtest of the Wechsler tests (WISC, WAIS, or the Wechsler Preschool and Primary Scale of Intelligence [WPPSI]), who score in the gifted range on the abstract visual reasoning section of the Stanford-Binet Fourth Edition, or who score in the superior range on any assessment of visual-spatial abilities (e.g., the Matrix Analogies Test, Raven's Progressive Matrices, the Mental Rotations Test, etc.) have documented giftedness in the spatial domain. High Block Design scores combined with significantly lower Digit Span scores, or Performance IQs significantly higher than Verbal IQs, are usually indicative of a visual-spatial pattern of learning.

A new instrument for students, teachers, and parents, the Visual-Spatial Identifier (VSI), is in the development stages. It is being constructed by an interdisciplinary group of psychologists, neuropsychiatrists, sociologists, reading specialists, gifted program coordinators, speech pathologists, artists, tutors, and parents. Thus far, they have generated thirty-seven positive characteristics of the visual-spatial learning style and 66 concomitant school problems have been generated. The descriptors comprise eight clusters: (1) visual rather than auditory; (2) spatial rather than sequential; (3) holistic rather than detailed; (4) focused on ideas rather than format; (5) pattern-seeking; (6) divergent rather than convergent; (7) sensitive; and (8) asynchronous (exhibiting large disparities between strengths and weaknesses) (Silverman, in press). The following are some sample questions from the student version, the VSI, Student Report:

1. I am an excellent visualizer.
2. I think primarily in images instead of words.
3. I need extra time to express my ideas.
4. I learn better from seeing than from listening.
   (Silverman, in press)

Three pilot studies of the instrument have been conducted to date, one with children and adults referred to the Gifted Development Center, one with children referred to a clinic for attentional deficits, and one with middle-school students who excelled in mathematics. Initial results indicate that there is considerable agreement between parental report and student self-report on the two different instruments and that the wording of some of the items is too complex for many children. The student self-report is currently under revision.

Spatial children appear to develop in a different manner from the norm. Normally, children progress at around age 9 from a phase of eidetic imagery to what has been considered a more sophisticated linguistic phase (Bruner, Goodnow, & Austin, 1966; Luria, 1961). Lohman (1994) asserted that "high-spatial individuals preserve in adulthood imagery abilities that are lost to most individuals as they mature" (p. 255) and that those with heightened imagistic abilities have a potential for "visual-spatial creativity of a high order" (p. 255). He suggested that high-level creativity is fostered in children who are slower in language development, who are homeschooled during their early school years, and who are furnished with construction toys, such as wooden cubes, geometric puzzles, and mechanical models. He went on to state, "Research suggests that the decline in the relative strength of visual-spatial abilities is not entirely due to disuse, but to their incompatibility with sequential modes of processing" (Lohman, 1994, p. 260). Bruner (1973) recommended programs that stimulate visual thinking and problem solving. And Lohman (1994) wistfully concurred: "I wonder what my life would be like had my education given as much attention to the development of my visual-spatial abilities as to my verbal abilities" (p. 263).

How do auditory-sequential learners learn best? Apparently, these students adapt and thrive in most educational environments. How do visual-spatial learners learn best? The following guidelines can assist teachers in adapting lessons to capitalize on visual-spatial strengths:

1. Present ideas visually on the chalkboard or on overheads. "A picture is worth a thousand words." Use rich, visual imagery in lectures.
2. Teach the student to visualize spelling words, math problems, and so forth. An effective method of teaching spelling is to write the word in large, colored print and present it to the student at arm's length, slightly above eye level. Have the student close his or her eyes, visualize the word, then create a silly picture of the word in his or her mind. Then have the student spell it backwards (this demonstrates visualization), then forwards, then write it once.
3. Use inductive (discovery) techniques as often as possible. This capitalizes on the visual-spatial learner's pattern-finding strength.
4. Teach the student to translate what he or she hears into images, and record those images using webbing, mind-mapping techniques, or pictorial notes.
5. Incorporate spatial exercises, visual imagery, reading material that is rich in fantasy, and visualization activities into the curriculum. Spatial conceptual-

ization has the ability to go beyond linear thinking because it deals more readily with immense complexities and the interrelations of systems.

6. To accommodate introverts, allow the introverted student to observe others before attempting activities. Stretch wait time after questions and have all students write answers before discussing them. Develop a signal system during class discussions that allows introverts to participate.

7. Avoid drill, repetition, and rote memorization; use more abstract conceptual approaches and fewer, more difficult problems.

8. Teach to the student's strengths. Help the student learn to use his or her strengths to compensate for weaknesses. Visualization and imagination are the visual-spatial learner's most powerful tools and should be used frequently.

9. Allow the student to use a computer for assignments and, in some subjects, for instruction. Teach the student how to use the computer keyboard effectively.

10. Give untimed power tests. Students with severe processing lags can apply to take their College Board examinations untimed if the disability has been documented through IQ and achievement testing within 3 years of the College Board exams and if teachers have provided extended time for the tests.

11. Give more weight to the content of papers than to format. Visual-spatial students often suffer from deficits in mechanics: spelling, punctuation, paragraphing, and so forth.

12. Allow the student to construct, draw, or otherwise create visual representations of a concept as a substitute for some written assignments.

13. If a bright student struggles with easy, sequential tasks, see if he or she can handle more advanced, complex work. Acceleration is more beneficial for such a student than remediation.

14. Expose the visual-spatial learner to role models of successful adults who learn in a similar manner. Many of the most celebrated physicists were visual-spatial learners. Biographical sketches of famous visual-spatial learners can be found in *The Spatial Child* (Dixon, 1983), *In the Mind's Eye* (West, 1991), and the spatial intelligence chapter in *Frames of Mind* (Gardner, 1983).

15. Be emotionally supportive of the student. Visual-spatial learners are keenly aware of their teachers' reactions to them, and their success in overcoming their difficulties appears directly related to their perception of their teachers' empathy.

Some good books on spatial learning are West's (1991) *In the Mind's Eye* and Dixon's (1983) *The Spatial Child*. For more detailed information on meeting the needs of spatial learners in the classroom, see Silverman (1989a, 1989b).

Although many highly gifted children prefer the visual-spatial approach to learning, they often can switch back and forth between the two modes easily and tend to rely on their well-developed sequential abilities when they cannot immediately apprehend a concept by means of spatial perception. Correlations have also been noted between visual-spatial learning preference and introversion (Dixon, 1983; Lohman, 1994; Riding, 1983; Silverman, 1989b). According to Lohman (1994), "Children who showed a preference for imagistic processing were much more likely to be introverted, whereas those who showed a preference for verbal elaboration were more likely to be extraverted" (pp. 256–257). The emergent pattern is that gifted spatial learners are likely to favor the visual modality, to be intuitive, to prefer perceiving to judging, and to be more introverted than extraverted. They tend to demonstrate high degrees of overexcitability, particularly imaginational, emotional, sensual, and psychomotor. Gifted sequential learners are more likely to favor the auditory modality and are equally apt to be introverts or extraverts. Most of them will be intuitive, but some will prefer sensing and a large number, particularly high-school students, will be organized, planful Js rather than organizationally impaired Ps. They will probably score higher on intellectual, emotional, and imaginational overexcitabilities than on sensual and psychomotor overexcitabilities.

It must be kept in mind that although these correlations hold for the majority of children assessed, some sequential learners prefer vision to audition, some spatial learners prefer audition to vision, and some visual-spatial learners are predominantly extraverted. There is also great variation in patterns of overexcitability. The most difficult children to diagnose are those who have weaknesses in both auditory and visual modalities. They are often labeled "kinesthetic learners," since they need concrete, tactile experiences to help them compensate for weaknesses in the major modalities.

School can be an unpleasant experience for visual-spatial learners. Yet, their learning style may be uniquely suited for our technological future (West, 1991). With appropriate detection of their learning style and classroom modifications, these students can be highly successful, particularly as they tackle more complex subject matter in high school and college. Visual-spatial learners show promise as future engineers, architects, pilots, mathematicians, scientists, computer programmers or technicians, entrepreneurs, artists, musicians, mechanics, human relations professionals, or spiritual leaders. They are the quintessential "late bloomers." Their chances of blooming are greater when they have teachers who recognize their promise and adapt teaching strategies to fit their learning style.

It would be ideal if all teachers could modify their teaching styles to take into account all 24 of Dunn and Dunn's (1975) environmental, sociological, physical, and psychological elements as well as the different learning needs of all 16 personality types on the MBTI and all the possible permutations and strengths of Dabrowski's five overexcitabilities. However, it might be simpler to start with the dichotomy between auditory-sequential learners and visual-spatial learners and assume that the current program is working effectively for the majority of the first group. The 15 strategies listed earlier in this section can be incorporated one at a time to observe their effectiveness.

Summary〜

What do the different variables of temperament, overexcitabilities, personality styles, modalities, and learning styles have in common? They all appear to be innate strengths that become preferred modes of dealing with information. Because they are preferred, they are continually strengthened through practice. There is some controversy regarding the degree to which students should be encouraged to develop their less preferred avenues of learning. In special education, the conventional wisdom is to teach to a child's strengths. Children enjoy learning more when they have the opportunity to build on their strengths. If, temperamentally, a young child has a tendency toward withdrawal, is slow to adapt, and has intense reactions, it is often effective to adapt to the child by allowing his or her mother to stay for the first week of kindergarten. A child with a high activity level, who is distractible and has a short attention span (three variables of temperament) is less likely to be successful in a classroom in which children sit for long periods of time than in a classroom with lots of action and activity. Of course, it is necessary for children to develop skills in areas that are not their strengths, but successful teachers capitalize on their students' temperaments and learning preferences while at the same time encouraging students to improve in their weak areas.

Timing is also an important consideration. When an introvert decides to overcome his or her fear of public speaking, the chances are that the student will be successful because he or she is internally ready for the challenge. However, when all students, regardless of type, are required to speak before large audiences, some introverts may be traumatized by the experience. An alternative approach is to allow the introverted student to videotape a prepared presentation or to present his or her speech to a small group of trusted friends instead of to the whole class. In this way, the desired skills are learned without the risk of damaging the child. Creative adaptations such as these provide a safe environment in which a student can grow and indicate respect for each student's individuality.

When gifted students are taught about temperament, overexcitabilities, personality types, and learning styles, they can assist their teachers in fine-tuning approaches so that they can learn more effectively. It takes more planning to individualize teaching strategies for differences in learning style, but a small investment in time results in rewarding, exciting classroom experiences for everyone.

References〜

Ackerman, C. M. (1993). *Investigating an alternate method of identifying gifted students.* Unpublished master's thesis, University of Calgary, Calgary, Alberta.

Ackerman, C. M. (in press). Identifying gifted adolescents using personality characteristics: Dabrowski's overexcitabilities. *Roeper Review.*

Ammirato, S. P. (1987). *Comparison study of instruments used to measure developmental potential according to Dabrowski's theory of emotional development.* Unpublished doctoral dissertation, University of Denver, Denver, CO.

Barbe, W. B., Swassing, R. H., & Milone, M. N. (1979a). *The Swassing-Barbe Modality Index: Zaner-Bloser Modality Kit.* Columbus, OH: Zaner-Bloser.

Barbe, W. B., & Swassing, R. H., with M. N. Milone. (1979b). *Teaching through modality strengths: Concepts and practices*. Columbus, OH: Zaner-Bloser.

Benbow, C. P. (1986). Physiological correlates of extreme intellectual precocity. *Neuropsychologia, 24,* 719–725.

Benbow, C. P. (1992). Mathematical talent: Its nature and consequence. In N. Colangelo, S. G. Assouline, & D. L. Ambroson (Eds.), *Talent development: Proceedings of the 1991 Henry B. and Jocelyn Wallace National Research Symposium on Talent Development* (pp. 95–123). Unionville, NY: Trillium.

Bireley, M. (1991). Learning styles: One way to help gifted adolescents understand and choose lifestyles. In M. Bireley & J. Genshaft (Eds.), *Understanding the gifted adolescent: Educational, developmental, and multicultural issues* (pp. 189–200). New York: Teachers College Press.

Black, J. D. (1980). Publisher's foreword. In Myers, I. B., with Myers, P. B., *Gifts differing* (pp. ix–xii). Palo Alto, CA: Consulting Psychologists Press.

Bogen, J. E. (1969). The other side of the brain. II: An appositional mind. *Bulletin of the Los Angeles Neurological Society, 34,* 135–162.

Boring, E. G. (1950). *A history of experimental psychology* (2nd ed.). Englewood Cliffs, NJ: Prentice-Hall.

Bradway, K. (1964). Jung's psychological types. *Journal of Analytical Psychology, 9,* 129–135.

Breard, N. S. (1994). *Exploring a different way to identify gifted African-American students*. Unpublished doctoral dissertation, University of Georgia, Athens, GA.

Bruner, J. S. (1973). *Beyond the information given*. New York: Norton.

Bruner, J. S., Goodnow, J. J., & Austin, G. A. (1966). *A study of thinking*. New York: Wiley.

Buerschen, T. (1995). *Researching an alternative assessment in the identification of gifted and talented students*. Unpublished research project, Miami University, Oxford, OH.

Calic, S. (1994). *Heightened sensitivities as an indicator of creative potential in visual and performing arts*. Athens: University of Georgia.

Card, C. N. W. (1994). *Discover the power of introversion: What most introverts are never told and extraverts learn the hard way*. Gladwyne, PA: C. O. Type and Temperament Press.

Carlson, N. R. (1995). *Foundations of physiological psychology* (3rd ed.). Boston: Allyn & Bacon.

Cattell, R. B. (1963). Theory of fluid and crystallized intelligence: A critical experiment. *Journal of Educational Psychology, 54,* 1–22.

Dabrowski, K. (1937). Psychological bases of self-mutilation. *Genetic Psychology Monographs, 19,* 1–104.

Dabrowski, K. (1964). *Spoleczno-wychowawcza psychiatria dziecieca* (2nd ed.) [Social-educational child psychiatry]. Warsaw: Panstwowy Zaklad Wydawnictw Szkolnych. (Original work published 1959)

Dabrowski, K., with A. Kawczak & M. M. Piechowski. (1970). *Mental growth through positive disintegration*. London: Gryf.

Das, J. P., Kirby, J., & Jarman, R. F. (1979). *Simultaneous and successive cognitive processes*. New York: Academic.

Dauber, S. L., & Benbow, C. P. (1990). Aspects of personality and peer relations of extremely talented adolescents. *Gifted Child Quarterly, 34,* 10-15.

Delbridge-Parker, L. (1988). *Two perspectives on gifted students: Time one of a longitudinal study of academically gifted Iowa students, and program evaluation of CY-TAG, a summer residential program for highly gifted seventh and eighth grade students*. Unpublished doctoral dissertation, Iowa State University, Ames.

Delbridge-Parker, L., & Robinson, D. C. (1989). Type and academically gifted adolescents. *Journal of Psychological Type, 17,* 66–72.

Dixon, J. P. (1983). *The spatial child*. Springfield, IL: Charles C Thomas.

Domroese, C. (1993). *Investigating an alternate method for identifying gifted students*. Research project, Oak Park Elementary School District #97, Oak Park, IL.

Doyle, Sir A. C. (1930). *The complete Sherlock Holmes*. New York: Doubleday. (Original work published 1892)

Dunn, R. (1983). Learning style and its relation to exceptionality at both ends of the spectrum. *Exceptional Children, 49*, 496–506.

Dunn, R., & Dunn, K. (1975). *Learning style inventory.* Lawrence, KS: Price Systems. (Revised edition, with G. Price, 1979)

Ely, E. (1995). *The overexcitability questionnaire: An alternative method for identifying creative giftedness in seventh grade junior high school students.* Unpublished doctoral dissertation, Kent State University, Kent, OH.

Falk, R. F., Manzanero, J. B., & Miller, N. B. (in press). Developmental potential in Venezuelan and American artists: A cross-cultural validity study. *Creativity Research Journal.*

Falk, R. F., Piechowski, M., & Lind, S. (1994). *Criteria for rating the intensity of overexcitabilities.* Unpublished manuscript, University of Akron, Department of Sociology.

Farris, D. (1991). *Type tales.* Palo Alto, CA: Consulting Psychologists Press.

Felder, R. F. (1982, October). *Developmental potential of chemical engineering and gifted education graduate students.* Paper presented at the 29th Annual Convention of National Association for Gifted Children, New Orleans, LA.

Gallagher, S. A. (1985). A comparison of the concept of overexcitabilities with measures of creativity and school achievement in sixth grade students. *Roeper Review, 8,* 115–119.

Gallagher, S. A. (1990). Personality patterns of the gifted. *Understanding Our Gifted, 3*(1), 1, 11–13.

Gardner, H. G. (1983). *Frames of mind: The theory of multiple intelligences.* New York: Basic Books.

Gazzaniga, M. S. (1985). *The social brain: Discovering the networks of the mind.* New York: Basic Books.

Geschwind, N., & Behan, P. (1982). Left-handedness: Association with immune disease, migraine, and developmental learning disorders. *Proceedings of the National Academy of Science, USA, 79,* 5097–5100.

Gottfried, A. W., Gottfried, A. E., Bathurst, K., & Guerin, D. W. (1994). *Gifted IQ: Early developmental aspects* (The Fullerton longitudinal study). New York: Plenum.

Guisewite, C. (1994). *Hallmark stickers.* Kansas City, MO: Hallmark Cards.

Hafenstein, N. L. (1986). *The relationship of intellectual giftedness, information processing style, and reading ability in young gifted children.* Unpublished doctoral dissertation, University of Denver, Denver, CO.

Hall, C. S., & Lindzey, G. (1970). *Theories of personality* (2nd ed.). New York: Wiley.

Harvey, S., & Seeley, K. R. (1984). An investigation of the relationships among intellectual and creative abilities, extracurricular activities, achievement, and giftedness in a delinquent population. *Gifted Child Quarterly, 28,* 73–79.

Helson, R. (1965). Childhood interest clusters related to creativity in women. *Journal of Consulting Psychology, 29,* 352–361.

Hoehn, L., & Bireley, M. K. (1988). Mental processing preferences of gifted children. *Illinois Council for the Gifted Journal, 7,* 28–31.

Hollingworth, L. S. (1939). What we know about the early selection and training of leaders. *Teachers College Record, 40,* 575–592.

Horn, J. L. (1976). Human abilities: A review of research theory in the early 1970s. *Annual Review of Psychology, 27,* 437–485.

Jackson, N. (in press). Strategies for modeling the development of giftedness in children: Reconciling theory and method. In R. Horowitz & R. Friedman (Eds.), *The gifted and talented: Theories and reviews.* Washington, DC: American Psychological Association.

Jackson, P. S. (1995). *Bright star: black sky. Origins and manifestations of the depressed state in the lived experience of the gifted adolescent. A phenomenological study.* Unpublished master's thesis, Vermont College, Norwich University, Norwich, VT.

Jung, C. G. (1938). *Psychological types or the psychology of individuation.* (H. G. Baynes, Trans.). London: Kegan Paul, Trench, Trubner & Co., Ltd. (Original work published 1923)

Kaufman, A. S. (1984). K–ABC and giftedness. *Roeper Review, 7,* 83–88.

Kaufman, A. S., & Kaufman, N. L. (1983). *Kaufman Assessment Battery for Children.* Circle Pines, MN: American Guidance Service.

Keefe, J. W., & Monk, J. S. (1986). *Learning style profile*. Reston, VA: National Association of Secondary School Principals.

Keirsey, D., & Bates, M. (1978). *Please understand me: Character and temperament types*. Del Mar, CA: Prometheus Nemesis Books.

Kolb, D. A. (1976). *Learning style inventory.* Boston: McBer.

Lawrence, G. (1982). *People types and tiger stripes: A practical guide to learning styles* (2nd ed.). Gainesville, FL: Center for Applications of Psychological Type.

Levy, J. (1980). Cerebral asymmetry and the psychology of man. In M. C. Wittrock (Ed.), *The brain and psychology* (pp. 245–321). New York: Academic.

Lewis, G. (1984). Alternatives to acceleration for the highly gifted child. *Roeper Review, 6*, 133–136.

Lohman, D. F. (1989). Human intelligence: An introduction to advances in theory and research. *Review of Educational Research, 59*, 333–373.

Lohman, D. F. (1994). Spatially gifted, verbally inconvenienced. In N. Colangelo, S. G. Assouline, & D. L. Ambroson (Eds.), *Talent development: Proceedings from the 1993 Henry B. and Jocelyn Wallace National Research Symposium on Talent Development* (pp. 251–264). Dayton, OH: Ohio Psychology Press.

Luria, A. (1961). *The role of speech in the regulation of normal and abnormal behavior*. New York: Liveright.

Luria, A. (1973). *The working brain: An introduction to neuropsychology* (B. Haigh, Trans.). New York: Basic Books.

Lysy, K. Z., & Piechowski, M. M. (1983). Personal growth: An empirical study using Jungian and Dabrowskian measures. *Genetic Psychology Monographs, 108*, 267–320.

MacKinnon, D. W. (1962). The nature and nurture of creative talent. *American Psychologist, 17*, 484–495.

MacKinnon, D. W. (1965). Personality and the realization of creative potential. *American Psychologist, 20*, 273–281.

Maker, C. J. (1975). *Training teachers for the gifted and talented: A comparison of models.* Reston, VA: Council for Exceptional Children.

Manzanero, J. (1985). *A cross-cultural comparison of overexcitability profiles and levels of emotional development between American and Venezuelan artists.* Unpublished master's thesis, University of Denver, Denver, CO.

Meckstroth, E. (1991, December). *Coping with sensitivities of gifted children.* Paper presented at the Illinois Gifted Education Conference, Chicago, IL.

Meisgeier, C., & Murphy, E. (1987). *Murphy-Meisgeier Type Indicator for Children.* Palo Alto, CA: Consulting Psychologists Press.

Miller, N. B., Silverman, L. K., & Falk, R. F. (1994). Emotional development, intellectual ability and gender. *Journal for the Education of the Gifted, 18*, 20–38.

Myers, I. B. (1962). *Manual: The Myers-Briggs Type Indicator*. Palo Alto, CA: Consulting Psychologists Press.

Myers, I. B., & McCaulley, M. H. (1985). *Manual: A guide to the development and use of the Myers-Briggs Type Indicator*. Palo Alto, CA: Consulting Psychologists Press.

Myers, I. B., with P. B. Myers (1980). *Gifts differing*. Palo Alto, CA: Consulting Psychologists Press.

Nelson, K. C. (1992). Kazimierz Dabrowski: Poland's gifted "outsider." In N. Colangelo, S. G. Assouline, & D. L. Ambroson (Eds.), *Talent development: Proceedings of the 1991 Henry B. and Jocelyn Wallace National Research Symposium on Talent Development* (pp. 362–364). Unionville, NY: Trillium.

Nixon, L. (1996). Factors predispositional of creativity and mysticism: A comparative study of Charles Darwin and Therese of Lisieux. *Advanced Development*.

Northern, J. L., & Downs, M. P. (1994). *Hearing in children* (4th ed.). Baltimore, MD: Williams & Wilkins.

O'Boyle, M. W., & Benbow, C. P. (1990). Enhanced right hemisphere involvement during cognitive processing may relate to intellectual precocity. *Neuropsychologia, 28*, 211–216.

Perrin, J. (1982). *Learning style inventory: Primary version*. Jamaica, NY: St. John's University, Learning Styles Network.

Piechowski, M. M. (1974). Two developmental concepts: Multilevelness and developmental potential. *Counseling Values, 18*(2), 86–93.

Piechowski, M. M. (1979). Developmental potential. In N. Colangelo & R. T. Zaffrann (Eds.), *New voices in counseling the gifted* (pp. 25–57). Dubuque, IA: Kendall/Hunt.

Piechowski, M. M. (1992). Giftedness for all seasons: Inner peace in a time of war. In N. Colangelo, S. G. Assouline, & D. L. Ambroson (Eds.), *Talent development: Proceedings of the 1991 Henry B. and Jocelyn Wallace National Research Symposium on Talent Development* (pp. 180–203). Unionville, NY: Trillium.

Piechowski, M. M. (1995, July). OE origins. *The Dabrowski Newsletter, 1*(4), 2–4.

Piechowski, M. M., & Colangelo, N. (1984). Developmental potential of the gifted. *Gifted Child Quarterly, 28,* 80–88.

Piechowski, M. M., & Cunningham, K. (1985). Patterns of overexcitability in a group of artists. *Journal of Creative Behavior, 19*(3), 153–174.

Piechowski, M. M., & Miller, N. B. (1995). Assessing developmental potential in gifted children: A comparison of methods. *Roeper Review, 17,* 176–180.

Piechowski, M. M., Silverman, L. K., & Falk, R. F. (1985). Comparison of intellectually and artistically gifted on five dimensions of mental functioning. *Perceptual and Motor Skills, 60,* 539–549.

Piirto, J. (1990). Profiles of creative adolescents. *Understanding Our Gifted, 2*(3), 1, 10–12.

Piirto, J. (1992). *Understanding those who create.* Dayton, OH: Ohio Psychology Press.

Plato's Republic. (1944). (B. Jowett, Trans.). New York: Vintage Books. (Original work published 1871)

Price, G. E., Dunn, K., Dunn, R., & Griggs, S. (1981). Studies in students' learning styles. *Roeper Review, 4*(2), 38–40.

Provost, J. A. (1988). *Procrastination: Using psychological type concepts to help students.* Gainesville, FL: Center for Applications of Psychological Type.

Rankel, M. D. (1994, October). Creativity through Dabrowski's eyes. *The Dabrowski Newsletter,* pp. 2, 4.

Renzulli, J. S., & Smith, L. H. (1978). *Learning styles inventory.* Mansfield Center, CT: Creative Learning Press.

Riding, R. J. (1983). Extraversion, field independence, and performance on cognitive tasks in twelve-year-old children. *Research in Education, 29,* 1–9.

Roedell, W. C., Jackson, N. E., & Robinson, H. B. (1980). *Gifted young children.* New York: Columbia University, Teachers College.

Rogers, M. T. (1986). *A comparative study of developmental traits of gifted and average children.* Unpublished doctoral dissertation, University of Denver, Denver, CO.

Rogers, M. T., & Silverman, L. K. (1988). Recognizing giftedness in young children. *Understanding Our Gifted, 1*(2), 5, 16–17, 20.

Rowe, M. B. (1974). Relation of wait-time and rewards to the development of language, logic, fate control: Part II. Rewards. *Journal of Research in Science Teaching, 11,* 291–308.

Runions, T. (1988). *The individualized school.* Unpublished manuscript.

Schiever, S. W. (1985). Creative personality characteristics and dimensions of mental functioning in gifted adolescents. *Roeper Review, 7,* 223–226.

Silver, H. F., & Hanson, J. R. (1978). *The Hanson-Silver Learning Preference Inventory.* Moorestown, NJ: Institute for Cognitive and Behavioral Studies.

Silver, H. F., & Hanson, J. R. (1980). *User's manual: The TLC Learning Preference Inventory.* Moorestown, NJ: Institute for Cognitive and Behavioral Studies.

Silverman, L. K. (1982). [Overexcitabilities of gifted education graduate students]. Unpublished raw data.

Silverman, L. K. (1983). Personality development: The pursuit of excellence. *Journal for the Education of the Gifted, 6*(1), 5–19.

Silverman, L. K. (1985). [Myers-Briggs Type Indicator scores for graduate students in gifted education]. Unpublished raw data.

Silverman, L. K. (1986). Parenting young gifted children. *Journal of Children in Contemporary Society, 18,* 73–87.

Silverman, L. K. (1989a). Invisible gifts, invisible handicaps. *Roeper Review, 12,* 27–42.

Silverman, L. K. (1989b). The visual-spatial learner. *Preventing School Failure, 34*(1), 15–20.

Silverman, L. K. (1993a). Counseling families. In L. K. Silverman (Ed.), *Counseling the gifted and talented* (pp. 151–178). Denver, CO: Love.

Silverman, L. K. (1993b). A developmental model for counseling the gifted and talented. In L. K. Silverman (Ed.), *Counseling the gifted and talented* (pp. 51–78). Denver, CO: Love.

Silverman, L. K. (in press). Toward the construction of an instrument to assess visual-spatial learners. In N. Colangelo & S. G. Assouline (Eds.), *Talent development: Proceedings from the 1995 H. B. and Jocelyn Wallace National Research Symposium on Talent Development.* Dayton, OH: Ohio Psychology Press.

Silverman, L. K., & Ellsworth, B. (1980). The theory of positive disintegration and its implications for giftedness. In N. Duda (Ed.), *Theory of positive disintegration: Proceedings of the third international conference* (pp. 179–194). Miami, FL: University of Miami School of Medicine.

Snow, R. E. (1981). Toward a theory of aptitude for learning: Fluid and crystallized abilities and their correlates. In M. P. Friedman, J. P. Das, & N. O'Connor (Eds.), *Intelligence and learning* (pp. 345–362). New York: Plenum.

Sorell, G. T., & Silverman, L. K. (1983). [Emotional development of women in mid-life]. Unpublished raw data.

Sternberg, R. J. (1985). *Beyond IQ: A triarchic theory of human intelligence.* Cambridge: Cambridge University Press.

Stewart, E. D. (1981). Learning styles among gifted/talented students: Instructional technique preferences. *Exceptional Children, 48,* 134–138.

Taylor, J. (Ed.). (1958). *Selected writings of John Hughlings Jackson.* New York: Basic Books. (Original work published 1932)

Terman, L. M., & Merrill, M. A. (1973). *The Stanford-Binet Intelligence Scale: Manual for the Third Revision Form L-M.* Boston: Houghton Mifflin.

Thomas, A., Chess, S., & Birch, H. G. (1968). *Temperament and behavior disorders in children.* New York: New York University Press.

Thorndike, R. L. (1963). *The concepts of over- and under-achievement.* New York: Columbia University, Teachers College.

Thorndike, R. L., Hagen, E. P., & Sattler, J. M. (1986). *The Stanford-Binet Intelligence Scale: Fourth edition.* Technical manual. New York: Riverside.

Tolan, S. S. (1995, May). *Honoring the mind.* Keynote address presented at the Hollingworth Center for Highly Gifted Children Conference, Boston, MA.

Watson, R. I. (1978). *The great psychologists* (4th ed.). Philadelphia: Lippincott.

West, T. G. (1991). *In the mind's eye: Visual thinkers, gifted people with learning difficulties, computer images, and the ironies of creativity.* Buffalo, NY: Prometheus Books.

Wittrock, M. C. (1978). Education and the cognitive processes of the brain. In J. S. Chall & A. F. Mirsky (Eds.), *Education and the brain* (77th yearbook of the National Society for the Study of Education, Part II, pp. 61–102). Chicago: University of Chicago Press.

Study Questions ⟿

1. Why are considerations of personality and learning style of importance in program development for both students and staff?

2. Describe at least three theoretical frameworks for understanding temperament. What are some differences between the gifted and the general population in relation to these models?

3. What should a teacher be sensitive to when planning instruction for a child with high intellectual overexcitability? For one with high emotional OE? For one with high psychomotor OE? Which types of OEs appear to correlate very highly with giftedness?

4. It appears that a preponderance of gifted students are either INFPs or INTPs. What are the characteristics that these acronyms represent? Can you identify at least one instructional adaptation that would relate to each dimension?
5. What are some differences between visual-spatial learners and auditory-sequential learners? Why are such learning characteristics important? Which group of learners is more likely to suffer if such differences go unrecognized?
6. How critical is the assessment of personality and learning style in working with the gifted? How might such data be used in tandem with intellectual assessment data to provide effective services?

Giftedness in Early Childhood

Ken Seeley

Recently, the mother of a 5-year-old girl called me looking for advice about finding a good school for her daughter. She had taken her daughter Tracey to the neighborhood public school "kindergarten roundup," where the children were screened prior to regular enrollment. She said Tracey had never been evaluated by a psychologist, but that she suspected she was very bright. When I asked what Tracey did that made her think that, I heard an incredible list of outstanding abilities. Tracey was talking in complete sentences when she was 18 months old, and she began reading before age 3. Her mother reported that Tracey now had an "adult vocabulary." When I asked what that meant, she reported that Tracey was able to do most newspaper crossword puzzles successfully. She also said that Tracey was good at playing cards and could fill in easily as a fourth for bridge with her mother's bridge club when one of the members was absent. When I asked what the school said after the kindergarten screening, the mother reported that the teacher was very excited about Tracey's skills, saying that Tracey knew all of her letters and could count to 100. That started the search for a school and ultimately a call to me as part of the search. Clearly, we all have a lot of work to do to find and nurture the Traceys of the world and to create appropriate educational opportunities.

As infants and toddlers, children often astound their parents with amazing feats of developmental growth. The parents can appreciate the rapid changes they observe in their children and often wonder, "Are they above normal or average?" Experts tell parents that their children are behaving in a particular "range of development" and provide percentile estimates typically tied, for infants and toddlers, to physical growth milestones and, for preschoolers, to language and social development. As a result of such broad developmental descriptions, many gifted children are undetected in early childhood unless their talent is prodigious and only emerge as gifted in the elementary-school years. Tracey's mother thought her child was a "little above average." Indeed, many parents of gifted young children think that their children are average and are intimidated by the myth that "all parents think their kids are gifted." The challenge of identifying giftedness in young children and then deciding how to nurture that talent is the focus of this chapter. The chapter presents the range of giftedness in early childhood and describes how educators can use a developmental approach to young children with high abilities.

The Views of Giftedness ⌇

Most definitions of giftedness include superior intellectual ability as a major component. However, a unitary view of giftedness—one that takes only intellectual ability into account—does not serve children well and particularly is a problem for young children, whose rapid and uneven development may confound normal measures of intellect. Most enlightened professionals today view giftedness and intelligence as multidimensional and manifested primarily as advanced development at early ages.

Most definitions of giftedness derive from studies that have compared groups of gifted children, often identified by IQ tests, with groups from a general population. The landmark work of Terman and his colleagues (Burks, Jensen, & Terman, 1930; Oden, 1968; Terman & Oden, 1947) laid the groundwork for current research methodologies, which typically limit the definition of giftedness among young children to IQ measures from age 2 on. As Tannenbaum (1992) observed,

> For inasmuch as IQ scores explain no more than 25% to 50% of the variance in scholastic achievement, and the earliest assessments of any kind explain no more than 10% to 50% of the variance in IQ, any attempt to connect children's beginning signs of cognition with eventual school performance must remain suspect. Yet there is no way to avoid reviewing evidence on the earliest correlates of IQ since these are virtually the only kinds of data presented in the research literature on symptoms of precocity among infants and toddlers. (p. 115)

Just as it is problematic to define giftedness only in terms of IQ, we cannot ignore this characteristic as an early indicator of high potential. Indeed, even Terman warned that gifted children demonstrated variability with respect to every trait measured in his sample. Terman and Oden (1947) stated that their subjects did not conform to unitary patterns of abilities and characteristics even though all of them had high IQ scores. For instance, in Terman's sample with average IQs of 151, only half learned to read before kindergarten.

We must also be sensitive to the fact that most studies of young children and their families have not well represented low income or diverse populations. Later in this chapter, a case study is presented of a program for high-ability young children in a low-income neighborhood.

Early Indicators of Giftedness ⁓

Terman (1926) reported that his sample of intellectually gifted children showed advanced development during infancy. For example, they walked and talked at earlier ages than other children. However, his attempts at correlating early developmental indicators with later IQ have not been confirmed by later studies. Willerman and Fiedler (1977) tested a sample of 114 four-year-olds with IQs of 140 and above and tested the children again at age 7 with the Bayley Scales. They then compared their performance on the Bayley Scales of Mental and Motor Development administered when the children were 8 months old. None of the developmental tasks on the Bayley were correlated with later IQ performance. Essentially, early development is not necessarily predictive of later intellectual ability. The Willerman and Fiedler study supported Bayley's (1955) earlier Berkeley Growth Study, which found that early developmental tasks such as motor coordination, memory, and discrimination do not predict IQ scores of youth at age 16 and 17 years.

More recent research tends to show that some early indicators of giftedness do appear in infancy. The characteristics of attention, alertness, and preference toward novel objects in the environment seem to relate to later intellectual talent (Fisher, 1990; Lewis & Brooks-Gunn, 1981; Storfer, 1990). Subsequent work by Lewis and Louis (1991) described the evolution of signs of talent from infancy through the preschool years. They found that as the child gets older, the indicators of giftedness become clearer and more stable. This is logical given that the children are easier to test with conventional measures because they have more language and cognitive skills. Some of the major characteristics of giftedness reported by these authors include:

- Attention
- Question frequency
- Advanced language
- Abstract thinking
- Memory
- Task motivation
- Persistence
- Social skills
- Curiosity
- Advanced humor
- Creative play
- Sensitivity to discrepancies

In addition to these characteristics, it is common to observe greater social-emotional maturity among young gifted children than other children. The research indicates that in choice of friends, play interests, socialization, and moral judgments, young gifted children operate at a much higher age expectancy (Janos & Robinson, 1985; Robinson & Noble, 1991) than children of average ability. Roedell (1980), who studied preschool children at the University of Washington, found that gifted children had higher levels of social understanding, as reported by self-assessment, and more mature views of friendship and social problem-solving than did average children. In most other areas of social-emotional development, she found that gifted preschoolers were within the same range of social behaviors as children with average intelligence. Other social characteristics that distinguish gifted young children were reported by Kitano (1985), who also studied a special preschool program. She found that gifted children were more competitive, independent, and task motivated than children of average intelligence.

Prodigious Talent ~

No discussion of gifted young children would be complete without some mention of child prodigies. In the mind of the general public, gifted young children conjure up a view of the prodigies who perform at the adult level of skill in their respective talent area. The exciting and magical image of Mozart performing for the kings of Europe at age 4 has come to characterize young gifted children. It is unfortunate for many young children with high potential that this yardstick is considered the standard for "truly gifted," for such a level of genius occurs in perhaps one in ten million children (Tannenbaum, 1992). It is unfair and unrealistic for parents or educators to expect this level of talent when evaluating young children. If the expectancy is so high, adults may dismiss early signs of giftedness as not outstanding enough to warrant attention. Although prodigies deserve special attention and sensitive planning, they are not at all typical of most young gifted children.

It appears that child prodigies are "born" with their particular talent, because very early in the child's development, the talent is very highly developed. Talent areas are typically in music, chess, mathematics, creative writing, and languages; they are rarely in visual art, science, or leadership. As with most gifted children, it is difficult to categorize prodigies into a set of predictable behavior patterns. Other than having a prodigious talent, they are very different in personality, temperament, family history, and personal interests. Feldman (1980) reported that prodigies exhibit in narrow areas advanced development that defies the norms anticipated by the Piagetian theory of "universal and sequential" development. Feldman (1986) also found that the prodigies he studied did not always pursue their talent area as adults. Some chose related fields and some went into entirely different fields of human endeavor.

The studies of prodigies make for interesting reading and offer fascinating case studies of human genius. Educators who are interested in this area should refer to the work of Feldman, cited earlier, and particularly to the works of Bamburger (1986), Montour (1976), Radford (1990), and Simonton (1988). The remainder of this chapter addresses the needs of and interventions for the majority of gifted young children, not the special cases represented by child prodigies.

Families of Young Gifted Children ~

Young children are particularly dependent on and close to their families, so it is important to discuss the influences of family background and interactions on the identification and development of giftedness. There is abundant evidence that early stimulation and interactive language between parents, caretakers, and children contribute to earlier language, reading, and cognitive skills for all young children. This is especially true for gifted children. Carew (1980), Klein (1993), and Moss (1990) found direct relationships between parent stimulation and the development of children's abilities in language, problem-solving, spatial, and artistic aptitudes.

Many children with high IQs come from middle- and upper-income families, as evidenced by many of the studies that report such findings (Barbe, 1955; Cattell, 1915; Hitchfield, 1973; Hollingworth, 1942; Terman & Oden, 1947). However, these studies are flawed by sample selection bias and testing bias that rewards children who have had rich and stimulating early language experiences. The information from the studies also fails to give an accurate representation of the high abilities of young children who come from low-income families and families with linguistic differences. Gifted children can be identified in all socioeconomic and ethnic groups.

Parents are the most well-informed sources of information about their children. To tap this information, educators can use numerous parent checklists, but basically educators of young gifted children need to interact with parents about their children in a way that uses the parents' experience as observers. After providing some basic characteristics of gifted children, they can merely ask parents if their children are gifted or ask about specific skill areas (Roedell, Jackson, & Robinson, 1980). Such informal interaction with the family can be very helpful in identifying giftedness in young children. Families are typically involved in identifying young gifted children because they observe something in their child that causes them to seek information. This early identification needs to be supported by professionals as a valid part of assessment, and it should be followed up with any further testing needed. Parents are very good informants. In the Seattle Project, which involved a longitudinal study of 300 gifted children who began schooling at the preschool level, researchers found a positive relationship between parent information and the children's test performance (Jackson & Robinson, 1977). Additionally, they found that parent information predicts the child's performance in later years. In summary, the family's role in the identification of young gifted children is absolutely essential.

The correlation between parents' education level and their children's intellectual ability and achievement is significant (Willerman & Fiedler, 1977). Also, families who read to their children regularly have a greater likelihood that the children will be early readers. There is no question that family background plays an important role in developing potential, but any children who are nurtured and read to in an environment that is warm and encourages verbal interaction and problem-solving will enjoy maximal development of their potential.

Identifying Young Gifted Children ~

For a variety of reasons, identification of young gifted children is fundamentally different from identification in older age-groups. There is some disagreement about whether the interpretation of early indicators remains stable into middle childhood. There is also wider and uneven development in this population than in older age-groups, as well as weaknesses in standardized performance tests, especially for special populations. These factors have led to the development of behavioral checklists that parents and educators can use to identify the early indicators of giftedness (Lewis & Louis, 1991; Robinson & Robinson, in press; Schwedel & Stonebrunner, 1983).

Rather than involving a "standard battery" of tests, the identification of young gifted children involves a more qualitative and interactive approach that has some standardized elements. The case has already been made for parent involvement as a primary source of information. Irwin and Bushnell (1980) recommended using observational approaches to assess young children. Such approaches can be used to:

1. Generate hypotheses about the child's strengths and challenges
2. Answer specific questions about the child
3. Develop a more accurate picture of the child's global comprehension and reasoning ability
4. Gain better understanding of both what the child knows and how the child uses what he or she knows
5. Evaluate or assess interactional behavior under a variety of conditions

The curriculum and instructional strategies outlined later in this chapter integrate observational methods both for the identification of gifted children and the ongoing planning for them.

Some basic assessment framework can be helpful in planning for the identification of giftedness in young children. The primary question about identification and assessment is, "For what purpose is the identification being made?" Is it because a parent is interested in obtaining more information about his or her child in order to prepare for long-term school planning? Perhaps the purpose is to qualify the child for a particular school program and to assure a good fit with that environment. It may be a school referral to determine a different class or pace of instruction for a child who is not being challenged in the present preschool setting. These are just some things to consider in planning with parents for a comprehensive assessment.

Going through some basic steps is the best way to devise the framework for assessment:

- *Step 1:* Begin with a parent interview to obtain developmental and anecdotal information about the child. Prior to the interview, parents should provide a developmental history and complete a behavioral checklist.
- *Step 2:* Make observations in natural settings as described earlier. The home or the child's school is usually the best place to observe "typical" behaviors.
- *Step 3:* Gather information from the child's teacher (if the child is enrolled in a preschool or child-care setting). As with the parent interview, behavioral

checklists completed before a live or phone interview with the child's teacher provide good background information.

- *Step 4:* Use some standardized and informal measures to get a more complete picture of the strengths and challenges of the child.
- *Step 5:* Aggregate the information into a picture of the child in the context of the home and the school in order to recommend the best methods to enhance the child's development immediately and for the longer term. The main purpose of assessment is to gather information for planning and decision-making. This final step is extremely important, as it affects many life decisions that parents and educators will make for the child.

Some discussion of standardized tests is in order because of the great deal of misinformation and mythology that have developed over the years with regard to researchers' attempts at defining and codifying "intelligence" in young children. The following are some of the myths about testing young children with IQ tests:

Myth: Young children cannot be tested because tests are not valid or reliable for early ages.

Response: There are standardized tests that are valid and reliable for many young children; and tests that are not valid and reliable should not be used for children of any age.

Myth: Verbal young children can score high on IQ tests causing false positives; that is, the tests will identify children as gifted who are not really gifted.

Response: If the test is valid and reliable, it will not give false positives. That is, children cannot do better than they are capable of doing. However, tests often give false negatives. Children do not always do as well as they are capable of doing for a variety of reasons, such as distractibility, testing environment, and lack of experience in test taking.

Myth: All parents think their children are gifted.

Response: Mounting evidence indicates that the reverse is true. Usually parents have very high expectations of their children's abilities before they are willing to even begin exploring the possibility of giftedness.

Specific examples of tests and procedures are given later in this chapter in the program case study. These examples are specific to the needs of a certain type of child and program in a diverse community. There is no magically prescribed test battery. Each child demands an appropriate, individualized assessment.

Early Childhood Programs ～

Quality programs designed to educate young children usually incorporate the best educational practices in the field. Early childhood is defined as birth to age 8, so the age span covers a series of developmental transitions—from home to preschool to kindergarten through the primary grades and, finally, to the middle grades at age 9. Typically, early childhood programs are child-centered, family-friendly, individualized, experiential, developmentally appropriate, warm, nurturing, attend to holistic needs of the child, and integrate theme-based curricula.

The long-standing philosophical position of early childhood educators has been to provide "developmentally appropriate practice." However, they have not been well informed about the potential for giftedness. Likewise, gifted educators have not been well informed about developmentally appropriate practice. The intersection of these two paradigms could greatly affect the education of young children (Barbour, 1993; Roedell, 1985). Unfortunately, developmentally appropriate practice has not had much impact on K–12 education; public education tends to neglect attention to development as the child gets older. For instance, it is not developmentally appropriate to have adolescents begin their school day at 7:30 A.M. with 50-minute periods in buildings with 3,000 students.

Many preschool programs for gifted children tend to use early extensions of programming models for older gifted children (e.g., Gardner's multiple intelligences, Bloom's taxonomy, the Vigotsky-Feuerstein model, and Renzulli's triad). A long-standing model program for the gifted is the Astor Program in New York, which has accepted 4-year-olds into kindergarten since 1974. Children are initially identified for this program by their parents and then tested using a Stanford-Binet IQ test. Specialized curricula and accelerated learning are used. The Astor Program is an excellent example of a model well-suited to children with high intellectual ability who would benefit from academic challenge in a developmentally oriented school. Children whose talents lie in different areas would benefit more from different programs. Many parents choose regular preschool options that allow children to move at their own pace, such as High Scope or Montessori (Hohmann, Banet, & Weikart, 1979). The best researched of those program options is High Scope, which is described in more detail in the following sections of this chapter as a cognitively oriented curriculum.

By continuing to draw parallels between gifted education and early childhood education, perhaps we can make some inroads into the longer term reform of these two educational specialties. To that end, the remaining section of this chapter is devoted to the adaptation of a curriculum and instructional model from early childhood education for gifted children. This model has been used in a program case study directed to a special population of high-ability children.

The Cognitively Oriented Curriculum ~

In the early 1960s the United States was facing major educational decline in its urban centers, with growing poverty, high juvenile crime rates, high numbers of school dropouts, and high teen pregnancy. The scene was similar to that in the 1990s. These conditions help justify looking to a very effective educational solution with over 30 years of experience and longitudinal research for our discussion of educating young children. What began as the Perry Preschool Project in Ypsilanti, Michigan, has become the foundation for national support of early childhood education. Although there are other successful models of early education, none has provided the same amount of longitudinal research to demonstrate its effectiveness as the High Scope Perry Preschool Project. The program designers were influenced by the work of J. McVicker Hunt (1963), described in Intelligence and Experience, and by the work of Jean Piaget (Piaget & Inhelder, 1969). The first major product of this early curriculum design was the instructional model called the Cognitively Oriented Curriculum (Weikart, Rogers, Adcock, & McClelland, 1971).

The Cognitively Oriented Curriculum, more commonly known as "High Scope," evolved during the 1970s from a teacher-directed instructional model to a child-directed learning environment. Driven by Piagetian theory, the teachers abandoned teaching developmental skills but developed a set of "key experiences" that allow children to invent their own understanding of life experiences. In the words of Banet, "The point of Piaget's epistemology is that children abstract underlying truths through active encounters with reality, not through active encounters with genetic epistemologists" (Hohmann, Banet, & Weikart, 1979, p. xv). This move from direct teaching to facilitating learning by empowering the learner to take charge is a powerful dynamic that characterizes both a good quality preschool and a good quality gifted education program. The intersection of gifted and early childhood education discussed earlier has its greatest likelihood for adoption through the High Scope Cognitively Oriented Curriculum. The values and cultures that form the foundations of both education specialties are extremely close.

Key Experiences

The building blocks of the Cognitively Oriented Curriculum are the key experiences, which are grouped into five areas: (1) active learning, (2) using language, (3) representing experiences and ideas, (4) developing logical reasoning, and (5) understanding time and space.

In key experiences in active learning, the child is:

1. Exploring actively with all the senses
2. Discovering relations through direct experience
3. Choosing materials, activities, and purposes
4. Acquiring skills with tools and equipment
5. Taking care of his or her own needs

In the area of using language, the child is:

1. Talking with others about personally meaningful experiences
2. Describing objects, events, and relations
3. Expressing feelings in words
4. Having his or her own spoken language written down by an adult and read back
5. Having fun with language: rhyming, creating stories, listening to stories and poems

In the area of representing experiences and ideas, the child is:

1. Recognizing objects by sound, touch, and smell
2. Imitating actions
3. Relating pictures, photographs, and models to real places and things
4. Role-playing, pretending
5. Making models out of clay, blocks, and other materials

In the area of developing logical reasoning for classification, the child is:

1. Investigating and labeling the attributes of things
2. Noticing and describing how things are the same and different
3. Describing things in several different ways
4. Describing the characteristics things do not possess
5. Holding more than one attribute in mind at a time
6. Distinguishing between "some" and "all"

In the area of developing logical reasoning through seriation, the child is:

1. Comparing sizes, weights, textures, lengths, widths, and so forth
2. Arranging several things in order along some dimension and describing the relations (the longest and shortest ones, etc.)

In the area of developing logical reasoning through number concepts, the child is:

1. Comparing number and amount
2. Comparing the number of items in two or more sets by matching them in one-to-one correspondence (Are there as many marbles as there are children in the room?)
3. Enumerating objects and counting by rote

In the area of understanding spatial relations, the child is:

1. Fitting things together and taking them apart
2. Rearranging sets of objects and observing and describing the spatial transformations (folding, twisting, tying, stacking, and so forth)
3. Observing things and places from different viewpoints
4. Experiencing and describing the position of things in relation to one another
5. Experiencing and describing relative distances among things and locations
6. Experiencing and representing his or her own body: how it is structured, what various body parts can do
7. Learning to locate things in the classroom, school, and neighborhood
8. Interpreting representations of spatial relations in drawings and pictures
9. Distinguishing and describing shapes

In the area of understanding time, the child is:

1. Planning and completing what he or she has planned
2. Describing and representing past events

3. Anticipating future events verbally and by making preparations
4. Starting and stopping an action on signal
5. Noticing, describing, and reporting the order of events
6. Experiencing and describing different rates of movement
7. Using conventional time units when talking about past and future events
8. Comparing time periods (short-long, new-old, and so forth)
9. Observing and reporting how clocks and calendars mark the passage of time
10. Observing and describing seasonal changes*

* Adapted from *Young Children in Action* by M. Hohmann, F. Banet, & D. Weikart, 1979, Ypsilanti, MI: High Scope Press. Used with permission of the author.

These key experiences, when adapted to learning pace and level, provide a framework for curriculum and instruction for gifted young children. There should be no attempt to prescribe ages for the activities, nor are they to be viewed as goals to be achieved and checked off. Rather, key experiences serve as the foundation for activities and materials in the learning environment. Gifted children could engage in these activities sooner and in greater depth than average-ability children. It is important to maintain the breadth of the experiences because they span the essential developmental tasks of early childhood. The adaptation of these ideas and activities for gifted young children can provide gifted educators with an outstanding developmentally based model that is supported by 30 years of research.

Cognitively Oriented Instruction

The cognitively oriented instructional model is best described as teacher-facilitated and child-directed. It takes a great deal of trust for educators to allow children to direct their own learning. It also takes a well-organized classroom that fosters independence and follows a learner-centered process and daily routine. Most cognitively oriented classrooms have learning centers with a broad spectrum of materials that are accessed independently by the children.

The simple instructional process suggested is *plan-do-review*. Before starting an activity, all children plan the time with the teacher, then they carry out their plan, and later they review what they did with the teacher. These learning habits are excellent ones for children to take to their later school experiences. During the "doing," or work, time, the teacher's role is to be a resource if needed and to record anecdotally what each child is doing in order to maintain progress records.

Whenever the idea of child-directed learning is proposed, teachers ask, "What if the child chooses the housekeeping area every day? How do we get balance?" The teacher must trust that the child will choose another activity area after a while. However, as facilitators, teachers can suggest other alternatives to the child and may take some individual time to introduce a new material to the child to open up new interests. The choice, however, still is with the child. As the High Scope staff suggest some balance between teacher-facilitated and child-directed activities, they strive to address the question, "How can the teaching staff provide the key experiences most supportive of learning and development for each child while acknowledging the child's own interests?" (Hohmann, Banet, & Weikart, 1979, p. 6).

Clayton Kids: A Program Case Study

The extensive background provided here and in the literature on the Cognitively Oriented Curriculum sets the stage for a program case study that provides a real-world example. Clayton Kids was founded in 1987 as a program for high-ability young children in a low-income neighborhood in Denver, Colorado. Many challenges were faced in initiating this program, identifying the children, selecting and training the staff, adapting the High Scope curriculum and instruction, arranging parent involvement, and planning for the long-term interests of the children.

Identifying the children began with the program initiators developing a close working relationship with Head Start centers and asking them to nominate their brightest stars, including those with possible hidden potential. The orientation of the Head Start staff involved a checklist and nomination form. If a child was nominated by a staff member or a parent, permission for assessment was obtained and the identification was begun. One assessor carried out all the necessary steps. The identification process typically followed these steps:

1. Review teacher or parent nomination
2. Obtain parent permission and give parent information about the new program
3. Observe the child in the Head Start classroom and record his or her behavior anecdotally
4. Administer individual tests, including the Raven's Standard Progressive Matrices, the CIRCUS battery (Educational Testing Service), and a play-based interview
5. Conduct a face-to-face parent interview to obtain family information and to explain the results of the testing and observations
6. Conduct a team staffing to review the identification data for all the children assessed and then to make final selections to obtain an initial class of 15 to 20 four- and five-year-old children.

Selecting and training the staff began with hiring the lead teacher, who would also be a trainer to all the new staff hired. Fortunately, a High Scope trainer/preschool teacher was found who brought both skills. Two teaching assistants were employed and trained by the lead teacher. They spent many hours obtaining materials to create a classroom with five learning centers: math, science, housekeeping, language, and art.

The adaptation of the Cognitively Oriented Curriculum went well after both the staff and students became acclimated to the new way of conducting learning. Initially, only the lead teacher was comfortable with child-directed learning. The children were accustomed to depending on their teacher to direct all activity. It took a while for the children to stop requesting, "Teacher, what do I do now?" Eventually, the children got into the routine of making their plan, carrying out their work, and then reviewing it with the teacher individually or during group time. It was equally difficult for the staff to refrain from direct teaching, particularly when the children kept requesting direction.

Having the learning centers and a daily routine that nurtured independence eventually got the staff and students into the mode of pursuing key experiences through the children's activities. Portfolios were developed for each child as part of their short-term and longer term work review process. Through the portfolios and reviews, children could see their own growth over time. The teacher's observational notes were also kept with the portfolios to remind the children of where they had been and where they might go next. In addition, the portfolios were the cornerstone of parent conferences.

The most powerful link to the children's homes was the home visitation program. One of the teaching assistants was assigned as the primary home visitor, but the teacher would also accompany the home visitor periodically for late afternoon or evening visits. The home visitor would assist the families with a variety of needs and also keep the focus of the visit on the child's learning and development. The home visitor supported the families with resources, referrals, and materials that could assist them with child discipline, with anger management, and with reinforcing educational experiences at home.

Planning for the long-term educational future of the children in the Clayton Kids program was both rewarding and frustrating. Clayton Kids was a half-day kindergarten program initially, and many of the children spent the other half of their day in a public school kindergarten nearby. After the children completed their kindergarten year, they would go on to regular school but would come back to an after-school program at Clayton. The long-term educational planning for these young children now carries them through elementary school with an adapted cognitively oriented, developmentally based curriculum. The next challenge is at the middle-school level.

This case study has been presented to illustrate that the determination and persistence of committed educators involved in a well-articulated comprehensive program can achieve great things for children. It was never easy, but the rewards of seeing both the children and their families grow over many years have made the struggles worthwhile. Long-term educational planning for gifted children is often missing in gifted education programs. Too often gifted preschools send the children on after they are "done" with preschool with little if any transition planning, let alone elementary-school planning. Clayton Kids is one success story of perseverance with a well-articulated program.

Summary ⁓

Young gifted children's needs often go unaddressed because the children are not identified until they are school age or older. This chapter has focused on some of the issues in early identification and has provided some guidelines for assessment, curriculum, and instruction. Moving from theory to practice, the chapter turned to a real-world model, Clayton Kids, a special population of gifted young children. The notion of working with key experiences in a developmentally based curriculum should provide an excellent foundation for undertaking program development for gifted children. If no early childhood gifted program is already in place, High Scope is a good place to begin planning. If an existing program is in place, High Scope offers a yardstick against which to test the current program for potential improvement.

When and whether to intervene in the life of a young gifted child will probably continue to be debated. The best approaches are found in how best to develop the potential of the child in the context of her or his family. Having options available for parents and their children can enhance the possibilities of the realization of that potential.

References ~

Bamburger, J. (1986). Cognitive issues in the development of musically gifted children. In R. Sternberg & J. Davidson (Eds.), *Conceptions of giftedness* (pp. 338–413). Cambridge: Cambridge University Press.

Barbe, W. B. (1955). Characteristics of gifted children. *Educational Administration and Supervision, 41,* 207–217.

Barbour, N. B. (1993). Early childhood gifted education: A collaborative perspective. In P. S. Klein & A. Tannenbaum (Eds.), *To be young and gifted* (pp. 145–147). Norwood, NJ: Ablex.

Bayley, N. (1955). *Berkeley growth study, Institute of Human Development.* University of California: Berkeley.

Burks, B., Jensen, D., & Terman, L. (1930). *The promise of youth: Follow-up studies of a thousand gifted children.* Stanford, CA: Stanford University Press.

Carew, J. (1980). *Experience and the development of intelligence in young children at home and in day care.* Monographs of the Society for Research in Child Development, 187.

Cattell, J. M. (1915). Families of American men of science. *Popular Science Monthly, 86,* 504–515.

Feldman, D. (1980). *Beyond universals in cognitive development.* Norwood, NJ: Ablex.

Feldman, D. (1986). *Nature's gambit.* New York: Basic Books.

Fisher, K. (1990). Interaction with infants is linked to later abilities. *Monitor,* April 1990, p. 10. Washington, DC: American Psychological Association.

Hitchfield, E. M. (1973). *In search of promise.* London: Longman Group Ltd.

Hohmann, M., Banet, F., & Weikart, D. (1979). *Young children in action.* Ypsilanti, MI: High Scope Press.

Hollingworth, L. (1942). *Children above 180 IQ.* New York: World Book.

Hunt, J. M. (1963). *Intelligence and experience.* New York: Basic Books.

Irwin, D. M., & Bushnell, M. (1980). *Observation strategies for child study.* Ft. Worth, TX: Harcourt & Brace.

Jackson, N. E., & Robinson, H. B. (1977). *Early identification of intellectually advanced children.* Annual report to the Spencer Foundation. Seattle: University of Washington, Child Development Research Group (ERIC ED 151095).

Janos, P. M., & Robinson, N. M. (1985). Psychosocial development in intellectually gifted children. In F. D. Horowitz (Ed.), *The gifted and talented: A developmental perspective* (pp. 149–195). Washington, DC: American Psychological Association.

Kitano, M. K. (1985). Ethnography of a preschool for the gifted: What gifted young children actually do. *Gifted Child Quarterly, 29,* 67–71.

Klein, P. S. (1993). Mediating the cognitive, social, and aesthetic development of precocious young children. In P. S. Klein & A. Tannenbaum (Eds.), *To be young and gifted* (pp. 222–245). Norwood, NJ: Ablex.

Lewis, M., & Brooks-Gunn, J. (1981). Visual attention at three months as a predictor of cognitive functioning at two years of age. *Intelligence, 5*(2), 131–140.

Lewis, M., & Louis, B. (1991). Young gifted children. In N. Colangelo & G. A. Davis (Eds.), *Handbook of gifted education* (pp. 365–381). Boston: Allyn & Bacon.

Montour, K. (1976). Three precocious boys: What happened to them? *Gifted Child Quarterly, 20,* 173–179.

Moss, E. (1990). Social interaction and metacognitive development in gifted preschoolers. *Gifted Child Quarterly, 34,* 16–20.

Oden, M. (1968). The fulfillment of promise: 40 year follow-up of the Terman gifted group. *Genetic Psychology Monographs, 77,* 3–93.

Piaget, J., & Inhelder, B. (1969). *The psychology of the child* (H. Weaver, Trans.). New York: Basic Books.

Radford, J. (1990). *Child prodigies and exceptional early achievers.* New York: Free Press.

Robinson, N. M., & Noble, K. D. (1991). Social-emotional development and adjustment of gifted children. In M. Wang, M. C. Reynolds, & H. J. Walberg (Eds.), *Handbook of special education: Research and practice* (Vol. 4, pp. 23–36). New York: Pergamon.

Robinson, N. M., & Robinson, H. B. (in press). *Teachers nurturing math talented young children.* Seattle, WA: Halbert B. Robinson Center for the Study of Capable Youth, University of Washington.

Roedell, W. C. (1980). Vulnerabilities of highly gifted children. *Roeper Review, 6*(3), 127–130.

Roedell, W. C. (1985). Developing social competence in gifted preschool children. *Remedial and Special Education, 6*(4), 6–11.

Roedell, W. C., Jackson, N. E., & Robinson, H. B. (1980). *Gifted young children.* New York: Teachers College Press.

Schwedel, A. M., & Stonebrunner, R. (1983). Identification. In M. B. Karnes (Ed.), *The underserved: Our young gifted children* (pp.195–213). Reston, VA: Council for Exceptional Children.

Simonton, D. K. (1988). *Scientific genius.* Cambridge: Cambridge University Press.

Storfer, M. D. (1990). *Intelligence and giftedness: The contributions of heredity and early environment.* San Francisco: Jossey-Bass.

Tannenbaum, A. (1992). Early signs of giftedness: Research and commentary. *Journal for the Education of the Gifted, 15,* 104–133.

Terman, L. M. (1926). *Genetic studies of genius: Vol. 1. Mental and physical traits of a thousand gifted children* (2nd ed.). Stanford, CA: Stanford University Press.

Terman, L. M., & Oden, M. (1947). *The gifted child grows up.* Stanford, CA: Stanford University Press.

Weikart, D., Rogers, L., Adcock, R. N., & McClelland, S. (1971). *The cognitively oriented curriculum.* Ann Arbor, MI: Campus Publishers.

Willerman, L., & Fiedler, M. (1977). Intellectually precocious preschool children. *Journal of Genetic Psychology, 131,* 13–20.

Study Questions ~

1. How is giftedness manifested in young children? What are developmental indicators of the gifted? What are social-emotional indicators? What are some traditional intellectual indicators?

2. How does the concept of the child prodigy relate to giftedness? Does that concept influence parental expectations regarding their own children?

3. What is the purpose of early identification of gifted children? What is an advisable strategy for executing such a process?

4. What are some considerations for optimal programming for gifted youngsters? What models in the literature illustrate quality programs at this level of development?

5. Why are disadvantaged gifted children less likely to be identified at young ages than their more affluent counterparts? Why is it important to focus special attention on this population?

5

Underachieving and Talented Learners with Disabilities

Ken Seeley

Peter is one of those children who has a disability that challenges teachers and parents. He is a bundle of contradictions. His oral verbal skills are above average, but at age 9 he is essentially a nonreader with almost no writing skills. His gross motor activity is excellent and his fine motor skills are about average for his age. Yet he does not do well in school on academic tasks and often exhibits behavior problems at school (although not at home). He has a keen interest in small engine repair and has built two go-carts from junk material. He knows all of the Indy 500 racers and can recite their track records and speeds with great accuracy from memory. Peter's label is "learning disability with attention deficit disorder." His performance IQ on the Wechsler Intelligence Scale for Children—Revised (WISC-R) is 128 with a verbal score of 90. Peter has been getting some help on his reading skills from the special education teacher and is making slow progress. His teacher recommends that he be put on Ritalin for his behavior problems in class. His parents have resisted because he is not a problem at home. Peter needs some specialized help, and he is not likely to get it in his current school. He is a child with gifts and disabilities that confound conventional educational approaches.

The term *gifted underachiever* is an ambiguous one. Gifted underachievers can be identified at all academic levels, although they are most frequently identified at the secondary level. To teachers, these students may seem lazy, uninterested, bored, rebellious, or generally irksome. They often are described in report cards as "capable of doing much better." The case can even be made that most gifted students could be identified as underachievers because they rarely are challenged sufficiently to match their potential level of achievement.

At the beginning of a discussion of the topic of gifted underachievers, it is helpful to review the definitions found in the literature. Table 5.1 lists sample definitions ranging from general to specific. Most authors agree that gifted underachieving students show significant discrepancy between academic performance (in class or on achievement tests) and tested intellectual ability in the upper range.

Table 5.1 ⁓
A Sample of Definitions of Underachieving Gifted Students

Authors	Definitions
Bricklin & Bricklin (1967)	Student whose day-by-day efficiency in school is much poorer than would be expected on the basis of intelligence
Fine (1967)	Student who ranks in the top third of intellectual ability but whose performance is dramatically below that level
Finney & Van Dalsel (1966)	Student who scored in the top 25% on the Differential Aptitude Test (DAT) in verbal-numerical score and whose grade point average (GPA) was below the mean for all students at the DAT level
Gowan (1957)	Student who performs 1 *SD* or more below his or her ability level
Newman (1974)	Student achieving significantly below the level statistically predicted by his/her IQ (GPA of C or below considered as significant)
Pringle (1970)	Student with IQ of 120 or above having educational or behavior difficulties
Shaw & McCuen (1960)	Student in upper 25% of the population on the Pinter General Ability Test (IQ over 110) who had earned a GPA below the mean of his/her class in grades 9–11
Thorndike (1963)	Student whose underachievement is measured in relation to some standard of expected or predicted achievement
Whitmore (1980)	Student who demonstrates exceptionally high capacity for academic achievement but is not performing satisfactorily for levels on daily academic tasks and achievement tests
Ziv (1977)	Student with a high IQ who has low grades in school

What Are the Causes of Underachievement? ∿

The research on underachievement has been inconsistent due to the variety of definitions used and the fact that variables have not been controlled from study to study. Sample selection has also varied widely. Tannenbaum (1983) summarized the research on underachievement by stating that:

> Underachievement should be regarded as a single symptom representing diverse etiologies. One type of underachiever fails to measure up to expectations because of overestimated general abilities; a second type possesses inadequate special aptitudes of any kind; a third type does not have the necessary drive, mental health, meta-learning habits or any other personality supports; a fourth type lacks the proper nurturance at home, at school and in the community; and a fifth type sinks into mediocrity through a series of misfortunes or distractions beyond anybody's control. Thus, the five factors that serve as links between potential and fulfillment are also clues to potential and failure. But it would be a mistake to assume that all underachievers suffer from all five handicaps. Each kind of deterrent can by itself make the difference between success and failure. (p. 224)

Whitmore (1980) described some of her research in a special program for underachieving gifted students in Cupertino, California. Student self-reports of the causes of their underachievement were used. The students indicated that the following factors at school contributed to their underachievement:

1. Perceived lack of genuine respect from teachers
2. A competitive social climate
3. Inflexibility and rigidity
4. Stress on external evaluation
5. The "failure syndrome" and criticism predominated except for those who were achieving and conforming
6. Constant adult/teacher control of the class
7. An unrewarding curriculum of textbook learning (pp. 192–193)

How Do We Find Underachievers? ∿

It is difficult to identify underachieving gifted students because they often perform at their grade level expectancy. Identification systems need to take into account this problem and look for less conventional signs of giftedness than academic performance and teacher nomination. Butler-Por (1987) suggested using a variety of procedures to look for giftedness, including:

1. Looking at discrepancies between high cognitive reasoning abilities and ordinary schoolwork mastery
2. Finding differences between high-interest topical reading and failure to complete general reading assignments
3. Observing task persistence at high levels of performance on topics of interest compared to ordinary or low motivation on schoolwork

4. Using teacher evaluation, student evaluation, and parent evaluation of strengths and weaknesses

These suggestions involve more than the typical assessment procedures used in the classroom, and if wide discrepancies are found, they should result in a referral for individual testing that might reveal high potential. Most learners perform unevenly across subject areas. What we are looking for is uneven performance that is significant based on the judgments of teachers, parents, and the students themselves. Examining this unevenness in greater detail is one of the best ways to begin discovering hidden potential.

Another approach to identifying gifted underachievers is to adopt an "at-risk" methodology (Seeley, 1993). This approach is borrowed from public health and has become popular in education as a means of identifying special populations of students who are at higher risk of school failure. It implies a strategy that has two major components: actively looking for "red flags" as signs of underachievement in all students, and taking special care in assessing abilities in the higher risk groups. With regard to the first component, the procedures suggested by Butler-Por, listed earlier, are good examples of the "red flags" or warning signs that might indicate a significant discrepancy between ability and potential.

The second component is to take more time and pay more attention to certain risk groups where potential may be overlooked. The most obvious group comprises those students with disabilities whom many would not think about as being potentially gifted. Typically, they might include low-income students, students of color, linguistically different students, delinquent students, discipline problems, girls, students with low motivation, and truants. Butler-Por (1991) added other risk groups, including unwanted children, children of divorce, and highly creative children. Special approaches and identification criteria need to be developed for each of these groups that go beyond nominations and testing. Strategies such as student and parent interviews, portfolio assessment, peer and community referral, and school and home observations should be employed.

Seeley (1987) interviewed 128 high-ability high-school students (upper quartile on nonverbal intelligence test) who were at risk for dropping out of school because of poor attendance, low grades, or behavior problems. Many already had dropped out but had returned to alternative schools. He also statistically analyzed the academic records of 2,000 middle-school students who were in the upper quartile in nonverbal intelligence. The latter students were studied to give a broader understanding of some of the causes of the at-risk conditions seen in the high-school sample.

Of particular interest is the finding that behavior and grades were reciprocally related. Not only did behavior problems cause poor grades, which was not surprising, but grading practices produced behavior problems. This vicious cycle caused underachievement for many students who failed in school not because of lack of mastery but, rather, because of lack of conformity to school rules.

Seeley's interview data clustered in five areas of concern: home/family, school environment, teachers, peer/social, and racial minority. Some of the more pertinent findings are as follows:

1. Ninety percent of the at-risk group were the middle or youngest children in their families.
2. Frequency of school change was a major factor in being at risk.
3. Teen pregnancy and drug use were not significant factors in the lives of these interviewees.
4. Teacher indifference was a major factor in poor achievement.
5. Competition with peers or family members was not influential.
6. Uneven academic performance was common.
7. The school treated minority students with behavior conflicts differently than it treated majority students, even though the characteristics of both groups were the same overall.
8. Family disruption (divorce, remarriage, separation) was twice as common as the normal expectancy.

The causes of underachievement are obviously multifaceted in scope and intensity. This discussion merely presents an overview of the problem. The final section about underachieving gifted students looks at intervention.

What Can We Do to Help Underachievers? ⌒

In planning intervention, it seems appropriate to abandon the medical model. If we were to address all of the research on the causes of underachievement, we would have to find specific prescriptions to ameliorate each cause. Although this goal is laudable, public education likely cannot provide the level of intensity necessary to achieve it. Rather, we should consider approaches to the general problem that suggest that schools be an inviting place, rather than a source of alienation and indifference, for underachievers. Alternative schools provide such an opportunity in many locales, but they should start earlier than the high-school–middle-school level.

To address the feelings of alienation and isolation among underachievers, a sense of "community" must be developed at school. Many mainstream students experience this feeling. Like most adolescents, underachieving students want to feel that they count in someone else's life. Their desire to find a caring environment at school also is tied to their need to be caring and giving about something important. School-sponsored community service options are excellent ways to involve students who might not choose pep club, football, or chorus as a means of feeling a part of the school community. Service projects within the school or community might offer an excellent opportunity for involvement.

Just as we need to modify our approaches to identification, we also need to change the educational strategies that we use when we teach gifted underachievers. The strategy should begin with constructing an individual learning plan built upon the following elements and action steps:

1. The assessment information from the identification procedures
2. The interest areas and strengths of the student
3. The family and home situation

4. The individual's personality factors of self-concept and motivation
5. The environmental risk factors causing the underachievement

Assessment Information. It is important to explain to the student and his or her family what the assessment information suggests. It may suggest that the student has a different learning style from the norm and would do well to study differently, or it may suggest the benefit of finding different teachers or even different schools. Most of all, it is important to not use the assessment to assign blame or emphasize weaknesses. Often the students or families blame themselves for not meeting expectations. Schools should also not be maligned for missing the potential in the student. The assessment is future directed and should bring about an appropriate course of action.

Interests and Strengths. Underachievers usually hear about their weaknesses or inadequacies. Even if they excel in one subject area, they often hear teachers say, "You are so good in math, why can't you do better in all your other subjects?" The individual learning plan should build on the positives and the special interests of the student. This is not to say that the other subject areas should be ignored but that an interest in rap music, for example, should be used to teach history or good skills in math should be capitalized on by teaching biographies of mathematicians. Most important, the student should help design the bridge from his or her interests to the academic requirements at school with the teacher's and parents' help.

Family and Home. The home is often seen as outside the province of education. Yet it is probably the greatest source for a solution to reducing the factors that put underachieving students at risk. Clearly, educators will not eliminate poverty or racism, but they can involve family members in planning with the student and the school to improve learning. Working with the family may involve home visits or special outreach to parents and family members. Setting up sibling or community study groups can be helpful, with the teacher on call by phone for questions or to come to the group occasionally as a consultant.

Self-Concept and Motivation. The literature on underachievement has abundant references to poor self-esteem and its behavioral manifestation of low motivation (Csikszentmilhalyi & Larsen, 1984; Delisle, 1990; Seeley, 1993; Whitmore, 1980). Although this relationship may explain causes, it does not necessarily lead to an intervention. In fact, the explanation often breeds a certain hopelessness about improving the learning of a student who is not motivated and feels academically incompetent. The explanation lets educators and parents off the hook when they can label the student as unmotivated. However, motivation is a state of mind that varies with the student's interests. It is not static and pervasive. It is also related to developmental levels.

Students go through periods of lower motivation. If school is boring and perceived by the student as being "dumb" assignments and busywork, the student will not be motivated to achieve. Educators cannot let the student off the hook. Personal responsibility and mutual respect are reasonable expectations for any student by the teacher or parent. Life is full of things that we are not motivated to do. If we can make work we do not want to do interesting or at least time limited, we can see greater achievement. Recognizing and celebrating the completion of achievement by a student who is not motivated is a good way to break the cycle.

Environmental Risk Factors. Resiliency factors are the counterpart to risk factors. Many risk factors for school failure cannot be changed, such as parents' educational level, living in low-income neighborhoods, and lack of community support for educational achievement. However, resiliency to these risk factors can be developed within a student by using many of the approaches suggested earlier in this chapter. An excellent way to build resilience is through the use of mentors for underachieving students. A good role model and a sustaining relationship with a caring adult outside the family can have tremendous impact. Social connections through youth groups, recreation, clubs, scouts, churches, and other community resources can also build resilience. Building these life skills in concert with building academic skills can help lead the gifted underachiever to realize greater potential.

If the goal is prevention of underachievement rather than remediation, we should begin intervention at the preschool level. Head Start programs have made a positive difference in preventing school failure for disadvantaged children, but more is needed for all young children with above-average potential. Early intervention as a means of addressing most educational problems has proven to be the best preventive approach. It is cost-effective and provides benefits for a smaller investment than is needed for later, more major remediation tasks.

Creating alternatives for middle-school students is also a good point to intervene. Middle school may be the last chance to break the cycle for many students who would otherwise become mediocre and just "get by" for the remainder of their secondary school years.

Overall, intervention programs for underachievers should focus attention on improving the self-esteem of these students regardless of their age. This point was nicely summarized by Whitmore (1980):

> Supportive strategies are those which affirm the worth of the child in the classroom and convey the promise of greater potential and success; [they are] yet to be discovered messages of the classroom environment that communicate to the child promises of belonging, finding acceptance, being affirmed as a valued and respected member of the group and being free to become the person he wishes to become—to realize his potential and develop his gifts. (p. 257)

Who Are the Gifted with Disabilities? ~

Children and youth who are both gifted and disabled share many of the problems of gifted underachievers. They are not likely to be identified by typical identification schemes. There is the widely held belief that children with disabilities cannot be gifted. Special education has traditionally used a medical model, which emphasizes finding the deficits and developing a remedial plan for those problem areas. These factors, in addition to the disability, put these students at risk of not being identified as gifted or educated appropriately.

To be called "disabled," children must meet specific state and federal guidelines. And to qualify for special education, the children must usually go through extensive assessment leading to a determination that special educational services are needed. Disabled children are different from underachievers in two ways. First, some are achieving at levels appropriate to their potential and so cannot be considered underachievers. Second, some disabled children are underachieving but the cause of underachievement is clearly attributable to the disability, and they are receiving special education services for compensatory or remedial skills.

The concept of disabled gifted may appear to be an oxymoron. Educators tend to view these two types of children as being at opposite ends of the education spectrum. That the characteristics of each type could reside in one child seems incongruous. But it is a phenomenon that has received long overdue attention in the past 20 years.

The special education obsession with the medical model approach to teaching disabled children has resulted in a focus on deficits rather than in a search for strengths. As such, a number of obstacles exist to finding these children. Whitmore and Maker (1985, pp. 14–21) discussed four of these major obstacles to identification:

Obstacle 1: Stereotypic expectations that disabled persons are below normal

Obstacle 2: Developmental delays, particularly in verbal areas, among disabled children, so their high intellectual ability usually goes undetected when using verbal tests with them

Obstacle 3: Incomplete information about the child, which results in overlooking areas of strength that might be displayed in nonacademic settings

Obstacle 4: No opportunity to demonstrate superior ability because of the highly verbal nature of school tasks and ability testing used in special education

Given these obstacles, it is a wonder that disabled gifted children are discovered at all. Greater use of nonverbal intellectual measures and tests of adaptive behavior have helped to some extent. Also, many disabled children whose verbal ability is intact, such as the blind or emotionally disturbed, can demonstrate superior intellect. But giftedness in the vast pool of learning disabled, deaf, and physically disabled is obscured by the disability. Specialized testing procedures are needed to find these children. These procedures usually encompass nonverbal measures of intellectual ability. Tests such as the Raven's Progressive Matrices or the performance section of the WISC–R can be used to identify abilities often masked by disabling conditions that limit verbal ability.

Every school district is required to have a "child-find" program to screen all children for disabling conditions when they enter school at kindergarten or through transfer. The child-find mechanism is also a good way to search for disabled gifted children. Early identification is crucial so that intervention can begin. Teachers of the gifted should call attention to this area of concern with their school's child-find coordinator and should look for high-potential children among those considered to be at risk in the screening process.

How Do We Serve the Gifted with Disabilities?~

The nature and extent of services needed for gifted children with disabilities will vary according to the child. Federal and state laws require that an individualized educational program (IEP) be formulated for each child placed in special education. Development of the IEP follows the assessment and staffing of the child and involves parents, special educators, and the building principal.

Teachers of the gifted should become resources to the team that develops the IEP. An intensive evaluation of the child's strengths serves as a vehicle for addressing the disabilities imposed by the handicap. In a team effort, the special education staff and the teacher of the gifted can work together in planning and implementing the IEP. The child with visual, hearing, or physical disabilities who is also gifted can use her or his intellectual strengths to learn compensatory skills. Gifted children with learning disabilities or behavior disorders also can use their superior intelligence to learn problem-solving or metacognitive strategies to help themselves cope with academic and social tasks required to be successful in school.

Learning disabilities are perhaps the most complex disabling conditions to impact high potential ability. Their causes are not known, and appropriate treatments are still evolving with mixed success. Generally, the approach to teaching gifted students with learning disabilities involves a thorough academic task analysis to find strengths and weaknesses. The strengths are used to help compensate for the weak areas. These students need to learn a lot of organizational skills, such as time management, note taking, tape recording of lectures, sequencing of topics, and basic writing skills.

The recent inclusion movement in special education has helped to increase the visibility of students with disabilities in general education classrooms. With this normalizing influence, we have seen a greater awareness among regular teachers of the potential strengths of students with disabilities. Thus far, there is no research to support a greater awareness of students who are both disabled and gifted as a result of inclusion, but many gifted programs are viewing inclusion as a strategy for the heterogeneous grouping of gifted with students with disabilities. While the inclusion movement may help to identify those who are gifted and disabled, it does not bode well for gifted students who continue to need specialized instructional groups and individual attention. The negative aspect of inclusion for students who are gifted and disabled is that they may not get the specialized attention they need from either gifted education or special education. Too often, inclusion means giving the general education teacher some training in special education and then assigning students with disabilities to his or her class with no other support. This dilution does a disservice to all involved.

As mentioned earlier, conventional approaches in special education often focus on remediating weaknesses rather than on developing compensatory strengths. Teachers of the gifted can supplement specialized instruction by using a student's strengths as a means of capturing the interests of the student and motivating him or her toward advanced study and task persistence.

The special education program typically has far more resources than does the gifted program and therefore has the potential to offer more extensive services to the disabled gifted than might be available to gifted underachievers. Social work services can be applied to the family to help family members work at home on improving the self-esteem of the child. Special education specialists can provide intensive individual services to teach remedial and compensatory skills. Finally, teachers of the gifted can provide the child with enriched and accelerated learning experiences to make learning both challenging and enjoyable. The old adage that "nothing succeeds like success" certainly holds true for these students. Teachers of the gifted can provide success experiences for disabled gifted learners by focusing on strengths and acknowledging and rewarding their advanced conceptual ability.

Summary ～

This chapter has discussed the complex problem of gifted underachievers and gifted children with disabilities. It provides an introduction to two often overlooked conditions that deserve attention from gifted educators and special educators. These children pose a serious paradox for education. By virtue of their giftedness, they often are not identified for any special services. To provide the most appropriate education, we must deal with this paradox through staff development, modified screening techniques, and team planning.

References ～

Bricklin, B., & Bricklin, P. (1967). *Bright child—poor grades: The psychology of underachievement*. New York: Delacorte.

Butler-Por, N. (1987). *Underachievers in school: Issues and intervention*. Chichester, England: Wiley.

Butler-Por, N. (1991). *Gifted children at risk of underachievement*. Unpublished paper, University of Haifa, Israel.

Csikszentmihalyi, M., & Larsen, R. (1984). *Being adolescent: Conflict and growth in the teenage years*. New York: Basic Books.

Delisle, J. (1990). *Underachieving gifted students* (ERI Digest No. E478). Reston, VA: Council for Exceptional Children.

Fine, B. (1967). *Underachievers—How they can be helped*. New York: Dutton.

Finney, B. C., & Van Dalsel, E. (1966). Group counseling for gifted underachieving high school students. *Journal of Counseling Psychology, 16*, 87–94.

Gowan, J. C. (1957). Dynamics of the underachievement of gifted children. *Exceptional Children, 24*, 98–101, 122.

Newman, R. (1974). *Groups in schools*. New York: Simon & Schuster.

Pringle, M. L. (1970). *Able misfits: A study of educational and behavior difficulties of 103 very intelligent children (IQs 120–200)*. London: Longmans.

Seeley, K. (1987). *High ability students at risk*. Denver: Clayton Foundation.

Seeley, K. (1993). Gifted students at risk. In L. Silverman (Ed.), *Counseling the gifted and talented* (pp. 263–278). Denver, CO: Love.

Shaw, M. C., & McCuen, J. T. (1960). The onset of academic underachievement in bright children. *Journal of Educational Psychology, 51,* 103–108.

Tannenbaum, A. J. (1983). *Gifted children.* New York: Macmillan.

Thorndike, R. L. (1963). *The concepts of over and underachievement.* New York: Columbia University, Teachers College, Bureau of Publications.

Whitmore, J. (1980). *Giftedness, conflict, and underachievement.* Boston: Allyn & Bacon.

Whitmore, J., & Maker, J. (1985). *Intellectual giftedness in disabled persons.* Rockville, MD: Aspen Systems.

Ziv, A. (1977). *Counseling the intellectually gifted child.* Toronto: University of Toronto.

Study Questions ⌇

1. How might we identify giftedness among deaf or blind children through cooperative efforts with special education personnel?

2. What effect might underachievement have on the emotional development of gifted learners?

3. How can parents help their children overcome underachievement?

4. How could you find strengths in a gifted child with learning disabilities that could be used to help capture and maintain his or her interest in academic areas?

5. How might you develop a team approach to intervention with gifted learners with disabilities with special education personnel?

6

Disadvantaged Learners with Talent

Joyce VanTassel-Baska

One of the most neglected populations among the gifted is the disadvantaged. This population is frequently overlooked for special programs by school districts whose identification procedures fail to find these students or whose standards for program entry are above the tested levels achieved by many of them.

Furthermore, even when such students are found and placed in programs, little attention is given to the background socioeconomic factors that may seriously affect their performance and their future achievements beyond the programs. Consequently, educators must focus more precisely on these questions: (1) Who are the disadvantaged gifted, and how do we find them? (2) What common and differential provisions should be made for them in schools? (3) What types of additional facilitation of talent development would be most useful to them?

Why Focus on the Disadvantaged Gifted?

Many educators and politicians would question the wisdom of targeting resources for such a small-incidence population. Studies have shown that the majority of gifted learners come from higher socioeconomic backgrounds (Sears & Sears, 1980; VanTassel-Baska & Willis, 1988). Thus, we are looking for a minority within the already limited population of gifted learners. There are important reasons, however, to pursue this issue:

1. Our sense of a low incidence rate of gifted among the disadvantaged is not substantiated, for the most part, by data. It is limited by the restrictions we place on the meaning of the term gifted. Historically, more students who

came from advantaged home and school backgrounds were identified as part of the gifted population. Yet, even when we look within restricted definitions based on standardized testing protocols, we find sizable numbers of students, such as 15.5% of an eight-state-region talent search, or some 2,800 students in seventh and eighth grade, who come from lower socioeconomic backgrounds (VanTassel-Baska & Chepko-Sade, 1986). The incidence rate of disadvantaged gifted learners may be far greater than we have assumed.

2. There is a clear underrepresentation of minority students, particularly African Americans, in gifted programs at the K–12 level of schooling. The disparity between minority representation in the general population and that in gifted programs is an issue that must be addressed in a sensitive way (Ford, 1995).

3. Colleges and universities, as well as selected professions, are still experiencing an underrepresentation of minorities capable of meeting entry standards.

4. The gap between low socioeconomic status (SES) and higher SES levels is widening, and, contrary to popular opinion, the upward mobility rate of lower SES levels is less than 3% (Sennett & Cobb, 1972). From 1972 to 1995, the percentage of individuals living below the poverty level has increased from 11.1% to 13.8%. However, poverty rates dropped in the United States between 1994 and 1995 by 1.6 million individuals (Baugher & Lamison-White, 1996). Nevertheless, current movement to a higher socioeconomic class is more difficult to assess. According to the National Education Longitudinal Study (NELS), only 9% of students in gifted programs were in the bottom quartile of family income, while 47% of program students were from the top quartile in family income (U.S. Department of Education, 1994).

5. The plight of the black family, which is experiencing an increasing rate of single parentage, teenage pregnancy, and high unemployment, points to a need for increased interventions for the children of these families that constitute the new poor. These children will compose a sizable segment of tomorrow's adult population.

6. Many have called gifted education "elitist," concerned with a group of learners not in need of special services given their advantaged status as students with high ability. Although such a charge clearly does not appreciate the importance of attending to individual differences in schooling regardless of the nature or type of difference, gifted educators should be cognizant of the charge. As a field, we must focus attention and resources on finding talented learners whose need may be more readily understood and then clarify the importance of providing a needs-based education to all who show exceptional promise.

Disadvantaged gifted learners do not, in fact, have the family or community resources to "make it on their own." This population of learners has the greatest need for programs and services that can help optimize their human potential and has the greatest risk of being forgotten in the context of both gifted and general education.

Who Are the Disadvantaged Gifted, and How Do We Find Them? ~

A 3-year study of key demographic features of disadvantaged gifted learners in the Midwest defined disadvantaged in purely economic terms (VanTassel-Baska & Willis, 1988). Other research efforts have considered the father's educational level and occupational status as the key variables (Jencks, 1972). Still other efforts within the field of gifted and general education have focused on minority status and cultural difference as the preconditions for being considered as part of the disadvantaged gifted population (Frasier, 1980). No one definition appears to be clearly accepted by the field. Perhaps the state of California has the best approach; the state's definition is an amalgam that takes into account any or all of the following factors: environmental, economic, linguistic, and social status.

Most studies on disadvantaged gifted populations have focused on four need areas related to identification and service:

1. The need to use nontraditional measures to identify them (Bernal, 1974; Bruch, 1978; Frasier, 1995; Torrance, 1971)
2. The need to recognize subcultural attributes and factors in deciding on identification procedures (Gay, 1978; Miller, 1974; Passow & Frasier, 1996; Samuda, 1975; Witty, 1978)
3. The need to focus on the student's strengths in nonacademic areas, particularly in creativity and psychomotor domains (Bruch, 1975; Torrance, 1977)
4. The need to create programs that address noncognitive skills and that enhance motivation (McClelland, 1978; Moore, 1978)

More recent work in identification spearheaded by U.S. Department of Education funding through the Javits Act has resulted in several projects that point toward some promising approaches to identification of this population. They include:

1. *The use of traditional tests.* Contrary to intuitive belief, traditional tests have been shown to be a valuable tool for identifying disadvantaged gifted populations. Individual intelligence tests offer valuable data on the ability of disadvantaged students, since new norms include appropriate samples of minority and low socioeconomic level populations. Achievement and aptitude measures also find many disadvantaged students, especially if cutoff score points are used less stringently for program inclusion. To ignore good standardized aptitude, achievement, and ability indices in the identification process would do more harm than good in identifying high-functioning students within this population.

2. *The use of nontraditional measures.* While traditional measures can continue to be supported for use with the disadvantaged, it also is helpful to employ nontraditional measures at the screening level of the process. The most promising of these measures appear to be the Raven's series of matrices and the Matrix Analogies Test, both of which are nonverbal, general ability measures. In one recent study, the Advanced Raven's Matrices was found to identify a significantly greater percentage of minority students than did a more traditional measure (Mills & Tissot, 1995). It appears to be especially promising as a screening tool (Mills, Ablard, & Brody, 1993). Less promising are creativity measures and checklists that lack good validity and reliability.

3. *The use of community nominations.* Community nominations appear to be as effective in finding disadvantaged gifted students at the screening level as parent inventories, hovering around 90% effectiveness (Ward, 1992). Such individuals as ministers, pediatricians, and social workers are in excellent positions to perceive high-functioning students in the neighborhood context. Using a formal tool with these individuals may assist school personnel in locating gifted students overlooked by teachers.

4. *The use of "tryout" approaches.* Several school districts employ an approach of delivering "gifted curriculum" to all students, typically at primary grade levels, for a period of several weeks and observing the behavioral reaction of the students to the challenge. The students' behaviors are noted by trained teachers, who then feed this information to a selection committee as an additional piece of information to support the identification of particular students. School district data in some contexts suggest that a greater number of disadvantaged students have been identified for gifted programs as a result of this approach (VanTassel-Baska, 1992).

5. *The use of profile analysis rather than matrix models.* Much has been written about the dangers of reducing identification data across measures to a single number and letting that number determine which students are placed in gifted programs (Feldhusen, Baska, & Womble, 1981; Frasier, 1995). A more equitable and personalized approach is the use of student profiles (Passow & Frasier, 1996). Early childhood researchers of disadvantaged gifted learners have stressed the importance of developmental portfolios as a tool for both identification and instruction (Wright & Borland, 1993). Such approaches assume that students, especially those from disadvantaged backgrounds, will evince uneven development. Therefore, the role of the selection committee is to look for peaks of performance in the overall data assembled and make judgments based on the range of functioning across measures rather than on an average of them.

A study conducted by the National Research Center on the Gifted and Talented at the University of Virginia indicated that current alternative assessment tools for identifying ethnically diverse and low-income gifted students, developed to be used in conjunction with multiple intelligences models, lack good validity data although reliability levels are acceptable. The researchers cautioned practitioners to evaluate carefully all instruments used to ensure that equitable practices are employed (Plucker, Callahan, & Tomchin, 1996).

Efforts to find these students have been further complicated by the confusion over whom to look for with what instrument. Several techniques have been tried with varying degrees of success. Yet the need to identify gifted students from disadvantaged populations—including culturally different, minority, low SES, and rural—is great. Some educators tend to focus on the debilities rather than the strengths of these populations. Others tend to view the job of the public school as that of raising skill levels to a minimum standard only and do not concern themselves with the larger job of educating students to levels of potential ability.

Selection and programming for gifted students in these categories should be a priority for all school districts. The discrepancy between their current instructional program and one that is appropriate to their ability is probably greater than for other populations of gifted students, perhaps with the exception of the highly gifted, some of whom also fall into these categories.

Some disadvantaged students undoubtedly will be chosen for gifted programs as a matter of course, because they will fall within the selection criteria. But much depends upon what criteria are used and how they are applied. If the criteria focus strongly on test scores and use rigid cutoffs, students from economically deprived or culturally different streams may be at a disadvantage. One alternative is to make the cutoff level more flexible to include students who are highly able but are within a standard deviation below the established cutoff on test scores. Many more disadvantaged learners probably will be included if this procedure is followed.

This alternative frequently becomes important after initial screening. If the community is 30% minority and if, after screening procedures for a gifted program have been completed, only 2% of the students selected are minority, the screening committee may wish to adjust the cutoff standards so that a larger proportion of minorities will be included.

Another alternative is to augment identification procedures with parent, teacher, or community checklists that cover special characteristics that have been noted for culturally different students who have been identified as gifted. Torrance (1977) listed 18 creative positives to look for among this group:

- Ability to express feelings and emotions
- Ability to improvise with commonplace materials and objects
- Ability to articulate well in role-playing, sociodrama, and storytelling
- Enjoyment of and ability in visual arts such as drawing, painting, and sculpture
- Enjoyment of and ability in creative movement, dance, dramatics, and so forth
- Enjoyment of and ability in music, rhythm, and the like
- Use of expressive speech
- Fluency and flexibility in figural media
- Enjoyment of and skills in group activities, problem-solving, and so forth

- Responsiveness to the concrete
- Responsiveness to the kinesthetic
- Expressiveness to gestures, body language, and so forth, and ability to interpret body language
- Humor
- Richness of imagery in informal language
- Originality of ideas in problem-solving
- Problem centeredness or persistence in problem-solving
- Emotional responsiveness
- Quickness of warm-up

Moreover, Bernal (1974) identified the following specific characteristics of the gifted Chicano child:

- Rapidly acquires English language skills once exposed to the language and given an opportunity to use it expressively
- Exhibits leadership ability, be it open or unobtrusive, with heavy emphasis on interpersonal skills
- Has older playmates and easily engages adults in lively conversation
- Enjoys intelligent (or effective) risk-taking behavior, often accompanied by a sense of drama
- Is able to keep busy and entertained, especially by imaginative games and ingenious applications, such as getting the most out of a few simple toys and objects
- Accepts responsibilities at home normally reserved for older children, such as supervising younger siblings or helping others do their homework
- Is "streetwise" and is recognized by others as a youngster who has the ability to "make it" in the Anglo-dominated society

Still another alternative is to state that every building in a school district will select for gifted programs the upper 3%, 5%, or 10% of its most talented students and then assume that the "levels of giftedness" from building to building will vary. Thus, a building that draws upon a group of economically deprived youngsters may identify a group of relatively "less gifted" (as indicated by standard test scores) youngsters than would a building that draws upon a more affluent population.

Passow and Frasier (1996) delineated key ideas for identifying minority students for gifted programs. They include:

1. Using multiple criteria that include inventories and checklists with traits corresponding to those found in gifted black populations
2. Using the diagnostic-prescriptive teaching approach to improving test performance, popularized by Feuerstein's notion of test-teach-test.
3. Broadening the data-finding procedures for students including such approaches as peer nomination, self-nomination, and assessments by personnel in addition to teachers

4. Considering broader ranges of scores for entrance into programs
5. Using standardized tests that have a history of effectiveness in identifying disadvantaged students

What Differential Provisions Are Needed? ~

Whether we are talking about minority students or poor white students from rural areas, one factor remains common to the members of each group—they reside outside the mainstream networks that provide knowledge about how to access educational advantage. This knowledge is crucial to the conversion of high aspirations into creative, productive achievement at various stages of development, particularly in providing families with the resources necessary to gain their own access to appropriate educational services and thereby to mobilize a community of parents to take responsibility for linking their high-potential children to available resources. Although schools can provide direct service programs for such atypical gifted learners, they typically are not in a position to act as strong resource linkers or to deliver knowledge about the process of talent development.

At their best, in-school programs have provided rigorous coursework comparable to the kind advantaged learners in the best school settings receive. At the same time, other school programs have focused on remediating skill deficits or offering programs in nonacademic areas such as the performing arts.

A national study of the prevalence of programs for disadvantaged gifted learners yielded data suggesting that limited efforts were in place for these learners (VanTassel-Baska, Patton, & Prillaman, 1991). A more recent study (Coleman & Gallagher, 1992) found that 38 states were focusing on these learners at the policy level.

As a result of surveying 25 districts that serve disadvantaged learners well, VanTassel-Baska (1992) identified the following interventions as effective:

1. Early and systematic attention to the needs of these children
2. Parental and family involvement in the educational program model
3. Effective school strategies (e.g., time on task, principal leadership)
4. Experiential and "hands-on" learning approaches
5. Activities that allow for student self-expression
6. Mentors and role models
7. Community involvement
8. Counseling efforts that address cultural values and facilitate talent development
9. Building on strengths and differential learning styles

Very few evaluation data are available regarding outcomes of special interventions for these learners. Those studies that have been conducted typically reflect modest gains. Several are described here. A 2-year instructional program focusing on reinforcing and extending disadvantaged gifted children's strengths was administered to "academically able" students. Instruction was given in language arts and math to the experimental groups. The largest achievement gains were in the math classes, suggesting that the approach used, flexible pacing without grade-level restrictions, can be an effective instructional practice (Mills, Stork, & Krug, 1992). More successes have been recorded for disadvantaged gifted learners in traditional gifted programs that employ common treatments across populations (Baska, 1989), suggesting that incremental gains can be made if the intervention is full-time over a span of years in school. A more recent study has documented that gifted minority students demonstrated higher achievement gains in gifted programs than in a general education classroom setting. No self-concept differences were discerned between minority and nonminority students as a result of placement in these programs (Cornell, Delcourt, Goldberg, & Bland, 1995).

What Do We Know About Effective Interventions? ~

In *Gifted Child Quarterly*, Bruch (1978) reviewed the available literature on culturally different gifted children and concluded that there were many gaps and that "no consistent plan for development of the culturally different gifted has been encompassed to date" (p. 383). In the same issue of *Gifted Child Quarterly*, devoted entirely to the disadvantaged gifted and gifted with disabilities, Torrance (1978) challenged his audience with the words, "It is time we did some genuine, serious research concerning the identification and development of the creative positives of minority/disadvantaged children" (p. 306).

Nevertheless, even today, studies on how disadvantaged gifted students are best served are relatively few. Progress is being made, however. One method of gaining insight into "what works" with the gifted disadvantaged is to broaden the concept to examine effective strategies for educating the disadvantaged in general.

For our purposes here, the term *disadvantaged* refers to economically disadvantaged, which includes large numbers of minority students. In 1985, minority groups made up nearly 20% of the population of the public schools in the United States. In that same year, approximately 31% of blacks and 29% of Hispanics were considered below poverty level (U.S. Bureau of the Census, 1986). Although highly visible in dropout, teen pregnancy, and special education counts, disadvantaged students continue to be underrepresented in programs for the gifted and college bound.

A study on social support systems for disadvantaged youth (VanTassel-Baska, Olszewski-Kubilius, & Kulieke, 1994) found that these students perceived themselves as less academically competent but more socially competent than their more advantaged peer group, suggesting that helping to foster a positive perception of academic ability is an essential part of programming for these students. In a related study, Olszewski-Kubilius and Laubscher (1996) found that the college adjustment of economically disadvantaged students was substantially aided by providing a counseling program to assist with concerns about functioning effectively in a challenging academic environment.

Early Intervention

Early intervention has been influential in reducing later academic problems for disadvantaged students (Ramey, Yeates, & Short, 1984; Seitz, Rosenbaum, & Apfel, 1985). Lazar (1981) reviewed the progress of children in Head Start programs. He concluded that participants in the preschool programs were significantly more likely to finish high school, stay out of special education, and complete school careers without retention. Similar findings were noted by Royce, Lazar, and Darlington (1983) in a study of children in preschool programs in the 1960s and 1970s. Lazar determined that the following characteristics related to positive outcomes: "the earlier the better," small adult-child ratio, parent participation, and service to families rather than just to the child.

Although it has been demonstrated that early intervention is effective, this does not imply that later intervention is useless. Kagan (1976) reminded us that even in a situation where slowing of development has taken place because of environmental factors, this slowing can be reversed if "the environment after infancy is beneficial to growth" (p. 103).

The National Excellence Report (U.S. Department of Education, 1994) emphasized early intervention as one of the keystones of the future of gifted education. The report noted:

> The nation must ensure that all children, especially economically disadvantaged and minority children, have access to an early childhood education that develops their potential. Young children need rich, varied learning opportunities and teachers and caregivers who look more for their strengths and potential rather than for their perceived weaknesses. (p. 27)

School and Classroom Environment

How, then, can a beneficial environment be best provided for disadvantaged learners in the schools? Research on school and classroom environment is extensive, and there is no reason to assume that effective school literature would not apply to disadvantaged learners as well as to the general population. In fact, much of this effort has centered on schools with sizable populations of lower SES students (Lezotte & Bancroft, 1985; Mann, 1985; Maskowitz & Hayman, 1976; Ornstein, 1983).

In an extensive review of what we know about educating disadvantaged learners, Ornstein (1983) included many controversial points of view. But he did cite several studies to indicate that the quality of the school is an important factor in outcomes for disadvantaged students. He listed leadership, supervision of teachers, teacher morale, emphasis on reading instruction, and communication with parents as important factors.

Murphy (1986) saw structured learning environments, emphasis on math and reading, staff development, parental involvement, and, again, active, motivated leadership as likely to be found in schools that are successful in teaching the disadvantaged. To these criteria, Mann (1985) added matching of instruction to the child's learning style and ensuring overlap between what is taught and what is tested. These issues have received theoretical support from other studies as well (Lezotte & Bancroft, 1985).

Recent efforts of the Accelerated Schools Project (Finnan, St. John, McCarthy, & Slovacek, 1996) have called for key environmental variables to be in place in order to promote learning, such as a vision for the school, working in teams on problems, and the assumption of a facilitative role by principals. It is premature to judge whether these school-wide change projects will have a positive impact on student learning and especially on the learning of the disadvantaged gifted.

Effective Teachers

Maskowitz and Hayman (1976) looked at the difference in styles between "best" teachers and first-year teachers of mostly lower SES junior-high students in a large northeastern city. These authors suggested that more successful teachers set a different climate, including more use of student ideas, more praise and encouragement, verbal recognition of student feelings, more time on task, and more activities per period. In spite of the now commonly accepted notion that active responding and time on task are closely related to learning, Stanley and Greenwood (1983) found that relatively little time to respond was given to the 93 elementary-school students they observed, and even less time was given to Title I students, who were already well behind academically. In his review of a direct instruction model, Becker (1977) stressed that the small-group situation for reading instruction increases verbal interaction with the teacher, provided that time is carefully structured, positive approaches are used to maintain student attention, and student progress is monitored regularly. In addition to these factors, effective teaching of disadvantaged gifted students needs to stress varied instructional approaches that address the preferred modes of learning of the students as well as instruction along more traditional lines.

Language

Becker (1977) also discussed another area frequently addressed in the preschool literature—language development. After evaluating the progress of thousands of students in the first to third grades for Project Follow Through, he concluded, "Words are the building blocks of education. Teach the English language" (p. 542).

Too often, educators have looked at language development as an obvious need in the early years but have abandoned it for individual specialty-area curricula in junior and senior high. Usova (1978) suggested techniques for motivating interest in reading with secondary disadvantaged students, including language-related methods, such as acting out reading material and reading aloud to students. The Upward Bound program, which assists high-school students in preparing for college, emphasizes language-based skills such as reading, composition, ethnic literature, and creative writing (Koe, 1980).

More recent work has focused on whole language instruction, yet studies have continued to document the greater effectiveness of basal approaches with the disadvantaged (Stahl & Miller, 1989). Such data, however, do not reflect the preferred model for use with the gifted, the Interdisciplinary Curriculum Model (ICM) (Van Tassel-Baska, in preparation). Data from classrooms using this model in language arts show significant gains for classrooms of predominantly disadvantaged students (VanTassel-Baska, in preparation).

Math and Science

As a group, disadvantaged minority students have not traditionally pursued advanced programming in math and science. Anick, Carpenter, and Smith (1981) noted that serious inequities exist in the math education of black and Hispanic students; that their achievement levels were considerably lower than the national average; and that differences from the larger population increased for each consecutive age-group. Their study also showed that although blacks appear to take less math than other groups, they report positive feelings about the subject. The authors concluded that motivation may not be a major problem and that general approaches used for all students would be appropriate for minorities. Lincoln (1980) suggested that disadvantaged students would learn best by the use of teaching tools in math and science and that those tools should be concrete objects known to the students outside of the school environment.

In a review of 24 studies done since 1975 on the participation and performance of minorities in math, Mathews (1984) concluded that research is scanty. However, her breakdown of the important factors of parent, student, and school influences is productive. Of special interest are indications that parents desire but often do not know how to help their children, that minority role models seem to have an effect on enrollment in math classes, and that lower SES youngsters may consider math to be lacking in utility.

In a recent study Yong (1992) found that African-American middle-grade students had positive math and science attitudes. This finding supports the need to encourage minority students at this level to continue with challenging work in these subject areas.

Compensatory Education

Cooley (1981) and Stickney and Plunkett (1982) presented varying points of view on the U.S. national compensatory education program, Title I. Cooley faulted the program for being difficult to evaluate. He was equally concerned about the confusion that develops when children are removed from the classroom to receive services and then may be found alternately eligible and ineligible from year to year.

Stickney and Plunkett (1982) cited overall improvement in achievement for Title I students. Of special note are the features of the program that seem to reflect solid educational practices suggested in their review and elsewhere. The four major components of programs that have been successful in enhancing achievement among disadvantaged students are that they (1) provide increased instruction time, (2) evaluate student progress with pre- and posttesting, (3) coordinate efforts among school personnel, and (4) extensively involve parents.

Counseling

The role of counseling in the education of the disadvantaged has been somewhat controversial. Some have argued that affective programming takes time away from cognitive instruction and expands the role of the school to encompass issues that are better dealt with in the family. Yet, a strong case has been made for the preventive mental health benefits of counseling in the schools (Pedro-Carroll, Cowen, Hightower, & Guare, 1986; Weissberg, Cowen, & Lotyczewski, 1983). Responses to problem-solving and cognitive therapy techniques have been especially positive (Kendall & Braswell, 1985; Shure & Spivak, 1982).

Several authors have noted that counseling with disadvantaged minorities is enhanced by the use of specific techniques addressed to those populations. Griffith (1977) suggested that the counselor show respect for the minority culture by learning about it and that contact between minority youth and high-achieving minority adults be facilitated. Exum (1983) cautioned nonminority counselors to be aware of the various stages minority children may undergo in their adjustments to racism. Colangelo and Lafrenz (1981) suggested that the counselor be aware of possible peer pressure not to succeed. According to Colangelo and Exum (1979), one of the ways in which minority children may differ greatly from one another is in the degree to which they would like to identify with or differentiate from their culture. Successful counseling programs will allow for the exploration of this issue without making assumptions that one direction is preferable or "healthier" than another.

Interventions for the Disadvantaged Gifted

In an interview with Draper (1980), Lopez and Payne emphasized that people are more alike than they are different. Therefore, much of what is already known about gifted education would apply to gifted minority groups. But they also cited research that suggested that disadvantaged minority students may have some specific strengths in spatial orientation, problem orientation, and artistic expression. At the same time, they mentioned several cultural norms that may serve to hold back gifted disadvantaged students. These include (1) the high degree of importance placed on social acceptance, (2) a tendency to reject solitary activity, and (3) sanctions against questioning cultural values.

Colangelo and Exum (1979) postulated that culturally different students are likely to have different learning styles that can be best accommodated in an individualized open environment. Thus, creating hands-on experiences and a gradual movement from a more structured to a less structured environment in the classroom can facilitate these students more successfully. Also recommended has been the use of mentors, community involvement, and early counseling to help broaden ideas on future career roles (Dunbaum & Russo, 1983).

The Ideal Program ～

Programs for disadvantaged gifted students are certainly not places for fostering stereotypes. Frasier (1979) aptly cautioned us not to assume that the disadvantaged are deprived of love or stimulation or that they are deficient in specific thought processes or language. Ideal programs would provide diverse opportunities for expression as well as for information gathering. They would allow for cultural differences in materials, curriculum, and, when possible, personnel (Clasen, 1979). They would address the whole child, including the development of basic building blocks for future life performance, such as learning the skills of problem-solving, decision-making, seeking assistance, discriminating relevant from irrelevant information, and developing self-direction and control (Frasier, 1979). Such programs would involve parents in the educational process and provide them with the knowledge, skills, and attitudes necessary to nurture their talented children.

Table 6.1 summarizes the research findings on successful interventions with disadvantaged learners, including the gifted, across several study areas. By

Table 6.1 ~
Topics and Successful Interventions
for Disadvantaged Students

Research Topics	Successful Interventions
Early intervention	Preschool programs Small adult-child ratio Parent participation Service to families
School and classroom environment	Motivated leadership/principal expectations Supervision of teachers Teacher morale Emphasis on reading instruction Communication with parents/parental involvement Instructional support Structured learning environments Staff development Matching of instruction to learning style/ diagnostic-prescriptive teaching
Effective teachers	Use of student ideas Praise and encouragement Verbal recognition of student feelings More time on task More activities per period

(continued)

(Table 6.1 continued)

Language	Teaching of the English language
	Acting out what is read
	Reading aloud
	Use of ethnic literature
	Creative writing
Math and science	Use of familiar concrete objects as teaching tools
	Use of minority role models
	Education of parents
	Focus on the value of math and science
Compensatory education	Increased instructional time
	Evaluation and monitoring of student progress (pre/post)
	Parental involvement
	Coordinated efforts by school personnel
Counseling	Teaching of problem-solving strategies
	Cognitive therapy techniques
	Mentors/role models
	Respect for minority culture and related issues
	Exploration of cultural identity issue
	Focus on future career roles
	Early intervention
	Community involvement
Disadvantaged gifted	Use of mentors
	Community involvement
	Early counseling
	Hands-on learning experiences

synthesizing these findings across types of study, we gain a clearer picture of some generic interventions that appear to work well, given the nature of the population.

These findings clearly identify some general directions for intervention with the disadvantaged gifted learner. It remains for the field of gifted education to address these areas in systematic program development efforts.

Key Issues in Addressing the Needs
of Disadvantaged Gifted Students ~

Based on what we know about the nature and needs of this population, we must be concerned about several issues if progress is to be made in increasing the number of disadvantaged gifted learners in gifted programs. These issues include the following:

1. Because sufficient evidence exists to suggest that low socioeconomic status plays an important role in how even highly able students may score on tests (VanTassel-Baska & Willis, 1988), we must view the home environment as a critical piece of information in understanding and interpreting the phenomenon of giftedness.

2. An equally important issue concerns gifted programs themselves. Some evidence suggests that lowering entrance scores in a rigorous program with well-defined expectations neither affects the student success rate appreciably nor affects the overall standards of the class (Olszewski, Kulieke, Willis, & Krasney, 1987). Consequently, we must carefully consider the "match" between identification and program in such a way that we are not excluding students who can succeed by arbitrarily establishing higher cutoff scores than necessary for the program intervention provided.

3. We must examine the purposes of existing gifted programs and what inferences can be made about levels or types of intellectual functioning required to participate. For example, if a given program requires students to engage in original production that requires rigorous high-level analytical and interpretive skills, only students with these "readiness" skills should be exposed to such a challenging intervention. If, however, the program provides only "mild" enrichment through, for example, a special unit on archaeology in which the expectations are open-ended, it is inappropriate to insist on high threshold scores for entry. Traditionally, we have not defined gifted programs well enough to justify the identification protocols that have been used to determine the programs' student populations. This mismatch can make our identification process appear capricious or arbitrary.

4. We also must examine whether we are maintaining a logical consistency in our procedures for addressing the needs of the disadvantaged gifted. If we are willing to entertain a multiple criteria model of identification as well as a quota system, are we equally willing to entertain the idea of multiple program options based on aptitude and interest? If we accept the premise that disadvantaged gifted students have different characteristics and needs from other gifted students, we also must accept the premise that differential programming for these students will be required in order to meet their differential needs.

This issue brings us to the point of asking the question, What program interventions do these students most need, and what are the implications of providing for the students differentially? Should gifted programs for such students be less academic, more creative, and more open-ended than programs for other groups of gifted learners? Or should all gifted students be immersed in a multifaceted set of program opportunities that allows for wide deviations among individual profiles? This is a central program issue that is much bigger than identification and is a critical area worth close scrutiny. To broaden identification criteria to include more disadvantaged students only to funnel them into a narrow conception of gifted program demands is to do the ultimate disservice—it is to attach a label that conveys the opposite impression from the reality of the program experience.

Given the set of issues just discussed, it is important that schools engage in ongoing discussions and program development efforts to serve disadvantaged gifted learners in their midst. Policy recommendations for working with these learners in school districts include the following (VanTassel-Baska, Patton, & Prillaman, 1991):

1. Ensure that disadvantaged gifted learners are cited in definitions of giftedness as a special population.
2. Initiate the use of multiple assessment measures that include traditional and nontraditional approaches.
3. Recognize and address the personalized needs of disadvantaged gifted learners, who share many commonalities with all gifted learners but may vary in significant ways, especially in their perception of social support.
4. Encourage the use of a "tryout" program for all students nominated to the gifted program in which responsiveness to differentiated classroom curriculum becomes a part of the selection paradigm.
5. Develop program prototypes for use with atypical gifted learners, recognizing differential aptitudes and interests.
6. Develop individual services such as tutoring, mentoring, and counseling for disadvantaged gifted learners.
7. Consider a "matching funds" model to encourage value-added services and scholarships for disadvantaged gifted students.
8. Collect systematic data on disadvantaged students served in gifted programs.

These issues are central to gaining an appropriate perspective on the involvement of disadvantaged and minority students in gifted programs. We need to examine our fundamental purposes for running such programs, our capacities to manage individual differences and needs within them, and our willingness to operate multiple program options and to define reasonable student outcomes. Only then will we be in a position as a field to do justice to this special population of learners.

Summary ~

This chapter has presented a definitional structure for examining the issue of disadvantaged gifted learners and has reviewed various approaches to identifying these learners. Furthermore, it has presented an overview of what we know about effective interventions with the disadvantaged. The concluding section has focused on important issues and concerns in building effective programs and services. Through systematic efforts to identify and nurture disadvantaged gifted learners, our society as a whole can accrue important benefits, and education can rightfully take credit for the progress.

References ∼

Anick, C. M., Carpenter, T. P., & Smith, C. (1981). Minorities and mathematics: Results from the national assessment of educational progress. *Mathematics Teacher, 74*(7), 560–566.

Baska, L. (1989). Are current identification protocols unfair to the minority disadvantaged student? In J. Maker & S. Schiever (Eds.), *Critical issues in gifted education* (pp. 226–236). Austin, TX: PRO-Ed.

Baugher, E., & Lamison-White, L. (1996). *Poverty in the United States: 1995.* (U.S. Bureau of the Census, Current Population Reports, Series P60–194). Washington, DC: U.S. Government Printing Office.

Becker, W. C. (1977). Teaching reading and language to the disadvantaged: What we have learned from field research. *Harvard Educational Review, 47*(4), 518–543.

Bernal, E. M. (1974). Gifted Mexican-American children: An ethno-scientific perspective. *California Journal of Educational Research, 25*(5), 261–273.

Bruch, C. B. (1975). Assessment of creativity in culturally different gifted children. *Gifted Child Quarterly, 19*(2), 164–174.

Bruch, C. B. (1978). Recent insights on the culturally different gifted. *Gifted Child Quarterly, 22*(3), 374–393.

Clasen, R. E. (1979). Models for the educational needs of gifted children in a multicultural context. *Journal of Negro Education, 48*, 357–363.

Colangelo, N., & Exum, H. H. (1979). Educating the culturally diverse gifted: Implications for teachers, counselors and parents. *Gifted Child Today, 6*, 23–24, 54–55.

Colangelo, N., & Lafrenz, N. (1981). Counseling the culturally diverse gifted. *Gifted Child Quarterly, 25*, 27–30.

Coleman, M., & Gallagher, J. (1992). *Report on state policies related to the identification of gifted students.* Chapel Hill, NC: Gifted Education Policy Studies Program. (ERIC Document Reproduction Service No. ED 344 368)

Cooley, W. W. (1981). Effectiveness of compensatory education. *Educational Leadership, 38*, 298–301.

Cornell, D., Delcourt, M., Goldberg, M., & Bland, L. (1995). Achievement and self concept of minority students in elementary school gifted programs. *Journal for the Education of the Gifted, 18*(2), 189–209.

Draper, W. (1980). The creative and gifted minority student: Related research, developmental and teaching strategies: Part 2. Interviews with Ambrocio Lopez and Charles Payne. *Creative Child & Adult Quarterly, 5*(3), 171–179.

Dunbaum, G., & Russo, T. (1983). Career education for the disadvantaged gifted: Some thoughts for educators. *Roeper Review, 5*(3), 26–28.

Exum, H. H. (1983). Key issues in family counseling with gifted and talented black students. *Roeper Review, 5*(3), 28–31.

Feldhusen, J., Baska, L., & Womble, S. R. (1981). Using standard scores to synthesize data in identifying gifted. *Journal for the Education of the Gifted, 4*(2), 177–185.

Finnan, C., St. John, E., McCarthy, J., & Slovacek, S. (1996). *Accelerated schools in action: Lessons from the field.* Thousand Oaks, CA: Corwin Press.

Ford, D. Y. (1995). Desegregating gifted education: A need unmet. *Journal of Negro Education, 64*(1), 52–62.

Frasier, M. M. (1979). Rethinking the issue regarding the culturally disadvantaged gifted. *Exceptional Children, 45*(7), 538–542.

Frasier, M. M. (1980). Programming for the culturally diverse. In J. Jordan & J. Grossi (Eds.), *An administrator's handbook on designing programs for the gifted and talented* (pp. 56–65). Reston, VA: Council for Exceptional Children.

Frasier, M. (1995). *A review of assessment issues in gifted education and their implications for identifying gifted minority students.* Storrs, CT: National Research Center on the Gifted and Talented.

Gay, J. (1978). A proposed plan for identifying black gifted children. *Gifted Child Quarterly, 22*(3), 353–360.

Griffith, A. R. (1977). A cultural perspective for counseling blacks. *Humanist Educator, 16*(2), 80–85.

Jencks, C. (1972). *Inequality.* New York: Basic Books.

Kagan, J. (1976). Resilience and continuity in psychological development. In A. M. Clarke & A. D. B. Clarke (Eds.), *Early experience: Myth and evidence* (pp. 97–121). New York: Free Press.

Kendall, P. C., & Braswell, L. (1985). *Cognitive behavior therapy with impulsive children.* New York: Guilford.

Koe, F. T. (1980). Supplementing the language instruction of the culturally different learner: Upward Bound program. *English Journal, 69,* 19–20.

Lazar, I. (1981). Early intervention is effective. *Education Leadership, 38,* 303–305.

Lezotte, L. W., & Bancroft, B. A. (1985). School improvement based on effective schools research: A promising approach for economically disadvantaged and minority students. *Journal of Negro Education, 54*(3), 301–311.

Lincoln, E. (1980). Tools for teaching math and science students in the inner city. *School Science & Math, 80,* 3–7.

Mann, D. (1985). Effective schools for children of the poor. *Education Digest, 51,* 24–25.

Maskowitz, G., & Hayman, J. T. (1976). Success strategies of inner city teachers: A year long study. *Journal of Educational Research, 69,* 283–289.

Mathews, W. (1984). Influences on the learning and participation of minorities in math. *Journal for Research in Math Education, 15*(2), 84–95.

McClelland, D. C. (1978). Managing motivation to expand human freedom. *American Psychologist, 33,* 201–210.

Miller, L. (1974). *The testing of black students: A symposium.* Englewood Cliffs, NJ: Prentice-Hall.

Mills, C., Ablard, K. E., & Brody, L. E. (1993). The Raven's Progressive Matrices: Its usefulness for identifying gifted/talented students. *Roeper Review, 15*(3), 185–186.

Mills, C. J., Stork, E. J., & Krug, D. (1992). Recognition and development of academic talent in educationally disadvantaged students. *Exceptionality: A Research Journal, 3*(3), 165–180.

Mills, C., & Tissot, S. (1995). Identifying academic potential in students from underrepresented populations: Is using the Raven's Progressive Matrices a good idea? *Gifted Child Quarterly, 39*(4), 209–217.

Moore, B. (1978). Career education for disadvantaged gifted high school students. *Gifted Child Quarterly, 22*(3), 332–337.

Murphy, D. M. (1986). Educational disadvantagement. *Journal of Negro Education, 55*(4), 495–507.

Olszewski, P., Kulieke, M., Willis, G., & Krasney, N. (1987). *A study of the predictors of success in fast paced classes and the validity of entrance scores.* Evanston, IL: Northwestern University, Center for Talent Development.

Olszewski-Kubilius, P., & Laubscher, L. (1996). Economically disadvantaged gifted students and their subsequent college adjustment. *Roeper Review, 18*(3), 202–208.

Ornstein, A. C. (1983). Educating disadvantaged learners. *Educational Forum, 47*(2), 225–247.

Passow, A. H., & Frasier, M. M. (1996). Towards improving identification of talent potential among minority and disadvantaged students. *Roeper Review, 18*(3), 198–202.

Pedro-Carroll, J., Cowen, E. L., Hightower, D. A., & Guare, J. C. (1986). Preventive intervention with latency-aged children of divorce: A replication study. *American Journal of Community Psychology, 14*(3), 277–290.

Plucker, J., Callahan, C., & Tomchin, E. (1996). Wherefore art thou, multiple intelligences? Alternative assessments for identifying talent in ethnically diverse and low income students. *Gifted Child Quarterly, 40*(2), 81–92.

Ramey, C. T., Yeates, K. O., & Short, E. J. (1984). The plasticity of intellectual development: Insights from preventive intervention. *Child Development, 55,* 1913–1925.

Royce, J., Lazar, I., & Darlington, R. B. (1983). Minority families, early education and later life chances. *American Journal of Orthopsychiatry, 53*(4), 706–720.

Samuda, R. J. (1975). *Psychological testing of American minorities: Issues and consequences.* New York: Dodd, Mead.

Sears, P., & Sears, R. (1980, February). 1528 little geniuses and how they grew. *Psychology Today*, pp. 28–43.

Seitz, V., Rosenbaum, L. K., & Apfel, N. H. (1985). Effects of family support intervention: A ten year follow-up. *Child Development, 56*, 376–391.

Sennett, R., & Cobb, J. (1972). *The hidden injuries of class.* New York: Random House.

Shure, M. B., & Spivak, G. (1982). Interpersonal problem solving in young children: A cognitive approach to prevention. *American Journal of Community Psychology, 10,* 341–356.

Stahl, S., & Miller, P. (1989). Whole language and language experience approaches for beginning reading: A quantitative research synthesis. *Review of Educational Research, 59*(1), 87–116.

Stanley, S. O., & Greenwood, C. R. (1983). How much "opportunity to respond" does the minority disadvantaged student receive in school? *Exceptional Children, 49,* 370–373.

Stickney, B. D., & Plunkett, V. R. L. (1982). Has Title I done its job? *Educational Leadership, 39*(5), 378–383.

Torrance, E. P. (1971). Are the Torrance Tests of Creative Thinking biased against or in favor of disadvantaged groups? *Gifted Child Quarterly, 15*, 75–80.

Torrance, E. P. (1977). *Discovery and nurturance of giftedness in the culturally different.* Reston, VA: Council for Exceptional Children.

Torrance, E. P. (1978). Dare we hope again? *Gifted Child Quarterly, 22*(3), 292–312.

U.S. Bureau of the Census. (1986). *Statistical abstract of the United States: 1987* (107th ed.). Washington, DC: U.S. Government Printing Office.

U. S. Department of Education Office of Educational Research and Improvement. (1994). *National excellence: A case for developing America's talent.* Washington, DC: Author.

Usova, G. (1978). Techniques for motivating interest in reading for the disadvantaged high school student. *Reading, 15*(1), 36–38.

VanTassel-Baska, J. (1992). *Planning effective curriculum for gifted learners.* Denver, CO: Love.

VanTassel-Baska, J. (in preparation). *Effects on disadvantaged gifted learners of the use of Interdisciplinary Curriculum Development (ICM) in language arts.*

VanTassel-Baska, J., & Chepko-Sade, D. (1986). *An incidence study of disadvantaged gifted students in the Midwest.* Evanston, IL: Northwestern University, Center for Talent Development.

VanTassel-Baska, J., Olszewski-Kubilius, P., & Kulieke, M. (1994). A study of self-concept and social support in advantaged and disadvantaged seventh and eighth grade gifted students. *Roeper Review, 16*(3), 186–191.

VanTassel-Baska, J., Patton, J., & Prillaman, D. (1991). *Gifted youth at risk.* Reston, VA: Council for Exceptional Children.

VanTassel-Baska, J., & Willis, G. (1988). A three year study of the effects of low income on SAT scores among the academically able. *Gifted Child Quarterly, 31*(4), 169–173.

Ward, T. (1992, May). *Identifying disadvantaged gifted learners.* Presentation at Project Mandala Conference, Williamsburg, VA.

Weissberg, R. P., Cowen, E. L., & Lotyczewski, B. S. (1983). The primary mental health project: Seven consecutive years of program research. *Journal of Consulting & Clinical Psychology, 51*(1), 100–107.

Witty, E. P. (1978). Equal educational opportunity for gifted minority children. *Gifted Child Quarterly, 22*(3), 344–352.

Wright, L., & Borland, J. (1993). Using early childhood developmental portfolios in the identification and education of young, economically disadvantaged, potentially gifted students. *Roeper Review, 15*(4), 205–210.

Yong, F. L. (1992). Mathematics and science attitudes of African-American middle grade students identified as gifted: Gender and grade differences. *Roeper Review, 14*(3), 136–140.

Study Questions ∿

1. How would you respond to the proposition that gifted learners who are economically disadvantaged need programs and services that are different from those for advantaged gifted learners?

2. Factors that narrow, inhibit, or distort one's self-perception of capacity are likely to impede the talent development process. How does this statement apply to the disadvantaged?

3. What definitional structure for disadvantaged gifted students would have the most meaning in school districts? Why?

4. If you were to recommend an approach for identifying disadvantaged gifted students in a given context, what procedures would you follow and why?

5. How might schools approach developing a special program for the disadvantaged gifted learner? Where should they begin?

6. Many talented people have come from disadvantaged backgrounds—Barbara Jordan, Maya Angelou, Stephen Leacock, and others. What issues about poverty are important to consider in working with disadvantaged gifted learners?

7

The Highly Gifted

Linda Kreger Silverman

Jeff was born 10 weeks premature, weighing 2 pounds 3 ounces, and was hospitalized for the first 7 weeks of his life. Beginning at 4 months, he suffered fevers as high as 106 degrees that lasted up to 3 days. While these factors would have put most infants at serious risk, Jeff spoke his first word at 9 months, learned all the letters of the alphabet in 1 week at 12 months, learned to count at 18 months, and was able to add and read several hundred words at the age of 2. By 3, he was reading second-grade books and performing multiple-digit addition and subtraction. By 4, he was reading fourth-grade books, multiplying, and dividing. By the age of 6, he was reading at a sixth-grade level and had mastered algebra. At 7 years old, he was achieving beyond the 12th-grade level in reading and was learning geometry and trigonometry.

Who are the highly gifted, and why is it necessary to discuss special provisions for this group in a textbook on the gifted? Simply stated, the highly gifted are those whose advancement is significantly beyond the norm of the gifted group. Although it would seem that these students are the ones most in need of gifted education, in a national study of identification procedures, exceptionally gifted and creative students were found to be a disadvantaged group at risk for being screened out of gifted programs (Richert, 1982). Even private schools for the gifted sometimes reject students for being "too gifted," because highly gifted children do not fit into the schools as well as mildly gifted children and require more work on the part of teachers. Some highly gifted students fail to qualify for programs that emphasize task commitment or evidence of creativity in their identification procedures. Others qualify but find the programs inadequate to meet their needs—a potential hazard in gifted programs that attempt to serve a large segment of the school population. Whatever the cutoff score for a program may be, the vast majority of qualified students cluster at the borderline for admission. Teachers almost universally gear instruction to the majority of the students in the group; this situation may leave the highly gifted child academically and socially isolated from others in the program.

These problems are partially created by the rudimentary nature of our classification system in the field of gifted education. Special education recognizes at least three degrees of developmental delay—mild, moderate, and profound—and prescribes interventions based on degree of severity (Grossman, 1977). We have not yet reached that level of sophistication in the field of gifted education, as indicated by the omnipresent query, "Is this child gifted or not?" The question of *how gifted* is usually not taken into account in programming. This single classification system creates strange bedfellows. Two children labeled "gifted" may be as different from each other in ability as a severely disabled child is from an average child.

Jeff, the child described in the vignette at the beginning of this chapter, had a measured IQ of 237+, with the plus sign indicating that no ceiling was reached; that is, he could have achieved a higher score if the test contained harder items. His score was well over 100 points higher than the scores required for placement in most gifted programs. However, he did not socialize well in a first-grade class for gifted students. To assist his adjustment, each day that he received a positive note from his teacher about his behavior, his mother rewarded him with his favorite activity: learning new chapters in a high-school physics book.

A number of factors have coalesced in the 1990s to make highly gifted children extremely vulnerable within the school system: (1) services for gifted students have been disbanded in many school districts; (2) IQ testing has come into question; (3) early identification of gifted children has come into disfavor (Office of Educational Research and Improvement, 1993); (4) the newer versions of the IQ tests have become speed tests with lower ceilings that do not differentiate highly gifted from modestly gifted children; (5) the concept of multiple intelligences has served to assist educators in seeing the talents of all children as being equal; (6) the school reform movement, in the name of egalitarianism, has abolished the practice of ability grouping and pressed for all students to study the same curriculum at the same rate in cooperative learning groups, regardless of individual differences (George, 1992). Without identification, a child like Jeff could be perceived as "behaviorally disordered," or having attention deficit disorder, instead of recognized as having very different abilities from his or her age peers (Silverman & Kearney, 1992b). Adaptations are essential to accommodate the special needs of exceptional children, whether they are developmentally delayed or developmentally advanced.

Provisions must take into account the strength of the children's abilities, their various talents and passions, and the asynchrony between their strengths and weaknesses; otherwise, instruction will be aimed at the lowest common denominator and the highly gifted will be poorly served. This chapter provides guidelines for identifying, assessing, and serving those students who vary significantly from the majority of identified gifted children in terms of degree of advancement.

Identifying the Highly Gifted ⁓

In keeping with the special education designations, it is possible to *roughly* categorize gifted children for school-based programs as mildly, moderately, and highly gifted. It must be kept in mind that testing is likely to generate underestimates rather than overestimates of a child's abilities, since competence always exceeds performance. One or two hours of examination will not reveal all that an individual knows. Conversely, it is practically impossible to achieve a higher score than one is capable of achieving. The segment of the population with the greatest potential for underestimation of ability is the highly gifted (Silverman, 1995), since their abilities often exceed the limits of the assessment instruments. The ranges of giftedness can be characterized as follows, where the numbers indicate individual IQ scores on most standardized tests:

mildly gifted	115–129	(1 *SD* beyond the norm)
moderately gifted	130–144	(2 *SD* beyond the norm)
highly gifted	145–159	(3 *SD* beyond the norm)
extraordinarily gifted	160+	(4 *SD* beyond the norm)

Individual intelligence tests are much better measures of abstract reasoning abilities than are group tests, and those children whose measured abilities are 3 standard deviations (*SD*) beyond the norm are sufficiently advanced from their age-mates to be considered highly gifted.

Another means of locating highly gifted children, other than through intelligence testing, is through the talent search programs originated by Julian Stanley (1990). In these programs students in seventh and eighth grade who achieve at the 95th or 97th percentile on grade-level achievement tests in reading and mathematics are eligible to take the College Board examinations (the Scholastic Aptitude Test [SAT] or the American College Testing Program [ACT]). Extremely precocious students can qualify in fifth or sixth grade. The talent searches provide an excellent view of what happens when we remove ceiling effects. Two 12-year-olds who achieve at the 97th percentile on grade-level achievement tests, for example, would appear fairly equivalent in ability. However, when they take the SAT, one may obtain a score of 780 on the Mathematics section while the other may achieve 420. The first student has already mastered algebra and geometry, whereas the test results of the second student demonstrate proficiency in pre-algebraic concepts. That student would not need the same degree of acceleration as the first.

In 1994, the average scores for college-bound seniors on the SAT were 423 on the Verbal (V) section and 479 on the Mathematics (M) section (these figures vary annually) (College Entrance Examination Board, 1994). High school seniors who attain scores in the high 600 range or above on either V or M could be considered highly gifted. The talent search programs usually select students who score 430 V or 500 M on the Scholastic Assessment Test–1 (SAT–1) in seventh or eighth grade to participate in special programs, such as college-level courses. These students may be thought of as moderately gifted. Students who score significantly above this range could be considered highly gifted. VanTassel-Baska (1984) designated students in the 530+ range as significantly advanced over other talent search participants and in need of additional provisions. This score represents a composite of V and M scores and is, therefore, a high estimate for Verbal and a low estimate for Mathematics scores. These figures would have to be adjusted for fifth and sixth graders, since 80-point to 90-point increases may occur from one year to the next in this age-group. The original talent search cutoff scores have been found useful for selecting students for high-powered, content-based programs; extrapolations for distinguishing highly gifted students from this group are yet to be tested by research.

As above-level tests, the SAT and ACT provide excellent, inexpensive methods of assessing the degree of advancement in verbal and quantitative abilities. Some drawbacks are that gifted girls are less likely to be identified than gifted boys with these instruments (Silverman, 1986b), the exams may be biased against lower income children (VanTassel-Baska, 1989), and seventh grade is late in the developmental sequence to identify high levels of giftedness, as highly gifted students need adaptations from the time they enter school.

If ability or aptitude testing is not available, another way to select highly gifted children is to provide above-grade-level achievement testing—that is, to test at least one level beyond the student's current grade placement. Students would qualify for programs for the highly gifted if their scores are one standard deviation beyond the mean of the gifted group in one or more areas on above-grade-level testing.

These methods are likely to identify academically precocious children, but they may miss children who are highly gifted in specific areas, such as the visual and performing arts, creative production, or ethical development. For such children to be identified and served, teacher judgment and parental report (including reports of developmental milestones) should supplement standardized assessment. Observational data can be collected to locate children whose production, precocity, or advancement in any area is noticeably beyond the level demonstrated by others enrolled in the gifted program.

Problems in Assessing the Highly Gifted

Assessment of the highly gifted is complex. Differences in scores obtained on various instruments are much greater for this group than for any other population. Discrepancies have been found in excess of 100 points (Silverman & Kearney, 1992b). The culprit is *ceiling effects*, which occur when the child's knowledge goes beyond the limits of the test. To paraphrase Julian Stanley (1990), assessing the highly gifted is like trying to measure individuals who are 6 feet tall with a 5-foot ruler. Because modern tests do not have items of sufficient difficulty, they fail to capture the full range of highly gifted children's abilities. There is no way of knowing how high a student's score might have been if the tests contained harder items.

To complicate matters, newer versions of the standardized intelligence scales generate substantially lower scores for gifted and highly gifted students than did previous versions. The Wechsler Intelligence Scale for Children—Third Edition

(WISC–III) manual indicates that scores in the gifted range derived from this measure are one to six points lower than scores derived from its predecessor, the Wechsler Intelligence Scale for Children—Revised (WISC–R) (Wechsler, 1991). When Sevier, Bain, and Hildman (1994) assessed students currently placed in gifted programs, they found that their WISC–III Verbal IQ scores were nearly 15 points lower, their Performance IQs were 7.6 points lower, and their Full-Scale IQs were 12.83 points lower than scores obtained for these students on the WISC–R. Forty percent of the group failed to attain 120 IQ on the WISC–III.

Another study compared IQ scores of 20 highly gifted children on the Stanford-Binet Intelligence Scale (Form L–M) and the WISC–III. The group attained scores in the 151–191 range on the Stanford-Binet L–M, with a mean of 173. On the WISC–III, their Full-Scale IQ scores ranged from 116–150, with a mean of 134. The highest score on the WISC–III was below the lowest score on the Stanford-Binet L–M, and only three of the children scored in the highly gifted range on the WISC–III, attaining Full-Scale IQ scores of 146, 148, and 150. The average discrepancy between the two scales was 37 points, and the differences ranged between 14 and 60 points. The greatest depression was seen in the Performance IQ scores, which ranged from 99 to 144, with a mean of 120. Only 6 of the 20 children attained Performance IQ scores sufficient to qualify them for placement in a gifted program (130 or above) (Silverman, 1995).

One cause of the lower Performance IQ scores is the substantially increased bonus points for speed on the WISC-III and the Wechsler Preschool and Primary Scale of Intelligence—Revised (WPPSI–R), as compared to earlier versions of these tests (Kaufman, 1992). Kaufman stated that if a 12-year-old student solved every Performance item correctly on the WISC–III but received no bonus points for speed, he or she would score below average on every subtest. He went on to say:

> The biggest negatives for gifted assessment are the new emphasis on problem-solving speed on the WPPSI-R [and] the substantially increased stress on performance time in the WISC-III compared to the WISC-R.... The speed factor will penalize gifted children who are as reflective as they are bright, or who tend to go slow for other non-cognitive reasons such as a mild coordination problem. (p. 158)

Given the state of the art of measurement, it is nearly impossible to tell just how gifted those students who score in the upper ranges on today's intelligence scales might be. There is no easy resolution to this problem. None of the current intelligence tests was designed with the highly gifted in mind. According to Hagen (Silverman, 1986a), items are purposely omitted from IQ tests if they can be solved only by gifted students.

The Stanford-Binet L–M remains the only instrument that was designed to differentiate highly gifted from moderately gifted children. It has a higher ceiling than other tests and serves as the prototype for above-level tests (Stanley, 1990); it is *untimed*, which makes it a fairer assessment of children with motor delays, reflective children, gifted children with learning disabilities, and gifted girls (Silverman & Kearney, 1992a); and it is more engaging for preschoolers (Canter, 1990; Vernon,

1987). However, because the Stanford-Binet L–M is considered outdated, many school psychologists refuse to recognize its validity. Plus, the scores derived from it are difficult to interpret, particularly in the highly gifted range.

In line with the talent search model, many psychologists who specialize in assessing the highly gifted have resorted to a two-step identification process. When children obtain ceiling scores (99th percentile) on any current instrument (e.g., 17, 18, or 19 on two or three subtests on the WPPSI–R, WISC–R, or WISC–III), they are retested on the Stanford-Binet L–M as an above-level assessment (Silverman & Kearney, 1989, 1992a). According to Rimm and Lovance (1992),

> The Wechsler IQ tests are used for initial testing because the subtest scores are viewed as important for curriculum-related decisions. When students are at or near the ceiling score on at least two subtests, the Clinic recommends further testing using the Stanford-Binet, Form L–M. (p. 101)

Some reservations psychologists might have about using the old Stanford-Binet are discussed elsewhere (Silverman & Kearney, 1992a, 1992b). However, it is important to note that it is not "unethical" to use a dated test. Stanley E. Jones, director of the Office of Ethics for the American Psychological Association, wrote:

> It would not be my reading that Principle 2.9 [Ethical Principles of Psychologists and Code of Conduct] would prohibit the use of any test for a purpose that can be defended. It does make it the responsibility of the psychologist to provide such a defense when using tests which are not obviously current. (S. E. Jones, personal communication to Sylvia Rimm, November 25, 1991)

Characteristics of the Highly Gifted ~

Highly gifted children may demonstrate developmental precocity early in life in such ways as early language development, asking complex questions, rapid learning ability, extensive vocabulary, unusual attention span, advanced abilities with puzzles or numbers, or teaching themselves to read while still toddlers. Complexity of thought and ability to understand abstract relationships may be manifested in startling ways.

The following example of developmental precocity comes from our case files at the Gifted Development Center in Denver. "A" turned pages in a book one by one at the age of 4 months. By 5 months, she had a four-word vocabulary. At 7 months she stood alone, climbed into chairs unassisted, and went up and down stairs by herself all day long. Her mother says she "was never a baby." At 2 she ordered her own meal in a restaurant, composed a song, swam across the swimming pool, and began riding a horse. By the age of 5, she was a capable photographer, switching among three different cameras with ease. She taught herself to play computer games and one day asked her mother to read her a high-school physics book. By 6, she was learning geometry and logic at home.

Her mother wrote: "I never taught 'A' anything.... I would put something out, and she would do it before I could teach her how." But school was an unending lesson in frustration for this child. In kindergarten, her teacher made fun of her precocity, saying things like, "What do you want to learn today...calculus?" A had trouble mixing with her classmates. She would come home from school crying, "I want to learn something. I want a challenge. I want school to be hard." Her first-grade teacher acknowledged that she was smart but said that she did not need more challenging material "because she doesn't finish her work early." The teacher discouraged A's mother from engaging a tutor for her to nurture her interests in geometry or advanced mathematics.

Exceptionally bright children have the same characteristics as other gifted children, but they may appear earlier in the developmental sequence or in an intensified manner. A good sense of humor, for example, is a mark of giftedness, but the degree of sophistication of that humor increases with ability. While playing under his mother's bed, one child spontaneously knocked on the bedsprings and asked, "Mommy, are you resting?" She replied, "Well, I'm trying to." He retorted, "Does that mean I'm under arrest?" This would have been amusing from a 9-year-old, but this boy was only 2 years old.

A major component of the learning style of children in this group is their ability to skip steps in learning and take giant intuitive leaps. They often surprise adults by arriving at insightful conclusions without being able to describe the steps they took to get there. "I just figured it out!" is a typical response. The need to show their work in a precise linear fashion is at cross purposes with their learning style. They may get a visual image of an intricate set of relationships and be unable to translate their thinking process in such a manner that others can follow it.

While their age-mates are comfortable working with concrete material, highly gifted children are more at home with abstractions. They may have difficulty concentrating on isolated fragments of information, analyzing bits of learning such as phonics, or memorizing facts. Yet they usually manipulate abstract symbol systems with ease and become animated when dealing with complex relations involving many variables. They are systems thinkers.

There are social ramifications to high levels of intelligence. The brighter the child, the more difficult it is for the child to find true peers. True peers are mental equals (Roedell, 1985), those who share common interests, understandings, and perspectives. A 5-year-old child who plays checkers, chess, Scrabble, and Monopoly will be unable to play these games with average or more modestly gifted 5-year-olds. Most 5-year-olds do not have a conception of rules. They make up the rules as they go along and then declare, "I win!" The highly gifted child is likely to say, "He cheats!" and refuse to play with age-mates.

The highly gifted also deal with complex moral issues at a very tender age. A 5-year-old said to her mother, "Mommy, did you kill that chicken? If you did, I'm not going to eat it." One 9-year-old refused to eat any living thing that had to die for him, which left very little for him to eat. More than one highly gifted child has become a vegetarian in a meat-eating family. The highly gifted tend to ask difficult questions, such as, "What is evil?" "Why is there violence?" "Is there a God?" "What happens when you die?" "How do we know we aren't part of someone else's dream?"

Their philosophical questions and moral concerns may or may not translate into moral actions. They can generate excellent ideas about solving social conflicts in cooperative ways (Roedell, 1985) and then bite someone on the leg right after the discussion. Social concern must fuse with experience and maturity before it will warm into consistent commitment to moral action. Yet, many highly gifted children are the protectors of children with disabilities, the elderly, or the infirm.

Differential Problem-Solving ∼

Jeff, the boy in the vignette at the beginning of this chapter attained a world-record score on the SAT-Mathematics assessment at the age of 8. When asked how he solved mathematics problems, he responded that he was able to do two mathematical operations simultaneously in his head and that "on a good day" he could do three (M. J. Morelock, personal communication, June 1994).

Discussion of the following two problems from different disciplines will illustrate the manner in which highly gifted children's problem-solving techniques vary from those used by average and modestly gifted children. In the first example, second graders are asked to balance the equation shown in Figure 7.1 by inserting two identical numbers into the empty squares.

A second grader of average intelligence might not be ready to understand the concept of balance. He or she might insert two 9s in the squares on the left side to make all the numbers the same, just like they are on the right side, failing to see the connection between the two sides. The mildly gifted child might tend to look for a formula to solve the problem. He or she might add all the numbers on the right, subtract 9, and divide the answer by 2 in order to derive the correct solution.

However, Justin, a highly gifted second grader, immediately apprehended the relationships among the numbers and was able to solve the problem in a unique way. He just looked at the problem and then wrote 39 in each of the squares. When asked

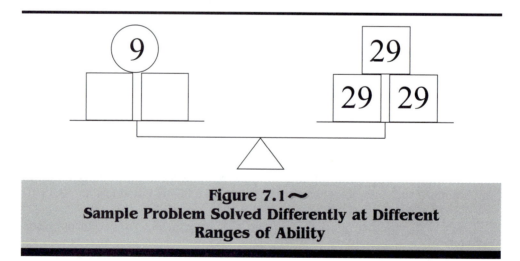

Figure 7.1 ∼
Sample Problem Solved Differently at Different
Ranges of Ability

how he arrived at the answer so quickly, he explained that 29 was 20 more than 9, so he split the 20 in half and added 10 to the other 29s. Intuitive leaps and recognition of abstract relationships served him better than an algorithmic solution with concrete numbers.

The second example is drawn from literature at the middle-school level. In his poem on loneliness, e. e. cummings portrayed a falling leaf through descending placement of the letters of the words "a leaf falls" and then simply wrote "loneliness." Average students notice that the pattern of the words graphically represents the leaf falling from the tree, and they may associate the poem with seasons of the year or the death of the leaf. Mildly gifted students look for a theme and begin to grasp the metaphor of life associated with the seasons. Highly gifted youngsters interpret the poem on many levels and see layers upon layers of meaning: The individual goes through life alone; death is an individual act; transitions in life are conducted alone; leaving the security of the known leads to loneliness; the fall from grace; and so on.

It is important to respond to the depth and intuitive insights of the highly gifted student rather than trying to get the child to adapt to the thought processes of others. When a spark of interest in an area is ignited, it needs to be nourished through increasingly more in-depth experiences in that area.

Provisions for the Highly Gifted ∿

We can use the normal curve of distribution of intelligence as a metaphor to help us understand the need for special provisions for the highly gifted beyond those available for moderately gifted children in the school environment. The basic curriculum, textbooks, and teaching methods were designed for the average group of learners. Average students may need concrete experiences and several repetitions of material in order for them to grasp it. The amount of drill, repetition, and review incorporated into the curriculum was designed for the average student.

As we move down the intelligence continuum, more drill and repetition are needed to get across even the simplest concepts, and the degree of complexity and abstraction that can be understood markedly decreases with each standard deviation (*SD*) of ability. At 1 *SD* below the norm (approximately 85 IQ), the child is considered a slow learner within a heterogeneous classroom, and programs such as remedial reading and mathematics are available. At 2 *SD* below the norm (approximately 70 IQ), the student qualifies *by law* for a complete individual diagnosis, staffing, and an individualized education program (IEP). Such children are included in general education classrooms whenever possible, but their academic needs are often met in resource rooms with specially certified teachers. At 3 *SD* below the norm (approximately 55 IQ), students may be in full-day placements with specially trained teachers and a curriculum specifically designed to meet their needs. At 4 *SD* below the norm or lower (approximately 40 IQ), children are often in special facilities or need a full-time aide in order to be placed in an "inclusion" setting.

Just as each standard deviation of ability is met with a different type of provision at the lower end of the intellectual spectrum, each standard deviation at the upper end of the spectrum requires unique consideration. As intelligence increases, so do abilities to deal with complexity, abstraction, and advanced concepts. The need for repetition dramatically decreases and the pace of instruction increases accordingly. At 1 *SD* above the norm (approximately 115 IQ), children are the fast learners in the general education classroom and profit from general enrichment activities. At 2 *SD* above the norm (approximately 130 IQ), individual diagnosis, certified teachers, resource rooms, special classes, and individualized programs are needed. For children 3 *SD* above the norm (approximately 145 IQ), full-day placements with specially trained teachers and a specially tailored curriculum actually provide the *least restrictive environment*. At 4 *SD* above the norm or higher (approximately 160 IQ), special facilities or mentors, or the flexibility to mobilize many provisions dependent on the specific needs of the child, may be needed.

The following provisions, or combinations of provisions, are suitable for highly gifted children. Some are also appropriate for moderately gifted children. If certain numbers of students are needed to make the creation of a particular option financially feasible, there is no harm in grouping moderately and highly gifted students together, provided that the instruction is kept at a sufficient pace to keep the highly gifted children challenged. Highly gifted students often develop leadership abilities in classes with moderately gifted peers, whereas they may remain isolated in a heterogeneous classroom (Hollingworth, 1926).

No matter which provisions are chosen, an individualized program is essential for highly gifted students. Lewis (1984) asserted:

> The higher the deviation above the mean, the greater the number of possible combinations and recombinations of abilities. No one highly gifted child can be expected to be like any other child with the same score. Therefore, no single-focus program, whether acceleration or any other design, can hope to adequately serve a population with such potentially complex profiles. (p. 134)

Provisions for the Highly Gifted

Individualized education programs	Mentors or tutors
Fast-paced, challenging courses	Special schools or programs
Self-contained classes	Community enrichment opportunities
Acceleration	Home teaching
University-based programs	Counseling

Individualized Education Programs

It would be wise to have an IEP for every highly gifted student to assess the student's strengths and needs and to determine collaborative means of meeting those needs. If possible, the IEP should be preceded by comprehensive individual assessment with a school psychologist in which not only intellectual capability is examined but also academic strengths, self-concept, social development, and student interests. An interview with the student should also precede the development of the IEP, since highly gifted students are often in the best position to tell us what they need for their optimal development. The IEP should represent the collaborative planning of administrators, parents, teachers, the school counselor, support personnel, and the student.

Acceleration

Acceleration is an appropriate response to a highly gifted student's accelerated pace of learning. Until recently, gifted children were automatically placed with children 1 or 2 years older, and the term *acceleration* was reserved for the type of advancement that we call "radical" today: 3 years or more of advancement. Research on the effects of acceleration supports it as a viable option, even in terms of social development (Benbow, 1991; Robinson & Noble, 1991). To determine if this option is right for a given student, *the student should be consulted*. This factor is critical. Ask the student! If the child wants to be accelerated, he or she will make a fine social adjustment, and vice versa.

University-Based Programs

The university is an excellent ally in the search for appropriate provisions for the highly gifted. The brightest students are often more at home and comfortable in a college setting than they are with their age-mates. It benefits the university to have these bright students on campus early, since they often select a campus with which they are familiar to complete their undergraduate education. Institutions of higher education have become involved in supplementing the education of the gifted in many creative ways, including Saturday, summer, and after-school *enrichment courses* for gifted children of all ages, taught by faculty, graduate students, or skilled community members; *laboratory schools* for gifted students on campus; *summer residential programs*, such as those that exist for Talent Search winners; *concurrent enrollment* programs, in which high-school students take college courses for both high school and college credit; *night or extension courses* to supplement offerings at the high school; early entrance programs, which enable students to enroll as full-time college students ahead of schedule; *advanced coursework offered by college faculty at the high school*; *mentorships*; and consolidated *high school/college programs*, such as at Simon's Rock College of Bard in Great Barrington, Massachusetts, in which students complete high school and college simultaneously.

Mentors

Mentors or tutors who work with students individually on their areas of interest are an excellent provision for the highly gifted. The mentor often has a powerful impact on the development of a talented young person. The brighter the child, the greater the need for an individualized approach. Mentors can be drawn from the community, college faculties, college students, and older gifted students.

Community Enrichment Opportunities

Parent groups can be encouraged to develop activities for highly gifted children to help them meet their social needs. In addition, community agencies, such as museums, galleries, planetariums, zoos, community schools, parks, and camps, often provide special opportunities for gifted students. Private agencies that offer special programs for gifted students, including computer camps, science schools, arts programs, archeological centers, music studios, centers for theater arts, and self-concept seminars, can also be found.

Homeschooling

Homeschooling was once the only option available for extraordinarily gifted children, and it is one that has yielded many eminent individuals. Among them are Albert Einstein, Pearl Buck, John Stuart Mill, Franklin Delano Roosevelt, and Andrew Wyeth (Kearney, 1988). Since the 1980s, homeschooling has been on the upswing, particularly in rural areas, where the services for gifted children are limited. Excellent guides to homeschooling with the highly gifted are available from Kearney (1984, 1988).

The more advanced the student, the more types of provisions should be considered. Determining which options to pursue at which points in a child's life can be a complex problem. A counselor who is familiar with the student, the family, and the available options can be particularly helpful to the family in selecting appropriate provisions.

Counseling

Asynchrony—uneven developmental patterns in the highly gifted—as well as the degree of difference from age of peers, creates a context in which counseling is needed as an important ongoing provision (Silverman, 1993). It may be nearly impossible for highly gifted children to conform their thinking to the ways in which others think. Some do not "group" well. Some have difficulty developing relationships with others. Some argue continuously because that is the way they learn. Some are intensely sensitive. Some have major discrepancies between their intellectual maturity and motor coordination and so appear "immature."

Those who are having difficulty with social relations need systematic instruction in developing friendships and building others' self-esteem. Bibliotherapy is helpful; several books feature gifted children, and others teach children about making friends (Silverman, 1993). Both gifted children and their parents may need counseling to cope with the child's intensity, sensitivity, or perfectionism. Parents usually need some counseling to adjust to the idea of raising a child who is so unique, and they need guidance in determining what to do. Within the school system there needs to be an advocate who appreciates the special needs and problems of highly gifted children. That person becomes a trusted friend for the child and the family—someone who can help them deal with the myriad of questions that plague them and who can help them sort the truth from the fiction.

Summary ～

The best program for highly gifted children involves a serious exploration of all existing possibilities with the assistance of an advocate who can help cut through the red tape. Cries of "she's too young," "you can't get credit for..." and "we don't allow..." need to be firmly met with "why don't we try..." Administrative support is essential to move a student into advanced experiences ahead of schedule. Parents and educators need to work together to change rules, regulations, and laws that prohibit or penalize advancement.

Our society offers very little support—financial, emotional, or educational—for the highly gifted child (Silverman & Kearney, 1989). A knowledgeable, caring individual in the school setting can make a sizable difference in the quality of life of the exceptionally gifted student. Many exceptionally gifted children have endured their school years in perpetual misery, but with the kind of awareness and services available today, these students can thrive and develop their potential for themselves and for society.

References ~

Benbow, C. P. (1991). Meeting the needs of gifted students through use of acceleration: An often neglected resource. In M. C. Wang, M. C. Reynolds, & H. J. Walberg (Eds.), *Handbook of special education, research and practice: Vol. 4. Emerging programs* (pp. 23–36). Elmsford, NY: Pergamon.

Canter, A. (1990). A new Binet, an old premise: A mismatch between technology and evolving practice. *Journal of Psychoeducational Assessment, 8*, 443–450.

College Entrance Examination Board. (1994). *National report on college bound seniors*. Princeton, NJ: Educational Testing Service.

George, P. (1992). *How to untrack your school*. Alexandria, VA: Association for Supervision and Curriculum Development.

Grossman, H. J. (Ed.). (1977). *Manual on terminology and classification in mental retardation* (rev. ed.). Washington, DC: American Association on Mental Retardation.

Hollingworth, L. S. (1926). *Gifted children: Their nature and nurture*. New York: Macmillan.

Kaufman, A. S. (1992). Evaluation of the WISC–III and WPPSI–R for gifted children. *Roeper Review, 14*, 154–158.

Kearney, K. (1984, May/June). At home in Maine: Gifted children and homeschooling. *G/C/T, 33*, 15–19.

Kearney, K. (1988, February). *Gifted children and homeschooling: Exploring the option*. Paper presented at the California Association for the Gifted 25th Annual Convention, San Jose, CA.

Lewis, G. (1984). Alternatives to acceleration for the highly gifted child. *Roeper Review, 6*, 133–136.

Office of Educational Research and Improvement. (1993). *National excellence: A case for developing America's talent*. Washington, DC: U.S. Government Printing Office.

Richert, E. S., with J. J. Alvino & R. C. McDonnel. (1982). *National report on identification: Assessment and recommendations for comprehensive identification of gifted and talented youth*. Sewell, NJ: Educational Improvement Center—South.

Rimm, S. B., & Lovance, K. J. (1992). The use of subject and grade skipping for the prevention and reversal of underachievement. *Gifted Child Quarterly, 36*(2), 100–105.

Robinson, N. M., & Noble, K. D. (1991). Social-emotional development and adjustment of gifted children. In M. C. Wang, M. C. Reynolds, & H. J. Walberg (Eds.), *Handbook of special education, research and practice: Vol. 4. Emerging programs* (pp. 57–76). Elmsford, NY: Pergamon.

Roedell, W. C. (1985). Developing social competence in gifted preschool children. *RASE, 6*(4), 6–11.

Sevier, R. C., Bain, S. K., & Hildman, L. K. (1994). Comparison of WISC–R and WISC–III for gifted students. *Roeper Review, 17*, 39–42.

Silverman, L. K. (1986a). An interview with Elizabeth Hagen: Giftedness, intelligence and the new Stanford-Binet. *Roeper Review, 8*(3), 168–171.

Silverman, L. K. (1986b). What happens to the gifted girl? In C. J. Maker (Ed.), *Critical issues in gifted education: Vol. 1. Defensible programs for the gifted* (pp. 43–89). Austin, TX: PRO-Ed.

Silverman, L. K. (Ed.). (1993). *Counseling the gifted and talented*. Denver, CO: Love.

Silverman, L. K. (1995). Highly gifted children. In J. Genshaft, M. Bireley, & C. L. Hollinger (Eds.), *Serving gifted and talented students: A resource for school personnel* (pp. 217–240). Austin, TX: PRO-Ed.

Silverman, L. K., & Kearney, K. (1989). Parents of the extraordinarily gifted. *Advanced Development, 1*, 41–56.

Silverman, L. K., & Kearney, K. (1992a). The case for the Stanford-Binet L-M as a supplemental test. *Roeper Review, 15*, 34–37.

Silverman, L. K., & Kearney, K. (1992b). Don't throw away the old Binet. *Understanding Our Gifted, 4*(4), 1, 8–10.

Stanley, J. C. (1990). Leta Hollingworth's contributions to above-level testing of the gifted. *Roeper Review, 13*, 166–171.

VanTassel-Baska, J. (1984). The talent search as an identification model. *Gifted Child Quarterly, 28*, 172–176.

VanTassel-Baska, J. (1989). The role of the family in the success of disadvantaged gifted learners. *Journal for the Education of the Gifted, 13*, 22–36.

Vernon, P. E. (1987). The demise of the Stanford-Binet scale. *Canadian Psychology/Psychologie Canadienne, 28*(3), 251–258.

Wechsler, D. (1991). *Manual for the Wechsler Intelligence Scale for Children III*. San Antonio, TX: The Psychological Corporation.

Study Questions ∽

1. Do you think that the highly gifted represent a special needs group within the gifted population? If so, why?
2. Have you ever worked with a highly gifted child? How was that child different from other gifted children?
3. How can the highly gifted be differentiated from more modestly gifted children in identification procedures?
4. What types of educational provisions are needed to serve the highly gifted?
5. How would you deal with the emotional and social ramifications experienced by your highly gifted students?

Girls of Promise

Joyce VanTassel-Baska

Much has been written about women as a special population to be singled out for attention under the rubric of gifted education (Callahan, 1979; Kerr, 1985; Reis, 1987; Silverman, 1986; Subotnik & Arnold, 1996). Yet very little has been attempted in the way of differentiation for this group of learners. In that sense, gifted women suffer the same neglect as do other populations with atypical needs among the gifted.

Who Are Gifted Girls? ∼

Who are these gifted girls? Basically, they make up half of the academically able population (VanTassel-Baska, 1983) and many times a disproportionate share of students who receive top grades and honors at the elementary and secondary levels in our schools. Evidence exists to suggest, however, that we lose many of these able women between high school and college as well as between a baccalaureate degree and advanced work leading to a professional career (Arnold, 1993). Thus, although the talent pool of gifted girls is relatively equal to that of gifted boys during the school years, there is a reduction of their numbers at each successive level of schooling and in high-level professional careers. Robinson and Noble (1991) described gifted girls as one of the most vulnerable special populations of gifted learners.

How Do We Identify Gifted Girls? ∼

Generally, the identification of gifted students is not differentiated by gender. Instead, traditional measures are used for all students, including intelligence tests, achievement and aptitude batteries, and nomination forms completed by teachers, parents, and others. Grade records also are frequently considered.

A logical question in a discussion of gifted girls is whether female students are being identified in equal numbers to male students for gifted programs. Some available data indicate that females are not being identified in equal numbers to males for special programs (Richert, 1982). Regional Talent Search data also support the conclusion that female students are underrepresented in secondary-level talent search programs and that even fewer choose to participate in on-campus programs. Among talent search participants in residential summer programs at one university, for example, during a 5-year period fewer than 40% of the attendees were women (VanTassel-Baska & Olszewski, 1989). At the elementary level, where more emphasis may be placed on achievement and grades, girls tend to outnumber boys in gifted program identification.

When we examine and compare achievement outcomes for girls and boys in specific areas of the curriculum, we tend to see significant differences in patterns of achievement based on gender. In the area of mathematics, boys and girls achieve at similar rates through the fifth-grade level. Beyond that level, however, boys outperform girls on math achievement and aptitude measures on an incremental basis (Maccoby & Jacklin, 1974). This differential achievement pattern is a fact, but its underlying causes are somewhat unclear. Some researchers have viewed the issue primarily in terms of participation in math programs; specifically, girls have a much lower participation rate in advanced math classes (Fennema & Sherman, 1977; Fox, 1977).

In today's society, participation in mathematics classes through the level of calculus is perceived to be an important base for mathematical competence for many professional careers, including many in the social sciences. Therefore, gifted girls who do not pursue this course-taking pattern are inadvertently opting out of career opportunities in many potential fields of interest. The same is true for advanced science classes, with gifted girls having a lower participation rate and a lower representation in related careers. A related area of concern is gifted girls' seeming avoidance of involvement with computers and computer science coursework (Lockheed & Frakt, 1984). Again, a lack of preference and participation in coursework leading to computer competence creates a serious gap in the preparation of gifted girls for later professional opportunities.

Other accounts of causes for these differences in mathematical achievement and aptitude also have been proposed by researchers. Benbow and Stanley (1980) argued that biological differences between the sexes may account for differential achievement patterns in mathematics. Waber (1977) explored the idea that the early maturation of girls in comparison to boys may account for differences in mathematical abilities, particularly those of a spatial nature. Eccles (1984) advanced the idea that girls' self-perception of not being good at math, even when achievement data confirm excellence in mathematics coursework, interferes with their ability to persevere with mathematics and its career paths. Fox (1980) found this perception to be particularly acute among gifted girls.

Regardless of the explanations put forth to explain the phenomenon of gender differences in math achievement, it seems appropriate to examine potential interventions that can positively affect the development of mathematical potential among gifted girls. As educators, we are in a position to help young gifted girls develop that potential, especially in light of the fact that strong evidence links confidence in learning mathematics to both math achievement and math course selection (Fennema & Sherman, 1977). Intervention might ameliorate the current situation and reduce the discrepancy between the sexes on this important dimension. Some supporting evidence exists that in schools where a conscious effort has been made to work with changing the attitudes of gifted girls, their parents, and counselors, gender differences in math and science achievement scores are negligible (Brush, 1980; Paulsen & Johnson, 1983).

Other research on gender differences has revealed key areas with which we should be concerned when designing interventions for gifted girls. Dweck (1986) noted a tendency among gifted girls toward low expectancies, avoidance of challenge, ability attributions for failure, and debilitation under failure. Thus, gender differences in motivational and personality patterns must be central issues in designing an effective intervention plan for gifted girls. Bandura and Dweck (1985) reported that measures of children's actual competence do not strongly predict their confidence in future attainments—a finding of particular relevance to gifted girls, whose discrepancy between actual and perceived competence was the greatest of any of the groups examined.

Gender Differences and Their Implications ~

Many recent studies have continued to examine the issues associated with gender differences. Wilson, Stocking, and Goldstein (1993) found that adolescent gifted girls chose courses in an intensive summer program that they believed would be challenging, were not offered at regular school, or were different, while gifted boys tended to choose courses they believed they would do well in or would be useful in their future careers or schooling. The authors suggested that gender-related preferences in curriculum options may already be in place by the end of elementary school.

Studies dealing with gender-based attribution theory have revealed some distinctions worthy of note. One study compared the causal attributions of gifted females for success and failure in math performance with those of gifted males and nongifted males and females (Cramer & Oshima, 1992). Students were compared across three different grade levels (third, sixth, and ninth grades) to assess developmental differences in their causal attributions. The authors concluded that intervention for gifted girls was necessary to remediate self-defeating causal attributions for math performance at these grade levels. Li and Adamson (1995) found that gifted girls attributed greater success and failure in the subjects of math, science, and English to effort and strategy than did boys. Gifted girls also showed greater confidence and interest in English than did boys.

Although the gap in achievement test scores between males and females seems to be decreasing, the gap that still remains seems largely attributable to differences in scores among the top 10% to 20% (American Association of University Women

[AAUW], 1992), giving educators of the gifted pause in respect to considering differential provisions to close the gap.

Studies in the area of gender differences in mathematics have found evidence of differential test performance and strategy use (Becker, 1990), differential performance on tasks requiring high-level problem-solving and conceptual understanding that had not been taught (Mills, Ablard, & Stumpf, 1993), and differential expectations of parents for perceived student success in doing mathematics (Dickens & Cornell, 1993), all favoring boys. Evidence also strongly suggests that girls may still face negative stereotyping in school and home environments (AAUW, 1992; Sadker & Sadker, 1994) and that families can impact both positively and negatively on the achievement goals of young women. The Sadkers' book, *Failing at Fairness* (1994), chronicles the many inequities experienced by girls in school, especially in the areas of curriculum materials that limit visual displays and text to male accomplishments and teacher behaviors that limit girls' articulation of ideas in class.

A lack of effective role models to encourage girls in nontraditional subjects also appears to be a problem. Girls attending special math, science, and technology schools who were surveyed regarding factors that were important in their decision-making process to apply to the schools (Callahan et al., 1996) cited parents, counselors, teachers, and personal recruitment contacts as important in their decision. In many cases, however, parents discouraged their daughters from applying. In other cases, teachers, counselors, and principals were cited as discouraging students from applying or enrolling by making derogatory comments about the school or the ability of the student. Students repeatedly mentioned extreme stress, pressure to succeed, and the necessity of abandoning any semblance of a social life as consequences of enrolling in the program. The decision to continue attending the school or to withdraw seldom involved counseling at the school, suggesting that schools need to strengthen their counseling resources.

One study revealed the need for appropriate female role models as girls mature. Spielhagen (1996), in an interview study of females from ages 9 to 26, found that older students were more independent of extrinsic reinforcement needs yet more in need of role models than younger subjects.

Subotnik and Arnold (1996) conducted case studies of 11 gifted scientists around the age of 30 who were participants in one of two longitudinal studies of talent development—either the Westinghouse Competition or the Illinois Valedictorian project. The study sought to identify key factors that determine the aspirations and attainments of talented individuals at the threshold of their careers. One interesting finding was that four key values influenced the subjects' decision-making about careers and personal life:

- Love of science
- Recognition of their intellectual ability for contributions to the field
- Opportunity for service to humanity, to create something useful
- Balanced emotional and professional life

In another study, Arnold (1993) found that gifted adolescent girls who were valedictorians of their high-school class tended to lower their expectations for school and career achievement in the years following graduation as conflicts of personal life and career collided. A more recent study by Reis (1995) documented a similar phenomenon with adult gifted women. Thus, preliminary evidence would suggest that the tension between career and personal life continues to cause problems for gifted girls all along the stages of development.

Callahan and Reis (1996) noted that research is still very limited on gifted girls as a special population and urged that the following research initiatives be pursued:

1. Single-sex classes in content areas in addition to mathematics and science
2. Study of the effect of gifted programs implemented in the primary grades on later achievement and attitudes
3. Study of the effect of counseling programs on such factors as underachievement, declining scores, and self-efficacy in math and science
4. Investigation into the reasons for the silence of girls in adolescence
5. Study of the impact of career programs that use such strategies as providing role models, specific tests, and other instructional programs, as well as in-service for parents and teachers

In a recent text highlighting the current research and thinking about gifted women, Arnold, Noble, and Subotnik (1996) presented a model for adult female talent development that takes into account three areas of impact: (1) the women's personality traits, family background, psychological resilience, and distance from the mainstream; (2) the opportunities that women need to act on linked to the talent domains of potential contribution; and (3) the spheres of influence that would affect high-level development—the personal through self-actualization and the public through either leadership or creative contribution to a field that one might term eminence. The authors cited many examples of barriers faced by gifted women, both internally constructed in the form of psychological feelings of inferiority and being an impostor and externally encountered in a lack of access to achievement areas and missed opportunities based on gender bias. They also cited persistent gender differences, reflected in the existing culture, that inhibit the attainment of high-level development in a chosen area for women. These differences coalesce around (1) problems with self-esteem, (2) problems with being marginalized in status settings, and (3) problems with balancing the demands of family and career with sufficient time to nurture the self.

Silverman (1993) highlighted the following gender issues that deserve attention in addressing the needs of promising girls in school and home contexts:

1. Gifted girls have a greater aptitude for social adaptability than gifted boys, which may be perceived as a strength in negotiating many troublesome social contexts but also may be a barrier to displaying their abilities in a way that will promote high-level achievement. Gifted boys, conversely, have a hard time hiding their abilities.

2. Gifted girls have a tendency to show decrements on traditional indices of ability with age. Silverman hypothesized that this situation is due to both the competitiveness of tests and the speed factor, noting that girls do not perform as well when those conditions are present.
3. Gifted girls experience the greatest difficulty in schooling at the key transition periods of preschool/kindergarten, third/fourth grade, and seventh/eighth grade. The last transition stage in particular is problematic, for girls are expected to display their abilities more fully, requiring greater effort, at a time when they are beginning to lose confidence in their abilities. As a result, their general self-image is negatively impacted.

What Differential Interventions Would Work with Gifted Girls? ~

The ability of the individual girl to monitor her own learning, to be an autonomous learner, appears to be a key variable in much of the gender research currently being done. If we can affect the motivation pattern of gifted girls and their often faulty perceptions of their own abilities, we can make progress in helping girls develop their potential at appropriate levels. It is also useful to consider Zinker's (1977) list of blocks to creativity, as they have a great deal of relevance to the plight of gifted girls noted in the research. Key blocks that relate to gifted girls include:

1. Rigidity-stereotyped reactions; overemphasis on traditions and on necessary conformity
2. Fear of failure and the unknown
3. Avoidance of frustration
4. Low self-evaluation—failure to see their own strengths

In planning interventions, it is important to view the problem of gifted girls as complex and to consider the use of multiple interventions. The implementation of various general approaches to effective interventions in a school setting to counteract the low aspiration level of many gifted females, as well as the blocks to development of their full potential, may be in order. Some of these interventions are described in the following sections.

Early and Consistent Identification and Programming

Among the problems we have with many special populations of the gifted are a late recognition of the problem and the implementation of a mild intervention to combat it. This "too little, too late" model certainly applies to gifted girls. We should begin at the primary level to work on the identified areas of need already delineated in this chapter. We cannot assume that outward displays of confidence in gifted girls at any stage of development mirror inward feelings of self-worth. Modifying inner perceptions of self is a long-term process, best begun early and integrated into the ongoing educational process in key domains of learning. Silverman (1986, 1993) suggested the following general approaches for parents in rearing gifted girls:

- Holding high expectations for their daughters
- Not purchasing sex-typed toys
- Avoiding overprotectiveness
- Encouraging high levels of activity
- Allowing their daughters to get dirty
- Instilling beliefs in their capabilities
- Supporting their interests
- Getting them identified as gifted during preschool years
- Finding gifted playmates for them to identify with and emulate
- Fostering an interest in mathematics outside of school
- Considering early school and college entrance and other opportunities to accelerate
- Encouraging them to take every mathematics course possible
- Introducing them to professional women in many occupations
- Having mother acknowledge her own giftedness
- Having mother work at least part-time outside the home
- Having daughters spend alone-time with father in "masculine" activities
- Having both parents share household duties equally
- Assigning chores to siblings on a nonsexist basis
- Discouraging the use of sexist language or teasing in the home
- Monitoring television programs for sexist stereotypes and discussing these with children of both sexes
- Encouraging siblings to treat each other equitably, rather than according to the traditional sex-role stereotypes they see outside the home

Counseling

Providing small-group and individual counseling sessions for gifted girls has been suggested by Fox (1980) as a strategy to encourage girls to take more mathematics courses before puberty. Indeed, counseling may be useful as a generalized strategy for developing female potential in a number of areas. Ascertaining the level of confidence that girls have of their ability and then working to bolster it in such sessions may provide them with a valuable service. The counseling may be conducted by a teacher, a school counselor, or even a parent. Group counseling could provide a strong sense of group identity among girls that would build toward an important networking function during the adolescent years. Silverman (1986, 1993) has recommended the use of support groups or seminars for gifted women beyond the high-school years. Topics for discussion in such counseling groups could include:

- Dealing with multiple interests and desires
- Entering a predominantly masculine profession
- Deciding whether to marry
- Deciding whether to have children

- Determining how to combine a career and a family
- Maintaining ego strength when one's choices bring censure from family or friends
- Supporting one another's achievements
- Understanding the impact of keeping one's own name or taking a married name in establishing one's professional identity
- Recognizing and appreciating the multipotentiality of one's giftedness
- Developing a big sister support system for younger gifted women
- Overcoming fears of success and fears of failure
- Combating dependency and conformity
- Believing in one's own abilities
- Learning that one can be successful without risking the loss of femininity
- Learning assertiveness-training techniques
- Learning to appreciate one's own work cycle and to judge one's accomplishments according to internal standards that take into account the many demands of multifaceted lives

Mentors as Role Models

Using successful females as adult role models is another strategy worthy of implementation. Women in professional life can provide elementary and high-school gifted girls with aspirations in line with their potential rather than in line with their family background and the roles their mothers play. These professional women also can provide assistance in thinking through the issues of how to balance a career and family life—still a major stumbling block for many gifted girls when thinking about long-term careers. Mentors can help girls set long- and short-term goals and make career decisions in light of the advantages and disadvantages of particular options.

In addition to adult role models, older gifted girls may be recruited to work with younger girls in various models and program configurations. High-school female gifted students can be wonderful role models for the prepuberty group of gifted girls in respect to course-taking issues as well as socialization and self-perception problems.

Career Development

Career development as an active intervention for gifted girls is an essential part of their schooling, probably from kindergarten through graduate school. Girls need to recognize their capacity and competence in a multitude of career areas. They also need to envision themselves engaging in such careers. Consequently, internships, as a part of career exploration, should prove very useful to them, as should career development models that stress options for serial careers, concurrent careers, and the creation of new careers. Gifted girls' concerns about having a family and balancing a career also have to be addressed. Discussing research on gifted women and what has contributed the most to their life satisfaction may be a useful tool in exploring these issues.

The Sears and Barbee research (1977) on gifted women at age 60 in the Terman sample revealed an interesting pattern of life satisfaction as it related to career. The happiest women in the Terman group were those who had a career and were single.

The least satisfied were the women who were housewives and did not have a career. Thus, gifted girls must understand the long-term impact and importance of finding a suitable career.

Female-Only Groupings, Classes, and Schools

Some evidence exists that female-only programs, especially in adolescence, can have a positive effect on gifted girls' attitudes toward themselves and their capacity for leadership in the future. Such programs can delay the social conflict about finding a mate or at least reduce its primacy in girls' thinking. The Program for Exceptionally Gifted Girls at Mary Baldwin College, for example, stresses advanced academic work that is challenging but also provides a nurturing context for developing leadership in the young women who attend. Programs for collegiate women at female-only colleges demonstrate excellent track records for placement of graduates in leadership positions. Undertaking within the gifted program a careful grouping strategy that encourages gifted girls working together on various aspects of learning can facilitate the positive development of leadership capabilities. This strategy is particularly important when implemented prior to puberty so that girls learn the strengths they possess devoid of the socialization pressure to hide them. Their strengths must be made manifest if they are to realize their presence.

Use of Teaching Models That Stress Connectedness, Independence, Creativity

Some research evidence indicates that teachers can influence the development of cooperative learning structures and independence among students, which can positively enhance girls' education (Serbin, 1984). Findings also support the contention that teachers give more attention, both of a positive and a negative nature, to boys than to girls (Good, Sikes, & Brophy, 1973). Working with teachers to stress individualized attention models can counteract the latter tendency. Using such strategies can clearly benefit both sexes in their development. Some examples of desired teacher strategies, juxtaposed with undesirable approaches to the same situation, are given in Table 8.1.

Use of Discipline-Specific Models That Value the Contributions of Women

The teaching of all subject matter can be handled in such a way as to recognize the achievements of women while stressing the problems women have encountered in being able to contribute in that area at particular stages in U.S. history or in particular areas of the world. Stressing the nature and extent of women's contributions is also important, particularly in male-dominated subjects such as math and science. Girls need to know that women have excelled in these areas—if not in equal numbers to men, at least in the level of the contribution made and recognition received, including the Nobel Prize. Having girls read biographies of famous women, instituting career days that reflect equal achievement by the two sexes, and selecting texts

Table 8.1 ～
Desirable and Undesirable Teacher Strategies

Desirable Teacher Strategy	Undesirable Teacher Strategy
Emphasis on utilizing all thinking skills (convergent, divergent, evaluative)	Emphasis on only convergent thinking with one right answer
Emphasis on problem-finding and problem-solving behavior	Emphasis on getting the answer
Emphasis on presentation of organizing concepts and ideas in each discipline of study	Emphasis on individual problems, isolated facts, or parts of a knowledge system
Use of concept mapping to encourage alternative ways of organizing information	Use of one process model for understanding an area of study

Use of teaching behavior that values thinking, such as:
   wait time
   students' processing of information
   follow-up questions that probe issues
    at a deeper level
	Use of teacher behavior that *discourages* thinking, such as:
	   ending discussions on right answer
	    formats
	   using right answers as the cue to proceed
	   rewarding quick response from a few
	    students

that treat gender issues in a balanced way can all contribute to classrooms in which girls can thrive. Use of reading materials that have girls as heroines, leaders, and inventors further enhances the possibility for positive self-image.

Family Education and Counseling

If we are serious about effecting changes in gifted girls' perception of self and in their development of self-esteem and confidence, intervention approaches must involve the girls' families. Mothers and fathers need to understand their roles in the process of helping young girls develop their potential. Only when the family begins to understand these issues can the collaborative effect of home and school begin to work in behalf of girls. Family needs are typically of two types: information needs and strategy needs. Parents need to know what the issues of subtle sexism are and how these can affect their gifted daughters. Parents also need to know what to do to combat bias and stereotyping, particularly within their own family.

Early Systematic Intervention in Mathematics and Science Programs

The issue of early intervention for gifted girls in critical areas such as mathematics and science cannot be overestimated. In a study conducted among members of the Association for Women in Mathematics, more than one third of the respondents indicated that they had an interest in mathematics as a career preference by age 11 (Luchins & Luchins, 1980). Consequently, prepubescent girls should be provided with career information and opportunities in math-related areas. Table 8.2 depicts major interventions that key individuals in the lives of gifted girls can make to effect positive self-perception and to provide the nurturance needed to continue with mathematics.

In a major summary of research and recommendations on influences in math achievement, Bearvais, Mickelson, and Pokay (1985) recommended that parents, teachers, and school personnel undertake the following actions to encourage girls in mathematics:

1. Provide more information on women and mathematics and discuss the value of mathematics in careers and in society at large.
2. Attribute girls' success in math to ability and interest, not just to hard work.
3. Be aware of one's own potential sex bias in regard to one's daughters' math abilities and expectations and openly encourage daughters to pursue math endeavors.
4. Employ cooperative teaming models in mathematics classes; use real-world problems to illustrate math concepts; and employ discovery learning techniques.
5. Consider math courses that promote the understanding of mathematics as a skill and stress the need for 4 years of mathematics in high school.

Use of Spatial Reasoning Strategies from K to 12

Studies have found differences between boys and girls in the area of spatial reasoning ability, with boys scoring higher on tests of this ability (Hyde, 1981). Teaching strategies that provide gifted girls with concrete experiences in visual spatialization tasks from an early age can address this issue. Such strategies include having girls play with building blocks, LEGOs, mechanical toys, and trucks. Given that studies of toy preference still support a tendency among girls to gravitate away from experiences like these, it is important to ensure their inclusion in a preschool program. In the early elementary years, girls should have ample opportunity to experience the following kinds of spatial tasks:

- Manipulating Cuisenaire rods and other materials to create models, solve problems, and so on
- Learning to use a typewriter/computer keyboard
- Learning LOGO on the computer
- Working matrix problems

Table 8.2. ~ Roles of Significant Others Influencing Gifted Girls		
Teachers Can	**Counselors Can**	**Parents Can**
Proactively talk about females who are mathematicians or mathematics-prone	Proactively counsel girls before puberty to take advanced math coursework	Set high expectations for female children regarding course-taking and success in mathematics
Assure girls they *can* do mathematics	Lay out detailed courses of study in mathematics to serve as a model	Seek information on excellent mathematics programs for girls and enroll daughters in them
Discourage stereotyping of math as a male subject	Discuss math anxiety issues with girls if or when they arise	Stress the competence of females in mathematics
Teach math in the context of social science experimentation	Provide career data that emphasize the central role of mathematics competency	
Teach math from a more conceptual framework, with linkages to other domains of inquiry		

- Learning visual patterns in math, science, art, poetry, and the like
- Manipulating shapes and colors in progressively more complex ways (tangrams)

By the time girls are ready to take geometry, they should have had myriad experiences that would ready them for dealing with three-dimensional figures, the rotation of figures in space, and the manipulation of patterns and designs for a desired effect. Without systematic intervention in this area, however, many gifted girls will not feel competent to handle geometry, a key course in the path to advanced mathematics and science training. Additionally, lack of competence in visual-spatial reasoning will continue to cause problems in other areas of endeavor as well.

Summary ~

Only when interventions such as those described in this chapter are undertaken are we apt to improve the number of gifted women obtaining the highest levels of education, commensurate with their ability. Evidence suggests that only 1 in 300 gifted women do so (Groth, 1969).

Aiding in the development of what is currently underutilized potential can be one of the most rewarding acts that educators can undertake. Clearly, gifted girls fall into the category of students with underutilized potential, as do other special populations that are not likely to succeed in representative numbers without personalized support. Given the nature of what gifted girls face as they move toward adulthood, it behooves educators to intervene appropriately to ensure that gifted girls develop their abilities commensurate with their potential. If this means providing a differential model of intervention, it should be done to the extent necessary to effect the desired results.

References ~

American Association of University Women. (1992). *The AAUW report: How schools shortchange girls*. Washington, DC: The American Association of University Women Educational Foundation.

Arnold, K. (1993). Academically talented women in the 1980's: The Illinois Valedictorian Project. In K. Hulbert & D. Schuster (Eds.), *Women's lives through time: Educated American women of the twentieth century* (pp. 393–414). San Francisco: Jossey-Bass.

Arnold, K., Noble, K., & Subotnik, R. (Eds.). (1996). *Remarkable women: Perspectives on female talent development*. Cresskill, NJ: Hampton Press.

Bandura, M., & Dweck, C. (1985). *Self-conceptions and motivation: Conceptions of intelligences, choice of achievement goals, and patterns of cognition, affect, and behavior*. Manuscript submitted for publication.

Bearvais, K., Mickelson, R., & Pokay, P. (1985). *Influences on sex equity in math achievement: Summary of research and recommendations*. Ann Arbor: University of Michigan, Bush Program in Child Development & Social Policy.

Becker, B. J. (1990). Item characteristics and gender differences on the SAT-M for mathematically able youth. *American Educational Research Journal, 27*(1), 65–87.

Benbow, C., & Stanley, J. C. (1980). Sex differences in mathematical ability: Fact or artifact? *Science, 210,* 1262–1264.

Brush, L. R. (1980). *Encouraging girls in mathematics*. Cambridge, MA: Abt Books.

Callahan, C. (1979). *The gifted and talented women*. In NSSE Yearbook on the Gifted and Talented. Chicago: University of Chicago Press.

Callahan, C. M., Adams, A. M., Bland, L. C., Moon, T. R., Moore, S. D., Perie, M., & McIntire, J. A. (1996). Factors influencing recruitment, enrollment, and retention of young women in special secondary schools of mathematics, science, and technology. In K. Arnold, K. D. Noble, & R. F. Subotnik (Eds.), *Remarkable women: Perspectives on female talent development* (pp. 243–260). Cresskill, NJ: Hampton Press.

Callahan, C. M., & Reis, S. M. (1996). Gifted girls, remarkable women. In K. Arnold, K. D. Noble, & R. F. Subotnik (Eds.), *Remarkable women: Perspectives on female talent development* (pp. 171–192). Cresskill, NJ: Hampton Press.

Cramer, J., & Oshima, T. C. (1992). Do gifted females attribute their math performance differently than other students? *Journal for the Education of the Gifted, 16*(1), 18–35.

Dickens, M. N., & Cornell, D. G. (1993). Parent influences on the mathematics self-concept of high ability adolescent girls. *Journal for the Education of the Gifted, 17*(1), 53–73.

Dweck, C. (1986). Motivational processes affecting learning. *American Psychologist, 41*(10), 40–48.

Eccles, J. (1984). Sex differences in mathematics participation. *Advances in Motivation & Achievement, 2*(2), 93–137.

Fennema, E., & Sherman, J. A. (1977). Sex related differences in mathematics achievement, spatial visualization, and affective factors. *American Educational Research Journal, 14,* 51–71.

Fox, L. H. (1977). The effects of sex role socialization on mathematics participation and achievement. In *Women and mathematics: Research perspectives for change* (NIE Papers in Education & Work No. 8). Washington, DC: National Institute of Education.

Fox, L. H. (1980). Conclusions: What do we know and where should we go? In L. H. Fox, L. Brody, & D. Tobin (Eds.), *Women and the mathematical mystique* (pp. 195–208). Baltimore, MD: Johns Hopkins University Press.

Good, T. L., Sikes, J. N., & Brophy, J. E. (1973). Effects of teacher sex and student sex in classroom inter- action. *Journal of Educational Psychology, 65*, 74–87.

Groth, N. (1969). *Vocational development for gifted girls: A comparison of career needs of gifted males and females between the ages of ten and seventy years.* Paper presented at American Personnel & Guidance Association.

Hyde, J. (1981). How large are cognitive gender differences? A meta-analysis using w2 and d. *American Psychologist, 36*, 892–901.

Kerr, B. (1985). *Smart girls, gifted women.* Columbus, OH: Ohio Psychology Press.

Li, A. K. F., & Adamson, G. (1995). Motivational patterns related to gifted students' learning of mathe- matics, science, and English: An examination of gender differences. *Journal for the Education of the Gifted, 18*(3), 284–297.

Lockheed, M. E., & Frakt, S. B. (1984). Sex equity: Increasing girls' use of computers. *Computing Teacher, 11*(8), 16–18.

Luchins, E. H., & Luchins, A. S. (1980). Female mathematicians: A contemporary appraisal. In L. H. Fox, L. Brody, & D. Tobin (Eds.), *Women and the mathematical mystique* (pp. 7–22). Baltimore, MD: Johns Hopkins University Press.

Maccoby, E. E., & Jacklin, C. N. (1974). *The psychology of sex differences.* Stanford, CA: Stanford University Press.

Mills, C. J., Ablard, K. E., & Stumpf, H. (1993). Gender differences in academically talented young stu- dents' mathematical reasoning: Patterns across age and subskills. *Journal of Educational Psychology, 85*(2), 340–346.

Paulsen, K., & Johnson, J. (1983). Sex role attitudes and mathematical ability in 4th-, 8th-, and 11th-grade students from a high socioeconomic area. *Developmental Psychology, 19*(2), 210–214.

Reis, S. (1987). We can't change what we don't recognize: Understanding the needs of gifted females. *Gifted Child Quarterly, 31*(2), 83–89.

Reis, S. (1995). Talent ignored, talent diverted: The cultural context underlying giftedness in females. *Gifted Child Quarterly, 39*(3), 162–170.

Richert, E. S. (1982). *National report on identification: Assessment and recommendations for compre- hensive identification of gifted and talented youth.* Sewell, NJ: Educational Improvement Center— South.

Robinson, N., & Noble, K. (1991). Socio-emotional development and adjustment of gifted children. In M. Wang, M. Reynolds, & H. Walberg (Eds.), *Handbook of special education: Research and practice* (pp. 57–76). London: Pergamon.

Sadker, M., & Sadker, D. (1994). *Failing at fairness: How America's schools cheat girls.* New York: Scribner's.

Sears, P., & Barbee, A. (1977). Career and life satisfactions among Terman's women. In J. C. Stanley, W. C. George, & C. H. Solano (Eds.), *The gifted and the creative: A fifty-year perspective* (p. 180). Baltimore, MD: Johns Hopkins University Press.

Serbin, L. (1984). Teachers, peers, and play preferences: An environmental approach to sex typing in the preschool. In S. Delamont (Ed.), *Readings on interaction in the classroom* (pp. 273–289). New York: Methuen.

Silverman, L. (1986). What ever happened to the gifted girl? In J. Maker (Ed.), *Critical issues in gifted education* (pp. 43–89). Rockville, MD: Aspen Systems.

Silverman, L. (1993). Social development, leadership, and gender issues. In L. Silverman (Ed.), *Counseling the gifted and talented* (pp. 291–327). Denver, CO: Love.

Spielhagen, F. R. (1996). Perceptions of achievement among high-potential females between 9 and 26 years of age. In K. Arnold, K. D. Noble, & R. F. Subotnik (Eds.), *Remarkable women: Perspectives on female talent development* (pp. 193–208). Cresskill, NJ: Hampton Press.

Subotnik, R. F., & Arnold, K. D. (1996). Success and sacrifice: The costs of talent fulfillment for women in science. In K. Arnold, K. D. Noble, & R. F. Subotnik (Eds.), *Remarkable women: Perspectives on female talent development* (pp. 263–279). Cresskill, NJ: Hampton Press.

VanTassel-Baska, J. (1983). Profiles of precocity. *Gifted Child Quarterly, 13*(4), 183–185.

VanTassel-Baska, J., & Olszewski, P. (Eds.). (1989). *Patterns of influence: The home, the self, and the school*. New York: Teachers College Press.

Waber, D. P. (1977). Sex differences in mental abilities, hemispheric lateralization, and rate of physical growth at adolescence. *Developmental Psychology, 13*(1), 29–38.

Wilson, J. S., Stocking, V. B., & Goldstein, D. (1993, April). *Gender differences in course selection criteria: Academically talented students in an intensive summer program*. Paper presented at the annual meeting of the American Educational Research Association, Atlanta, GA. (ERIC Document Reproduction Service No. ED 369 721)

Zinker, J. C. (1977). *Creative process in gestalt therapy*. New York: Brunner/Mazel.

Study Questions ⌇

1. What are some of the factors in the larger society that may interfere with gifted girls as they attempt to develop their talents?

2. What approaches to program intervention might be most effective with gifted girls at various stages of development? How might you defend your perspective?

3. What issues must gifted girls consider in choosing a career?

4. What if you had a 12-year-old daughter who was good at mathematics but superior in the humanities and enjoyed writing poetry more than anything else? How would you counsel her in regard to taking mathematics courses?

5. What are the costs and benefits of providing single-sex classes or schools or both?

6. What is the appropriate role for the schools in addressing the needs of gifted girls? For parents? For others in the community?

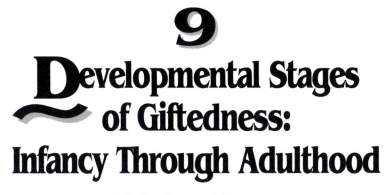

9

Developmental Stages of Giftedness: Infancy Through Adulthood

Linda Kreger Silverman

Jay's favorite activities are reading books, watching videos, and visiting museum exhibits about exotic animals, specifically Mesozoic era dinosaurs; Cenozoic era mammals, especially carnivores; Cambrian period sea creatures; and sea reptiles. His favorite books are any and all dinosaur books, *Animal World Atlas*, and *Peter Rabbit*. Jay is 4 years old.

Exceptional ability does not begin when a child is identified as gifted, nor does it end when a student exits a gifted program or graduates from school. The phenomenon, like retardation, involves inherent differences in development from birth through maturity. Developmental differences between gifted children and their age peers piqued the interest of such early leaders in psychology as William Stern (1910/1911), Lewis Terman (1914), and Leta Hollingworth (1930). Although much of the current literature focuses on school-based performance of academically talented students, there has been a continuous undercurrent of interest in the developmental aspects of giftedness, including the development of special talents (e.g., Bloom, 1985; Csikszentmihalyi, Rathunde, & Whalen, 1993; Feldman, 1992; VanTassel-Baska, 1996); the development of creativity (e.g., Albert, 1983; Feldman, 1982; Gardner, 1993; Goertzel, Goertzel, & Goertzel, 1978; Piechowski, 1978; Simonton, 1994; Wallace & Gruber, 1989); career paths of individuals identified as gifted in childhood and adolescence (e.g., Hollinger & Fleming, 1993; Kaufmann, 1981; Subotnik & Arnold, 1994); and the social and emotional development of gifted accelerates (e.g., Janos & Robinson,

1985; Richardson & Benbow, 1990; Robinson & Noble, 1991; Swiatek & Benbow, 1991). Case studies of exceptionally gifted children (e.g., Gross, 1993; Hollingworth, 1942; Morelock, in press) have illuminated the unique developmental issues of this population. Although only a few prospective studies have been conducted comparing gifted children's development with that of their less able age peers, these studies reveal consistent differences between gifted children and unselected children at various stages in development (e.g., Gottfried, Gottfried, Bathurst, & Guerin, 1994; Hitchfield, 1973; Humphreys & Davey, 1988). Findings from the Fullerton Longitudinal Study indicated that "gifted and nongifted children develop at different levels from infancy through adolescence" (Gottfried et al., 1994, p. 61). To obtain a comprehensive view of the nature of giftedness, therefore, one must go beyond the classroom to the home life, the infant and preschool years, the social and emotional aspects at each stage of development, gender issues, and the challenges presented in adulthood.

Infancy and Toddlerhood ⌇

How early in life do the developmental differences of gifted children begin to be manifested? In a study conducted by Gogel, McCumsey, and Hewett (1985), nearly half of the 1,039 parents of identified gifted children suspected that their children were gifted before their toddlers were 2 years old. White and Watts (1973) noted that children who are either unusually rapid or unusually slow in their development show signs of their exceptionality as early as 18 months of age. These findings were recently confirmed in the Fullerton Longitudinal Study (Gottfried et al., 1994):

> Differences in level of intellectual performance between the gifted and nongifted children emerged on the psychometric testing at 1.5 years and maintained continuity thereafter. However, the earliest difference was found on receptive language skills at age 1 year. Differences in receptive and expressive language skills were consistently found from infancy onward....
>
>   There were reliable signs of potential intellectual giftedness in the course of early development. (pp. 84–85)

Some signs of developmental advancement may be seen in newborns, such as preference for the novel over the familiar, high newborn cry counts, and alertness (Robinson, 1993). Berché Cruz (1987) found higher glucose absorption in gifted infants than their age peers, as well as faster progression from reflexive to intentional behavior. The Fullerton group asserted that parents are "perceptive of their children's developmental position as early as infancy" (Gottfried et al., 1994, p. 83), and some, according to Louis and Lewis (1992), make judgments about their children's abilities within the first 48 hours of life.

The amazing range of children's development becomes vivid when one observes extraordinarily gifted young children. In Rogers' (1986) study, a parent reported that her 7-month-old infant "was watching 'Sesame Street' so intently that when he finally fell asleep he was still watching and just fell over backwards" (Rogers &

Silverman, 1988, p. 5). One of the children in our case files at the Gifted Development Center held his head up and pulled his chest up by pushing with his arms almost from birth; he waved "hello" at 2 months of age. Another said "hi" at 4 months of age. A third spoke in sentences and had a vocabulary of over 250 words at 14 months; by the age of 2 she could put together a 60-piece puzzle. A 17-month-old girl was able to recite a 60-page beginning reader, *Go Dog, Go*, from memory.

Recognizing Giftedness

The three most frequent indicators of even moderate levels of giftedness in infants and toddlers appear to be early attention, memory, and advanced language development (Tannenbaum, 1992). Over 90% of the parents in Rogers' (1986) study described their children as having an excellent memory and advanced vocabulary development. In studies at the Gifted Development Center, the earliest signs of giftedness reported by parents of mildly, moderately, and highly gifted children were:

- Unusual alertness in infancy
- Less need for sleep in infancy
- Long attention span
- High activity level
- Smiling or recognizing caretakers early
- Marked need for attention and stimulation
- Intense reactions to noise, pain, frustration
- Advanced progression through the developmental milestones
- Extraordinary memory
- Rapidity of learning
- Early and extensive language development
- Fascination with books
- Curiosity; asks many questions (Silverman, 1997)

Children who display approximately three fourths of the characteristics of giftedness usually test in at least the mildly gifted range (>120 IQ) (Silverman, 1992). In one study, 86% of the children whose parents endorsed three fourths of the characteristics of giftedness tested above 120 IQ (Silverman, Chitwood, & Waters, 1986). In a later replication, 84% of 1,000 children whose parents said they exhibited three fourths of the gifted characteristics tested in the superior range (>120 IQ). The Seattle Project (Roedell, Jackson, & Robinson, 1980), the Fullerton Longitudinal Study (Gottfried et al., 1994), and Louis and Lewis (1992) also found parents to be good judges of giftedness in their preschoolers. Sixty-one percent of 118 preschool children whose parents suspected that they were gifted tested above 132 IQ on the Stanford-Binet Intelligence Scale (Form L–M) (Louis & Lewis, 1992).

Gifted children differ markedly from one another in temperament, interests, talents, skills, and rate of advancement; therefore, it would be inappropriate to expect any gifted child to exhibit all of the characteristics of giftedness. Although the characteristics presented earlier in this chapter appear to differentiate gifted from nongifted children in the majority of cases, so far there does not appear to be a correlation between the number of characteristics or specific characteristics endorsed by parents and the degree of precocity beyond 120 IQ (Silverman, Chitwood, & Waters, 1986). One exception may be sleep patterns: In Gaunt's (1989) study, parents of highly gifted children reported that their children needed less sleep than the amount parents of moderately gifted children reported.

In addition, it must be kept in mind that not all gifted children demonstrate abilities early. Visual-spatial learners are often late bloomers (see Chapter 3). Their reading and language development may not develop as quickly as their skills in investigation, construction, mechanics, and solving puzzles or mazes. Many gifted children have dual exceptionalities, such as giftedness combined with weak audition, vision, or motor coordination. Children with a history of recurrent ear infections may develop expressive language at a slower rate than their healthier siblings. And then there are introverted children who understand everything they hear but choose not to speak until they have perfected the linguistic system. One child's first "word" was "Charlie, will you please pass the salt?"

Parenting the Gifted

What is it like to raise a gifted infant? In a word, exhausting! The composite picture of the infancy of gifted children obtained from over 2,000 families would indicate that parents get more than they bargained for when they give birth to precocious babies. Sleepless nights seem never ending, colic often comes with the territory, and a desire for novelty (Fagan & McGrath, 1981; Lewis & Brooks-Gunn, 1981) and constant stimulation are the norm (Silverman & Kearney, 1989). Gifted infants tend to be both highly active and highly reactive—intense balls of energy who have as great an impact on their environment as their environment has on them (Robinson, 1993). There may exist many calm, placid gifted infants who sleep a lot and do not need much attention, but they do not often come to the attention of clinicians.

It is possible that gifted young children are at higher risk for allergic reactions, ear infections, and other immune-related deficiencies (Benbow, 1986). They seem to be wired for action, more tense than other babies, and more susceptible to respiratory and gastrointestinal stress. Several researchers have hypothesized that the gifted come equipped with supersensitivity of the nervous system, like a finely wired thoroughbred, which enables them to assimilate extraordinary amounts of sensory stimuli (Blackburn & Erickson, 1986; Cruickshank, 1963; Silverman, 1993; Whitmore, 1980).

Gifted toddlers are delightful in their advanced progression through the developmental milestones, their curiosity, their conceptual development, and their facility with language, but their precocity can also be embarrassing. Stories abound of small children reading the menus at restaurants or the labels on all the cans at the grocery store amidst the disbelieving and disapproving stares of other customers. Katheryn Kearney (1992) related a particularly embarrassing incident reported by one of the families with whom she worked:

> At a time when most two year olds are content to name items in the supermarket, Andrew had already initiated extensive discussions with his mother at home about the nutritional value of various products. As they were proceeding down the cereal aisle,

Andrew, seated in the grocery cart, spied three middle-aged women selecting sugared cereals with artificial colors. Before Andrew's mother knew what had happened, three startled women turned around to see the two year old standing up in the grocery cart, shaking his finger, and lecturing, "Put those back! Put those back! Don't you realize that cereal is bad for you? It is mostly sugar, and contains artificial flavors and colors!" (p. 9)

When to Identify

The evidence that developmental precocity is observable in the first years of life leads to the question, "When is it optimal and appropriate to identify gifted children?" Typically, schools wait until third or fourth grade, and some educators insist that identification is not possible, valid, or appropriate in the preschool or primary grades. However, if developmentally advanced children are viewed as children with special needs—a legitimate branch of exceptional education—then the question, "When is it optimal to identify any exceptional child?" must be raised. The answer for every other special education population is quite clear: "As early as possible." Why? Because the unequivocal importance of *early intervention* with the disabled and disadvantaged has been impressed upon the American psyche. However, early intervention is also essential in the development of talent (Bloom, 1985) and in the optimal emotional, social, moral, spiritual, and intellectual development of precocious children.

Numerous methods are used to assess developmental delay in newborns, and methods are even available to detect it prenatally in order to facilitate early intervention. Current research indicates that giftedness is identifiable and measurable by 18 months of age and probably much earlier in the highly gifted, who perform astounding feats almost from birth. Developmental advancement conceivably could be detected in utero, but efforts in this direction are unlikely to be supported in today's political climate. It is remarkable that so many educators feel children cannot or should not be identified as gifted during the early years (Office of Educational Research and Improvement, 1993) when psychology has demonstrated both the feasibility and wisdom of early identification of children with atypical developmental patterns, whether delayed or advanced.

Preschool and Primary Years

The challenges of the first few years of life are greater for parents than for their gifted children. But eventually most parents accommodate to the unusual developmental schedules of their young gifted children. It is the next few years that seem to take the greatest fortitude for both gifted children and their parents. These are the years when children in our society are required to adapt to group norms, and social comparison begins to play an enormous part in the formation of children's self-concepts. Gifted preschoolers and kindergarten-aged children, like their age peers, define themselves through their first social interactions, and if the gap between their development and that of their playmates is too great, they have difficulty adjusting. As

Terman (1931) stated, "Precocity unavoidably complicates the problem of social adjustment" (p. 579).

The child who asks a thousand questions a day is not likely to fit in very well in the context of school. It is difficult for a child to relate socially when his or her fund of knowledge and interests far surpasses those of classmates (Hollingworth, 1931). Three-year-old Antoine wanted to bring his favorite video to preschool, but the teacher thought the other children wouldn't like the ballet "The Nutcracker Suite." Antoine retorted that the children would *love* the characters in it! At the age of 4, Antoine made a model of Mars to take to school for show-and-tell and the following week tried to explain the meaning of a black hole to the class. When his classmates did not understand the difference between implosion and explosion, he used the example of import versus export. Antoine was puzzled about why the children did not seem interested.

Being different is a problem in childhood. Young children—even gifted ones— do not have the capacity to comprehend differences between themselves and others. They have difficulty understanding why other children do not think the way that they do. They equate differentness with being "strange" or unacceptable, and this becomes the basis of their self-concept. A common scenario recounted by parents is that their buoyant, confident, exuberant toddler gradually becomes subdued and uncertain during the preschool and primary years. One parent wrote,

> Alice is doing all she can to blend in and not stand out as different. She does not ask all the questions she used to. Alice is not the same person she was before she started going to school. Before she started kindergarten she had an insatiable quest for more knowledge.
>   We are concerned because we think she is a bright child who is turning off.

These descriptions of Antoine and Alice typify the differences often observed in the social development of gifted girls and gifted boys during their earliest years in school. Young boys frequently persist in sharing their knowledge with the other children regardless of the others' lack of interest, whereas girls are more likely to hide their advanced knowledge. Undaunted by his classmates' reactions to the two moons of Mars, Antoine followed up with a dissertation on black holes; Alice just stopped asking questions and tried to blend in with her age peers.

Young gifted boys appear to have greater difficulty than gifted girls in relating to children who are not at their own developmental level. They think the games of average children are "silly" or "babyish." A gifted 5-year-old boy with an 8-year-old mind will typically get angry when the other children do not follow the rules; he is unable to comprehend that his age-mates are not mentally ready to understand the meaning of rules. His own games tend to be highly organized and sophisticated (Hollingworth, 1931). If the other children cannot relate to his games, or if they laugh at him or reject him, he may conclude that there is something wrong with him (Janos, Fung, & Robinson, 1985) or he may reject the other children.

The enhanced ability of gifted girls to perceive social cues and their early programming in the critical importance of social acceptance enable them to learn more easily than boys how to modify their behavior to fit into a group (Kerr, 1994; Silverman, 1986). If a girl's social group is mentally much younger than she is, she will frequently don the mental attire of her friends and soon be imperceptible from them in thought, manner, and achievement. The girl's chameleon qualities are her saving grace in social situations, but they are also her greatest handicap in the development of her abilities.

If gifted children have early contact with others like themselves, they do not come to see themselves as different or "weird." They are able to make friends easily with others who think and feel as they do, who communicate on their level and share their interests. Association with true peers at an early age facilitates social development and prevents social alienation. "The word peer," according to Roedell (1989), "refers to individuals who can interact on an equal plane around issues of common interest" (p. 25). Many gifted children have different sets of peers for different activities. Roedell stressed the importance of true peer interaction for gifted children:

> While adaptation is important, gifted young children also need the give-and-take of interactions with others of equal ability, where they can find acceptance and understanding, the keys to the development of successful social skills and positive self-concept. (p. 26)

(See Chapter 4 in this volume for an in-depth discussion of methods for identifying and serving gifted children in early childhood.)

The Middle Years ~

Common folklore holds that by third grade the slower children will somehow manage to catch up to the faster ones, and much classroom practice is based on this misconception. Psychology, however, tells a different story. LeFrancois (1981) summarized a basic principle of development: "Development usually proceeds at the rate at which it started" (p. 89). Therefore, children who start out in the fast lane developmentally generally maintain that lead over time. Robinson (1993) elaborated:

> Not only do groups of children who were identified by their parents as advanced tend to attain high test scores, those children's scores tend to *remain* high over time, even though individual scores may vary up or down. Such findings suggest that, on average, advanced ability tends to maintain its rapid pace of development. This evidence substantiates the notion that early giftedness, or rapid development, also *predicts* the subsequent rate of development. (p. 511)

In the Fullerton Longitudinal Study, "gifted children were significantly more likely to obtain extremely superior scores" on three different achievement tests at ages 5, 6, 7, and 8 (Gottfried et al., 1994, p. 96).

However, it must be kept in mind that gifted children do not develop evenly in all areas (see Chapter 4). Even within a skill area, such as reading, gifted children vary in the degree to which they master specific subskills. Some of the precocious readers followed by Jackson and Kearney (1994) tested in the average range in reading by fourth or fifth grade, but for the group as a whole "performance levels on reading, language, and mathematics achievement were all high" (p. 497) with median scores in the 85th to 95th percentile range. Jackson and Kearney's research substantiated the findings of the Fullerton study that there tends to be continuity in development.

> Recent research suggests that, as early as the first year of life, children differ from one another in the efficiency with which they process information and learn about their world. This elementary processing efficiency appears to contribute to the development of intelligence and, perhaps, various forms of gifted performance (Jackson & Kearney, 1994, p. 495).

Differential rates of development continue to widen the gap between gifted children and their age-mates over time. Figure 9.1 shows the different developmental trajectories of gifted and average children. Notice that at no time do the trajectories converge; on the contrary, each year they diverge to a greater extent. The 4-year-old with a 6-year-old mind becomes an 8-year-old with a 12-year-old mind.

Intelligence tests document the rate at which a gifted child's mental development races ahead of his or her age mates'. When IQ scores are not available, the child's reading level can be used as a rough estimate of precocity. Many third- and fourth-grade gifted students have standardized achievement scores four grade levels beyond their current grade placement. They are capable of mastering much more advanced information than their classmates at a much more rapid rate than they are being taught. Good education actually expands the differences between gifted children and other students at their grade level. If a gifted student is capable of gaining two grade levels in reading or mathematics each year, and that opportunity is provided, the gifted student will diverge more from his or her classmates at the end of the year than at the beginning. The aim of education should be to meet the individualized needs of students rather than to close the gap between slower and faster learners.

Differences in rate of development do not tell the entire story. Children who develop in an atypical fashion are not just moving along the same track as other children at a faster or slower pace. Qualitative differences also exist in the complexity of thought and the emotional intensity of gifted individuals. A number of researchers have addressed this issue:

> The difference is not mere precocity, not just "getting there sooner." The child who deals with abstract concepts early brings those concepts to bear on all later experience. This different, more complex way of processing experience creates essentially different experience. The result is that the differences, far from shrinking as the child develops, are likely to grow larger. (Tolan, 1995, pp. 15–16)

> Gifted children are in many ways like other children, but there exists a basic difference in the *quality* of their thinking and feeling. While they progress through Piaget's stages in the same manner as other children, their progression appears to be accelerated, and, in addition, their thought processes within a stage of development are significantly more complex. (Roeper, 1995, p. 44)

> One of the basic characteristics of the gifted is their intensity and expanded field of their subjective experience. The intensity, in particular, must be understood as a quali-

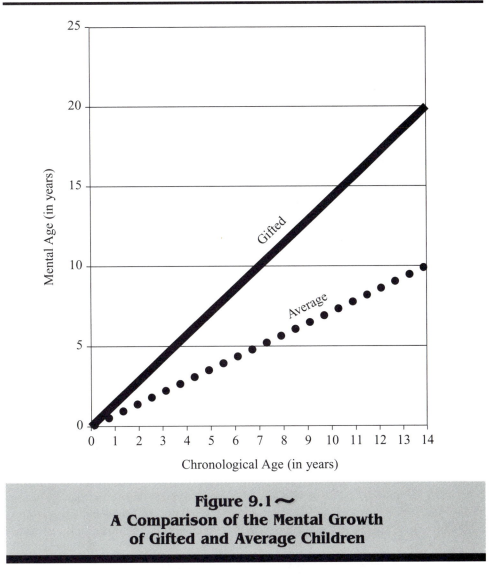

Figure 9.1 ∼
A Comparison of the Mental Growth
of Gifted and Average Children

tatively distinct characteristic. It is not a matter of degree but of a different quality of experiencing. (Piechowski, 1992, p. 181)

Gifted children are naturally drawn to activities geared toward abstract and complex thought. The intensity of this phenomenon leads us to speculate that it is undergirded by a structural and/or functional difference in brain development resulting in neurological requirements for a specific quality and level of stimulation. Thus, the gifted child is driven to extract from the environment the degree and quality of stimulation and the type of socioculturally-evolved structural support required for the development of higher psychological processes. Why? We don't know, but we need to find out. (Morelock, cited in Silverman, 1995b, p. 5)

The middle years are a time of mastery, a time in life when children delight in learning (Erikson, 1950). If gifted children are asked to sit still and be patient while the other children attempt to "catch up" to them, their natural progress will be retarded, their motivation undermined, and they will feel punished for their developmental precocity. In reality, there is no way for children developing at different developmental rates to eventually learn at the same rate (Benbow & Stanley, in press). The illusion that they will do so leads to destructive educational practices for gifted students.

Social Concerns

The advanced cognitive development of gifted children in the middle years has ramifications in the social arena as well. As Terman noted,

> The child of eight years with a mentality of twelve or fourteen is faced with a situation almost inconceivably difficult. In order to adjust normally such a child has to have an exceptionally well-balanced personality and to be well nigh a *social genius* [italics added]. The higher the IQ, the more acute the problem. (Terman, 1931, p. 579)

Sixty years of research on highly gifted children confirms Terman's observations (Dauber & Benbow, 1990; Robinson & Noble, 1991). The greater the difference between the child's abilities and the abilities of others in his or her social group, the greater the potential for loneliness and problems in social adjustment.

Whereas most of their age-mates are obsessed with following rules, gifted children in the middle years tend to question them. They understand that rules are invented and can be changed to fit circumstances, so they often test the limits of a rule's application with endless what-ifs. In addition to annoying most adults, the behavior can cause social isolation. Conformity is important in upper-elementary peer groups, and gifted children who question the rules have a difficult time socially. Boys begin to judge one another on the basis of athletic ability, and girls begin to judge one another on more encompassing criteria—"like us" or "not like us." Nine-year-old girls place a high premium on conformity and are quick to ostracize any girl they perceive as different. Bell (1989) reported that by fourth grade, gifted girls start to lose confidence and lower their effort and expectations. The crisis that awaits most girls in preadolescence (American Association of University Women, 1992; Pipher, 1994) can occur at age 9 for early maturing gifted girls. Lifelong patterns of underachievement may be seeded during this phase of development. But prior to this crisis, gifted girls often believe in themselves, exude self-confidence, and are willing to demonstrate their capabilities. Kerr (1994) provided the following rich description:

> Like birds in spring, they are in their most colorful phase. Later on, they will blend in, perhaps so much that their gifts might never be spotted. But for this brief time of childhood, gifted girls may be enthusiasts, scholars, clowns, and dreamers. Few educators or psychologists have studied the gifted female in this bright and florid phase, from preschool to junior high. (pp. 109–110)

Gender-Identification Issues

During the stage of development in which girls prefer the company of other girls and boys seem particularly allergic to girls, gifted boys and girls often break the rules and befriend children of the opposite sex. Many gifted girls secretly wish they were boys or openly defy group norms, earning themselves the label "tomboy." The word "tomboy," according to Pipher (1994), "conveys courage, competency and irreverence" (p. 18); it represents a brief respite from the female role. There are many advantages to choosing to be a tomboy rather than adopting a more feminine demeanor. Tomboys learn a great deal about being a "team player," which serves them well in the corporate environment or in male-dominated professions in adult life. The desire to be male may stem from observing the greater freedom allowed to boys (Clark, 1992) and the greater status afforded adult males (Kerr, 1994). In addition, many gifted girls and boys exhibit cross-gender characteristics and interests (Silverman, 1986) and are more comfortable with the opposite sex than with members of their own.

Gender identification is more problematic for gifted boys than it is for gifted girls. Whereas being a tomboy is generally considered healthy for preadolescents, or at least tolerated in most modern families, being called a "sissy" is quite another matter (Alvino, 1991). Derogatory names for elementary-school boys often contain aspects of femininity. Boys in upper elementary grades define their maleness as the opposite of femaleness; by third or fourth grade, they are expected to summarily reject all aspects of themselves that are considered "feminine" or face serious peer rejection. This places the sensitive, compassionate, nurturant gifted boy in conflict with his peer group and endangers the concept of his masculinity. Gifted boys need sensitive adult male role models in their lives so that they can learn to honor and retain the feminine aspects of themselves. Some researchers contend that these aspects are important for the development of a man's creative potential (Dellas, 1980; MacKinnon, 1962).

Gifted boys and girls need to be encouraged to develop in an androgynous manner—that is, to value traits in themselves that are both "masculine" and "feminine." The blending of masculine and feminine traits appears to be correlated with high self-esteem in adolescent females (Hollinger, 1983; Hollinger & Fleming, 1993) and higher creativity in adolescent males (Dellas, 1980). Too much emphasis on sex-role stereotyping is likely to be damaging to both genders.

Preadolescence ⁓

Caught between childhood and adulthood, the preadolescent undergoes profound physiological and psychological changes. According to Erik Erikson (1950), puberty is the beginning of the adolescent search for identity. Self-concept is a major issue for all children during this stage of development; it is likely to take precedence over the need for achievement. For these reasons, the essence of middle-school philosophy is the nurturance of children's self-concept. However, the complexities of giftedness have not been taken into account in the equation, and the well-intended formulas for healthy development of middle schoolers can often be counterproductive for gifted preteens.

Being Out-of-Sync

In addition to all the bodily changes, fears, and social comparisons that affect all individuals during this period of development, gifted young people must cope with dramatic differences in the rates of their own internal development. A 12-year-old boy with the mind of an 18-year-old, coupled with the physique and athletic prowess of a 10-year-old, has a unique set of issues. Part of the boy has already entered older adolescence, complete with existential angst about the meaning of his existence, career concerns, questions about which college to attend, strong desires for independence, awareness of the condition of the world he is inheriting, and fear that he is helpless to make a difference. Part of the boy holds tenaciously to childhood, is awkward, is ashamed that his own physical attributes and skills compare unfavorably to more mature peers, is unable to contemplate dating, is overwhelmed at the thought of becoming an adult, and takes refuge in books. Gifted preteens are a mass of contradictions. One 11-year-old insisted vehemently to his parents that he was too old to be told what time to go to bed but wanted to be tucked in at night. A 12-year-old boy stepped off an airplane with his calculus book in one hand and his Curious George in the other.

Kline and Short (1991) found that feelings of discouragement and hopelessness peaked for gifted boys during junior high school. "During junior high," they wrote, "gifted boys have increased feelings of depression, worry and loneliness. Additionally, they deal with more thoughts about not wanting to live, even to the point of thinking how to end their lives" (pp. 186–187). In another study, more than half the gifted boys polled admitted hiding their abilities in order to fit in with their peers (Alvino, 1991). The psychic pain experienced during this preadolescent period may be sufficient to cause gifted males to disconnect emotionally for the remainder of their lives.

The dilemmas for girls of this age appear to be just as acute (Pipher, 1994). A turning point for many gifted girls occurs during middle school or junior high school, when they leave the bright hopes of childhood behind. Without warning, their confidence fades and is replaced with self-doubt and lowered aspirations (Orenstein, 1994). Several recent books describe the crippling aspects of the culture in which American girls come of age (e.g., American Association of University Women, 1992; Eagle & Colman, 1993; Orenstein, 1994; Pipher, 1994; Sadker & Sadker, 1994), and all refer, either directly or indirectly, to the tragedy of being a smart girl in today's society. The term "schoolgirl" is an insult other students hurl at studious middle-school girls who value their intelligence; many feel it is second only to "slut" in terms of its potential to degrade (Orenstein, 1994). Gifted girls are likely to deny their intelligence and downplay their abilities because the costs of expressing them are too high. Orenstein (1994) described the dilemma the girls face as follows:

> Girls like Lindsay and Suzy are the biggest losers: gifted girls, who best combine tractability with superior performance, receive less attention from their teachers, and often their talents are overlooked entirely.... Liz Muney...discovered that boys were referred to her twice as often as girls for special testing, precisely because giftedness is seen as aberrant, and girls strive to conform.... The social pressure, Liz Muney says, has prompted innumerable Weston girls to repudiate their intelligence (as well as their self-esteem) and drop out of the district's gifted program. (p. 36)

In clinical interviews, gifted women often recall their middle-school years as nightmarish:

> A soft-spoken young woman...remembered middle school as a smart girl's torture chamber. "No one would speak to me," she said. "I wouldn't even go into the cafeteria for lunch. Long tables stretched the length of the whole room, but wherever I sat, people acted as if I wasn't in the right place. It wasn't so much cliques as a long social scale, and I couldn't figure out where I was supposed to fit." (Sadker & Sadker, 1994, pp. 92–93)

The vulnerability of gifted girls during junior high school has been reported again and again in the literature (Bell, 1989; Buescher & Higham, 1989; Casserly, 1979; Silverman, 1995a). Noble (1987) summed up the situation, "The pre-adolescent peer group tends to reject a girl who appears to be too smart or too successful" (p. 371).

What Can Make a Difference?

The university-sponsored talent search programs have been the salvation of countless gifted seventh and eighth graders. Numerous gifted teenagers have reported how desperately lonely they were, how ashamed they felt of their differences, until they met other students like themselves at a summer gifted program on a nearby college campus. Contrary to the widely held belief that associations with other gifted students prevent youth from adjusting to the "real world," their ability to relate to heterogeneous groups *increases* when they have the opportunity to associate with others like themselves. Higham and Buescher (1987) reported that there is a carry-over effect from the positive social experiences of preadolescents in summer enrichment programs to their regular school experiences: The students felt more comfortable and socially adept as a result of their summer experiences. Once they have found friends who truly appreciate them, laugh at their jokes, and enjoy their company, their self-confidence increases in other situations. They demand less from average peers because they know that somewhere someone likes them just the way they are. One boy wrote:

> I think CTY [the Center for the Advancement of Academically Talented Youth] completely changed my outlook on everything. I used to try to fit in and be like everybody else but CTY taught me that I could be my own person and be as wacky or crazy as I want to be, and people would still like me, and if they don't, I don't care. I'm much happier now and have more friends than before. (Leviton, 1994, p. 18)

The high-powered academic offerings completed by gifted students in summer and after-school, university-sponsored enrichment programs call into question some basic assumptions about the intellectual growth potential of middle schoolers. Most middle schools present gifted students with an underchallenging, excruciatingly slow-paced curriculum; in contrast, studies over the past 25 years have demonstrated that gifted 13-year-olds can devour an entire year of high-school mathematics, chemistry, physics, biology, or Latin, or a full semester of college-level physics, logic, computer science, astronomy, or psychology, in *3 weeks* during a summer talent search program (Benbow & Stanley, in press; Lynch, 1992; Stanley & Stanley, 1986). (See Chapter 16.)

Gifted preteens light up when they talk about their summer enrichment experiences. They describe feeling more intellectually stimulated, more motivated, and more accepted than they have ever felt in their lives. Some say that they live for summers, and many lament, "Why can't school be like this all year 'round?"

Adolescence ～

Adolescence is an interesting period in the lives of the gifted and may be quite different from what parents expect. In many respects, gifted children enter adolescence much earlier than their peers. They may begin to experience existential angst in elementary school, wondering about the meaning of life and their place in the scheme of things. Some gifted girls mature physically at an accelerated rate, beginning menses at age 9 or 10. And many gifted children have such a strong need for self-reliance that they may fight the battle for independence with their parents (and win it) well before the onset of adolescence. However, independence brings with it adult awareness and responsibilities, and when gifted youth are faced at adolescence with the imminence of adulthood, many retreat into younger behavior patterns, clinging desperately to their rapidly vanishing childhood freedom. So while their age-mates are pressing their parents for more and more autonomy, gifted adolescents may be moving, at least temporarily, in the opposite direction. Buescher (1989) described adolescence for gifted youth as follows:

> The first real surge of feeling different or separate from their families in adolescence...seems to trigger a kind of large scale retreat, moving these students in reverse, past the normal reactive or rebellious activities of adolescence back into a "clingy" stage of apparent *undifferentiated* childhood. For example, some bright 13 and 14 year olds who once bristled with surety and confidence sometimes begin to act indecisive, incapable of even the simplest solution. (p. 16)

It is difficult to make generalizations about gifted teens, since each story is unique and the years encompassed are so vast. It seems that as gifted youth reach adolescence they are carving out paths that set them apart not only from average adolescents, but also from other gifted teens. One student may be highly studious, have clear interests and goals, and be determined to attain those goals. The student may set aside athletics and dating in favor of academic pursuits. Another may be working just as hard to attain social acceptance, and schoolwork takes a back seat to this developmental goal. The least popular student in the school tends to be the brilliant, studious, nonathletic boy (Cramond & Martin, 1987; Tannenbaum, 1962), and many gifted young men manage to convince themselves that popularity is not important to them. However, girls find it more difficult to devalue popularity, for a number of reasons, including their greater need for affiliation (Gilligan, 1988), the constraints imposed by the female peer group (Pipher, 1994; Silverman, 1986), and fear that lack of popularity means that they will be doomed to spend the rest of their lives alone.

The search for identity tends to take different forms in males and females. Young men become increasingly aware that they must choose a meaningful career in order to survive in the adult world. Their identity may become fused with their career goals. They are likely to build walls to protect themselves from feeling vulnerable:

> By high school age, it appears that most gifted boys decide to emphasize career success. They relegate emotional and relational themes to a lower order of priority. They do not rely on relationships as much as they did when they were younger for feelings of self-worth and confidence. It appears they decide to shut the door on the emotional insecurity of their junior high experience and put a shield over their vulnerability, suppressing their potential for experiencing feelings and having rewarding relationships. This is a different position than that taken by gifted females in senior high school for whom relationships take a primary place in their value constellation. (Kline & Short, 1991, p. 187)

Indeed, young women tend to be more focused on relationships, acting on the conviction—conscious or unconscious—that their survival depends upon their attractiveness. Dieting is a preoccupation for the majority of female adolescents (Sadker & Sadker, 1994), and their caloric intake may be insufficient to support the strenuous mental effort required to attain high grades in difficult subjects. Excessive dieting can also cause lack of interest in, and energy for, schoolwork, and it can lead to depression or worse. Eating disorders claim the lives of 150,000 young women annually (Sadker & Sadker, 1994). Yet, little is done to discourage teenage girls from dieting.

Emotions are costly, and gifted males and females are blessed with an overabundance of intense emotional energy (Piechowski, 1992). Alvino (1991) suggested that gifted boys are not permitted to develop or express their emotionality in healthy ways, and that this can lead to explosive competitiveness, excessive perfectionism, and insecurity: "It is as though their sense of self-worth and means of obtaining love and affection inextricably are tied to their accomplishments. This can reach tragic proportions" (p. 176). It is important for gifted adolescents, males and females alike, to learn how to deal effectively with the strength of their emotional reactions.

Family Life

Pipher (1994) asserted that parents who are strict but loving "have teenagers who are independent, socially responsible and confident" (p. 83). She warned that too much parental control circumscribes and thwarts the development of a young person's potential, but too little control leaves adolescents with too much personal freedom, which can have disastrous consequences in today's world. Families must strike a difficult balance between security and freedom.

Families that treat the 16-year-old-going-on-24 more like an adult than a child have much less strife than families in which the parents hold onto the reins too tightly. It is helpful for parents to keep in mind that their role needs to shift during their children's adolescence. Instead of being responsible for their children and protecting their welfare, they need to shift the balance of responsibility to the young adults in their care. Doing so will provide the best preparation for their children for adult life and will provide the basis for lifelong friendship between parents and their offspring. Family meetings, in which everyone has a share in decision-making, serve as one way of moving out of old roles, teaching young people the art of negotiation, and establishing new patterns of family dynamics (Silverman, 1992).

Social Development

By late adolescence, most gifted children have weathered the storm and have made life decisions about who they are and what they will do with their lives. Radically accelerated students spend their adolescence in college atmospheres in which they are expected to have adult-like judgment, and in fact, they do (Benbow, 1991; Robinson & Noble, 1991). Although, at first blush, it may seem that placing an underage student in a college atmosphere is pushing his or her social and emotional adjustment well beyond reason, the research consistently shows that students who enter college at as young an age as 14 have excellent social development that is maintained over time (Benbow, 1991; Janos & Robinson, 1985; Robinson & Noble, 1991). The social and emotional adjustment of no other group of students has been studied so thoroughly. There is no research to support the popular contention that children are more socially adjusted when they are kept with age peers throughout their school experience.

Whereas some gifted students are clear in late adolescence about the career paths they wish to engage in, others need more time to decide. A liberal arts education, at least for the first 2 years of undergraduate school, allows time to explore the larger questions, time to appreciate the interconnectedness of disciplines, and time to savor what is left of childhood before the responsibilities of adulthood ensue.

By the end of high school and the beginning of college, the gifted young adult may be wrestling with profound questions about the meaning of his or her existence (Kerr, 1991). When struggling to find his or her own set of values, the gifted young adult may temporarily reject the values of his or her parents and peers. After a period of questioning and exploration, however, most gifted adolescents adopt the values of their parents (LeFrancois, 1981). A few follow a different path, entering into a lifelong search for a deeper reality. The search may take them down a more introspective, contemplative path. Instead of identifying with the values of their immediate peer group, they may find themselves identifying with the plight of humanity. They may immerse themselves in the study of philosophy or comparative religions until they can construct a sense of order and meaning in their lives. This path has been described by Dabrowski (1964, 1972) and his colleagues (Dabrowski & Piechowski, 1977).

Adulthood ⌇

Giftedness does not cease when children grow up. For adults, society tends to use the term *gifted* to describe only those individuals whose accomplishments have won recognition. But the same characteristics that parents observed in their 1-year-olds continue to be exhibited in them when they are 20, 40, or 60. Abstract reasoning, rapid learning, curiosity, awareness (the sequel to alertness), fascination with books, unusual sleep patterns (Tolan, 1994), high energy, marked need for stimulation, extensive vocabulary, and intense reactions are all part of the adult experience of being gifted. The only trait that does not survive older adulthood very well is excellent memory.

This emerging viewpoint on giftedness in adults suggests that throughout the lifespan the gifted face unique social, emotional, moral, and spiritual issues (Silverman, 1990). Although it may appear that development is complete by the time an individual attains adulthood, a number of theorists (e.g., Dabrowski, Erikson, Loevinger, Kegan, Maslow) described stages of adult development according to various criteria. Dabrowski's theory, more than any of the other frameworks, has been applied to the study of gifted adults (see Piechowski, 1978, 1992; Silverman, 1990, 1993, 1995b). Through this lens, the moral and emotional development of the gifted can be tracked, as well as their progress toward self-actualization.

In a collection of articles on giftedness in adults, Tolan (1995) made the case that giftedness is more than just developmental precocity:

> If giftedness is merely an artifact of rapid progress through normal developmental stages, it could be destined to fade when others "catch up" or even move beyond.
> If, on the other hand, it is a quality of mind that creates a genuinely unusual developmental trajectory, it would be a stable attribute, remaining with the individual throughout life whether outwardly evident or not....
> What is different about the gifted individual is his or her mind. Not understanding that mind makes it virtually impossible to honor the self.... From childhood to adulthood, to be themselves, to value and honor themselves and lead fulfilled lives, gifted adults must understand and come to terms with their own—unusual—minds. (pp. 14, 19)

Tolan's position echoes the early wisdom of Terman (1931), who perceived giftedness as a high degree of intelligence or the..."ability to see relationships and to think in abstract terms." (p. 569)

> The possession of this ability in high degree enables one to solve difficult problems, to adjust to complicated situations having novel elements, and to acquire extensive command of thought or behavior symbols in the form of language. Intelligence in this sense has to do with the higher mental processes. (p. 569)

Although this perspective has been censored by the media (Snyderman & Rothman, 1988) and has been eschewed by educators in favor of more egalitarian conceptions, the fact remains that the degree of abstract intelligence does vary among human beings and that significantly more or less of it—which we call "exceptionality"— exerts a profound impact on every aspect of an individual's development throughout life.

Summary ~

Giftedness involves a developmental trajectory that is differentiated in many respects from the norm. The path leads to unusual life experiences at each stage in the life cycle, complicating the processes of social and emotional development. The problems are magnified by societal anti-intellectualism and confining gender roles. Gifted boys and girls appear to be at considerable risk of damage to their self-esteem at various points in their development, particularly preadolescence. Positive interventions for the gifted include parental support, early identification, grouping with other gifted peers, university-sponsored enrichment programs, adult role models, mentors, and self-recognition in adulthood. It is sometimes painful, sometimes glorious, to be exceptional; it helps to have guides to light the path throughout the journey into adulthood.

References ~

Albert, R. S. (Ed.). (1983). *Genius and eminence: The social psychology of creativity and exceptional achievement*. London: Pergamon.

Alvino, J. (1991). An investigation into the needs of gifted boys. *Roeper Review, 13*, 174–180.

American Association of University Women. (1992). *The AAUW report: How schools shortchange girls. Executive summary*. Washington, DC: The American Association of University Women Educational Foundation.

Bell, L. A. (1989). Something's wrong here and it's not me: Challenging the dilemmas that block girls' success. *Journal for the Education of the Gifted, 12*, 118–130.

Benbow, C. P. (1986). Physiological correlates of extreme intellectual precocity. *Neuropsychologia, 24*, 719–725.

Benbow, C. P. (1991). Meeting the needs of gifted students through use of acceleration: An often neglected resource. In M. C. Wang, M. C. Reynolds, & H. J. Walberg (Eds.), *Handbook of special education, research and practice: Vol. 4. Emerging programs* (pp. 23–36). Elmsford, NY: Pergamon.

Benbow, C. P., & Stanley, J. C. (1996). Inequity in equity: How "equity" can lead to inequity for high-potential students. *Psychology, Public Policy, and Law, 2*(2), 249–292.

Berché Cruz, X. (1987, August). *Developmental differences in gifted and average children*. Paper presented at the Seventh World Conference on Gifted and Talented Children, Salt Lake City, UT.

Blackburn, A. C., & Erickson, D. B. (1986). Predictable crises of the gifted student. *Journal of Counseling and Development, 9*, 552–555.

Bloom, B. S. (Ed.). (1985). *Developing talent in young people*. New York: Ballantine.

Buescher, T. M. (1989). Adolescent passages: Building relationships beyond the family, Part II. *Understanding Our Gifted, 1*(6), 16–17.

Buescher, T. M., & Higham, S. J. (1989). A developmental study of adjustment among gifted adolescents. In J. VanTassel-Baska & P. Olszewski-Kubilius (Eds.), *Patterns of influence on gifted learners: The home, the self, and the school* (pp. 102–124). New York: Teachers College Press.

Casserly, P. L. (1979). Helping able young women take math and science seriously in school. In N. Colangelo & R. T. Zaffrann (Eds.), *New voices in counseling the gifted* (pp. 346–369). Dubuque, IA: Kendall/Hunt.

Clark, B. (1992). *Growing up gifted: Developing the potential of children at home and at school* (4th ed.). New York: Macmillan.

Cramond, B., & Martin, C. E. (1987). Inservice and preservice teachers' attitudes toward the academically brilliant. *Gifted Child Quarterly, 31*, 15–19.

Cruickshank, W. M. (1963). *Psychology of exceptional children and youth* (2nd ed.). Englewood Cliffs, NJ: Prentice-Hall.

Csikszentmihalyi, M., Rathunde, K., & Whalen, S. (1993). *Talented teenagers: The roots of success and failure*. New York: Cambridge University Press.

Dabrowski, K. (1964). *Positive disintegration*. London: Little, Brown.

Dabrowski, K. (1972). *Psychoneurosis is not an illness*. London: Gryf.

Dabrowski, K., & Piechowski, M. M. (1977). *Theory of levels of emotional development* (Vols. 1 & 2). Oceanside, NY: Dabor Science.

Dauber, S. L., & Benbow, C. P. (1990). Aspects of personality and peer relations of extremely talented adolescents. *Gifted Child Quarterly, 34*, 10–15.

Dellas, M. (1980). Counselor role and function in counseling the creative student. In J. C. Gowan, G. D. Demos, & C. J. Kokaska (Eds.), *The guidance of exceptional children* (2nd ed., pp. 87–93). New York: Longman.

Eagle, C. J., & Colman, C. (1993). *All that she can be: Helping your daughter maintain her self-esteem*. New York: Simon & Schuster Fireside Book.

Erikson, E. H. (1950). *Childhood and society*. New York: Norton.

Fagan, J. F., & McGrath, S. K. (1981). Infant recognition memory and later intelligence. *Intelligence, 5*, 121–130.

Feldman, D. H. (Ed.). (1982). *Developmental approaches to giftedness and creativity*. San Francisco: Jossey-Bass.

Feldman, D. H. (1992, January). Intelligences, symbol systems, skills, domains, and fields: A sketch of a developmental theory of intelligence. In H. C. Rosselli & G. A. MacLauchlan (Eds.), *Proceedings of the Edyth Bush Symposium on Intelligence: Theory into practice* (pp. 83–95). Tampa: University of South Florida.

Gardner, H. G. (1993). *Creating minds*. New York: Basic Books.

Gaunt, R. I. (1989). *A comparison of the perceptions of parents of highly and moderately gifted children*. Unpublished doctoral dissertation, Kent State University, Kent, OH.

Gilligan, C. (1988). Prologue: Adolescent development reconsidered. In C. Gilligan, J. V. Ward, & J. M. Taylor with B. Bardige (Eds.), *Mapping the moral domain: A contribution of women's thinking to psychological theory and education* (pp. vi–xxxix). Cambridge, MA: Harvard University Press.

Goertzel, M. G., Goertzel, V., & Goertzel, T. G. (1978). *Three hundred eminent personalities*. San Francisco: Jossey-Bass.

Gogel, E. M., McCumsey, J., & Hewett, G. (1985, November/December). *G/C/T*, Issue Number 41, 7–9.

Gottfried, A. W., Gottfried, A. E., Bathurst, K., & Guerin, D. W. (1994). *Gifted IQ: Early developmental aspects. The Fullerton longitudinal study*. New York: Plenum.

Gross, M. U. M. (1993). *Exceptionally gifted children*. London: Routledge.

Higham, S. J., & Buescher, T. M. (1987). What young gifted adolescents understand about feeling "different." In T. M. Buescher (Ed.), *Understanding gifted and talented adolescents: A resource guide for counselors, educators, and parents* (pp. 77–91). Evanston, IL: Northwestern University, Center for Talent Development.

Hitchfield, E. M. (1973). *In search of promise*. London: Longman.

Hollinger, C. L. (1983). Counseling the gifted and talented female adolescent: The relationship between social self-esteem and traits of instrumentality and expressiveness. *Gifted Child Quarterly, 27*, 157–161.

Hollinger, C., & Fleming, E. S. (1993). Project CHOICE: The emerging roles and careers of gifted women. *Roeper Review, 15*, 156–160.

Hollingworth, L. S. (1930). Personality development of special class children. *University of Pennsylvania Bulletin. Seventeenth Annual Schoolmen's Week Proceedings, 30,* 442–446.

Hollingworth, L. S. (1931). The child of very superior intelligence as a special problem in social adjustment. *Mental Hygiene, 15*(1), 1–16.

Hollingworth, L. S. (1942). *Children above 180 IQ Stanford-Binet: Origin and development.* Yonkers-on-Hudson, NY: World Book.

Humphreys, L. G., & Davey, T. C. (1988). Continuity in intellectual growth from 12 months to 9 years. *Intelligence, 12,* 183–198.

Jackson, N. E., & Kearney, J. M. (1994). Relations between post-kindergarten reading precocity and later achievement in language arts and mathematics: A longitudinal study. In N. Colangelo, S. Assouline, & D. L. Ambroson (Eds.), *Talent development: Proceedings of the 1993 Henry B. and Jocelyn Wallace National Research Symposium on Talent Development* (pp. 495–498). Dayton, OH: Ohio Psychology Press.

Janos, P. M., Fung, H. C., & Robinson, N. M. (1985). Self-concept, self-esteem, and peer relations among gifted children who feel "different." *Gifted Child Quarterly, 29,* 78–82.

Janos, P. M., & Robinson, N. M. (1985). Psychosocial development in intellectually gifted children. In F. D. Horowitz & M. O'Brien (Eds.), *The gifted and talented: Developmental perspectives* (pp. 149–195). Washington, DC: American Psychological Association.

Kaufmann, F. A. (1981). The 1964–1968 Presidential Scholars: A follow-up study. *Exceptional Children, 48,* 164–169.

Kearney, K. (1992). Life in the asynchronous family. *Understanding Our Gifted, 4*(6), 1, 8–12.

Kerr, B. A. (1991). *A handbook for counseling the gifted and talented.* Alexandria, VA: American Association for Counseling and Development.

Kerr, B. A. (1994). *Smart girls two: A new psychology of girls, women and giftedness.* Dayton, OH: Ohio Psychology Press.

Kline, B. E., & Short, E. B. (1991). Changes in emotional resilience: Gifted adolescent boys. *Roeper Review, 13,* 184–187.

LeFrancois, G. R. (1981). *Adolescents* (2nd ed.). Belmont, CA: Wadsworth.

Leviton, M. (1994). My best summer. *Understanding Our Gifted, 6*(4), 18.

Lewis, M., & Brooks-Gunn, J. (1981). Visual attention at three months as a predictor of cognitive functioning at two years of age. *Intelligence, 5*(2), 131–140.

Louis, B., & Lewis, M. (1992). Parental beliefs about giftedness in young children and their relation to actual ability level. *Gifted Child Quarterly, 36,* 27–31.

Lynch, S. J. (1992). Fast-paced high school science for the academically talented: A six-year perspective. *Gifted Child Quarterly, 36,* 147–154.

MacKinnon, D. W. (1962). The nature and nurture of creative talent. *American Psychologist, 17,* 484–495.

Morelock, M. J. (in press). The child of extraordinarily high IQ from a Vygotskian perspective. In R. C. Friedman & B. M. Shore (Eds.), *Talents within: Cognition and development.* Washington, DC: American Psychological Association.

Noble, K. D. (1987). The dilemma of the gifted woman. *Psychology of Women Quarterly, 11,* 367–378.

Office of Educational Research and Improvement. (1993). *National excellence: A case for developing America's talent.* Washington, DC: U.S. Government Printing Office.

Orenstein, P. (1994). *SchoolGirls: Young women, self-esteem, and the confidence gap.* New York: Anchor.

Piechowski, M. M. (1978). Self-actualization as a developmental structure: A profile of Antoine de Saint-Exupery. *Genetic Psychology Monographs, 97,* 181–242.

Piechowski, M. M. (1992). Giftedness for all seasons: Inner peace in time of war. In N. Colangelo, S. G. Assouline, & D. L. Ambroson (Eds.), *Talent development: Proceedings of the 1991 Henry B. and Jocelyn Wallace National Research Symposium on Talent Development* (pp. 180–203). Unionville, NY: Trillium.

Pipher, M. (1994). *Reviving Ophelia: Saving the selves of adolescent girls.* New York: Ballantine.

Richardson, T. M., & Benbow, C. P. (1990). Long-term effects of acceleration on the social-emotional adjustment of mathematically precocious youths. *Journal of Educational Psychology, 82,* 464–470.

Robinson, N. M. (1993). Identifying and nurturing gifted, very young children. In K. A. Heller, F. J. Monks, & A. H. Passow (Eds.), *International handbook of research and development of giftedness and talent* (pp. 507–524). Oxford: Pergamon.

Robinson, N. M., & Noble, K. D. (1991). Social-emotional development and adjustment of gifted children. In M. C. Wang, M. C. Reynolds, & H. J. Walberg (Eds.), *Handbook of special education, research and practice: Vol. 4. Emerging programs* (pp. 57–76). Elmsford, NY: Pergamon.

Roedell, W. C. (1989). Early development of gifted children. In J. VanTassel-Baska & P. Olszewski-Kubilius (Eds.), *Patterns of influence on gifted learners: The home, the self, and the school* (pp. 13–28). New York: Teachers College Press.

Roedell, W. C., Jackson, N. E., & Robinson, H. B. (1980). *Gifted young children.* New York: Columbia University, Teachers College.

Roeper, A. (1995). Some thoughts about Piaget and the young gifted child. In *Annemarie Roeper: Selected writings and speeches* (pp. 39–44). Minneapolis, MN: Free Spirit.

Rogers, M. T. (1986). *A comparative study of developmental traits of gifted and average youngsters.* Unpublished doctoral dissertation, University of Denver, Denver, CO.

Rogers, M. T., & Silverman, L. K. (1988). Recognizing giftedness in young children. *Understanding Our Gifted, 1*(2), 5, 16–17, 20.

Sadker, M., & Sadker, D. (1994). *Failing at fairness: How America's schools cheat girls.* New York: Scribner's.

Silverman, L. K. (1986). What happens to the gifted girl? In C. J. Maker (Ed.), *Critical issues in gifted education: Vol. 1. Defensible programs for the gifted* (pp. 43–89). Rockville, MD: Aspen Publications.

Silverman, L. K. (1990). The emotional development of the gifted over the life-span. In D. Ventis & J. VanTassel-Baska (Eds.), *Proceedings of symposium on the developmental potential of the gifted* (pp. 59–73). Williamsburg, VA: College of William and Mary.

Silverman, L. K. (1992, October). How parents can support gifted children. *CEC/ERIC Bulletin,* pp. 6–8. (ERIC Digest No. EDO-ED-92-5, #E515)

Silverman, L. K. (1993). The gifted individual. In L. K. Silverman (Ed.), *Counseling the gifted and talented* (pp. 3–28). Denver, CO: Love.

Silverman, L. K. (1995a). To be gifted or feminine: The forced choice of adolescence. *The Journal of Secondary Gifted Education, 6,* 141–156.

Silverman, L. K. (1995b). The universal experience of being out-of-sync. In L. K. Silverman (Ed.), *Advanced development: A collection of works on giftedness in adults* (pp. 1–12). Denver, CO: Institute for the Study of Advanced Development.

Silverman, L. K. (1997). Family counseling with the gifted. In N. Colangelo & G. A. Davis (Eds.), *Handbook of gifted education* (2nd ed., pp. 382–397). Boston: Allyn & Bacon.

Silverman, L. K., Chitwood, D. G., & Waters, J. L. (1986). Young gifted children: Can parents identify giftedness? *Topics in Early Childhood Special Education, 6*(1), 23–38.

Silverman, L. K., & Kearney, K. (1989). Parents of the extraordinarily gifted. *Advanced Development, 1,* 41–56.

Simonton, D. K. (1994). *Greatness: Who makes history and why.* New York: Guilford.

Snyderman, M., & Rothman, S. (1988). *The IQ controversy, the media and public policy.* New Brunswick, NJ: Transaction Books.

Stanley, J. C., & Stanley, B. S. K. (1986). High school biology, chemistry, and physics learned well in three weeks. *Journal of Research in Science Teaching, 23,* 237–250.

Stern, W. (1910). Das ubernormale kind. *Der Saemann, 67*–72. (Translated and reprinted in 1911 as The supernormal child, *Journal of Educational Psychology, 2,* 143–148, 181–190.)

Subotnik, R. F., & Arnold, K. D. (1994). *Beyond Terman: Contemporary longitudinal studies of giftedness and talent.* Norwood, NJ: Ablex.

Swiatek, M. A., & Benbow, C. P. (1991). Ten-year longitudinal follow-up of ability-matched accelerated and unaccelerated gifted students. *Journal of Educational Psychology, 83,* 528–538.

Tannenbaum, A. J. (1962). *Adolescent attitudes toward academic brilliance.* New York: Bureau of Publications, Columbia University, Teachers College.

Tannenbaum, A. J. (1992). Early signs of giftedness: Research and commentary. *Journal for the Education of the Gifted, 15,* 104–133.

Terman, L. M. (1914). Precocious children. *Forum, 52,* 893–898.

Terman, L. M. (1931). The gifted child. In C. Murchison (Ed.), *A handbook of child psychology* (pp. 568–584). Worcester, MA: Clark University Press.

Tolan, S. S. (1994). Psychomotor overexcitability in the gifted: An expanded perspective. *Advanced Development, 6,* 77–86.

Tolan, S. S. (1995). Discovering the gifted ex-child. In L. K. Silverman (Ed.), *Advanced development: A collection of works on giftedness in adults* (pp. 13–20). Denver, CO: Institute for the Study of Advanced Development.

VanTassel-Baska, J. (1996). The talent development process in women writers: A study of Charlotte Bronte and Virginia Woolf. In K. Arnold, K. D. Noble, & R. F. Subotnik (Eds.), *Remarkable women: Perspectives on female talent development* (pp. 295–316). Creskill, NJ: Hampton Press.

Wallace, D. B., & Gruber, H. E. (1989). *Creative people at work: Twelve cognitive case studies.* New York: Oxford University Press.

White, B. L., & Watts, J. C. (1973). *Experience and environment* (Vol. 1). Englewood Cliffs, NJ: Prentice-Hall.

Whitmore, J. R. (1980). *Giftedness, conflict, and underachievement.* Boston: Allyn & Bacon.

Study Questions ⌇

1. Is there a drop-off in the phenomenon of giftedness as a child becomes an adolescent? As an adolescent becomes an adult? What are the implications for the school? For society?

2. What are some of the challenges gifted students face that reflect the gender bias of our society? Is one group more adversely affected by such biases than others?

3. Why is the role of parents of such importance in discussing the developmental stages of giftedness?

4. What are some of the behaviors that are manifested in gifted infants and/or toddlers? What is the relationship between precocious development and later identification in the gifted range?

5. Do all gifted children bloom early? What are some factors that affect the evidence of early precocity?

Introduction to
Part Two

Serving Talented Learners
in Special Programs

This section of the book explores the important interrelationships between the differential characteristics and needs of the gifted population and the provisions that are responsive to those differences. As such, the section represents an important treatment of the issue of differentiation at the level of program approach. Chapters in this section tie together the most important dynamics of program development, namely, identification, program options, acceleration, grouping, and evaluation, with individual analyses of each feature. Moreover, two chapters focus on secondary program concerns. The final chapter, on comprehensive program development, reflects on how these key elements can fit together in a pattern of rich opportunity for gifted and talented learners in school.

Chapter 10 explores both cognitive and affective aspects of gifted and talented learners, noting the importance to educators and parents of seeing these differential characteristics as the basis for appropriate differential education for these students. Behaviors associated with giftedness act as a catalyst for proactive responses in both home and school settings. The chapter also examines the relationship between behavioral characteristics, educational needs, and programming implications, thus setting the stage for all the chapters that follow.

The Feldhusen chapter on identification and assessment (Chapter 11) states that the purpose of identifying gifted students is to enable schools to provide educational opportunities that will maximize their cognitive and affective growth and support the development of their talents. Identification facilitates the match between the student and the most appropriate program that is available. If no program or special accommodation is planned, identification is a bankrupt process.

The chapter also addresses a number of concepts and issues related to the identification of gifted students, including (1) giftedness is a continuous variable, not a discrete phenomenon, (2) children develop differently, so the identification process should be seen as fluid rather than as a one-time opportunity, and (3) no identification process is error-proof. Because of ceiling effects, problems with validity and reliability, concerns about special populations, and so forth, care needs to be exercised in the selection and aggregation of diagnostic information.

Feldhusen notes that conducting validity studies on how students do in the programs for which they are selected is vital to reviewing the identification process that is in place. It is often helpful to have a diagnostic-identification committee that can track the decision-making process and refine ongoing identification approaches.

Chapter 12, on elementary program models, describes a variety of special options offered to provide educational services for gifted elementary school students. Although research shows that gifted children thrive and learn best in special classes where they are homogeneously grouped for most of their academic instruction, philosophical and organizational constraints make it necessary to consider a range of intervention models.

Models that emphasize enrichment are very popular and a number of them provide for levels of enrichment that ensure that no student is unchallenged. Some exemplary models built on the enrichment framework include the Enrichment Triad/Revolving Door Model advanced by Renzulli and Reis, the Individualized Program Planning Model of Treffinger, and Feldhusen's Purdue Three-Stage Model proposed in conjunction with Kolloff and Moon.

Like enrichment models, acceleration models may be individualized or delivered through grouping arrangements. All models of acceleration require some preliminary assessment of the youth's current knowledge base and rate of learning. Once these factors have been determined, options include placement in advanced classes (a third grader in fourth-grade math), early admission to kindergarten, and grade skipping. Guidelines are presented in the chapter to help educators make decisions about such accelerative approaches. Special full-time, self-contained classes for the gifted are able to encompass their needs for both acceleration and enrichment. Although research shows that inclusion typically does not result in differentiated instruction for gifted children, the literature does identify discrete general education classrooms that have demonstrated modest success. Guidelines are offered to identify the teacher behaviors that support this alternative.

Feldhusen's chapter on programs and services at the secondary level (Chapter 13) provides an eclectic overview of several key options. Whereas elementary programming for the gifted tends to be somewhat generic, the focus at the secondary level should recognize the differentiation of abilities and seek to bring some cohesion to the integration of each child's strengths, interests, and personality. Specific educational and career goals emerge in this phase of development and can be used to design educational services that address the students' longer term needs. Enriched and accelerated academic coursework, extracurricular activities, and opportunities in the broader community are important elements of program development at the secondary level.

At the middle-school level, Feldhusen asserts, major differences in philosophy between general education and gifted education proponents have the potential to emerge. The current emphasis on cooperative learning and detracking does not maximize the learning potential of gifted preadolescents. However, there are many areas of convergence between these two educational movements. Both advocate the utilization of a nongraded approach, differentiation of learning objectives and instructional strategies, creative expression by students, and emphases on inquiry, problem-solving, and higher level cognitive skill development.

The major components of gifted program development at the secondary level cited in the chapter are (1) counseling services, (2) special classes, (3) accelerated learning opportunities, (4) extracurricular learning experiences, (5) foreign language instruction, (6) art and cultural experiences in the school and community, and (7) formal and informal learning experiences in the community and beyond school time. Feldhusen notes that secondary counseling must be particularly comprehensive and include academic planning, goal-setting, career education and mentoring, and personal and social development.

The VanTassel-Baska chapter on issues and problems in secondary programming for gifted students (Chapter 14) outlines the different organizational parameters of a comprehensive gifted program at that level. The author cites a number of issues that affect how school systems choose to program for the gifted at the secondary level. The focus broadens from general ability, which is frequently a focus in elementary programming, to embrace specific areas of talent that can be addressed through core subject matter at secondary levels. Cocurricular activities tend to be more abundant.

Because of the importance of academic planning and course selection or program placement decisions at the secondary level, counseling is considered to be the linchpin of successful programming. Identification of career preferences and dispositions can also be a valuable activity at this juncture to help guide decision-making and to make connections to appropriate mentors or internships. VanTassel-Baska discusses curricular enhancements, including inter- and intradisciplinary courses, heightened emphasis on critical thinking, reasoning, and research embedded in content domains, and involvement in contests and competitions.

She also acknowledges some common problems in secondary program work. Among the problems in effecting positive change at the secondary level are difficulties in scheduling, an overreliance by teachers on predigested content, inappropriate requirements and expectations for gifted students, lack of sufficient differentiation, and program fragmentation. To overcome such obstacles, the author suggests that administrators understand the need for and be committed to systemic change.

The Benbow chapter on grouping intellectually advanced students (Chapter 15) presents the strong case for using flexible grouping patterns with the gifted based on need. In spite of the current trend to abolish ability grouping, convincing research exists that supports its effectiveness with gifted learners when coupled with differentiated curricula appropriate to their needs. Several forms of ability grouping can accomplish these ends: XYZ grouping, within-class grouping, cluster grouping, cross-grade grouping, special classes, and special schools. These last two models tend to be used more frequently at the high-school level than earlier, and Advanced Placement classes are a common approach for college-bound adolescents.

Recent empirical work by Page and Keith (1996) has confirmed that homogeneous grouping improves the achievement of high-ability youth, especially high-ability minority youth; is not harmful to low-ability students' (or any group of students') achievements, aspirations, or self-perceptions; and is favored by classroom teachers. In addition, such grouping experiences help gifted youngsters to establish more realistic self-concepts, having the effect of deflating their sense of their abilities, and provide a better match between the developmental readiness and needs of students and the instruction that is received. Since comparable data are not available to support the countervailing arguments for heterogeneous grouping, Benbow concludes that the current educational climate is responding to a political agenda that espouses equity over excellence.

Benbow's chapter on acceleration (Chapter 16) reminds us of the centrality of this intervention approach in effective programming for the gifted. Acceleration is critical for gifted students in attaining excellence in our educational system and has a long, time-honored history of use. It is the practice best supported by research, showing significant academic benefits, and it has been shown to contribute to positive socio-emotional adjustment as well. Also labeled curricular flexibility, acceleration puts competence above age in dictating an appropriate educational menu for a student. There are a variety of adjustments that can be made in the student's program to support exposure to content and skills in line with the student's readiness. Some of the options cited in the chapter include (1) early admittance to school, (2) grade skipping, (3) content acceleration, (4) fast-paced classes, (5) telescoping or compressing curricula, (6) the use of Advanced Placement courses, and (7) a variety of models that ensure access to dual enrollment, early college admission, or alternative secondary placements.

Benbow cautions, however, that students should be assessed for acceleration on an individual basis and notes that guidelines are available to educators considering placement or program alternatives. Moreover, acceleration has been shown to work best when combined with other educational options designed to meet the learning needs of gifted students.

In Chapter 17, on evaluating programs for the gifted, Seeley perceives program evaluation as a function that involves the collection and analysis of information for decision-making. Program evaluation is usually the responsibility of an administrator or program coordinator but may be delegated to the instructional staff in some school districts. The previously conducted needs assessment may be pivotal to the evaluation process, as it provides data upon which programs are built or expanded. If an initial needs assessment suggests the development of a program in critical thinking, for instance, the evaluation should include a component that shows whether or not a program was developed to respond to this need and the impact of the program on critical-thinking levels of participants. Seeley notes that evaluation is not expected to meet the threshold requirements of research (i.e., one need not scientifically "prove" that the program was responsible for the learning gains), but it should attend to both process and outcome indicators. He cautions, however, that instruments should be selected or developed with an awareness of issues of validity and reliability as well as an awareness of how the information will be able to be aggregated meaningfully. When designing an evaluation, it is important to consider the following factors: (1) context, (2) audience, (3) decision questions, (4) usefulness of data, and (5) ethical considerations. Seeley strongly suggests that the groundwork for an evaluation be laid during the planning phase of a program, with provisions set in place for the collection of relevant data at key junctures during implementation.

In the final chapter in this section (Chapter 18), Van Tassel-Baska pulls together the major stages of the program development process into a model for use in schools. Coordinators of programs for gifted students need to adopt such a model to ensure ongoing and responsible programs that continue to grow and improve. The chapter delineates the various factors essential to operating a dynamic program. It discusses the need for a strong philosophical orientation and definitional stance as a frame of reference for needs assessment work. It links identification approaches to choice of models, to issues of teacher selection, to training, and to curriculum development. It specifies the relationship of counseling needs to community resource utilization. It addresses the issues of monitoring and evaluation and of enacting a plan of action to document change. All of these elements constitute important aspects of effective program management. Each is addressed in the chapter, accompanied by sample planning forms for easy use by practitioners.

References ~

Page, E. B., & Keith, T. Z. (1996). The elephant in the classroom: Ability grouping and the gifted. In C. P. Benbow & D. Lubinski (Eds.), *Intellectual talent: Psychometric and social issues* (pp. 192–210). Baltimore, MD: Johns Hopkins University Press.

10

Characteristics and Needs of Talented Learners

Joyce VanTassel-Baska

Much of the foundational work in creating a field of gifted education has been based on the articulation of the characteristics and needs of gifted children. Early pioneers of this movement, such as Lewis Terman (1925) and Leta Hollingworth (1926), did much to aid our understanding of these children in the context of behavioral characteristics, and case study research has additionally refined our understanding. Witty (1930), Benbow and Stanley (1983), Tannenbaum (1983), and others also have sought to identify differences within the gifted population with respect to family backgrounds, special aptitudes, ability levels, and temperament. In more recent years, scales for rating behavioral characteristics (Renzulli, Smith, White, Callahan, & Hartman, 1976) have attempted to quantify the relative presence or absence of some of these key behavioral indicators.

The characteristics and needs of gifted children also have played an important role in defining appropriate interventions for gifted learners in schools. Classroom teachers frequently make inferences about curriculum that flow directly from the observation of a stated behavior (see Table 10.1). In this way, an "optimal match" might be made between the learner's strength area and a curricular opportunity.

Psychologists also have begun to analyze individual test results for appropriate interventions to suggest to parents and educators for providing more extensive work in specific areas of strength. Table 10.2 presents a menu of ideas developed at the Center for Gifted Education at the College of William and Mary (1993) for matching student ability with appropriate options.

This chapter discusses some of the most significant characteristics and needs of the gifted child so the reader can more readily come to appreciate the nature of these

Table 10.1 ∼
Characteristics of Gifted Learners and
Curriculum Implications

Characteristics of the Gifted Learner	Curriculum Implications
Reads well and widely	Individualize a reading program that diagnoses reading level and prescribes reading material based on that level Form a literary group of similar students for discussions Develop critical reading skills Focus on analysis and interpretation in reading material
Has a large vocabulary	Introduce a foreign language Focus on vocabulary building Develop word relationship skills (antonyms, homonyms, and so on)
Has a good memory for things heard or read	Have student present ideas on a topic to the class Have student prepare a skit or play for production Build in Trivial Pursuit activities
Is curious and asks probing questions	Develop an understanding of the scientific method Focus on observation skills
Is an independent worker and has lots of initiative	Focus on independent project work Teach organizational skills and study skills
Has a long attention span	Assign work that is long-term Introduce complex topics for reading, discussion, and project work
Has complex thoughts and ideas	Work on critical thinking skills (analysis, synthesis, evaluation) Develop writing skills
Is widely informed about many topics	Stimulate broad reading patterns Develop special units of study that address current interests
Shows good judgment and logic	Organize a field trip for the class Prepare a parent night Teach formal logic
Understands relationships and comprehends meanings	Provide multidisciplinary experiences Structure activities that require students to work across fields on special group/individual projects Organize curriculum by issues and examine those issues from different perspectives (e.g., poverty—economic, social, personal, education views)
Produces original or unusual products or ideas	Practice skills of fluency, flexibility, elaboration, and originality Work on specific product development

Note: From *Comprehensive Curriculum for Gifted Learners* (2d ed.) (pp. 158–159) by J. VanTassel-Baska (1995). Boston: Allyn & Bacon. Used by permission.

Table 10.2 ~
Individual Instruction Plan Menu for the Gifted Child

The following recommendations are intended for consideration by those who know the child well and can make informed decisions about the relevance and practical application of a curriculum recommendation to an individual child's aptitude, interest, and needs.

Language Arts

Reading
1. Use an inquiry-based study of appropriate children's literature (e.g., *Junior Great Books* program).
2. Select biographies and books in the content areas (including subjects dealing with multicultural issues) for supplementary reading.
3. Encourage and provide time to pursue free reading based on student interests.
4. Individualize a reading program that diagnoses reading level and prescribes reading material based on that level.
5. Form a literary group of students with similar interests for discussions of books read.
6. Provide literature that is broad-based in form (myths, nonfiction, biography, poetry, etc.), rich in language, and provides role models for emulation.
7. Utilize children's literature that involves finding solutions to scientific, environmental, and mathematical problems or mysteries.
8. Encourage participation in library-based programs.
9. Introduce students to new genres of books (e.g., science fiction).
10. Provide the opportunity for author study by having the child read several books by the same author.
11. Provide the opportunity for topic study by having the child read several books on the same topic and contrasting authors and writing styles.

Writing
12. Use a writing program that encourages elaboration and incorporation of ideas from literature into stories.
13. Develop expository writing skills.
14. Encourage extracurricular experiences that are language-based, such as school paper or yearbook.
15. Encourage personal journal writing.
16. Encourage use of a wide variety of words in writing through the use of thesaurus and dictionary.
17. Suggest keeping a journal for "word of the day" or "word of the week."
18. Encourage parents to transcribe child's stories at home.
19. Have students draw pictures to illustrate their stories and develop titles for them.

(continued)

Table 10.2 continued

20. Use tape recorders to initially record a story and have students transcribe it later.
21. Encourage free story building; provide students with a set of givens (character, plot pieces, a setting).
22. Have students respond in writing to a piece of music, a picture, or a poem presented in class.
23. Allow young students the freedom to write without requiring accurate spelling and grammar.
24. Provide opportunities for students to read written work out loud to individuals or to small groups of students.
25. Encourage child to submit written work for publication to children's magazines.
26. Have student attend available creative writing opportunities (e.g., special courses or writing camps).
27. Teach the writing process: prewriting, organizing, writing, editing, and rewriting.
28. Use writing skills across the curriculum.
29. Teach word processing.

Verbal Expression
30. Include experiences in foreign language in the curriculum.
31. Use storytelling techniques.
32. Teach debating skills.
33. Focus on vocabulary building.
34. Develop word relationship skills (e.g., analogies, antonyms, homonyms).
35. Allow for oral reports before the class.
36. Encourage child to join debate team.
37. Provide opportunities for student to speak in public settings.
38. Encourage theater club participation.
39. Provide the opportunity for the child to act out what is read.
40. Teach oral presentation skills.

Math
41. Focus on developing spatial skills and concepts through geometry and other media.
42. Focus on problem-solving skills with appropriately challenging problems.
43. Have student use calculators and computers as tools in the problem-solving process.
44. Focus on logic problems that require deductive-thinking skills and inference.
45. Emphasize mathematical concepts more and computational skills less.
46. Emphasize applications of mathematics in the real world through creation of special projects.
47. Emphasize algebraic manipulation.
48. Focus on the use of probability, estimation, statistics, and computer technology.

(continued)

Table 10.2 continued

49. Apply mathematical concepts across the curriculum, for example, by having the child read and report on a book about a famous mathematician, assess the mathematical challenges of planning a Civil War battle, or study a unit on the history of mathematics.
50. Facilitate the child's attendance at career seminars in math.
51. Utilize a diagnostic-prescriptive approach to mathematics that allows the student to move at a fast pace and not be subject to instruction in skills already learned.
52. Begin college preparatory courses as soon as possible.
53. Teach the creative process in mathematics, including problem-finding and problem-solving.
54. Encourage the student to participate in math-related challenges, such as Mathematics Olympics, Math Counts, Virginia Math League, and the Great Computer Challenge.
55. Allow student to substitute the five most difficult problems in a set for the 10 easiest.
56. Provide manipulatives such as pattern blocks, tangrams, and Cuisenaire rods.
57. Utilize computer-assisted drawing programs.
58. Assist the student in developing her or his own computer programs dealing with problem-solving skills.
59. Provide opportunities for the study of computer technology.

Science
60. Provide opportunities to visit museums of science and natural history.
61. Provide reading material that suggests experiments the child can try; provide a balance between text and activities.
62. Help the child develop a scientific hobby like birdwatching, shell collecting, gardening, or electronics.
63. Provide opportunities for naturalistic observation at the beach, mountains, or local pond.
64. Provide well-made scientific toys.
65. Provide basic tools, such as a magnifying glass, binoculars, and a camera.
66. Assist the child in selecting biographies and autobiographies about scientists.
67. Consider summer science camp experiences.
68. Provide opportunities for interacting with practicing scientists.
69. Place a strong emphasis on the inquiry process.
70. Emphasize topics that place science in the context of human decision-making and social policy.
71. Teach skills that help children to define a problem, make a hypothesis, and draw implications from data.
72. Teach the child to conduct literature searches.
73. Use open-ended questioning techniques.

(continued)

Table 10.2 continued

74. Foster the use of collaborative techniques by allowing students to work in small groups.
75. Establish a science mentorship program.
76. Explore educational programming at community facilities such as the National Aeronautics and Space Administration and Continuous Electron Beam Accelerator Facility.
77. Suggest that the student volunteer in a hospital, doctor's office, veterinary clinic, or science museum.
78. Review each December issue of *Scientific American* for science books for children.
79. Focus on problems that require deductive-thinking skills and inference.
80. Teach critical-thinking skills.

Social Studies
81. Provide opportunities for students to develop timelines.
82. Teach visual spatialization techniques.
83. Teach mapping strategies.
84. Teach metacognition.
85. Use puzzles and mazes.
86. Develop understanding of cultures.
87. Study the development of cities.
88. Develop geography and mapmaking skills.
89. Develop cultural literacy around important historical events in American history and world history.
90. Develop an understanding of global interdependence.
91. Analyze primary documents, including the Declaration of Independence.
92. Teach critical-thinking skills.
93. Assist the child in selecting reading in history, biography, and historical fiction.
94. Foster discussion of social and environmental issues.

Creativity/Aesthetics
95. Practice skills of fluency, flexibility, elaboration, and originality.
96. Work on specific product development.
97. Have the student prepare a skit or play for production.
98. Provide art appreciation opportunities.
99. Provide music opportunities.
100. Provide dramatic instruction.
101. Provide opportunities for dance and movement.
102. Teach role-playing.
103. Provide "collage" experience across art, music, literature.

(continued)

Table 10.2 continued

104. Introduce various artistic forms.
105. Introduce various musical forms.
106. Use biographies of creative people.
107. Teach creative problem-solving.
108. Use brainstorming.
109. Provide exhibition space for student products.
110. Provide opportunities to illustrate school publications.
111. Allow the child to create new endings for stories read.
112. Encourage the exploration of creative arts careers through library and guidance programs and contact with community members in the creative arts.
113. Suggest that the child illustrate original stories.
114. Consider providing an artist mentor.
115. Provide unstructured activities, allowing the student to choose the medium of expression.

Leadership/Social Skills
116. Encourage leadership skills through work with small groups in academic settings.
117. Encourage leadership skills through work with student government, safety patrol, or other school organizations and community groups such as Scouts, book clubs, or religious institutions.
118. Explore leadership training programs for precollegiate students at local colleges and universities.
119. Assist the child in selecting biographies and autobiographies about high achievers.
120. Provide monitored opportunities for involvement in volunteer or social service work in the community or at school.
121. Provide the opportunity for the student to explore people-oriented careers through mentorships, on-site observations, career fairs, and research.
122. Provide support for the child as he or she copes with the inevitable frustrations and challenges in working with others to accomplish a goal.
123. Encourage the exploration of service-oriented summer experiences such as camp counseling, recreation program assistance, or hospital volunteer work.

Note: Developed by the Center for Gifted Education, College of William and Mary, 1993. Used by permission.

children. Furthermore, the chapter addresses those characteristics and needs in the framework of both cognitive and affective domains and draws implications for educational practice.

Characteristics of Gifted Children ~

Cognitive Characteristics

Gifted children display atypical behaviors in the cognitive arena from an early stage of development. If proper nurturance occurs in the environment, these characteristics continue to expand as the children grow older. When nurturance is not present, however, many of these characteristics can act as negative forces to learning or can be hidden because of a gifted child's vulnerability. When considering the cognitive characteristics of gifted children, one must bear in mind the following:

1. Not all gifted children will display all of the characteristics.
2. There will tend to be a range among gifted children in respect to each characteristic.
3. These characteristics may be viewed as developmental in the sense that some children may not display them at early stages of development but may at later stages. Others may manifest the characteristics from a very early age.
4. Characteristics of the gifted tend to cluster and thus constitute different profiles across children as the combination of characteristics varies.
5. Characteristics may reveal themselves only when students are engaged in an area of interest and aptitude.

The following cognitive characteristics provide a basis for differentiating programs and services for gifted students in schools.

Ability to Manipulate Abstract Symbol Systems The gifted child exhibits a facility for learning systems such as language and mathematics at an earlier age than is typical. Children with gifted potential usually become known to parents and teachers by their skills in manipulating language or numbers. Less apparent are abilities to solve puzzles and to use figural analogies or other kinds of nonlanguage systems. Available resources that enhance those skills early on are crucial to the development of superior talent. Thus, prodigies such as Bobby Fisher, who benefited from mentoring at the Manhattan Chess Club, and Wolfgang Mozart, who inherited a genetic predisposition and an environmental context for music from Leopold Mozart, are examples of people for whom talent and a supportive milieu resulted in eminence.

Power of Concentration The gifted child who is absorbed by a science project or other arcane subject is like the absentminded professor at the adult level. Both display a high degree of concentration and an ability to focus on a problem for a considerable period of time. The reality is that long-term application and concentration in an area of interest are important components for gifted children to cultivate. An enduring interest or curiosity in some field that produces expert-level knowledge may be satisfying for its own sake as an avocation or may become the foundation of a career. The MacArthur fellows (Cox, Daniel, & Boston, 1985) represent persons who have been rewarded for sustained contribution over an extended period of time in various fields. Such rewards speak to the recognition of promising work in society.

Unusually Well-Developed Memory Memory is the sine qua non for the acquisition of information. Many gifted students from an early age have a phenomenal memory for data they have been exposed to only once. One young boy at age 3 had memorized all the license plates, house numbers and telephone numbers in his neighborhood. Another young girl at age 4 could recite "The Night Before Christmas" in its entirety after only one practice session.

Although it is a central aspect of intelligence, memory can be trivialized into spelling contest activity or other demonstrations and feats that have few long-term implications and little usefulness. Memory of events that are connected by historical significance and related to other social, economic, and cultural change has more meaning than does memory of a series of dates with little connection.

Early Language Interest and Development The gifted child often exhibits precocious development in language and has a strong interest in reading from an early age. Cases of early reading from as young as 2½ years are not uncommon. One study documented that early reading was apparent by age 5 in 80% of children later identified as gifted learners (VanTassel-Baska, 1983). The early reader has become less of an anomaly in our society in recent years for a number of reasons, some related to decreasing family size, others to older parents who are career-established and able to devote more time and attention to home teaching. Television programming that includes "Sesame Street" and "The Electric Company" also may positively influence the reading skills children bring to school. Thus, this characteristic alone may be less predictive of gifted behavior than it once was, yet it is still moderately predictive of later advanced reading behavior (Mills & Jackson, 1990).

Children whose language extends well beyond reading into a fascination with words and word relationships, with using language in speech and writing, are exhibiting important indicators of verbal aptitude.

Curiosity The gifted child displays a strong need to know and to understand how the world works. From early childhood on, this child craves to make sense of the world, and adults who treat these questions with respect and provide information appropriate to the needs of the child help build in him or her a personality orientation that seeks to discover the world.

Curious children ask questions frequently, and often these questions are on adult subjects fundamental to the large issues of life, such as "How was the world created?" or "Where did I come from?" or "Why do people die?" This level of question illustrates the advanced level of thought in which such children engage, an important indication of advanced development.

Reconstruction of the world or internalization of personal knowledge that comes about in learning is a long-term process that can be damaged by insensitive parents or teachers. Thus, the teacher who "turns on" the child's curiosity is usually remembered long afterward as part of a pivotal educational event.

Preference for Independent Work   The gifted child has a natural propensity for working alone, for figuring things out on his or her own. This trait reflects enjoyment in constructing an internal schema to solve problems rather than a tendency toward antisocial behavior. At age 13, Robert attended one of the eastern summer Talent Search programs at a major university. On entering the class, the instructor asked each of the students what he or she hoped to accomplish. Robert answered that he wished to complete algebra and trigonometry so that he could take Advanced Placement (AP) calculus in the fall. The instructor replied that all Robert needed to do was finish two math books, whereupon Robert said, "Give me the books." He finished both algebra and trigonometry with a 97+ grade average for the summer. He then took AP calculus as a high-school freshman and, because of a tragedy in the instructor's family, stepped in to teach the last 10 weeks of the course. Needless to say, Robert's independent work habits contributed significantly to his early accomplishments.

Multiple Interests   The gifted child has a large storehouse of information that interacts with good memory skills as well as with wide-ranging interests. Adrienne was a 5-year-old child in first grade who appeared highly able, so it seemed reasonable for the teacher to discuss with Adrienne the concept of birds as linear descendants of dinosaurs. Even so, the girl's response, "Oh, you mean like Archaeopteryx," did come as a surprise. Similarly, after she was given an aquarium for her fourth birthday, she became an "ichthyologist" who could explain differences between skates and other fish to her older brothers. When asked about her favorite books, she spoke of an interest in science fiction and in H. G. Wells's *War of the Worlds*, which Adrienne had read four times. This was the same child who was criticized by her teacher for being inattentive to the spelling lesson from the second-grade curriculum. Thus, the characteristic of having multiple interests may be missed or go unappreciated in gifted children if activities used with them do not allow for open exploration in a variety of areas.

Ability to Generate Original Ideas   The gifted child can generate novel ideas on his or her own or in collaboration with others. In some gifted children this ability is manifested predominantly in one area, but for others the creative response is marked in several types of endeavor. John was a published poet in fourth grade partly because of his teacher's encouragement and partly by virtue of the writing talent search in his large school system. His science fair project was an example of programming subtleties with numbers. Lien and Phillip collaborated successfully as 10-year-olds on building a model city, complete with electricity.

These cognitive characteristics are typical of intellectually gifted students but may need to be considered in tandem with characteristics related to specific curriculum applications. For example, mathematically precocious children may be best identified using the following list of behaviors:

- Early curiosity and understanding about the quantitative aspects of things
- Ability to think logically and symbolically about quantitative and spatial relationships
- Ability to perceive and generalize about mathematical patterns, structures, relations, and operations
- Ability to reason analytically, deductively, and inductively
- Ability to abbreviate mathematical reasoning and to find rational, economical solutions
- Flexibility and reversibility of mental processes in mathematical activity
- Ability to remember mathematical symbols, relationships, proofs, methods of solution, and so forth
- Ability to transfer learning to novel solutions
- Energy and persistence in solving mathematical problems
- Mathematical perception of the world

Thus, cognitive strengths may be discerned by observing students at work in a given area of learning.

Affective Characteristics *Need for counseling —*

The following affective characteristics provide another important lens through which to view the developing gifted child. This set of indicators provides information about the social and emotional development often seen in gifted children.

Sense of Justice   Gifted children display a strong sense of justice in their human relationships. At later ages they generally are attracted to causes that promote social equality. This characteristic reflects a general concern for others and also a concern that the world work in a humane way.

At age 6, Renee wanted to protest the nuclear waste dump disposal procedures in her community. She made up signs, organized her friends, and carried off a "kids" march.

Altruism and Idealism   Gifted children in general display a helping attitude toward others that may manifest itself in wanting to serve, to teach, or to tutor other children. They also may want to volunteer at a hospital or a senior center in the community. They may become very supportive of parents or older adults, taking on a caregiving stance. The altruism and idealism that gifted children exhibit frequently lead to involvement in service organizations or leisure activities that can consume large amounts of energy. This is a socially desirable direction when balance is maintained with the child's growth and when those activities promote goals that the parents can appreciate or at least accept. The sensitivity and insight these children bring to working with others, coupled with their altruism and idealism, can become a basis for later career decisions as well.

Sense of Humor   Gifted children often have the ability to recognize or appreciate the inconsistencies and incongruities of everyday experience. The relatively large knowledge base they possess allows them to perceive those instances more quickly than their age-mates do. A sense of humor and a playfulness with ideas attest to the gifted child's ability to interpret the world in what may be a less threatening manner. Humor can defuse many painful experiences and subtly point up foibles with less damage to the self-esteem of the child or of others. Humor also can be used for self-deprecation and self-defense, leading some gifted children to become known as the class clown or stand-up comic. Because this use of humor may mask a deep sense of alienation, it may be cause for concern.

Emotional Intensity   Just as gifted children are more able cognitively, they frequently experience emotional reactions at a deeper level than their age peers do. The death of a pet, for example, caused days of grieving for Dylan. The ability to emote within a dramatic framework makes gifted children good candidates for theater productions. Their sensitivity to nuances of expression and use of language is an asset in that activity. That same asset can become a liability when other children find they can provoke a reaction that brings negative attention to the child. The hyper-sensitivity of gifted children in the general education classroom is a phenomenon that troubles many parents. The homogeneous grouping of high-ability children academically and socially potentially places them in a more accepting environment that reduces the temptation for attack by their age-mates. The opportunity to share experiences for these children and the reduction of the isolation they may have felt in a general education classroom should be viewed as some of the more important benefits of the grouping/identification process.

Early Concern About Death   A concern with death or mortality often emerges early in the thoughts of gifted children. Responding to these concerns, and helping these children understand and accept the life-cycle process, is an important role for educators and parents and is one that must be approached and treated with maturity. Learning to use their cognitive strength to view the natural process apart from the emotional impact and stress that accompany the death of loved ones will be an important part of the emotional growth of gifted children. Respect for and celebration of life should be part of this process. The discovery of intergenerational relations through tracing the family tree and coming to know the events in the lives of forebears also offer a good perspective and a sense of identity for the child.

Perfectionism   Many gifted children display characteristics of perfectionism. These children focus undue energy on doing everything perfectly and become disturbed if they or others in their environment make mistakes. Sally became incensed when she received a 98% on her paper because of a punctuation error. She immediately asked the teacher if she could redo the paper. Ed reacted very sullenly when members of his group could not answer the quiz bowl questions he considered easy.

In our enthusiasm to encourage a child to do his or her best work, we may cross a line that causes the child to internalize perfectionistic tendencies. A realistic acceptance of error in people and in the world and of the imperfection of our own knowledge should temper the judgments a child is likely to make. The unrealistic fear and anxiety that can accompany perfectionism may hinder growth or result in guilt that works against the child's maximal development. Growth should be toward excellence, not perfection—a subtle distinction that teachers and parents must appreciate when working with the gifted child.

High Levels of Energy   Gifted children often display high energy in the conduct of play and work. This energy can be observed in the ability to accomplish a great deal of work in a short time or in highly tuned verbal or psychometric activity.

In fourth grade, Lenore decided on her own to work on homonyms one weekend, after having been introduced to them in school on Friday. She discovered over 450 by careful dictionary work and proudly brought her list to school on Monday.

The high energy levels that gifted children bring to school tasks can be misinterpreted as hyperactivity by teachers who are not sensitive to rapid learning styles. Using the child's energy for productive purposes requires channeling it into meaningful tasks and encouraging persistence in working toward short- and long-term goals. The resulting motivation for achievement and success then will reinforce the child's identity and self-esteem. Positive use of high energy is a critical part of gifted children's emotional development so that boredom, frustration, and a tendency toward hostile outlets for the energy do not develop.

Strong Attachments and Commitments   The gifted child frequently forms strong attachments to one or two friends who may be a few years older or to an adult figure. And these children, as they develop, form equally strong attachments to their work.

Laurel, at age 12, has maintained only two strong friendships. But these friendships were begun at age 2 and have continued to evolve. Winston, now in college, corresponds regularly with a drama teacher he became close to as a seventh grader.

Providing opportunities for role modeling of an ego ideal or hero can help the gifted child use his or her strong attachments to begin to formulate a long-range focus toward adult life goals. Mentors can provide a view of the adult world that will help a gifted child understand the commitment required for vocational success. Gifted children also tend to form unusually strong attachments to "the idealized self" that have to be balanced with the reality of human development over time.

Aesthetic Sensitivity   The gifted child's appreciation of complexity often is expressed through aesthetic sensitivity. The "unity in variety" that is integral to works of art provides intellectual and emotional satisfaction in ways that are surprisingly comprehensible to young gifted children. Lisa was writing poetry and illustrating it at age 5, with her first book completed by age 7. The multilayered analysis required for interpreting works of art appeals to the gifted child and presents an excellent opportunity for demonstrating an interdisciplinary view of knowledge. Opportunities that enhance perceptual processes through music, dance, and drama are appropriate ways to stimulate gifted children and address their needs in this area.

These affective characteristics are crucial to understanding the personality structure of the gifted child. Yet each set of characteristics—the cognitive and affective—explained independently is less powerful than seeing them merged into an integrated structure. Silverman (1993) conceptualized the cognitive and affective characteristics of the gifted as corresponding characteristics, each understood as a reflection of the other. This integration of the nature of gifted children is a useful tool for addressing their needs in a more holistic and effective way.

Needs of Gifted Children ~

An important way to view the needs of the gifted child is through the lens of behavioral characteristics. In so doing, we can translate these characteristics into a set of educational needs that schools might address. Tables 10.3 and 10.4 summarize the linkage of key cognitive and affective characteristics, respectively, to learning needs and to curriculum interventions for the gifted.

Many times, gifted children appear to be "out of sync" for their age when we consider the normal development expected at any given age in cognitive, emotional, and physical realms. The mythical "norm" has become a benchmark that schools use; however, it may fit very few students in any case and is especially pernicious when applied to the gifted. The ceiling effect of the regular grade curriculum and the distorted notion of the child's ability based on the narrow-range sampling of standardized testing obscure a realistic view of gifted children. This situation is compounded by the fact that gifted children share many characteristics with all children; they may excel intellectually but be more typical in respect to physical or emotional development.

The match of ability to curriculum that maximizes opportunities of choice and development has ostensibly become the cornerstone of educational planning for all students. Gifted students have a right to such an optimal match of curriculum and ability without their parents having to create elaborate explanations of need. The need can easily be discerned from student behavior in the classroom. The characteristics of gifted children described in this chapter are relatively easy to recognize if educators are looking for such indicators, especially in young children before the behaviors have "gone underground" in favor of more socially accepted ones.

Too frequently, the school's resources and priorities become ordered on the basis of "obvious need," which usually means failure or some other negative attribute. Because gifted students do not have trouble with the core curriculum, they are ignored while others are served, and when the problems of mismatch become troubling, the home or parents are blamed. Arguments against providing for the gifted are many, but they usually constitute excuses to maintain the status quo and reduce parental complaints.

Gifted children often have large variability in their profiles, which leads to attacks on their "weak" or average areas as evidence of "ungiftedness." Overlooking the strengths of these children and the implications for change in curriculum is a

Variability in profiles

Table 10.3∼
The Relationship of Characteristics, Learning Needs, and Curriculum for the Gifted (Cognitive)

Characteristic	Learning Need	Curriculum Inference
Ability to handle abstractions	Presentation of symbol systems at higher levels of abstraction	Reorganized basic skills curriculum Introduction of new symbol systems (computers, foreign language, statistics) at earlier stages of development
Power of concentration	Longer time frame that allows for focused in-depth work in a given area of interest and challenge	Diversified scheduling of curriculum work "Chunks" of time for special project work and small-group efforts
Ability to make connections and establish relationships among disparate data	Exposure to multiple perspectives and domains of inquiry	Interdisciplinary curriculum opportunities (special concept units, humanities, and the interrelated arts) Use of multiple text materials and resources
Ability to memorize and learn rapidly	Rapid movement through basic skills and concepts in traditional areas; more economical organization of new areas of learning	Restructured learning frames to accommodate capacities of these learners (speed up and reduce reinforcement activities) New curriculum organized according to its underlying structure
Multiple interests; wide information base	Opportunity to choose area(s) of interest in schoolwork and go into greater depth within a chosen area	Learning center areas in the school for extended time use Self-directed learning packets Individual learning contracts

Table 10.4~
The Relationship of Characteristics, Learning Needs, and Curriculum for the Gifted (Affective)

Characteristic	Learning Need	Curriculum Inference
Need for justice, fair play	Understanding of the complexity of issues associated with justice	A course study curriculum of humankind Study of court cases (judicial opinion) Bill of Rights/Constitution as sources of understanding
Altruism	Opportunities to help others matched with understanding needs of family and personal needs	Work with younger gifted children Study of the role of religion in televangelism from a review of newspaper articles and presidential campaigns Study of Puritans and early American religion
Humor	Opportunity to appreciate various forms of humor; use of humor for positive and negative purposes	Political cartooning in perspective Satire in Greek drama Clowns; pathos/bathos
Interest in death and mortality	Appreciation of human life cycle	*Roots* model for genealogy Use of curriculum that takes a life-span perspective
Perfectionism	Acceptance of human fallibility as a natural event	Heisenberg principle of indeterminism Understanding of statistical probability Safe risk-taking activities that allow students to fail

(continued)

Table 10.4 continued

High energy	Focus of attention to make best use of that energy	Psychomotor outlets for sublimation Gradual lengthening of learning increments Variety of experiences
Commitment	Realistic assessment of talent and process necessary to achieve	Mentoring Counseling toward goal in systematic fashion
Aesthetic sensitivity	Development of skills as an observer or performer	Exposure to the fine arts from various periods of history Opportunities for interrelated arts curriculum

much easier strategy than addressing the needs of their giftedness because there already are mechanisms in place for giving additional time to the "weaknesses."

Another strategy of schools as gatekeepers consists of making the criteria for identification so cumbersome or restrictive that only a few children are found to qualify. This strategy allows the schools to have an identifiable program for public relations purposes and at the same time keeps the number of students small enough to maintain the status quo in regular classrooms.

A common problem related to the peaks and valleys of development for the gift- *asynchrony* ed is the contrast of rapid cognitive development with less rapid physical maturation. Accelerating students as an accommodation to rapid mental growth by placing them with older students is a common school strategy that has been employed during the years. Because cognitive and physical maturation rates operate separately, this acceleration can highlight the differential in unrealistic ways. Thus, the child who can think through problems but not write them fast enough for the final test is penalized for writing and not thinking.

The narrow range on grade standardized achievement tests that schools use for accountability also has become a problem for the gifted. Little diagnostic or teaching information is to be derived from 95th percentile and above scores, and gifted children are characteristically in this group on such measures. The school's explanation of these scores usually points to the excellence of its teaching and programs rather than to the problem inherent in a test that was too easy in the first place to provide useful information on superior learners. A more realistic testing procedure should be used that provides data that can be used to tailor the curriculum to the gifted child's needs.

Summary ~

This chapter has delineated important characteristics and needs of gifted learners. Schools and parents must provide appropriate experiences to nurture these characteristics and needs. Thus, the case for gifted education in schools must rest on a firm foundation of differential characteristics. The following understandings emanate from appreciating the nature of gifted children:

1. Gifted students, like other populations that deviate significantly from what we call the norm for learning, have learning needs that require a special education program. Characteristics such as varied interests, intense curiosity, and the ability to manipulate abstract symbol systems all point to the need for a responsive school environment.
2. Most gifted learners will not develop their potential commensurate with their capacity without careful nurturance—some of which must be provided by the home and greater community and some by the schools. Data on dropout rates among the gifted, the lack of funding for and servicing of low-income students who have promise, and serious problems with underachievement among that population all point to areas of need.
3. A general education program does not respond adequately to such specialized needs because of an undue emphasis on basic skills taught from basal texts.
4. Change in schools is slow and reactive in nature, and innovative efforts are frequently diffused. Consequently, seeking positive change with a targeted group of learners whose performance outcomes can be impacted most greatly provides a safe testing ground for efforts ultimately to be used with larger segments of the school population.

Gifted education seeks to enable and empower exceptional learners to engage in meaningful experiences that will help develop their initial promise, both for the sake of themselves and of society. Gifted education also seeks to use what is learned from successful work with the gifted to make positive changes in schools for all learners.

References ~

Benbow, C. P., & Stanley, J. (1983). *Academic precocity*. Baltimore, MD: Johns Hopkins University Press.

Center for Gifted Education, College of William and Mary. (1993). *A menu of opportunities for gifted learners*. Williamsburg, VA: Author.

Cox, J., Daniel, N., & Boston, B. O. (1985). *Educating able learners: Programs and promising practices*. Austin: University of Texas Press.

Hollingworth, L. (1926). *Gifted children*. New York: World Press.

Mills, J. R., & Jackson, N. E. (1990). Predictive significance of early giftedness: The case of precocious reading. *Journal of Educational Psychology, 82*(3), 410–419.

Renzulli, J. S., Smith, L. H., White, A. J., Callahan, C. M., & Hartman, R. K. (1976). *Scales for the rating of behavioral characteristics of superior students*. Mansfield Center, CT: Creative Learning Press.

Silverman, L. (1993). *Counseling the gifted and talented*. Denver, CO: Love.

Tannenbaum, A. (1983). *Gifted children*. New York: Macmillan.

Terman, L. (1925). *Genetic studies of genius* (Vol. 1). Stanford, CA: Stanford University Press.

VanTassel-Baska, J. (1983). Profiles of precocity: The 1982 Midwest talent search finalists. *Gifted Child Quarterly, 27*(3), 139–144.

Witty, P. (1930). *A study of one hundred gifted children*. Lawrence, KS: Bureau of School Service & Research.

Study Questions ⁓

1. How do the particular needs of gifted children pose special challenges for schools?
2. What approaches could teachers reasonably explore when gifted children are not producing or flourishing in school?
3. What are some of the problems inherent in labeling children as gifted? How might sensitive educators deal with these problems?
4. How can we involve parents more effectively in recognizing and acting on the observed characteristics of their children?
5. How might the affective characteristics of gifted children be supported in the home? In the school? In society?
6. Individual profiles of gifted children typically reveal differential mixes of cognitive and affective characteristics. What might we infer from this situation with regard to identification and programming in schools?

11

Identification and Assessment of Talented Learners

John F. Feldhusen

Identification of gifted and talented youth is the process through which we attempt to become aware of students whose abilities, motivational patterns, self-concepts, and creative capabilities are so far above average that differentiated educational services are needed if they are to make the full educational progress indicated by their potential (Brandwein, 1980). We assume that all youth have a right to educational services that will meet their needs, be adapted to their personal characteristics, and help them achieve to the highest possible level of their potential. Identification systems that merely enable us to label or categorize "gifted" youth are of no value and are potentially harmful. The basic purpose of identification is to guide the educational process and serve youth (Feldhusen, Hoover, & Sayler, 1990).

In many schools, the identification process has gone astray (Alvino, McDonnel, & Richert, 1981; Feldhusen, 1991; Feldhusen, Asher, & Hoover, 1984), especially when identification has become an end in itself (Henry, 1994). In other schools, educational services for the gifted are severely limited or nonexistent. Additionally, the identification process can exacerbate problems of elitism. This chapter reviews some of the major issues and concerns related to identification and assessment, suggests some methods of dealing with those issues, and presents a general set of guidelines for the identification and assessment processes.

Some Issues and Concerns ~

Validity and Appropriateness

A major issue in identification of gifted and talented youth is validity of the identification process with respect to program goals and services (Feldhusen & Jarwan,

1993). The identification process must be appropriate for selecting youth who need and will profit from a particular program service. The Future Problem Solving program (Flack & Feldhusen, 1983) is one example of an excellent service offered in many gifted programs. Verbal skills and abilities, a high degree of motivation, creative capacity, and good independent study skills might be seen as appropriate abilities and characteristics of youth who need and would profit from that program. A valid identification process, then, would include assessment of the nominee's strengths in each of those areas. Assessment of math and science abilities as represented in standardized achievement test scores would be less relevant and could render the process invalid. The use of language achievement tests and creativity and study skill scores to identify youth for accelerated algebra classes might be equally questionable. In summary, the identification process should select youth whose needs, abilities, and characteristics fit the goals or nature of the program service to be offered (Feldhusen, 1991).

Programs at the early childhood level might identify generally gifted children who can profit from a general set of stimulating educational experiences. As children move through the elementary grades, however, their talents begin to crystallize and become focused in specific areas. Increasing attention must be paid with age to students' abilities and characteristics, matching them to appropriate and valid educational experiences (Bloom, 1985; Feldhusen, 1994; Gagné, 1993).

Talent Versus Giftedness

In early childhood, some children are seen as generally bright, precocious, or gifted. By ages 3 to 5, however, some of them begin to show special kinds of ability: verbal, logical, spatial, musical, and so forth. The pattern of development is toward increasingly specific talents or abilities. Schools can search for talents from the late elementary years (grades 4–6) onward in the areas of academic, artistic, vocational, interpersonal, and psychomotor-kinesthetic abilities (Feldhusen, 1995b). As youth progress through middle school and high school, the major goal is to help them discover and understand their own talents, select appropriate educational experiences, and set career goals related to their talents (Achter, Lubinski, & Benbow, 1996).

Parent Input

Another issue of concern in identification of the gifted is parent input to the process. There is a myth that all parents think their children are gifted. In truth, few parents think their children are gifted or want to label their children as gifted. Moreover, few parents are willing to single out their children from age peers by labeling them gifted. Whether this comes about because of subcultural cautions against elevating oneself above the group or an unrealistic "child prodigy" image of giftedness, parents do not readily accept the label. They do begin to seek special remediation when they come to view the school's curriculum as substandard or lacking challenge for their child or begin to hear rumblings of the child's negative attitudes toward peers and school. The label at that point seems a lesser evil though it carries the stigma of hubris (Rimm, 1994).

Nevertheless, parents do have a great amount of knowledge that is relevant to the identification process. They may not know the technical jargon of the gifted field, but they do know a great deal about the abilities, motivation, self-concept, and creative capacity of their children. Furthermore, they see their children in free behavior situations and less restrictive environments than the classroom. They often have information on hidden talents of which teachers are totally unaware that can be extremely valuable in the identification process (Robinson, 1993).

Through rating scales, questionnaires, or open-ended instruments, parents can provide information concerning their children's reading habits, vocabulary, hobbies, interests, motivation, creative behavior, and self-views. All of this information can be valuable in the identification process. The ASSETS scale developed in Grand Rapids, Michigan, is one published example of an instrument used to gain parent input in identification (ASSETS, 1979). Table 11.1 shows another instrument, an open-ended nomination scale, that can be used to secure parent input for the identification process. It is important that established scales be used, since parents may not be well informed about critical talent indications.

Combining Assessment Data

A major challenge in identification occurs when those who are carrying out the identification process wish to combine data from several sources for a unitary or syn-

---

Table 11.1 ～
Parent Nomination Form

Child's Name_____ Grade_____

Parent's Name_____

Address_____ Zip_____

1. What are some things you have observed in your child's behavior that lead you to believe that he/she should be in the special program for high-ability children?

2. What problems, if any, is he/she having in school as a result of the high ability?

3. Describe briefly your child's reading habits, patterns, and levels at home.

4. Describe briefly your child's major interests, hobbies, art activities, and so on.

5. Describe any projects or studies your child has done (if not covered in Item 4).

6. Please give any other information about your child that you believe is relevant to his/her abilities or interests.

---

thesized evaluation of a child. Obviously, scores derived from different types of scales (e.g., percentiles, IQs, stanines, and Z scores) cannot simply be added together. Must we settle for a subjective, intuitive combination?

One answer, widely applied in the gifted field, is to use a simplified standardization process as represented in a matrix. All of the scores are converted to a simple 5-level or 10-level scale without regard to the variance of individual measures and then summed to derive a gross index of giftedness. Table 11.2 is an illustration of such a matrix. Each test score is converted to a 1–5 score, and then those numbers are added to get a total giftedness score (Baldwin, 1984).

Feldhusen and Jarwan (1993) detailed the serious weaknesses of such matrix approaches and argued that a standardized score approach be used instead. They advocated that all input variables be converted to T scores and then combined, argu-

Table 11.2
Baldwin Identification Matrix

Assessment Items	Scores				
	5	4	3	2	1
1. Cognitive Abilities Test	140+	139–130	129–120	119–110	109–100
2. Metropolitan Achievement (percentile)—Reading	95%ile	94–90%	89–85%	84–80%	79–75%
3. Metropolitan Achievement—Math	sta. 9	8	7	6	5
4. Renzulli Leadership	40	39–35	34–30	29–25	24–20
5. Renzulli Creativity	40	39–35	34–30	29–25	24–20
6. In-school Psychomotor	5	4	3	2	1
7. Renzulli Motivation	36–34	33–30	29–26	25–22	21–18
8. Renzulli Learning	32	31–28	27–24	23–20	19–16
9. Teacher recommendation	5	4	3	2	1
Column Tally of Checks					
Weight	x5	x4	x3	x2	x1
Add Across	+	+	+	+	+

TOTAL SCORE

Note: From "The Baldwin Identification Matrix" by A. Y. Baldwin (1978) in *Educational Planning for the Gifted.* Reston, VA: Council for Exceptional Children. Reprinted by permission.

ing that that approach is a more reliable way of synthesizing data. A standard score expresses the variability within the group's real scores that is consistent with the technical data presented for other tests.

Probably the best argument for the standard score is the ease of computation with a computer because such programs are now included as part of software packages. The availability of personal computers and user-friendly software has become a major benefit for recordkeeping and assessment. In addition, computers have become part of the early home experiences of children. Teachers of the gifted must familiarize themselves with these tools if only to keep pace with the children in their classes.

Another serious problem with all matrix approaches and score combinations is the tendency to settle for a global identification of giftedness and to fail to delineate youths' specific talents (Feldhusen, 1995b; Howley, Howley, & Pendarvis, 1995). It is clear from the recent research of Csikszentmihalyi, Rathunde, and Whalen (1993) that the most critical aspect of early talent development is the process by which youth and their parents become increasingly aware of the child's specific talents and seek educational experiences that are appropriate for those talents.

One-Shot Versus Continuing Assessment

Identification often is viewed as a one-time process, particularly if it seeks simply to identify, label, and categorize youth as gifted or nongifted. Developmental psychology and the common sense of school personnel, however, indicate that children grow and children change. Most assuredly, their talents and abilities undergo processes of differentiation and specialization as they move through the elementary grades and into high school. Thus, the identification process demands periodic reassessment (Csikszentmihalyi et al., 1993).

Reassessment should not be oriented to the question of whether the child is still gifted. Rather, it should seek to identify changing abilities or characteristics and the emergence of more specialized talents. Furthermore, it should ask whether the student has special needs, related to the area(s) of talent, for which new or different educational services are needed.

Reliability

Reliability means accuracy in measurement. The reliability of test scores, rating scales, observation data, and other measures used in assessing gifted youth varies tremendously. Some degree of imprecision is always present, of course. Scores derived from intelligence and achievement tests are likely to be highly reliable. Other measures, such as nomination procedures, rating scales, creativity tests, and self-concept inventories, are likely to be low or very low in reliability. This means that if the assessment is repeated or done by another examiner, the scores may differ substantially. This is a central problem with current performance and portfolio assessment approaches.

Technical manuals provided by test publishers and reviews such as those found in the *Mental Measurement Yearbook* (Kramer & Conoley, 1992) provide information on the reliability and validity of most of the widely used standardized tests. Although this information is not available for some tests, it is the ethical obligation of the author or publisher to provide accurate data about the test's psychometric properties and information about the norming process. Rating scales, self-concept inventories, and observation systems seldom provide technical information; yet they often are used as part of the selection process. Users of such informal measures have a similar obligation to secure their own reliability estimates through test-retest, split-half, or interrater-interscorer analyses. Knowing the reliability of tests or other assessment procedures allows for estimates of the accuracy of the identification process (Jarwan & Feldhusen, 1993). Reliability must be present to a high degree for the identification process to be fair.

Ceiling Effect and Off-Grade-Level Testing

When the form of test for a child's age level is too easy or does not give the child a chance to show the full range of his or her ability, the ceiling effect may be operating. When students are given standardized achievement tests at their grade level, those who are very high achievers may score at the 95th percentile or greater and a "ceiling effect" may be obscuring their true achievement. Because the child has missed very few test questions to arrive at this score, those errors could have been the result of careless mistakes, computer errors, or an imperfect test form rather than lack of knowledge. A more reliable picture of the child's achievement could be obtained through a sample of more difficult items. Ideally, a well-written test in which the child obtains correct scores on only half the items would give a better picture of true achievement.

A well-known solution to this problem is the procedure called off-grade-level, or above-level, testing. In this procedure a level of test higher than the child's age or grade level is selected; it is hoped that the test will be sufficiently challenging so that the child will have an opportunity to display the highest level of his or her ability.

Thousands of children now participate in off-grade-level testing at the middle-school or junior-high level by taking the College Board Scholastic Aptitude Test, an instrument not ordinarily administered until the junior or senior year of high school (VanTassel-Baska, 1985). Presumably the test will be at such a high level that these younger students will all be able to display their highest levels of ability. Even in this form of radical off-grade-level testing, however, a few youngsters score at the perfect (800) level. They seemingly need an even higher form of off-grade-level test to adequately assess their talents and abilities.

Identifying Students from Special Populations

Jenkins-Friedman, Richert, and Feldhusen (1991) documented the special problems of underrepresentation of minority and disadvantaged children and those with learning disabilities in gifted programs. Traditional identification procedures often fail to detect the gifts or special talents of these youth. Many of the projects funded by the Jacob K. Javits Gifted and Talented Students Education Act of 1988 address these concerns and have shown remarkable success with alternative identification procedures that focus on youth talents rather than traditional academic-intellectual gifted-ness (Berger, 1992). Shore, Cornell, Robinson, and Ward (1991) suggested that for special populations we should (1) use tests that are less dependent on the English language, (2) use tests that identify a broad range of talents, (3) use a variety of pro-cedures, and (4) look at assessment results as units, not combined in a matrix. Special efforts to identify youth from special populations can be successful in over-coming underrepresentation.

Evaluation Procedures

Does the identification process in use at a school select youth properly? Does it iden-tify boys and girls who need special gifted program services? Will those who are selected do well in the special programs? Will those who are selected go on to high-level success in their life careers? Will they go on to college and to advanced degrees? These are questions we must answer through research, evaluation, and dissemination procedures. Often, the identification process is taken for granted; educators simply assume that it is selecting the students who can benefit most from the program.

In reality, the identification process ought to undergo periodic validity evaluation. Such evaluation should be done to determine if the process is bringing into the program the youth who have need for its services, especially those who will profit and grow as a result of receiving the services and will go on to use their potential to achieve at lev-els commensurate with their superior ability. Validity evaluation procedures involve gathering data concerning the performance or achievement of youth in the program and data on their achievements after they leave the program. Do they go on to college, to graduate training, to advanced degrees, to significant achievement in their fields?

Feldhusen and Jarwan (1995) conducted a study of identification-selection methods used by state-supported residential schools for talented youth. Their methodology, which used regression analysis, can serve as a model for validating identification measures and procedures. Essentially, the method answers questions regarding the predictive validity of selection measures in relation to later perfor-mance or achievement in a program.

Many identification procedures fail to bring into the program youth who need its services, who would perform well, and who would achieve high-level success if given the opportunity. A variety of assessment supplements and experimentation can be used to overcome this problem, but the problem is not easily dealt with by school personnel. Coordinators of programs, however, should be aware of the situation and attempt to minimize its dangers by vigilance in searching for and assessing poten-tially gifted youth. The safest error direction is false positive—that is, youth who are selected but really are not qualified. Most programs will not likely harm them. The greatest risk is to be left out when the program may be just the stimulus needed to motivate a student.

Performance or Potential?

Currently, the process of identifying gifted and talented youth is based primarily on assessments of how well the youth are performing in tasks relevant to the areas of giftedness and talent. All test procedures are measures of performance; they are not measures of some hidden, innate, or basic capacity. All of the tasks included in intelligence and aptitude tests involve learned behaviors. Nevertheless, two kinds of inferences are often made from the tests. First, intelligence test scores are used as an index to infer innate capacity. Second, test scores such as those yielded by the Scholastic Aptitude Test are considered a good indicator or prediction of how well a student will learn or perform some time in the future.

The point to be made is that all assessments of ability or aptitude are measures of current performance levels and that their major value is in identifying youth who might profit from special gifted program services and go on to higher level success and achievement. Interpretation of test scores as representing innate abilities leads to misconceptions of giftedness as fixed and unchanging (Dweck, 1986). Realistically, however, without nurture, abilities may decline, whereas with nurture they may increase. Identifiers of gifted and talented youth must develop an understanding of the nature and uses of ability and aptitude scores and use them properly in the identification process.

Tryout as Identification

The identification process cannot achieve perfect reliability, primarily because it cannot be more reliable than the tests, rating scales, and observation data on which it is based. To counteract the dangers of low reliability in identification procedures, program coordinators should view tryout in programs as an extension of the identification process and offer tryout opportunities to as many borderline youth as possible.

Vygotsky's (1978) theoretical formulation of the "zone of proximal development" suggests that test scores reveal only a current level of achievement and seem to imply readiness for just the next small step forward in learning as appropriate instruction. However, the "zone of proximal development" also suggests that some youth—notably, the gifted and talented—may be ready to learn new and advanced material far beyond the level of readiness indicated by an achievement test. Thus, real learning opportunities with advanced and fast-paced instruction may reveal more than tests about the levels of talent of gifted youth, especially if the tests used had low ceilings.

Observation of students' performance in programs can provide valuable supplementary information to assess potential giftedness. Performance or learning in programs is one of the major criteria for evaluating identification predictors. Youth who perform well in a program are most directly demonstrating one desired criterion for gifted programs. To the extent that students succeed in a program, we can be sure of the good predictive validity of the identification process.

Karnes (1987) described an approach to the identification of gifted youth that combines training that alerts teachers to the characteristics of the gifted with training in how to structure classroom activities that optimize the opportunity for potentially gifted youth to demonstrate their talent or ability. The system is particularly effective in identifying gifted youth from culturally different backgrounds.

The Nature of Giftedness~

Parents and teachers often erroneously believe that the administration of tests and other measures will result in explicit identification of youth as gifted and talented or not gifted. Gifted youth often are perceived as categorically different human beings, much like people's perceptions of youth who have diseases or disabilities. Thus, parents and teachers have been heard to ask if a particular child who seems to be precocious or bright is "really and truly gifted." The question seems to imply that some individuals are geniuses and others are pseudogifted and that, if tested, rated, and observed properly, a gifted child will be clearly seen as gifted.

In truth, all types of giftedness and talent correspond to psychological characteristics and abilities that are continuous variables. The characteristics exist at some level in all human beings; they vary in intensity or level in each; and the abilities differ within each gifted individual. Thus, all living persons have some level of intelligence, as well as some adaptability, some ability in numerical or quantitative operations, and some ability for reasoning.

But some youth can reason more rapidly and accurately with complex, abstract material, whereas others have limited reasoning capacity, can deal only with simple, concrete material, and are slow in reasoning. Furthermore, some youth have high mathematical reasoning ability but limited ability in verbal reasoning tasks, and vice versa. They differ in levels of different abilities within themselves. The identification process must take these conditions into account.

In a major national survey of identification procedures in the United States, Richert, Alvino, and McDonnel (1982) found widespread variability from city to city in the tests used, the cutting levels, and the general process of identification. Thus, definitions vary, and we should recognize that giftedness is a varying concept.

Identification of gifted and talented youth might most appropriately be seen as a process in which highly able youth are helped in delineating or becoming aware of their own special talents and aptitudes (Feldhusen, 1995a). Csikszentmihalyi et al. (1993), in their study of talented teenagers, found that those who progressed well in developing their talents were marked by a growing awareness and understanding of their own talents. Hence, students should be involved in discussing the data that contributed to their identification.

Proposed Identification Procedures~

Procedures for identifying the gifted and talented must be closely linked to the nature of the available program services, as discussed earlier in this chapter. Talents differ, assessment procedures differ, and different program services minister to different talents. In the broadest sense, elementary program services differ in their mathematical, verbal, and artistic orientation. Later, as youth move into junior high and high school, their talents become quite specialized in science, mathematics, languages, literature, social studies, music, art, dance, and so on (Saunders, 1982). The identification process must increasingly recognize specialization of talent, and it must be fine-tuned to fit the talent domain of a potentially gifted youth. The following, for example, might be the set of criteria used to identify the gifted for an honors English class in a middle school:

1. The Purdue Academic Rating Scale for English
2. The Cognitive Abilities Test verbal score
3. A teacher recommendation
4. The total language score from the Iowa Test of Basic Skills
5. A grade average from previous language arts courses

But the set of selection criteria for an honors mathematics class (algebra in seventh or eighth grade) might be as follows:

1. The Purdue Academic Rating Scale for mathematics
2. A teacher recommendation
3. The Cognitive Abilities Test quantitative score
4. The total mathematics score from the Iowa Test of Basic Skills
5. A grade average from previous math courses

In each case, the selection or identification criteria are theoretically and, it is hoped, empirically related to the area of talent for which youth are being selected. In essence, the identification process assesses the relative precocity of students in a specific academic talent domain.

Nomination/Screening

The initial stage of identification may consist simply of a call for informal nominations. Parents, teachers, counselors, and gifted youth may be invited to submit the names of students they view as gifted or talented. Tables 11.1, 11.3, 11.4, and 11.5 present illustrative nomination forms to be completed, respectively, by parents, the student, peers, and teachers. Before nominations are requested, in-service workshops concerning the nature and characteristics of the gifted and talented should be held for teachers so that they will have an accurate understanding of the type of youth being sought (Borland, 1989). The rating scales themselves also can provide guidance to nominators by focusing on salient characteristics of nominees. Rating scales, however, often are not used until a second stage, after initial nomination procedures have been completed and have generated a pool for further assessment.

Further screening can be carried out through examination of available test scores in school files. Scores for IQ, reading readiness, and standardized achievement tests are typically found in the files. An inspection of those files can serve to identify students in the top 5%–10%. These names, along with the file scores, can be added to the existing list of nominees.

The process of securing nominations from relevant persons and from school files yields a list of nominees, many of whom are mentioned repeatedly. A particular child might be nominated by two teachers, the parents, and a counselor, as well as by high IQ and achievement scores. The greater the number of nomination sources, the greater is our confidence that a youth is indeed talented and merits further con-

Table 11.3~
Student Self-Nomination Form

Name_____ Date_____

Address_____ Grade_____

_____

Phone (   ) _____ Birth Date_____

1. In what areas do you have special talent or ability?

2. In which subjects or courses do you do superior work?

3. What are the areas, topics, or activities in which you have special or strong interests?

4. Describe a project, product, or performance that you have done or created in which you excelled.

5. How many hours per week do you spend in voluntary reading?

6. What are your areas of special interest in reading?

7. Why do you want to be in the special program?

Students in our special program are expected to strive for excellence in all their work and to work harder than they normally do in regular classes. If you agree with this expectation, sign your name below.

_____
Name

sideration. If resources permit, however, all youth who have at least one nomination source should be assessed. It is important to ensure that students who are very strong in only one area not be excluded from consideration for more targeted programming that addresses their needs.

Assessment

The next stage in the identification process is to secure additional information that will aid in determining the youth's talents or giftedness and his or her fit with particular services. Tests, rating scales, and other observations should be selected to match the potential abilities of the youth and the nature of the program services.

Table 11.4~
Peer Nomination Form

1. Who are some kids who always seem to have a lot of good ideas?

2. Who are some kids who can write really good stories or scripts?

3. Who are some kids who seem to come up with far-out, crazy, or very unusual ideas?

4. Who are some kids who draw really well?

5. Who are some kids who are really good logical thinkers?

6. Who are some kids who are really good at solving problems?

7. Who are some kids who do really good work in science?

Table 11.5~
Teacher Nomination Form

Student's Name_____ Grade_____

Teacher's Name_____ Date_____

1. What are some things you have observed in this student's behavior or schoolwork that lead you to believe that he/she should be in a special program for high-ability children?

2. What problems, if any, is he/she having in school as a result of the high ability?

3. Describe briefly the student's reading habits, patterns, and levels.

4. Describe briefly the student's major interests, hobbies, art activities, and so on.

5. Describe any special projects or studies this student has done (if not covered in number 4).

6. Please give any other information about this student that you believe is relevant to his/her abilities or interests.

Feldhusen (1993) reviewed a wide variety of test instruments that could be used in assessing youth for selection in gifted programs.

For a pullout program in which students will receive instruction related to the language arts, creativity, research, and independent study, the following data might logically be secured:

1. Language arts standardized achievement test scores
2. Teacher ratings of the child's reading and writing skills
3. Motivation assessment using the motivation scale developed as part of Renzulli et al.'s Scales for Rating the Behavioral Characteristics of Superior Students (Renzulli, Smith, White, Callahan, & Hartman, 1976).
4. Creativity assessment using the Torrance Tests of Creative Thinking (Torrance, 1974).

For a leadership and personal-social development program, the following data might be secured:

1. A self-concept scale
2. Leadership assessment using the leadership scale developed by Renzulli et al. (1976) as part of the Scales for Rating the Behavioral Characteristics of Superior Students
3. IQ score from a group test
4. Sociogram information

For an accelerated mathematics program, the following three items might be particularly applicable:

1. Mathematics achievement test scores
2. Grade average in previous mathematics courses
3. Rating on the Purdue Academic Rating Scale for mathematics

The Purdue Academic Rating Scales (Feldhusen et al., 1990) are a series of five rating scales, each consisting of 15 items, focusing on signs of superior academic performance in mathematics, science, English, social studies, and foreign languages. The scales were designed for the identification of secondary students for honors, Advanced Placement, seminar, and accelerated classes.

Assessment should typically focus on two or more of the four domains of psychological functioning that relate to giftedness: (1) talents and abilities, (2) creative capacity, (3) self-concept, and (4) motivation. Test instruments are used to assess many talents and abilities, but some talents, especially in the arts, are typically assessed through expert judgment of students' performance or products. Creative capacity may be assessed using test instruments or rating scales. Self-concept usually is assessed using self-rating inventories such as the Piers-Harris Children's Self-Concept Scale (Piers & Harris, 1969), the ME Scale (Feldhusen & Kolloff, 1981), or the Harter Self-Perception Profile (Harter, 1982, 1985). Motivation can be rated with one of the Renzulli scales (Renzulli et al., 1976), or it can be inferred from achievements or products that the nominee has produced.

Assessment of intelligence is often carried out with children at the elementary-school level with the Wechsler Intelligence Scale for Children—Revised (Wechsler, 1974) or the Stanford-Binet Intelligence Scale (Thorndike, Hagen, & Sattler, 1986). Assessment of general intelligence is most appropriate with children at the early childhood, primary, and upper grade levels in cases in which the program is a broad, general instructional service. Intelligence tests are also used in making decisions concerning early admission or grade advancement.

In addition, valuable assessment information can be secured through interviews and from essays written by nominees. From essays, inferences can be drawn concerning writing skills, interests, and motivation. They were used, for example, in a career education project for the gifted conducted by Moore, Feldhusen, and Owings (1978) to assess the motivation and goals of nominees. The nominees were asked to write a paper setting forth their own short- and long-range personal goals. In the same project, nominees were interviewed to assess their oral-verbal abilities, social poise, and motivation/enthusiasm.

One school uses the following interview questions to assess gifted students' readiness to participate profitably in elementary, full-time, self-contained gifted classes:

1. Tell me about your reading. How much time do you spend in voluntary reading each day? Do you like to read? What are your favorite books?
2. Do you like to work hard and study hard in school? Do you like to do homework? Have you got a lot of energy? Do you like to work on one project for a long time?
3. Do you get a lot of good ideas? Do you get unusual or "far-out" ideas? Do you like to write down your ideas?
4. What hobbies do you have? Do you like to do projects? Do you have collections? What are your interests?
5. Do you like to work with kids who have a lot of good ideas? Who are good thinkers? Who can solve problems easily and quickly?
6. What are your major goals in school? What do you want to accomplish? What do you want to do when you finish school?

While an interview may be a relatively laborious task, it nevertheless can yield valuable information in understanding gifted and talented youth. It can also provide useful information for program planning and for the design of individual educational services.

Combining Data

All the data from tests, rating scales, product assessment, interviews, and the like, should be drawn together into a folder for each nominee. Scores relevant to a particular program service for which a nominee is being considered should be standardized, preferably by conversion to T scores. They then can be added together, weighted (if there is a rationale for increasing or reducing the power of each score in the combination), and a total score derived. Feldhusen, Baska, and Womble (1981) presented a detailed plan for combining standardized scores.

In some instances, program assignments might be made on the basis of a single test score. For example, children may be selected for an accelerated mathematics program on the basis of the mathematics score from the Scholastic Aptitude Test. In such cases, the single score is highly relevant to the area of program service.

Diagnostic-Assessment Committee

The final decision-making in the selection of youth for program services should be a professional judgment, preferably made by a diagnostic-assessment committee. The decision should be dictated neither by a test score nor by some total or combination score. The cutoff level can be established, and for youth who score well above that level, the committee's decision may be perfunctory. For all the scores that are lower than the cutoff level but within the standard error of measurement for the scales used, committee judgment is necessary. In reaching a decision, the committee can take into account any other relevant information. Although relatively subjective, the committee's decision nevertheless should be based on sound professional judgment with due regard to the potential errors or lack of reliability in all the assessment-identification procedures.

In some instances, the committee should be able to make a decision for tryout of a possibly talented youth in a program service. Such a recommendation is often relevant when youth are being selected for early admission or grade advancement. When doubt or uncertainty exists about the decision, the student's performance during the trial period should determine if the student can handle the demands of the new assignment and profit from the experience.

Continuing Student Evaluation as Identification

Students who have been placed in a program service (e.g., a full-time, self-contained class, a pullout program, an accelerated math class, an Advanced Placement [College Board, 1995] class, or a Future Problem Solving program) should be evaluated periodically to determine their progress and ascertain if the identification decision was sound. Are the students progressing well? Does the service meet some of their needs? The diagnostic-identification committee should receive this type of information periodically (e.g., every 6 to 9 weeks), and the committee should make decisions concerning the desirability of a gifted youth's continuation in the program, withdrawal from the program, or reassignment to another program service.

In a sense, the identification process should be continuous and designed to help gifted youth come to know and understand their own talent strengths. This understanding can come from periodic review of new test data and performance or achievement measures with a counselor. Awards and recognitions, grades in courses, and participation in talent searches can also provide valuable information about emerging talents and their potential link to career goals.

Repeated evaluation to determine if a child is gifted or not seems to be of little value. The critical issue is determining if the child has continuing special educational talents and needs that cannot be served in a general education classroom and whether the special program service is meeting those needs.

Summary ⁓

The purpose of the identification process in gifted education is to identify youth whose abilities, motivation, self-concept, interests, and creative talents are so much greater than average that special education program services are needed to meet their needs. All youth have a right to educational programs that will help them achieve their highest potential. Program services for the gifted should be designed to fit each child's unique talents and needs. Because parents know their own children better than anyone else, their input should be a vital part of the identification process.

Identification should be a continuing effort. It should not be viewed as a one-time assessment. Children's performance in a program should be used to verify or contradict the results of tests and rating scales. Reliability and validity of the tests and rating scales are crucial to the process. Giftedness is not a unique diagnostic category; rather it denotes children whose talents are markedly higher but not fundamentally different from those of other children.

In practice, identification of the gifted begins with a nomination/screening process that seeks to find all possibly gifted youth. An assessment process should follow in which various measures are administered to determine the levels of a youth's special talents and abilities. After all the data have been gathered, a diagnostic-assessment committee should review the data, determine whether each nominee has special needs because of superior talent or ability, and suggest the appropriate educational service. Programs for gifted students should consist of a variety of services that can be used selectively to fit their special characteristics and needs.

At the secondary level, identification becomes a selection process. Gifted youth may have been generally identified to become part of a talent pool, but to identify youth qualified for specific program services, such as an honors class or a seminar, specific selection criteria should be used. Those selection criteria must clarify youths' special talents, aptitudes, and interests to assure that the program services selected will best enhance the youths' overall talent development.

References ∼

Achter, J., Lubinski, D., & Benbow, C. (1996). Multipotentiality among the intellectually gifted: "It was never there in the first place, and already it's vanishing." *Journal of Counseling Psychology, 43*(1), 65–76.

Alvino, J., McDonnel, R. C., & Richert, S. (1981). National Survey of identification practices in gifted and talented education. *Exceptional Children, 48*, 124–132.

ASSETS. (1979). *User's guide to A.S.S.E.T.S.* Holmes Beach, FL: Learning Publications.

Baldwin, A. Y. (1984). *Baldwin Identification Matrix 2 for identification of gifted and talented.* Unionville, NY: Trillium.

Berger, S. L. (Ed.). (1992). *Programs and practices in gifted education.* Reston, VA: Council for Exceptional Children.

Bloom, B. S. (Ed.). (1985). *Developing talent in young people.* New York: Ballantine.

Borland, J. H. (1989). *Planning and implementing programs for the gifted.* New York: Teachers College Press.

Brandwein, P. R. (1980). On the search for the gifted. *Roeper Review, 3*, 2–3.

College Board. (1995). *A guide to the advanced placement program.* New York: Author.

Csikszentmihalyi, M., Rathunde, K., & Whalen, S. (1993). *Talented teenagers: The roots of success and failure.* New York: Cambridge University Press.

Dweck, C. S. (1986). Motivational processes affecting learning. *American Psychologist, 41*(10), 1040–1048.

Feldhusen, J. F. (1991). Identification of gifted and talented youth. In M. C. Wang, M. C. Reynolds, & H. J. Walberg (Eds.), *Handbook of special education: Research and practice* (pp. 7–22). New York: Pergamon.

Feldhusen, J. F. (1993). Assessment tools for counselors. In L. K. Silverman (Ed.), *Counseling the gifted and talented* (pp. 239–259). Denver, CO: Love.

Feldhusen, J. F. (1994). Talent identification and development in education. *Gifted Education International, 10,* 10–15.

Feldhusen, J. F. (1995a). Talent development vs. gifted education. *The Educational Forum, 59*(4), 346–349.

Feldhusen, J. F. (1995b). *Talent identification and development in education (TIDE)* (2nd ed.) Sarasota, FL: Center for Creative Learning.

Feldhusen, J. F., Asher, J. W., & Hoover, S. M. (1984). Problems in the identification of giftedness, talent or ability. *Gifted Child Quarterly, 28,* 149–156.

Feldhusen, J. F., Baska, L. K., & Womble, S. R. (1981). Using standard scores to synthesize data in identifying the gifted. *Journal for the Education of the Gifted, 4,* 177–185.

Feldhusen, J. F., Hoover, S. M., & Sayler, M. F. (1990). *Identification and education of the gifted and talented at the secondary level.* Unionville, NY: Trillium.

Feldhusen, J. F., & Jarwan, F. A. (1993). Identification of gifted and talented youth for educational programs. In K. A. Heller, F. J. Monks, & A. H. Passow (Eds.), *International handbook of research and development of giftedness and talent* (pp. 233–251). New York: Pergamon.

Feldhusen, J. F., & Jarwan, F. (1995). Predictors of academic success at state-supported residential schools for mathematics and science: A validity study. *Educational and Psychological Measurement, 55*(3), 505–512.

Feldhusen, J. F., & Kolloff, M. B. (1981). ME: A self-concept scale for gifted students. *Perceptual and Motor Skills, 53,* 319–323.

Flack, J. D., & Feldhusen, J. F. (1983). Future studies in the curricular framework of the Purdue three-stage model. *G/C/T, 27,* 1–9.

Gagné, F. (1993). Constructs and models pertaining to exceptional human abilities. In K. A. Heller, F. J. Monks, & A. H. Passow (Eds.), *International handbook of research and development of giftedness and talent* (pp. 69–87). New York: Pergamon.

Harter, S. (1982). The perceived competence scale for children. *Child Development, 53,* 87–97.

Harter, S. (1985). *Manual for the self-perception profile for children.* Unpublished manuscript, University of Denver, Denver, CO.

Henry, W. A. (1994). *In defense of elitism.* New York: Doubleday.

Howley, C. B., Howley, A., & Pendarvis, E. D. (1995). *Out of our minds: Anti-intellectualism and talent development in American schooling.* New York: Teachers College Press.

Jarwan, F. A., & Feldhusen, J. F. (1993). *Residential schools of mathematics and science for academically talented youth: An analysis of admissions programs.* Storrs, CT: National Research Center on the Gifted and Talented.

Jenkins-Friedman, R., Richert, E. S., & Feldhusen, J. F. (1991). *Special populations of gifted learners: A book of readings.* Unionville, NY: Trillium.

Karnes, M. L. (1987). Bringing out Head Start talents: Findings from the field. *Gifted Child Quarterly, 31*(4), 174–179.

Kramer, J. J., & Conoley, J. C. (Eds.). (1992). *The eleventh mental measurements yearbook.* Lincoln: University of Nebraska Press.

Moore, B. A., Feldhusen, J. F., & Owings, J. (1978). *Professional career exploration program for minority and/or low income gifted and talented high school students.* West Lafayette, IN: Purdue University Education Department.

Piers, E. V., & Harris, D. B. (1969). *The Piers-Harris Children's Self-Concept Scale.* Nashville, TN: Counselor Recordings & Tests.

Renzulli, J. S., Smith, L. H., White, A. J., Callahan, C. M., & Hartman, R. K. (1976). *Scales for Rating the Behavioral Characteristics of Superior Students.* Wethersfield, CT: Creative Learning Press.

Richert, E. S., Alvino, J. J., & McDonnel, R. C. (1982). *National report on identification.* Sewell, NJ: Educational Improvement Center—South.

Rimm, S. B. (1994). *Keys to parenting the gifted child.* Hauppauge, NY: Barrow's.

Robinson, N. M. (1993). Identifying and nurturing gifted, very young children. In K. A. Heller, F. J. Monks, & A. H. Passow (Eds.), *International handbook of research and development of giftedness and talent* (pp. 507–524). New York: Pergamon.

Saunders, R. J. (1982). Screening and identifying the talented in art. *Roeper Review, 4,* 7–10.

Shore, B. M., Cornell, D. G., Robinson, A., & Ward, V. S. (1991). *Recommended practices in gifted education.* New York: Teachers College Press.

Thorndike, R. L., Hagen, E. P., & Sattler, J. M. (1986). *The Stanford-Binet Intelligence Scale (4th ed.). Technical manual.* New York: Riverside.

Torrance, E. P. (1974). *Torrance Tests of Creative Thinking.* Bensenville, IL: Scholastic Testing Service.

VanTassel-Baska, J. (1985). The talent search model: Implications for secondary school reform. *National Association for Secondary School Principals Journal, 69*(482), 39–47.

Vygotsky, L. S. (1978). *Mind in society: The development of higher psychological processes.* Cambridge, MA: Harvard University Press.

Wechsler, D. (1974). *Wechsler Intelligence Scale for Children—Revised.* New York: Psychological Corp.

Study Questions ~

1. What major sources of information should be tapped in identifying gifted and talented youth?
2. What is meant by reliability of test scores?
3. What is the ceiling effect? What is off-grade-level testing?
4. When we identify gifted youth, are we assessing accomplishment or potential?
5. What is giftedness?
6. Why are interviews useful in identifying the gifted and talented?
7. Should identification of the gifted and talented be a one-time process? Why or why not?

12
Programs and Services at the Elementary Level

John F. Feldhusen

Gifted programs are alternative administrative structures for bringing curriculum and instruction to gifted and talented youth (Feldhusen, 1986b). These structures do not properly constitute a delivery system, for that implies that the curriculum is simply a body of skills and knowledge imposed upon gifted youth. Rather, the curriculum might best be viewed as an organized set of skills and content that gifted youth can experience or interact with generatively to develop their own knowledge schemas, understandings, and skills (VanTassel-Baska, 1993). The program model is the system that facilitates interaction of gifted youth with curriculum to produce learning.

All learning in a gifted program occurs within either planned or unplanned environments. If the environment is planned, it is a part of the program model (Maker & Nielson, 1995). All learning yields products, at least in the sense that learning always implies a residual effect that enables a learner to behave (cognitively, verbally, socially, emotionally) in some new way. Of course, the concept of product advocated by Maker (1982) and Renzulli and Reis (1986) is a concrete entity that results from the research and project activity of gifted youth. Whatever the product residual, the learning activities that result in products are a part of the program model.

Programs for the gifted and talented may be designed for faster delivery of content, for delivery of more content, for examining content in greater depth, or for dealing with more complex and higher levels of subject matter. All of these approaches are essentially accelerative in nature and are based on efforts to fit instruction to the precocity of students. Other programs for the gifted and talented also may seek to provide alternatives that will enrich the learning experiences and allow students to study topics that fit their interests. Enrichment programs often seek to provide instruction in subject matter appropriate to the children's grade level but to also allow the study and investigation of supplementary content. Still other programs attempt to provide instruction that individually and explicitly fits the achievement levels, ability, interests, and learning style of the gifted student. This last approach, individualization, is called "diagnostic prescriptive" by VanTassel-Baska et al. (1988) or an "individually prescribed" program model by Treffinger (1986). Perhaps the best overall approach to programming for the gifted and talented is a combination of these three approaches.

This chapter describes program arrangements and organized models to help gifted and talented youth at the elementary level achieve the goals and objectives of the curriculum.

Comprehensive Program Models ~

Enrichment

A number of systematic enrichment program models have been developed, such as the Enrichment Triad/Revolving Door Model advanced by Renzulli and Reis (1986), the Individualized Program Planning Model (IPPM) of Treffinger (1986), the Purdue Three-Stage Model advocated by Feldhusen and Kolloff (1979, 1986) and Moon and Feldhusen (1991), the talent development models presented by Renzulli (1994) and Feldhusen (1995), and the Autonomous Learner Model presented by Betts (1986). All of these models provide relatively comprehensive plans for identification and program services for gifted children that are essentially enriching in nature. They were selected for description here because they are illustrative of a large number of models that seek to enrich learning experiences for gifted youth.

The Renzulli model is possibly the most comprehensive in its extensive treatment of identification, administration, staff training, and program delivery structure (Renzulli, 1994; Renzulli & Reis, 1986). There are three types of program experience.

1. Type I enrichment involves general exploratory experiences, which expose students to "new and exciting topics, ideas and fields of knowledge that are not covered in the regular curriculum" (Renzulli & Reis, 1986, p. 237). The actual activities include field trips, speakers, learning centers, readings, audiovisual materials, minicourses, museum programs, artistic performances, and so forth. Some Type I activities are offered to all children, not just the gifted.

2. Type II enrichment, group training activities, consists of activities designed to develop cognitive and affective processes. The activities can be offered to all children, not just the gifted.

3. Type III enrichment calls for individual and small-group investigations of real problems. Special identification procedures are used to select children for Type III enrichment—especially through observation of "action information," or overt behavior of the child that reflects current interests, motivation, or behavior related to a specific topic or project. Type III enrichment

activities usually are carried out in a special resource room and directed by a special resource teacher who is trained to work with gifted youth.

The Treffinger (1986) Individualized Program Planning Model stresses the intensive use of information gathered during the identification process to plan individualized programs of study for the gifted based on their talents, strengths, and interests. The model also seeks to develop independence and self-direction skills in the gifted. IPPM focuses attention on how to deal with or provide for the gifted in general classrooms. Treffinger presented a wide variety of potential program services for the gifted. In this model, the entire staff receives extensive training to learn how best to provide for the diverse needs of the gifted.

The Purdue Three-Stage Model developed by Feldhusen and Kolloff (1979, 1986) is essentially an enrichment model and is most often delivered as a pullout program. The three-stage model is implemented in many schools as the Program for Academic and Creative Enrichment (PACE) (Kolloff & Feldhusen, 1981). The model is implemented in resource rooms with small groups of 8 to 15 gifted children. During stage one, the children follow a curriculum focusing on thinking skills and basic subject matter content, meeting at least 2 periods a week and preferably 1 full day a week. The thinking skills and content are taught at a high level and fast pace appropriate for the gifted.

During stage two, broader and more concrete strategies are taught. These include library skills, creative problem-solving, future studies, and research skills, all of which pave the way to stage three activities, which are project-oriented applications in students' areas of personal interest. During stage three, students work on research projects and developmental tasks, and these efforts result in presentations, products, or performances. Stage three simulates real-life creative productivity.

The Autonomous Learner Model developed by Betts (1986, 1991) attempts to meet the academic, social, and emotional needs of the gifted while setting the goal of independence or autonomy so that the gifted will become responsible for their own learning. It probably is best characterized as an enrichment model. The model offers time for (1) orientation to the self as a gifted person and to program opportunities; (2) enrichment activities such as investigations, cultural activities, and field trips; (3) seminars on futurism, problems, and controversial issues; (4) individual development of learning skills, career knowledge, and interpersonal abilities; and (5) in-depth study in individual and group projects and mentorships. This model is particularly strong in its focus on the individual or personal development of gifted students.

Individualization

When pullout models are used, there is danger that gifted children will languish and lose motivation in the general classroom where they spend most of their time because all or most of the activities are too low level or slow paced (Feldhusen & Kroll, 1991). All children learn best when learning involves challenge and offers success. Thus, if the gifted are served in a general classroom, instruction must be individualized and thereby adjusted to their skill levels (Feldhusen, 1993a, 1993b).

Alternatively, cluster grouping (Hoover, Sayler, & Feldhusen, 1993) can be used to bring all the gifted in a grade level together from several rooms into one room with a teacher who is able and willing to differentiate instruction to fit the level and pace of the cluster while also dealing with all of the other children at their differing levels of ability in the classroom. A cluster usually consists of three to seven children in an otherwise heterogeneous classroom (Hoover, Sayler, & Feldhusen, 1993).

In the cluster-group or individualized approaches, the use of individualized educational programs (IEPs) (Feldhusen, 1986a), developed cooperatively by the gifted coordinator and the general classroom teacher, can be a useful mechanism to induce specific planning and teaching activities appropriate for the gifted. Classroom teachers need special in-service preparation to learn how to assess children's levels of abilities in the different subjects, to eliminate or reduce activities in which they are already competent, and to plan for higher level and faster paced instruction.

Acceleration

Gross (1993) documented well the precocity of gifted and talented children. All of the children she studied were achieving and functioning intellectually at levels far beyond what would be normative for their chronological ages. Yet schools, and teachers in particular, were often reluctant to acknowledge the precocity or to make any modifications in the curriculum. Fred, for example, learned to read fluently before age 3, but when he entered school his teachers ignored his advanced reading ability and provided only the regular curriculum. Cassandra was also verbally highly precocious, and her school, too, made very little provision for her precocity.

The most appropriate provisions for such academically advanced children are exactly the same as would be provided for children who are advanced in art or music—that is, opportunities to work at levels appropriate to their achievement or ability levels. Ungraded schools provide such an opportunity, but they are still comparatively rare. Adjustments can also be made in general classroom practice with the techniques of compacting, as described by Reis and Purcell (1993). The general classroom teacher assesses a child's skill level and frees those who are gifted from the normative level of curriculum and instruction and the regularly expected activities. Such children are then provided new instructional material at appropriate levels.

Yet another programmatic approach is to assess the child's level of readiness for new work in a particular subject and place those who are advanced in a higher level grade or classroom for that subject matter. The child remains in his or her general classroom for the majority of the time during the school day, leaving the room each day, for example, just for mathematics or reading at a higher grade level.

Some children are so far advanced in their basic skills and knowledge that acceleration to a higher grade level is necessary (VanTassel-Baska, 1986). After reviewing the literature on early admission of precocious children to school, Proctor, Black, and Feldhusen (1986) concluded that early admission is desirable for many gifted children. Many gifted children have reading skills or numerical ability (or both) before they enter school. They should be admitted to kindergarten or first grade ahead of schedule. Research indicates that if they are carefully screened and evaluated, they will thrive on the accelerated school learning experience (Feldhusen, 1992).

Feldhusen, Proctor, and Black (1986) also presented guidelines for grade advancement of precocious children. From a comprehensive review of the research on grade advancement, and from their personal experiences in consulting on grade advancement cases, the authors concluded that failure to advance children who are ready may be harmful to their social-emotional-academic development. These authors presented guidelines for decision-making in grade advancement case studies, which include the following steps:

1. A comprehensive psychological evaluation of the child's intellectual functioning, academic skill levels, and social-emotional adjustment should be conducted by a psychologist.
2. Intellectually, the child should have an IQ of 125 or greater or have a level of mental development greater than the mean for the grade he or she desires to enter.
3. Academically, the child should demonstrate skill levels greater than the mean of the grade desired. If the child is high in several skill levels but low in one area, the child may be advanced to the appropriate grade if private tutoring is provided in the area of weakness.
4. Socially and emotionally, the child should be free of any serious adjustment problems. In some cases, however, serious adjustment problems may result from inappropriately low grade placement. In such cases, the problem may be alleviated by grade advancement.
5. Physically, the child should be in good health. The child's size should be considered only to the extent that competitive sports may be viewed as important in later years.
6. The psychologist should determine that the child does not feel unduly pressured by his or her parents to advance. The parents must be in favor of grade advancement, but the child should express the desire to move ahead.
7. The receiving teacher or teachers must have positive attitudes toward the acceleration and be willing to help the child adjust to the new situation. If a receiving teacher is hostile or pessimistic, another receiving teacher should be located or the move should not be made.
8. Public school teachers are sometimes unduly pessimistic about children's social-emotional maturity. They might confuse a precocious child's misbehavior that is caused by dissatisfaction with inappropriate instruction with immaturity. Judgments about a precocious child's maturity therefore should include input from parents and the psychologist.
9. Midyear and year-end grade advancements appear to be equally successful. Midyear advancements may be more desirable because the teachers may more easily confer about how best to help the child make a smooth transition.

10. All cases of grade advancement should be arranged on a trial basis. A trial period of 6 weeks should be sufficient. The child should be aware that if the trial period does not go well, he or she may ask to be returned to the original grade.
11. Care should be exercised to not build up excessive expectations from grade advancement. The child should not be made to feel he or she is a failure if the experience does not go well. Alternatively, some precocious children are so advanced in their intellectual and academic skills that 1 year of advancement may still leave them bored in school. For a few precocious children, additional advancements may be necessary.
12. Grade advancement decisions should be made by a committee consisting of an administrator, a teacher, and a counselor or school psychologist. Examination of the research literature reveals that acceleration contributes to academic achievement. No negative effects on social or emotional development have been identified. If adjustment problems occur, they tend to be minor and temporary in nature. Conversely, failure to advance a precocious child may result in poor study habits, apathy, lack of motivation, and maladjustment.

Southern and Jones (1991) compiled reports from a number of researchers on grade advancement in their book *The Academic Acceleration of Gifted Children*. The book offers many suggestions and cautions for school personnel and parents.

It is imperative that gifted and talented youth have good opportunities to advance to higher levels of instruction when they are ready so that there can always be a degree of challenge and newness in their school experience. Teachers often worry excessively about possible social damage as a result of grade advancement, but a large body of research (Shore, Cornell, Robinson, & Ward, 1991) shows clearly that if grade advancement is carried out carefully following reasonable guidelines there will be no social difficulties. Indeed, the research shows that the child will profit from the academic progress and motivational development.

Serving the Gifted in General Classrooms

Many gifted children will remain in the general classroom and receive no special instruction of any kind. The model set forth by Feldhusen (1981, 1993a, 1993b) offers general classroom teachers clear guidelines for differentiating instruction for gifted children while serving all children well. The model emphasizes the following:

1. Frequent evaluation of performance levels in basic skills areas
2. Extensive use of a variety of individualized instructional materials that permit individual progress
3. Daily planning by children of appropriate learning activities
4. Instructional units and learning centers in which students can access materials by themselves
5. Effective recordkeeping that permits a teacher to monitor each student's progress

6. Instructional emphasis on teaching children to be independent and self-directing
7. Cluster seating to encourage cooperative learning among children

Feldhusen (1981) evaluated her model while it was being developed and found it to be effective in producing higher levels of achievement, favorable attitudes, and good motivation in gifted children.

Special, Full-Time, Self-Contained Classes for the Gifted

Gifted children thrive and learn best in special classes where they are together on a daily basis for all or most of the school day. In many schools that offer special classes for the gifted, these children join the other students for art, music, physical education, and playground (recess) so that social interaction among children of all ability levels will be facilitated. Feldhusen and Treffinger (1985) noted that interest in special classes for the gifted was growing because pullout models were failing to meet their academic needs. Special classes are also more cost-effective. Pullout classes always involve added cost, but special classes simply involve regrouping gifted children into a class of typical size for the school and having one teacher serve them just as one teacher would serve a mixed group of the same number of students.

After surveying programs for the gifted in U.S. schools, Cox, Daniel, and Boston (1985) concluded that pullout classes are often weak and ineffective. They called for stronger offerings such as special classes, especially for the highly gifted. Belcastro (1987) also presented a substantial argument concerning the weaknesses of enrichment and pullout program models, asserting that they often fail to meet the basic need of the gifted, which is instruction at an appropriate pace and level.

VanTassel-Baska, Willis, and Meyers (1989) conducted a study of full-time, self-contained classes for gifted students and found very positive effects. Feldhusen and Sayler (1990) conducted a statewide study of such classes in Indiana and also found very positive results for student motivation, attitudes, and achievement. Feldhusen (1991a, 1991b) argued that such classes are the best arrangement for highly gifted students, especially because they profit so much from working with other gifted students.

Other Options

A variety of other options, such as the following, are offered at the elementary level as special services for gifted and talented children:

- Seminars
- Special computer classes
- Junior Great Books program
- Future Problem Solving
- Foreign language instruction
- Career education, mentors, and role models
- After-school, Saturday, and summer enrichment classes
- Special classes in art, music, and dance

All of these options can be of value to gifted and talented students if the options are taught at a sufficiently high level and pace to constitute a real challenge. If the gifted return to general classes taught at the normative level and pace for all students, however, they will languish, learn how to get by without effort, or become systematically demotivated toward school learning. After reviewing the wide variety of extra-school program options that are available to gifted and talented youth in the United States and Europe, Goldstein and Wagner (1993) concluded that there are a multitude of opportunities to enhance the learning and cognitive development of gifted and talented youth. Thus, the crucial problem is how to provide appropriate, challenging learning experiences for the gifted at the elementary level in school on a daily basis in basic subject matter as well as in the supplementary learning experiences.

Seminars Seminars for the gifted are conducted in some elementary schools. Kolloff and Feldhusen (1986) described a number of seminar programs operating in schools in the Midwest and listed the following as typical characteristics of more successful seminars:

1. An organized, regularly scheduled class
2. Much time for discussion, small-group work, and student presentations
3. A focus on a theme or concept, when relevant
4. A goal of teaching thinking skills, library skills, research skills
5. A focus, when relevant, on personal-social development and understanding of giftedness
6. In-depth projects
7. Incorporation of career education, when appropriate
8. Incorporation of art and cultural experiences

Career Education, Mentors, and Role Models Career education for the gifted helps these students come to understand their career potentials, talents, abilities, and limitations and helps them to know better the nature and demands of higher level occupations (Feldhusen & Kolloff, 1979; Moore, Feldhusen, & Owings, 1978). It may consist of classroom experiences exploring the self, occupational specifications, and educational programs leading to the occupations. It also may offer mentoring experiences (Ellingson, Haeger, & Feldhusen, 1986), which provide more explicit and intimate understandings of target occupations.

Feldhusen and Gassin (1991) studied the impact of a Saturday program for gifted and talented students on their knowledge and understanding of their own talents, interests, career planning, and educational goals. They found the program highly successful in helping the students understand their own talents and interests and moderately successful in helping them develop educational and career plans. Explicit educational programs are needed for gifted and talented youth to help them learn earlier about high-level careers that fit their talents and interests and the educational routes to those careers.

Gifted and talented students can learn about potential careers that are related to their talent strengths from role models, mentors, and the study of heroes (Pleiss &

Feldhusen, 1995). The work of Bandura (1986) reminds us of the powerful roles played by role models in shaping adolescent and adult social and professional behavior. Feldhusen (1986a), in his studies of highly talented youth, also noted the powerful impact of role models on youth talent development. Career education surely involves much academic and affective learning through school and guidance services, but in addition, role models, mentors, and heroes are vital parts of the career education and career development processes.

Opportunities in the Arts Special opportunities in the arts are needed for artistically talented children and for intellectually gifted children who are not destined for high-level careers in the arts but who wish to pursue competence in an art form avocationally. Several different models are being developed in connection with gifted programs to assure advanced art experiences for the gifted and talented (Clark & Zimmerman, 1987; Haroutounian, 1993). The major goal is to assure that art opportunities are not relegated to a secondary or nonexistent status while academic and intellectual program services predominate.

Clark and Zimmerman (1994) reviewed research and theory on talent development in the visual arts and concluded that a paucity of information exists to guide program development and that there is confusion in the language used to describe art programs. However, in their 1984 book, these authors described several program arrangements, such as special grouping, accelerated classes, and out-of-school programs, that could be used to provide special instruction for artistically talented students.

Extra-School Academic Learning Experiences Programming for elementary gifted students should include extra-school or beyond-school learning experiences. Counselors or program coordinators should lead the effort to guide gifted children to these experiences. Saturday programs are widely available (Feldhusen & Sokol, 1982), as are summer programs (Feldhusen & Clinkenbeard, 1982). These experiences give gifted youth special opportunities for advanced and fast-paced instruction, for exploring areas of special interest, for working in areas of study related to their talents, and for working with other precocious youth in challenging learning experiences.

Feldhusen (1991c) described program models for Saturday and summer experiences for gifted and talented youth and argued that such programs can provide challenging experiences, opportunities to work with other talented youth, in-depth and fast-paced study, and exposure to stimulating and knowledgeable teachers. In addition, Goldstein and Wagner (1993) inventoried a wide variety of competitions that can provide valuable learning experiences for talented youth.

Extra-School Cultural Experiences Extra-school cultural experiences provide opportunities for gifted and talented youth to learn about artistic and cultural resources that can enrich their lives. Eisner (1985) argued that through aesthetic and cultural experiences we do more than simply enjoy the experience; we come to better know or understand the world around us. Early introduction to aesthetic and cultural experience establishes receptivity to and enthusiasm for the arts in gifted youth.

These extracurricular activities include going to concerts, plays, art exhibits, historical restorations, or museum programs and then having an opportunity to discuss them. A group of gifted youth who attend a play may be provided with an opportunity to discuss the drama with the cast following the performance. Other gifted programs may provide discussion opportunities before and after a cultural experience in a seminar-like setting.

The program model developed by Betts (1985) offers a good example of cultural activities incorporated into a program for gifted youth. The model advocates visits to museums, plays, concerts, and other cultural events followed by opportunities for youth to meet performers or staff and discuss with them the aesthetics of the experiences (Albert, 1990).

Foreign Language Learning   Foreign language learning also provides invaluable experiences for gifted youth (Garfinkel, Allen, & Neuharth-Pritchett, 1993; Garfinkel & Prentice, 1985; VanTassel-Baska, 1982). Such experience should begin in the elementary grades and lead to early enrollment in foreign language classes in high school. Learning a foreign language enhances gifted students' grasp of their own native language, provides an extended perspective on the function of language in our lives, readies gifted youth for a multicultural future, and provides insights about differences among cultures. VanTassel-Baska (1987) delineated several program models for the verbally able in which teaching Latin is combined with teaching a second language. She suggested that learning Latin enhances learning generally in the language arts.

Summary ~

Various program models are available to provide sound curriculum experiences for gifted and talented youth at the elementary level. The best models provide accelerated, enriched, and challenging learning experiences that help gifted youth clarify their talent strengths and potential and give them opportunities to move ahead to higher levels of learning at a pace that fits their abilities. Maker and Nielson (1995) presented comprehensive descriptions of 15 instructional models that can be used to guide program and curriculum development in gifted education at the elementary level. The models are characterized by high-level cognitive approaches, in-depth investigations and projects, stress on problem-solving, conceptual learning, and development of creative products. Program developers at the elementary level have access to ample resources in the material presented in this chapter and in Maker and Nielson (1995) to create excellent programs for gifted and talented children.

References ~

Albert, R. S. (1990). Identity, experiences, and career choice among the exceptionally gifted and talented. In M. A. Remco & R. S. Albert (Eds.), *Theories of creativity* (pp. 13–34). Newbury Park, CA: Sage.

Bandura, A. (1986). *Social foundations of thought and action: A social cognitive theory.* Englewood Cliffs, NJ: Prentice Hall.

Belcastro, F. P. (1987). Elementary pullout program for the intellectually gifted—boon or bane? *Roeper Review, 9*(4), 4–11.

Betts, G. (1985). *The Autonomous Learner Model for the gifted and talented*. Greeley, CO: ALP's Publications.

Betts, G. T. (1986). The Autonomous Learner Model for the gifted and talented. In J. S. Renzulli (Ed.), *Systems and models for developing programs for the gifted and talented* (pp. 27–56). Mansfield Center, CT: Creative Learning Press.

Betts, G. (1991). The Autonomous Learner Model for the gifted and talented. In N. Colangelo & G. Davis (Eds.), *Handbook of gifted education* (pp. 142–153). Boston: Allyn & Bacon.

Clark, G. A., & Zimmerman, E. D. (1984). *Educating artistically talented students*. Syracuse, NY: Syracuse University Press.

Clark, G. A., & Zimmerman, E. D. (1987). *Resources for educating artistically talented students*. Syracuse, NY: Syracuse University Press.

Clark, G. A., & Zimmerman, E. (1994). *Programming opportunities for students gifted and talented in the visual arts*. Storrs, CT: National Research Center on the Gifted and Talented.

Cox, J., Daniel, N., & Boston, B. O. (1985). *Educating able learners, Programs and promising practices*. Austin: University of Texas Press.

Eisner, E. (1985). Aesthetic modes of knowing. In E. Eisner (Ed.), *Learning and teaching the ways of knowing* (84th yearbook of the National Society for the Study of Education, Part 2) (pp. 23–26). Chicago: University of Chicago Press.

Ellingson, M. K., Haeger, W. W., & Feldhusen, J. F. (1986). The Purdue Mentor Program: A university-based mentorship experience for gifted children. *Gifted Child Today, 9*(2), 2–5.

Feldhusen, H. J. (1981). Teaching gifted, creative, and talented students in an individualized classroom. *Gifted Child Quarterly, 25*(3), 108–111.

Feldhusen, H. J. (1993a). *Individualized teaching of gifted children in the regular classroom*. West Lafayette, IN: STAR Teaching Materials.

Feldhusen, H. J. (1993b). Individualized teaching of the gifted in regular classrooms. In C. J. Maker (Ed.), *Critical issues in gifted education* (Volume 3, pp. 263–273). Austin, TX: PRO-Ed.

Feldhusen, J. F. (1986a). A new conception of giftedness and programming for the gifted. *Illinois Council for the Gifted Journal, 5,* 2–6.

Feldhusen, J. F. (1986b). Policies and procedures for the development of defensible programs for the gifted. In C. J. Maker (Ed.), *Critical issues in gifted education, defensible programs for the gifted* (pp. 235–255). Rockville, MD: Aspen Publications.

Feldhusen, J. F. (1991a). Full-time classes for gifted youth. *Gifted Child Today, 14*(5), 10–13.

Feldhusen, J. F. (1991b). Gifted students must have time together in learning activities at their level and pace. *Images, 5*(2), 2–3, 12–13.

Feldhusen, J. F. (1991c). Saturday and summer programs for the gifted and talented. In N. Colangelo & G. A. Davis (Eds.), *The handbook of gifted education* (pp. 197–207). Boston: Allyn & Bacon.

Feldhusen, J. F. (1992). Early admission and grade advancement. *Gifted Child Today, 15*(2), 45–49.

Feldhusen, J. F. (1995). *Talent identification and development in education (TIDE)* (2nd ed.). Sarasota, FL: Center for Creative Learning.

Feldhusen, J. F., & Clinkenbeard, P. R. (1982). Summer programs for the gifted: Purdue's residential programs for high achievers. *Journal for the Education of the Gifted, 5*(3), 178–184.

Feldhusen, J. F., & Gassin, E. A. (1991). Career development, impact of a Saturday program on the career development of gifted youth. *Prufrock Journal, 3*(2), 22–24.

Feldhusen, J. F., & Kolloff, P. B. (1979). An approach to career education for the gifted. *Roeper Review, 2*(2), 13–17.

Feldhusen, J. F., & Kolloff, P. B. (1986). The Purdue Three-Stage Model for gifted education at the elementary level. In J. S. Renzulli (Ed.), *Systems and models for developing programs for the gifted and talented* (pp. 126–152). Mansfield Center, CT: Creative Learning Press.

Feldhusen, J. F., & Kroll, M. D. (1991). Boredom or challenge for the academically talented. *Gifted Education International, 7*(2), 80–81.

Feldhusen, J. F., Proctor, T. B., & Black, K. N. (1986). Guidelines for grade advancement of precocious children. *Roeper Review, 9*(l), 25–27.

Feldhusen, J. F., & Sayler, M. F. (1990). Special classes for academically gifted youth. *Roeper Review, 12*(4), 244–249.

Feldhusen, J. F., & Sokol, L. (1982). Extra-school programming to meet the needs of gifted youth: Super Saturday. *Gifted Child Quarterly, 26*(2), 51–56.

Feldhusen, J. F., & Treffinger, D. J. (1985). *Creative thinking and problem solving in gifted education.* Dubuque, IA: Kendall/Hunt.

Garfinkel, A., Allen, L. Q., & Neuharth-Pritchett, S. (1993). Foreign language for the gifted: Extending affective dimensions. *Roeper Review, 15*, 235–238.

Garfinkel, A., & Prentice, M. (1985). Foreign language for the gifted: Extending cognitive dimensions. In P. B. Westphal (Ed.), *Meeting the call for excellence in the foreign language classroom* (pp. 43–49). Lincolnwood, IL: National Textbook.

Goldstein, D., & Wagner, H. (1993). After-school programs, competitions, school olympics, and summer programs. In K. A. Heller, F. J. Monks, & A. H. Passow (Eds.), *International handbook of research and development of giftedness and talent* (pp. 593–604). New York: Pergamon.

Gross, M. V. (1993). *Exceptionally gifted children.* London: Routledge.

Haroutounian, J. (1993). Identifying talent in the performing arts. *Spotlight: Newsletter of the Visual and Performing Arts Division of the National Association for Gifted Children* (June, 1994), 8–12.

Hoover, S. M., Sayler, M. F., & Feldhusen, J. F. (1993). Cluster grouping of gifted students at the elementary level. *Roeper Review, 16*(1), 13–15.

Kolloff, P. B., & Feldhusen, J. F. (1981). PACE (Program for Academic and Creative Enrichment): An application of the three-stage model. *G/C/T, 18*, 47–50.

Kolloff, P. B., & Feldhusen, J. F. (1986). Seminar: An instructional approach for gifted students. *Gifted Child Today, 9*, 2–7.

Maker, C. J. (1982). Curriculum development for the gifted. Rockville, MD: Aspen Publishers.

Maker, C. J., & Nielson, A. B. (1995). *Teaching models in education of the gifted* (2nd ed.). Austin, TX: PRO-Ed.

Moon, S. M., & Feldhusen, J. F. (1991). Identification procedures: Bridging theory and practice. *Gifted Child Today, 14*(l), 30–36.

Moore, B. A., Feldhusen, J. F., & Owings, J. (1978). *The professional career exploration program for minority and/or low income gifted and talented high school students.* Washington, DC: U.S. Department of Health, Education, and Welfare, Office of Education.

Pleiss, M. K., & Feldhusen, J. F. (1995). Mentors, role models, and heroes in the lives of gifted children. *Educational Psychologist, 30*(3), 159–169.

Proctor, T. B., Black, K. N., & Feldhusen, J. F. (1986). Early admission of selected children to elementary school: A review of the research literature. *Journal of Educational Research, 80*, 70–76.

Reis, S. M., & Purcell, J. H. (1993). An analysis of content elimination and strategies used by elementary classroom teachers and the curriculum compacting process. *Journal for the Education of the Gifted, 16*, 147–170.

Renzulli, J. S. (1994). *Schools for talent development.* Mansfield Center, CT: Creative Learning Press.

Renzulli, J. S., & Reis, S. M. (1986). The enrichment triad/revolving door model: A schoolwide plan for the development of creative productivity. In J. S. Renzulli (Ed.), *Systems and models for developing programs for the gifted and talented* (pp. 216–266). Mansfield Center, CT: Creative Learning Press.

Shore, B. M., Cornell, D. G., Robinson, A., & Ward, V. S. (1991). *Recommended practices in gifted education.* New York: Teachers College Press.

Southern, W. T., & Jones, E. D. (1991). *The academic acceleration of gifted children.* New York: Teachers College Press.

Treffinger, D. J. (1986). Fostering effective, independent learning through individualized programming. In J. S. Renzulli (Ed.), *Systems and models for developing programs for the gifted and talented* (pp. 429–460). Mansfield Center, CT: Creative Learning Press.

VanTassel-Baska, J. (1982). Results of a Latin-based experimental study of the verbally precocious. *Roeper Review, 4*(4), 35–37.

VanTassel-Baska, J. (1986). Acceleration. In C. J. Maker (Ed.), *Critical issues in gifted education, defensible programs for the gifted* (pp. 179–196). Rockville, MD: Aspen Publishers.

VanTassel-Baska, J. (1987). A case for the teaching of Latin to the verbally able. *Roeper Review, 9*(3), 159–161.

VanTassel-Baska, J. (1993). Theory and research on curriculum development for the gifted. In K. A. Heller, F. J. Monks, & A. H Passow (Eds.), *International handbook of research and development of giftedness and talent* (pp. 365–386). New York: Pergamon.

VanTassel-Baska, J., Feldhusen, J. F., Seeley, K., Wheatley, G., Silverman, L., & Foster, W. (1988). *Comprehensive curriculum for gifted learners: An integrative approach.* Boston: Allyn & Bacon.

VanTassel-Baska, J., Willis, G., & Meyers, D. (1989). Evaluation of a full-time class for gifted students. *Gifted Child Quarterly, 33*(1), 7–10.

Study Questions ~

1. What would you include in an elementary program model for the gifted and talented?
2. Contrast any two elementary models.
3. How can we accelerate gifted and talented students?
4. How can the gifted be served in general classrooms?
5. How can we serve the gifted in the arts?
6. Why is foreign language study important in educating the gifted and talented?

13

Programs and Services at the Secondary Level

John F. Feldhusen

By the time gifted and talented youth reach the middle-school level and preferably no later than in high school, they should have a clear awareness and understanding of their talent areas and should no longer view themselves as generally gifted. Achievement test results, grade averages in different subjects, and some special examinations such as the Scholastic Aptitude Test, which is often taken in seventh or eighth grade as part of the regional talent searches (VanTassel-Baska, 1984), provide assessments of academic strengths or emerging talents. Music and art lessons, and awards in relevant competitions, indicate talent potential in those areas. Grades, prizes, and project recognition in vocational classes reveal manifest talent in some of those classes, and youth opportunities for leadership roles, tutoring younger students, or community caregiving indicate talent in intra- and interpersonal domains. Thus, students should be beginning the process of integrating their strengths, interests, and personality, as they understand them, toward some long-range educational and career goals (Csikszentmihalyi, Rathunde, & Whalen, 1993).

Programs and services for talented youth in middle school and high school should offer an abundance of opportunities for students to enroll or participate in a diversity of classes and activities that are related to their emerging talents and pointed toward their career goals. Stanley (1978a) referred to the ideal program as a smorgasbord of opportunities. Feldhusen (1983) has described it as an eclectic approach. Ideally, young people and their parents look to courses in school, extracurricular activities, and opportunities in the broader world around them for good educational experiences.

Table 13.1 shows some potentially good services for talented youth at the middle- and high-school levels. These talent development services or experiences may differ widely from school to school in both availability and scope. Selection of the services should be planful and grow out of the students' understanding of their own talents and goals.

Programs for gifted and talented youth at the middle- and high-school level should be designed to meet their special educational needs. Students should receive instruction at a level and pace commensurate with their levels of achievement and the speed at which they are able to learn. Minds grow when confronted with intellectual challenge and good teaching.

A list of basic needs that is not unique to gifted and talented youth but that sets forth what may be regarded as the fundamental requisites for optimum development of precocious or highly able youth follows:

Table 13.1 ∼
Gifted Program Services

Junior-High or Middle-School Services	High-School Services
Counseling	Counseling
Group	Group
Individual	Individual
Honors classes	Honors classes
Future Problem Solving	Advanced Placement classes
Junior Great Books	Foreign language instruction
Odyssey of the Mind	Seminars
Career education	Mentorships
Seminars	Internships
Mentors	Concurrent college enrollment
Advanced Placement or college classes	College classes in high school
Acceleration	Special opportunities
Math	Art
Science	Music
English	Drama
Special opportunities	Dance
Art	Special projects for the vocationally talented
Music	Debate
Drama	Correspondence study
Dance	Independent study
Special projects for the vocationally talented	
Foreign language instruction	
Correspondence study	
Independent study	

1. Achievement of basic skills in language and mathematics as early as they are ready
2. Learning experiences throughout the school years that are accelerated in level and pace
3. Learning experiences and counseling that helps them grow in their understanding of their own talents, abilities, and interests
4. Encouragement and guidance to become self-managing, self-directing, autonomous leaders
5. Opportunities to develop their knowledge bases to the fullest extent possible through reading, good teaching, and access to information-transmitting technologies
6. Opportunities to work and learn with other gifted and talented youth for better social and emotional development and motivation to excel
7. Experiences in high-level problem finding and solving, creative thinking, decision-making, and other complex cognitive processes
8. Supportive counseling and guidance to facilitate the development of good personal and social adjustment

Middle-School Programs ~

Meeting the needs of gifted and talented youth in the middle-school years may be particularly difficult because of the conflicting educational goals, values, or philosophies of specialists in gifted education and specialists in middle-school education. The conflict is exacerbated by conflict between gifted education specialists and cooperative learning proponents, who are also influential in determining middle-school policies and practices. At one extreme is the neo-Marxist orientation of Oakes, Quartz, Gong, Guiton, and Lipton (1993), who have argued that "we will need to replace many of the competitive, individualistic, and bureaucratic norms embedded in current practice, and existing political relations" (p. 461). Elsewhere, Oakes (1985) cited the Marxist authors Bowles and Gintis (1976) to support her arguments for revolutionary reform in education. At the other end of the spectrum are gifted educators who see the middle school as a place where all students can achieve to their highest individual potential, where both competitive and cooperative learning experiences can be used to motivate students, and where norms or standards of excellence are used as guides to the improvement of instruction for all students. They believe that all students should be allowed or assisted educationally to rise to educational challenges in the curriculum as rapidly as they are able and be urged to achieve at a maximum level of excellence.

Rosselli (1990) analyzed the tenets and philosophy of the middle-school movement, focusing on organization, school climate, curriculum, and teaching methods. She concluded that a number of tenets in the movement can be used as guides to sound practice for gifted students as well as all others. She lists 37 fundamental practices as characterizing the middle-school movement, eight of which are commensurate with the philosophy of gifted education:

- Utilization of a nongraded approach
- Encouragement of creative ideas by students
- Specific opportunities for gifted students
- Curriculum emphasizing exploratory study
- Differentiation of objectives according to ability
- Emphasis on inquiry, problem-solving, and higher level cognitive skills
- Differentiation of methods according to ability
- Progression according to student ability

Rosselli suggested that the explicit incorporation of these tenets or practices into a middle-school's philosophy statement would do much to reduce or totally remove the frequent conflict that otherwise arises between a middle-school orientation and gifted education.

Gallagher, Coleman, and Nelson (1995) surveyed 317 middle-school educators about their views or beliefs concerning middle-school ideology, cooperative learning, and gifted education. They found considerable disagreement among advocates of the three positions but a great deal of agreement that there is little collaborative effort among proponents of the three positions. The major areas of disagreement had to do with ability grouping and labeling children as gifted. The educators in this study expressed particular concern about lack of challenge in cooperative learning, use of gifted students as "junior teachers," and lack of any opportunities in middle-school programs for gifted students to work together on advanced curriculum appropriate to their levels of achievement and needs.

Tomlinson (1995) carried out an intensive, qualitative study of one middle-school program. She found that many teachers simply did not know how to differentiate curriculum and instruction to meet the needs of talented youth, nor did they know how to challenge them at a level commensurate with their abilities. Management of differentiated instruction was a particular challenge for teachers who were used to teaching a common lesson from a common text at one level for all students, regardless of student diversity. Clearly, teachers need instruction and models on how to differentiate curriculum and instruction for gifted as well as less able students.

Coleman (1995) cited resolutions from both the National Middle School Association and the National Association for Gifted Children that recognize the special needs of gifted and talented children. Her list of the 10 shared goals of middle-school philosophy and gifted education as delineated by Alexander and George (1981) follow:

1. To meet varied affective needs of students
2. To allow each student to work at his or her own pace and level of learning
3. To use team teaching and planning
4. To use an exploratory curriculum in the classroom
5. To develop and use interdisciplinary curricula in the classroom
6. To use outcome-based assessment or mastery learning
7. To emphasize thinking strategies and decision-making within the curriculum

8. To allow teacher/student relationships to be more intimate, and to provide students with "families" within school
9. To have teachers serve as facilitators of learning rather than disseminators of knowledge
10. To extend learning beyond the textbook.

These goals provide a remarkably acceptable philosophy to guide program development for gifted and talented youth in middle schools. However, as an overriding goal Alexander and George stressed the need for grouping gifted and talented students in their areas of special talent (e.g., mathematics, science, art) and for the provision of advanced and fast-paced curricula in such classes.

Thus, it appears that the philosophy of middle schools and gifted education can come together in ways that honor the spirit of both initiatives, if flexible grouping practices can be maintained.

High-School Programs ⌇

High-school programs for gifted youth must offer a wide variety of classes and extracurricular activities to meet the emergent talents, interests, and learning styles of gifted students (Feldhusen, 1995). The educational, career, personal, and social goals of adolescents are approaching the young adult level, and the diversity of talents that characterize the gifted as well as all youth place great demands on schools to meet individual needs.

A number of models for secondary programs have been proposed (Renzulli, 1986). Generally, all the models call for accelerated learning experiences, special advanced classes or opportunities to take advanced levels of classes early, opportunities to participate in extracurricular activities related to student interests, and enriched or extended learning opportunities in academic, artistic, athletic, and personal-social domains.

Some talented youth will be fortunate enough to have rich learning experiences at magnet schools for artistic or academically talented students, at residential schools for the gifted, or at private schools for academically talented youth. Others find these experiences through early college admission or International Baccalaureate programs. All such programs and schools routinely provide advanced, enriched, and fast-paced instruction that affords the ideal level of challenge to meet the needs of gifted and talented youth and should be implemented in all high schools.

Major Areas of Service

Ideally, there should be a coordinator of talent development for the gifted program at the secondary level who works closely with the counseling staff and teachers, planning and coordinating the special program services for students with high levels of talent. The major areas with which the coordinator is concerned are (1) counseling services, (2) special classes, and (3) accelerated learning opportunities. Other areas of concern are (4) art and cultural experiences in the school and community, (5) foreign language instruction, (6) extracurricular learning experiences, and (7) formal and informal learning experiences in the community and beyond school time. These areas of concern are delineated more fully in the remainder of this chapter and in Figure 13.1.

Counseling Counselors who are trained in gifted and talented education can play a vital role in a school's talent development program beginning with the talent identification process. Students who have superior abilities profit little from simply being identified as gifted. Counselors can work with the gifted coordinator, talented youth, and teachers in selecting, administering, and interpreting tests and rating scales to help students grow in awareness and understanding of their own talents. Counselors can also help them clarify and set academic, career, personal, and social goals and provide information concerning educational opportunities to facilitate talent development (VanTassel-Baska, 1993). A "growth plan" developed by Feldhusen (1995) can be used with talented youth to help them conduct a self-assessment, personal goal-setting, and planning for their educational futures.

Counselors can also work with talented students to help them better understand the unique issues and problems of personal and social development they may face. Peer pressure, relationships with parents, boredom in school, managing multiple talents and interests, personal time management, and relating to teachers are some of the special concerns of highly talented youth that counselors can address in small group sessions. The purpose, of course, is to help the students learn to cope with problems and develop positive self-esteem (Silverman, 1993).

Career education and mentoring experiences fall into the domain of counseling concerns and can be dealt with by counselors in concert with the program coordinator (Haeger & Feldhusen, 1989). Feldman (1986) suggested that talented students need and profit from being able to see experts or star performers at work. At one end of the spectrum, they can read about people operating in their domains of talent and experience their careers vicariously. At the other end of the spectrum, they can experience an internship where they actually are on the job amidst people who are practicing in a career area of interest to them. Thus, they can come to have firsthand knowledge of a prospective career domain and opportunities to test their own talents and interest for goodness of fit with that domain.

The counselor, in cooperation with the school psychologist, can also work with talented students who experience more severe adjustment problems. Robinson and Noble (1991) reported that problems of adjustment are most likely to occur among very highly gifted youth. The problems may include severe depression, extremely negative peer pressures, or stress due to academic pressures to be excellent in all areas of the school curriculum.

It is important to stress that counselors should have special training in the nature and nurture of talent. They should also be enlisted to work with the whole school staff in developing a better understanding of talent development processes.

Special Classes The major offering for gifted and talented students in most secondary programs is special academic classes. Such classes may be offered to students who have been identified as generally gifted, students who have been identi-

	1. Counseling Services	1. Talent identification 2. Education counseling 3. Career counseling 4. Personal counseling

2. Advanced Placement Classes	1. Open to students in top 10% 2. Grades 9–12

3. Honors classes	1. English 2. Social studies 3. Biology

	4. Seminars	1. In-depth study 2. Self-selected topics 3. Career education 4. Affective activities 5. Thinking, research, and library skills 6. Presentations

5. Career Education	1. Mentors
	2. Seminar experience
	   A. Study of careers
	   B. Study of self
	   C. Educational plans

6. Acceleration	1. Begin algebra in Grade 7 2. Enroll in English and social studies courses early 3. Open science courses to early admission

	7. The Arts	1. Art 2. Drama 3. Music 4. Dance

8. Extra-School Learning Experiences	1. Saturday school 2. Summer classes 3. Correspondence study

9. Extra-School Cultural Experiences	1. Concerts, plays, exhibits 2. Field trips 3. Museum programs

	10. Foreign Languages	1. Latin or Greek 2. French or Spanish 3. German or Oriental

11. Vocational Programs	1. Home economics 2. Agriculture 3. Business 4. Industrial arts

Figure 13.1 ∼
An Eclectic Program Model for Secondary-Level Gifted

fied as having strong talents in a particular academic or artistic area, or students who have been nominated by teachers familiar with their abilities in the relevant area. Selection for enrollment in a special academic class should be determined from indications of motivation and interest from students themselves, by an examination of students' grades in previous courses in the specific domain or academic area, and by scores from achievement and aptitude tests if available. It is probably undesirable at the secondary level to do a general assessment of a student and place him or her in all available special classes. Many students will be well qualified for one or two special classes but not for a full regimen of such classes.

There are three major forms of special classes: honors, Advanced Placement, and seminars. Honors classes may be offered in any of the traditional middle- and high-school disciplines, such as English, history, biology, chemistry, algebra, and French. The classes are expected to operate at a higher level of intellectual discourse than general education classes, to involve more discussion, to require more homework, and to present greater academic challenges to students. The curriculum is expected to be differentiated and typically to cover more ground than a general education class.

In Advanced Placement classes, the curriculum syllabi and final examinations have been developed by the College Board. Students who pass the final examination at a sufficiently high level have completed work equivalent to a college course and may, upon presenting a transcript to a college or university, receive college credit and be excused from taking the course when they enroll at a college.

Seminars are intensive academic classes in which gifted and talented students are led by teachers in in-depth study of selected, advanced topics. Students assume much greater leadership in structuring the goals and direction of the seminar than they do in other classes. Seminars are typically small, involve much library research, and are devoted chiefly to in-depth discussions. Dixon (1995) described a seminar class in English literature for verbally talented youth at the Indiana Academy for Mathematics, Science, and the Humanities. The students studied literature that would ordinarily be addressed at the college level and engaged in a variety of creative interactions and discussions in their pursuit of in-depth understanding of the ideas presented in the literature. From their study of seminars offered in seven different school-based gifted programs, Kolloff and Feldhusen (1986) found that all the seminars were characterized by high intellectual levels of academic content, an abundance of student-teacher interaction, general use of in-depth research, and much focus on higher level thinking skills. Just as seminars are used as scholarly enterprises at colleges and universities, the seminars Kolloff and Feldhusen studied provided powerful academic challenges and experiences for participants.

In studies conducted of secondary school student and teacher attitudes toward honors academic classes (Feldhusen & Kennedy, 1989; Feldhusen & Sayler, 1990), a high percentage of students (94%) reported that they felt most highly motivated to study and learn when they were in honors classes. Many of the students complained about the boring, slow pace and the low curriculum level of general education classes. Ninety-seven percent of teachers in two school districts judged that the honors classes had very positive effects on gifted students' achievement, and 86% said that honors classes had very positive effects on their students' motivation. It is also note-worthy that 66% of these teachers felt students in general education classes had bet-ter chances to learn when gifted and talented youth were removed and placed in hon-ors classes. Sixty-three percent of the honors class teachers also felt that their teach-ing in general education classes was improved as a result of their teaching in honors classes.

Special honors, Advanced Placement, and seminar classes appear to offer gift-ed and talented students solid learning experiences at a level, speed, and depth appro-priate to their needs. They also provide the conditions for intrinsic motivation and the development of self-efficacy.

Acceleration Curriculum and instruction in general education and even honors and Advanced Placement courses may not be advanced enough nor taught at a suf-ficiently fast pace to meet the needs of highly precocious students. Furthermore, in many schools few such courses can be offered. Therefore, it is necessary to think of advanced placement in a broader sense and to seek acceleration to courses at higher levels that offer curriculum and learning experiences closer to or commensurate with gifted and talented students' levels of readiness. When precocious students are left in regular, slow-paced classes with teachers who provide no higher level challenges, some or many of them may slow down, adapt to the norm, and lose their motivation to strive for excellence.

Brody and Benbow (1987) studied youth who had been given accelerated oppor-tunities for learning in school and found that acceleration resulted in many desirable outcomes. Accelerated youth were not social recluses but rather were participants in extracurricular programs, had many friends, and liked their school experiences. Southern and Jones (1991) reported some cautions in the use of acceleration, but suggested that advancing gifted students to their levels of instructional readiness leads to generally desirable outcomes, including increased or sustained motivation to learn.

Critics of academic advancement often note the potential harm to students' social adjustment but rarely ask questions about the social damage of being held back with intellectually incompatible peers or peers who exert negative pressure (Brown, Clasen, & Eicher, 1986). Julian Stanley (1978b), an internationally recog-nized researcher on gifted and talented students, referred to our failure to use acad-emic advancement in the title of one of his publications as "Educational Non-Acceleration: An International Tragedy." Stanley (1978a) is also well known for his instructional method of continuous progress for talented youth: diagnostic testing followed by prescriptive instruction (DT-PI). The method is clearly accelerative in that testing is used to establish a student's readiness level for new instruction, and instruction is then given at that level.

Academic advancement may be most vital for youth who are talented in mathe-matics. A number of new methods for acceleration in mathematics have come out of the Study of Mathematically Precocious Youth (SMPY) at Johns Hopkins University

(Stanley, 1979). For example, algebra, traditionally taught in ninth grade, was found to be highly teachable to precocious seventh graders. Now algebra is taught to seventh graders and to students enrolled in summer programs at colleges and universities all over the United States. Many public and some private schools also offer algebra and other advanced mathematics courses one to three years earlier than was traditional, and in individual cases of highly precocious youth such courses have been offered even earlier. David, for example, took calculus in sixth grade in his local high school and earned straight A's.

Academic advancement is possible and desirable in all areas of the curriculum—not just mathematics—for talented, precocious youth. It is desirable, however, to ascertain through assessment the particular areas in which students demonstrate precocity and to advance their programs only in those areas of the curriculum in which they are highly precocious. Sally, for example, took the Scholastic Aptitude Test in eighth grade and scored 670 on the quantitative part of the test. She had already taken algebra and geometry and was ready for advanced algebra and trigonometry. She was enrolled in the latter classes and earned straight A's.

Verbally precocious students can and should move forward to advanced levels of English and social studies, and students precocious in mathematics and/or science should be able to take biology, chemistry, physics, and advanced mathematics classes in their freshman and sophomore years of high school. Verbally precocious students can also be enrolled in more than one foreign language class at a time or be allowed to begin formal language study earlier than traditional assignment might dictate.

Moreover, talented youth can be advanced academically by taking college courses while they are in high school (Feldhusen & Cobb, 1989) or by entering college early (Stanley & McGill, 1986). Excellent programs for admission to college after the sophomore year of high school have been in operation at Simon's Rock College and at North Texas State University and by all accounts have been highly successful. Sayler (1994) studied a group of early entrants at Purdue University and found that their experiences were generally positive and successful.

All forms of academic advancement are viable and desirable educational alternatives for highly precocious students. Assessment can give us good insights about the students' levels of readiness. Successes in advanced educational experiences sustain and build the academic motivation of talented students and help them to develop a strong sense of self-efficacy (Schunk, 1991).

Art and Cultural Experiences All talented youth should be provided with early and continuous exposure to the arts and cultural experiences (Eisner, 1985). For those who are particularly talented in one of several art areas, the exposure must be translated into intensive educational or learning experiences. Many academically talented students also have substantial art talents. Those talents may be in visual or performing arts (Clark & Zimmerman, 1987; Haroutounian, 1993).

Cultural experiences lead to what is often called art appreciation. Through the experiences of attending operas, visiting art exhibits, going to concerts, or viewing ballet with adults who respond to the aesthetics of the art, children become sensitized and receptive to the beauty and joy of artistic experiences. Their appreciation can be enhanced by attending lectures and taking courses on the appreciation of arts. Art constitutes a way of knowing (Eisner, 1985) and affords youth a set of concepts, skills, and aesthetic capability that can enhance their career productivity and enjoyment of life. All gifted and talented youth, whether they are talented in art areas or not, should have abundant opportunities to grow at home and at school in the realm of aesthetics. (See Chapter 25 for specific curriculum ideas.)

Some talented youth will exhibit precocity in mastering one or more of the art forms. This precocity should be nurtured in a direct way. American artist Georgia O'Keeffe, for example, showed incipient art talent at age 5 (Lisle, 1980). Her mother recognized her talent potential and began a long-term effort to provide her with lessons and classes to meet her need for higher level training in visual art. Rachel Carson (1962) showed great literary talent when she published a story at age 7. Mozart was able to play complex musical compositions before age 5; his father, also a great musician, acknowledged and nurtured his budding talent.

As a response to precocity, schools can provide advanced lessons in visual arts and music. Tutors and private lessons are often invoked by parents and schools to provide early stimulation and training. Students precocious in the arts also need special teachers. Bloom (1985) described such teachers as being masters or experts in their art forms, demanders of hard work and practice, and guides toward excellence and creative achievement in their area of expertise.

Art classes, art lessons, and cultural experiences for talented students should be offered under the aegis of a school's gifted and talented program; art talent identification, consisting of observations, auditions, product evaluations, portfolios, and rating scales, should be directed by the gifted coordinator in concert with art teachers.

Foreign Language Instruction Some students have special talent in verbal-linguistic activities and are unusually adept in learning foreign languages (Garfinkel, Allen, & Neuharth-Pritchett, 1992). Learning foreign languages also seems, in turn, to enhance general verbal ability (VanTassel-Baska, 1981). Thus, opportunities for the study of foreign languages should begin early in the elementary school and lead to early admission to high-school language courses while students are still in middle school.

Verbally talented students also benefit from having the linguistic base of an ancient language, preferably Latin. Because language is learned easily and rapidly during the elementary-school years, such students should have access to the learning of Latin at that time. A major impediment, however, may be finding a teacher well qualified to teach Latin. Andrea, a tenth grader, is in second-year Latin, having previously been tutored by her mother in first-year Latin. She loves the course and is expressing a strong sense of self-efficacy in learning a foreign language.

Skill in one or more foreign language can enhance one's productivity in other realms. In sciences and business fields there is now much international interaction and exchange of information and activity. This work can be more creatively carried forward when participants are fluent in one another's languages. Today's enhanced ease of travel, computerized information exchanges, faxes, e-mail, and inexpensive means of voice and visual communication all facilitate contact between people speaking different languages. Talented students can best be readied for careers in the 21st century by providing them with opportunities to learn one or more languages in addition to their native tongue.

Extracurricular Opportunities in School   Clubs and other school organizations, as well as competition, can provide excellent opportunities for talent development. Math Olympics, Future Problem Solving, Chess Club, Odyssey of the Mind, Junior Great Books, Future Farmers of America, and a host of other extracurricular activities afford opportunities for a variety of talents to be nurtured.

Most youth clubs and organizations offer abundant opportunities for leadership talent to be manifested and developed (Feldhusen & Richardson, 1991; Karnes & Chauvin, 1984). Other talents in the realms of organizational ability, planning, public relations, use of computers, business, and so forth, can also be exercised and developed in the context of extracurricular clubs and organizations.

For many students in small rural schools with limited curriculum offerings in academic subjects and no special honors or Advanced Placement courses, extracurricular activities may offer the only significant opportunity to work with other students who share similar talents and interests. Gifted and talented students need and profit from such opportunities to work, study, and socialize with one another.

Extra-School Learning Experiences   Students who live in medium-sized and large cities, in particular, are likely to have access to an abundance of talent development resources beyond the school in which they are enrolled. These may include college and university courses, lectures, lab work, professional mentors, libraries, workshops, museums, institutes, industrial research labs, performing arts centers, theaters, nature preserves, and so forth. Not only can these resources be tapped, but their staff members can be accessed as mentors or guides in internships. Parents and students can be guided to these resources by counselors, teachers, and coordinators of gifted and talented programs.

Personal Growth Planning   Csikszentmihalyi, Rathunde, and Whalen (1993) found that teenagers whose talents are developing well will carry out a process of self-analysis to differentiate or identify their own talent strengths as a prelude to each stage of educational and career planning. Betts (1986) urged that we engage gifted and talented youth in goal-setting to help them attain a clearer sense of their short- and long-term future activities. The development of an individual growth plan by such students engages them in reviewing their talents, abilities, achievements, aptitudes, interests, and learning styles. In addition, it involves them in planning short- and long-term personal, social, academic, and career goals and guides them in selecting courses, extracurricular activities, and resources in the broader community to facilitate their talent development and achievement of goals.

The growth planning process is typically carried out formally once a year in the spring. The plan is developed by the students in consultation with their parents. They typically work in groups of 15 to 20 for a total time of 4 to 8 hours. The growth plan provides an excellent opportunity to help gifted and talented students articulate their talents, interests, and learning styles with goals and educational activities that will help them achieve optimum development of their talents.

The International Baccalaureate as a Secondary Gifted Program

Poelzer (1994) reviewed the development of the International Baccalaureate program. Designed to bring a common curriculum to multinational students living in countries throughout the world, the underlying philosophy of the program is to develop the whole student with challenging and in-depth learning experiences through a general and comprehensive curriculum at the precollege level. The program's curricular depth and breadth is seen in the fact that International Baccalaureate (IB) students must take one course from each of the following areas during the program: (1) Language A (first language), (2) Language B (second language), (3) Study of Man in Society (History, Geography, Economics, Philosophy, Psychology, or Social Anthropology), (4) Experimental Sciences (Chemistry, Biology, Physics, Physical Science, Experimental Psychology, Environmental Systems), (5) Mathematics (Higher Level Mathematics, Mathematics and Computing), and (6) a sixth subject (Art/Design, Music, Computer Studies, Classical Languages). Typically, IB courses are at the university freshman or sophomore level. Examinations are offered after the first year of study.

IB students also take a course called Theory of Knowledge, which is highly interdisciplinary and emphasizes critical thinking. The program culminates in an intensive scholarly experience called the Extended Essay, which involves an in-depth and independent study of a topic followed by the writing of an essay of about 4,000 words. In addition, IB students are required to participate in a creative, aesthetic, or social service project for approximately a half day a week for a year.

The IB program has grown rapidly and now operates in schools in over 50 countries throughout the world. Its success is attributable to the high standards of the curriculum and the quality of instruction. The essay and the oral examinations that are used provide excellent opportunities for gifted students to realize their full potential.

Summary ∼

Programs for gifted and talented students at the secondary level should offer breadth, depth, and diversity of educational experiences. During the middle-school and high-school years, students' specific talent strengths are more clearly identified, and students need to be provided with advanced and in-depth study in those areas. However, they also need a sound general education and to identify their emerging strengths. Thus, the ideal program offers a wide range of educational experiences as described in this chapter. The ultimate goal is a commitment on the part of gifted and talented students to the development of their own talents with a clear understanding of their own talent areas, interests, and personal styles. They need help from parents, teachers, and counselors during the high-school years, as well as from mentors or role models who can show the full scope of intellectual, personal, and social attributes of the professionals or artists these students hope to become.

References ⌇

Alexander, W., & George, P. (1981). *The exemplary middle school*. New York: Holt, Rinehart, & Winston.

Betts, G. T. (1986). Development of emotional and social needs of gifted individuals. *Journal of Counseling and Development, 64*(9), 587–589.

Bloom, B. S. (1985) (Ed.). *Developing talent in young people*. New York: Ballantine Books.

Bowles, S., & Gintis, H. (1976). *Schooling in capitalist America*. New York: Basic Books.

Brody, L. E., & Benbow, C. P. (1987). Accelerative strategies: How effective are they for the gifted? *Gifted Child Quarterly, 31*(3), 105–110.

Brown, B. B., Clasen, D. R., & Eicher, S. A. (1986). Perceptions or peer pressure, peer conformity dispositions, and self-reported behavior among adolescents. *Developmental Psychology, 22,* 521–530.

Carson, R. (1962). *Silent spring*. Boston: Houghton Mifflin.

Clark, G. A., & Zimmerman, E. D. (1987). *Resources for educating artistically talented students*. Syracuse, NY: Syracuse University Press.

Coleman, M. R. (1995). Middle schools and their impact on talent development. *The Middle School Journal, 26*(4), 47–56.

Csikszentmihalyi, M., Rathunde, K., & Whalen, R. (1993). *Talented teenagers*. New York: Cambridge University Press.

Dixon, F. (1995). The gifted in secondary literature programs. *Understanding Our Gifted, 7*(4), 4–5.

Eisner, E. (1985). Aesthetic modes of knowing. In E. Eisner (Ed.), *Learning and teaching the ways of knowing* (84th yearbook of the National Society for the Study of Education, Part 2) (pp. 23–36). Chicago: University of Chicago Press.

Feldhusen, J. F. (1983). Eclecticism: A comprehensive approach to education of the gifted. In C. P. Benbow & J. C. Stanley (Eds.), *Academic precocity: Aspects of its development* (pp. 192–204). Baltimore, MD: Johns Hopkins University Press.

Feldhusen, J. F. (1995). Talent development as the alternative in high school gifted programs. *Understanding Our Gifted, 7*(4), 1, 11–14.

Feldhusen, J. F., & Cobb, S. J. (1989). College courses count for high school credit. *G/T Indiana, 1*(6), 3.

Feldhusen, J. F., & Kennedy, D. M. (1989). Effects of honors classes on secondary students. *Roeper Review, 11*(3), 153–156.

Feldhusen, J. F., & Richardson, W. B. (1991). *Leadership education: Developing skills for youth*. Unionville, NY: Trillium.

Feldhusen, J. F., & Sayler, M. F. (1990). Special classes for academically gifted youth. *Roeper Review, 12*(4), 244–249.

Feldman, D. H. (1986). *Nature's gambit: Child prodigies and the development of human potential*. New York: Basic Books.

Gallagher, J. J., Coleman, M. R., & Nelson, S. (1995). Perceptions of educational reform by educators representing middle schools, cooperative learning, and gifted education. *Gifted Child Quarterly, 39*(2), 66–76.

Garfinkel, A., Allen, L. Q., & Neuharth-Pritchett, S. (1992). Foreign language for the gifted: Extending affective dimensions. *Roeper Review, 15*(4), 235–238.

Haeger, W. W., & Feldhusen, J. F. (1989). *Developing a mentor program*. East Aurora, NY: DOK Publishers.

Haroutounian, J. (1993). Identifying talent in the performing arts. *Spotlight, 3*(2), 8–12.

Karnes, F. A., & Chauvin, J. C. (1984). *The leadership skills activities manual*. East Aurora, NY: DOK Publishers.

Kolloff, P. B., & Feldhusen, J. F. (1986). The seminar: An instructional approach for gifted students. *Gifted Children Today, 9*(5), 2–7.

Lisle, L. (1980). *Portraits of an artist: A biography of Georgia O'Keeffe*. New York: Seaview Books.

Oakes, J. (1985). *Keeping track: How schools structure inequality*. New Haven, CT: Yale University Press.

Oakes, J., Quartz, K. H., Gong, J., Guiton, G., & Lipton, M. (1993). Creating middle schools: Technical, normative, and political considerations. *The Elementary School Journal, 93*(5), 461–480.

Poelzer, G. H. (1994). *An empirical study of international baccalaureate students in the sciences*. Unpublished doctoral dissertation, Purdue University, West Lafayette, IN.

Renzulli, J. S. (Ed.) (1986). *Systems and models for developing programs for gifted and talented*. Mansfield Center, CT: Creative Learning Press.

Robinson, N. M., & Noble, K. D. (1991). Social-emotional development and adjustment of gifted children. In M. C. Wang, M. C. Reynolds, & H. J. Walberg (Eds.), *Handbook of special education: Research and practice* (pp. 67–79). London: Pergamon.

Rosselli, H. C. (1990). *Gifted education and the middle school movement: A position paper*. Tampa, FL: University of South Florida.

Sayler, M. F. (1994). Early college entrance: A viable option. In J. B. Hansen & S. M. Hoover (Eds.), *Talent development: Theories and practice* (pp. 67–79). Dubuque, IA: Kendall/Hunt.

Schunk, D. H. (1991). Self-efficacy and academic motivation. *Educational Psychologist, 26*, 207–231.

Silverman, L. K. (1993). *Counseling the gifted*. Denver, CO: Love.

Southern, T., & Jones, E. D. (1991). *Acceleration: Issues and answers*. New York: Teachers College Press.

Stanley, J. C. (1978a). SMPY's DT-PI model: Diagnostic testing followed by prescriptive instruction. *Intellectually Talented Youth Bulletin, 4*(10), 7–8.

Stanley, J. C. (1978b, November/December). Educational non-acceleration: An international tragedy. *G/C/T, 3*, 2–5, 53–57, 60–64.

Stanley, J. C. (1979). The study and facilitation of talent for mathematics. In A. H. Passow (Ed.), *The gifted and the talented: Their education and development* (78th yearbook of the National Society for the Study of Education) (pp. 169–185). Chicago: University of Chicago Press.

Stanley, J. C., & McGill, A. M. (1986). More about young entrants to college: How did they fare? *Gifted Child Quarterly, 30*(2), 70–73.

Tomlinson, C. A. (1995). Deciding to differentiate instruction in middle schools: One school's journey. *Gifted Child Quarterly, 39*(2), 77–87.

VanTassel-Baska, J. (1981). *Results of a Latin-based experimental program for the verbally precocious*. Unpublished doctoral dissertation, University of Toledo, Toledo, OH.

VanTassel-Baska, J. (1984). The talent search as an identification model. *Gifted Child Quarterly, 28*(4), 172–176.

VanTassel-Baska, J. (1993). The roles of educational personnel in counseling the gifted. In L. K. Silverman (Ed.), *Counseling the gifted* (pp. 181–200). Denver, CO: Love.

Study Questions ~

1. Why is it important to assess students' strengths and interests when planning secondary education experiences?

2. What are some controversial aspects of the current philosophy of middle-school education? How do these ideas support or contradict gifted education philosophy? Identify some strategies that would reduce societal resistance to programs for gifted students.

3. What major service components should be incorporated into secondary programs for gifted students? Why is counseling seen as the glue that holds these services together?
4. What is the International Baccalaureate program? How is it comparable to Advanced Placement coursework?
5. Are honors and Advanced Placement classes sufficiently accelerated for all gifted youth? Who might be ill-served by such placements?

14

Key Issues and Problems in Secondary Programming

Joyce VanTassel-Baska

While many issues in gifted education are the same across all levels of schooling, some clearly have greater significance at the secondary level than at earlier levels of education. Many factors affect how gifted education is viewed and implemented at the secondary level. Secondary schools have a different organizational structure from elementary schools. Teachers at the secondary level tend to be subject matter oriented and trained to address student needs within those parameters. The size of secondary schools tends to be large, and the physical plants can be sprawling. Ancillary services such as counseling, social work, and the use of library/media centers have a substantive foothold in the organizational pattern. For the first time in the schooling pattern, students have choices in what courses they will take and when they will take them. Students at various age and competency levels can select from a complex schedule of options. Additionally, extracurricular options abound, addressing various interest areas and social needs. Based on a typical teaching load of five classes and 150 students per day, teachers tend to see students as groups rather than as individuals. Whole-group instruction is the norm. Teachers are organized into departments rather than being a part of a loosely construed team. And the segmentation of secondary schools is punctuated by the sound of the bell, announcing beginnings and ends of learning frames. Whereas the middle-school movement has attempted to break down the rigidity of such an organizational pattern, most manifestations of it persist at the secondary level in many school districts; even where middle-school organization has brought about teaming, flexible scheduling, and greater student choice, high schools in the same districts have made very few, if any, changes.

Given these distinctive features of secondary schools, it is not surprising that programs for the gifted would fare differently in these contexts than in the elementary context. Limited attention has been given to the specific development of secondary programs for the gifted at the individual school level, although historically such programs represent some of our most important models at the city, regional, and statewide levels. Much of the work at the secondary level has focused on models to be tried (Betts, 1988; Feldhusen, 1989; Reis & Renzulli, 1989; Silverman, 1993). Evidence of efficacy for secondary programming is limited to Advanced Placement data and curriculum materials effectiveness (Welch, 1984). However, promising case studies have been conducted on selected secondary programs (Cox, Daniel, & Boston, 1985). Moreover, with the establishment since 1980 of 12 specialized secondary schools for the gifted, a much stronger emphasis has been placed on collecting research data on the effectiveness of specific programs as well as on the achievements of the graduates of such institutions. Most of these schools routinely provide annual reports listing the accomplishments of graduates. Typically, the graduates accrue more honors than students attending regular secondary schools, enter more prestigious institutions, and receive more scholarships.

This chapter highlights trends and issues affecting secondary programs for the gifted at their current stage of program evolution.

Broadened Conception of Giftedness ⌇

The conception of intellectual giftedness yields to more domain-specific considerations in secondary schools than at earlier levels. Gifted students at the secondary level have developed strong aptitudes and interest preferences that affect their choices of areas of learning. A study of subject matter preferences of junior-high students who scored high on the Scholastic Aptitude Test (SAT) revealed a strong preference for mathematics and science study over any other areas (VanTassel-Baska, 1986). These preferences tend to be the basis on which important learning is likely to occur. Student aptitude, interest, and opportunity to learn in-depth content come together at this stage of development more powerfully than at any prior time in a gifted student's life. Thus, the premise of general advanced development that is used to define giftedness during the elementary years broadens at the secondary level to embrace specific areas of talent across the spectrum of human abilities—from artistic to mathematical to athletic to leadership talent. A secondary-school program for the gifted can entertain all of these areas and more through a multiple options approach (Feldhusen, 1995; Feldhusen, Hoover, & Sayler, 1990).

Without a way to integrate curriculum options across content areas, most secondary programs for the gifted rely on core content as the framework for program delivery. This phenomenon has both advantages and disadvantages from a student perspective. On the positive side, students with a particular talent for mechanical drafting, for example, will be able to have that talent addressed. On the negative side, however, the child who is intellectually talented across academic and other areas must pick and choose separate courses that may not address his or her conceptual needs' and, may be forced to miss out on certain offerings that would be profitable due to scheduling problems.

The conception of giftedness also shifts toward an adult model of creative productivity at secondary level. Advanced development alone may not guarantee success at this level of schooling. The application of skills through homework assignments is now a staple of the program, and ability must converge with effort for success to be maintained. The conceptual level of material becomes more abstract, too, so that even able students must persevere to understand. Therefore, the nonintellective qualities of motivation and task commitment become more important in the full picture of giftedness.

Also, for the first time, students who are talented in the arts, leadership, vocational, or psychomotoric areas have outlets for their talent through special classes as well as cocurricular structures. Both identification and programming for multiple areas of giftedness become much more likely at the secondary level because the context is available to support talent development.

Interactive Influences on the Talent Development Process ⁓

Secondary schools are forced to come to grips with the complexity of talent development that arises in adolescence. Indicators of development must move beyond assessing mere competency in verbal and mathematical areas to the recognition of distinct student profiles on several continua. Ability differences must be considered in light of different experiences, motivation, personality, and achievement within the population of gifted learners. The influence of home background and earlier schooling patterns may become visible issues as well as the characteristics of self. The role of significant others, especially peers, also intensifies at this stage of development (VanTassel-Baska & Olszewski-Kubilius, 1989).

The importance of recognizing these interactive forces in the development of adolescent programs for the gifted cannot be overstated. Frequently, secondary teachers bemoan the fact that a gifted student lacks motivation or initiative regarding ideas. At this stage of development, gifted students become defined not by their ability alone but also by their work habits and attitudes, built up over the preceding 7 years of schooling. Thus, the nonproductive gifted student is a major problem at the secondary level, a problem requiring a different set of interventions than those found to be appropriate for productive gifted learners (Rimm, 1995).

As secondary educators, we need to recognize the potent effects of early schooling impacts and the context of the home environment on the gifted learner. Csikszentmihalyi and Larsen (1984) found that the nonconstructive use of leisure time at home characterized underachieving, and not achieving, gifted youth. Researchers of underachievement have consistently recommended various forms of counseling and tailored programming to respond to this problem

(Colangelo, 1993; Rimm, 1995). Thus, secondary schools must move toward a delivery system that recognizes important differences among gifted learners with respect to their nonintellective traits.

Multiple Options and Multiple Ways of Interpreting Success~

Secondary schools specialize in a cafeteria model of education, where students select from a menu of required courses and electives twice a year. For gifted learners, this model provides opportunities frequently not available to them at earlier levels of schooling. Additionally, at the secondary level, just as in adult life, success depends on one's productivity, metacognitive skills, and display of diligence as well as on one's test performance. Performance-based success is another accepted model at this level of schooling, as seen in musical performances, dramatic productions, quiz bowls, and student council debates. Increasingly, secondary schools must provide multiple options that allow for differential measures of success. Table 14.1 lists a set of options with an appropriate indicator of success next to each. Such a model allows for greater flexibility in programming and evaluation of efforts so that students may be perceived as successful in many different ways.

Table 14.1~
Performance-Based Success Options

Option	Criteria for Success
Advanced Placement (AP)	A score of 3 or above on the AP test High-level performance in classroom contexts
Creative writing	A written product that is published A written product that satisfies a set of predetermined criteria
Mentorship	Development of a career plan Satisfactory completion of a self-directed study
Seminar on global interdependence	Peer reviews of debates held High-level performance in shared inquiry model of discussion Product assessment

Identification Practices ~

Partly because of the domain-specific nature of secondary-school organization and partly because of the use of more reliable and valid methods of assessment than at earlier levels (since individual intelligence tests are infrequently used for identifying students in the elementary grades), secondary programs for the gifted have the capacity to assess significant differences in learner capacity among the gifted and talented population. The most widespread example is the testing of middle-school students on the SAT, which allows educators to perceive important differences in verbal and mathematical abilities among able learners. Other instruments, such as the Differential Aptitude Test (DAT), provide profiles of individual student strengths and weaknesses across a range of aptitude areas. Such testing allows for a more complete assessment of students that can be used for counseling purposes as well as curriculum planning. More recently, tests related to values and career preferences have yielded important data for more effective planning of gifted secondary programs. Career preference and value profiles have even been shown to differ considerably among gifted students, with the differences being discernible as early as seventh grade (Achter, Benbow, & Lubinski, 1996).

A recent study of the most effective approaches to identifying students for specialized residential high schools found that high-school grade records and SAT scores were the best predictors of success in the program (Feldhusen & Jarman, 1995). Interviews and selection committee ratings were found to be of no value as predictors. The SAT and grades reflect on student aptitude and effort, two major components in being successful in secondary gifted programs. Clinical judgment has been shown consistently to be much less useful as an identification practice. Thus, the combination of SAT scores and grades better captures the predictor variables for success at this level of schooling than any other practices, a finding comparable to those of studies done at the college level.

A Confluent Model of Intervention Approaches ~

The need for enrichment, acceleration, and counseling of gifted students is much more readily accepted in secondary programs than in elementary contexts. At the secondary level, counseling becomes the glue by which the gifted program holds together, since the school counselor is the major point of contact for parents and students to engage in academic planning. Recruitment for special classes and proper guidance into and out of selected options become important functions in the operation of secondary gifted programs. Secondary staff also tend to have little difficulty with the concept of acceleration since the dominant programs at this level of schooling have traditionally been of this nature—namely, honors and Advanced Placement coursework, both models implying that students are working at least one grade level beyond placement in the particular subject area. And enrichment opportunities also abound in these settings, sometimes through the seminar model, other times through a special course elective, and still other times through special cocurricular options.

The critical issue for secondary schools, it seems, is how to ensure that the gifted program is integrated, so that students feel there is a core program and various opportunities within it. It is very easy for secondary gifted programs to become fragmented and departmentalized rather than coherent and schoolwide.

Thus, secondary schools may find it worthwhile to spend more time discerning not just aptitude areas of gifted students but also preferences and dispositions toward certain types of careers. This service at the middle-school or junior-high level would accomplish three important goals:

1. It would provide a basis for affective secondary program planning from grades 8 to 12.
2. It would provide parents with a basis for understanding their child's strengths and areas of interest, which would help them make decisions about extracurricular opportunities such as Saturday and summer programs and camps.
3. It would provide gifted program planners with important data on potential options to be provided as well as providing a more substantial basis for possible internship and mentorship opportunities.

Interdisciplinary and Intradisciplinary Curriculum ⟿

In many of the best secondary programs, a healthy tension exists between providing quality programs within the disciplines and providing opportunities across the disciplines. Interdisciplinary work is enhanced by block scheduling, team teaching, and interdepartmental planning. However, the quality and experience of the teaching staff are the final determinents of the effectiveness of such efforts. Concept-based and problem-based curricula both have become popular ways for secondary schools to increase interdisciplinary work.

Although such interdisciplinary approaches to curriculum development have enjoyed recent popularity, traditional secondary programming for gifted learners has frequently included opportunities for cross-disciplinary studies in areas like American Studies, humanities, special seminars (on topics like ecology), and the philosophy course that anchors the International Baccalaureate program (Poelzor, 1994). Such interdisciplinary options have frequently evolved out of the commitment of secondary teachers to work together on course planning and delivery. Rarely have they worked well without a team teaching approach.

Just as valuable for gifted learners and perhaps a necessary precursor to gaining depth of knowledge and understanding about ideas, issues, and themes is a thorough exploration of ideas within a particular discipline. What are the most important ideas that frame our understanding of science in today's world? This and other questions are the basis for a substantive course of study for the gifted called Search for

Solutions, developed by Judson (1980), which is appropriate for junior-high gifted learners. Use of the major concepts outlined in *Science for All Americans* (Rutherford & Ahlgren, 1994) provides another concept-based approach to teaching science at the secondary level.

The issue for secondary gifted programs becomes how to develop a strong conceptual orientation to existing content-based courses and also move toward a more integrative model of curriculum and instruction across disciplines. Each task is important and feeds the other in shaping important curriculum experiences for gifted learners.

Teaching Thinking Skills Within Content Areas ⌇

At no level should thinking skills be more wedded to content than at the secondary level of gifted programs. The major problem appears to be with the terminology used. The teaching of literature, for example, requires having the student analyze and synthesize ideas, make inferences, determine authors' tones, and evaluate arguments. These thinking skills are unarguably important, yet they do not necessarily correspond to an existing thinking skills paradigm. Discipline-specific models of thinking, such as that just described for the teaching of literature, are frequently used in gifted programs and include many of the same types of thinking operations used in more generic models.

There are several strategies that developers of secondary programs might consider for embedding thinking skills for the gifted into content areas. One is to consider carefully what are the relevant mental processes used in a given area of study. In literature, for example, the relevant mental processes might be defined as the following:

- Making inferences
- Interpreting and creating analogies
- Using deductive and inductive reasoning
- Evaluating arguments
- Discerning the author's purpose

In the area of mathematics, thinking skills might be viewed as metacognitive approaches to solving problems. Relevant mental processes might include those in the following set:

- Looking for a pattern
- Guessing and testing
- Making a model
- Conducting a random search
- Working backwards
- Setting up an equation

In science, the most important mode of thinking is the scientific process. Thus, students would learn how to:

- Select a problem
- Study the problem
- Make hypotheses
- Collect data
- Analyze and interpret data
- Draw conclusions and test their relevance to the problem
- Make implications

As these examples demonstrate, the translation of thinking skills into content areas will vary by discipline both in terminology and in the nature of the thinking required. One challenge in secondary-level programming is to define and clarify the nature of thinking in each discipline and then to discuss commonalities across disciplines that can help make the teaching of thinking as interdisciplinary as possible.

One model of thinking that works well for secondary classrooms is the Paul model of reasoning (1992). This model treats thinking and reasoning as an interrelated set of processes that may be used whenever students need to reason something through. Paul's elements of reasoning include issues or problems, assumptions, points of view, inferences, data or evidence, implications and consequences, and concepts. Table 14.2 illustrates the utility of this model in examining issues in English, math, and science at the secondary level. Unlike some models, this one focuses students' thinking beyond discipline-specific content and into more interdisciplinary terrain.

The inclusion of a thinking skills model in secondary programming is consistent with our understanding of the research on thinking, namely:

1. Thinking is highly complex, made up of many skills, processes, and attitudes.
2. Thinking is dependent on student discourse for improvement. That is, students must interact in a meaningful, focused way in order for thinking to occur.
3. Thinking is integrated and interrelated in application. We rarely use only one thinking skill to deal with real-world issues and problems. Rather, how well we engage in several thinking skills and processes together determines the quality of our thinking.
4. Thinking involves the development of an inquiring mind as well as the mastery of certain skills and processes. Students must learn to approach all new data or stimuli with curiosity, openness, intellectual courage, honesty, and integrity.
5. Thinking is domain-specific; thus, it is best taught in the context of content. The use of the Paul model, for example, allows teachers at secondary levels in all the subject areas to find the appropriate applications rather than insisting the model be "force fit" in exactly the same way for each subject matter area.

Table 14.2~
Reasoning in the Content Areas

Reasoning Elements	Language Arts	Math	Science
Issues/Problems	Should libraries withhold books based on reader's age?	Should all students be required to take algebra?	Should new technology be controlled?
Concepts	Censorship Development Role of libraries in society	Mathematics in the real world Student learning needs	Societal control Range of technology Applications
Assumptions	That limited censorship is acceptable to protect the young	That algebra is a necessary subject for students to function in the world of work	That technological applications can be harmful to society
Data/Evidence/ Reasons	1. Yes, to be sure students are developmentally ready to experience a given text. 2. No, because gifted students are ready on an earlier development continuum and therefore should not be denied access.	1. Yes, because algebra is basic to daily functioning. 2. No, because it is too abstract for some students to acquire during high school.	1. Yes, because uses of new technology have been abused in the past, such as with the H-bomb and Agent Orange. 2. No, because new technology is found to be very useful in treating disease.
Implications, Consequences	If yes, gifted students may be denied access to materials for which they are ready.	If yes, algebra courses may be watered down to accommodate all learners.	If no, technological applications could be used to harm major segments of the population.

6. Thinking depends on a rich knowledge base. Although students can complete thinking skill exercises without deep learning of a content area, they cannot think effectively without having rich stimuli to think about. Thus, it is important to ensure that students learn enough about a content area to be able to manipulate it in different ways conceptually.

Although little evidence exists of the effectiveness of specific thinking skills programs (Sternberg & Lubart, 1993), evidence does suggest that teaching thinking as procedural knowledge to be internalized can promote advanced learning (Marzano, 1993).

Involvement in Contests and Competitions〜

A profusion of competitive opportunities for secondary gifted students has sprung up over the past several years. Following general societal trends, many of these options have emerged in the areas of mathematics and science, such as Math Counts, Math-letes, Talent Search, Math Olympiad, JETS, and science fairs. Other types of abilities are also recognized through competitive events. Future Problem Solving bowls, Odyssey of the Mind, and Young Authors are just a few of these other contest opportunities. These contests become an integral part of many gifted secondary programs with class time spent on preparation.

Extracurricular options also provide an important forum for competitive opportunities. Writing clubs, chess clubs, and debate tournaments all flourish at the secondary level as important avenues of talent development, avenues that are rarely available in the more limited elementary setting. These options should become an important emphasis for all secondary gifted programs since they may provide the best pure link between student aptitude and interest.

Yet, the extent to which contests and competitions become the substance of the programming for gifted students is clearly an issue. In many school districts, contests and their materials become the curriculum for gifted students. Where this occurs, program planners are being shortsighted in the sense that competitions should grow out of students' developing skills, concepts, and attitudes that need to be embedded in their regular subject matter curriculum. When growth in skills necessary to do well in competition is not fundamental to classroom work, the competition model has appeared to many districts to be a suitable substitute. Yet it is not, since such contests operate according to a narrow conception of learning, based only on the goals and procedures of each specific contest. Thus, if they are used as a curriculum model, student learning is unnecessarily limited as well. For example, Odyssey of the Mind expects student teams to invent a solution to a given problem. The goal is to challenge students' ingenuity and creativity, and the elaborate procedures require students to work toward that end. Although interesting and useful as an activity, it is hardly substantial enough to base a whole curriculum around, nor does it engage students in learning a knowledge base or being able to think in a number of different ways.

Another issue related to contests and competitions is their acceptability as positive forces in the lives of gifted students. Some researchers have noted that competition with its concomitant evaluative results diminishes intrinsic motivation and thus negatively affects student development (Amabile, 1993; Clinkenbeard, 1991). When competitions are used excessively or inappropriately, these concerns may be valid. But there is also evidence that competitions that provide students with a sense of their own mastery of a field at key stages of development and after age 10 appear to be facilitative in developing an internal standard of excellence (Bloom, 1985). Thus, the role of contests and competitions in secondary programs for the gifted needs to be carefully examined and thought through; yet they appear to have an important place in the overall development of gifted students.

Use of an Effective Counseling Model ~

At the secondary level, strong counseling models have emerged that focus on three key areas of gifted students' development. These areas are psycho-social development, with counseling delivered through small-group or individual clinical approaches; academic planning, with counseling typically delivered collaboratively with departments; and career counseling, handled through special seminars and scheduled field trips. In exemplary secondary programs for the gifted, a particular counselor is designated as the counselor of the gifted and works with all of that population as part of his or her overall job assignment. Occasionally, another faculty member assumes the role of counselor of the gifted and performs similar functions (Colangelo & Peterson, 1993).

Counseling models at the secondary level need to stress the importance of academic planning to ensure that gifted students are encouraged to explore an appropriate array of program and service options in school (VanTassel-Baska, 1993). Department chairpersons can assist in this process by collaborating on the discussion of course options, conducting career days in each discipline, and building relevant levels of Scholastic Aptitude Test items into their curricular plans.

Counseling becomes an issue at secondary levels when it is not taken seriously as a service to be rendered for gifted populations. The needs of the gifted are different enough from those of other students that separate counseling provisions are essential. For academic planning purposes alone, these students need assistance earlier and more consistently as their capacity to handle advanced work continues to expand. Most gifted students should enter college with Advanced Placement credits in at least two subject areas and be provided with assistance in getting scholarships as well as in selecting an appropriate college for their abilities and interests. These are basic expectations for service to this population, yet many schools do not provide the counseling necessary to ensure such outcomes.

Collaborative Relationships with Other Agencies ⌇

Successful secondary programs for the gifted have major outreach programs in place that create networks of opportunities for these learners in the larger community. Vehicles for such opportunities may be mentorships, internships, or independent study. Behind all such efforts is the important recognition that the school cannot possibly meet all of the needs of gifted learners by itself no matter how many options are offered or how good the staff are. Also, because individual variation among gifted students reaches a heightened level in adolescence, more tailored responses to interests and strength areas, such as are available through outreach programs, are necessary.

Collaborative relationships with universities and other community-based institutions constitute another realm of service delivery in programs for the gifted. These relationships validate the important recognition that although schools can provide some direct services to the gifted very well, other services are better brokered. Museology programs such as those in the Chicago Public Schools, which are held in conjunction with 24 of the city's museums, are testimony to the power of community-based opportunities for the gifted run off-site during the academic day. Mentorship programs such as those run through the Virginia Governor's Schools offer secondary students intense involvement with professionals for a semester of work. Dual enrollment programs, where high-school students take college courses during the day in areas of aptitude and need, are active at many universities. The future of diversified secondary programs demands more such collaborative efforts in school districts of all sizes.

The Issues of Middle School and the Gifted ⌇

The battle in secondary education over the role of the grades leading up to high school has impacted gifted education in many ways that have been detrimental to the middle-school movement as well as to the development of gifted students at those stages of development. Many aspects of the middle-school movement are in tune with the needs of the gifted: an affective component that stresses connectedness to others, an interdisciplinary curriculum that connects subject matter areas, teacher and student teaming that promotes greater cohesion among staff and students, and more student-initiated opportunities (Erb, 1994). All of these aspects, if they are undertaken with an eye to the individual differences within a middle-school population, can be important aspects of gifted programming (Coleman & Gallagher, 1995). Yet middle-school philosophy also calls for heterogeneous grouping, less emphasis on rigorous academics, and more socialization, all of which blur individual differences. Moreover, even the best middle schools have not made significant positive changes at the classroom level, where the best intentions of the initiative could reap results (VanTassel-Baska, Bailey, & Hammett-Hall, 1995). As with so many efforts in education, if the middle-school movement efforts were enacted in a judicious manner, they might prove successful for most students, including the gifted. But because they are implemented with great rigidity or in a haphazard way, they stand little chance of benefiting anyone. Currently, no studies have been done that document the effectiveness of the middle-school model as it has been proposed.

For gifted students, there is a particular need for caution around the model, for it assumes two problematic areas of belief. One is that middle-school students need to focus more on a social-emotional development agenda than on an academic one. The other belief is that middle-school students are not ready for rigorous academic work and therefore can benefit from studies that are high in interest but low in academic value. Such assumptions are erroneous with regard to gifted middle-school populations, who have entered formal operational thinking. For them, the middle-school years are a crucial time for more advanced and rigorous academic work. Moreover, the strongest evidence for the value of accelerated content comes from the talent search programs targeted for seventh and eighth graders (VanTassel-Baska, 1996).

Thus, the issues surrounding the middle-school model must be carefully negotiated in school districts to ensure that gifted students receive appropriate level programs and services that are commensurate with their readiness.

Linkages with General Education ~

Whereas elementary programs for the gifted resemble special education models, secondary programs derive their substance and flavor primarily from general education. A recent example of this phenomenon includes gifted education's response to the focus on math and science education initiatives in the fabric of the general educational community. Although little impact has occurred at the elementary level, secondary schools have responded with new courses, increased use of Advanced Placement courses in these content areas, and construction of special math-science centers for the gifted. Another outcome of this trend has been the increase in residential schools for the gifted with math and science as the banner for existence. Illinois and Maryland have mounted such efforts within the past 5 years. Massachusetts, Virginia, Indiana, and Florida have all drafted extensive plans for creating such entities as well.

Currently, academic-year, state-funded residential programs that offer gifted students the opportunity to live and learn together in one setting exist in 12 states. Many more states and universities offer summer residential opportunities that last from 3 to 6 weeks to qualified gifted secondary students. The proliferation of such programs has raised a host of issues not encountered before in this field. Some of the key questions surrounding such opportunities include:

- How healthy is it for gifted students to associate only with intellectual peers in such a situation?
- How can such schools determine the mental state of students before they are accepted so that students with a history of mental disturbances do not partici-

pate in such programs or, if they do, may receive the level of assistance necessary to function?

- Does the more interdisciplinary approach to teaching and learning employed at these schools prove to be more beneficial than the Advanced Placement approach over time?
- Does the advanced nature of exposure to the technology and expertise of the field in these programs render much of related college work trivial or unexciting?

All of these questions remain to be answered satisfactorily. Evaluation reports on such programs attest to parent and student perception of superior academic and social outcomes, but the data are often anecdotal in orientation (Kolloff, 1991).

Problems in Effecting Positive Change at the Secondary Level ᨑ

The issues in secondary education of the gifted that have been discussed in this chapter point the way toward greater possibilities for expanding gifted programs and services at an important level of the schooling process. Just as there are promising signs, however, there are also problems indigenous to secondary schools that cause difficulties in advancing such programs. These problems may be characterized as follows.

- *The difficulty in creating flexibility in scheduling.* Scheduling difficulties are the reasons most frequently cited by secondary administrators for why new courses cannot be instituted, block scheduling cannot be enacted, students cannot add needed classes, and so forth. These responses are truly an example of administrative convenience taking precedence over student need. One way to combat the realities of these difficulties is for gifted program coordinators to review the master schedule at least a year ahead of time and map out the parameters needed for gifted programs, such as double periods, block scheduling for interdisciplinary work, independent work options, and new courses in the planning stages that will need to be scheduled. By laying out all the variations at once and asking for changes early, the coordinators heighten their likelihood of success.
- *The difficulty in bridging the focused content perspective held by many secondary teachers to other curriculum orientations.* A problem frequently ascribed to secondary teachers is an overfondness of content at the expense of students. This tendency to want to deliver content at all costs is natural enough, and for gifted students it can be a real blessing after years of pablum. However, it also can be a problem if secondary teachers are not flexible with regard to how content is delivered. The use of learning strategies that augment and enhance what they are teaching is essential. Encouraging student involvement and the articulation of their understanding is a staple of good secondary teaching. Thus, if programs for the gifted are to be successful, regular in-service training for secondary teachers on content-based approaches to delivery are essential. Particularly useful are approaches that promote student thinking out loud.

• *Inappropriate requirements and expectations for gifted students.* Secondary-level gifted programs have frequently been charged with having too high expectations in relation to the quantity of work expected of the students, as well as with assigning work of a repetitive nature and assigning work inappropriately and the timing around its being assigned. Since we know that homework is an important aspect of gifted student learning (Walberg, 1991), secondary gifted program teachers are correct in assigning homework. However, guidelines for gifted program homework may be in order. These guidelines should ensure that students are given no more than one major project or research paper per quarter across all classes, that they be given no more than 30 minutes of homework nightly per academic class (or 2½ hours of homework per week per academic class), and that the homework assignments assess student understanding of a concept learned that day. If such guidelines were developed, the charge of uneven expectations might be dissipated. Equally insidious to those programs that give too much homework are the gifted programs that give no homework and do not hold students accountable for actual learning. These misguided programs do real damage to student development, self-discipline, and responsibility for learning.

• *Lack of differentiation in honors-level classes.* Secondary programs have also been charged with providing exactly the same work in honors classes that is provided in general classes, the only variation being the textbook used and the quantity of homework assigned. Although this problem can be alleviated by the diverse strategy approaches already cited in this chapter, further work is needed to improve honors classes. The materials used need to extend beyond one selected text. The level of curriculum expectations needs to be adjusted upwards with Advanced Placement tests used as a guide in the subject areas. More emphasis on generative work needs to be incorporated. Study groups need to be formed for special projects, and group work in the classroom needs to be encouraged. All of these approaches taken together would move secondary honors classes toward greater differentiation from general classes.

• *Teachers being textbook bound.* The problem of gifted program teachers being textbook bound is not limited to secondary-level teachers. One study found that 95% of the time, gifted teachers were working out of basic texts at all levels of learning (Apple, 1991). Yet it is a different kind of problem to combat at the secondary level, since teachers' perception of the core curriculum is embedded in the choice of text. Strategies to move beyond textbooks include the selection of supplementary material at the same time textbooks are adopted, the use of primary source documents, the use of trade books, the use of biography in all subject areas, and the regular employment of reference materials in the classroom. All of these approaches can loosen the stranglehold of a one-textbook mentality.

• *Falling into a cycle of seat work.* Seat work at any level can be deadly, but when executed as a daily staple in gifted programs at the secondary level, it can reinforce student passivity in the learning enterprise, the opposite of what is desired. One way to combat this problem is to ask teachers to divide every class period into at least two segments—one active and one passive. Thus, students may write for half a period and discuss for the other half, or they can conduct lab experiments for half a period and collaborate in teams on findings for the other half. Such variation in student engagement is critical to enhancing good learning. Obviously, exceptions will occur, such as on testing days or on days when a writing assignment or discussion takes the whole period, but in general a balance between types of activities is desirable.

  • *Program fragmentation resulting from lack of coordination of the gifted student's curriculum plan.* Program fragmentation is a special concern in gifted education at the secondary level. Because of the scope of students' programming at that level, it is difficult to ensure that all aspects of a student's plan fit together well. As noted earlier in this chapter, the school counselor or gifted program coordinator needs to ensure cohesion in a student's program. Such a strategy implies that several program options exist for students based on aptitude and interest and that these options are articulated over the years in school. If such a template does not exist in a school program, then it needs to be developed so that students and parents both can understand how the gifted program will provide services across the duration of the secondary-school experience.

Many of the problems cited with regard to secondary programs for the gifted can be perceived as generic to the secondary-school experience. Studies have consistently noted the difficulty in effecting change at the secondary level of schooling because of the complexity of the organizational structure and the lack of appropriate in-service training programs offered to high-school personnel (Sarason, 1993; Siskin & Little, 1995). Consequently, an effective model of school change must take into account the school as a complex social system (Senge, 1990) and the instructional and organizational behavior of teachers in the classroom as central emphases for effecting the desired changes (Shachar, 1996).

An excellent model that can be adapted for use in secondary programs focuses on four stages in the process of effecting change: learning what to do, learning how to do it, expanding the change process in the school, and institutionalizing the change (Shachar, 1996). Moreover, it emphasizes the importance of role clarification for principals, subject matter coordinators, teachers, and students in the process. Table 14.3 reflects the specific applications of the model by role function and stage in the change process.

Summary ⌇

The issues and problems cited in this chapter clearly are not insurmountable, and successful secondary programs for the gifted are testimony to what a committed corps of educators are capable of doing when the will is stronger than the perceived obstacles in the environment. Thus, secondary programs for the gifted hold great promise for fulfilling many of the important tenets of gifted education that have consistently been espoused but too rarely enacted.

	Table 14.3~ A Four-Stage Working Model for Instructional Change in Secondary Schools			
	Stage 1: Learning What to Do	Stage 2: Learning How to Do It	Stage 3: Expanding the Change Process in the School	Stage 4: Institutionalizing the Change
Principal	Defining the principal's role as facilitator for changing teaching methods in school	Setting up a schedule for collaborative planning by teachers	Expanding the use of the new instructional methods; facilitating the development of new methods of evaluation	Establishing the new instructional methods as a norm in school life
Subject Matter Coordinators	Defining the role of coordinators; acquiring the necessary skills to lead collaborative planning by teachers	Leading team planning; sharing observations of classrooms and drawing conclusions	Developing teamwork and planning alternative ways of student evaluation	Ongoing assessment of goals and means of the new instructional methods
Teachers	Introducing the new instructional methods; some initial implementation	Collaborative planning of lessons; implementation with peer observations	Ongoing team planning and implementation; developing new ways of evaluation	Using the new methods of teaching and evaluating regularly
Students		Initial exposure to new learning methods	Developing the skills for cooperative and self-regulated learning	Mastering different learning techniques and social skills

Note: Reprinted from "Developing New Traditions in Secondary Schools: A Working Model for Organizational and Instructional Change" by H. Shachar, 1996, *Teachers College Record, 97*, p. 566.

References ∾

Achter, D., Benbow, C., & Lubinski, D. (1996). Multipotentiality among the intellectually gifted: "It was never there in the first place, and already it's vanishing." *Journal of Counseling Psychology, 43*(1), 65–76.

Amabile, T. (1993). *The social psychology of creativity*. New York: Springer-Verlag.

Apple, M. W. (1991). The culture and commerce of the textbook. In M. W. Apple & K. Christian-Smith (Eds.), *The politics of the textbook* (pp. 22–40). New York: Routledge.

Betts, G. (1988). Profiles of the gifted and talented. *Gifted Child Quarterly, 32*(2), 248–253.

Bloom, B. (1985). *Developing talent in young people*. New York: Ballantine.

Clinkenbeard, P. (1991). Unfair expectations: A pilot study of middle school students' comparisons of gifted and regular classes. *Journal for the Education of the Gifted, 15*(1), 56–63.

Colangelo, N. (1993). A comparison of gifted underachievers and gifted high achievers. *Gifted Child Quarterly, 37*(4), 155–160.

Colangelo, N., & Peterson, J. (1993). Group counseling with gifted children. In L. Silverman (Ed.), *Counseling the gifted* (pp. 111–129). Denver, CO: Love.

Coleman, M., & Gallagher, J. (1995). The successful blending of gifted education with middle schools and cooperative learning: Two studies. *Journal for the Education of the Gifted, 18*(4), 362–384.

Cox, J., Daniel, N., & Boston, B. (1985). *Educating able learners: Programs and promising practices*. Austin: University of Texas Press.

Csikszentmihalyi, M., & Larsen, R. (1984). *Being adolescent: Conflict and growth in the teenage years*. New York: Basic Books.

Erb, T. (1994). The middle school: Mimicking the success routes of the information age. *Journal for the Education of the Gifted, 17*(4), 385–406.

Feldhusen, J. (1989). Effects of honors classes on secondary students. *Roeper Review, 11*(3), 153–156.

Feldhusen, J. (1995). Talent development during the high school years. *Gifted Education International, 10*(2), 60–64.

Feldhusen, J. F., Hoover, S. M., & Sayler, M. F. (1990). *Identifying and educating gifted students at the secondary level*. Unionville, NY: Trillium.

Feldhusen, J., & Jarman, F. (1995). Predictors of academic success at state-supported residential schools for mathematics and science: Availability study. *Educational and Psychological Measurement, 55*(3), 505–512.

Judson, H. (1980). *Search for solutions*. Baltimore, MD: Johns Hopkins University Press.

Kolloff, P. (1991). Special residential high schools. In N. Colangelo & G. Davis (Eds.), *Handbook of gifted education* (pp. 209–215). Needham Heights, MA: Allyn & Bacon.

Marzano, R. (1993). *Cultivating thinking in English and the language arts*. Urbana, IL: National Council of Teachers of English.

Paul, R. (1992). *What every thinking person needs to know*. Sonoma, CA: Critical Thinking Foundation.

Poelzor, G. H. (1994). *An empirical study of international baccalaureate students in the sciences*. Unpublished doctoral dissertation, Purdue University, West Lafayette, IN.

Reis, S., & Renzulli, J. (1989). The secondary triad model. *Journal for the Education of the Gifted, 13*(1), 55–77.

Rimm, S. (1995). *Why bright kids get poor grades: And what you can do about it*. New York: Crown.

Rutherford, J., & Ahlgren, A. (1994). *Science for all Americans*. New York: Oxford University Press.

Sarason, S. (1993). *The case for change: Rethinking the preparation of educators*. San Francisco: Jossey-Bass.

Senge, P. M. (1990). *The fifth discipline: The art and practice of the learning organization*. New York: Doubleday.

Shachar, H. (1996). Developing new traditions in secondary schools: A working model for organizational and instructional change. *Teachers College Record, 97*(4), 549–568.

Silverman, L. (1993). *Counseling the gifted and talented*. Denver, CO: Love.

Siskin, L., & Little, J. W. (1995). *The subject in question: Departmental organization and the high school*. New York: Teachers College Press.

Sternberg, R., & Lubart, T. (1993). Creative giftedness: A multivariate investment approach. *Gifted Child Quarterly, 37*(1), 7–15.

VanTassel-Baska, J. (1986). Effective curriculum and instructional models for talented students. *Gifted Child Quarterly, 30*(4), 164–169.

VanTassel-Baska, J. (1993). Academic counseling for the gifted. In L. Silverman (Ed.), *Counseling the gifted and talented* (pp. 201–214). Denver, CO: Love.

VanTassel-Baska, J. (1996). The contribution of the talent search to gifted education. In C. Benbow & D. Lubinski (Eds.), *From psychometrics to giftedness: Essays in honor of Julian Stanley* (pp. 214–224). Baltimore, MD: Johns Hopkins University Press.

VanTassel-Baska, J., Bailey, J., & Hammett-Hall, K. (1995). Case studies of promising change schools. *Research in Middle Level Educational Quarterly, 19*(2), 89–116.

VanTassel-Baska, J., & Olszewski-Kubilius, P. (Eds.). (1989). *Patterns of influence: The home, the self, and the school.* New York: Teachers College Press.

Walberg, H. (1991). Does homework help? *School Community Journal, 1*(1), 13–15.

Welch, W. (1984, March). *Women in science: Perceptions of secondary school students.* Paper presented at the annual meeting of the National Association for Research in Science Teaching, New Orleans, LA.

Study Questions ⌇

1. What are some of the organizational variables at the secondary level that facilitate gifted programming? What are some that hinder it?

2. What are some of the differences in the conceptualization of giftedness at the secondary level? How do these differences relate to identification procedures? In what way are these differences related to assessment strategies?

3. What are the roles of counseling in the implementation of gifted programs at the secondary level? How does academic counseling differ from career counseling? How do they complement each other?

4. What is the role of Advanced Placement in secondary gifted programming? How can secondary programming be developed beyond Advanced Placement?

5. What current educational assumptions about middle-school education are highly detrimental to the gifted population? What can be done to ensure that the needs of the gifted are met at this critical juncture in their schooling?

6. What do you think are the most significant problems related to gifted education at the secondary level? What could you, as an educator, do to ameliorate these conditions? How would an understanding of the change process help shape the steps you might take in this regard?

15

Grouping Intellectually Advanced Students for Instruction

Camilla Persson Benbow

This chapter discusses one of the most effective means for meeting the needs of intellectually talented students, perhaps the most ideal (Feldhusen, 1991a, 1991b): grouping students for instruction on the basis of competence.

Within any age-group and any subject matter, there is a wide range in achievement as well as in the rate at which new material can be mastered. The range is as wide as that for any physical attribute, such as hair color or height. Effective teaching is responsive to these individual differences, as will be discussed later, and instructional grouping is one means of being responsive that is favored by classroom teachers (ERIC, 1988) and strongly supported by research (Kulik, 1992a, 1992b). Yet instructional grouping is currently out of favor within a large portion of the educational community. Jeannie Oakes, for example, claimed:

> During the past decade, research on tracking and ability-grouped class assignments has provided striking evidence that these practices have a negative impact on most children's school opportunities and outcomes. Moreover, the negative consequences of these practices disproportionately affect low-income, African-American and Latino children. (Oakes & Lipton, 1992, p. 448)

Robert Slavin, another strong advocate of detracking, noted: "I am personally opposed to ability grouping, and, particularly in the absence of any evidence of positive effects for anyone, I believe that between-class ability grouping should be greatly reduced" (Slavin, 1990b, p. 506). In a later publication, Slavin (1995) contended:

Ability grouping by its nature works against democratic and egalitarian norms, often creates racial or ethnic divisions, risks making terrible and long-lasting mistakes, and condemns many children to low-quality instruction and low-quality futures. If there were strong educational justification for ability grouping, the situation might be different.... Let's work toward schools that can do a better job with all of our children. (p. 221)

We are being told by these authors and others that we should detrack our schools, and many schools are indeed responding. However, the empirical evidence supporting the views of detracking advocates is meager at best. The detracking policies being proposed are often a reflection of politics rather than the result of a careful examination of the results of empirical research. The following quotation by Oakes is telling: "We will need to replace many of the competitive, individualistic, and bureaucratic norms embedded in current practice, and existing political relations" (Oakes, Quartz, Gong, Guiton, & Lipton, 1993, p. 461).

Nonetheless, a consequence is that instructional grouping is being abandoned and programs for the gifted are being dismantled across the country (Benbow, 1992b). Such programs are quickly becoming an endangered species (Silverman, 1994). They are being condemned as further privileges bestowed on the already privileged (see, e.g., Berliner & Biddle, 1995) rather than being recognized as a necessary response to the different learning needs of children who learn differently and at a faster pace.

Why have politics turned against grouping and programs designed to respond to the educational needs of gifted children? Benbow and Stanley (1996) claimed that the movement is the result of an extreme form of egalitarianism currently operating within American society. In American society the pendulum seems to swing between an emphasis on equality and an emphasis on developing excellence, instead of both being viewed as ideals (Gardner, 1961, 1984). The pendulum has now swung so sufficiently far toward equality that the popular viewpoint is against excellence. Because this conflict has strong implications for the formation and understanding of educational policy (and hence the use of grouping), it will be explored in more detail in the next section, which is based on Benbow and Stanley (1996).

Excellence Versus Equity: An Unnecessary Tension

Excellence versus equity is one of the most difficult tensions permeating American society and its schools (Gardner, 1961, 1984). According to Gardner (1961, 1984), who was U.S. secretary of health, education, and welfare from 1965 to 1968, chairman of the National Urban Coalition, and founder of Common Cause, there are two hopes driving American society. These are the faiths in individual achievement (or excellence) and equality. With regard to the former, American society functions on the belief "that everyone would be free to perform at the level of his or her ability, motivation, and qualities of character and be rewarded accordingly" (Gardner, 1984,

p. 22); people should have the opportunity to develop excellence and be able to go where their talents take them. With regard to the latter, American society is driven by its commitment to equality, the premise that all "men" are created equal. To foster that equality, legislation and programs exist that provide "unequal treatment of unequals in order to make them more equal." This is the philosophy that supports Head Start and Chapter 1 programs in our schools.

It is critical for schools to focus on both equality and excellence. Fostering both should be seen as not only challenges for but goals of American public education (Gardner, 1961, 1984; Singal, 1991). Disadvantaged minority children attending inner-city schools operate in environments that make it extremely difficult to learn. For children consigned to schools in such environments, the question is not why they are not learning but how some manage to learn and move ahead despite the many obstacles. Moreover, students with developmental disabilities or students who demonstrate less readiness to learn need extra assistance. That is only fair. Consequently, much attention has been focused on how to educate children arriving at school from disadvantaged backgrounds or with disabilities. Such children need dedicated teachers and a sound curriculum; they also need a safe school environment and parental support (Lykken, 1995). It is only equitable that they be provided with resources so that they, too, can develop to their full potential and become well-functioning citizens. This contention is consistent with the country's notions of excellence and equity. The challenge here is visible and clear even if the solutions have been difficult to decipher.

Another challenge for American education is less visible. It involves nurturing the talents or challenging and stretching the intellectual propensities of America's highly able students. They, too, need a chance to develop their full potential. Unfortunately, many intellectually advanced students are not receiving this opportunity (Archambault et al., 1993; Westberg, Archambault, Dobyns, & Salvin, 1993). Collectively, and to the surprise of many, the gifted constitute America's largest group of underachievers (Reis, 1989). Perhaps even more surprising is that the relatively poor standing of American students in international comparisons of mathematical and scientific achievement is primarily the result of the relatively poor performance of America's brightest students, not its average students (Benbow & Stanley, 1996; Berliner & Biddle, 1995; Herrnstein & Murray, 1994). Moreover, few people realize that the achievement of gifted students in the United States is not only well below the level of their own potential but is also below the achievement levels of previous generations of gifted students. It is the achievements of previous generations of gifted students that formed the basis for the following controversial conclusion in *A Nation at Risk* (National Commission on Excellence in Education, 1983): "Each generation of Americans has outstripped its parents in education, in literacy, and in economic attainment. For the first time in the history of our country, the educational skills of one generation will not surpass, will not equal, will not even approach, those of their parents." Not fully developing the talents of America's gifted students has grave implications for our country's ability to economically compete with other industrialized nations (Bishop, 1989; Boissiere, Knight, & Sabot, 1985;

Rivera-Batiz, 1992; Singal, 1991), especially as progress becomes more dependent upon technological advances and sophisticated levels of thinking and reasoning.

These assertions may cause confusion for many people, for intellectually precocious students give the appearance of performing well. They appear to be doing well because the criteria schools employ to demonstrate that outcomes have been achieved are too shallow for use with highly able students. Most assessment instruments used to measure educational outcomes and achievement have low ceilings, a concept that was discussed in Chapter 11. They do not have sufficient "top" to capture the full scope of these students' capabilities and potential achievement. Their use is akin to measuring students' achievement in arithmetic by probing only their ability to do addition and subtraction, ignoring the fact that some students should be able, given their abilities, to multiply and divide. It appears that we, as educators, are satisfied by the fact that the students can add and subtract and are not worried about the few who could multiply and divide as well. That is, gifted students give the appearance of performing well because we do not ask much from them. We do not consider or measure what gifted students ought or could know if they were performing at a level commensurate with their demonstrated competencies.

Progress of society depends upon our ensuring that the distribution of educational resources is equitable and fosters excellence. Yet, as noted earlier, we seem to develop policies viewing excellence and equity as polarized incompatibilities of a zero-sum game, excellence *versus* equity, not excellence *and* equity. When excellence is of concern, we become too competitive. When equity is of concern, as it is currently and was in the 1960s, we dismantle programs designed to develop excellence (Sykes, 1995; Tannenbaum, 1979). We become hostile to gifted students, even highly achieving minority students. Australia gives a name to this trend, which some call coercive egalitarianism (Schroeder-Davis, 1993) or Ressentiment (Friedenberg, 1962): "cutting down the tall poppies." No one should stand out (Sykes, 1995). Yet, as Silverman (1994) stated, "holding back the brightest students will not magically help the slower ones; *bringing the top down does not bring the bottom up*" (p. 3).

The misguided view of so many people today reflects a changed meaning of equality. We equate equality with identity (Mayr, 1963). Hence, today we strive for sameness in educational outcomes rather than for providing equal opportunities to develop differing potentialities. Educational outcomes have become a metric for human worth. Yet human dignity and worth should be assessed only in terms of those qualities of mind and spirit that are within the reach of every human being (Gardner, 1961, 1984).

Extreme egalitarianism (Benbow & Stanley, 1996), then, coupled with the insistence of many schools to use the same curriculum at the same pace with all students has led to a situation where many of the brightest students, especially bright minority students, are being treated inequitably because they are not provided with an appropriate education. As Gregory Anrig, former president of the Educational Testing Service, asserted, American schools have devoted so much energy to bringing up the bottom that they have failed to challenge students at the top ("Top Students," 1991). Consequently, gifted students are being deprived of opportunities to develop their potential. We need to restore a better balance between America's two strivings, educational equity and excellence (Gardner, 1961, 1984).

Interestingly, improving the education that intellectually capable students receive, and hence restoring balance, does not necessitate large, increased expenditures by schools. Such improvement need not be made at the cost of any other group of students. The main requirement is administrative flexibility. Yet, even if there were a price tag, would it not be a fair proposition to suggest that at least 10% of the funding that currently goes toward special education be earmarked for the special needs of gifted students (Belin, 1995) rather than the current low level of 2 cents out of every $100 spent in education (Brimelow, 1994; Sykes, 1995)?

Individual Differences in Abilities

Unfortunately, expecting equal educational outcomes is not realistic. The expectation belies robust findings from developmental and educational psychology and behavior genetics, which have revealed large individual differences in the rate of learning of schoolchildren and have concluded that at least half of these differences are due to genetic variation (see, e.g., Bayley, 1955, 1970; Bouchard, 1993; Bouchard, Lykken, McGue, Tellegen, & Segal, 1990; George, Cohn, & Stanley, 1979; Keating, 1975; Keating & Schaefer, 1975; Keating & Stanley, 1972; Pedersen, Plomin, Nesselroade, & McClearn, 1992). Not everyone is well equipped to master calculus or differential equations, create beautiful pieces of art, or have an excellent batting average. Moreover, the rate of learning for each child varies considerably as a function of content area (verbal, numerical, and spatial) (Ackerman, 1987; Carroll, 1985; Humphreys, 1979; Snow, Kyllonen, & Marshalek, 1984). As was concluded in the *Prisoners of Time* report: "If experience, research, and common sense teach nothing else, they confirm the truism that people learn at different rates and in different ways with different subjects.... Some students take three to six times longer than others to learn the same thing" (National Education Commission on Time and Learning, 1994, pp. 7, 15). These individual differences in rate of learning lead to differential academic outcomes, even among the intellectually able (Benbow, 1992a; Chauncey & Hilton, 1965; Harmon, 1961).

It has been known for some time, for example, that younger students in a particular grade tend to possess more knowledge about key academic topics than older students in the same grade and that approximately 10% of 12th graders under 18 years of age have more scientific knowledge than the average college senior (Learned & Wood, 1938). In addition, bright students can achieve well not only in subjects at their grade placement but also at much higher levels. In homogeneously grouped classes, where the curriculum is differentiated on the basis of content and pace, 13-year-old students in the top 1% in abilities relevant to academic excellence (e.g., mathematical, spatial, or verbal reasoning) can, from three intensive weeks of schooling, assimilate and retain a full school year of high-school biology, chemistry, Latin, physics, or math (see, e.g., Lynch, 1992; Stanley & Stanley, 1986). They also can master a full semester of college freshman-level English, logic, computer science, psychology, and so forth, in the same amount of time. They do this routinely in summer programs for gifted students and have done so for almost 25 years (Stanley, 1973). Such homogeneously grouped classes are discussed later in this chapter.

Responding to these individual differences and allowing for differential outcomes does not create elitism, a frequent charge against programs for gifted students. Indeed, just the opposite is true (Allan, 1991). Hollingworth (1930), reporting on research findings from studies of ability grouping, noted: "Conceit was corrected, rather than fostered, by the experience of daily contact with a large number of [academic] equals" (p. 445). As a matter of fact, decline in academic self-concept has been documented as a result of participation in gifted programs (Gibbons, Benbow, & Gerrard, 1994). This decline should not be viewed as negative, however. Gifted students' self-concepts become more realistic through such experiences (Robinson & Noble, 1991). Moreover, when gifted students are appropriately served, they develop an enhanced ability to get along with their age-mates (Gross, 1993).

Further, effective teaching involves providing the "optimal match" (Durden & Tangherlini, 1993; Hunt, 1961; Robinson & Robinson, 1982; Robinson, Roedell, & Jackson, 1979; Vygotsky, 1962), that is, posing problems to an individual student that appreciably exceed the level that student has already mastered. Too-easy problems lead to boredom, too-difficult problems lead to frustration. Neither promote optimal learning nor motivation to learn. According to Carroll (1989), "Available evidence suggests that when the variables of quality instruction and opportunity to learn are properly managed, the variable of student perseverance—willingness to learn—will take care of itself" (p. 30). The following adaptation of a quote by Thomas Jefferson sums things up well: There is nothing so unequal as the equal (same) treatment of unequals (people with differing abilities).

We need to provide *all* children with an equal opportunity to learn and to develop to their full potential. A "one-size-fits-all" educational system is not effective and hence not equitable. Equity should be viewed as equal access to an *appropriate* education. In the words of Sirotnik (1983): "Quality of schooling includes not only time-on-task, but time well spent" (p. 26). And, as Gardner (1984) stated, "The good society is not one that ignores individual differences but one that deals with them wisely and humanely" (p. 92). Instructional grouping is one means of being responsive to individual differences in ability to learn.

Homogeneous Grouping Versus Detracking ∾

As mentioned earlier, at this juncture in American education, the concept of homogeneously grouping students according to ability for instruction is unfashionable (Deutsch, 1993; Oakes, 1985, 1990; Slavin, 1987, 1995). Detracking is pursued due to beliefs or assertions that ability grouping produces inequalities in student opportunities and outcomes (Brewer, Rees, & Argys, 1995; Page & Keith, 1996). The evidence to support such a view is striking, however, by its almost complete absence (Allan, 1991; Brewer, Rees, & Argys, 1995; Page & Keith, 1996; VanTassel-Baska,

1992). There is "remarkably little support for detracking efforts" (Brewer, Rees, & Argys, 1995, p. 211). Rather, scholarly reports and meta-analyses of the grouping literature are strongly in support of the practice of homogeneous grouping (Allan, 1991; Feldhusen, 1989, 1991c; Feldhusen & Moon, 1992; Gamoran, 1986; Gamoran & Berends, 1987; Kulik & Kulik, 1982, 1987, 1992; Page & Keith, 1996; Rogers, 1991).

The key work cited as supporting the need for detracking is Slavin's (1987, 1988, 1990a, 1990b) "best-evidence" syntheses. Although the work is cited to support the contention that grouping harms some students, it should be noted that these syntheses did not result in a conclusion that any students were harmed. It should also be noted that Slavin's methods have been criticized (Benbow & Stanley, 1996). Slavin studied grouping in isolation (i.e., grouping without curricular modifications) and excluded gifted students from his analyses (see, e.g., Allan, 1991). Grouping students without differentiating the curriculum is rather pointless (see Gallagher, 1995; Robinson, 1990).

Moreover, some of the arguments in support of detracking attribute differential educational outcomes to instructional practices rather than to the equally plausible alternative of differences in behaviors that students themselves bring to the learning setting that affect the nature of the instruction (Gamoran, Nystrand, Berends, & LePore, 1995). For example, is it appropriate to focus on grouping as the critical variable when students in higher level classes complete more assignments than students in lower level classes?

Other arguments against ability grouping include that (1) it negatively affects students' self-concepts by stigmatizing those who are in the lower groups and inflating the self-worth of those placed in higher groups, (2) most adult experiences do not occur in homogeneous groups and hence students need to learn to interact with all types of people, (3) students of lesser ability may profit from learning with and from those who are more advanced, and (4) grouping segregates students along ethnic and socioeconomic lines. The research shows, however, that inclusion (or heterogeneous grouping) lowers the academic self-concepts of low-ability students (Wilson, 1992), whereas homogeneous grouping lowers the academic self-concept of high-ability students (Gibbons et al., 1994). These findings are just the opposite from what the attackers of grouping claim. As for later life experiences occurring in homogeneous groups, it needs to be pointed out that people choose careers on the basis of ability and interests (Lofquist & Dawis, 1969, 1991). People work in quite homogeneous groups, and many of one's friends come from the work setting. We also mate assortatively. That is, we choose partners and friends who are similar to us on the basis of ability. Hence, life for adults is much more homogeneous than it is for children. As for the educational benefits for low-ability students who are able to interact with their high-ability counterparts, it needs to be pointed out that we model our behaviors after those whom we perceive to be similar to ourselves (Schunk, 1987). Struggling students do not choose high-ability students to be their role models.

Yet grouping does tend to produce classes that are somewhat segregated on the basis of ethnic and socioeconomic backgrounds. This is not because students are selected into high- or low-ability groups on the basis of race or socioeconomic status (SES), but rather it is because race and SES are associated with ability and demonstrated achievement. The solution is to make sure that no student is overlooked when forming high-level classes and that grouping does not take place in all school activities, but only for those where it makes sense (i.e., in core academic subjects).

Given this discussion, the reader might think that it is only the gifted child community that advocates for homogeneous grouping. This is not the case. Within special education, as well, concern is being raised about detracking (Kauffman, 1993).

The Empirical Support for Grouping ~

What does the research indicate about homogeneous grouping? Page and Keith (1996) captured the situation well when they drew the conclusion from their empirical study and analysis of the literature that homogeneous grouping improves the achievement of high-ability youth, especially high-ability minority youth; is not harmful to low-ability students' (or any group of students') achievement, aspirations, or self-perceptions; and is favored by classroom teachers. It is also favored by adults who were themselves identified as gifted when children (Benbow, 1995). Further, research indicates that grouping is most effective when the curriculum is differentiated and especially if the class is an accelerated or fast-paced class. Students in accelerated classes have been shown to gain in grade-level competencies at twice the typical rate, and those in enriched classes have been shown to gain at a rate that is 50% higher (Kulik, 1992a, 1992b; also see Table 15.1). In the words of Kulik (1992b, pp. 6–7):

Table 15.1 ~
Ability Grouping and the Gifted

Study Types	Context	Value-Added Gains
XYZ classes (51 studies)	Differential placement; no differential treatment	1-month gain for high-ability students
Cross-grade Within-class grouping (14 studies/11 studies)	Partial differential placement; differential treatment	2–3 months for all groups
Accelerated classes (23 studies)	Differential placement and treatment	1 year
Enriched classes (25 studies)	Differential placement and treatment	4–5 months

In typical evaluation studies, talented students from accelerated classes outperform non-accelerates of the same age and IQ by almost one full year on achievement tests. Talented students from enriched classes outperform initially equivalent students from conventional classes by four to five months on grade equivalent scales.

One might ask what the effect would be if detracking took hold and homogeneous grouping were entirely eliminated. Kulik (1992b) asserted the following:

> The damage would be the greatest, however, if schools, in the name of detracking, eliminated enriched and accelerated classes for their brightest learners. The achievement level of such students falls dramatically when they are required to do routine work at a routine pace. No one can be certain that there would be a way to repair the harm that would be done if schools eliminated all programs of acceleration and enrichment. (pp. 6–7)

As concluded by the National Education Commission on Time and Learning (1994, p. 31), grouping children by age should become a thing of the past. The commission noted that it makes no more sense to put a computer-literate second grader in Introduction to Computers than it does to place a recent Hispanic immigrant in Introductory Spanish. Both should be placed at their current level of accomplishment.

Rationale for Homogeneous Grouping ~

Homogeneous grouping has been with us for over 100 years. Initially, groups were informally formed and consisted of students who were at approximately the same level of the curriculum and maintained the same pace of learning. Following the work of Gessell in the 1940s, however, ability grouping became restricted to involve only those students of the same age.

Why was ability grouping implemented? Ability and achievement grouping, rather than grouping by age alone, is effective because (1) it provides a better match between the developmental readiness and needs of a given student and the instruction he or she receives, (2) students differing in ability respond differently to various educational strategies or teaching methods, (3) students learn better when they work with other students at their level of competence or just slightly above (as in sports, where one's game improves when one plays with an equally skilled or a slightly better partner), (4) grouping provides a challenge for students to excel or forge ahead, and (5) grouping makes teaching easier by restricting the range of ability or achievement.

What should be of concern to educators is what is appropriate to teach and how to teach it, to what students, and when. In this regard, it is important to keep in mind that intellectually advanced students benefit more from instruction that gives them considerable responsibility for organizing and interpreting information than from tightly structured lessons. Less able children, conversely, need more concrete and less abstract presentations with lesser amounts of information conveyed (Cronbach, 1989; Snow, 1986).

Instructional grouping also can provide a better social environment for children, at least for gifted children; they are with children for part of the day who are more like themselves academically and ones who are more likely to understand their needs, humor, and vocabulary (Lubinski & Benbow, 1995). Participation in an ability-grouped program reduces deliberate underachievement among the gifted; in such a group they have less need to deny their abilities for peer acceptance. There is no one in the group to make fun of them.

Forms of Ability Grouping∿

There are several forms of ability grouping: XYZ grouping, within-class grouping, cluster grouping, cross-grade grouping, special classes (e.g., seminars, fast-paced classes, Advanced Placement classes), and special schools.

XYZ grouping occurs when students in the same grade are split into high-, middle-, and low-ability groups based on performance or achievement, often determined through testing. In XYZ grouping, students are differentially placed into groups on the basis of achievement but the treatment is not necessarily differentiated (often it is not). That is, all students are subjected to the same curricula. XYZ grouping is a form of tracking. Not surprisingly, this approach to grouping yields little if any educational advantages for gifted students (Kulik, 1992b). When the curriculum is adjusted to respond to the differences in ability, the gain for gifted students is much greater.

Within-class grouping occurs when students within the same class are grouped for instruction according to their achievement. There are three primary means to accomplish this type of grouping: (1) mastery learning, (2) individualized instruction, and (3) regrouping by subject. The latter is the most common form of within-class grouping and involves placing students into three or more levels. The students in each level study material from different textbooks that are at different levels. The curriculum is differentiated for the various groups. Gains for low-, middle-, and high-ability groups have been demonstrated from this approach, with students averaging 1.2 years of academic progress in a school year.

Cluster grouping is a type of within-class grouping. In this situation several of the talented students or even all of the talented students are placed with a teacher who will respond to their needs by differentiating the curriculum for them. Winebrenner and Devlin (1991) suggested that four to six gifted students should make up a cluster. Through cluster grouping, students can have their instructional needs met all the time, not just in the 1- to 2-hour pullout experience that is often provided by schools. This practice fits well with the philosophy of inclusion found within special education.

Cross-grade grouping occurred first as part of the Joplin plan in Missouri in the 1950s. As part of cross-grade grouping, students in several grades, for example fourth through sixth, have arithmetic, or another course, offered at the same time of day. Several instructional groups are formed on the basis of the students' demonstrated achievement, without regard to the students' grade level. That is, all the students in the grades involved are rearranged into as many groups as there are teachers; the groups are homogeneous as to demonstrated level of achievement. Instruction is geared to be responsive to the level and needs of the group. Other forms of cross-grade grouping include special classes or seminars, where students of different grade levels are drawn together for an experience. The benefits of cross-grade grouping are similar to those obtained from within-class grouping.

Special fast-paced classes in mathematics were developed and pioneered in 1972 by Julian C. Stanley (Stanley, Keating, & Fox, 1974). In 14 months, a group of eighth-grade students were able to master 4.5 years of high-school mathematics. At the end of the 14 months they were prepared to study calculus. Subsequent attempts produced equally startling results (see, e.g., Bartkovich & George, 1980; Bartkovich & Mezynski, 1981). After demonstrating that fast-paced classes worked well in mathematics regardless of whether the class was conducted over the full academic year or during a brief time in the summer (Benbow, Perkins, & Stanley, 1983; Swiatek & Benbow, 1991), the concept was expanded to other domains. Now, as noted earlier, it is a rather routine option for talented students. These classes are offered as part of summer programs for gifted students at Iowa State University and at similar programs across the country (e.g., at Duke, Hopkins, Northwestern, Purdue, and the University of Denver). Most students enjoy the experience and then become motivated to speed up their educational progress in other domains (Benbow, Lubinski, & Suchy, 1996). Fast-paced classes also have been offered as part of general education programs (see, e.g., Lunny, 1983). In such classes, a group of students master 2 years of mathematics, for example, during a single school year.

The Advanced Placement (AP) program, which has been offered by the College Board since 1955, gives able and motivated high-school students the opportunity to study the material for one or more college-level courses and then, depending on their examination results, to receive upon matriculation to college advanced standing and/or course credit. The AP program provides schools with course descriptions in about 30 disciplines, such as biology, calculus, physics, psychology, Latin, art, and computer science. These course descriptions, prepared by committees of high-school and college teachers, are frequently updated and can be obtained at minimal cost by writing to College Board Publications, P.O. Box 2815, Princeton, NJ 08541.

The committees designing the course descriptions also are responsible for preparing a rigorous, 3-hour, comprehensive examination in each of the respective subject areas. The Educational Testing Service (ETS) administers these examinations each May for a fee for which the student is responsible. Readers, staff drawn from various high schools and colleges, then assemble to grade the exams using a 5-point scale, determining the degree to which the student is qualified to receive college credit for his or her work. The 5-point scale is as follows: 5 = extremely well qualified (or an A+ in a college course); 4 = well qualified (or an A in a college course); 3 = qualified; 2 = possibly qualified; and 1 = no recommendation.

It is up to the college that the student enters to decide whether and how it will recognize the student's work, with each college having its own guidelines. Yet scores of 4 or 5 are generally accepted by even the most selective colleges; usually a score of 3 is sufficient to obtain credit. As a matter of fact, many colleges are more lenient in providing advanced standing and/or credit for work completed through the AP program than they are for providing transfer credit. Finally, students should be made aware of the fact that the completion of AP coursework will enhance their college applications. Such work can provide the edge needed to obtain admittance into selective colleges.

It is often assumed that only seniors can take AP exams or that students can take them only if they have been enrolled in the relevant AP course. These assumptions are inaccurate. Students of any age can take the AP exams, and students can study the material on their own and then try to receive college credit through examination.

Students benefit when high schools offer AP courses that prepare them for these examinations and also provide much needed intellectual stimulation. For those small high schools where there are not enough students to fill AP classes, independent study arrangements for the few students ready for such work can be instituted. Under the supervision of a teacher, students can study on their own at the AP level. Such independent study arrangements should be in lieu of taking a lower level class in the same subject and follow closely the guidelines contained in the AP syllabus.

The benefits of conducting an AP class are rich. Plus, such classes provide intellectual stimulation and possible college credit to the students enrolled. AP courses have been found to be one of the most effective means for meeting the educational needs of gifted students. Of the available programs, the AP program is among the best (Benbow, 1991).

Special high schools created for gifted students across the country are examples of excellent homogeneous grouping (Benbow & Stanley, 1996). Perhaps the best known of these are the Bronx High School of Science, Stuyvesant High School, and the Hunter College School for the Gifted, which are all public, nonresidential schools located in the New York City area that have been in existence for many years. Similar to these New York City schools is the Thomas Jefferson School of Science and Technology in Fairfax County, Virginia. It, however, is a rather new creation.

Starting in the 1970s, a new type of special school for the gifted began to appear—the residential special high school. The first was the North Carolina School of Science and Mathematics (NCSSM), a residential state-supported high school. It consists of only the 11th and 12th grades and has demonstrated much success (Eilber, 1987). Student outcomes are exceptional. Subsequently, residential high schools similar to NCSSM have been created in Louisiana, Illinois, Indiana, Alabama, Oklahoma, and several other states (Stanley, 1987).

There is another tradition of special high schools, which is based upon early entrance to college. Early entrance colleges, which can be considered a type of special high school, have been established where students enter either without the high-school diploma or by being a young high-school graduate. The first such early-entrance program took place at the University of Chicago but eventually was abandoned and replaced for a while in the 1960s with a program at Shimer College in Mt. Carroll, Illinois. The first successful program of this kind, in terms of longevity, is Simon's Rock Early-Entrance College in Massachusetts. It admits students a year or two shy of completing their high-school requirements. The Program for the Exceptionally Gifted of Mary Baldwin College (a school for women only) in Staunton, Virginia (Stanley, 1995a), and the 1-year Clarkson School of Clarkson University (Kelly, 1989) in Potsdam, New York, have followed Simon's Rock's lead and are of the same general type of special school.

Another form of the special high school for gifted students was created in 1988 with the founding of the state-chartered Texas Academy of Mathematics and Science (TAMS) (Stanley, 1991). About 200 highly selected boys and girls enter the academy after completing 10th grade, living in their own special residence hall on campus with some restrictions because of their age. They take a rigorous, required set of *college* courses in the sciences, as well as some social science and humanities courses, in order to earn a high-school diploma. In the fall of 1995, a school somewhat similar to TAMS was established at West Georgia College (Stanley, 1995b). Students enter after the 10th or 11th grade and complete the graduation requirements of their own high school *in absentia* via college courses.

All of these types of special high schools constitute strong examples of full-time grouping of gifted learners.

Summary ⚊

Currently, homogeneous grouping is under attack. Yet the scientific evidence clearly supports the practice of homogeneous grouping. Homogeneous grouping in its various forms enhances the achievement of gifted students, especially gifted minority students, and does not detract from the achievement of students placed in lower or middle ability groups (see Table 15.1). The National Research Center on the Gifted and Talented, through Kulik (1992b), published several guidelines relevant to ability grouping (Piirto, 1994). With them, I draw this chapter to a close.

Guideline 1: Although some school programs that group children by ability have only small effects, other grouping programs help children a great deal. Schools should, therefore, resist calls for the wholesale elimination of ability grouping.

Guideline 2: Highly talented youngsters profit greatly from work in accelerated classes. Schools should, therefore, try to maintain programs of accelerated work.

Guideline 3: Highly talented youngsters also profit greatly from an enriched curriculum designed to broaden and deepen their learning. Schools should, therefore, try to maintain programs of enrichment.

Guideline 4: Bright, average, and slow youngsters profit from grouping programs that adjust the curriculum to the aptitude levels of groups. Schools should try to use ability grouping in this way.

Guideline 5: Benefits are slight from programs that group children by ability but prescribe common curricular experiences for all ability groups. Schools should not expect student achievement to change dramatically with either the establishment or elimination of such programs. (Piirto, 1994, p. 65)

References ~

Ackerman, P. L. (1987). Individual differences in skill learning: An integration of psychometric and information processing perspectives. *Psychological Bulletin, 102*, 3–27.

Allan, S. (1991). Ability-grouping research reviews: What do they say about grouping and the gifted? *Educational Leadership, 48*(6), 60–65.

Archambault, F. X., Westberg, K. L., Brown, S. W., Hallmark, B. W., Zhang, W., & Emmons, C. L. (1993). Classroom practices used with gifted third and fourth grade students. *Journal for the Education of the Gifted, 16*(2), 103–119.

Bartkovich, K. G., & George, W. C. (1980). *Teaching the gifted and talented in the mathematics classroom*. Washington, DC: National Education Association.

Bartkovich, K. G., & Mezynski, K. (1981). Fast-paced precalculus mathematics for talented junior-high students: Two recent SMPY programs. *Gifted Child Quarterly, 25*, 73–80.

Bayley, N. (1955). On the growth of intelligence. *American Psychologist, 10*, 805–818.

Bayley, N. (1970). Development of mental abilities. In P. H. Mussen (Ed.), *Carmichael's manual of child psychology* (Vol. 1, pp. 1163–1209). New York: Wiley.

Belin, D. W. (1995, May 21). More money is needed for the gifted and talented. *Des Moines Register*, p. 2C.

Benbow, C. P. (1991). Meeting the needs of gifted students through use of acceleration: An often neglected resource. In M. C. Wang, M. C. Reynolds, & H. J. Walberg (Eds.), *Handbook of special education* (Vol. 4, pp. 23–36). Elmsford, NY: Pergamon Press.

Benbow, C. P. (1992a). Academic achievement in mathematics and science between ages 13 and 23: Are there differences among students in the top one percent of mathematical ability? *Journal of Educational Psychology, 84*, 430–441.

Benbow, C. P. (1992b). Progress in gifted education—everywhere but here! *Gifted Child Today, 15*(2), 2–8.

Benbow, C. P. (1995, May). *Our future leaders in science: Who are they and can we find them early?* Paper presented at the Wallace National Research Symposium on Talent Development, Iowa City, IA.

Benbow, C. P., Lubinski, D., & Suchy, B. (1996). Impact of the SMPY model and programs from the perspective of the participant. In C. P. Benbow & D. Lubinski (Eds.), *Intellectual talent: Psychometric and social issues* (pp. 266–300). Baltimore, MD: Johns Hopkins University Press.

Benbow, C. P., Perkins, S., & Stanley, J. C. (1983). Mathematics taught at a fast pace: A longitudinal evaluation of SMPY's first class. In C. P. Benbow & J. C. Stanley (Eds.), *Academic precocity: Aspects of its development* (pp. 51–78). Baltimore, MD: Johns Hopkins University Press.

Benbow, C. P., & Stanley, J. C. (1996). Inequity in equity: How "equity" can lead to inequity for high-potential students. *Psychology, Public Policy, and Law, 2*, 249–292.

Berliner, D. C., & Biddle, B. J. (1995). *The manufactured crisis: Myths, fraud, and the attack on America's public schools*. Reading, MA: Addison-Wesley.

Bishop, J. H. (1989). Is the test score decline responsible for the productivity growth decline? *American Economic Review, 79*, 178–197.

Boissiere, M., Knight, J. B., & Sabot, R. H. (1985). Earnings, schooling, ability, and cognitive skills. *American Economic Review, 75*, 1016–1030.

Bouchard, T. J., Jr. (1993). The genetic architecture of human intelligence. In P. A. Vernon (Ed.), *Biological approaches to the study of human intelligence* (pp. 33–93). Norwood, NJ: Ablex.

Bouchard, T. J., Lykken, D. T., McGue, M., Tellegen, A., & Segal, N. (1990). Sources of human psychological differences. *Science, 250*, 223–228.

Brewer, D. J., Rees, D. I., & Argys, L. M. (1995). Detracking America's schools: The reform without cost? *Phi Delta Kappan, 77*(3), 210–215.

Brimelow, P. (1994, November 21). *Disadvantaging the advantaged*. Forbes, pp. 52–57.

Carroll, J. B. (1985). Exploratory factor analysis: A tutorial. In D. K. Detterman (Ed.), *Current topics in human intelligence: Vol. 1. Research methodology* (pp. 25–58). Norwood, NJ: Ablex.

Carroll, J. B. (1989). The Carroll Model: A 25-year retrospective and prospective view. *Educational Researcher, 18*, 26–31.

Chauncey, H., & Hilton, T. L. (1965). Are aptitude tests valid for the highly able? *Science, 148*, 1297–1304.

Cronbach, L. J. (1989). Lee J. Cronbach. In G. Lindsey (Ed.), *A history of psychology in autobiography* (Vol. 3, pp. 62–93). Stanford, CA: Stanford University Press.

Deutsch, M. (1993). Educating for a peaceful world. *American Psychologist, 48*, 510–517.

Durden, W. G., & Tangherlini, A. E. (1993). *Smart kids: How academic talents are developed and nurtured in America*. Seattle, WA: Hogrefe & Huber.

Eilber, C. R. (1987). The North Carolina School of Science and Mathematics. *Phi Delta Kappan, 68*, 773–777.

ERIC. (1988). *Measuring teacher attitudes toward mainstreaming*. (ERIC Document Reproduction Service No. ED 289 885)

Feldhusen, J. F. (1989). Synthesis of research on gifted youth. *Educational Leadership, 46*(6), 6–10.

Feldhusen, J. F. (1991a). Full-time classes for gifted youth. *Gifted Child Today, 14*(5), 10–13.

Feldhusen, J. F. (1991b). Gifted students must have time together in learning activities at their level and pace. *Images, 5*(2), 2–3,12–13.

Feldhusen, J. F. (1991c). Susan Allan sets the record straight. *Educational Leadership, 48*(6), 66.

Feldhusen, J. F., & Moon, S. M. (1992). Grouping gifted students: Issues and concerns. *Gifted Child Quarterly, 36*(2), 63–67.

Friedenberg, E. Z. (1962). The gifted student and his enemies. *Commentary, 5*(33), 410–419.

Gallagher, J. J. (1995). Comments on "The reform without cost?" *Phi Delta Kappan, 77*(3), 216–217.

Gamoran, A. (1986). Instructional and institutional effects of ability grouping. *Sociology of Education, 59*(4), 185–198.

Gamoran, A., & Berends, M. (1987). *The effects of stratification in secondary schools: Synthesis of survey and ethnographic research*. Madison, WI: National Center on Effective Secondary Schools.

Gamoran, A., Nystrand, M., Berends, M., & LePore, P. C. (1995). An organizational analysis of the effects of ability grouping. *American Educational Research Journal, 32*, 687–715.

Gardner, J. W. (1961). *Excellence: Can we be equal and excellent too?* New York: Harper.

Gardner, J. W. (1984). *Excellence: Can we be equal and excellent too?* (rev. ed.). New York: Norton.

George, W. C., Cohn, S. J., & Stanley, J. C. (1979). *Educating the gifted: Acceleration and enrichment*. Baltimore, MD: Johns Hopkins University Press.

Gibbons, F. X., Benbow, C. P., & Gerrard, M. (1994). From top dog to bottom half: Social comparison strategies in response to poor performance. *Journal of Personality and Social Psychology, 67*, 638–652.

Gross, M. U. M. (1993). *Exceptionally gifted children*. London: Routledge.

Harmon, L. R. (1961). High school backgrounds of science doctorates. *Science, 133*, 679–688.

Herrnstein, R. J., & Murray, C. (1994). *The bell curve: Intelligence and class structure in American life*. New York: Free Press.

Hollingworth, L. S. (1930). Personality development of special class children. University of Pennsylvania Bulletin. *Seventeenth Annual Schoolmen's Week Proceedings, 30*, 442–446.

Humphreys, L. G. (1979). The construct of general intelligence. *Intelligence, 3*, 105–120.

Hunt, J. M. (1961). *Intelligence and experience*. New York: Ronald Press.

Kauffman, J. M. (1993). How we might achieve the radical reform of special education. *Exceptional Children, 60*(1), 6–16.

Keating, D. P. (1975). Precocious cognitive development at the level of formal operations. *Child Development, 49*, 276–280.

Keating, D. P., & Schaefer, R. A. (1975). Ability and sex differences in the acquisition of formal operations. *Developmental Psychology, 11*, 531–532.

Keating, D. P., & Stanley, J. C. (1972). Extreme measures for the exceptionally gifted in mathematics and science. *Educational Researcher, 1*, 3–7.

Kelly, G. F. (1989). The Clarkson School: Talented students enter college early. In S. M. Elam (Ed.),

Prototypes: An anthology of school improvement ideas that work (pp. 86–90). Bloomington, IN: Phi Delta Kappa Foundation.

Kulik, C. C., & Kulik, J. A. (1982). Effects of ability grouping on secondary school students: A meta-analysis of evaluation findings. *American Educational Research Journal, 19*, 415–428.

Kulik, J. A. (1992a). Ability grouping and gifted students. In N. Colangelo, S. Assouline, & D. L. Ambroson (Eds.), *Talent development: Proceedings of the 1991 Henry B. and Jocelyn Wallace National Research Symposium on Talent Development* (pp. 262–266). Unionville, NY: Trillium.

Kulik, J. A. (1992b). *An analysis on the research on ability grouping: Historical and contemporary perspectives*. Research-Based Decision Making Series. Storrs, CT: National Research Center on the Gifted and Talented.

Kulik, J. A., & Kulik, C. C. (1987). Effects of ability grouping on school achievement. *Equity and Excellence, 23*, 22–30.

Kulik, J. A., & Kulik, C. C. (1992). Meta-analytic findings on grouping programs. *Gifted Child Quarterly, 36*(2), 73–77.

Learned, W. S., & Wood, B. D. (1938). *The student and his knowledge: A report to the Carnegie Foundation on the results of the high school and college examinations of 1928, 1930, and 1932.* New York: Carnegie Foundation for the Advancement of Teaching.

Lofquist, L. H., & Dawis, R. V. (1969). *Adjustment to work.* New York: Appleton-Century-Crofts.

Lofquist, L. H., & Dawis, R. V. (1991). *Essentials of person-environment-correspondence counseling.* Minneapolis: University of Minnesota Press.

Lubinski, D., & Benbow, C. P. (1995). Optimal development of talent: Respond educationally to individual differences in personality. *Educational Forum, 59*, 381–392.

Lunny, J. F. (1983). Fast-paced mathematics classes for a rural county. In C. P. Benbow & J. C. Stanley (Eds.), *Academic precocity: Aspects of its development* (pp. 79–85). Baltimore, MD: Johns Hopkins University Press.

Lykken, D. (1995). *The antisocial personality.* Hillsdale, NJ: Erlbaum.

Lynch, S. J. (1992). Fast-paced high school science for the academically talented: A six-year perspective. *Gifted Child Quarterly, 36*, 147–154.

Mayr, E. (1963). *Animal species and evolution.* Cambridge, MA: Harvard University Press.

National Commission on Excellence in Education. (1983). *A nation at risk: The imperative for educational reform.* Washington, DC: U.S. Dept. of Education.

National Education Commission on Time and Learning. (1994). *Prisoners of time.* Washington, DC: U.S. Government Printing Office.

Oakes, J. (1985). *Keeping track: How schools structure inequality.* New Haven, CT: Yale University Press.

Oakes, J. (1990). *Multiplying inequalities: The effects of race, social class, and tracking on opportunities to learn math and science.* Santa Monica, CA: Rand.

Oakes, J., & Lipton M. (1992). Detracking schools: Early lessons from the field. *Phi Delta Kappan, 73*, 448–454.

Oakes, J., Quartz, K. H., Gong, J., Guiton, G., & Lipton, M. (1993). Creating middle schools: Technical, normative, and political considerations. *The Elementary School Journal, 93*(5), 461–480.

Page, E. B., & Keith, T. Z. (1996). The elephant in the classroom: Ability grouping and the gifted. In C. P. Benbow & D. Lubinski (Eds.), *Intellectual talent: Psychometric and social issues* (pp. 192–210). Baltimore, MD: Johns Hopkins University Press.

Pedersen, N. L., Plomin, R., Nesselroade, J. R., & McClearn, G. E. (1992). A quantitative genetic analysis of cognitive abilities during the second half of the life span. *Psychological Science, 3*, 346–353.

Piirto, J. (1994). *Talented children and adults: Their development and education.* Columbus, OH: Merrill.

Reis, S. M. (1989). Reflections on policy affecting the education of gifted and talented students: Past and future perspectives. *American Psychologist, 44*, 399–408.

Rivera-Batiz, F. L. (1992). Quantitative literacy and the likelihood of employment among young adults in the United States. *Journal of Human Resources, 27*, 313–328.

Robinson, A. (1990). Cooperation or exploitation? The argument against cooperative learning for talented students. *Journal for the Education of the Gifted, 14*, 9–27, 31–36.

Robinson, H. B., Roedell, W. C., & Jackson, N. E. (1979). Early identification and intervention. In A. H. Passow (Ed.), *The gifted and the talented: Their education and development* (pp. 138–154). Chicago: University of Chicago Press.

Robinson, N. M., & Noble, K. D. (1991). Social-emotional development and adjustment of gifted children. In M. G. Wang, M. C. Reynolds, & H. J. Walberg (Eds.), *Handbook of special education in research and practice* (Vol. 4, pp. 57–76). New York: Pergamon Press.

Robinson, N. M., & Robinson, H. B. (1982). *The optimal match: Devising the best compromise for the highly gifted student.* San Francisco: Jossey-Bass.

Rogers, K. B. (1991). *The relationship of grouping practices to the education of the gifted and talented learner: Executive summary* (Report No. 1). Storrs, CT: National Research Center on the Gifted and Talented.

Schroeder-Davis, S. (1993). Coercive egalitarianism: Subverting achievement through neglect and hostility. *Gifted Education Press Quarterly, 7*(1), 2–9.

Schunk, D. H. (1987). Peer models and children's behavioral change. *Review of Educational Research, 57,* 149–174.

Silverman, L. K. (1994, April 20). *Gifted education: An endangered species. Empowering Partnerships Fulfilling Potential.* Indiana Association for the Gifted.

Singal, D. J. (1991, November). The other crisis in American education. *Atlantic Monthly,* pp. 61–74.

Sirotnik, K. A. (1983). What you see is what you get—consistency, persistency, and mediocrity in classrooms. *Harvard Educational Review, 53,* 16–31.

Slavin, R. E. (1987). Ability, grouping, and student achievement in elementary schools. *Review of Educational Research, 57,* 293–336.

Slavin, R. E. (1988). Synthesis of research on grouping in elementary and secondary schools. *Educational Leadership, 46*(1), 67–77.

Slavin, R. E. (1990a). Ability grouping, cooperative learning, and the gifted. *Journal for the Education of the Gifted, 14,* 3–8.

Slavin, R. E. (1990b). Ability grouping in secondary schools: A response to Hallinan. *Review of Educational Research, 60,* 505–507.

Slavin, R. E. (1995). Detracking and its detractors: Flawed evidence, flawed values. *Phi Delta Kappan, 77*(3), 220–221.

Snow, R. E. (1986). Individual differences and the design of educational programs. *American Psychologist, 41,* 1029–1034.

Snow, R. E., Kyllonen, P. C., & Marshalek, B. (1984). The topography of ability and learning correlations. In R. J. Sternberg (Ed.), *Advances in the psychology of human intelligence* (Vol. 1, pp. 47–104). Hillsdale, NJ: Erlbaum.

Stanley, J. C. (1973). Accelerating the educational progress of intellectually gifted youths. *Educational Psychologist, 10,* 133–146.

Stanley, J. C. (1987). State residential high schools for mathematically talented youth. *Phi Delta Kappan, 68,* 770–773.

Stanley, J. C. (1991). A better model for residential high schools for talented youth. *Phi Delta Kappan, 72,* 471–473.

Stanley, J. C. (1995a, October). Gifted children grow up. *CHI News* (Support Society for Children of High Intelligence, London), pp. 15–20.

Stanley, J. C. (1995b). Three or four years of schooling in two. *World Business Review, 5*(4), 41.

Stanley, J. C., Keating, D. P., & Fox, L. H. (Eds.). (1974). *Mathematical talent: Discovery, description, and development.* Baltimore, MD: Johns Hopkins University Press.

Stanley, J. C., & Stanley, B. S. K. (1986). High school biology, chemistry, and physics learned well in three weeks. *Journal of Research in Science Teaching, 23,* 237–250.

Swiatek, M. A., & Benbow, C. P. (1991). A ten-year longitudinal follow-up of participants in a fast-paced mathematics course. *Journal for Research in Mathematics Education, 22,* 138–150.

Sykes, C. J. (1995). *Dumbing down our kids: Why America's children feel good about themselves but can't read, write or add.* New York: St. Martin's.

Tannenbaum, A. J. (1979). Pre-Sputnik to post-Watergate concern about the gifted. In A. H. Passow (Ed.), *The gifted and the talented: Their education and development* (78th yearbook of the National Society for the Study of Education) (pp. 5–27). Chicago: University of Chicago Press.

Top students subjects of ETS study. (1991, fall). *Teaching Exceptional Children, 71.*

VanTassel-Baska, J. (1992). Educational decision making in acceleration and grouping. *Gifted Child Quarterly, 36*(2), 68–72.

Vygotsky, L. S. (1962). *Thought and language.* Cambridge, MA: MIT Press.

Westberg, K., Archambault, F., Dobyns, S., & Salvin, T. (1993). *An observational study of instructional and curricular practices used with gifted and talented students in regular classrooms.* Storrs, CT: National Research Center on the Gifted and Talented.

Wilson, M. (1992). *Children's academic self-perceptions: The influences of social comparison and classroom setting.* Unpublished doctoral dissertation, Department of Psychology, Iowa State University, Ames, IA.

Winebrenner, S., & Devlin, B. (1991). *Cluster grouping fact sheet.* Lombard, IL: Phantom Press.

Study Questions

1. What are six main forms of ability grouping, and what are the differences between them?
2. What form of grouping has shown the most dramatic gains for gifted students?
3. What is the postsecondary payoff for taking Advanced Placement classes and scoring well in them?
4. What is the empirical basis for discarding ability grouping in the schools? What arguments exist to support this position?
5. What is the empirical basis for supporting ability grouping? Why is this organizational arrangement experiencing reduced popularity?
6. What is the nature of the relationship between grouping strategies and differentiated curricula with regard to learning gains?

16

Acceleration as a Method for Meeting the Academic Needs of Intellectually Talented Children

Camilla Persson Benbow

In 1991 the Educational Council Act (PL 102-62) established the National Education Commission on Time and Learning (NECTL) to conduct a comprehensive review of the relationship between time and learning in our nation's schools. In the resulting report, titled *Prisoners of Time* (National Education Commission on Time and Learning ([NECTL], 1994), the commission made the following conclusions and recommendations.

> If experience, research, and common sense teach nothing else, they confirm the truism that people learn at different rates, and in different ways with different subjects. (p. 7)

> Research confirms common sense. Some students take three to six times longer than others to learn the same thing. (p. 15)

> Under today's practices, high-ability students are forced to spend more time than they need on curriculum developed for students of moderate ability. Many become bored, unmotivated, and frustrated. They become prisoners of time. (p. 15)

> Students deserve an education that matches their needs every hour of the school day, not just an hour or two a week. Pull-out programs are a poor part-time solution to a serious full-time problem. (p. 15)

> Fix the Design Flaw: Use Time in New and Better Ways. We recommend that the state and local boards work with schools to redesign education so that time becomes a factor supporting learning, not a boundary marking its limits. (p. 31)

Fixing the design flaw means that grouping children by age should become a thing of the past. It makes no more sense to put a computer-literate second grader in *Introduction to Computers* than it does to place a recent Hispanic immigrant in *Introductory Spanish*. Both should be placed at their level of accomplishment. (p. 31)

In the case of genuinely exceptional students who meet these requirements [i.e., high performance standards for high-school graduation] while very young, schools should offer them the opportunity to take advanced courses. (p. 31)

Above all, fixing the flaw means that time should be adjusted to meet the individual needs of learners, rather than the administrative convenience of adults. (p. 31)

These conclusions provide a strong rationale for the use of educational acceleration with children who are academically advanced or intellectually talented (Benbow, 1991). Moreover, these recommendations from *Prisoners of Time* are a much needed antidote to current schooling practices, which are characterized by a one-size-fits-all mentality to curriculum development and by a strong concern for bringing up the bottom. U.S. schools frequently fail to challenge students at the top ("Top Students," 1991). As a result, the achievement of the most able students in the U.S. lags far behind that of their counterparts in other industrialized nations; it is also well below both the level of the students' own potential and the achievement levels of previous generations of academically advanced U.S. students (Benbow & Stanley, 1996). The wide use of acceleration by schools could greatly help in turning this trend around. It is one especially effective means of putting excellence back into education. Thus, this chapter describes what acceleration is and how it can be used to provide a challenging education for gifted students.

Brief History of Acceleration in Our Schools ~

Acceleration is one of the most time-honored program adaptations (Gallagher, 1985; Passow, 1996). Although research reports on acceleration have been issued since at least 1928 (e.g., Lincoln, 1929; Washburne & Raths, 1928), acceleration was used, with some frequency, long before then in the one-room schoolhouses of the 18th and 19th centuries (Otto, 1950). The year 1862 is frequently marked as the year in which the first formal accelerated program was implemented. In that year the St. Louis schools began promoting students who were well ahead of their classmates academically. The use of acceleration by schools quickly spread, gaining increasing popularity until about 1920 (Brody & Stanley, 1991). At that point the trend reversed, and for 50 solid years enthusiasm for acceleration waned. By 1970 acceleration had become an educational practice of the past, essentially unheard of and certainly not used much in our schools. Yet that situation was to change in 1971. In that year Julian C. Stanley began his now long-standing debate with the schools of this country to open up or create more accelerative opportunities for bright students (Passow, 1996; VanTassel-Baska, 1996). Now, as we approach the 21st century, acceleration is gaining in popularity again and can be seen in our schools even if only in limited ways.

Although the utilization of acceleration by this nation's schools has been and continues to be rather spotty, the empirical research in support of acceleration cannot be characterized as such. Several reviews of the vast literature on acceleration (e.g., Benbow, 1991; Daurio, 1979; Gallagher, 1996; Robinson, 1983), as well as meta-analyses (Kulik & Kulik, 1984, 1992), have clearly demonstrated that acceleration works in both the long-term and the short-term (U.S. Department of Education, 1986). Decades of research have clearly shown that acceleration is a "best practice" (Benbow, 1991; Boatman, Davis, & Benbow, 1995). VanTassel-Baska (1989) stated, "Of all the interventions schools provide for the gifted, acceleration is best supported by research" (p. 25). Intellectually talented students who are accelerated in grade placement perform as well as talented but older students already in those grades; they also show almost a year's advancement over talented same-age nonaccelerates (Kulik & Kulik, 1984). Moreover, differences between accelerates and nonaccelerates, favoring the accelerates, can be detected as much as 50 years later (Cronbach, 1996). Gowan and Demos (1964) summed up the situation succinctly when they stated, "Accelerated students do better than non-accelerated students matched for ability" (p. 194).

As for the question of whether acceleration negatively affects a student's social and emotional development, the answer, based on much research, is a firm no. There is no evidence to show that acceleration detracts from social and emotional development (Richardson & Benbow, 1990). Moreover, accelerated students and their parents view acceleration positively. Keating (1979) captured the situation well: "As for the socio-emotional concerns, it seems time to abandon them unless and until some solid and reliable evidence is forthcoming that indicates real dangers in well-run programs" (p. 218). Indeed, many people have actually argued that not accelerating a gifted child who desires it is detrimental to the child's social and emotional development.

What Is Acceleration? ⌒

Acceleration is simply deciding that competence rather than age should be the criterion for determining when an individual obtains access to particular curricula or academic experiences. This principle is endorsed and used unquestioningly in the arts and in athletics. Few piano classes or skiing lessons, if any, are designated for only 8-year-olds, for example. Grouping for instruction according to age is unheard of in these domains. Instead, instructors try to figure out what the child knows and does not know and then begin working with them at a level slightly above their demonstrated level of mastery, the level at which people learn best according to much research in educational and developmental psychology (Benbow, 1991). Concern is not raised about such placement according to competence in these areas. So why do we worry so much about placement according to competence when the domain is reading or math? Putting all children of the same age in the same reading group is akin to buying the same size shoe for all students of the same age. People do not come that neatly packaged. We vary greatly at every age in size, physical and intellectual development, maturity, and so forth. If education is to be effective, educators need to respond to these differences (Benbow & Lubinski, 1994; Lubinski & Benbow, 1995).

A problem, however, is that many people believe acceleration is just another word for grade skipping. Yet acceleration is much more than that. It is also not meant to be used in isolation. The goal is to develop a combination of accelerative options, enrichment options, and out-of-school opportunities that reflect the best possible alternative for educating a specific child. This approach has been labeled curricular flexibility (Benbow & Stanley, 1983).

What does acceleration or curricular flexibility consist of? It includes:

- *Early admittance to school* (Proctor, Feldhusen, & Black, 1988). This is one of the best options for meeting the needs of gifted students whose advanced abilities are evident at an early age. It allows the student to enter school with a peer group with whom he or she will remain. It is also the least disruptive strategy for social and academic development. An example of an individual taking advantage of this option is Peter. At age 4 his IQ was found to exceed 140. He was already reading and doing basic mathematics. Although it was agreed that the appropriate placement for Peter was kindergarten, which is where he was placed, many of his basic skills were more highly developed than most of his classmates. His needs were handled through content acceleration and individual tutoring, options described later in this chapter. Now at age 20 Peter is about to graduate from college, Phi Beta Kappa, with a degree in physics. When asked how he felt about his acceleration, he was glad that it had happened. The biggest problem that he encountered because he was young for his grade was not having a driver's license until his senior year—well after all of his other friends. Yet the saving of time in school was well worth the temporary inconvenience, he said.
- *Grade skipping* (Feldhusen, Proctor, & Black, 1986). When most people hear the word acceleration, they assume grade skipping. Indeed, that is a common form of acceleration. Grade skipping is especially recommended for highly gifted students who are advanced in all subjects relative to their classmates or for those gifted students who just missed the age cutoff for school entrance or were held back by their parents for a year because they were close to the age cutoff. Grade skipping is most effective when implemented at a natural transition point in schools. For example, a good time to skip a grade is the year before there is a transition to a new school. That is, the recommendation may be made to have a child skip sixth grade if he or she will transition to middle school the next year. The child will thus be put into an environment where all children have made a new transition to a different school with different students. The accelerated child will, thereby, not be so conspicuous and will enter a grade with students for whom old friendship cliques have already been disrupted and new ones are ready to form. Tia, for example, skipped ninth grade—her last year of junior high school. Tia had exceptional scores on the

Scholastic Aptitude Test (SAT) when she took it as a 13-year-old. Both her verbal and math scores exceeded 600. Tia was also old in relation to her classmates. Her parents had waited a year before entering her into school. So, in essence, the grade skipping only brought her up to a level where she should have been in the first place. Not surprising (but a bit to her parents), Tia flourished through acceleration. She graduated from high school one of the top students in her class and is now majoring in chemical engineering in college. Tia continues to develop her abilities. For some individuals with highly exceptional talents, skipping more than one grade might be warranted. Colin was one such child. His parents discovered him reading *Time* magazine at age 5, being unaware until that time that he was able to read. (They had assumed that he was just looking at the pictures in *Time*.) Because of a late birthday, his school entrance was delayed by a year. Eventually, however, he regained that year and more. Colin ended up skipping grades 7, 9, and 10. Now, more than 20 years later, Colin is a distinguished professor in economics at a highly prestigious institution.

- *Entering college early with or without a high-school diploma* (Brody & Stanley, 1991; Eisenberg & George, 1979; Janos, Robinson, & Lunneborg, 1989; Robinson & Janos, 1986; Stanley & Benbow, 1983). This accelerative option may seem extreme, but it should be kept in mind that most high schools will award a high-school diploma after completion of 1 year of college. Richard serves as an example. After much consultation and agonizing over whether it was the right thing for their son, Richard's parents decided to allow him to leave high school at the end of 11th grade. His high school could offer Richard very little. Yet Richard could not graduate from his high school because he had not taken a year of American Government, a 12th-grade course required for graduation. His high school, by the way, adamantly opposed this early transition to college. Nonetheless, Richard went to college early and in his first year there was named the best physics student of the year and received other academic recognitions as well. One of the courses that Richard took in college was American Government. That allowed him to complete the requirements for his high-school diploma. Although Richard did receive his high-school diploma a year after he left high school, the school refused to allow him to participate in the graduation ceremonies. He sat in the audience and watched his friends graduate.

- *Entering a college early-entrance program* such as Simon's Rock College, the Texas Academy of Math and Science (Stanley, 1991), Mary Baldwin College, or the Transition Program at the University of Washington (Noble & Drummond, 1992; Robinson, 1996). These programs, although they vary widely in their philosophy and approach, are designed to meet the needs of students who are ready for college work but would like to be part of a peer group who have made the same decision to leave high school early. Many students complete these programs and then transfer to another university where they eventually obtain their baccalaureate. Some of the programs are able to grant high-school diplomas as well. Ingrid, for example, had exhausted her high-school curriculum after having attended accelerated summer and academic-year programs for several years. She needed college-level science and mathematics courses, but a suitable arrangement was difficult to negotiate for her in her hometown. Ingrid and her parents, therefore, decided that an early-entrance program was best for her overall, and she entered Simon's Rock at age 16. She has done well there, academically and socially, and is now planning to transfer to another university to complete her bachelor's degree.

How do students in general respond to such programs? Some selected quotes from students, contained in Noble and Drummond (1992), provide a glimpse of the students' feelings. The students who are quoted had been enrolled in the University of Washington's Transition Program, which admits highly capable 14-year-olds to a 1-year transition program that is followed by 4 years of college. Perhaps most telling is the following quote: "We were thrown out of the roles that we had occupied all through school, and forced to work for our grades. We learned how to fail. It was hard and painful at times, but I think it was also necessary. I also learned a lot socially. It was a whole new ball game because none of us was cast in the role of the class brain anymore, or we didn't have to work hard not to be cast that way because we were all pretty much in the same boat academically." One student's answer to the question of what are the best and worst things about entering college early also was revealing: "The best thing is being able to critically think about what you're doing and not accept things as they are. The worst is that everything about what I wanted to do used to be very clear, but now there are lots of ideas running through my head. All options seem to be a little bit improper or gray. I'm always unsatisfied and can't answer questions about how things are going or what I'm going to do with my life. Essentially the best thing is also the worst." Finally, in response to the perennial question "But what about the prom?" one student summed up the general feeling well: "If that's the most important thing about high school, why should I go?"

- *The International Baccalaureate (IB) Program.* The IB program is designed to facilitate admission to colleges and universities around the world. In the United States, students who complete the IB program have mastered two languages and are frequently allowed to enter college with sophomore standing. (For a more complete description, see Chapter 13, p. 237.)
- *Content acceleration* (Kolitch & Brody, 1992). This idea, taking a course (e.g., Algebra 1) 1 or 2 years earlier than typical, is a simple one. If a student is reading at the level of the fourth graders in his or her school but is placed only in the second grade, the student should be allowed to take reading with the fourth graders. Similarly, if the student is ready for algebra in seventh grade, that student should be allowed to take algebra with the eighth graders. In some school systems, an advanced middle-school student might go to the high school in the morning or for first period for the classes he or she needs and then return to the middle school for the remaining classwork. Take, for example, Claire, who

had finished Algebra I as part of a fast-paced summer program for gifted students. (Fast-paced summer programs are described later in this section.) She was ready to take either Algebra II or geometry but neither course was available at her middle school. Her school arranged for her to take geometry at the high school during first period and then return to the middle school for the rest of the day.

- *Taking college courses on a part-time basis while in secondary school or dual enrollment in high school and college* (Solano & George, 1976). This idea is very much like the one just presented. The only difference is that with the present option students take advantage of *college-level* curricula available at a local college, community college, or university. Students often take such courses either to replace a high-school course that is not sufficiently challenging or to obtain access to advanced coursework not available at their high school. Take, for example, Brandon. He had completed the entire math curriculum at his high school but was not ready to go to college. He decided to take a class on differential equations at the local university. One of his class periods during the day was designated for this course. Two other students, twin brothers, who also were not quite ready to leave high school, enrolled in the closest university to meet their needs for advanced mathematics and science. They enrolled in differential equations and physics for physics and engineering majors. To get to class, they obtained a school driving permit and drove themselves! They were only 15 at the time but, nevertheless, were among the top students in their college classes.

- *Taking special fast-paced classes during the summer or academic year* (Bartkovich & George, 1980; Durden, 1980; Stanley & Stanley, 1986; Swiatek & Benbow, 1991; VanTassel-Baska, 1983). There are many summer programs offering fast-paced courses across the United States. Some of the larger programs are sponsored by Johns Hopkins University (Center for the Advancement of Academically Talented Youth—CTY), Duke University (Talent Identification Program), Northwestern University (Center for Talent Development), Purdue University (Gifted Education Resource Institute), Iowa State University (Office of Precollegiate Programs for Talented and Gifted), the University of Iowa, and the University of Denver (Rocky Mountain Talent Search). In these programs, students who as seventh graders scored at the level of college-bound, high-school seniors on the SAT or the American College Test (ACT) study one topic in depth and at a fast pace so that they cover a semester of college work or a year of high-school work in about 3 weeks. The first such fast-paced class, in mathematics, was created by Julian Stanley and began in June 1972. After years of refining the process in mathematics, Stanley moved on to pioneer fast-paced classes in the sciences and humanities. Students can master in 3 weeks a year of high-school physics, a year or two of precalculus mathematics, a semester of writing at the college level, or even a semester of college philosophy. Kurt, an exceptionally bright young man (his SAT–M score as an eighth grader was at the top of the scale), actually managed in 3 intensive weeks to demonstrate mastery of the entire high-school sequence of precalculus mathematics (Algebra I through functions) and, thus, was ready for calculus in the following school year.

Long-term evaluations of programs offering fast-paced classes have been extremely positive (see, e.g., Benbow, Lubinski, & Suchy, 1996; Swiatek & Benbow, 1996). Some excerpts from the student questionnaires used for the evaluation of these programs by Benbow, Lubinski, and Suchy (1996) might best give the flavor of the findings: "Creating a 3-6 week haven for gifted to learn with and from one another." "Seeing so many other people like me.... It helped me gain confidence in who and what I am." "Enabled me to meet three other women who were gifted and whose achievements continue to encourage me in terms of my future." "Finally, the chance to learn at the pace and intensity I had always longed for."

- *Completing 2 years of a subject in 1 year*. With this option, the student doubles up on courses in 1 year in order to subsequently reach higher level coursework. Gwen, for example, had scored 500 on the SAT–M as a seventh grader (the average score for a college-bound senior is almost 500). Yet she had been unable to take algebra at her middle school. Thus, in order to reach a level of math that was more challenging and to be able to complete calculus in high school, she enrolled in Algebra II and geometry concurrently.
- *Telescoping curricula*. With telescoping curricula, schools provide students with the means of completing, for example, 4 years of high school in 3 years or completing, say, the third- and fourth-grade curriculum in the same year.
- *Compressing curricula*. Here, the curriculum is compressed or compacted in such a way that it can be completed by gifted students in much less time (Reis et al., 1993; Stanley, 1978). One means of doing this is to allow students to skip those units in which they have already attained mastery. If, for example, a student can solve correctly four of the five most difficult math problems in a chapter, the student can be allowed to skip that chapter and go on to the next, with the procedure repeated for subsequent chapters. Alternatively, diagnostic testing can be used to determine what the student knows and does not know in a subject matter area; then, the student is taught only those concepts that he or she has not already mastered (Benbow, 1986; Stanley, 1978). In the fast-paced mathematics classes pioneered by the Study of Mathematically Precocious Youth (SMPY), for example, a standardized algebra test is used to determine what concepts a student has not mastered, and then instruction is focused only upon those concepts. It is through this diagnostic testing followed by prescriptive instruction (DT-PI) that Kurt was able to cover 4 years of high-school mathematics and Amy a full year of algebra in just 3 weeks. They came to the fast-paced mathematics class with different knowledge bases and rates of learning, and the instructors responded by developing individualized, compressed learning experiences that enabled each of them to optimize the amount learned.
- *Taking Advanced Placement (AP) courses and examinations* (Zak, Benbow, & Stanley, 1983). AP courses, which are different from honors courses, are col-

lege-level courses taught in high school that may garner college credit for the student if his or her final AP exam scores are sufficiently high. There are approximately 30 different AP courses that high schools can offer. The Advanced Placement program provides to schools, at no cost or at a nominal cost, syllabi and complete instructions for conducting AP courses. At the end of an AP course, students must take an AP examination, administered by the Educational Testing Service (ETS), and score well if they are to become eligible for college credit. Peter, for example, took several AP classes in high school and was able to enter college with advanced standing due to his high performance on the AP exams. Jill had done well on so many AP exams, some for which she only studied rather than taking a formal course, that she was able to enter a selective college as a sophomore.

Many professionals in gifted education view AP courses and exams as the best program option high schools can provide to their gifted students. Research has shown that students who completed AP courses had better academic records in college, graduated from college with more honors, engaged in more leadership activities, and took more advanced courses in college than students of equal ability who did not complete AP courses (Willingham & Morris, 1986).

- *Individual tutoring in advanced subject matter* (Stanley, 1979). Sometimes it is not practical or advisable to accelerate a gifted student or to further accelerate a gifted student who had earlier been accelerated. In such cases, how can one attend to the student's learning needs to ensure that the student receives an education that is commensurate with his or her abilities? Individual tutoring is one option. This tutoring could be provided by a college student, an older and more advanced gifted student, a senior citizen, or a teacher. Peter, the student described in the discussion about early admittance to school, had entered school early. Yet by third grade he had exhausted the math of even the most advanced curricula offered for his age. His parents had concerns about accelerating him further at that time, partly because Peter was shy and hence had difficulty making new friends. The solution in this case was to provide individual tutoring in mathematics once per week. The tutor was a college student. That way Peter continued to be stimulated in mathematics but could remain with his peers and friends.
- *Earning a master's degree simultaneously with the bachelor's degree.* This option is increasingly being offered by colleges and universities. It is especially attractive to gifted students who enter college with advanced standing and have a desire to obtain depth in training in one area. Trudy, for example, managed in 4 years to earn, concurrently, her bachelor's and master's degrees in computer science at Johns Hopkins University. She then entered industry to work.
- *Joint B.A./M.D. or B.A./Ph.D. programs.* Programs such as these exist but are relatively rare. This option is attractive to students who enter college firmly knowing what career they would like to pursue and eager to complete their

training rapidly. These may be students who received a broad education in high school through AP courses, the International Baccalaureate program, honors classes/seminars, or college classes. Their professional training would then proceed in a fashion that more closely resembles the system in Europe.

Stanley called the accelerative options a smorgasbord of accelerative opportunities (Stanley & Benbow, 1982). The idea is to help a gifted child select a combination of accelerative opportunities that will provide an education commensurate with his or her abilities. Some students choose none of the options or just one, whereas others select a combination of approaches. For example, Tia accelerated in mathematics and enrolled in a fast-paced summer program (twice) before she skipped a grade. Peter, in addition to receiving tutoring and entering school early, took AP classes in high school, enrolled in six fast-paced classes over the course of three summers, and took departmental exams to obtain college credit for some of his high-school work. Paul and Mary skipped several grades and managed to earn their high-school diplomas before entering college at age 14. The possible combinations are endless.

An in-depth exploration of one of the cases mentioned earlier—Colin, who was found reading *Time* at age 5—will illustrate how acceleration can work in the life of a gifted youngster. When Colin entered school, his primary teachers found him to be very bright and allowed him to work ahead. By the second grade, he was doing fourth- or fifth-grade work. At the end of the second grade, his family moved and advanced work ceased for a while. His schooling proceeded uneventfully until the fifth grade, when Colin was sent to a science academy for a few hours each week to learn about computers. Yet it was not long before Colin had exhausted the academy's resources, and his parents were forced to seek some professional advice. It was decided that it would be best for Colin to skip seventh grade, enroll in a fast-paced mathematics class, and take a college computer science course on release time from school. Colin fully agreed. Within 14 months, Colin completed not only eighth grade but 4.5 years of precalculus mathematics and, with a final grade of A, his first college course. With these impressive accomplishments behind him, it was decided that Colin should skip both the 9th and 10th grades. He then completed high school in 2 years. His high-school years were active and full of extracurricular activities, including chess club and the "It's Academic" quiz team. By the time Colin entered college at age 14, he had earned 34 credits of advanced standing. This enabled Colin to finish his bachelor's degree in quantitative studies in five semesters, and he graduated less than a month after his 17th birthday. One might have thought that tackling college at this pace might have meant little room for extracurricular activities. But Colin was quite active in college, especially on the school newspaper and in varsity golf. Colin went on to graduate school and earned an Ph.D. in economics. For several years after he received his Ph.D., he was offered and took several professorial positions at various prestigious schools. Currently, Colin is a full professor at a highly prestigious institution, having become a full professor at the young age of 32. Colin exemplifies, perhaps to the utmost degree, what the strategic use of acceleration can facilitate or accomplish.

In sum, acceleration essentially consists of providing to younger gifted students resources, curricula, or programs that were designed and are being used for older students (Benbow & Stanley, 1983). It is simply grouping for instruction without regard for age and is consistent with basic research findings revealing that gifted students are precocious or developmentally advanced (Dark & Benbow, 1990, 1991, 1994; Elkind, 1988). Acceleration interventions are incredibly cost-effective and are practical even for rural areas where high-ability students are often scarce (Benbow, 1991).

Guidelines for Using Acceleration

VanTassel-Baska (1986), Proctor et al. (1988), and Brody and Stanley (1991) developed sets of recommendations, not prescriptions, to guide the decision-making process for implementing acceleration. Some flexibility, of course, must be allowed to respond to individual differences and differing circumstances.

Selection of Students

The first recommendation is to study the nature of the gifted students who are candidates for acceleration. What are their characteristics? For grade acceleration, they should:

1. Have the ability to manipulate abstract symbol systems far better than their peers.
2. Be at least in the upper 2% of the general population in terms of general ability, which in terms of IQ would mean an IQ score of 130 or more (Gallagher, 1975; Terman & Oden, 1947). The further the child is from the typical entering age for the grade, the higher the IQ score needs to be. If the gifted child is close to the age cutoff, the IQ need not be as exceptional.
3. Be functioning intellectually and academically above the mean of the desired grade. As an example, early entrants to college should have college admissions test scores (SAT or ACT scores) that match or exceed the averages for the particular institution the student chooses to attend.
4. Not be underachievers.
5. Have exhausted the challenging opportunities available within their school or grade.
6. Have received a comprehensive psychological report attesting to their superior intellectual functioning, academic maturity or readiness, and social and emotional maturity.
7. Be free of any serious adjustment problems, socially and emotionally, and demonstrate a desire to learn.
8. Not be under pressure to accelerate.
9. Be entering a classroom where the receiving teacher is positive about the acceleration.

In addition, it may be useful to consider the students' physical size (Hildreth, 1966; Hollingworth, 1942; Morgan, 1957, 1959; Terman & Oden, 1947) and parental attitudes toward acceleration (Morgan, 1957, 1959).

For advancement other than grade acceleration, the criteria can be less stringent. Nevertheless, the child needs to demonstrate:

1. Advanced abilities in the subject area in which the advancement will take place (e.g., the child should be mathematically precocious if he or she is to be placed in a higher mathematics class or in a fast-paced class)
2. Motivation and desire to do accelerated work
3. An understanding of the implications of content acceleration or telescoping
4. Good achievement in current schoolwork

Although the fourth recommendation in each of these lists seems to imply that gifted underachievers should not be accelerated, at times acceleration is the appropriate course of action. In certain circumstances, a lack of challenge in school is pivotal in leading to underachievement. For such underachievers, acceleration may be an appropriate intervention (Rimm & Lovance, 1992; Whitmore, 1980).

Enhancing Effectiveness of Acceleration

Other recommendations have been provided in the area of enhancing the effectiveness of acceleration. There are several means whereby the positive effects of acceleration can be ensured or even enhanced. To make acceleration a more positive experience for students, educators may want to consider the following:

1. Accelerating more than just one student
2. The need for program modifications in addition to acceleration (e.g., career counseling, enrichment, independent study, mentorships, teaching higher order thinking skills, or teaching problem-solving)
3. Selecting a teacher who endorses acceleration, has the ability to modify the curriculum appropriately for gifted learners, exhibits an advanced knowledge base, and has good classroom management skills
4. Implementing acceleration on a trial basis
5. Accelerating students at natural transition points, that is, between rather than within schools
6. Having students complete some college or advanced high-school-level coursework (e.g., AP courses) if they are to enter college early
7. Arranging opportunities for students to interact socially with older students, prior to acceleration, to ensure that they will feel comfortable with their new peer group
8. Helping and advising students to avoid publicity and avoid discussing their age with their new peer group

Exemplary Programs

Providing further recommendations, VanTassel-Baska (1986) described and delineated the characteristics of exemplary acceleration programs. Grouping, individualization, in-depth enrichment, counseling, and discussion opportunities were vital components of these programs. Specifically, the program administrators tended to be cognizant of and attendant to the following:

1. The affective needs of the students
2. The students' needs for peer interaction and discussion
3. The necessity of reorganizing the curriculum to make it appropriate for the gifted, including teaching higher level thinking skills and providing means of compressing the curriculum
4. The usefulness of selecting materials that organize subject matter according to its structural and/or thematic nature
5. The need for diversity in teaching and learning experiences

In sum, acceleration works best when combined with other educational options designed to meet the learning needs of gifted students. How it is implemented relates to its outcomes.

Summary ~

This chapter began with a quotation from the *Prisoners of Time* report, which was prepared by the National Education Commission on Time and Learning. The commission recommended that the time devoted to mastering curricula should be adjusted to meet the needs of individual learners. Some students need more time, and others need less. Acceleration is a means by which educators can adjust (1) the time that gifted students require to demonstrate mastery of the curricula presented to them, and (2) the time used to introduce certain curricula. Acceleration is simply placement according to competence, a principle that goes unquestioned in athletics and in the arts.

Acceleration, moreover, comes in many different forms, which can be broadly characterized as grade skipping, content acceleration, and telescoping. It is an approach to teaching curricula that is flexible in regard to age and pace. Of all the services provided to gifted children, it has been shown to be the most effective (Kulik & Kulik, 1992; VanTassel-Baska, 1989). Lubinski and Benbow (1995) called the practice of avoiding the use of acceleration malpractice. Indeed, it does constitute a form of educational malpractice. To create excellence in education, we need to provide acceleration opportunities to more intellectually talented students.

References ~

Bartkovich, E. G., & George, W. C. (1980). *Teaching the gifted and talented in the mathematics class-room*. Washington, DC: National Education Association.

Benbow, C. P. (1986). SMPY's model for teaching mathematically precocious students. In J. S. Renzulli (Ed.), *Systems and models in programs for the gifted and talented* (pp. 1–25). Mansfield Center, CT: Creative Learning Press.

Benbow, C. P. (1991). Meeting the needs of gifted students through acceleration: A neglected resource. In

M. C. Wang, M. C. Reynolds, & H. J. Walberg (Eds.), *Handbook of special education* (Vol. 4, pp. 23–36). Elmsford, NY: Pergamon.

Benbow, C. P., & Lubinski, D. (1994). Individual differences among the gifted: How can we best meet their educational needs? In N. Colangelo, S. G. Assouline, & D. L. Ambroson (Eds.), *Talent development* (Vol. 2, pp. 83–100). Dayton, OH: Ohio Psychology Press.

Benbow, C. P., Lubinski, D., & Suchy, B. (1996). The impact of the SMPY model and programs from the perspective of the participant. In C. P. Benbow & D. Lubinski (Eds.), *Intellectual talent: Psychometric and social issues* (pp. 266–300). Baltimore, MD: Johns Hopkins University Press.

Benbow, C. P., & Stanley, J. C. (1983). Constructing educational bridges between high school and college. *Gifted Child Quarterly, 27,* 111–113.

Benbow, C. P., & Stanley, J. C. (1996). Inequity in equity: How "equity" can lead to inequity for high-potential students. *Psychology, Public Policy, and Law, 2,* 249–292.

Boatman, T. A., Davis, K. G., & Benbow, C. P. (1995). Best practices in gifted education. In A. Thomas & J. Grimes (Eds.), *Best practices in school psychology* (Vol. 3, pp. 1083–1096). Washington, DC: National Association of School Psychologists.

Brody, L. E., & Stanley, J. C. (1991). Young college students: Assessing factors that contribute to success. In W. T. Southern & E. D. Jones (Eds.), *The academic acceleration of gifted children* (pp. 102–132). New York: Teachers College Press.

Cronbach, L. J. (1996). Acceleration among the Terman males: Correlates in mid-life and after. In C. P. Benbow & D. Lubinski (Eds.), *Intellectual talent: Psychometric and social issues* (pp. 179–191). Baltimore, MD: Johns Hopkins University Press.

Dark, V. J., & Benbow, C. P. (1990). Mathematically talented students show enhanced problem translation and enhanced short-term memory for digit and spatial information. *Journal of Educational Psychology, 82,* 420–429.

Dark, V. J., & Benbow, C. P. (1991). Differential enhancement of working memory with mathematical and verbal precocity. *Journal of Educational Psychology, 83,* 48–60.

Dark, V. J., & Benbow, C. P. (1994). Type of stimulus mediates the relationship between working memory performance and type of precocity. *Intelligence, 19,* 337–357.

Daurio, S. P. (1979). Educational enrichment versus acceleration: A review of the literature. In W. C. George, S. J. Cohn, & J. C. Stanley (Eds.), *Educating the gifted: Acceleration and enrichment* (pp. 13–63). Baltimore, MD: Johns Hopkins University Press.

Durden, W. J. (1980). The Johns Hopkins program for verbally gifted youth. *Roeper Review, 2,* 34–37.

Eisenberg, A. R., & George, W. C. (1979). Early entrance to college: The Johns Hopkins experience. *College and University, 54,* 109–118.

Elkind, D. (1988). Acceleration. *Young Children, 43,* 2.

Feldhusen, J. F., Proctor, T. B., & Black, K. N. (1986). Guidelines for grade advancement of precocious children. *Roeper Review, 9,* 25–27.

Gallagher, J. J. (1975). *Teaching the gifted child* (2nd ed.). Boston: Allyn & Bacon.

Gallagher, J. J. (1985). *Teaching the gifted child* (3rd ed.). Boston: Allyn & Bacon.

Gallagher, J. J. (1996). Educational research and educational policy: The strange case of acceleration. In C. P. Benbow & D. Lubinski (Eds.), *Intellectual talent: Psychometric and social issues* (pp. 83–92). Baltimore, MD: Johns Hopkins University Press.

Gowan, J. C., & Demos, G. D. (1964). *The education and guidance of the ablest.* Springfield, IL: Charles C Thomas.

Hildreth, G. H. (1966). *Introduction to the gifted.* New York: McGraw-Hill.

Hollingworth, L. S. (1942). *Children above 180 IQ Stanford-Binet: Origin and development.* Yonkers, NY: World Book.

Janos, P. M., Robinson, N., & Lunneborg, C. E. (1989). Markedly early entrance to college: A multi-year comparative study of academic performance and psychological adjustment. *Journal of Higher Education, 60,* 496–518.

Keating, D. P. (1979). The acceleration/enrichment debate: Basic issues. In W. C. George, S. J. Cohn, & J. C. Stanley (Eds.), *Educating the gifted: Acceleration and enrichment* (pp. 217–220). Baltimore, MD: Johns Hopkins University Press.

Kolitch, E. R., & Brody, L. E. (1992). Mathematics acceleration of highly talented students: An evaluation. *Gifted Child Quarterly, 36,* 78–86.

Kulik, C. C., & Kulik, J. A. (1992). Effects of ability grouping on secondary school students: A meta-
analysis of evaluation findings. *American Educational Research Journal, 19,* 415–428.

Kulik, J. A., & Kulik, C. C. (1984). Effects of accelerated instruction on students. *Review of Educational
Research, 54,* 409–425.

Lincoln, E. A. (1929). The later performance of under-aged children admitted to school on the basis of
mental age. *Journal of Educational Research, 19,* 22–30.

Lubinski, D., & Benbow, C. P. (1995). Optimal development of talent: Respond educationally to individual differences in personality. *Educational Forum, 59,* 381–392.

Morgan, A. B. (1957). Critical factors in the academic acceleration of gifted children: Hypotheses based
on clinical data. *Psychological Reports, 3,* 71–77.

Morgan, A. B. (1959). Critical factors in the academic acceleration of gifted children: A follow-up study.
Psychological Bulletin, 5, 649–653.

National Education Commission on Time and Learning. (1994). *Prisoners of time.* Washington, DC: U.S.
Government Printing Office.

Noble, K. D., & Drummond, J. E. (1992). But what about the prom? Students' perceptions of early college entrance. *Gifted Child Quarterly, 36,* 106–111.

Otto, H. J. (1950). Elementary education—III. Organization and administration. In W. S. Monroe (Ed.),
Encyclopedia of educational research (pp. 367–383). New York: Macmillan.

Passow, A. H. (1996). Acceleration over the years. In C. P. Benbow & D. Lubinski (Eds.), *Intellectual talent: Psychometric and social issues* (pp. 93–98). Baltimore, MD: Johns Hopkins University Press.

Proctor, T. B., Feldhusen, J. F., & Black, K. N. (1988). Guidelines for early admission to elementary
school. *Psychology in the Schools, 25,* 41–43.

Reis, S. M., Westberg, K. L., Kulikowich, J., Caillard, F., Hebert, T., Plucker, J., Purcell, J., Rogers, J. B.,
& Smith, J. M. (1993). *Why not let high ability students start school in January? The curriculum
compacting study.* Storrs, CT: National Research Center on the Gifted and Talented.

Richardson, T. M., & Benbow, C. P. (1990). Long-term effects of acceleration on the social and emotional adjustment of mathematically precocious youth. *Journal of Educational Psychology, 82,*
464–470.

Rimm, S. B., & Lovance, K. J. (1992). The use of subject and grade skipping for the prevention and reversal of underachievement. *Gifted Child Quarterly, 36,* 100–105.

Robinson, H. B. (1983). A case for radical acceleration: Programs of the Johns Hopkins University and
the University of Washington. In C. P. Benbow & J. C. Stanley (Eds.), *Academic precocity: Aspects
of its development* (pp. 139–159). Baltimore, MD: Johns Hopkins University Press.

Robinson, N. (1996). Acceleration as an option for the highly gifted adolescent. In C. P. Benbow & D.
Lubinski (Eds.), *Intellectual talent: Psychometric and social issues* (pp. 169–178). Baltimore, MD:
Johns Hopkins University Press.

Robinson, N., & Janos, P. (1986). Psychological adjustment in a college-level program of marked academic acceleration. *Journal of Youth and Adolescence, 15,* 51–60.

Solano, C. H., & George, W. C. (1976). College courses and educational facilitation for the gifted. *Gifted
Child Quarterly, 20,* 274–285.

Stanley, J. C. (1978). SMPY's DT-PI model: Diagnostic testing followed by prescriptive instruction.
Intellectually Talented Youth Bulletin, 6, 1–2.

Stanley, J. C. (1979). How to use a fast-pacing math mentor. *Intellectually Talented Youth Bulletin, 6,* 1–2.

Stanley, J. C. (1991). A better model for residential high schools for talented youth. *Phi Delta Kappan,
72,* 471–473.

Stanley, J. C., & Benbow, C. P. (1982). Educating mathematically precocious youth: Twelve policy recommendations. *Educational Researcher, 11*(5), 4–9.

Stanley, J. C., & Benbow, C. P. (1983). Extremely young college graduates: Evidence of their success.
College and University, 58, 361–371.

Stanley, J. C., & Stanley, B. K. S. (1986). High-school biology, chemistry, or physics learned well in three
weeks. *Journal of Research in Science Teaching, 23,* 237–250.

Swiatek, M. A., & Benbow, C. P. (1991). A ten-year longitudinal follow-up of participants in a fast-paced mathematics course. *Journal for Research in Mathematics Education, 22,* 138–150.

Swiatek, M. A., & Benbow, C. P. (1992). Nonintellectual correlates of satisfaction with acceleration. *Journal of Youth and Adolescence, 21,* 699–723.

Terman, L. M., & Oden, M. H. (1947). The gifted child grows up: Twenty-five years' follow-up of a superior group. In *Genetic studies of genius* (Vol. 4). Stanford, CA: Stanford University Press.

Top students subject of ETS study. (1991, fall). *Teaching Exceptional Children, 71.*

U.S. Department of Education. (1986). *What works.* Washington, DC.

VanTassel-Baska, J. (1983). Illinois state-wide replication of the Johns Hopkins Study of Mathematically Precocious Youth. In C. P. Benbow & J. C. Stanley (Eds.), *Academic precocity: Aspects of its development* (pp. 179–191). Baltimore, MD: Johns Hopkins University Press.

VanTassel-Baska, J. (1986). Acceleration. In C. J. Maker (Ed.), *Critical issues in gifted education* (pp. 179–198). Rockville, MD: Aspen Publications.

VanTassel-Baska, J. (1989). Appropriate curriculum for gifted learners. *Educational Leadership, 46,* 19–27.

VanTassel-Baska, J. (1996). Contributions of the talent-search concept to gifted education. In C. P. Benbow & D. Lubinski (Eds.), *Intellectual talent: Psychometric and social issues* (pp. 236–245). Baltimore, MD: Johns Hopkins University Press.

Washburne, C., & Raths, L. (1928). Selection of under-age children for entrance into school. *Educational Administration and Supervision, 14,* 185–188.

Whitmore, J. R. (1980). *Giftedness, conflict, underachievement.* Boston: Allyn & Bacon.

Willingham, W. W., & Morris, M. (1986). Four years later: A longitudinal study of Advanced Placement students in college. In *College Board Reports No. 86-2.* New York: College Board.

Zak, P. M., Benbow, C. P., & Stanley, J. C. (1983). AP exams: The way to go! *Roeper Review, 6,* 100–101.

Study Questions ~

1. What is acceleration? Do you think it is an appropriate alternative for gifted students? Why or why not?

2. What is the research evidence on acceleration?

3. What arguments are prevalent among educators to discourage the use of acceleration practices? Is acceleration an expensive program or placement adjustment for schools to make? Explain your answer.

4. How many acceleration options can you describe? Can you articulate the differences between them? What, for instance, is the difference between telescoping and content compression?

5. What are some considerations in making the decision to accelerate a student?

6. What steps can be taken to enhance the effectiveness of the use of acceleration?

7. How do you feel about acceleration? Describe any concerns you may have about the practice and the basis for your concerns.

17

Evaluating Programs for the Gifted

Ken Seeley

Dr. Stern, the director of curriculum for a mid-sized school district, has just called in the school district's coordinator of gifted education to explain that some board members and a few principals think the district's funding for gifted children could be better spent on enrichment for all students. After all, she said, "the gifted children always get all the extra attention and academic goodies." The gifted coordinator pled his case that the current program is addressing important needs and that to do away with it would actually hinder the growth of the gifted students. Dr. Stern agreed that an evaluation of the gifted program might be in order and asked the coordinator to work with the teachers of the gifted to design an evaluation plan. The future of the program would depend on the outcome of the evaluation.

As stated by Renzulli (1975), "The general purpose of evaluation is to gather, analyze and disseminate information that can be used to make decisions about educational programs" (p. 2). In any discussion of evaluation, we must examine the area of decision-making, given that we rarely encounter situations in which only one simple decision is to be made. In fact, evaluation provides information for a series of interactive decisions that are typically directed toward program improvement. The decisions themselves also should be subject to evaluation, for evaluation and decision-making continue to intertwine in the evolution of a program. Evaluation is the "bottom line" for creating defensible programs.

Hunsaker and Callahan (1993) studied current practices in the evaluation of gifted programs by securing and analyzing program evaluation reports from three sources: (1) the professional literature, (2) an appeal to professionals through journals, newsletters, and conferences, and (3) a mass mailing to state-level coordinators and local districts. Although several hundred responses ensued, only 70 reports were suitable for analysis. Among their findings were the following:

- A majority of reports made summative findings, but only a third addressed formative issues.
- Over half of the evaluations were conducted by internal evaluators (role unspecified).
- Students, teachers, and parents were the primary sources of information.
- Simple descriptive techniques were used in almost two thirds of the evaluations; multiple data analysis techniques were used in fewer than half.
- Only one fourth of the reports included recommendations with accompanying activities and timelines for implementation.

A major concern brought to light by this study is the paucity of reports that were made available, perhaps due to the nonexistence of such reports in the field.

The importance of evaluation components was highlighted by Callahan and Caldwell (1995):

> We need to evaluate whether the school system has identified the right children for a particular type of differentiation, whether the curriculum is in place to deliver the differentiation, whether the curriculum is appropriately differentiated, whether the teachers are appropriately trained and have the skills to deliver the curriculum, and whether the students achieve the goals of the curriculum. (p. 1)

Who Should Conduct Evaluations? ~

Many think that evaluation is the province of administrators and that teachers should not be involved. Nevertheless, because evaluation affects the future of the gifted program (and sometimes its continued existence), teachers now are taking a leadership role in carrying out effective evaluation. At certain times in the evolution of programs, it may also be helpful to have someone from outside help the gifted staff and administration with the evaluation. Callahan (cited in Kirschenbaum, 1993, p. 29) commented on the utility of bringing in an evaluation expert at four key junctures in the development of a gifted program—(1) at the beginning, so that the groundwork for evaluation is incorporated into the planning, or when major changes are being considered, (2) after a program has been operating for 4 or 5 years, when an outside perspective may offer some freshness, (3) when a drastic change occurs because of new administrative personnel or an influx of money, and (4) when there is a groundswell of criticism or when key support is beginning to erode. The program staff should request help from an outside consultant in transferring his or her expertise into the existing system so that future outside services will be unnecessary. In this way, the consultant functions in a "teaching" capacity, and the gifted program avoids creating a dependency on outside services.

The appropriate person(s) to conduct the evaluation depends upon many factors, such as audience, level of sophistication needed, and scope. But teacher input is vital. As those closest to the program and its students, teachers bring the best understandings of what is going well and what should be improved.

How Does a Needs Assessment Relate to Evaluation? ∾

Scriven and Roth (1978) stated that "needs assessment is absolutely fundamental to evaluation: There is no way to do a complete evaluation without knowing (or at least making a reasonable guess) about what clients or consumers need" (p. 1). A needs assessment is the logical first step in program development and program evaluation. Even if a gifted program has been in place for a number of years, a periodic needs assessment is important. Needs change, as do programs and services within schools.

Developing and maintaining a special program depends on administrators and staff being able to demonstrate that gifted students' needs are being met in the existing program. Also necessary is to demonstrate how these needs are being met and at what level. Thus, needs form the base and rationale for the efficacy of the program. As such, the needs typically underlie the evaluated goals and objectives.

Educators often need information about gifted education before they can rate their attitudes toward certain approaches to it. It is strongly recommended that any needs assessment be preceded by some staff development activity so that the assessment reflects informed choices about preferences. For example, because of the prevailing negative attitudes toward acceleration, educators must be informed about the positive aspects, particularly as they are supported by research and practice.

Table 17.1 presents an outline of the steps to follow in carrying out an effective needs assessment. The three major areas of the table correspond to the major elements of a needs assessment. The first element, determining the current status of the program, will provide a starting place for identifying the major concerns and evaluation questions that the needs assessment might identify. The second element, determining the approach to the needs assessment, will identify who might be contacted and how one might gather information. The final element, describing the actual content of the needs assessment, would vary depending upon the situation. The major areas to tap are identified. It must be recognized that we cannot evaluate everything in a program. The best way to limit the scope of the evaluation is through a needs assessment, which helps to clarify the most important or urgent concerns.

What Is the Difference Between Research and Evaluation? ∾

The implicit basis of research is comparison. Research requires approaches that are different from evaluation approaches. Research designs necessitate comparisons in order to control variables. Statistical analysis is also required to account for variance

Table 17.1 ∼
Outline for a Needs Assessment

I. Current status of gifted programs
  A. Pilot programs?
  B. Administrative commitment?
  C. Any staff development?
  D. Type of student assessments? Portfolios? Standardized tests?

II. Approach
  A. Surveys for all administrators
    1. Central office instructional administrators
    2. Building principals
    3. Teachers
    4. Parents
  B. Structured interviews
    1. All curriculum coordinators
    2. Assistant superintendents for instruction
    3. At least 50% of principals

III. Content of needs assessment
  A. Essential elements of a definition of "gifted"
  B. Philosophy and attitudes
    1. Toward acceleration
    2. Toward enrichment
    3. Toward general education teacher role
    4. Toward giftedness
    5. Toward IQ testing and identification
  C. Program prototype preferences
    1. Rating of major options
    2. Amount of time for special instruction
    3. Amount of regularly funded staff time commitment
    4. Space commitment for program
    5. Materials budget support
    6. Parent involvement
  D. Staff development
    1. Released time for teachers
    2. Administrator involvement in training
  E. Community resources already developed
    1. School partnership with community
    2. Community volunteer program in schools
    3. Service learning opportunities for students
  F. Leadership role for principal
    1. Organizing building-level planning
    2. Initiating parent education activities
    3. Demonstrating commitment to past educational innovations

or relationships that may exist in comparing groups or approaches. Certainly research is needed, and it can be included as part of an evaluation design. But different standards must be used in designing research than in designing evaluation. If decision-makers want a comparative study, research is required with all of its attendant standards and procedures. Research usually is more time-consuming and costly to carry out than is evaluation.

An evaluation design should be conceptualized as an integral part of the program development so that each facet of evaluation relates to program objectives or anticipated outcomes. Evaluation provides decision-making information regarding how close a program comes to its predetermined standards. Any discrepancies allow decision-makers to address program improvement needs.

The critical issue in differentiating research from evaluation appears when evaluators attempt to answer research questions with evaluation designs not intended to provide research data. Decisions are then based on designs that did not adequately control variables or adequately analyze comparative data. The classic example of a research question that uses evaluation designs, with unsuccessful answers, is "Is enrichment better than acceleration for gifted students?" A comparative study must be done to answer this question.

What Instrumentation Is Needed for Evaluation? ~

The instruments needed to gather data for evaluation have a broad definition for the purposes of this discussion. They can range from a structured interview with parents to a test of student mastery. The purpose of instruments is to measure and describe a condition or level of performance. They also include a means to record data in some systematic manner.

Critical issues with regard to instrumentation and measurement for evaluation reside in two areas. The first issue is the *appropriateness* of the instrument to provide pertinent and meaningful information for the evaluation. The second issue is the *interpretation and presentation of data* gathered by the instrument.

The field of gifted education is replete with teacher-made evaluation instruments. These typically survey students, parents, teachers, mentors, and administrators to gain their perceptions of the gifted program. These data are aggregated into a report upon which decisions are made concerning program modification and maintenance. Often these "soft" data are supplemented with "hard" data from standardized tests of achievement, intelligence, and creativity.

Although such a framework for evaluation is sound conceptually, the measurements are too often done with instruments that are subject to a good deal of measurement error. The soft data from teacher-made surveys can provide excellent descriptive information for program administrators, but these global data are too often interpreted as specific. Groups of respondents are compared to each other using different instruments, which results in measurement error. For instance, a student may respond to the survey item, "How did you like the unit on computer-based retrieval systems? (Rate 1–5.)" The parents might be asked to respond to, "Rate your child's attitudes toward computer usage. (Rate 1–5.)" Although these items are similar in some ways and provide some descriptive data, they are different enough that comparisons should not be made. Yet we find mean scores extrapolated from such samples of the population and decisions made on the basis of these scores. Such measurement errors affect the quality of the evaluation.

Even hard data from standardized measures are subject to misuse and misinterpretation. In gifted education we continue to wrestle with balancing hard data against soft data. Hard data comprise test scores and quantifiable measures. Soft data usually consist of observations, rating scales, and professional judgments. With the advent of so-called authentic assessment, we add student products gathered into portfolios of work as more soft data. The ceiling effects of achievement tests and the variations and biases of intelligence tests and creativity tests also confound decision-making.

This discussion is not intended to dissuade anyone from using both soft and hard data in evaluating programs. Rather, we must attend to the measurement problems inherent in using any kind of instrument and guard against sweeping generalizations upon which important decisions are to be made. We must use all the data we can gather to create defensible programs for gifted children. But the measurement and interpretation must be done well with good instruments that attend to the focus of the evaluation and to the audience for the evaluation. Principles of *validity* and *reliability* should be addressed for all instruments. Local norms that attend to these principles can be established for frequently used instruments.

What Constitutes Excellence in Evaluation? ~

Stufflebeam and Webster (1983) provided an excellent taxonomy of different models of evaluation. The authors distinguished between pseudo-evaluations, which they described as evaluations politically controlled or manipulated for public relations reasons; quasi-evaluations, which provide data that are helpful but independent of worth; and true evaluations, which assess worth. Within the category of true evaluations, they identified six models. The first two models, accreditation and policy studies, are not specific to program evaluation, but the last four models provide a useful framework for conceptualizing approaches to program-specific evaluation efforts. These four models, their distinguishing purposes, and their pioneering developers are delineated in Table 17.2.

Guidelines for these evaluation models, which represent a synthesis of ideas and concepts from other major authors in education evaluation (Gage, 1970; Stake & Denny, 1969; Stufflebeam, 1971) as well as from Stake, Stufflebeam, and Webster are presented in Table 17.3. These guidelines constitute a comprehensive model for excellence in evaluation of educational programs. The primary areas to be addressed in planning comprehensive education evaluation are (1) the context of the evaluation, (2) the audience for the evaluation, (3) the classes of decisions to be made, (4) the usefulness of evaluation information, and (5) ethical considerations. These areas

Table 17.2 ∼
A Taxonomy of Evaluation Models

Model No.	Model Type	Purpose	Pioneer
1	Decision-oriented studies	To provide a knowledge and value base for making and defending decisions	Cronbach, Stufflebeam
2	Consumer-oriented studies	To judge the relative merits of alternative goods and services	Scriven
3	Client-centered studies	To foster understanding of activities and how they are valued in a given setting and from a variety of perspectives	Stake
4	Connoisseur-based studies	To critically describe, appraise, and illuminate an object	Eisner, Guba

Note: Adapted from *An Analysis of Values-Orientation Study Types (True Evaluation)* (pp. 39–40)

should guide the formulation of evaluation objectives, design, instrumentation, data gathering, and dissemination of results.

Context

Context of the evaluation refers to the setting, including people and program. Front-end analysis by the evaluator is necessary to determine attitudes of the audience toward the evaluation process. These attitudes can determine the accuracy of data sources and the level of openness to evaluation information. The context also attends to variations within and between programs. Rarely is a program not impacted by other programs. The interactive effects of programs should be part of the context description. Finally, the roles and goals of the evaluator and audience have to be made explicit during the course of the evaluation. The audience may expect a summative evaluation (a final report) when a formative evaluation (work-in-progress description) would be appropriate.

Audience

The audience for the evaluation greatly affects the formulation of the evaluation design. If the audience is homogeneous, with similar information needs, the steps of gathering and reporting data are easier and more focused. If there are a number of different audiences, the design should differentiate objectives, methods, and reporting procedures.

Table 17.3~
Model Guidelines for Evaluation

Major Areas	Subcomponents	Comments
1. Context of the evaluation	1.1 *Attitudes* toward evaluation	1.1 Evaluation raises anxiety and often negative attitudes.
	1.2 *Variations* within and between programs	1.2 Programs being evaluated are rarely homogeneous within themselves.
	1.3 *Roles and goals* of evaluator and audience	1.3 There must be a good match between evaluator and audience.
2. Audience for the evaluation	2.1 *Single-channel reporting* to a person or group with the same information needs.	2.1 Having a homogeneous audience simplifies the process of identifying decisions, sources of information, and appropriate reporting procedures.
	2.2 *Multichannel reporting* to several audiences	2.2 Several audiences require separate considerations based on information needs for decisions.
3. Classes of decisions	3.1 *Intervention* information for decisions	3.1 This is information for yes-no decisions. Is intervention needed?
	3.2 *Reaction* information for decisions	3.2 Information from evaluation data must allow for easy retrieval and reaction to a decision request.
	3.3 *Planning* information for decisions	3.3 Planning decisions require a broad information base for viable alternatives.
	3.4 *Adoption* information for decisions	3.4 Adoption decisions are based on known, effective alternatives to be applied to local conditions.

(continued)

Table 17.3 continued

	3.5 *Individual vs. group decisions* requiring different evaluation data	3.5 Individual decision information is attained with some certainty. Group decisions require attention to various levels and types of information for members of the group.
4. Usefulness of evaluation information	4.1 *Scientific nature* of data to assist credibility	4.1 The validity and reliability of the data should be made clear.
	4.2 *Relevance* of data to make information obtained useful	4.2 To be relevant, the data must apply to contingencies in meeting program objectives.
	4.3 *Significant* data important in making decisions	4.3 Data must be weighted for importance to specific conditions.
	4.4 *Scope* of data to cover evaluation problems	4.4 Scope of the evaluation must key on its major elements related to necessary decisions.
	4.5 *Credibility* as perceived by the audience from the information	4.5 The evaluator must consider the audience's cognitive and affective response to the evaluation data.
	4.6 *Timeliness* as a major factor in usefulness of data	4.6 Time has three dimensions in evaluation: lag time (time between information need and information availability), time points (specific times when data are needed), and readiness (when the audience is most open to receive information).

(continued)

Table 17.3 continued

	4.7 *Efficiency* of evaluation data (financial value of information related to its usefulness)	4.7 The value of data to be gathered must be weighted based on the cost of obtaining the information. Priorities must be set by evaluator working with audience.
5. Ethical considerations	5.1 *Candor* to ensure accuracy and completeness of information	5.1 The evaluator should avoid unsupported judgments and biases and be candid with the audience.
	5.2 *Confidentiality*	5.2 The evaluator must be sensitive to when confidentiality can be and should be guaranteed in sharing evaluation data.
	5.3 *Scientific caution* to guide interpretation or inferences from data reported	5.3 Limitations on inferences from the evaluation must be a part of the final evaluation report.

Classes of Decisions

Classes of decisions to be made from the evaluation are important determiners of methodology. Some decision-makers may need to know only if intervention in a program is needed or not needed. Other decision-makers may want the evaluation to produce a pool of data that can be drawn on for a specific reaction to a decision request. Such a data pool is important for planning decisions that require a number of alternatives. Adoption decisions, based on data from successful programs in place elsewhere that could be transported for adoption locally, are often necessary. Data for individual decision-makers can be directed to the decision-maker's needs, but when decisions are to be made by groups, the evaluator must attend to various levels and types of information required by group members.

Usefulness of Information

The usefulness of evaluation information is perhaps the hallmark of good evaluation practice. Too often evaluation is an "add-on" activity to meet minimal accountability demands. In such situations, decisions are based on limited information from selective sources that do not represent relevant constituencies.

To be useful, evaluation data must be valid and reliable. The scientific nature of the data gathering and analysis lends credibility to the results. The information obtained should be relevant to the audiences in its application to program decisions. The most precise evaluation data are useless if they do not translate into effective decisions significant to program management. The evaluator must assist the audience in weighing the significance of data when applied to specific conditions. Audiences tend to infer significance to specific situations from data that are not directly applicable. These types of inference error result in poor decisions. The scope of the evaluation must be sufficiently broad to address the evaluation problems. Credibility of the data must be considered from both cognitive and affective dimensions. It is important for evaluation information to be well founded, but sensitivity to its impact on people should guide the format in which it is reported. Timeliness is another important component of how useful the evaluation data are viewed. The information should be available when needed for decision-making but also reported when the audience is most open to receive it.

The final component of usefulness of the evaluation is efficiency. Often evaluation demands exceed resources. The evaluator must assist the audience in setting priorities with attendant costs, so that the most useful information can be gathered for the best financial value.

Ethics

Ethical considerations must overlay all aspects of program evaluation. To this end, three areas should be considered: candor, confidentiality, and scientific caution. *Candor* requires openness and accuracy in gathering and reporting data. *Confidentiality* may have to be assured when providing certain information to different audiences. *Scientific caution* has to be a part of the interpretation in order to limit inferences. Even the best instruments and statistical designs have limitations. Cautions must be clearly stated when reporting data.

How Do We Get Started? ~

To illustrate how program administrators can get started in program evaluation, an overall view of an evaluation system is presented in Table 17.4. What is done to get started and how to follow through on each step are outlined. Figure 17.1 presents a flow chart of evaluation activities that graphically represents this process.

How Do We Make Evaluation Meaningful? ~

The best way to make evaluation meaningful is to be sure to look at program outcomes as part of the process. Too often, evaluation looks only at inputs or processes in the program, such as how many children were served in the advanced math seminar. We need to go one step further to answer the question, "What happened as a result of the math seminar?" When we take that step, we begin to address outcomes and provide meaning. If our evaluation produces accurate data, we can be

Table 17.4~
Overview of an Evaluation System

Before You Start	When You Get Started	After You Get Started	Down the Road
Justify the need for this type of program.	Start small and add on later.	Have faith in your decisions and choices.	Use a variety of instruments to check on your perceptions of how the program is going:
Review school district procedures for starting pilot programs.	Allow enough lead time to bring all those involved along with you as you go.	Keep thorough, accurate records of the process used and the students' progress.	Rating scales Checklists Observation systems Questionnaires Logs
Gather input from *all* publics who will be affected by this program. (What are their concerns and interests?)	Continually check your perceptions with one or more of the easy feedback techniques.	Document with lots of pictures, graphs, diaries, and so on.	Interview schedules Anecdotal records Inventories
Write an evaluation plan with readily observable activities that anyone can follow.	Identify those things that should be changed, and make appropriate recommendations.	Get a good idea of the costs in terms of time, money, people involvement, and so on.	Using a "buddy system," exchange visits with people involved in another program and see if you can verify their perceptions of that program.
	Be on guard for little problems that can grow into bigger problems a little later.	Make some judgments about the program as implemented in comparison to the intended program.	Change those things that need to be changed to make the program effective ad efficient.
		Make changes according to pupil needs and building-level priorities.	Prepare appropriate information to support the continuation of your program and allow others to adopt some or all of your model.

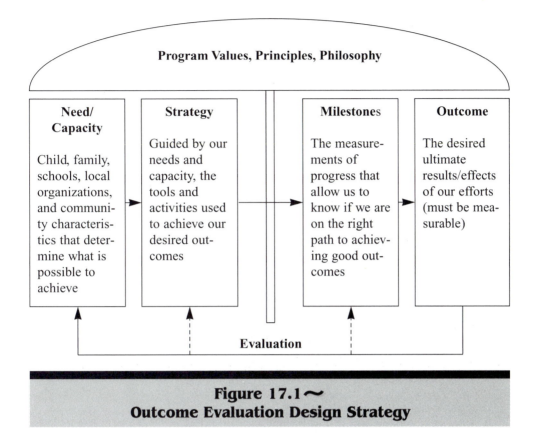

Figure 17.1 ~
Outcome Evaluation Design Strategy

sure it is meaningful if we interpret the data in three ways suggested by Williams (1996, p. 14):

1. As *performance information,* which tells us how much progress we are making toward outcomes
2. As *predictive information,* which guides us into the future based on current or past performance
3. As *early warning information,* which alerts us to changes or shifts that will likely create a problem if not corrected.

Figure 17.1 shows the essential ingredients of an outcome-based evaluation. The umbrella must be the program values, principles, or philosophy. The evaluation process addresses four areas under the umbrella: needs and capacities of the program, its strategies, which must match the needs and the desired outcomes, the milestones or benchmarks that we might use to look at interim progress, and finally, the measurable outcomes.

Summary ～

An evaluation of programs for the gifted begins with a needs assessment and continues through the development of the program. Evaluation monitors program development in order to inform decisions along the way. Sometimes consultants from outside the program are needed to assist in evaluation, but teachers of the gifted always should be intimately involved in the process.

The model guidelines for evaluation presented in this chapter should help practitioners view the major considerations in evaluation design and implementation. These also can be used as a means of structuring an evaluation when using outside resources. Whatever strategies are used, the best way to give meaning to evaluations is to use an outcomes orientation.

References ～

Callahan, C. N., & Caldwell, M. S. (1995). *A practitioner's guide to evaluating programs for the gifted.* Washington, DC: National Association of Gifted Children.

Gage, G. (1970). Distribution of information. In C. F. Paulson (Ed.), *A strategy for evaluation design.* Salem: Oregon State System of Higher Education.

Hunsaker, S. L., & Callahan, C. M. (1993). Evaluation of gifted programs: Current practices. *Journal for the Education of the Gifted, 16*(2), 190–200.

Kirschenbaum, R. J. (1993). An interview with Carolyn M. Callahan: Part 2. *Gifted Child Quarterly, 37*(3), 28–33.

Renzulli, J. (1975). *A guidebook for evaluating programs for the gifted and talented.* Ventura, CA: Office of the County Superintendent of Schools.

Scriven, M., & Roth, J. (1978, spring). Needs assessment, concept and practice. *New Directions for Program Evaluation, 1,* 1–11.

Stake, R. E., & Denny, T. (1969). Needed concepts and techniques for utilizing more fully the potential of evaluation (pp. 83–131). In R. W. Tyler (Ed.), *Educational evaluation: New roles, new means* (68th yearbook of the National Society for the Study of Education, Part 2). Chicago: University of Chicago Press.

Stufflebeam, D. L. (1971). *Educational evaluation and decision-making.* Itasca, IL: F. E. Peacock.

Stufflebeam, D., & Webster, W. (1983). An analysis of alternative approaches to evaluation. In D. Stufflebeam & W. Webster (Eds.), *Evaluation models* (pp. 23–43). Boston: Kluwer.

Williams, H. S. (1996). *Innovating, 6*(2), 9–24.

Study Questions ～

1. Why should teachers of the gifted be involved in evaluating programs?
2. What kind of research could be done to help answer questions as part of an evaluation design?
3. What kind of program decisions might be made as the result of a good evaluation?
4. What could be some common problems in attempting to evaluate too much, too soon?
5. How can program evaluation make programs for the gifted more defensible during times of budget cuts?

18

A Comprehensive Model
of Program
Development

Joyce VanTassel-Baska

Program development efforts for the gifted require careful planning, development, and implementation. Research on local program efforts (Borland, 1989; Cox, Daniel, & Boston, 1985) has documented the need for systematic comprehensive program development to ensure adequate services to gifted learners. The Pyramid Project, a Richardson Foundation 7-year funded effort to enhance gifted programs, advocated multilevel service delivery, which would differentiate the nature of the population to be served through multiple options. Other program development resources have also supported the need for organizing and planning the gifted program in a systematic manner (Hunsacker & Callahan, 1993; Jordan & Grossi, 1980).

In the 1990s there is some evidence that gifted programs have moved to a maintenance mode of operation and in some contexts, without the support of state mandates, have been cut back (Purcell, 1995). Recent evaluations of two large state programs point to the lack of well-developed comprehensive articulated programs and services (Avery & VanTassel-Baska, 1995; Seeley & VanTassel-Baska, 1995). Moreover, local evaluation data, even in progressive school districts, reflect a similar picture of limited growth (Avery & VanTassel-Baska, in preparation). Yet strategic plans developed by state groups belie such a situation, heralding a new era of gifted program activity and suggesting important initiatives for the future (e.g., State of Maryland Task Force, 1994) with advocacy work on the rise (Berger, 1990). On the surface, these situations seem contradictory. Yet they reflect a fundamental issue in the evolving canvas of gifted education as a field. That is, whenever the existence of programs is in question and the threat of funding cuts looms, the emphasis on proactive work in program development suffers. While the problems that have beset the field in the 1990s may be among the worst in the history of gifted education— denunciation of separate gifted programs as elitist and interfering with an "inclusion" and reform agenda—program efforts have been crippled for decades by lack of sufficient funding and support for the enterprise. Thus, it may not be surprising that the state of program development is so limited and fragmentary at all levels.

Yet there is reason for hope. The Javits Act, responsible for much national program development activity from 1989 forward, still survives in a federal environment that is generally hostile toward several education programs. National advocacy continues to be provided through the efforts of national organizations, such as the National Association for Gifted Children (NAGC) and Council for Exceptional Children (CEC). Some mandated service states have increased allocations to gifted programs in recent years, and selected local districts have made major progress toward program improvement.

Important issues that have arisen from this current phase of program development activity may be characterized in the following way:

1. We need a clearer recognition of the interrelated nature of the program development enterprise. What we offer in a staff development program, for example, should have a direct and deliberate impact on program improvement. We do not have the time or resources for work that is "interesting" but unrelated to program goals.

2. We need a better understanding of program improvement mechanisms that appear to be out of control. Two areas are particularly troubling—scheduling and contact time. If we have no control over the structure of a program, over the consistent learning time for which gifted students are engaged, then we are in no position to move the program forward in a meaningful way.

3. We need stronger program designs that have not only goals but also student outcomes that can be assessed annually. The paucity of evaluation data in the field (Hunsacker & Callahan, 1993) speaks to a real lack of carefully planned and implemented designs. There appears to be almost a lack of will on the part of educators to move programs to this very critical next stage of development and implementation.

4. We need a clearer assessment of the day-to-day operations of gifted programs. Coordinators at local and state levels appear to be unaware of specifically what teachers of the gifted are delivering to their students. Hence, ideas for program improvement tend to come from the fads of the time, not the realities of district gifted classrooms.

5. We need data on gifted student performance in programs. It is difficult to argue a case for more funding, program enhancements, or new initiatives without some evidence that the program has mattered in respect to student learning. Although perceptual and attitudinal data of various constituent groups, including students, parents, and teachers, are good public relations

tools, the substance of a case for program expansion rests with documenting student learning results in a meaningful way. Too few gifted programs currently are in a position to do this.

Thus, the program development model presented in this chapter has direct meaning for programs in process that need to be improved and strengthened. Further, because good programs continue to evolve over time, the fundamental stages of program development described herein should be revisited periodically to ensure that program vitality will remain and growth will occur.

School districts have to consider many factors in developing programs for the gifted. One such factor is the *community*. How will it respond to such a program initiative? A second factor is the *institution of school* itself. How will the institution respond to the change process being undertaken? A third factor is the *students to be served*. What programs and services will best match their current and future needs? Another factor is *school personnel*. Who can best implement school programs, and how will they gain staff acceptance? Various publics and social contexts must be understood before meaningful program development in gifted education can occur.

To gain insight into those client groups and social contexts, this chapter delineates specific steps that might be taken in the program development process, many of which take into account the aforementioned factors. These steps represent the whole integrative process of program development. The ordering of the steps represents a deliberate attempt to illustrate the relative importance of some tasks occurring early in the process rather than later. Many of the steps can and should be worked on simultaneously.

Aspects of Program Development~

Set Up a Steering Committee and Establish a Basic Philosophy and Definition of the Population to Be Served

For a district to discuss philosophical attitudes and possible barriers to establishing programs for the gifted, it is essential that a representative testing ground be established. A steering committee made up of members from key groups is one way of determining the "threshold of tolerance" for gifted programs and of providing help in actual program planning. At a minimum, members should represent these areas within the district structure:

- Administration (central and building)
- Teachers
- Parents
- Students identified as gifted (junior-high-school age and older)
- Pupil personnel services (counselor, social worker, preferably psychologist)

It would also be desirable to have representation from the business, arts, and professional communities.

The steering committee might address the following questions and thus agree on a general programmatic thrust:

1. What group of gifted students is most in need of special programming within our district: intellectual, creative, artistic?
2. What are their needs from a programmatic point of view: more in-depth work in academic areas, more creative projects, more independent work?
3. What organizational approaches to a program would be appropriate: a separate center or magnet school, part-time grouping in individual buildings, grouping within the general education classroom?
4. At what grade level(s) should the program begin, and how great a span should it encompass initially?

Work at this phase should culminate in a formal district philosophy statement that features fundamental understanding about gifted students and their services in the school district. Emanating from this philosophy should be a clear definition of gifted students to be served and programmatic approaches to be employed.

The findings of the steering committee should also be used to conduct the second step in planning—a formal needs assessment. In a sense, the steering committee will have brought data forward in an informal manner that would document the need for such a program. But a formal assessment of needs is also important.

Conduct a Needs Assessment

Scriven and Roth (1973) characterized needs as gaps between actual and satisfactory conditions. Needs assessments, then, must distinguish between wants and needs as well as carefully examine the following issues:

- Incremental versus maintenance needs
- Short-term versus long-term needs
- Superficial versus deep needs
- Performance needs versus treatment needs
- Severe versus slight needs
- Temporary versus permanent needs
- Specific versus generic needs

The understanding of student and program needs, and then of the interaction of student data and program data, derived from a needs assessment will lead to informed decisions about a planned gifted program. The aggregation of data from the various sources usually provides a good indication of people's thinking about gifted education. The extent to which planners can rely on the data to guide program development likely will depend on the importance the district places on responding to perceived needs. Even if a program coordinator does not develop programs in the areas suggested, the needs assessment still provides important information for baseline purposes.

Boyd (1992) advocated for a broad data collection effort at this stage of program development including:

- Determining general district demographics on population, community, facilities, personnel, and budget
- Determining national and state gifted policies
- Collecting local data on the gifted population and programs

Student needs can be determined by surveying students, teachers, and perhaps parents. It usually is easiest to provide those being surveyed with a list of "typical" needs of gifted students, such as the following (VanTassel, 1979), and ask respondents to indicate, in order, those needs they think are most important:

1. To be challenged by activities that enable them to operate cognitively and affectively at complex levels of thought and feeling
2. To be challenged through opportunities for divergent production
3. To be challenged through group and individual work that demonstrates process/product outcomes
4. To be challenged by discussions with intellectual peers
5. To be challenged by experiences that promote understanding of human value systems
6. To be challenged by the opportunity to see interrelationships in all bodies of knowledge
7. To be challenged by special courses in their area of strength and interest that accelerate the pace and depth of content
8. To be challenged by greater exposure to new areas of learning within and without the school structure
9. To be challenged by the opportunity of applying their abilities to real problems in the world of production
10. To be taught the following process skills in the context of meaningful content:
    a. critical thinking
    b. creative thinking
    c. research
    d. problem-solving
    e. coping with exceptionality
    f. leadership

The needs most frequently identified from this list can be clustered for purposes of establishing goals and objectives for student programs.

One also can identify a sampling of students who are considered gifted or talented and then examine their current classroom experiences to determine the extent of the gap between what these youngsters are capable of doing and what they actually are doing. For example, what kinds of assignments are they being given? What is the overall cognitive level of the discussions in which they are taking part? To what extent are these students given opportunities to work independently? To what extent are they grouped with other students within the classroom who have similar abilities and interests? To answer these questions, one person or a team probably will have to talk to the teachers and make classroom observations. Interviewing the students or, in the case of young children, their parents may be a good technique. Written survey forms also may be used.

To obtain answers to the following questions, one could call together a group of teachers and administrators interested in gifted education:

1. What should be the goals of a program?
2. What should be the overall program model?
3. How should the program be organized?
4. What should be the content focus of the program: academic areas (if so, which one[s]), interdisciplinary areas (if so, which content cluster)?
5. Who should be involved in the program: teachers, administrators, parents, psychologists, counselors?
6. To what extent should they be involved and for what specific purpose (e.g., psychologists for testing only)?

Another important approach to needs assessment is to ascertain what the district program currently is doing to address the needs of these learners, how extensively it is being done, and where the gaps are. One should start from the premise that any given school district is providing some important aspects of gifted program services. The needs assessment function, then, is to determine the discrepancy between what is provided now that is appropriate and what more should be provided. The discrepancy "gap," as it is called, can be seen as the core area for proposed program development activities. The following program options might be viewed as categories to be explored:

1. Academic courses (e.g., honors, Advanced Placement)
2. Independent study, mentoring, seminars
3. Accelerative options
4. Extracurricular services (e.g., Future Problem Solving, Odyssey of the Mind, Junior Great Books, debate, science club, astronomy club)
5. Counseling services (e.g., meetings with gifted/talented students individually or in small groups, individualized education programs, career education, vocational education, or anything especially designed for gifted and talented students)
6. Community services (e.g., college classes, museum programs, Saturday classes, cultural opportunities, library programs)
7. By-mail options (correspondence, Duke program, Northwestern program, and so on)
8. Foreign language classes
9. Summer program options

Once a needs assessment has been completed, a coordinator can be appointed for the new program development effort. In a large district, one member of the staff may assume this role; in smaller districts, it may fall to the already designated gifted program coordinator.

Appoint a Coordinator for the Program Development Effort

Even in a small district, having one person in charge of planning a program initiative will save considerable time in implementing it. At an initial stage of program development, the coordinator might focus on the following tasks:

- Assembling the needs assessment data and using them to develop a program plan, including goals, objectives, and types of appropriate activity for students
- Developing a plan for technical assistance (what are the training needs?)
- Developing and implementing an identification process

Several months will be necessary for completing these tasks, which are critical to a successful program. These tasks should be an ongoing part of the coordinator's duties, which also include conducting meetings with relevant groups about the program, working on curriculum development, developing and implementing the evaluation component, and acting as a gifted resource conduit within and without the district. The coordinator also should be responsible for all relevant reports and public relations work conducted about the program.

A local coordinator has to have enough authority to carry out these responsibilities. For this reason, selection of a coordinator is important. His or her ongoing duties will require a certain finesse in working with people, in understanding how to set up programs, and in acquiring a working knowledge of gifted education.

In addition to these qualities, the coordinator should possess the following:

- Coursework in gifted education (depending on the state, anywhere from 6 to 24 hours may be considered necessary)
- Experience in working with gifted children directly, either in a small group in a general education classroom or in a special program
- Administrative experience or coursework (or both) that reflects an understanding of how schools operate and how innovation occurs

Many districts have treated the gifted program as an "add-on" administrative duty. Such a situation does not bode well for program development activity, for a person split across programs cannot undertake new initiatives very well. If this is the situation in a local district, hiring one person for a short time to engage in only gifted program development would appear to be justified.

Delineate Program Model and Service Alternatives

From the needs assessment information, the coordinator and steering committee should develop concept papers that present alternative program models to be considered. Chapters 12 and 13 explore such models in depth. An outline for such a concept paper might include:

1. Summary of assessment data
2. Nature of population to be served
3. Overall program philosophy and approach

4. Major goals and objectives
5. Curricular areas to be explored
6. Grouping approach to be used
7. Program organization and schedule
8. Staff development models
9. Evaluation approach
10. Budget considerations

With budgetary constraints' being a reality in most local school districts, it is advisable for the coordinator and steering committee to work out alternative budgets based on alternative approaches to programming. By doing so, the superintendent and the board of education will be able to easily see the effects of different amounts of funding.

Resources that aid in the process of comparing general program models (Renzulli, 1986), teaching models (Maker, 1985), and curriculum models (VanTassel-Baska, 1993) are available. Yet the task of tailoring such models for a given school district must rest with the steering committee and the coordinator of the program.

Initiate a Staff Development Plan

For a gifted program to be implemented successfully, all people in the district must be aware of its existence and purpose. In addition, individuals working closely with the program need a more in-depth understanding of the nature and needs of gifted children and the interventions to be implemented with them. Current research evidence suggests that the more training teachers receive in working with gifted learners, the better the results for enhanced performance (Hansen & Feldhusen, 1994; Reis & Westberg, 1994). In addition, the sharing of information from different gifted programs can be extremely profitable. Thus, a staff development plan should address at least three levels:

- Level One: Awareness
  This level may best be accomplished through brochures, newsletters, and workshops. The information should be available to all educational personnel and parents as well as to key community leaders. Content should focus on the who, what, and why of the district gifted program as well as provide information on the general characteristics and needs of gifted children.
- Level Two: Developmental
  This level of technical assistance may be accomplished through extended workshops and group consultations. It should be available primarily to individuals working directly with the gifted program. Content should focus on specific developmental issues, such as how to assess individual student needs; what are specific project models for working with students who are gifted in, for example, language arts, and how to teach critical thinking to the gifted.
- Level Three: Reflective
  This level of technical assistance may be accomplished through a seminar approach. Seminars should be available to educators who have been integrally

involved with the program for at least 1 year and should attempt to involve several districts for purposes of exchanging information. The seminars should focus primarily on strengths and weaknesses in gifted programming and should be conducted as problem-solving workshops by a consultant with group process skills.

Ideally, the staff development plan should also include minimum expectations for participants at each level. For example, at the awareness level, participants should gain information about the gifted program that can be documented. At level two, participants should be able to demonstrate competency in the specific content and process areas on which the training has focused. At level three, participants should be able to analyze the program and make recommendations for modification based on seminar discussions. Excellent resources for program planners at this stage are the Summer 1986 special issue of *Gifted Child Quarterly* devoted entirely to articles on staff development and the Summer 1994 issue devoted to teacher training issues.

Develop and Implement an Identification Process

Some experts in the field might argue that the identification of gifted students should occur earlier in the process of planning than suggested here. However, the program and the selected population must match in a defensible fashion. Unfortunately, it is easy to identify a population you cannot serve if the nature of the program and the resources available to carry it out are not in place first. Therefore, it may be appropriate in some instances not to identify students until a program plan has been worked out.

Given that identification was discussed in depth in Chapter 11, only an outline of key issues is presented here. The following factors should be carefully considered by local program developers when designing and implementing an identification process:

- Use objective and subjective data. Recommendations should be balanced by tests that document performance or potential or both.
- Use multiple criteria in the process. Developmental levels of the student population should guide which criteria are most appropriate. For example, use of parent nomination and inventory procedures for young children has proved very effective (Ehrlich, 1984; Robinson, 1996; Roedell, Jackson, & Robinson, 1980). At later stages of development, self-nomination and special aptitude measures are useful (VanTassel-Baska & Strykowski, 1987). According to Gallagher and Gallagher (1995), the three most frequently used criteria for programs for the intellectually gifted are teacher recommendations, achievement tests, and intelligence instruments.
- Develop an identification process. Once you have determined the criteria for consideration, you must create a system for determining selection. Will all criteria weigh equally? How will selection be determined? Who will be involved? Feldhusen, Baska, and Womble (1981) suggested a conversion to standard scores as one approach to aggregating data.

- At the screening level, include criteria that are easily accessible, such as scores on annual achievement tests, IQ tests on file, and so on.
- Ensure the cooperation of classroom teachers; it is critical to the program's success. Teacher recommendations may be time-consuming, but they are an important part of the process.
- Be sure the instruments used for the selection of students are appropriate to the nature of the program and defensible in terms of identifying giftedness. For example, if you are going to initiate an advanced math program for sixth graders, math scores on achievement and aptitude tests are more important to consider than are IQ test scores. Research evidence (Lupkowski-Shoplik & Assouline, 1993; Stanley, 1981) and common sense suggest the feasibility of such an approach.

In addition, attention should be focused on the following factors (Callahan, Tomlinson, & Pizzat, 1993; Mills, Ablard, & Brody, 1993):

- Use of instruments that tap into different talents and abilities
- Choice of instruments that are sensitive to the inclusion of underrepresented groups
- For secondary students, development of a system of identification that is distinctive from the model used at the elementary level
- Use of a two-stage approach—screening followed by identification—implying the use of different instruments appropriate for the specific stage of the process

The selection process should also allow for discussion among educators and for "trying out" the various ways of thinking about how best to collect the data. Identification is a human process, not a numbers game. Consequently, having a selection committee review and discuss procedures as well as individual cases seems appropriate. Although some school districts might argue that this "messing around" is not a clean process, it is an honest one that takes seriously the issue of cutting arbitrarily on the continuum of human abilities.

Once students have been selected, meetings should be scheduled with them and their parents to discuss the nature of the program. "Permission to participate" forms should be collected from parents and "commitment forms" from students. This approach is a good way to gain early acceptance and responsibility for the program from those who will be most affected by it.

Decide on a Curriculum Development Plan

Curriculum development for the gifted means integrating the major successful approaches to serving gifted students into proposed programs. The Integrated Curriculum Model (ICM) is one approach to doing that. The model recognizes the importance of fusing the components of content, higher order process, and resultant products as well as major concepts and issues into a curriculum whole (VanTassel-Baska, 1995).

Some of these components may be perceived as more important than others depending on the program model(s) selected. For example, a model of accelerated content would place a great emphasis on content organization, whereas districts using an enrichment triad approach might focus more on classroom management and instructional strategies. As another example, work with the multiple intelligences model would imply heavy concentration on the model as the primary vehicle for planning and generating curriculum. Thus, the focus of a curriculum plan may depend on the general direction selected for the program model. No one model has been judged superior, and most offer interesting, productive approaches for working with gifted students. In fact, many programs attempt a synthesis approach and cull the best from each model to develop a curriculum plan. (For a complete treatment of curriculum content issues, see Chapters 19–25.)

All gifted program curricula should employ good teaching strategies, some of which are more conducive to certain kinds of programs. For example, inquiry teaching is an effective technique in social studies and English—courses in which discussion is a key component—whereas it may not be as helpful in foreign language or mathematics, in which application of skills is the overriding concern. In the final analysis, strategies for working with the gifted are more heavily predicated on understanding individual and group needs than on demonstrating special techniques. But at a minimum, a teacher of the gifted should have in his or her arsenal the ability to do inquiry teaching, ask good discussion questions, organize small groups and independent work, and lecture effectively.

Another important aspect of curriculum development is choice of selected materials and resources. Because there are no such things as "gifted materials," it is useful to examine criteria for selecting materials appropriate for use with gifted learners. Program coordinators should consider the following:

- Materials should be grounded in an important knowledge base so that gifted students can learn and reflect on the important understanding about that knowledge base.
- Materials should be attuned to the national content standards.
- Materials should be geared to an appropriate reading level, slightly above the gifted students' tested level.
- Materials should stimulate discussion opportunities in small groups through the inclusion of good higher level questions.
- Materials should be varied, offering diverse points of view and representing multiple media.
- Materials should be geared to complex thought processes, especially the development of analytical and evaluative skills.
- Materials should be organized around key issues, themes, and ideas within or across domains of inquiry or should represent the underlying structure of a given discipline.
- Materials should be supplementary and not the substance of the program.

More specific criteria for selecting materials for gifted programs in the areas of science and language arts have been developed for use by school districts (Johnson, Boyce, & VanTassel-Baska, 1995; VanTassel-Baska, Johnson, & Boyce, 1996).

Select Teachers

Teacher selection is an extremely important step in program development, because the teacher has been found to be the most important factor in whether a program benefits gifted students (Borland, 1989; Renzulli, 1977). Consequently, the school district should have its selection committee establish a protocol for deciding who will teach the gifted program. Such a committee also may be used to interview candidates if this procedure becomes part of the selection model. Generally teachers tend to nominate themselves for consideration in such programs. Self-nomination is a desirable part of the process, but other factors also should be considered. Certain qualities are essential for a teacher of the gifted:

- Good academic record. The prospective teacher of the gifted need not be as gifted as many of the students, but he or she cannot be borderline average either.
- Keen interest in at least one academic or creative area.
- The ability to be flexible in terms of time, pace, materials, instructional patterns, and so forth.
- A good sense of humor.
- Strength. The prospective teacher should be a strong individual who is not easily intimidated or threatened by able learners.

Borland (1989) offered a few other characteristics that teachers of the gifted should have. According to Borland, they:

- Should possess a considerable amount of general intelligence.
- Should have a strong educational background in at least one substantive discipline.
- Should consistently demonstrate a hunger for learning.
- Should frequently say, "I don't know."
- Need a solid sense of personal security.
- Should be tolerant of diversity, originality, and off-beat responses to questions and assignments.
- Should be well organized and well structured in their teaching.
- Should have some formal education in the nature, needs, and education of the gifted.
- Should possess effective counseling skills.

To continue to shape an exemplary program, these teachers also must be energetic and creative. More complete lists of teacher characteristics are available from several sources (Gallagher & Gallagher, 1995; Maker & Nielson, 1996).

A process for teacher selection could incorporate the following steps:

1. Accept self-nomination through an application form.
2. Study the records of those who apply, keeping in mind the key characteristics just cited.
3. Observe candidates in the classroom, using a list of instructional behaviors deemed appropriate to classrooms for the gifted (see Table 18.1).

Table 18.1 ~
Instructional Process Goals

In a gifted program, the teacher will:

1. Conduct group discussions.
2. Select questions that stimulate higher level thinking.
3. Use varied teaching strategies effectively.
4. Utilize critical-thinking skills in appropriate contexts.
5. Encourage independent thinking and open inquiry.
6. Understand and encourage student ideas and student-directed work.
7. Demonstrate understanding of the educational implications of giftedness.
8. Utilize creative-thinking techniques.
9. Utilize problem-solving techniques.
10. Synthesize student assessment data and curriculum content effectively.

Note: The Martinson-Weiner scale has been adapted to link these goals to an assessment tool.

4. Interview top candidates individually or by committee.
5. Select according to criteria developed within the parameters of district policy.

Implement the Program

Start-up times for gifted program initiatives vary, but allowing 12 months is advisable—6 months to plan the program and another 6 months to implement a pilot effort. Planning is essential in making the program work, but too long a time expended for this effort can dampen enthusiasm and support. Moving into the program implementation phase is important. Curriculum can be developed during the program as long as the overall conceptual ideas are in place and teachers feel comfortable working with the students. Ideally, spring and summer planning with fall implementation is best, but winter implementation following first-semester planning also can work.

The first 6 weeks of implementation yield much information crucial to program continuance. The following problems are apt to occur or will surface, if they are going to, at this time:

- Selection of students who do not fit the program
  Possible solution: Have in place a policy to facilitate moving students in and out of programs. Such a policy should be in place when the program is set up, and parents and students should be informed about this policy at the orientation session. It is important to suggest an alternative to these students, such as meetings with a counselor or special projects.
- Disenchantment of teachers who "lose" students to the program
  Possible solution: Keep such teachers carefully informed of what is happening

in the program, how their students are progressing, and how the teachers can help.

- Students' feelings of being overwhelmed/overworked
  Possible solution: Delineate student expectations at the orientation meeting, including estimates of extra time involvement. Listen to concerns and try to help. Sometimes the gifted program represents the first time a student has been challenged, and therefore he or she may not know how to cope. Let some time pass.
- Teachers' feelings of being overwhelmed/overworked
  Possible solution: More planning is a good remedy for this problem. New programs are energy-draining, but they should not make excessive demands. Another approach might be to allow teachers some additional time off for planning and for attending sharing sessions with other educators in gifted programs.

A frequently overlooked aspect of program implementation is careful monitoring of the classroom. Some key strategies for classroom monitoring include:

1. Asking teachers to keep daily logs of what worked and what did not work.
2. Videotaping selected classroom lessons.
3. Scheduling weekly meetings to define learning events.
4. Observing classes firsthand, using a structured form.

Evaluate the Program

Program evaluation is too frequently an afterthought in programs for the gifted. Limited data exist on program effectiveness and those that do exist frequently lack utility to the users (Callahan & Caldwell, 1995).

For an administrator, evaluation is important because it aids in improving programs and in making decisions about program worth and desirability on an ongoing basis. It is especially important to evaluate gifted program efforts carefully because of the tenuousness of long-term financial commitment to such programs by school boards. Good data alone will not necessarily maintain a program, but they are facilitative.

Two kinds of data should be collected: *student data* and *program data*. In designing a gifted program evaluation, structure questions that you want answered about the program, such as:

- How have students benefited from this program?
- Have students met the planned objectives? Why or why not?
- How well does the identification process work?
- How effective is the staff development component?

Such questions should be incorporated into a format that allows for appropriate instrumentation selection, timetables for data collection, and data collection procedures. The format also should allow for involvement by key persons in the process. A balanced concern for student growth data and program process data is an important consideration. (See Chapter 17 for an in-depth discussion of the evaluation topic.)

Use Community Resources

Although many local educators may not view the community as an essential component of successful gifted program development, it is a tremendous resource that can be used to enhance any gifted program. A key to community involvement is to identify important contacts and develop a resource directory. These contacts can come from civic and professional organizations, many of which are highly predisposed toward helping gifted education.

Other important contacts come through universities. University personnel tend to be approachable about helping with gifted programs because of their natural interest in gifted students. They are a good source for establishing mentorships. School district personnel also can be tapped for program development. Curriculum specialists and pupil personnel workers are often willing to work on some aspect of the gifted program.

In recent years, business partnerships and consortia have become important means of involving communities in program development. Research facilities and museums also make excellent resource partners.

Structure a Counseling Component

The need for gifted students to receive counseling help already has been cited (also see Chapter 27). Too many gifted students currently receive incidental counseling at best, which ill prepares them to make decisions about their school program or to focus on career options. It also fails to prepare them to cope with being gifted.

School counselors should be involved with the gifted program and encouraged to meet with the students in small groups on a regular basis. Some of the issues of coping that a counselor can explore with identified gifted students include those addressed by the following questions, which capitalize on affective aspects of being gifted:

- How do you feel different from others? Knowing that each person is unique, how can you cope with the ways in which you feel different?
- What do you perceive to be your strengths and weaknesses? How can you capitalize on and minimize them, respectively?
- Why do you often like to work alone? When do you prefer not to, and why?
- How do you handle criticism? Do you feel "picked on" when suggestions are made to you?
- Do you feel confident about your ability? How do you "practice" it with others?
- Do you criticize yourself for mistakes? How do you feel when you make mistakes?
- Do you like to lead others? In what kind of enterprise?
- How do you make decisions?
- What information resources can you access to answer college-planning questions? Career-planning questions?

The school counselor or other designated person can work with identified gifted students at least twice a month in a group setting to explore these kinds of issues. Counselors also should provide special programs, perhaps once a month, addressing school and career opportunities based on the perceived needs of the groups.

Sometimes teachers and program coordinators would like to be involved with this aspect of the gifted program. They should be encouraged to participate, for much can be learned about gifted children from informal sessions.

Develop Gifted Program Policy

New programs represent change in a school district. Consequently, no program development effort will be successful unless the change process is accounted for and addressed in a deliberate way. Not only are we, as gifted educators, interested in individuals "changing," but we also are interested in the school system changing. Consequently, there is a need to develop policies at the local level that will facilitate the ongoing growth of the gifted program. A sample list of policies on acceleration and grouping has been developed by VanTassel-Baska (1992) and is summarized here. Such a list is highly applicable at the local level.

Acceleration Policies for the Gifted Learner
1. Each learner is entitled to experience learning at a level of challenge. For gifted learners, this implies the opportunity for continuous progress through the basic curriculum based on demonstrated mastery of prior material. In all planned curriculum experiences for the gifted, care must be taken to ensure that students are placed at their optimum instructional level. This level may be determined by diagnostic testing, observation of mastery, or performance-based assessments.
2. Gifted learners should be afforded the opportunity to begin school-based experiences based on readiness and to exit them based on proficiency. Thus, both early entrance and early exit options should be provided. Gifted learners are best served by school systems that are flexible about when and where learning takes place. Some students will benefit most from a prereading program at age 4; other students may be best served by college opportunities at age 16. Individual variables must be honored in an overall flexible system of implementation.
3. Some gifted learners may profit from telescoping 2 years of education into one or by bypassing a particular grade level. Provision for such advanced placement should be made based on individual student demonstration of capacity, readiness, and motivation. Grade-level placement should be determined by many factors beyond age. Tailoring learning levels, as well as bypassing them, is another important way to ensure implementation of this policy.

Grouping Policies for the Gifted Learner
1. Grouping of the gifted should be viewed as a fundamental approach to serving them appropriately rather than merely as an organizational arrangement.

Grouping gifted students is a basic program provision that should be used in tandem with other provisions, such as curriculum modification, alternative choice of materials, and learning centers.

2. Grouping strategies for the gifted should remain flexible, based on individual needs of both identified and nonidentified learners. Dyads, small instructional groups, cooperative learning groups, and the seminar model all provide important alternatives for teachers to employ, depending on the learning task and the readiness of the learner to engage in it.

3. Gifted learners should have the opportunity to interact with others at their instructional level in all relevant core areas of learning in the school curriculum. Usually, this would imply, at the least, instructional grouping in reading and mathematics at the elementary level and special subject area classes and Advanced Placement classes at the secondary level. Grouping for science and social studies instruction is also advocated.

4. Gifted learners should be grouped according to special interest areas with other learners who share those interests. Opportunities for small-group project work should involve students interested in the same topics or problems. Students would then need instruction in the process to be employed in their investigation or a model for constructing their own line of investigation.

5. Gifted learners should have the opportunity for independent learning based on both their ability and interest.

Such policies provide a foundation for integrating gifted education more successfully into major reform movements such as inclusion and the middle-school movement (Coleman & Gallagher, 1992).

Enact a Change Model

No gifted program will survive or grow if its central actors do not understand the role of change in schools. Change theory has dominated many of the current discussions on school reform. Fullan's (1991) view of change as a positive dynamic relationship occurring both top down and bottom up is useful for school-based work. Senge's model (1991) of systemic change also offers important ideas for addressing change in a systems context. Senge enumerated five major *disciplines* associated with bringing about meaningful change: personal mastery, team learning, mental models, shared vision, and the resultant learning organization that emerges out of such individual and shared responsibility for growth.

Additionally, it is helpful to review the basic elements involved in the process of change. Key aspects of the process of change in schools include the following:

1. Change generally must be viewed as desirable by relevant constituencies.
2. At least a few people must be committed to change.
3. Change must be planned for and implemented systematically.
4. Change must be monitored.
5. Change requires skilled leadership at each stage of the process.
6. Change is slow but steady.

7. Positive change represents growth in individuals and systems.
8. The critical unit for implementing change is the individual school.

The goal of local policy development concerning gifted education is to ensure that the gifted program becomes integrated with the general education programs at all appropriate levels of decision-making. In this way it will come to be viewed as a part of the school system program, not as a "frill" or "extra." Boards of education must understand gifted education programs as a part of the total fabric of quality education for all. Policy development and enactment provide the mechanisms for creating such an understanding.

Develop and Activate a Plan of Action

The aspects of program development that have been described in this chapter are important interactive pieces in institutionalizing a model program effort for gifted learners (see Figure 18.1). Neglect or deletion of any of these elements can have a deleterious effect on the program in its formative stages. Furthermore, as local programs grow and expand, more opportunities for using this program development cycle, albeit in tailored form, will emerge. Sound program development practices are essential for building defensible programs for the gifted and in keeping them going. Yet this is not meant to be a linear model. Rather, it is a simultaneity model in which individual elements constitute clusters of ongoing activities and individual program developers make decisions on an appropriate plan of action for proceeding. Formats for such plans may vary, but typically they include the following components:

1. Area to be addressed (for example, counseling, policy, identification)
2. Tasks to be undertaken
3. Responsibility
4. Timeline for completion
5. Documentation of progress (agendas, minutes of meetings held, products such as brochures, and so on)

Table 18.2 provides a sample plan of action form. Only when an action plan is developed will progress be made in the program development process. Knowing what to do and how to do it are only part of program development. Activating a plan of action that involves others is a key to a successful venture in this area.

Program Articulation

Program articulation is central to meaningful program development practices (Tyler, 1958). The term program articulation refers to the development of appropriate offerings for gifted students on a K–12 basis, with planned curriculum experiences that allow for progressive development of both content and process skills. To examine the issue intelligently, however, one must look at the components in the educational enterprise that affect the ability of schools to carry out such efforts.

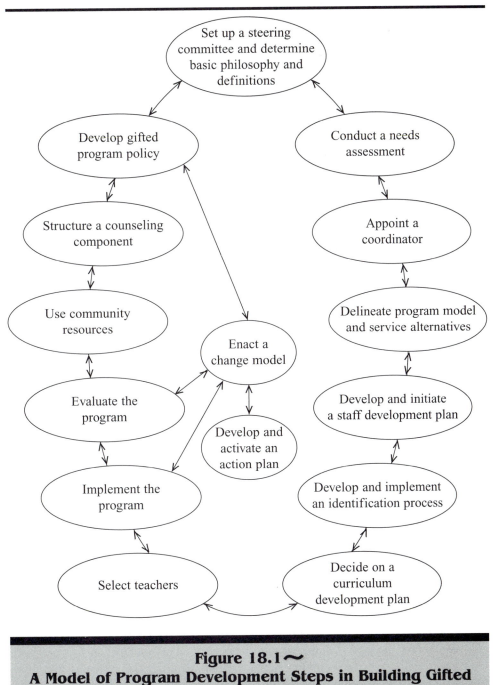

Figure 18.1 ～
A Model of Program Development Steps in Building Gifted
Education Programs at the Local Level

Table 18.2~ "Plan of Action" Form						
What problems or issues have to be addressed? (What?)	What solution options should be considered? (What?)	Option feasibility (Costs/ Benefits?)	Processes for change (How?)	Respon- sibility (Who?)	Timeline (When?)	Documen- tation of progress

Components Affecting Program Articulation

A major assumption that underlies the ability to carry out program articulation is that schools are willing to accept a primary role for developing individual academic potential. To implement an articulation plan effectively, schools must modify their basic educational program to meet the academic needs of gifted students. In so doing, schools must be willing to abandon a chronological-age basis for determining curriculum skill levels and examine instead a *competency-based model* for progress. (Although many educators purport to employ a continuous progress model, in reality their efforts are usually related to steps taken for slower students only.)

A second ingredient of good program articulation is that identification of gifted children occurs when they enter the school district, usually at the kindergarten level. The argument frequently given for not identifying at this age is that the tests available to measure giftedness are not reliable or valid for such young children. Recent studies (Robinson, 1996; Roedell, Jackson, & Robinson, 1980) have indicated, however, that several effective tools can be used in combination for successful identification of young children. Obviously, no identification system at entry will identify all gifted children who could profit from later programming, so provision for an ongoing identification procedure is essential. But from the articulation perspective, *early programming* is critical for ensuring appropriate skill development and excitement for learning.

A third component underlying articulation is that schools must have some provision for *grouping* gifted children in the academic areas. Carrying out an articulated program with gifted students who are not grouped frequently or for reasonable periods of time is almost impossible. Thus, effective grouping must be employed to make an articulation plan workable.

Another aspect of program articulation is the need for *self-pacing* of the gifted in the core content areas in which the program is offered. Self-pacing in the field of gifted education is also known as content acceleration and modification, in which the scope and sequence of instruction in reading, mathematics, science, and social studies for gifted students are programmed from kindergarten through the secondary level. Especially important, given the learning rate differences and intellectual power of gifted students, are the use of (1) a diagnostic-prescriptive approach over time to assure that the learning is progressive; (2) a conceptually organized curriculum that compresses content into major schemas, systems, and matrices for ease in mastering important knowledge areas; and (3) a teacher who facilitates and monitors progress in relationship to student mastery.

An articulation plan also has to address the integration of *process skills, special projects, mentorships, internships, and other modifications* of the overall curriculum for these students into the traditional subject matter provided within the context of the school. Working on process skills within the traditional domains of knowledge to ensure that gifted students both master them and are able to transfer that mastery to applicable areas makes the most sense.

Assumptions About Teachers and Teaching

Program articulation also carries certain assumptions about the selection of and training procedures for teachers who work with gifted students. To facilitate conceptual learning in the gifted, the teacher must understand a given domain of knowledge well enough to organize it effectively for able learners and be able to develop advanced-level work for them. Even elementary teachers of the gifted need good content mastery so they can work effectively with the gifted in the various areas. A teacher working with the mathematically gifted at the elementary level, then, would require high-level ability and training in mathematics as well as demonstrated effectiveness with gifted students at a given age level. A differentiated staffing pattern within the traditional elementary school could be an effective strategy for obtaining appropriate staff for such programs.

Use of Confluent Approach

Finally, program articulation implies a sustained confluent approach to meeting the needs of the gifted population. The strategies of acceleration, enrichment, and counseling all have their part in the delivery of an appropriate program effort. A carefully conceived long-range plan that incorporates all of these issues can be effected in any school district that is willing to expend the effort on behalf of gifted students.

Cost-Effectiveness ⌇

Programs for the gifted may be entering a new cycle with regard to how educators perceive their benefits. More than ever before, cost-effectiveness is an issue in educational programming. Because of general cuts in educational funding at federal, state, and local levels, special programs, including those for the gifted, are being examined more critically.

In a discussion of cost-effectiveness, one must first ask what constitutes an effective gifted program. There are perhaps two ways to respond to that question. One is to cite the limited research available on the evaluation of gifted programs (Gallagher, Weiss, Oglesby, & Thomas, 1982). Another is to cite the standards used to judge exemplary programs on a statewide basis (*Illinois Exemplary Program Handbook*, 1979). To be judged effective by the first approach, a program must demonstrate specific benefits to students in the areas of cognitive and/or affective growth. Few programs have found their way into the literature through such an evaluative perspective. The one sustained evaluation effort in this area, conducted over the past 20 years, is the work of the Study of Mathematically Precocious Youth at Johns Hopkins University, where student growth gains have been impressive.

With regard to the second approach, the standards for what constitutes an effective program for the gifted are more general. Yet, taken as a whole they may be helpful in determining the issue of effectiveness. The standards used for identifying exemplary programs in the Illinois study (*Illinois Exemplary Program Handbook*, 1979) were as follows:

1. That identification of gifted students (a) focus on the top 5%–8% of a school population; (b) use appropriate instrumentation based on the nature of the program planned; (c) utilize a balance between objective criteria, such as tests, and subjective criteria, such as teacher recommendations and peer inventories; and (d) provide an ongoing process for inclusion of eligible students
2. That the program have appropriate objectives and activities for the nature and needs of the population selected
3. That teaching strategies stress the use of higher level thinking processes, problem-solving techniques, discussions, and high-quality student products
4. That appropriate measures be taken to select and train the best teachers available for the specific program to be implemented and that community resources be utilized
5. That programs provide comprehensive articulation for students across grade levels and subject areas as need indicates
6. That materials be selected and used in accordance with program objectives
7. That the school and community demonstrate involvement with the program through regular interaction in activities such as parent education seminars, board meetings, and special workshops
8. That the program evaluation be comprehensive, utilizing appropriate instru-

mentation to document student growth, attitudes of significant publics, and efficacy of program processes

Classroom observation, interviews, and the review of pertinent documents constituted the strategies used by the Illinois teams to ascertain if self-nominated school districts were operating exemplary gifted programs.

If these standards are reasonable for determining whether a gifted program is effective, what are the criteria to be used in assessing a program's cost-effectiveness? Given that 80% of any program budget is usually allocated for personnel costs, a gifted program should have in place a plan for the flexible use of existing human resources in order to keep costs under control. Several strategies can be employed:

- Grouping and scheduling
- Differentiated staffing
- Planned use of community volunteers
- Extended school day and year

Summary ~

Developing and activating programs and services for gifted learners are important enterprises that are ongoing and dynamic in nature. One gifted program will not meet the needs of all gifted learners in a given school district, nor will activation of all the program development elements described herein guarantee a sufficient effort. Only as we continue to work at the individual and collective aspects of the program development cycle are we likely to build the quality programs we envision. The building process also takes time. Years of effort usually are required to establish and fine-tune a program of quality. Gifted program developers should view the task of program development as a major undertaking that is full of challenges and frustrations on the way to creating a "willed future" for gifted learners.

References ~

Avery, L., & VanTassel-Baska, J. (1995). *Evaluation report on the Greenwich School District's Talented and Gifted (TAG) Program*. Williamsburg, VA: The College of William and Mary, Center for Gifted Education.

Avery, L., & VanTassel-Baska, J. (in preparation). *Making evaluation work: One school district's experience with gifted programs*.

Berger, S. L. (1990). *Supporting gifted education through advocacy*. Reston, VA: Council for Exceptional Children. (ERIC Digest No. E494)

Borland, J. (1989). *Planning and implementing programs for the gifted*. New York: Teachers College Press.

Boyd, L. N. (1992). The needs assessment—who needs it? *Roeper Review, 15*(2), 64–66.

Callahan, C. M., & Caldwell, M. S. (1995). *A practitioner's guide to evaluating programs for the gifted*. Washington, DC: National Association for Gifted Children.

Callahan, C. M., Tomlinson, C. A., & Pizzat, P. M. (Eds.). (1993). *Contexts for promise: Noteworthy practices and innovation in the identification of gifted students*. Charlottesville: University of Virginia, National Research Center on the Gifted and Talented.

Coleman, M. R., & Gallagher, J. (1992). *Middle school survey report: Impact on gifted students*. Chapel Hill: North Carolina University, Gifted Education Policy Studies Program.

Cox, J., Daniel, N., & Boston, B. (1985). *Educating able learners*. Austin: University of Texas Press.

Ehrlich, V. (1984). *The Astor program for young gifted children: 10 years later*. Unpublished report.

Feldhusen, J. F., Baska, L. K., & Womble, S. R. (1981). Using standard scores to synthesize data in identifying gifted. *Journal for the Education of the Gifted, 4,* 177–185.

Fullan, M. (1991). *The new meaning of educational change*. Toronto, Canada: Ontario Institute for Education.

Gallagher, J., & Gallagher, S. (1995). *Teaching the gifted child* (4th ed.). Boston: Allyn & Bacon.

Gallagher, J., Weiss, P., Oglesby, K., & Thomas, T. (1982). *Report on education of gifted: II. Surveys of education of gifted students*. Chapel Hill: University of North Carolina, Frank Porter Child Development Center.

Hansen, J. B., & Feldhusen, J. F. (1994). Comparison of trained and untrained teachers of gifted students. *Gifted Child Quarterly, 38*(3), 115–121.

Hunsacker, S. L., & Callahan, C. M. (1993). Evaluation of gifted programs: Current practices. *Journal for the Education of the Gifted, 16*(2), 190–200.

Illinois Exemplary Program Handbook. (1979). Springfield: Illinois Office of Education.

Johnson, D. T., Boyce, L. N., & VanTassel-Baska, J. (1995). Science curriculum review: Evaluating materials for high ability learners. *Gifted Child Quarterly, 39*(1), 36–43.

Jordan, J., & Grossi, J. (1980). *An administrator's handbook on designing programs for the gifted and talented*. Reston, VA: Council for Exceptional Children.

Lupkowski-Shoplik, A., & Assouline, S. (1993). Identifying mathematically talented elementary students: Using the lower level of the SSAT. *Gifted Child Quarterly, 37*(3), 118–123.

Maker, J. (1985). *Teaching models in gifted education*. Rockville, MD: Aspen Systems.

Maker, J., & Nielson, A. (1996). *Curriculum development and teaching strategies for gifted learners* (2d ed.). Austin, TX: PRO-Ed.

Mills, C., Ablard, K. E., & Brody, L. E. (1993). The Raven's Progressive Matrices: Its usefulness for identifying gifted/talented students. *Roeper Review, 15*(3), 185–186.

Purcell, J. H. (1995). Gifted education at a crossroads: The program status study. *Gifted Child Quarterly, 39*(2), 57–65.

Reis, S. M., & Westberg, K. L. (1994). The impact of staff development on teachers' ability to modify curriculum for gifted and talented students. *Gifted Child Quarterly, 38*(3), 127–135.

Renzulli, J. (1977). *The enrichment triad model: A guide for developing defensible programs for the gifted and talented*. Mansfield Center, CT: Creative Learning Press.

Renzulli, J. (Ed.). (1986). *Systems and models for developing programs for the gifted and talented*. Mansfield Center, CT: Creative Learning Press.

Robinson, N. (1996, May). *Development of abilities in young math talented children: A two-year longitudinal study*. Paper presented at the annual meeting of the American Educational Research Association, New York, NY.

Roedell, W., Jackson, N., & Robinson, H. (1980). *Gifted young children*. New York: Teachers College Press.

Scriven, M., & Roth, J. (1973). Needs assessment: Concept and practice. *New Directions for Program Evaluating, 1,* 1–11.

Seeley, K., & VanTassel-Baska, J. (1995). *A survey of programs and services in the state of Florida*. Tallahassee, FL: State Department of Education.

Senge, P. (1991). *The fifth discipline*. New York: Doubleday.

Stanley, J. (1981). Using the SAT to find intellectually talented seventh graders. *College Board Review, 122,* 3–7.

State of Maryland Task Force. (1994). *Renewing our commitment to the education of gifted and talented students: An essential component of educational reform. Recommendations for gifted and talented education in Maryland*. Baltimore: Maryland State Department of Education.

Tyler, R. (1958). *Principles of curriculum and instruction*. Chicago: University of Chicago Press.

VanTassel, J. (1979). A needs assessment model for gifted education. *Journal for the Education of the Gifted, 2*(3), 141–148.

VanTassel-Baska, J. (1992). Educational decision-making on acceleration and grouping. *Gifted Child Quarterly, 36*(2), 67–71.

VanTassel-Baska, J. (1993). *Comprehensive curriculum for gifted learners.* Boston: Allyn & Bacon.

VanTassel-Baska, J. (1995). The development of talent through curriculum. *Roeper Review, 18*(2), 98–102.

VanTassel-Baska, J., Johnson, D. T., & Boyce, L. N. (Eds.). (1996). *Developing verbal talent.* Boston: Allyn & Bacon.

VanTassel-Baska, J., & Strykowski, B. (1987). *An identification resource guide on the gifted and talented.* Evanston, IL: Northwestern University, Center for Talent Development.

Study Questions ⌇

1. How might various aspects of the program development process be organized effectively in a school district?
2. What school district and community variables must be taken into account when developing a gifted program?
3. What types of barriers inhibit gifted program development in school districts? How might they be overcome?
4. If you were a school superintendent, how would you proceed with gifted program development? What would be your major concerns?
5. Evaluate the advantages and disadvantages of competing program models, identification models, and curriculum models. What direction appears most feasible?
6. What other programs in a school district might provide useful information for studying and understanding gifted program development?
7. We have difficulty articulating gifted programs for the transitions from elementary to middle school and from middle school to high school. What are some ways to enhance program cohesion at these transition points?
8. What arguments would you put forth to have local schools provide further funding for gifted programs?
9. What problems might be encountered in building an exemplary gifted program?

Introduction to
Part Three

Providing Effective Curriculum and Instruction for Gifted and Talented Learners

This section focuses on organizing curriculum and delivering it to gifted and talented learners at the classroom level. Moving beyond the general provisions noted in part two, this section of the book emphasizes the important role of curriculum in shaping the talent development process. Specifically, it examines the broad-based tasks of teaching thinking skills and encouraging creativity in various contexts over a span of years. It lays out the predominant teacher strategies and methods found effective with gifted and talented learners and links them to major program approaches. The section also explores curriculum emphases by subject matter areas, weaving in new work based on the content standards in mathematics, science, social studies, language arts, and the arts and humanities.

The introductory chapter in this part (Chapter 19), by VanTassel-Baska, provides a context for understanding important issues in structuring a curriculum for gifted and talented learners. New research on learning, coupled with a domain-specific view of intelligence, affects how we serve these learners in important ways. The chapter outlines major approaches to serving the gifted in classrooms, emphasizing the need for an integrated model that addresses the many faces of giftedness noted in part one. The chapter also provides a history of curriculum development in the field and cites new work on effective interventions.

The Feldhusen chapter on strategies and methods (Chapter 20) describes approaches that expert teachers use in their work with gifted students. The elements that make a teacher an expert are derived from the work of Sternberg and Horvath (1995) and include possession of a comprehensive knowledge base, efficiency in using it, and insight into problem solving. Underlying the deployment of all strategies is a recognition of the importance of a diagnostic/prescriptive model (Stanley, 1978), which ensures that the instruction builds on the student's current information base and level of functioning.

Feldhusen cites research suggesting that the organizational models that group gifted students homogeneously for instruction in core curriculum offer the best opportunity for addressing their educational needs in both cognitive and affective domains. With this in mind, major strategies and methods highlighted for use in the gifted classroom include the following:

- Opening and warm-up exercises that engage students in a challenging cognitive activity
- Lectures, lecturettes, teacher presentations, and explanations that present the current conceptions of fundamental ideas in the discipline and induce students to think critically and creatively
- Reading and homework that advance the students' understanding of the concepts, expose them to primary sources, and enhance their self-regulatory skills
- Evoking intrinsic motivation through creating interest, relating new information to previously learned material, modeling enthusiasm for the subject matter, and commending specific achievements
- Discussions, questioning, and dialogue that challenge and extend the students' thinking skills and help them to incorporate new ideas into their schematic frameworks
- Small-group projects, seminars, and debates that provide opportunities for in-depth and collaborative work and reinforce extemporaneous thinking skills
- Library and empirical research that illustrates the importance of problem definition and the use of the scientific reasoning processes

For gifted students served in the general education classroom, Feldhusen suggests that teachers select appropriate materials and monitor student mastery to ensure continuous progress as the major provisions employed.

The VanTassel-Baska chapter on creativity (Chapter 21) acknowledges that developing creativity in gifted students is a goal in gifted education programs across the United States. The construct of creativity has relevance for identification, programming, and assessment practices, yet common measurement instruments are not able to discern creativity from intelligence at the upper ranges. In fact, many researchers believe that creativity is best understood as an aspect of giftedness, not separate from it. Like intelligence, creativity displays itself through prodigious development in younger children and progresses toward quality adult-level products or performances over time.

Most contemporary views of creativity recognize the interrelationship of a variety of forces in influencing its development in individuals. Personal, social, and educational variables all play a role. VanTassel-Baska synthesizes the current research on the development of creativity into a matrix that identifies four categories of factors: internal, external, facilitating processes, and personal catalysts.

Despite the popularity of creativity programs for the gifted, the body of research on the effectiveness of direct teaching of creativity skills remains unconvincing. Many instructional materials are not grounded in a theoretical model, and programming strategies that view creativity as a set of specific skills appear to account for limited variance in creative behavior. In addition, much of the content of creativity programs is relevant for all populations of students, not just the gifted. VanTassel-Baska outlines steps schools can take to nurture creativity within the context of domain-specific programs and strategies that can be undertaken by parents.

Feldhusen's chapter on thinking skills (Chapter 22) stresses the importance of providing gifted students with instruction on much higher and more complex levels of thinking at an earlier point in the educational experience than for other learners. Although the real world requires the ability to use thinking skills in the context of specific disciplinary or cross-disciplinary domains and although emerging evidence suggests that the nature of thinking may differ from one discipline to another, evidence exists that the teaching of thinking skills is a helpful and enlightening process that complements student understanding. Models of thinking skills are particularly useful for ensuring that the curriculum for the gifted emphasizes agility and depth in applying information to novel and/or productive ends in society.

Feldhusen treats critical thinking, creative thinking, and metacognition as three frameworks for conceptualizing thinking processes or skills. Critical thinking can be defined as reflective and reasonable thinking directed toward an end belief or action, whereas creative thinking (or divergent thinking) emphasizes skills such as fluency, flexibility, originality, and elaboration in realistic contexts and in the disciplines. Metacognition, or how one thinks about and shapes one's own thinking processes, enhances the ability to think critically and creatively. Feldhusen highlights several models that address these three thinking components.

Each of the final three chapters in this section explores the major emphases necessary for providing sound programs for gifted and talented learners in specific disciplines of knowledge: mathematics and sciences, social studies and language arts, and arts and humanities. In mathematics, emphasis, based on a review of research, should be placed on early access issues, on instructional grouping, and on various approaches to acceleration. These are seen as the most effective ways of serving gifted students in this content area. The science emphasis is more broad-based, focusing on advanced content, science process, interdisciplinary opportunities, problem finding, problem solving, and the need for collaboration in worthwhile scientific endeavors. Technology is addressed as a sophisticated instructional tool to aid in the integration of learning as well as a major part of student research.

In the social studies area, gifted and talented learners need to appreciate the role of history, civics, and geography in understanding their world. The emphasis in this subject area is on integrating the ideas and issues that frame the discipline. An inquiry-based teaching approach that allows ready exploration of real-world problems has been found to be effective. Examples of law-based curricula are included in the social studies discussion to illustrate these emphases. In the language arts, the emphasis is placed on making appropriate choices in the study of literature, on the development necessary for mastering various forms of writing, especially expository modes, and on the importance of oral communication and language study as a formal part of the language arts curriculum.

Finally, in the arts and humanities, the emphasis for gifted and talented learners is on the integration of form and meaning as seen within, as well as across, the arts areas. Collaboration across arts areas is encouraged as is solid integration of aesthetics into the intellectual fabric of the gifted curriculum. A model is presented that emphasizes the relatively equal importance of communication, continuity, criticism, and creation in apprehending the artistic products of a world culture.

References ⌇

Stanley, J. C. (1978). SMPY's DT-PI model: Diagnostic testing followed by prescriptive instruction. *Intellectually Talented Youth Bulletin, 4*(10), 7–8.

Sternberg, R. J., & Horvath, J. A. (1995). A prototype view of expert teaching. *Educational Researcher, 24*(6), 9–17.

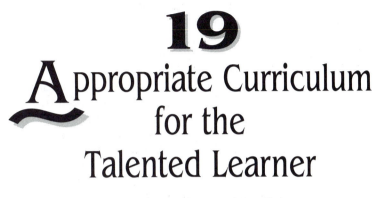

Appropriate Curriculum
for the
Talented Learner

Joyce VanTassel-Baska

No area of emphasis within gifted education better captures its core concepts than does the area of curriculum. Notions of differentiation of services are linked directly to the curriculum intervention provided. Thus, to espouse programs for the gifted is to advocate a differentiated curriculum based on the nature of the learner (see Chapter 10). Such differentiation, given the new content standards in all disciplines that stress higher order thinking and processing skills and interdisciplinary approaches, turns on several fundamental adaptations:

1. The *level* of the curriculum must be sufficiently advanced to interest and challenge the gifted learner.
2. The *pace* at which the curriculum is offered must be adjusted to accommodate both faster and slower rates, depending on the nature of the curriculum challenge.
3. The *complexity* of the curriculum should reflect the capacity of the gifted learner to engage in simultaneous rather than linear processing of ideas.
4. The *depth* of the curriculum should allow gifted learners to continue exploring an area of special interest to the level of an expert.

Current research on learning informs the current work in curriculum for the gifted. Research on expertise, on domain-specificity, on understanding, and on various models of intelligence all add to our ability to plan effectively for this special population.

Research on expertise has shown that experts and novices differ in metacognitive and executive control of cognition. Experts typically spend a greater proportion of their solution time trying to understand the problem to be solved. Novices, in contrast, typically invest less time in trying to understand the problem and more in actually trying out different solutions (Lesgold, 1984). While novices and experienced nonexperts seek to reduce problems to fit available methods, true experts seek progressively to elaborate on current understanding, continually working on the leading edge of their own knowledge and skill (Bereiter & Scardamalia, 1993).

The expertise studies relate directly to our understanding of gifted learners. Because gifted learners have attained automaticity of certain basic content skills earlier than other learners, they have the learning time to invest in more advanced and complex concepts and skills. These studies also coalesce with our understanding of gifted adolescents' preference for complexity (Csikszentmihalyi, Rathunde, & Whalen, 1993). Several studies of gifted students attest to the need for a sufficiently high challenge level in the curriculum, tasks tailored to interests, and choice over activities (Middleton, Littlefield, & Lehrer, 1992; VanTassel-Baska, 1992).

The idea that giftedness in the context of school represents domain-specific developmental advancement that varies both intrapersonally and interpersonally is well accepted by researchers (Howe, 1990; Keating, 1991; Matthews, 1993). It is also consistent with older (Stanley, 1997) and newer (Feldhusen, 1995; Gardner, 1991) conceptions of talent development. Moreover, studies of creativity (see Chapter 21) have suggested that creativity is built upon content acquisition and mastery and that it may be futile or deceptive to try to measure it in children separate from a field in which they display unusual competence (Feldman, 1991). Thus, in addressing issues of curriculum for gifted learners and the programs that undergird them, it is useful to acknowledge the importance of domain-specificity as a point of departure for effective planning.

Curriculum areas carry with them their own distinct approaches to learning in respect to style, techniques, and the habits of mind necessary to do the work (Gardner & Boix-Mansilla, 1994). Gaining such an understanding of the disciplines is the task of educators in an age of reform, just as it is valuable to expose students to the interdisciplinary connections that are possible to forge. Yet deep understanding in specific areas is necessary for meaningful cross-disciplinary work to occur.

In gifted education, one promising approach to linking identification, instruction, and assessment is the application of the triarchic theory to work in various subject domains (Sternberg & Clinkenbeard, 1995). A sample matrix of such applications is presented in Table 19.1. Although research results are tentative, the use of such approaches may allow us to employ more tailored and individualized approaches with gifted students based on tested differences in types of ability.

As one examines the issue of appropriate curriculum for the gifted, several questions deserve to be asked. These questions should be considered before moving into curriculum development.

Table 19.1 ～
Triarchic Theory Applied to Student Instruction and Assessment Methods

	Analytic	Creative	Practical
Psychology	Compare Freud's theory of dreaming to Crick's.	Design an experiment to test a theory of dreaming.	What are the implications of Freud's theory of dreaming for your life?
Biology	Evaluate the validity of the bacterial theory of ulcers.	Design an experiment to test the bacterial theory of ulcers.	How would the bacterial theory of ulcers change conventional treatment regimens?
Literature	In what ways were Catherine Earnshaw and Daisy Miller similar?	Write an alternative ending to *Wuthering Heights* uniting Catherine and Heathcliff in life.	Why are lovers sometimes cruel to each other and what can we do about it?
History	How did events in post-World War I lead to the rise of Nazism?	How might Truman have encouraged the surrender of Japan without A-bombing Hiroshima?	What lessons does Nazism hold for events in Bosnia today?
Mathematics	How is this mathematical proof flawed?	Prove how catastrophe theory might be applied to psychology.	How is trigonometry applied to construction of bridges?
Art	Compare and contrast how Rembrandt and Van Gogh used used light in...	Draw a beam of light.	How could we reproduce the lighting in this painting in the same actual room?

1. What should be the *content* of the curriculum for the gifted? Should it be different in substance from the curriculum of other learners or merely organized differently? Should the national content standards guide curriculum development for the gifted or should the curriculum proceed on a path distinctive from them?

2. How do we treat the cognitive processes of critical and creative thinking, problem solving, and decision making—as content in themselves or as overlays to existing content areas?

3. Can we define with precision and integrity what we mean by "differentiating" the curriculum for the gifted?

4. For what group of learners are we planning curricular experiences—only high achievers or a broader base of students who may vary in their profiles to the extent that a planned set of experiences may not be responsive to their needs?

5. How can we sequence curriculum experiences in such a way as to provide maximum learning for the gifted?

6. How can we best effect curriculum change for the gifted in schools—by developing and implementing new curriculum, by training, or by monitoring curriculum implementation?

We have not successfully been able to settle on workable answers to these questions in the past, but new theories and research efforts applied to practice bode well for the future. As we educate the gifted for the year 2000, it is clearly time to tackle these questions with renewed vigor.

Research on Curriculum for the Gifted ~

Research on appropriate curriculum for gifted children is fairly recent. Until the *Sputnik* era of the late 1950s—which resulted in programs that addressed specific content areas—few ideas about differentiated curriculum for the gifted had been studied systematically. Even though special classes had been in operation since 1919 in selected locations such as New York and Cleveland, the actual differences in instructional strategies, content, or materials between these and other classes were not examined. Grouping based on intelligence and achievement was the predominant strategy employed, and curriculum outlines and, sometimes, units were prepared for use with identified gifted students (Hall, 1956; Hollingworth, 1926).

In the 1960s and 1970s, educators in the field of the gifted conceptualized some general principles about appropriate curriculum for gifted children. Ward (1961) developed a theory of differential education for the gifted that established specific principles around which an appropriate curriculum for the gifted could be developed. Meeker (1969) used the Guilford structure of intellect to arrive at student profiles highlighting areas of strength and weakness so that curriculum planners could build a gifted program to improve weak areas. Curriculum workbooks were structured specifically to address appropriate curriculum in the areas of memory, cognition, convergent thinking, divergent thinking, and evaluation. Renzulli (1975) focused on a differentiated curriculum model that moved the gifted child from enrichment exposure activities through training in thinking and research skills into a project-oriented program that dealt with real problems to be solved. Gallagher and Gallagher (1995) stressed content modification in the core subject areas of language arts, social studies, mathematics, and science. Stanley, Keating, and Fox (1974) concentrated on a content acceleration model to differentiate programs for the gifted.

More recent writings (e.g., Maker & Nielson, 1996) have stressed a confluent approach to differentiation of curriculum for the gifted that includes both acceleration and enrichment strategies. Passow (1982) formulated seven cardinal curriculum principles that reflect content, process, product, behavioral, and evaluative considerations. VanTassel-Baska (1993b) developed an outline of 20 aspects of good curriculum for the gifted that emphasize the confluence of advanced content, process/product, and concept/theme dimensions of a curriculum into an Integrated Curriculum Model (ICM) that has been tested in science and language arts classrooms nationally. Data from two preliminary studies indicate that gifted learners taught the curriculum developed from this model outperform controls in higher level thinking skill task demands (VanTassel-Baska, Johnson, Hughes, & Boyce, 1996; VanTassel-Baska, Bass, Ries, & Poland, in press).

State of the Art ∼

In examining the state of the art with respect to gifted curriculum, one is struck by the abstract broadness of the principles compared to the one-dimensionality of the practice. To implement appropriate curriculum for gifted students, there must be concern for the translation of theoretical principles into good practice in a holistic manner so that education of the gifted is complete, not fragmented. This can be accomplished if we focus on the core elements to be addressed:

1. Gifted children learn at a different rate from other children, and accommodation of that rate is crucial to their development (Keating, 1976). Furthermore, differences in rate or pace can be so great that they necessitate differences in kind, not merely degree, of instruction (Ward, 1961).

2. Gifted children crave *depth* in key areas of learning. Educators have addressed this need through "enrichment," which tends to be a superficial add-on to the curriculum. The issue of depth cannot be addressed by this type of approach. It can, however, be addressed by examining key areas of learning in terms of their essence, core, and inherent concepts and exploring with gifted children through Socratic means what these key concepts are and how they relate to all areas of learning. Appropriate learning materials for such work include *Ascent of Man*, by Jacob Bronowski (1973); *Connections,* by James Burke (1978); and *Civilization,* by Kenneth Clark (1969).

3. Gifted children need the challenge and stimulation of being together for at least part of every school day, with expectation levels set high enough to stretch their potential ability to realize them. Setting high expectation levels does not imply more work at low levels of difficulty but, rather, unending work at complex levels of operation. In that sense, meaningful work for the gifted is that which creates more questions that require exploration and leads to continued study on an individual or small-group basis. These expectations can be set and worked on only in a climate in which children have similar levels of ability and understanding. Therefore, grouping of gifted children becomes essential.

4. Gifted children need programs and services during the entire span of years that they are in school. Their giftedness frequently manifests itself by age 3 and requires nurturance on a regular basis from that time forward. Thus, K–12 articulated planning and programming for all gifted students is essential.

Once these basic elements have been understood, we can begin to examine the areas of learning that are most facilitative for gifted students.

Traditional Content Learning ⌇

The myth persists that some semblance of a program is better than no program at all. Once students are in a gifted program, they tend to respond favorably to it, regardless of its structure or focus. Consequently, we sometimes are hard-pressed to show that the *nature* of a particular treatment has made a difference, as opposed to the mere fact that some treatment occurred. Even positive evaluations overall may be more a manifestation of the Hawthorne effect than of "significant difference."* Gifted programs, just by their existence, often offer emotional and motivational support for many gifted children, who then "take off" on their own.

However, as we become more knowledgeable about identifying talent at early ages, we must plan for programmatic intervention much more carefully and consistently. Solid research has shown that mathematical talent and foreign language ability can be developed most economically through an accelerative mode (Keating, 1976; Stanley et al., 1974; VanTassel-Baska, 1981). Primarily descriptive studies have implied that enrichment is useful to a student's fuller understanding of the world (Gallagher & Gallagher, 1995). We have teachers who are trained to teach content. We may have teachers who can teach creative processes. We know that schools are organized to handle gifted children best within content areas (especially at grades 7–12). Based on these observations, it seems prudent to build a foundational program for gifted students within the basic domains of knowledge—the sciences, mathematics, the humanities, the social sciences, and the behavioral sciences.

---

* The Hawthorne effect refers to the positive effect brought about by the act of experimentation itself, based on a set of studies conducted at the Hawthorne plant of the Western Electric Company by researcher Elton Mayo from 1923 to 1932.

Curriculum Conceptualization

Why should curriculum for the gifted be conceptualized within the framework of the basic domains of knowledge? To satisfy gifted students' need for depth, exposure to these traditional areas of learning is essential, not only to develop and refine proficiency skills in verbal and quantitative areas but also to allow for expanded growth into related disciplines and interdisciplinary studies. A firm understanding of a field of inquiry must precede "creative dabbling." Gifted writers have thoroughly mastered techniques of writing and have refined their skills through repeated practice. The "creative" aspect of writing demands a high level of proficiency in the skill and repeated use of both ends of the writing implement before a product can be perceived as art. By the same token, gifted students benefit greatly from curriculum experiences that go beyond and across the traditional content areas in order to acquire an integrated understanding of knowledge. Curriculum for the gifted should connote the literal meaning of the Latin root for the term *education*—a "leading out" from one point in experience to view the larger perspective.

A curriculum that does not have a strong content base or focus has little richness. In reality, identifying aptitude that corresponds to a content area such as mathematics or the verbal arts is far easier than conceptualizing programming in another fashion. Specific content areas provide the appropriate match for specific aptitudes. We would not think of providing a child with high musical aptitude a program in futuristics or an independent study in building an electrical car. Yet, similarly inappropriate practices frequently are applied to students who have readily identifiable aptitudes in specific academic areas. Students with high mathematical aptitude should receive a strong program in mathematics concepts and systems. Students with high verbal abilities should be provided programs in foreign language, rich literature, and writing.

I do not intend to imply that serving the gifted appropriately requires only a direct match to a specific identified aptitude area. In the minds of most educators of gifted students, much more is needed. The research base on the positive effects of this approach with precocious students, however, is impressive (Durden, 1979; Lynch, 1992; Stanley et al., 1974). Yet, this deceptively simple approach of matching aptitudes to curriculum offerings rarely occurs in the average elementary school in this country and is subverted at the middle-school and high-school levels by inflexible scheduling and programming.

Misconceptions in Teaching Traditional Content

Perhaps traditional content domains have been passed over in curricular work in the education of the gifted because of several misconceptions. One of these is that the gifted study these content areas in their general school program, and therefore the gifted should have a "special" curriculum. Unfortunately, the content that the gifted receive in the general school program is minimal compared to what they are capable of learning. If content were rearranged and restructured around a conceptual framework, the gifted could master whole content areas in half the time currently spent.

Such a compression of content facilitates proficiency and the learning of conceptual wholes. It also allows more time for gifted learners to pursue related areas of interest. For example, the gifted may master all the principles of English grammar and syntax in less than 4 weeks of instruction in any given year. By demonstrating this proficiency on a criterion-referenced test, they then can begin to apply that knowledge to their specific areas of language interest: a course in Latin, a workshop in composition writing, a debate team. Instead, we tend to introduce grammar in minute sections, drag it out over 12 years of English instruction, and never present it so that the gifted have the opportunity to grasp the total linguistic picture or to learn new language systems.

Another misconception is that content acceleration merely means moving through the same material faster. In reality, good content acceleration allows for faster pacing of well organized, compressed, and appropriate learning experiences for the gifted. Real enrichment for the gifted in the content areas can occur only if a fast-paced compressed model is utilized. Otherwise, content is trivialized or disconnected to what is happening in the general program. We can focus on teaching logic as an enrichment topic for the gifted in math, but we must be prepared to accelerate and compress it to accommodate the gifted learner. Thus, enrichment topics define a content focus, not an appropriate treatment.

A third misconception concerning the use of content areas with gifted students is that there are areas of learning outside the traditional subject matter that are more important for them to explore for purposes of developing their potential creativity. Yet, creativity without subject matter competency has no meaning (Feldman, 1991; Stanley, 1980). Creative mathematicians in real life must be proficient in mathematics before they can apply math principles and concepts in new and diverse ways. Even in applied areas of endeavor such as engineering, medicine, and education, conceptual proficiency in core content domains of knowledge is critical.

Thinking Skills Learning⁓

If accelerative and in-depth experiences are provided to the gifted as an initial curriculum modification, the development of skills in critical or creative thinking and research can merge with each area to be studied. By their nature, good critical and creative thinking experiences are adaptable with respect to content, age level, and the experience of participants. These experiences tend to be presented through teaching strategies that create diverse and motivated responses. Their purpose is primarily to provide a prelude to analytical and creative endeavors, regardless of type, and to open up children to fuller expression of their potential (Feldhusen & Kolloff, 1978). Because this is the case, restructuring and infusing a program with these aspects of the curriculum is easier than sacrificing traditional content areas or treating the experiences as an add-on to the curriculum.

Development of process skills in students should be viewed as basic to their curriculum and should begin as soon as they enter school. These "basics for the gifted" would reflect practice in the following skill areas:

- Critical thinking
- Creative thinking
- Problem finding and problem solving
- Research
- Decision making

Each of these skills should be linked directly to a content domain. Thus, gifted students might learn problem solving in mathematics, critical thinking in literature, and decision making in history. Skill development in all five areas is stressed on a hierarchical K–12 basis. This approach appears to be promising in light of the lack of research on process programs that demonstrate transfer of these skills to content dimensions after the skills have been mastered in isolation (Perkins & Salomon, 1989).

Learning Concepts ~

Conceptual learning for the gifted puts a premium on providing students with a good scaffolding of important concepts that constitute the structure of each discipline as well as providing them with important pathways between disciplines so that separate aspects of knowledge are understood as being integrated. A conceptual approach to curriculum focuses on large organizational themes and issues in order to frame the curriculum at an appropriate level. This approach allows for maximum applications in various domains. Some major concepts used frequently in curriculum development work are:

- Change
- Systems
- Models
- Patterns
- Origins
- Signs and symbols
- Power

New learning theory research postulates that declarative knowledge is best taught through a concept approach. Such learning is crucial to understanding any discipline, and in each discipline no more than 8 to 14 concepts should be taught across a K–12 continuum (Marzano, Brandt, Hughes, Jones, Presseisen, Rankin, & Suhor, 1988). The emphasis in concept learning is on depth, interdisciplinarity, and understanding important ideas within a discipline. Gifted students are in an excellent position to benefit from such a curriculum approach since it honors their capacity to make connections among bodies of knowledge easily and to deal effectively with abstractions and complexity of thought (VanTassel-Baska, 1995).

Modifications of curriculum that employ a concept orientation typically teach a core set of generalizations about the concept through carefully selected applications. Student learning is then assessed on depth of understanding of how the chosen concept may be applied to different knowledge areas. Table 19.2 illustrates this point.

Table 19.2~
Illustration of a Concept-Based Approach
to Curriculum Development

Concept: Systems	Concept: Change
Generalizations	*Generalizations*
1. Systems have identifiable elements.	1. Change is pervasive.
2. Systems have definable boundaries.	2. Change is linked to time.
3. Most systems receive input in the form of material or information from outside their boundaries and generate output to the world outside their boundaries.	3. Change may be perceived as systematic or random.
4. The interactions of a system's elements with one another and their response to input from outside the system combine to determine the overall nature and behavior of the system.	4. Change may represent growth and development or regression and decay.
	5. Change may occur according to natural order or be imposed by individuals or groups.
Applications to Science	*Applications to Language Arts*
	Students will be able to:
A. Students will be able to analyze several systems during the course of the unit. These include the "problem system," defined by the boundaries of the area affected by the acid spill; the stream ecosystem (into which the acid flows); and the transportation system (which is disrupted by the acid spill). In addition, all experiments set up during the course will be treated as systems.	A. Understand that change is pervasive.
B. For each system, students will be able to use appropriate systems language to identify boundaries, important elements, input, and output.	B. Illustrate the variability of change based on time.
C. Students will be able to analyze the interactions of various system compo-	C. Categorize types of change, given several examples.

(continued)

Table 19.2 continued

nents with one another and with input into the system, both for the real-world systems and for the experimental systems.

D. Based on their understanding of each system's functioning, students will be able to predict the impact of various approaches to the cleanup of the acid spill on each relevant system.

E. Students will be able to transfer their knowledge about systems in general to a newly encountered system. In the final assessment activity, students will be given a new system to analyze in the same way that they have analyzed the systems in the unit.

D. Interpret change as progressive or regressive in selected works.

E. Demonstrate the change process at work in a piece of literature.

F. Analyze social and individual change in a given piece of literature.

Applications to Technology

Computer systems

Applications to Technology

Technological advances as societal changes

Applications to Mathematics

Number systems

Applications to Mathematics

Tessellations as change in form

Applications to Social Sciences

Transportation systems; social, political, and economic systems

Applications to Social Sciences

Cycles and trends in social, political, and economic life

Note: From Science and Language Arts Curriculum Units prepared by the Center for Gifted Education, College of William and Mary.

Product Development ⁓

Much emphasis in the gifted curriculum has been placed on students' generating real-world products. That has been a core feature of differentiating the curriculum for them in schools (Renzulli, 1975, 1995), and very popular models in the field have been based on this emphasis (Delcourt, 1994; Moon & Feldhusen, 1994). Self-selected or mutually negotiated projects between teacher and learner that lead to meaningful products might be best viewed in the context of a student's total curriculum experience. As such, the emphasis on meaningful project work in content areas is well placed, as it allows students the opportunity to create on their own and to apply and expand ideas learned in class.

As with any approach, overuse of project work and product development can become a detriment to a gifted curriculum, especially if it consumes large amounts of instructional time and is not well grounded in a discipline. The opportunities provided for generative open-ended learning, however, are important outcomes to be anticipated.

Learning the Arts ⁓

Certainly gifted children need the rigor of an advanced program in a content area in which they excel, coupled with an emphasis on critical and creative thinking and research. In addition to these components, gifted children need experiences in the arts for development of high intellectual potential, and they need such training as early as kindergarten. A good gifted program should incorporate the arts, both in terms of developing performance skills and developing aesthetic judgment throughout the education continuum. For students with special abilities in these areas, intensive training may be most appropriate.

Why the arts? Real enrichment, it can be argued, consists of offering new awareness about the world that has a deep relevance to the individual. Surely the arts can offer this in a way that other fields cannot, for the arts tap into the emotional center of human beings (Eisner, 1984). We are responsive to art and music and the performing arts because we are human, and they touch us as human beings. The immense difference one senses in live performance versus the electronically filtered reproduction of a recording makes the point eloquently.

What we know about the nature of gifted children would lead us to include in the gifted curriculum a strong component in the arts. Their high-level differential characteristics such as high-level sensitivity, keenness of perception, and ability to understand interrelationships and grasp meanings (Clark, 1980) all reflect a need for exposure to aesthetic experiences that allow for further development of these traits. In addition, research studies on eminence have pointed to the passion for and importance of the arts displayed by individuals who are exceptional in fields other than artistic endeavor (Cox, 1926; Goertzel & Goertzel, 1962).

Teaching the arts to the gifted is also particularly critical in developing an understanding of self and others, based on the interrelationship of thoughts and feelings. All of the arts offer a medium for understanding the congruence of ideas and emotions. The arts provide direct access to emotional response, but through a rational process and presentation. The arts can be a vehicle for developing aesthetic judgment, thus offering many opportunities for the acquisition of evaluation skills. Setting criteria to measure the value of art objects, a piece of music, or a performance enables gifted students to act as "critics" and to develop the intellectual framework for this kind of effort.

Offering an arts component in a curriculum for the gifted can be a good stimulus for some students to begin the formal study of a particular area. For example, a student may wish to pursue musicology as a result of early music experiences. Another may wish to intern in a museum to learn the job of curator. Thus, career exploration can be merged with serious study in a specific area of interest.

The arts also lend themselves well to the development of meaningful projects, not only in terms of conceptualization but also in terms of the actual mode of presentation. Children who have experienced theater are more apt to try to create it than those who have not. Similarly, children exposed to the visual arts are more apt to employ them in a creative product. Consequently, product development can be enhanced greatly by systematic work in the arts.

Relating various areas of the arts in some manner also offers to gifted children an excellent opportunity to analyze and synthesize information in the aesthetic domain. It builds on their strong ability to grasp interrelationships and comprehend meaning at high levels. Deliberately planned experiences that use "forced association" as a technique work well in the arts and begin to move children toward free association among other arts experiences. At junior-high and high-school levels, the interrelationships can take the form of a humanities program in which the arts are seen as an avenue to other fields, such as philosophy, history, and literature.

Values Education～

Most people would agree that high-level ability that is not directed in socially constructive ways may be socially dangerous. Thus, curriculum for the gifted should include components of values education through which students can learn to examine their own values as well as the values of others. Some research has suggested that gifted students often are concerned about the moral and ethical dimensions of questions (Gallagher & Gallagher, 1995). Therefore, the study of competing value systems would serve to enhance the understanding of an area of identified interest. Assuming that gifted students often become the leaders of tomorrow, the moral, social, and ethical dimensions of topics seem particularly relevant as an area for study in its own right or infused into other aspects of learning.

Additional Services and Programs～

This chapter has stressed traditional content, process skills, concepts, and the arts as key components in an ideal curriculum for the gifted. Other special services and programs uniquely appropriate for this population are needed as well. Areas such as counseling, career education, and mentorships should be considered.

Counseling

Counseling is not usually considered a part of curriculum, yet it is a service that provides the key framework that allows the curriculum delivery system to work for gifted students. Therefore, counseling services become a curricular concern.

Particularly at middle-school and high-school levels, counseling (or lack of it) determines what courses and level of courses the students will take. For gifted students to receive appropriate curriculum, they must be informed about specific courses that address their area(s) of strength. In addition, gifted students should have the opportunity to learn to understand and cope with their exceptionality in small-group sharing sessions, receive training in decision-making skills, and be provided with alternative choices involving course taking, colleges, and careers (VanTassel-Baska, 1990).

Counseling for the gifted should occur throughout the span of their school years. Although coping skills may be most critical at the elementary level, academic counseling becomes important by junior high school, as decisions often have to be made four years in advance. Choices of what college to attend and what career to pursue become important counseling issues by ninth grade and should be reflected in a specific structured program provided by the school. Parent involvement in all aspects of the counseling program is essential, as is the use of teachers to perform the counseling function. Utilization of counseling specialists may be necessary in the case of gifted youths who experience unusual difficulty in adjustment, achievement, and other school-related issues.

Career Education

Concern for career education for gifted individuals stems from their natural profusion of abilities in regard to life's alternatives. Because many of these students are good at so many kinds of tasks, to focus attention and energy on one line of endeavor is sometimes difficult and even painful for them. Career education can enhance their powers of decision making by enabling informed choices based on assessments of strength, interest, and values (Hoyt & Hebeler, 1974). Furthermore, the gifted can learn to appreciate the uniqueness of their potential through recognizing life themes as a basis for career choice (Silverman, 1993).

By the same token, some gifted students are very sure at an early age about the career avenue they wish to pursue. Career education can supplement these students' avid interest in a field by providing internship experiences in the desired career area as early as junior high school. In addition, it can help both student and parent plan ahead for educational experiences that would be most profitable, given the student's clarity of choice. Many times, irrelevant requirements can be avoided if the course of study is well defined (VanTassel-Baska, 1993a).

Mentorships

Much of the research on eminent persons clearly points to the profound influence of a single tutor, friend, or family member on the gifted child (Bloom, 1985; Cox, 1926; Goertzel & Goertzel, 1962). Both as an aid to cognitive learning and for emotional support, the one-to-one relationship has provided special benefits for the development of exceptional potential.

Although the tutorial approach may be ideal, it is hardly practical for schools to consider for more than a few students and rather difficult for parents to implement on their own. But creating the opportunity for gifted children to experience a mentor relationship even on a limited basis can be facilitative to their development (Pleiss & Feldhusen, 1995).

Creating a mentorship experience requires two fundamental steps: (1) developing a resource bank of adults in the community who have an interest in working with gifted students and who have high-level expertise in a particular area, and (2) identifying students who can profit from exposure to these adults and who share similar abilities and interests with the chosen mentor. A structured mentorship program can focus on a contract between student and mentor for completion of specific tasks or a project over a predetermined time period (Cox & Daniel, 1983; Ellington, Haeger, & Feldhusen, 1986). Other collaborative opportunities can develop out of the working relationship that is established, such as an "apprenticeship" situation in a research laboratory, a joint publication, or a shared presentation at a professional meeting.

Key Issues in Development and Implementation of Curriculum ~

A curriculum for the gifted must be more than the sum of the components just discussed. It must represent an interaction between the content dimension, the instructional dimension, and the logistical dimension. Although this chapter has been concerned primarily with the content dimension, certain logistical issues that provide the framework and setting for the delivery of content as well as certain instructional issues merit comment.

Principles and Instructional/Logistical Implications

The curriculum committee of the Leadership Training Institute conceptualized seven principles about the gifted curriculum that contain instructional and logistical implications (Passow, 1982):

1. The content of curricula for the gifted should focus on, and be organized to include, more elaborate, complex, and in-depth study of major ideas, problems, and themes that integrate knowledge within and across systems of thought.
2. Curricula for the gifted should allow for the development and application of productive thinking skills to enable students to reconceptualize existing knowledge and generate new knowledge.
3. Curricula for the gifted should enable them to explore constantly changing knowledge and information and develop the attitude that knowledge is worth pursuing in an open world.
4. Curricula for the gifted should encourage exposure to, selection of, and use of specialized and appropriate resources.
5. Curricula for the gifted should promote self-initiated and self-directed learning and growth.

6. Curricula for the gifted should provide for the development of self-under-standing and the understanding of one's relationships to persons, societal institutions, nature, and culture.

7. Evaluations of curricula for the gifted should be conducted in accordance with prior stated principles, stressing higher level thinking skills, creativity, and excellence in performance and products.

Borland (1989) cited the following issues as essential to developing curriculum for the gifted. Curriculum:

1. Must be developed from a systematic study of a body of knowledge
2. Must identify what basic knowledge, declarative and procedural, students need to learn
3. Must be logically structured in a scope and sequence to promote mastery
4. Must be differentiated from the mainstream curriculum
5. Must employ good instructional design
6. Must be articulated with core curriculum

VanTassel-Baska (1993b) provided the checklist of curriculum principles given in Table 19.3, some of which represent general curricular considerations and some of which represent specific ones deemed appropriate for the gifted.

Scope and Sequence

Good curriculum must reflect progressive development in both skill and content are-nas (Borland, 1989; Tyler, 1958) and as such, appropriate pacing and diversity must be maintained. Student interest should be a prime input factor in modifying curric-ular units and teacher expectations with regard to the expansion of educational and cultural opportunities for gifted students.

The curriculum should reflect provisions for accelerating skill building in the areas of reading, writing, research, the use of computers and scientific apparatus, and mathematical problem solving. It should demonstrate well-planned sequential development of increasingly difficult content and processes and include materials and activities that will provide for the development of skills in group and individual problem solving and decision making. Interdisciplinary curriculum units should pro-vide for conceptual development over time. Themes such as humankind's search for identity, the question of authority, and the concept of unity could be explored at sev-eral grade levels with more sophisticated objectives at each succeeding level.

The scope of full-time curriculum for the gifted should be broad-based and as comprehensive as possible, given the level of ability and interest of the students. At the same time, curriculum experiences must be carefully structured to promote max-imum learning in specific aptitude areas.

Differentiation

Most gifted programs, it is generally agreed, may be distinguished from general edu-cation programs by placing more emphasis on the following curriculum considera-tions:

Table 19.3~
Checklist of Curriculum Principles for Use in Developing Gifted/Talented Programs

General Principles

☐ 1. Continuity—a well-defined set of learning activities that reinforce the specified curriculum objective

☐ 2. Diversity—provisions for alternative means to attain determined ends within a specified curricular framework

☐ 3. Integration—integrative use of all abilities, including cognition, emotion, and intuition

☐ 4. Substantive learning—inclusion of subject matter, skills, products, and awareness that are of consequence to the learner and to the discipline

☐ 5. Consistency with good teaching/learning methodologies—inclusion of varied teaching practices that allow for motivation, practice, transfer of training, and feedback

☐ 6. Interaction with peers and significant others—provisions to learn about and meet with individuals who share same and different talents/gifts

☐ 7. Value system—inclusion of consistent opportunities to develop and examine personal and societal values and to establish a personal value system

☐ 8. Communication skills—development of verbal and nonverbal systems and skills to discuss, share, and exchange ideas

☐ 9. Multiple resources—provision of a variety of material and human resources as part of the learning process

Specific Principles for Gifted Curriculum

☐ 1. Appropriateness—curriculum based on assessment of abilities, interests, needs, and learning styles of gifted students

☐ 2. Openness—elimination of preset expectations that limit the learnings within the curricular framework

☐ 3. Independence—provisions for some type(s) of self-directed learning

☐ 4. Complexity—provision for exposure to systems of knowledge, underlying principles and concepts, and key theories about what students study

☐ 5. Interdisciplinary learning—provisions for transfer of learning to other domains of knowledge, new situations, and so on

☐ 6. Decision making—provisions for students to make some appropriate/relevant decisions regarding what is to be learned and how

☐ 7. Creation/re-creation—provisions to apply the creative process to improve and modify one's creations and to challenge prevailing thought and offer more appropriate solutions

(continued)

Table 1.3 continued

- ☐ 8. Timing—appropriation of time span for learning activities that is consistent with characteristics of gifted learners for shorter/longer allotments
- ☐ 9. Accelerated/advanced pacing of content—provision for quickness and aptness of gifted students to master new material
- ☐ 10. Economy—compressed and streamlined organization of teaching material to match learning capacity of gifted students
- ☐ 11. Challenge—provision for a sophisticated level of learning experience that requires gifted learners to stretch their understandings

1. *The principle of economy* seeks to delete or compress a gifted student's basic curriculum in content skills that he or she has mastered independently or can master quickly if the organization of content focuses on concept mastery. Thus, a student who comes to school reading holistically would not be expected to spend kindergarten and first grade in reading readiness programs or heavy phonics training. Rather, a reading program would be devised focusing on developmental reading skills such as vocabulary, comprehension, and interpretation. Phonics work would be organized into a set of skills for quick mastery by this student.

2. *Concentration on higher level thinking skills and concepts* is an important tool for the gifted student as a producer rather than a consumer of knowledge. Application of skills such as critical and creative thinking is essential for meaningful work in any context.

3. *Concentration on the interrelationships among bodies of knowledge* focuses on depth in the curriculum plan developed for the gifted. Based on Ward's (1961) theory of differential education for the gifted, it establishes the concept of content integration by schemas and systems for the gifted as the highest order of importance.

4. *Exposure to nontraditional school subjects* provides gifted students with challenging areas of traditional liberal arts curriculum not typically offered in elementary and secondary schools, such as logic, law, and philosophy. Early exposure and training in foreign language at the elementary level also could be an offering in this context.

5. *Self-directed learning* enables gifted students to develop responsibility and take charge of their own learning and growth. Upon demonstrating such responsibility, students will have access to more program options of an independent nature.

6. *Commitment to future learning*. Gifted students must become sensitive to the knowledge explosion and the impact of technology on the task of learning, with the view that learning will be a fulfilling, lifelong pursuit.

The resultant curriculum, then, is more complex, more open-ended, and focuses at a more abstract level of thought than is typical of school-based curriculum for all learners. These features of differentiation are still critical today to attend to in the context of educational reform.

Grouping

Most educators who work with the gifted believe that the practice of putting young-sters of similar abilities, interests, and learning styles together for large portions of time is extremely beneficial. Gifted youngsters enjoy more than almost anything else the opportunity to exchange ideas among themselves without fear of being laughed at or scorned. Some programs group youngsters only periodically or for a certain time each day. However, extensive grouping by interest and ability is needed for gift-ed students to fully develop their potential. Recent research supports the contention that grouping gifted students together enhances their achievement and positive atti-tude toward the subject matter (Kulik & Kulik, 1992). For a complete treatment of this issue, see Chapter 15.

Instructional grouping enables students to grow in ways that are not possible under other arrangements, and this approach allows a program to reveal its effec-tiveness much more readily. The historical development of gifted programs high-lights the strong relationship between the longevity of a program and its grouping patterns. Both the Cleveland Major Work Program and the Bronx High School of Science have survived for more than 50 years and employ full-time grouping of gift-ed students in all academic areas. Comprehensive programs for the gifted should uti-lize instructional grouping strategies as frequently as possible to enhance continuity of individual student progress in curriculum areas as well as the continuity and effec-tiveness of the overall program.

Curriculum Articulation

Any school district that takes on the task of developing a gifted program must care-fully develop an overall articulation plan that allows for identification of its gifted population at the kindergarten level and offers appropriate curriculum for that pop-ulation on a K–12 basis. In many districts, funds do not exist to implement a total program in any given year, but total articulation can be accomplished within a rea-sonable span of time. An example might be a 3-year plan in which K–3 students and identified high school students receive programming during year 1, students in grades 4-6 receive programming in year 2, and those in grades 7–8 in year 3. In this way, all students identified in year 1 will receive appropriate services from the point of identification, yet the district will have an opportunity to stagger its program implementation.

Curriculum articulation of this kind is important for several reasons:

1. Once a student has been identified and offered a program at any given level, he or she has the right to expect that it will continue on the same basis.
2. Because content acceleration is and should be a facet of curriculum for the gifted, students should not have to return to a level of work less than their state of advancement.

Table 19.4 ～
Essential Curriculum Components for Gifted Students

Acceleration, Compression, and Reorganization of Content Based on Proficiency (examples)

K–3	4–6	7–8	9–12
Reading Mathematics Science Social studies Literature/language arts	Reading Mathematics Science Social studies Literature/language arts	Access to high school coursework In selected content areas including mathematics, foreign language, English study, social studies, science	Access to upper-level high school and/or college courses Advanced Placement courses according to strength areas Foreign language instruction—third and fourth year of a foreign language

Infusion of Process Skills and Nontraditional Content (examples)

K–3	4–6	7–8	9–12
Problem-solving strategies Science experimentation via computers Expository and creative writing Creative dramatics Introduction of foreign languages Development of critical and creative thinking skills Learning of basic research skills on topics of interest	A computer literacy program Foreign language instruction Research projects Theater arts Junior Great Books Man: A Course of Study (MACOS)	Foreign language instruction (second year) A course in logic Selective reading and discussion groups Humanities course Computer programming Advanced research projects	Art appreciation Music appreciation Leadership Psychology Anthropology Urban planning Political science Law Creativity

Integration of Curriculum Experiences According to Ideas, Issues, and Themes (examples)

K–3	4–6	7–8	9–12
Change as reflected in the conventions of society (shelter, clothing, food) Signs and symbols that make up our world (words, traffic signs, language gestures)	Change as reflected in the development of major cultures in respect to art, language, inventive mathematics Symbol systems (languages, mathematics, sign language)	Change as reflected in the development of major cultures The development of a symbol system (codes, computer language)	Change as reflected in the development of major cultures Symbol systems as represented in the real world (abstract mathematics, genetic patterns, literary symbols)

3. Growth gains and attitude changes can be adversely affected by curriculum coming too late in a student's career or stopping in the middle.

An Ideal Curriculum for the Gifted ～

Table 19.4 incorporates all the curricular components discussed in this chapter. It highlights the need for content specialization. It attends to the need for acceleration, enrichment, and other special services in educating the gifted. It recognizes the role of thinking skills in developing students' potential, and it provides appropriate experiences in the arts. It demonstrates progressive and sequential development of broad curriculum areas on a K–12 basis and suggests the need for comprehensive services across the span of school years. It highlights differentiation issues in an integrated fashion. It may serve as a guide for schools and parents in making sound educational decisions around curriculum alternatives for gifted and talented students.

The table also provides examples of topics/courses that might be offered at a grade-level cluster. Sequence of a topic or content area is suggested across clusters by section. The intent of the table is to suggest ideas and principles discussed in this chapter, not to prescribe for any given school program.

Summary ～

This chapter has contended that a content-based curriculum is the core of any program for gifted and talented students. It has argued for including traditional subject matter areas taught from a process and concept perspective as well as experiences in the arts. It has demonstrated that conceptual learning and enrichment in the content areas must be accompanied by appropriate content acceleration allowing for both pacing and depth. It has asserted the need for a facilitative grouping model to accommodate a full range of comprehensive articulated programs and services to gifted students at all grade levels.

References ～

Bereiter, C., & Scardamalia, M. (1993). *Surpassing ourselves: An inquiry into the nature and implications of expertise.* Chicago: Open Court.

Bloom, B. (1985). *Developing talent in young people.* New York: Ballantine.

Borland, J. (1989). *Planning and implementing programs for the gifted.* New York: Teachers College Press.

Bronowski, J. (1973). *Ascent of man.* Boston: Little, Brown.

Burke, J. (1978). *Connections.* Boston: Little, Brown.

Clark, B. (1980). *Growing up gifted.* Columbus, OH: Charles E. Merrill.

Clark, K. (1969). *Civilization.* New York: Harper & Row.

Cox, C. M. (1926). *Genetic studies of genius* (Vol. 2). Stanford, CA: Stanford University Press.

Cox, J., & Daniel, N. (1983, September–October). The role of the mentor. *G/C/T,* 54–61.

Csikszentmihalyi, M., Rathunde, K., & Whalen, S. (1993). *Talented teenagers: The roots of success and failure.* Cambridge: Cambridge University Press.

Delcourt, M. (1994). Characteristics of high level creative productivity: A longitudinal study of students identified by Renzulli's three-ring conception of giftedness. In R. Subotnik & K. Arnold (Eds.),

Beyond Terman: Contemporary longitudinal studies of giftedness and talent (pp. 401–436). Norwood, NJ: Ablex.

Durden, W. (1979). The Johns Hopkins program for verbally gifted youth. *Roeper Review, 2*(3), 34–37.

Eisner, E. (1984). *Educational evaluation.* London: Falmer Press.

Ellingson, M., Haeger, W., & Feldhusen, J. (1986, March–April). The Purdue mentor program. *G/C/T,* 2–5.

Feldhusen, J. (1995). Talent development: The new direction in gifted education. *Roeper Review, 18*(2),

Feldhusen, J., & Kolloff, M. (1978). A three-stage model for gifted education. *G/C/T, 1,* 53–58.

Feldman, D. H. (1991). Why children can't be creative. *Exceptionality Education Canada, 1*(1), 43–51.

Gallagher, J., & Gallagher, S. (1995). *Teaching the gifted child* (4th ed.). Boston: Allyn & Bacon.

Gardner, H. (1991). *The unschooled mind: How children think and how schools should teach.* New York: Basic Books.

Gardner, H., & Boix-Mansilla, V. (1994). Teaching for understanding—within and across the disciplines. *Educational Leadership, 51*(5), 14–18.

Goertzel, V., & Goertzel, M. (1962). *Cradles of eminence.* Boston: Little, Brown.

Hall, T. (1956). *Gifted children: The Cleveland story.* Cleveland, OH: World Publishing.

Hollingworth, L. (1926). *Gifted children.* New York: World Book.

Howe, M. J. A. (1990). *The origins of exceptional abilities.* Oxford: Basil Blackwell.

Hoyt, K., & Hebeler, J. (1974). *Career education for the gifted and talented.* Salt Lake City, UT: Olympus.

Keating, D. (1976). *Intellectual talent: Research and development.* Baltimore, MD: Johns Hopkins University Press.

Keating, D. (1991). Curriculum options for the developmentally advanced: A developmental alternative to gifted education. *Exceptionality Education Canada, 1,* 53–83.

Kulik, J. A., & Kulik, C. C. (1992). Meta-analytic findings on grouping programs. *Gifted Child Quarterly, 36*(2), 73–77.

Lesgold, A. (1984). *Human skill in a computerized society.* Austin, TX: Psychonomic Society.

Lynch, S. J. (1992). Fast-paced high school science for the academically talented: A six-year perspective. *Gifted Child Quarterly, 36*(3), 147–154.

Maker, J., & Nielson, A. (1996). *Curriculum development and teaching strategies for gifted learners.* Austin, TX: Pro-Ed.

Marzano, R. J., Brandt, R. S., Hughes, C. S., Jones, B. F., Presseisen, B. Z., Rankin, S. C., & Suhor, C. (1988). *Dimensions of thinking: A framework for curriculum and instruction.* Alexandria, VA: Association for Supervision and Curriculum Development.

Matthews, D. J. (1993). Linguistic giftedness in the context of domain-specific development. *Exceptionality Education Canada, 3*(3), 1–23.

Meeker, M. (1969). *The structure of intellect: Its interpretations and uses.* Columbus, OH: Charles E. Merrill.

Middleton, J. A., Littlefield, J., & Lehrer, R. (1992). Gifted students' conceptions of academic fun: An examination of a critical construct for gifted education. *Gifted Child Quarterly, 36*(1), 38-44.

Moon, S. M., & Feldhusen, J. F. (1994). The program for academic and creative enrichment (PACE): A follow-up study ten years later. In R. Subotnik & K. Arnold (Eds.), *Beyond Terman: Contemporary longitudinal studies of giftedness and talent* (pp. 375–400). Norwood, NJ: Ablex.

Passow, A. H. (1982). *LTI committee report.* Unpublished report, National/State Leadership Training Institute of the Gifted and Talented.

Perkins, D. N., & Salomon, G. (1989). Are cognitive skills context-bound? *Educational Researcher, 18,* 16–25.

Pleiss, M. K., & Feldhusen, J. F. (1995). Mentors, role models, and heroes in the lives of gifted children. *Educational Psychologist, 30*(3), 159–169.

Renzulli, J. (1975). *The enrichment triad.* Mansfield Center, CT: Creative Learning Press.

Renzulli, J. S. (1995). *Building a bridge between gifted education and total school improvement: Talent development research-based decision making series 9502.* Storrs, CT: National Research Center on the Gifted and Talented. (ERIC Document Reproduction Service No. 388 013)

Silverman, L. (1993). *Counseling the gifted and talented.* Denver, CO: Love.

Stanley, J. (1980). On educating the gifted. *Educational Researcher, 9,* 8–12.

Stanley, J. (1997). Varieties of intellectual talent. *Journal of Creative Behavior, 31*(2), 93–119.

Stanley, J., Keating, D., & Fox, L. (1974). *Mathematical talent: Discovery, description, and development.* Baltimore, MD: Johns Hopkins University Press.

Sternberg, R. J., & Clinkenbeard, P. R. (1995). The Triarchic Model applied to identifying, teaching, and assessing gifted children. *Roeper Review, 17*(4), 255–260.

Tyler, R. (1958). *Principles of curriculum and instruction.* Chicago: University of Chicago Press.

VanTassel-Baska, J. (1981, June). A comprehensive model of career education for gifted and talented. *Journal of Career Education,* 325–331.

VanTassel-Baska, J. (1990). *A practical guide to counseling the gifted in a school setting.* Reston, VA: Council for Exceptional Children.

VanTassel-Baska, J. (1992). Educational decision making on acceleration and grouping. *Gifted Child Quarterly, 36*(2), 68–72.

VanTassel-Baska, J. (1993a). Academic counseling for the gifted. In L. Silverman (Ed.), *Counseling the gifted* (pp. 201–214). Denver, CO: Love.

VanTassel-Baska, J. (1993b). *Comprehensive curriculum for gifted learners* (2nd ed.). Boston: Allyn & Bacon.

VanTassel-Baska, J. (1995). The development of talent through curriculum. *Roeper Review, 18*(2), 98–102.

VanTassel-Baska, J., Bass, G., Ries, R., & Poland, D. (in press). A national pilot study of science curriculum effectiveness for high ability students. *Gifted Child Quarterly.*

VanTassel-Baska, J., Johnson, D. T., Hughes, C., & Boyce, L. N. (1996). A study of language arts curriculum effectiveness with gifted learners. *Journal for the Education of the Gifted, 19*(4), 461–480.

Ward, V. (1961). *Educating the gifted: An axiomatic approach.* Columbus, OH: Charles E. Merrill.

Study Questions ~

1. What is meant by the term *comprehensive curriculum*? Why is such a curriculum needed for gifted learners?

2. What aspects of a curriculum should be differentiated for gifted learners? Provide a rationale for each.

3. In what ways could grouping be considered a curriculum issue?

4. Evaluate the importance of articulating a curriculum for K–12.

5. What if you were to select appropriate curricula for a given group of gifted learners? What would be the most important criteria to consider in the process?

6. Why has modification of traditional curricula for the gifted been less popular than other approaches?

20

Strategies and Methods for Teaching the Talented

John F. Feldhusen

The primary characteristic of gifted and talented youth is precocity, and thus all of our efforts to teach them well must take into account their advanced levels of achievement and their ability to learn more rapidly than youth of low or average ability. They also have higher levels of long-term memory ability, a more rapid and effective ability to retrieve information from long-term memory, and a higher aptitude to create or deal with complex concepts and arrays of information.

This chapter focuses on the methods and strategies expert teachers use in their work with gifted and talented students. It is often difficult to separate curriculum from teaching or instruction. In this chapter, I refer to curriculum as all specifications and plans for subject matter that exist prior to the beginning of instruction. That is, it is all the declarative and procedural knowledge specified in goals and objectives as well as in delineations of information, concepts, principles, skills, attitudes, and so forth, to be learned. Methods and strategies refer to the approaches and techniques used by teachers in live and direct interactions with students with the purpose of helping students achieve the goals and objectives specified in the curriculum.

John Bailey teaches a special fourth-grade class for highly gifted students. On Friday his goal was to help his students learn how to analyze current events and to see relationships between current events in different parts of the world. Bailey opened the discussion by asking his students to identify what they considered to be some of the major events going on in countries around the world. From the class of 23 students, nine offered responses, mentioning such events as minor wars in Africa, car bombings in the Middle East, and trade wars in Asian countries. He then asked the class to point out similarities and differences between the events in different countries. Five students who had not participated in the first phase and seven of those who had contributed in the first phase were involved in this new phase of the discussion. The discussion proceeded with occasional new guiding questions from Bailey. In the concluding part of the discussion, he asked the gifted students to speculate about future developments related to internecine strife in African countries. Three hands shot up, all with the intent of asking the teacher what internecine meant. None of the three had been heard from before. Five students participated in the final part of the discussion, three of whom had not been heard from before. The entire session was videotaped and then viewed and evaluated by myself and four other specialists in gifted education. Although they were unanimous in their agreement that Bailey had done an excellent job of leading this group of gifted students in this learning experience, Bailey observed that the students were generally a highly verbally gifted group and that they had had a lot of discussion experience. He also noted that they were avid readers of newspapers and weekly news magazines. Thus, they came to the discussion extremely well prepared.

Alec Wilden teaches a high-school honors biology class. On the day we observed his class, his goal was to help his students learn how to initiate and design experiments with large insects. He divided the class into small groups of four and gave each group a Madagascar cockroach. Their opening task was to observe and study the cockroach carefully and to brainstorm all the questions they could think of about the cockroach. He then circulated from group to group offering guidance and answering questions. We noted that each of the six groups was a beehive of on-task verbal behavior. Each group quickly selected a recorder, and ideas and questions flowed freely. After about 15 minutes, Wilden asked the groups to go over their observations and questions and evaluate which would be of greatest interest and value for further study or experimentation. He suggested an upper limit of approximately 10. The discussion in each group was even more animated than before as the students argued for and against items on the list. However, in about 10 minutes all the groups had achieved consensus on their pared-down lists.

In the final phase of the lesson, Wilden asked the groups to begin to design an experiment or study that would address some of their questions. One student expressed his enthusiasm for this phase by rolling up his sleeves and saying, "Wowee, let's go!" This entire class session had also been videotaped, and the same five experts in gifted education who had evaluated the fourth-grade class also viewed this tape. We concluded that the teacher had done an excellent job with this group of gifted high-school students. Teacher Alec Wilden, however, was reluctant to take much credit, assuring us that this group of gifted students were all high in verbal, quantitative, and analytical abilities. He told us that the major challenge in teaching these gifted students was to keep up with the advanced pace they set and the challenging ideas and questions they came up with. He also noted that they were almost all highly motivated to learn and metacognitively competent to guide themselves in learning activities.

These descriptions set the stage well for the discussions that follow in this chapter about teaching methods and strategies for gifted and talented students. Both of the teachers had specific curricular goals and subject matter that they wished to address in the lessons we observed, and both had some specific methods and strategies that they had carefully selected to help students achieve the goals. Both had been teachers for 6 or more years and thus had become proficient, even relatively automated, in selecting methods that would be best suited to the particular group of students and the specific goals.

Sternberg and Horvath (1995) proposed that there are three major dimensions to expert teaching: the knowledge base, efficiency in using it, and insight in solving problems. The knowledge base includes a comprehensive grasp of the content or subject matter of one's field or fields of teaching and practical, procedural knowledge about how to operate effectively as a teacher in a school. The efficiency component refers to the teacher's smooth, automatic functioning in a school setting and includes skill at monitoring student learning and behavior as well as evaluating student progress and learning. Finally, the insight dimension refers to the teacher's ability to solve problems that arise in the classroom or in working relationships with fellow teachers. The insight dimension also includes the ability to anticipate problems and head them off or solve them before they become major impediments.

Any effort to delineate instructional strategies for gifted and talented youth must take these components into account. It is also crucial that teachers know the specific levels of precocity or achievement of the students in particular areas of the curriculum. Although a general measure of intelligence, represented by g, provides an overall index of a child's ability, it does not provide the instructional guidance needed for each specific subject matter. The diagnostic/prescriptive model for instruction pioneered by Julian Stanley (1978) and now used in summer programs for the gifted is, however, a basic and sound guide to the strategies needed to teach gifted and talented youth well.

It is also necessary to address the problem of the instructional milieu in which teaching strategies are to be implemented. The ideal is a classroom of youth who are all at relatively similar levels of achievement in a given subject such as mathematics, science, social studies, English, foreign language, home economics, accounting, agriculture, or computer programming. However, an alternative milieu is often one, two, three, or four high-achieving youth within a general education classroom containing children of all levels of ability. Thus, this chapter first addresses the former as represented by Advanced Placement classes, honors classes, and full-time self-contained classes at the elementary level or any similar arrangement in which the entire class is made up of precocious youth. Later it addresses the mixed, or inclusion, classroom. Strategies the teacher can or should use in each situation are discussed. In both situations it is assumed that the teacher has had or is getting special training in the nature and nurture of gifted and talented youth.

It is anticipated that the procedures, methods, and strategies set forth in this chapter will be used by teachers with increasing efficiency as they move toward becoming expert teachers. There may be a number of different styles that characterize the expert teacher of the gifted, but all who rise to the stature of expert teacher will have mastered the three dimensions of teaching delineated by Sternberg and Horvath (1995).

Opening and Warm-Up for Classes with Gifted Students ⁓

An ideal opening strategy for gifted, honors, or Advanced Placement classes is to engage students' minds quickly in an intellectual task. Far too many class sessions begin with a dreary litany of announcements and housekeeping duties. Boredom, and sometimes misbehavior, set in rapidly. Far preferable is a warm-up activity based on the lesson or goal for the day. Warm-up activities can often be of a brainstorming or problem-solving nature. For example, as a warm-up for their study of Darwin's voyage on the *Beagle*, gifted students might be asked to imagine themselves setting off on a voyage by ship around the world and to select all the books and compact disks (CDs) they would want to take with them. Or as a warm-up in a chemistry class, gifted students might be asked, prior to their study of a unit on toxic chemicals and their impact on the environment, to speculate on the problems that would exist today if DDT had not been banned. In a math class on numerical bases, gifted students might be asked to speculate about the impact of base two on the computer industry. In an honors business education class studying personnel selection policies, the teacher might confront the students with brief descriptions of five job applicants for a managerial position and ask the students to select the best and most highly qualified applicant keeping in mind also what they have previously learned about federal regulations on fairness in hiring.

Such warm-up, opening, and problem-solving activities are designed by teachers of gifted students to engage their minds in a challenging cognitive activity right at the beginning of a class period. The activities are open-ended so that multiple ideas or solutions are possible. Furthermore, they are selected to lead to the main area of study for the day and to be tied to the curriculum and goals of study. They are also meant to be mentally challenging, to press gifted students to think hard about complex intellectual material. Finally, they are designed to draw students into the area of study, to turn their minds from conflicting interests, and above all to motivate their interest and desire to engage in further study of the area in question.

Lectures, Lecturettes, Teacher Presentations, and Explanations ⁓

By virtue of their superior verbal abilities, many gifted and talented youth are regularly able to learn from discourse or oral communication from teachers. The most efficient modes for the communication of abstract information, concepts, principles, theories, and illustrations are oral and written messages. Snow (1989) showed that high-ability youth prefer learning experiences involving complex and abstract material whereas less able children need more concrete and less abstract presentations with lesser amounts of information conveyed.

There is almost a fetish among teachers about the value of hands-on experiences in learning, even among teachers of gifted and talented youth. However, as Mezynski, Stanley, and McCoart (1983) showed, highly able youth can learn abstract concepts in physics, chemistry, and calculus without the usual laboratory experience. They can deal with more material and process it well when it is at an advanced level, is presented more rapidly, ideas are dealt with, and their extensive vocabularies can be used to process abstract concepts and principles.

Some degree of hands-on experience is appropriate for younger gifted youth, but as gifted students advance through middle school and high school, their increasing verbal and abstract conceptual ability should be exercised in appropriate lecture experiences, thereby better readying them for the still higher level of abstract lecturing they will face in college. Teachers of gifted and talented youth should present lectures in which they explain and give illustrations of ideas. Lecturettes or short presentations are most appropriate at the elementary level, but they can increase in length as grade level increases. Lecturers should be dynamic, expressive, and enthusiastic, and thereby evoke interest in the field of study. Above all, the teacher's lectures should present the best current conceptions of fundamental ideas. The lectures should move rapidly but always with abundant opportunity and encouragement for students to ask questions, advance their own observations, and organize ideas into complex understandings.

The expert teacher has, as noted earlier, a strong knowledge base in the subject matter and in the methodology of lecturing. Well-designed overhead transparencies, videotapes, and models should be used to enhance the oral messages. The lecturette or lecture can be followed by discussion, small-group work on problems or tasks growing out of the lecture, or dramatic techniques such as simulations, role-playing, or mock trials when appropriate. Supporting or summary print material should also be used to enhance the lecture as well as computer programs that reinforce the lecture material.

Talking at gifted students is not an effective strategy. Rather, the teacher as thinker and knowledgeable person should model intellectual processing (Bandura, 1990). Inducing gifted and talented students to think creatively, critically, and evaluatively is the goal. Gifted and talented students need teachers who model, inspire, stimulate, and motivate them to use their minds to the fullest, most challenging extent possible. Minds grow through the challenges of thinking.

Lectures and lecturettes afford excellent opportunities for teachers to impart important information to gifted and talented students and to model thinking skills and processes. Learning through auditory perception is fundamental to all interactive intellectual activity. Ideally, teachers will use the lecture or lecturette to emphasize or highlight very important issues, concepts, and problems, not simply to transmit perfunctory information that could more readily be transmitted through printed materials. The lecture can also be interactive, so that students can call for clarification from time to time, add their own insights to those being presented by the teacher, and/or be a mutual inquiry-thought process between the teacher and the class.

Reading and Homework ~

The reading load in classes for gifted students should be more extensive and involve more complex and abstract material than would typically be used with students of average or low ability. Advanced Placement courses (College Board, 1995) confront talented youth with college-level text and reading material, and they have been shown to thrive on it. Thousands of able American youth now take courses at colleges and universities while in high school and some even take such courses while in middle school (Feldhusen, 1983). The teacher's strategy is to select materials that address course goals at abstract and complex levels and help students master the materials or derive the conceptional understanding intended by the authors.

In classes for gifted and talented youth, especially in verbally oriented courses in English, social studies, and the arts, there should be substantial reliance on large reading assignments or offerings. Ideally, course syllabi will offer both required and optional reading lists. There should also be an extensive reliance on the selection of books and articles that represent primary sources from leaders in the field of study, which is often material that would be considered college level. Many standard textbooks used in middle and high schools offer only survey types of information, and the reading levels are often far too low for gifted and talented youth. Thus, care should be taken to select reading materials that are challenging and that expose gifted students to the best thinking in the fields of study.

Homework for gifted students should call for good metacognitve or self-regulatory skills, and teachers of gifted and talented youth can help them learn those skills. Homework may consist of readings, written response to readings, writing papers, solving complex verbal problems, or writing essays. In all such activities, the steps of preplanning, monitoring oneself while work is in progress, and evaluating one's products call for special study skills that are often somewhat unique to the subject matter or discipline. However, teachers of gifted and talented youth can teach the general skills to classes as a whole and help individuals with varying learning styles to master the skills in ways that accommodate their individual styles of learning (Dunn, Dunn, & Treffinger, 1992).

Gifted and talented students must learn to be self-directing in their learning and work experiences as a prelude to their eventual roles as professionals, artists, and business leaders. In adulthood, creative productivity comes about when knowledgeable people are self-motivated or intrinsically motivated (Nicholls, 1992) to pursue creative and productive goals without a "boss" to direct them. They can acquire such ability through early self-directing, self-guiding experiences with teachers and mentors who give them freedom and openness as well as intellectual support to test their own exploratory motivations.

The term *homework* should be used to denote all learning, project, problem-solving, planning, designing, and writing activity that can be carried out not only at home but also in libraries, in computer labs, in school study rooms, and at other meeting places. Reading assignments and student-initiated reading experiences feed into the "homework" activities. The entire process calls for ideational fluency and a great deal of general cognitive activity. The best gifted programs have teachers whose strategies of instruction include much focus on rich reading resources and creative "homework" experiences.

Motivation, Goal Setting, Self-Efficacy ~

The teacher's major motivational goal for gifted and talented students is to evoke their intrinsic motivation in the topics of study and to help them develop a sense of self-efficacy or competence in intellectual activity in the domains of study (Schunk, 1994). Intrinsic motivation, in this context, refers to interest in and a desire to learn the school curriculum because of the qualities or merits of the material itself and its relatability to things students already know or want to know about. Extrinsic motivation, in contrast, assumes students' lack of interest in the subject matter or their lack of desire to see its value in relation to their own needs or interests. Extrinsic motivation is evoked by threats such as of low grades or punishment, by offering rewards or payoffs to students, or by setting up competitive conditions in which failure threatens student egos.

The ideal strategy obviously is to evoke intrinsic motivation in gifted and talented students—that is, to induce or elicit interest, enthusiasm, or love for the subject matter being studied so that they will plunge into learning activities with enthusiasm and self-commitment. For a number of reasons gifted and talented students probably have a head start toward intrinsic motivation: Most of them have superior entry knowledge bases in the subject matter areas; they are more capable of dealing with the abstract and complex nature of the school curriculum; they arrive with stronger senses of self-efficacy or competence; and they are often more capable than students of average ability in using metacognitive and self-regulating approaches to their studies and learning activities.

Teacher strategies that evoke intrinsic motivation include avoidance of excessive use of rewards, payoffs, and incentives; minimizing competition in daily learning activities, reserving competition experiences to extra-classroom events such as the Mathematics Olympiad or Odyssey of the Mind; and stressing the inherent value, importance, or interest of the subject matter at hand. One effective opening strategy is to relate new subjects or areas of study to things the students already know or have previously studied. Relatability leads to meaningfulness and in turn to intrinsic motivation.

Intrinsic motivation is also evoked by teachers' modeling of their love and enthusiasm for the topics of study. Teachers' expressions of enthusiasm and excitement can have profound effects on student behavior and motivation (Bandura, 1988). In contrast, dull repetition and monotonous teaching lead to loss of intrinsic motivation and often to coercive or threatening teacher behavior, which in turn evokes, at best, extrinsic motivation or, worse, the loss of all motivation among gifted and talented students.

It is also clear that a desirable teacher strategy is to involve gifted and talented students in goal setting as a mechanism for inducing intrinsic motivation. After the preliminary introduction of new topics, teachers can allot specific time blocks in which students formulate goals they would like to achieve in their further study of the topics. The goals often focus on learning activities as well as products. These goals then serve as intrinsic guides and motivators of student learning.

Further, student motivation can be enhanced by evoking in students a sense of self-efficacy or competence. Indeed, self-efficacy draws on a sense of competence (Schunk, 1991a; Schunk, 1991b) or competence motivation (White, 1959). It represents ideal intrinsic motivation in that a sense of competence leads to a nondefensive approach to new learning. Students begin such study with a high degree of confidence in their ability to deal with the challenges of new topics and new learnings. Self-efficacy is best induced when students experience repeated successes in learning the subject matter, when teachers point out or note their successes or achievements, and when students can metacognitively evaluate their own efficacy in the learning situation. Research in this area has shown that the appropriate teacher strategy for building a sense of self-efficacy is to commend specific achievements rather than to praise students in general ways (Schunk, 1991). When recognizing student achievements, teachers should delineate accomplishments or activities that were well done. They might use words such as the following: "This is an excellent paper. Your dialectical arguments were very persuasive." "Your solution to these simultaneous equations was very well conceived and parsimonious." "This is a well-designed experiment. It will provide an ideal test of your hypothesis."

Teaching students metacognitive and self-regulating skills can also enhance their motivation to learn. Metacognitive skills include planning, monitoring behavior in progress, and evaluating ends or products of learning. Self-regulating behaviors include self-observation, self-judgment, and self-reaction. Gifted and talented students who have developed good metacognitive and self-regulating skills experience increases in intrinsic motivation and in confidence in new and ongoing learning situations. It is a good teacher strategy to teach and encourage students to use metacognitive skills and self-regulatory behaviors during all learning experiences.

Most gifted and talented youth profit from explicit training in *time management, study, and goal setting skills*. Because they are often multitalented and enthusiastic about many areas of study, they may have trouble setting priorities and may develop habits of dabbling in many areas of study, failing to pursue any in-depth. Furthermore, because they are typically fast learners, they may fail to develop sound skills for the management of their daily lessons and assignments. Indeed, some gifted and talented youth have so much trouble with study skills and time management that they literally become underachievers (Rimm, 1995). Thus, special short courses in study skills, time management, goal setting, and prioritizing activities can be very profitable for gifted and talented students. There are a number of published programs on the market that teachers can use in teaching these skills.

Teachers of gifted and talented students must address the issues of intrinsic motivation, self-efficacy, goal setting, and metacognition if they are to prepare their students to become the self-propelled leaders, innovators, and creators of the future. Without such efforts, the topics of study often become boring and drudgery to be covered and forgotten. With strong intrinsic motivation, gifted and talented students acquire love and enthusiasm for learning that transfers into adult creative productivity.

Constructivism as Strategy~

A relatively new movement in education called constructivism (Brooks & Brooks, 1993) stresses the critical need for active student cognitive engagement in all learning situations. The constructivists argue that students must develop their own cognitive schemas or understandings of conceptual material studied in school by exploring, problem solving, inquiring, examining, analyzing, creating, synthesizing, and so forth. Through such active cognitive activity students develop their own unique cognitive structures or representations of material being studied. According to the constructivists, meaningful learning occurs only when students have ample time for in-depth cognitive study of new material (Wheatley, 1989).

From this perspective, the appropriate teaching strategy is to bring students into contact with conceptual material, provide opportunities for in-depth exploration or study of it, and induce intrinsic motivation or interest in the material. Constructivist-oriented teachers often have their students work in small groups of three or four with minimum directions from the teacher. Students are expected to develop their own, often idiosyncratic, understandings. However, these teachers have an abiding faith that understandings gained though such activity will lead to greater clarity in the students' conceptual grasp of the material, that the students will remember the concepts better, and that their understanding will transfer more effectively or be more usable in the future.

When Allen Jenkins, a mathematics teacher at Skyline School, arrived at the point in the curriculum where his students were learning about trapezoids, he divided his class into six groups, four with five students each and two with four each. The students gathered around tables and were shown a picture of a trapezoid with the length of its sides indicated. Their task was to find as many ways as possible to calculate the area of the trapezoid. After allowing the students a period of time to work, during which he circulated from group to group, often offering hints or cues, Jenkins began to call on groups to come forward and show, on a large-scale drawing, how they would do the calculations. Our observation of this class indicated that every student seemed to be engaged in the activity. It was also obvious, as we circulated, that some students were clearly the leaders while others contributed little. Later, in conversation with Jenkins, we learned that the brightest, most mathematically talented students in the class not only tended to be the leaders in all such activities but were also the verbally talented ones who most often presented solutions to the class.

The constructivist approach is most clearly usable in high-ability classes because the students are able to operate cognitively at the high level the method dictates. Archconstructivists would probably argue that the lesson just described was too highly structured and thus was not a good example of constructivism being used in the classroom. In fairness to the teacher, who purports to be a constructivist, it should be noted that on another visit to his classroom we saw his class simply examining different two-dimensional shapes and trying to form generalizations about them. That might have been a clearer illustration of a constructivist approach to a lesson.

The constructivists remind us of several important aspects of appropriate strategy for teaching gifted and talented students. First, the active engagement of students in the learning process must be cognitive or mental engagement, not just a lot of hands-on busywork. Second, gifted and talented students have tremendous capacity to develop their own understandings and conceptual schemas. Thus, our strategy as teachers must be to guide them toward more complex and elaborate syntheses of knowledge, to see more extensive connections, and to formulate more diverse configurations of knowledge. Finally, the appropriate motivational techniques are those that evoke intrinsic motivation and interest in the curriculum under study as well as a sense of self-efficacy.

Discussions, Questioning, and Dialogue ~

Our ultimate goal as teachers should be to help students become competent thinkers as individuals and when working in groups. How well we lead discussions, pose thought-evoking questions, and engage students in intellectual dialogues will determine how well that goal is realized. Through discussions, responses to good questions, and engagement in dialogues, all involving classroom discourse, students' cognitive processing mechanisms are activated, and cognitive growth occurs as the students learn how to think critically and creatively and develop new conceptual schemes and understandings in their long-term memory.

Socratic dialogue is used by some teachers to examine or analyze, in consummate detail, arguments presented in literature and to test the validity of the arguments. Often both inductive and deductive reasoning are employed in search of the truth of ideas. Hegelian dialectic is another useful approach to the search for truth and validity. It involves the identification of the thesis of a document, the evocation of all the contrary theses to the thesis, and resolution in dialogue. Hegelian dialectic is an excellent approach to the discussion of literature.

Creative or divergent questions, such as the following, are also often used to teach gifted and talented students how to think speculatively in discussion: "What if the South had won the Civil War? How would our lives be different today?" "What if Shakespeare had written essays and poetry but no plays? How would the field of dramatic literature be different today?" "What are all the ways by which we could find the area of a trapezoid?" "What is the most unique or original approach you can think of for reforming American schools?" These creative questions call for fluent, original, flexible, or elaborative responses, all of which will aid in the development of creative thinking capacities.

Whereas teacher-designed questions often dominate classroom discourse, gifted and talented students should also be engaged in designing the questions and leading discussions of the whole class as well as of small groups. The students can be taught all the mechanisms presented in this section to guide their efforts in formu-

lating questions. They can also learn that it is through questioning, probing, dialectic, and dialogue and through their own participatory leadership in discussion that
they become knowledge seekers and acquirers.

Discussions, dialogues, and discourse in the classroom are fundamental mechanisms for student cognitive growth and the development of metacognitive control
mechanisms (McKeachie, 1994). Skillful teachers of the gifted formulate good questions, encourage and help students to formulate their own questions, and guide the
classroom discussions that engage their students in high-quality, thoughtful learning
activities. Students of low and average ability are often bored by high-level intellectual discussions (Feldhusen & Kroll, 1991), and Oakes (1985) has shown that students in low-track classes often exhibit negative and disruptive behaviors that make
it impossible to carry on orderly and productive classroom discussions. However,
spirited discussions should always characterize special classes for gifted and talented youth. Teachers can learn to become good leaders of discussion. They can employ
a number of specific techniques (McKeachie, 1994) to enhance student participation
and effectiveness. However, none is more important than the teacher's command or
mastery of the subject matter or discipline he or she is teaching.

Small-Group Projects, Seminars, Debates ⌇

Small-group projects and problem-solving activities are another excellent teaching
strategy for work with gifted and talented youth. They are capable of a high degree
of initiative in identifying problems and designing projects and in doing so can be
engaged in the highest and most complex levels of cognitive activity. Although there
has been much support of so-called cooperative learning in mixed-ability groups
(Slavin, 1990), for gifted and talented youth such small-group or cooperative learning activity appears to be most effective and productive when the members of the
group are all of high or very high ability (Robinson, 1990). When gifted and talented youth work together on problems and project activities in groups of three to five
students, the intellectual challenge, the advanced levels of subject matter content,
and the higher levels of thinking skills all result in far greater achievement and substantial enhancement of interest and motivation.

Seminar-like classes also afford opportunities for gifted and talented youth to
delve into the subject matter far more deeply than they can in regular classes (Dixon,
1995; Kolloff & Feldhusen, 1986). Seminars are usually composed of small groups,
rarely exceeding 15 students, and there is often a high level of student initiative in
selecting topics for study and in the types of learning activities used to achieve the
goals. The teacher's role is less directive and much more facilitative than in other
classes. Students are likely to make presentations of their research or projects, do a
great deal of reading or research, and be very active in class discussions. The seminar format is ideal for special classes involving gifted and talented youth.

Debates offer gifted and talented youth excellent opportunities to deal with
complex, abstract cognitive themes, concepts, and principles. In a debate there is a
major resolution that evokes an issue or problem for study. Library research and

reading are the basic beginning activities that lead to the clarification of issues and problems as well as to insights or assertions about the topic at hand. Students simultaneously clarify and delineate the problem domain as they accrue information about the resolution and organize it into meaningful patterns and schemas. The process of learning is clearly that favored by the new constructivism (Brooks & Brooks, 1993) and widely used in new approaches to the teaching of mathematics and science and to a lesser extent English and social studies. Versatility or openness of thought is required as students learn the position they are to take in the debate. The presentation is then planned and later delivered before an audience. The extemporaneous nature of the presentation calls for thinking clearly on one's feet.

Following the completion of all debate presentations, rebuttals are presented. In a rebuttal, students must respond in detail to the contradictory ideas presented by fellow debaters. Since the debate event may be repeated in several places and on several occasions, following each debate the debaters reflect on and clarify their own strong and weak points, seek new information, and ready their arguments for the next debate. Overall, the instructional strategy of debate affords ample opportunities for cognitive growth and the enlargement of talented students' knowledge bases.

Library and Empirical Research ~

Gifted and talented students should also have ample time and opportunity for learning how to design and conduct both *library* and *empirical research* and for learning how to use computers and other technologies in these activities. A course in research methods, preferably at the college level, would be ideal for all gifted and talented youth beginning at the middle-school level and proceeding to more advanced levels in high school and in the undergraduate years of college. Courses in statistics and psychometrics in the high school and early college years would also provide gifted and talented youth with invaluable skills for research, project, and other creative activities. Development of youths' creative talents can be enhanced by providing them with accelerated opportunities to learn the investigatory skills employed by scholars, researchers, artists, and scientists.

Writing for Publication ~

Writing for publication is a valuable culmination activity for student projects, research, experiments, and artistic endeavors. In addition to providing experience in the technical and artistic aspects of writing, the activity can involve the thrill of risk taking and the thrill of getting one's message out to a large audience. Writing for publication often means that one's work will be reviewed and evaluated by leaders in a field. Following publication there may be rejoinders in the form of letters to the editor. The whole experience provides an introduction to the world of creative production, be it in the arts, business, the sciences, or the professions. Talented youth may begin to see that they have the capability of developing ideas that can influence the world around them in some way. Thus, writing for publication is an ideal creative experience for talented youth.

Use of Technologies

A final strategy that has become vital in gifted and talented programs is the use or infusion of technologies and computers in all aspects of teaching. Members of the new generation of youth in gifted and talented programs are highly computer literate. They know how to use the Internet. They are familiar with CD ROM. They have E-mail addresses. Their potential sophistication with the computer as a communication and processing tool is immense. Thus, teachers' efforts in all the strategies discussed so far demand that schools, classrooms, and teachers be able to operate effectively in the information-processing age (Beasley, 1994).

Strategies for Full-Time Self-Contained Classes

School personnel often fail to understand the basic needs of gifted and talented youth and thus often offer inappropriate and weak enrichment when challenging, high-powered academic instruction is needed. Feldhusen (1989) listed four basic characteristics of talented youth that, in turn, should delineate or guide our approaches to the design of instruction. According to Feldhusen, talented youth are:

1. Far ahead of their age-grade peers in mastery of basic skills
2. Able to learn much more rapidly than children of average ability
3. More adept in dealing with complex concepts and abstractions
4. Highly advanced in thinking skills

These special characteristics of talented youth lead to or call for instructional adaptations that can best be carried out in a full-time, self-contained classroom at the elementary level and in special honors, accelerated, advanced, or elective classes at the middle- and high-school levels. In such classes, the teacher can select curriculum at a level appropriate to the precocity of the students, move more rapidly in teaching it (typically taking one-half the time used in a general education classroom), select much more conceptually complex and abstract curriculum content, and expect or require students to do more higher level thinking as a part of the learning process.

The specific strategies to be used in implementing such an approach to instruction for highly able or talented youth are guided by an awareness that talented youth also need time working together. That is, from a social-emotional point of view, they profit greatly from the mutual acceptance and support they receive in homogeneous groups of talented peers. In other settings, talented youth are confronted with much negative and adverse peer pressure because of their academic prowess, precocity, and speed and ease of learning (Brown, Clasen, & Eicher, 1986; Brown & Steinberg,

1989). Many, especially girls and minority youth, succumb to the pressure and portray themselves as of average ability. Others who are more determined to develop their talents maintain their academic posture and intellectual activity and end up loners or social outcasts. Special classes, however, offer the loners, the outcasts, and the "nerds" the opportunity to make friends with equally talented youth who share their interests and accept them as they are. Research by Feldhusen and Sayler (1990) at the elementary- and middle-school levels and by Feldhusen and Kennedy (1989) at the middle- and high-school levels showed that special classes for talented youth are highly effective in meeting their academic and affective needs. Thus, it appears that gifted and talented youth should be grouped together in special classes whenever possible (Feldhusen & Moon, 1992). They should also, however, have opportunities to work with youth of average and low ability so that they can develop social skills and interactive abilities for a wide variety of social and career-defining situations. That mixing can occur in art, music, intramural athletics, recess time, clubs, and social events.

Specific teaching strategies for the special classes should include challenging lectures, small-group project and problem-solving activities, seminar-like classes, discussions, debates, designing and conducting library and empirical research, substantial reading assignments, the teaching of specific thinking and metacognitive thinking skills, study of time management skills, writing for publication, public presentations of project and research results, and the use of appropriate and related technologies in all aspects of instruction.

Strategies for Teaching the Gifted in General Education Classrooms ~

Recent research (Archambault et al., 1993; Westberg, Archambault, Dobyns, & Slavin, 1993) indicates that in general education classrooms there is little or no adaptation or individualization for gifted and talented youth. The instructional offering is not differentiated. All students study the same material at the same level and the same rate of speed. Several researchers have recently offered instructional strategies for individualizing the offering in a mixed, heterogeneously grouped classroom (Feldhusen, 1993; Milgram, 1989; Winebrenner, 1992), and cluster grouping of gifted and talented students in mixed-ability classrooms has also been quite widely used (Hoover, Sayler, & Feldhusen, 1993).

Individualizing the offering, the strategy of individualization, means that the teacher assesses the achievement levels of students from time to time and provides new curricula that are at the right next level for each student. Thus, continuous progress is possible for each student in the classroom. From another point of view, as Feldhusen (1993) pointed out, there is less emphasis on formal assessment and more on finding appropriate starting levels and then letting children progress through the curriculum as rapidly as they wish. The teacher, of course, monitors their progress carefully to make sure that they are not covering the material superficially. That means that the teacher does a lot of informal assessment by watching and talking with students while they are at work, providing corrective or formative feedback, and encouraging or reinforcing their progress. In this way students' good and continuous progress will build their sense of self-efficacy (Schunk, 1991a, 1991b) and their motivation to set high-level achievement goals.

Cluster grouping means that the teacher, or someone else, has explicitly identified the gifted and talented youth in the classroom. The teacher is then committed to spending some time working with the cluster and giving those students some differentiated and higher level curriculum materials. One advantage of cluster grouping over the pure individualization approach is that the teacher can work with, say, four to six students at a time rather than just one student at a time. Furthermore, working together in a cluster, gifted and talented youth can help one another a great deal and often make much better progress than they would working alone. Schools that use cluster grouping often group all the identified gifted and talented students in a grade level into one of the several rooms at that grade level and expect the teacher to differentiate instruction for the cluster group as much as possible or as much as seems appropriate. In many of the states in the United States there is an expectation that teachers have or get special training in gifted and talented education and/or have earned a special endorsement or certification in gifted education.

In both the individualized approach and cluster grouping it is clear that teachers need special, advanced, and more cognitively complex curriculum material for carrying out instruction with gifted and talented youth. That may simply mean that they have access to text material at higher grade levels, or it may mean that they have access to specially designed material for gifted and talented instruction (VanTassel-Baska, 1992). With good instructional materials teachers can put gifted and talented youth to work either individually or in a cluster group and assist them as necessary in learning the material.

In both individualized and cluster grouping approaches gifted and talented youth are likely to spend much or some part of each class period working with other students who have not been identified as gifted or talented. That is a valuable part of the school experience for them and for all students. Ideally, there will be no explicit singling out, labeling, or categorizing of gifted and talented youth in the classroom as gifted or talented. Such labeling often leads to undesirable peer pressure and ostracization. Skilled teachers can make it possible for all students to feel successful in classroom activities without singling out a few to be the stars.

Summary ⌇

Teachers of gifted and talented youth can use a number of strategies to provide valid and effective instruction in special classes and in regular, mixed-ability classrooms. All of the strategies are designed to actively involve these students in thinking about and solving problems raised in the instructional material or the curricula of the different disciplines of study. Good learning activities for gifted and talented youth engage the students' minds at the highest levels of their capabilities and help them become effective thinkers and problem solvers.

References ∼

Archambault, F., Westberg, K., Brown, S., Hallmark, B., Zhang, W., & Emmons, C. (1993). Classroom practices used with gifted third and fourth grade students. *Journal for the Education of the Gifted, 16*(2), 103–119.

Bandura, A. (1988). Self-regulation of motivation and action through goal systems. In V. Hamilton, G. H. Bower, & N. J. Frijda (Eds.), *Cognitive perspectives on emotion and maturation* (pp. 37–61). Dordrecht, The Netherlands: Kluwer Academic Publications.

Bandura, A. (1990). Reflections on nonability determinants of competence. In R. J. Sternberg & K. Kolligian, Jr. (Eds.), *Competence considered* (pp. 315–362). New Haven, CT: Yale University Press.

Beasley, W. A. (1994). Gopher, World Wide Web, and Wide Area Information Servers: Three Internet services for the gifted education community. *Gifted and Talented International, 9*(2), 47–51.

Brooks, J. G., & Brooks, M. G. (1993). *In search of understanding: The case for constructivist classrooms.* Alexandria, VA: Association for Supervision and Curriculum Development.

Brown, B. B., Clasen, D. R., & Eicher, S. A. (1986). Perceptions of peer pressure, peer conformity dispositions, and self-reported behavior among adolescents. *Developmental Psychology, 22,* 521–530.

Brown, B. B., & Steinberg, L. (1989, November). How bright students save face among peers. *Newsletter, National Center on Effective Secondary Schools*, pp. 2–4.

College Board. (1995). *Advanced placement.* Princeton, NJ: College Board.

Dixon, F. (1995). Tactics: The gifted in secondary literature programs. *Understanding Our Gifted, 7*(4), 4–5.

Dunn, R., Dunn, K., & Treffinger, D. (1992). *Bringing out the giftedness in your child.* New York: Wiley.

Feldhusen H. J. (1989). Why the public schools will continue to neglect the gifted. *Gifted Child Today, 12*(2), 55–59.

Feldhusen, H. (1993). Individualized teaching of the gifted in regular classrooms. In C. J. Maker (Ed.), *Critical issues in gifted education* (Vol. 3, pp. 263-273). Austin, TX: Pro-Ed.

Feldhusen, J. F. (1983). Eclecticism: A comprehensive approach to education of the gifted. In C. P. Benbow & J. C. Stanley (Eds.), *Academic precocity: Aspects of its development* (pp. 192–204). Baltimore, MD: Johns Hopkins University Press.

Feldhusen, J. F., & Kennedy, D. M. (1989). Effects of honors classes on secondary students. *Roeper Review, 11*(3), 153–156.

Feldhusen, J. F., & Kroll, M. D. (1991). Boredom or challenge for the academically talented. *Gifted Education International, 7*(2), 80–81.

Feldhusen, J. F., & Moon, S. M. (1992). Grouping gifted students: Issues and concerns. *Gifted Child Quarterly, 36*(2), 63–67.

Feldhusen, J. F., & Sayler, M. F. (1990). Special classes for academically gifted youth. *Roeper Review, 12*(4), 244–249.

Hoover, S. M., Sayler, S., & Feldhusen, J. F. (1993). Cluster grouping of gifted students at the elementary level. *Roeper Review, 16*(1), 13–15.

Kolloff, P. B., & Feldhusen, J. F. (1986). The seminar: An instructional approach for gifted students. *Gifted Children Today, 9*(5), 2–7.

McKeachie, W. J. (1994). *Teaching tips* (9th ed.). Lexington, MA: D. C. Heath.

Mezynski, K., Stanley, J. C., & McCoart, R. F. (1983). Helping youths score well on AP examinations in physics, chemistry, and calculus. In C. P. Benbow & J. C. Stanley (Eds.), *Academic precocity: Aspects of its development* (pp. 86–112). Baltimore, MD: Johns Hopkins University Press.

Milgram, R. M. (Ed.). (1989). *Teaching gifted and talented learners in regular classrooms.* Springfield, IL: Charles C Thomas.

Nicholls, J. G. (1992). Students as educational theorists. In D. H. Schunk & J. L. Meece (Eds.), *Student perceptions in the classroom* (pp. 267–286). Hillsdale, NJ: Erlbaum.

Oakes, J. (1985). *Keeping track, how schools structure inequality.* New Haven, CT: Yale University Press.

Rimm, S. (1995). *Why bright kids get poor grades.* New York: Crown.

Robinson, A. (1990). Cooperation or exploitation? The argument against cooperative learning for talented students. *Journal for the Education of the Gifted, 14*(1), 9–27.

Schunk, D. H. (1991a). *Learning theories: An educational perspective*. New York: Macmillan.

Schunk, D. H. (1991b). Self-efficacy and academic motivation. *Educational Psychologist, 26,* 207–231.

Schunk, D. H. (1994). Self-regulation of self-efficacy and attributions in academic settings. In D. H. Schunk & B. J. Zimmerman (Eds.), *Self-regulation of learning and performance* (pp. 75–99). Hillsdale, NJ: Erlbaum.

Slavin, R. E. (1990). *Cooperative learning, theory, research, and practice*. Englewood Cliffs, NJ: Prentice-Hall.

Snow, R. E. (1989). Aptitude treatment interaction as a framework for research on individual differences in learning. In P. L. Ackerman, R. J. Sternberg, & R. Glaser (Eds.), *Learning and individual differences* (pp. 13–59). New York, NY: W. H. Freeman.

Stanley, J. C. (1978). SMPY's DT-PI model: Diagnostic testing followed by prescriptive instruction. *Intellectually Talented Youth Bulletin, 4*(10), 7–8.

Sternberg, R. J., & Horvath, J. A. (1995). A prototype view of expert teaching. *Educational Researcher, 24*(6), 9–17.

VanTassel-Baska, J. (1992). *Planning effective curriculum for gifted learners*. Denver, CO: Love.

Westberg, K. L., Archambault, F. X., Dobyns, S. M., & Slavin, T. J. (1993). The classroom practices observation study. *Journal for the Education of the Gifted, 16*(2), 120–146.

Wheatley, G. H. (1989). Instructional methods for the gifted. In J. Feldhusen, J. VanTassel-Baska, & K. Seeley (Eds.), *Excellence in educating the gifted* (pp. 261–275). Denver, CO: Love.

White, R. W. (1959). Motivation reconsidered: The concept of competence. *Psychological Review, 66*(5), 297–333.

Winebrenner, S. (1992). *Teaching gifted kids in the regular classroom*. Minneapolis, MN: Free Spirit.

Study Questions ~

1. What are some characteristics of gifted students that justify the need for differentiated teaching strategies and methods?

2. Is one type of organizational or grouping model preferable? If so, identify the model and describe why it is advantageous.

3. What are the three elements of expert teaching? How do they interact to create an effective teacher?

4. What are four or five strategies that are particularly effective for use with groups of gifted students? Defend why they are effective based on your understanding of the population.

5. Is there a relationship between the use of these strategies and the popular philosophy of constructivism? How do they complement one another? Is hands-on learning an important component of gifted education?

6. What strategies are critical for use in the inclusive classroom? What advantages make cluster grouping more attractive than pure inclusion for gifted students?

21
Creativity and the Gifted

Joyce VanTassel-Baska

To give a fair chance to potential creativity is a matter of life and death for any society. This is all-important, because the outstanding creativity of a fairly small percentage of the population is mankind's ultimate capital asset.

—Toynbee (1964)

Creativity as a construct of interest to the field of gifted education has a long and rich history. The goal of many, if not most, gifted programs is to develop the potential of identified gifted students in such a way that they later become creative producers in the real world of the professions. Einstein believed that imagination is a more valuable quality than knowledge. This view is generally held by gifted educators as well. We tend to devalue traditional academic achievers in favor of more original, nonconforming thinkers and producers, and finding creatively gifted individuals and nurturing them through specialized programs has been a major mission of the field since the early 1950s.

Definitions ~

Various definitions of creativity and the creative characteristics of individuals exist. J. P. Guilford, a major contributor in the field of creativity research, described creativity as being grounded in the ability to manipulate ideas in fluent, flexible, elaborate, and original ways. His view, embodied in the structure of intellect model and cited in his now famous American Psychological Association presidential address (Guilford, 1950), sees creativity as not related to specific domains but as more exogenous and transferable in its manifestations of mental manipulations. The work of Paul Torrance is based strongly on this perspective as well (Torrance, 1967; Torrance & Myers, 1970).

Getzels and Csikszentmihalyi (1977), in a classic longitudinal study of art students, found creative productivity in later life to be highly related to problem-finding ability during student days. Thus, creativity has also come to be associated with problem-finding behavior (Runco & Nemiro, 1994). Sternberg's view of creativity is strongly linked to insight, a quality that has been found in various studies to distinguish the creative products of subjects (Sternberg, 1985). Ochse (1990), after reviewing the lives and works of many creative producers, declared that the most important distinguishing characteristic they possessed was the desire and proven ability to work hard at their chosen profession. That link of work ethic and creative accomplishment had been noted earlier by Berry (1981).

Amabile (1983) viewed creativity as a composite of three factors: knowledge in a given domain, creativity-relevant skills, and intrinsic motivation to contribute to a field of knowledge. Table 21.1 reflects this combinational view. In Amabile's view, creativity requires extensive knowledge preparation in a given field.

Feldhusen (1995) expanded on Amabile's view to include a strong emphasis on metacognitive skills as an aspect of creativity-relevant skills. His review of the research led him to see three factors as most relevant:

Table 21.1 ～
Amabile View of Creativity

Domain-Relevant Skills	Creativity-Relevant Skills	Task Motivation
Include:	Include:	Include:
Knowledge about the domain Special skills required Special domain-relevant "talent"	Appropriate cognitive style Implicit or explicit knowledge of heuristics for generating novel ideas Conducive work style	Attitudes toward the task Perceptions of own motivation for undertaking the task
Depend on:	Depend on:	Depend on:
Innate cognitive abilities Innate perceptual and motor skills Formal and informal education	Training Experience in idea generation Personality characteristics	Initial level of intrinsic motivation toward the task Presence or absence of salient extrinsic constraints Individual ability to cognitively minimize extrinsic constraints

Note: From *The Social Psychology of Creativity* (p. 68) by T. Amabile, 1983, New York: Springer-Verlag.

1. A set of strategies or metacognitive skills for processing new information and for using the knowledge base that one has acquired
2. A large and fluent knowledge base and mastery of skills in a particular domain
3. A set of attitudes, dispositions, motivations, and so forth, acquired from parents, teachers, mentors, peers, and personal experiences that predispose and orient the individual to search for alternatives, new configurations, or uniquely appropriate solutions

Ochse (1990) defined creative people as those who have been recognized by expert opinion as having contributed something of original value to the culture and deliberately excluded those who simply live unconventional lives or who are creative in classroom-type or test tasks. More recent approaches to decisions about who is creative have centered on the societal validation of experts in the field of the quality of creative products generated.

Jensen (1996) cited three criterion measures of interest in this respect: (1) overt production, meaning the sheer number of publications and patents of an individual, (2) professional recognition awards, and (3) peer judgment. He viewed the creative act as made up of several parts, including the individual's processing ability and dispositional characteristics, how his or her ideas are translated, the social context for engaging in creative behaviors, and the social context for executing creative work. The combination of these parts, however, still results in creative undertakings that vary by degree as well as kind. By contrast, Bandura (1986) offered a more pragmatic view of societal validation, noting that the most acceptable innovations are those that meet the criterion of low cost/high benefit compatibility with existing sociotechnical systems and those that have low complexity. It would seem that innovations meeting these criteria are at a lower level than those typically acclaimed as creatively productive.

Trait Views

Trait-specific definitions of creativity have also been an important part of the history of creativity in the field of gifted education, with a strong emphasis placed on the characteristics of the creative personality as the chief set of indicators of what creativity looks like. The same characteristics, as well as others, have been found in the psychiatric literature describing developmentally advanced individuals in terms of their overexcitability (Dabrowski & Piechowski, 1977; Piechowski, 1984). A sample list (Barron, 1969; Runco, 1993b) of characteristics constituting the creative personality follows:

- Independent in attitude and social behavior
- Dominance
- Introversion
- Tolerance for ambiguity
- Openness to stimuli; wide interests

- Self-acceptance
- Intuitiveness
- Flexibility
- An asocial attitude; unconcern for social norms; risk-takers
- Social presence and poise
- Radicalism; rejection of external constraints
- Ability to fantasize and toy with ideas
- Aesthetic and moral commitment to work

There has been much debate about whether creativity and giftedness are separate phenomena. In a landmark study, Getzels and Jackson (1968) found that highly creative people were a distinct group from highly intellectual people above the IQ range of 120. Most research supports the notion that not all gifted individuals are highly creative and not all creative individuals are highly gifted. However, it is widely recognized that significant overlap exists—witness Renzulli's definition of giftedness, which excludes those children who do not display evidence of creativity (Renzulli & Smith, 1980). Indeed, the interplay between cognitive and personality factors has been perceived as the new landscape of creativity research (Runco, 1993a).

Process Views∼

Gardner's view of creativity expressed in *Creating Minds* (1993) is based on three factors and their interrelationships: the relationship between the child and the master, the relationship between an individual and the work in which he or she is engaged, and the relationship between an individual and other persons in his or her world. Two dominant themes emerged from Gardner's analytic study of the lives of Freud, Picasso, Stravinsky, Eliot, Graham, and Gandhi: (1) the role of intensive social and affective forces that surround creative breakthroughs, and (2) the personal sacrifices made somewhat willingly by creative individuals in the pursuit of their work. Like Amabile and others, Gardner saw creativity as wedded to thorough, often precocious mastery of a field, but he also argued that an intuitive understanding of ideas obtained in childhood is important to creative discovery.

Sternberg and Lubart (1993) presented a model of creativity that considers six factors: intelligent processes, knowledge, thinking styles, personality, motivation, and environment. They suggested that educating the creatively gifted should focus on the following elements:

1. Encouraging children to find, define, and redefine problems rather than solve presented problems
2. Teaching the flexible use of knowledge
3. Encouraging role-making and global styles of thought rather than rule-executing and local styles
4. Teaching children to tolerate ambiguity as they strive for creative solutions to problems, to persevere, and to take sensible risks in their work

5. Teaching children to focus on their tasks rather than the potential rewards
6. Changing classroom environments to encourage and reward students' creative work

They acknowledged the role of knowledge acquisition as being necessary for creative work in a given area and suggested that a strong knowledge base also helps in resource concentration and the production of high-quality work.

Feldman's view of creativity is grounded in an appreciation of prodigies, and what young, highly competent individuals in a field of study are like and capable of doing. He found that by the age of 10, prodigies have many times mastered the level of expertise in a field of study associated with adult performance, that prodigies are present in most fields even though they seldom are systematically sought out, and that prodigious development is dependent on early sustained interest of the child and support both in the family and from external resources (Feldman, 1988). Society, then, must be ready to recognize and support the talent area in order for the creative development of prodigies to be sustained.

Piirto's (1992) view of creativity is based on her firsthand knowledge and experience with creative artists of various types, but perhaps most of all with writers. To Piirto, creative performance in the arts involves a combinational pattern of personal, social, and educational variables. High-level intellectual promise is coupled with attendance at the right liberal arts college, the establishment of a coterie of other people equally committed to the enterprise, and the personal need to achieve based on life experiences. *Piirto*

In current creativity research, the search for how cognitive and personality variables interact appears to be of strong interest. Jensen (1996) acknowledged the importance of ideational fluency, access to a wide relevance horizon, and suspension of critical judgment as key variables in creative work along with mental energy, defined as noncognitive cortical arousal. Rothenberg (1993), who studied the process of Janusian thinking as a way of understanding creativity, noted that creativity involves a process of two disparate elements occupying the same mental space and then being brought together in the act of articulation. Dudek (1993) viewed primitive drive coupled with a cognitive search for symbolic solutions as a defining feature of creative people. This interplay of affect and cognition appears to be a distinctive sign of creativity at work. Weisburg (1986) viewed creativity as multidimensional, heavily dependent on organizing past experience in novel ways, and linked to inclination and concentration to produce.

In other recent theoretical work on creativity, Eysenck (1993) posited that psychoticism is a central trait of high creativity in individuals. Similarly, Simonton (1995) showed highly creative people to be higher than normal on a psychopathology scale but lower than psychotics. Barron (1969) added that psychoticism is held in check by ego strength in creative individuals who are functioning at high levels. Psychoticism has been correlated with aggressive, cold, egocentric, impersonal, impulsive, anti-social, unempathetic, creative, and tough-minded traits—traits that are often cited in research on creativity.

The cognitive aspect of Eysenck's (1993) theory revolves around intelligence as a search process to bring together ideas from memory in novel ways to solve problems, with both speed of information processing and error rate being relevant to the success of the search. Eysenck also linked creativity to a cognitive style he called "over-inclusiveness," noting that 50% of creative achievement can be explained by scores on a word association test. His theory further posits that creativity is more related to temperament than cognition, to personality traits rather than cognitive abilities.

Eysenck's view of the concept of creativity is also revolutionary in that he saw creativity as highly genetically based and irregularly distributed among the population, making it difficult to consider as a variable of interest in school-based programs. Support for his perspective on creativity as unique achievement with an irregular pattern of distribution has come from studies of highly creative people in various fields that showed that a small percentage of individuals are responsible for the majority of work in the fields. For example, only one scientist out of 10,000 would produce 100 papers. Only 10% of scientists are responsible for 50% of the total works published. Only 16 composers are responsible for half the pieces heard in modern repertoire. Jensen (1996), however, explained this J-curve phenomenon as resulting from the synergy of several constructs that are normally distributed making up creativity. From a societal point of view, Martindale (1993) has contended that creative achievement is maximized when egotism and individualism pervade a society—in other words, when social psychoticism is high. This view appears to have its roots in Arieti's (1976) notion of a permissive society that is open to individual divergence.

Based on these various theories and ways of seeing creativity, it may be useful to consider the model described in Table 21.2 as a way of synthesizing the current research. The table examines four major aspects of the development of creativity:

1. Internal factors that include intelligence, personality, psychoticism, and energy
2. External factors that take into account domain-specific variables, educational variables, and social-cultural variables
3. Facilitating processes that are relevant to creative production, such as ideational fluency, novelty, cognitive style, insight, use of imagery, and metacognitive strategies
4. Personal catalysts that are both internal and external in orientation that work together to create drive, such as task motivation, disposition to achieve, crystallizing experiences, and significant paragons or mentors

These four aspects, then, must work in a synergistic way to result in high-level creative productivity and significant contribution to a field. The complexity inherent in the developmental process of creativity and the complex interplay of various forces point to a phenomenon that will continue to tantalize researchers for some time to come. In the meantime, our current understanding of theories underpinning

Table 21.2~
The Development of Creativity

Internal Factors	External Factors	Facilitating Processes	Personal Catalysts
Intelligence (Getzels & Jackson, 1968)	Domain-Specific Variables • field-readiness • opinion of experts • acceptance of ideas (Feldman, 1988; Csikszent-mihalyi, 1990)	Ideational Fluency (Guilford, 1957)	Task Motivation (Amabile, 1983)
Personality Variables (Barron, 1969; Runco, 1993b; Taylor & Holland, 1962)	Educational Variables • learning relevant skills (Amabile, 1983) • developing a rich knowledge base (Glaser, 1985)	Originality, Novelty (Eysenck, 1993)	Disposition to Achieve (Albert, 1989)
Psychoticism (Eysenck, 1993)	Family Variables • wobble effect (Albert, 1989)	Cognitive Style (Eysenck, 1993)	Crystallizing Experiences (Walters & Gardner, 1986)
Energy (Jensen, 1996)	Social-Cultural Variables • absence of war • open society • societal valuing of relevant domain • social context that nurtures creative expression (Arieti, 1976; Tannen-, baum, 1983)	Insight and Intuition (Sternberg, 1988)	Significant Paragons or Mentors (Simonton, 1994)
		Use of Imagery (Dudek & Marchand, 1983)	
		Metacognitive Strategies (Perkins, 1981; Feldhusen, 1995)	

creativity provides little practical assistance in deliberate attempts to develop it, especially in young students whose knowledge base and experiences are more limited than those of older individuals.

The Demographics of Creativity ~

Based on the work of the historiometrist Simonton (1984), we know that a few creative people account for the major creative products of a society at a given time. For example, 20% of musical compositions played today can be attributed to three composers—Mozart, Beethoven, and Bach. Ochse (1990) discussed the issue of quantity and quality of production among the creative as well, noting that quality appears to result from quantity because of the incremental nature of creative work over time (Campbell, 1960). In other words, the more experience one has in an area, the more likely that relevant insights will occur about that area that might lead to creative products of high quality.

Highly creative individuals tend to be only or firstborn children (Albert, 1980) and to come from professional homes where they are exposed to intellectual ideas and materials (Zuckerman, 1977). In a study by Walberg and Redding (1989), creative productivity was found to be nurtured by a home curriculum that stressed conversation, discussion of reading and television, and peer activities. Yet in the homes of highly creative children, Albert (1969) also found what he called a "wobble effect," a decided lack of total cohesion, with pressure sometimes placed on the creative child to succeed.

Intrinsic Motivation and Creativity ~

Much work on motivation theory has direct relevance for understanding creativity. Amabile (1983) saw intrinsic motivation as central to doing creative work. Csikszentmihalyi (1990) viewed intrinsic motivation as essential to experiencing optimal learning in any domain and in any culture. He described an intrinsic motivation pattern, which he called "flow," as having the following characteristics:

1. Individual is faced with tasks he or she can do
2. Individual is able to concentrate on those tasks
3. Task has clear goals and immediate feedback
4. Individual experiences deep involvement in the task to the exclusion of everyday life issues
5. Concerns for self disappear
6. Sense of time is altered

Creative individuals appear to be those having sufficient intrinsic motivation to engage for prolonged periods of time in the act of creating.

Insight and Creativity ⌒

Early on, creative thought was considered somehow "magical," many times because the connections between what was currently accepted and what was discerned by a creative person in a given field were not easily followed by an average person. Mental leaps, as Perkins (1981) called them, had to be taken. The fields of science, mathematics, and technology are loaded with examples of mental insights that occurred at a propitious but seemingly unusual time for the creator. Table 21.3 documents some of these more astounding insights and the context of discovery.

Yet studies of insight (e.g., Perkins, 1981; Sternberg, 1985) have shown that deep immersion in a problem over time coupled with the serendipitous recognition of an analogy and one's reasoning through it can lead to insight. These studies present a less mysterious view of insight than we might like to believe.

Perkins' work on creativity is useful for thinking about the construct in terms of school-based programs for the gifted. He noted the following principles:

1. Creativity involves traits that make a person creative; the act of creativity calls for traits and behaviors that are not intrinsically creative, such as planning and abstracting.
2. Creativity requires four fundamental acts: planning, abstracting, undoing, and making means into ends.
3. The guiding force that creates a product is purpose or intent.
4. Creating is a process of selecting among many possible outcomes by using such approaches as noting opportunities and flaws, directed remembering, reasoning, looking harder, setting work aside, using schemata, and problem finding.
5. Creativity involves a style, values, beliefs, and tactics that specially favor selecting for a creative product.

Perkins' work would suggest the need for gifted programs to develop depth of student learning in key areas of aptitude and interest coupled with an environment that encourages thoughtful planning and working through projects if continued cre-

Table 21.3 ⌒
Relationship of Context to Creative Discovery

Creator	Circumstance	Creative Insight
Archimedes	Taking a bath	Volume displacement
Poincaré	Stepping onto a bus	Fuchsion function
Darwin	Reading Malthus	Explanation of evolution
Watson and Crick	Recalling a dream	DNA (deoxyribonucleic acid)

ative efforts are to occur. One of the benefits of such instruction may be building confidence for continued creative efforts (Delcourt, 1993), since systems that support autonomy and self-esteem also increase innovative achievement (Mumford & Gustafson, 1988).

Adversity and Creativity ⌇

Many researchers interested in the study of eminent personalities have hypothesized a connection between creativity and adversity (Albert, 1983; Piirto, 1991; Therivel, 1993; VanTassel-Baska, 1989, 1996). This hypothesis views creative production as emanating from a set of drives brought about by traumatic experiences in youth, crystallizing experiences at critical periods, or preconditions of personality and/or disability that might affect a particular outlook on life. Goertzel and colleagues (Goertzel & Goertzel, 1962; Goertzel, Goertzel, & Goertzel, 1978) found that a high number of the 300 eminent personalities they studied had a much higher than normal rate of troubled backgrounds, including family breakups, deaths of siblings, and alcoholism. Some professions appeared particularly overrepresented by eminent people with such adversities. Generals, political leaders, and writers all had uncommonly high adversity profiles.

Simonton (1994) noted the tendency of eminent individuals toward a higher psychopathic profile than less productive gifted individuals. In a study of the writers Brontë and Woolf, VanTassel-Baska (1996) proposed that mental instability and a high-strung nature were added reasons for those women to turn to writing, as writing offered relief and an outlet for such symptoms. Jamison (1995) found intense creative states with many features of hypomania present in close to 90% of her sample of creative artists and writers. Such interpretations lend support to Freud's view that the unconscious sublimation of energy generated by instinctual drives into creative work is responsible for the progress of civilization. Obviously, later psychologists such as Adler, Rank, and Maslow considered creativity much more closely linked to positive drives of mentally stable people to improve and move toward a more self-actualized state. Rogers, too, linked creativity to something positive, characterizing it as being open to experience (Ochse, 1990).

The adversity view of creativity obviously contrasts sharply with the supportive family model that is usually perceived as a fundamental part of the talent development process (Bloom, 1985). However, even in cases of creative people with high adversity profiles, at least one family member has usually been found supportive of the individual, and family played an important part in the lives of such eminent people.

Identification of the Creatively Gifted ⌇

There has been a flurry of interest in the identification of students who are creatively gifted, as opposed to those who are more traditionally academically gifted. Such efforts, however, have not proven very successful, for current research has shown that (1) it is difficult to discern creativity as a distinct phenomenon from general intellectual giftedness at the upper ranges (Venable, 1994), typically students scoring above 120 on an IQ measure, and (2) most creativity tests lack content validity (Baer, 1994). Wakefield (1992) found artistic competence to be a better predictor of creativity in art than creativity test scores.

Tannenbaum (1983), in an extensive review of research on creativity, noted that issues of identifying creativity are plagued by methodological problems that call into serious question the use of such instruments to make decisions about inclusion or exclusion for gifted programs. Moreover, he concurred with Gallagher (1966) that creativity is best understood as an aspect of giftedness, not separate from it, and that both terms should be used synonymously since giftedness is best reflected in performance and productivity. Newer approaches to identifying creativity among student populations have focused sharply on the following considerations:

1. Demonstration of competence in a particular domain or performance area
2. The use of portfolios, performance tryouts, and exhibits of work to make judgments
3. The use of panels of experts in the specific domain under consideration to make decisions about the relative quality of the products

Thus, there appears to be a clear shift away from general assessments of creative potential and toward more specific approaches to identifying creative potential in specific domains. Tannenbaum (1983) summarized our understanding of the problems in assessing creativity by noting that divergent thinking tests are limited, that correlations between creativity test scores and IQs vary from near-zero to moderately positive and significant, and that correlations between IQ and proficiency in the different divergent thinking skills vary widely.

Use of Creativity Instruments with Disadvantaged Gifted Populations

Much work in the field of gifted education has focused on ways to identify more students as gifted from underrepresented populations, including low-income and minority students and those with learning disabilities. One approach to such identification has been the use of nontraditional tests, such as creativity tests that purport to tap into fluid abilities not always readily apparent on an IQ test but important to an understanding of intelligence (Carroll, 1993). Although many special projects have used and continue to advocate the use of a creativity measure to find such children (Lopez, Esquivel, & Houtz, 1993), little empirical evidence exists to show the validity or predictive value of creativity measures in such a process. Clear evidence suggests that they do identify some students not found through the use of standardized measures, but the program success of such students has not been systematically studied. The use of work samples and tryout strategies for identifying these special populations appears to be more promising at this stage of our understanding of the issues.

18 Creative Positives (handwritten annotation in left margin)

Torrance and Safter (1986) and Bernal (1981), among other researchers, have identified creative traits found among special populations. Their lists of behavioral characteristics have been used to some extent in searching out underrepresented groups, especially African and Hispanic Americans. The validity and reliability of such checklists, however, has not been well established.

The Teaching of Creativity ~

Regardless of whether one identifies students as creatively gifted, it is generally accepted in the field of gifted education that all gifted students can benefit from the direct teaching of creativity-relevant skills. Indeed, recent research on the use of creative problem solving (CPS) and problem-based learning (PBL) lends support to the idea that all students can benefit from such instruction (Schack, 1993; VanTassel-Baska, Bass, Ries, & Poland, in press). Borland (1988) demonstrated that ideational fluency in particular is a skill that can be successfully taught to groups of gifted students and is highly correlated with intelligence.

Yet the body of research on the teaching of creativity is hardly convincing. Tannenbaum (1983), in his comprehensive review of creativity programs, concluded that creativity training is successful in the short run for the specific skills it purports to develop. We know little, however, about long-term impacts or transfer to other contexts. More current research suggests that generic creative thinking skills do not transfer to any domain in which they were not taught (Perkins & Salomon, 1989).

Rose and Linn (1984), in a meta-analytic study of long-term creativity programs, found that training accounted for no more than 22% of the variance in creative behavior. Feldhusen and Clinkenbeard (1986) reviewed instructional materials designed to teach creativity and found that much of the material was not based on a theoretical model of creativity or subjected to any rigorous evaluation or research study. They found evidence of instructional effectiveness for only three programs.

Less direct approaches to facilitating creativity are, however, apparently successful. The role of mentors and significant others has been cited often in the literature as highly relevant to helping individuals become creative producers (Feldhusen & Pleiss, 1994). Along these lines, Simonton (1994) made an interesting distinction between individuals who are creative in the arts and those who are creative in the sciences. For scientific creativity to develop, mentoring appears to be an important part of the process; for artistic creativity to flourish, the role of a nonpersonal paragon, an individual who can be emulated from afar, appears to be the more critical model. Further, Simonton showed that although mentors and paragons may be important to the attainment of creative potential, it is in the master-apprentice relationship that the growth appears to take shape rather than through any form of direct teaching. Mentors provide a strong emotional support base as well as being a model of high-level functioning in a field. It is this dual perspective of feeding both the affective and cognitive needs of students that makes the relationship so satisfactory and in many instances successful.

Walters and Gardner (1986) have identified crystallizing experiences—the occurrence of life events that serve as markers to how an individual may focus his or her life's work and resultant productivity—as an important aspect contributing to creative achievement. Gruber (1981) noted that for Darwin that crystallizing experience was the year he spent at sea on the *Beagle*. In the teaching of creativity, there may be much to be said for the provision of high-powered experiences outside the classroom that are intensive enough to affect students in profound ways. Many internship and summer program experiences now provided to gifted students appear to have just this kind of impact.

Moreover, some limited recent evidence suggests that educational programs based on a creativity model may in fact facilitate the ongoing aspect of the creativity process. Two nascent longitudinal studies have attempted to link creatively oriented gifted programs to later adult productivity. Delcourt (1994) studied 18 secondary students who were identified by Renzulli's Three Ring Conception of Giftedness and were provided with Type III enrichment activities three years after completing a creatively oriented gifted program. All of the students were found to be satisfied with the nature and extent of the project work with which they were engaged. Moon and Feldhusen (1993) studied 23 students who participated for at least three years in an enrichment program using the Purdue Three-Stage Model of creative development. They found that all of the students planned to attend college and 78% planned to undertake graduate training. The study noted that aspiration levels for girls were tempered by interest in marriage and children.

Other types of study designs have been used in attempts to correlate creative performance in adulthood with creativity test scores in childhood. Cramond (1994), for example, studied the lifetime productivity of individuals identified at elementary ages by the Torrance Tests of Creative Thinking as having creative potential. Results demonstrated that lifetime creative achievement was moderately correlated with the test scores. Two other variables were found also to have important correlational value: an enduring future career image during childhood and a mentor at some time.

Torrance (1993), in a related study, reported on two exceptional cases of "beyonders" who outperformed any prediction of their success in the adult world. He found that these individuals possessed such characteristics as love of work, perseverance with tasks, lack of concern with being in the minority, enjoyment of working alone, and immersion in work-related tasks. It is interesting to note that all of these characteristics are highly related to the ethics of intrinsic motivation, individualism, and work.

Implications of Creativity Research for Schools ⌒

Because the research evidence appears to be limited in supporting the pursuit of separate identification of creative children and in supporting separate programs, devoid of content, that teach to only creative thinking and problem solving, the best course of action for schools to take seems to be to provide the following kinds of options within the scope of their existing gifted programs:

1. Encourage creative expression in all gifted programs, ensuring that students generate new ideas in product development.
2. Provide rigorous and deep subject matter content in areas in which gifted students show specific aptitude and interest.
3. Provide ways to put gifted students in direct contact with practicing professionals.
4. Encourage the reading of biographies of eminent individuals in students' fields of interest and aptitude.
5. Provide academic counseling assistance so that individual student profiles may be considered in making summer program or camp decisions.
6. Demonstrate that the school is a social context that values creative thought by creating schoolwide outlets for creative work, such as a school newspaper, journals, books, photography, and other art-form exhibits.
7. Provide in-service training to teachers on ways to enhance creative thought in each subject area, especially by using heuristics like creative problem solving and problem-based learning.
8. Enhance student metacognition by regularly asking students to plan, monitor, and assess their own progress in the classroom.
9. Encourage creative work within students' individual aptitude and interest areas.
10. Use active involvement strategies in the classroom that give voice to creative thoughts, such as role-playing, oral problem solving, and dramatic skits.
11. Offer extracurricular activities that address talent areas not found in the school curriculum, such as chess, dramatics, debate, and writing.

While these suggestions are rather general in orientation, they are in keeping with major elements of the research in the field of creativity. Moreover, they are well within the realm of what schools *can* do if they wish to promote the development of creativity in their student population. Keeping in mind that the creative development of an individual is highly complex and long term, schools should put themselves in a position of facilitating such development rather than either impeding it or trying to address its development in a very direct way.

Implications of Creativity Research for Parents ~

Perhaps more than schools, parents are in a position to facilitate the development of creativity in their children by helping them develop over time the knowledge base, skills, and attitudes cited earlier in this chapter as contributing to high creative development. Many of the strategies they can use are parallel to those schools can use for developing talent. They might include the following:

1. Locate other children who share your child's interests and abilities. Get to know their parents and create opportunities for the children to act out their creative interests.
2. Find an older student or an adult who shares your child's interests and who may act as a mentor over time.
3. Enroll your child in university-based summer programs or camps as his or her areas of interest develop.
4. Provide a wide range of extracurricular offerings that may stimulate interest in your child.
5. Provide enriching experiences that provide creative outlets, such as music, art, dance, or drama lessons.
6. Model your own creative interests in the home and teach them to your child when and if appropriate.
7. Take your child to museums of all types; explore exhibits and discuss them as a family.
8. View selected television programs with your child and discuss them as a family.
9. Conduct "conversations" with your child on current events, current reading, or interesting ideas at least once a day.
10. Listen with interest to your child's ideas; create a context in the home where openness to ideas is valued.

If parents take an active role in promoting creative development in their children, the combined efforts of school and home can begin to demonstrate a true accumulation of positive acts that can only facilitate the future development of gifted students toward greater creative productivity.

Summary ～

The nurturance of creativity within the context of domain-specific gifted programs and the context of the home environment seems highly supportable from what we know about creativity. Can we identify creativity in childhood separate from giftedness? It appears highly doubtful. Thus, our resources should be directed toward finding high-functioning students who can profit from an integrated approach to addressing their giftedness and talents that includes an emphasis on creativity-relevant skills and attitudes.

References ～

Albert, R. (1969). Genius: Present-day status of the concept and its implications for the study of creativity and giftedness. *American Psychologist, 24*(8), 743–753.

Albert, R. (1980). Family positions and the attachment of eminence: A study of special family positions and special family experiences. *Gifted Child Quarterly, 24*(2), 87–95.

Albert, R. (1983). *Genius and eminence: The social psychology of creativity and exceptional achievement.* Elmsford, NY: Pergamon.

Albert, R. (1989). Independence and the creative potential of gifted and exceptionally gifted boys. *Journal of Youth and Adolescence, 18*(3), 221–230.

Amabile, T. M. (1983). *The social psychology of creativity*. New York: Springer-Verlag.

Arieti, S. (1976). *Creativity: The magic synthesis*. New York: Basic Books.

Baer, J. (1994). Why you shouldn't trust creativity tests. *Educational Leadership, 51*(4), 68–77.

Bandura, A. (1986). *Social foundations of thought and action: A social cognitive theory*. Englewood Cliffs, NJ: Prentice-Hall.

Barron, F. (1969). *Creative person and creative process*. New York: Holt, Rinehart, & Winston.

Bernal, E. (1981, August). *Intelligence tests on trial*. Discussion presented at "Intelligence Tests on Trial: Larry P. and PASE," a symposium held at the meeting of the American Psychological Association, Los Angeles, CA.

Berry, C. (1981). The Nobel scientists and the origins of scientific achievement. *British Journal of Sociology, 32*, 381–391.

Bloom, B. S. (1985). *Developing talent in young people*. New York: Ballantine.

Borland, J. (1988). Cognitive controls, cognitive styles, and divergent production in gifted preadolescents. *Journal for the Education of the Gifted, 11*(4), 57–82.

Campbell, D. T. (1960). Blind variation and selective retention in creative thought as in other knowledge processes. *Psychological Review, 67*, 380–400.

Carroll, J. B. (1993). *Human cognitive abilities: A survey of factor and analytic studies*. Cambridge, MA: Cambridge University Press.

Cramond, B. (1994). The Torrance Tests of Creative Thinking: From design through establishment of predictive validity. In R. Subotnik & K. Arnold (Eds.), *Beyond Terman: Contemporary longitudinal studies of giftedness and talent* (pp. 229–254). Norwood, NJ: Ablex.

Csikszentmihalyi, M. (1990). *Flow*. New York: Harper Perennial.

Dabrowski, K., & Piechowski, M. M. (1977). *Theory of levels of emotional development* (Vols. 1 & 2). Oceanside, NY: Dabor Science.

Delcourt, M. A. B. (1993). Creative productivity among secondary school students: Combining energy, interest, and imagination. *Gifted Child Quarterly, 37*(1), 23–31.

Delcourt, M. A. B. (1994). Characteristics of high-level creative productivity: A longitudinal study of students identified by Renzulli's Three-Ring Conception of Giftedness. In R. Subotnik & K. Arnold (Eds.), *Beyond Terman: Contemporary longitudinal studies of giftedness and talent* (pp. 401–436). Norwood, NJ: Ablex.

Dudek, S. Z. (1993). Creativity and psychoticism: An overinclusive model. *Psychological Inquiry, 4*(3), 190–192.

Dudek, S. Z., & Marchand, P. (1983). Artistic style and personality in creative painters. *Journal of Personality Assessment, 47*(2), 139–142.

Eysenck, H. J. (1993). Creativity and personality: Suggestions for a theory. *Psychological Inquiry, 4*(3), 141–178.

Feldhusen, J. F. (1995). Creativity: A knowledge base, metacognitive skills, and personality. *Journal of Creative Behavior, 29*(4), 255–266.

Feldhusen, J. F., & Clinkenbeard, P. M. (1986). Creativity instructional material: A review of research. *Journal of Creative Behavior, 20*(3), 153–182.

Feldhusen, J. F., & Pleiss, M. K. (1994). Leadership: A synthesis of social skills, creativity, and histrionic ability? *Roeper Review, 16*(4), 293–294.

Feldman, D. (1988). *Nature's gambit*. New York: Teachers College Press.

Gallagher, J. (1966). *Research summary in gifted child education*. Springfield, IL: Office of the Superintendent of Public Instruction.

Gardner, H. (1993). *Creating minds*. New York: Basic Books.

Getzels, J. W., & Csikszentmihalyi, M. (1977). *The creative vision*. Chicago: University of Chicago Press.

Getzels, J., & Jackson, P. (1968). *Creativity and intelligence: Exploration with gifted students*. New York: Wiley.

Glaser, R. (1985). *Education and thinking: The role of knowledge*. Pittsburgh, PA: University of Pittsburgh, Learning Research and Development Center.

Goertzel, V., & Goertzel, M. G. (1962). *Cradles of eminence*. Boston: Little, Brown.

Goertzel, V., Goertzel, M. G., & Goertzel, T. (1978). *Three hundred personalities: A psychosocial analysis of the famous*. San Francisco: Jossey-Bass.

Gruber, H. (1981). *Darwin on man: A psychological study of scientific creativity*. Chicago: University of Chicago Press.

Guilford, J. P. (1950). Creativity. *American Psychologist, 5*, 444–454.

Guilford, J. P. (1957). *The relations of creative-thinking aptitudes to non-aptitude personality traits: Studies of aptitudes of high-level personnel*. Los Angeles: University of Southern California, Psychological Laboratory.

Jamison, K. R. (1995). *Touched with fire: Manic depressive illness and the artistic temperament*. New York: Macmillan.

Jensen, A. R. (1996). Giftedness and genius: Crucial differences. In C. P. Benbow & D. Lubinski (Eds.), *Intellectual talent: Psychometric and social issues*. Baltimore, MD: Johns Hopkins University Press.

Lopez, E. C., Esquivel, G. B., & Houtz, F. (1993). The creative skill of culturally and linguistically diverse gifted students. *Creativity Research Journal, 6*(4), 401–412.

Martindale, H. (1993). Psychoticism, degeneration, and creativity. *Psychological Inquiry, 4*(3), 209–211.

Moon, S. M., & Feldhusen, J. F. (1993). Accomplishments and future plans of high school seniors who participated in an elementary enrichment program. *Roeper Review, 15*(3), 176–178.

Mumford, M. D., & Gustafson, S. B. (1988). Creativity syndrome: Integration, application, and innovation. *Psychological Bulletin, 103*(1), 27–43.

Ochse, R. (1990). *Before the gates of excellence: The determinants of creative genius*. Cambridge, MA: Cambridge University Press.

Perkins, D. N. (1981). *The mind's best work*. Cambridge, MA: Harvard University Press.

Perkins, D. N., & Salomon, G. (1989). Are cognitive skills context-bound? *Educational Researcher, 18*, 16–25.

Piechowski, M. (1984). Developmental potential of the gifted. *Gifted Child Quarterly, 28*(2), 80–88.

Piirto, J. (1991). Encouraging creativity in adolescents. In J. Genshelf & M. Bireley (Eds.), *Understanding gifted adolescents* (pp. 104–122). New York: Teachers College Press.

Piirto, J. (1992). *Understanding those who create*. Dayton, OH: Ohio Psychology Press.

Renzulli, J., & Smith, L. (1980). An alternative approach to identifying and programming for gifted and talented students. *Gifted Child Today, 15*, 4–11.

Rose, L. H., & Linn, H. (1984). A meta analysis of long term creativity training programs. *Journal of Creative Behavior, 18*, 11–22.

Rothenberg, R. (1993). Creativity—complex and healthy. *Psychological Inquiry, 4*(3), 217–221.

Runco, M. A. (1993a). Creativity, casuality, and the separation of personality and cognition. *Psychological Inquiry, 4*(3), 221–225.

Runco, M. A. (1993b). Divergent thinking, creativity, and gifted. *Gifted Child Quarterly, 37*(1), 16–22.

Runco, M. A., & Nemiro, J. (1994). Problem finding, creativity, and giftedness. *Roeper Review, 16*(4), 235–241.

Schack, G. (1993). Effects of a creative problem-solving curriculum on students of varying ability levels. *Gifted Child Quarterly, 37*(1), 32–38.

Simonton, D. K. (1984). *Genius, creativity, and leadership*. Cambridge, MA: Harvard University Press.

Simonton, D. K. (1994). *Greatness: Who makes history and why*. New York: Guilford.

Simonton, D. K. (1995, November). *The Terman thesis: Giftedness and/or genius*. Invited presentation at the National Association of Gifted Children Convention, Tampa, FL.

Sternberg, R. (1985). *Beyond IQ*. New York: Cambridge University Press.

Sternberg, R. J. (Ed.). (1988). *The nature of creativity: Contemporary psychological perspectives*. New York: Cambridge University Press.

Sternberg, R. J., & Lubart, T. I. (1993). Creative giftedness: A multivariate investment approach. *Gifted Child Quarterly, 37*(1), 7–15.

Tannenbaum, A. (1983). *Gifted children*. New York: Macmillan.

Taylor, C. W., & Holland, J. L. (1962). Development and application of tests of creativity. *Review of Educational Research, 32*(1), 91–102.

Therivel, W. (1993). The challenged personality as a precondition for sustained creativity. *Creativity Research Journal, 6*(4), 413–424.

Torrance, E. P. (1966). *Torrance tests of creative thinking.* Bensenville, IL: Scholastic Testing Service.

Torrance, E. P. (1967). *Education and the creative potential.* Minneapolis, MN: University of Minnesota Press.

Torrance, E. P. (1993). The beyonders in a thirty-year longitudinal study of creative achievement. *Roeper Review, 15*(3), 131–139.

Torrance, E. P., & Myers, R. E. (1970). *Creative learning and teaching.* New York: Dodd, Mead.

Torrance, E. P., & Safter, H. T. (1986). Are children becoming more creative? *Journal of Creative Behavior, 20*(1), 1–13.

VanTassel-Baska, J. (1989). Factors that characterize the developmental path of eminent individuals. In J. VanTassel-Baska & P. Olszewski-Kubilius (Eds.), *Patterns of influence: The home, the self, and the school* (pp. 146–162). New York: Teachers College Press.

VanTassel-Baska, J. (1996). The process of talent development. In J. VanTassel-Baska, D. T. Johnson, & L. N. Boyce (Eds.), *Developing verbal talent* (pp. 3–22). Boston: Allyn & Bacon.

VanTassel-Baska, J., Bass, G., Ries, R., & Poland, D. (in press). A national pilot study of science curriculum effectiveness. *Gifted Child Quarterly.*

Venable, B. (1994). *A philosophical analysis of creativity measurement.* (ERIC Document Reproduction Service No. ED 374 140)

Wakefield, J. F. (1992, February). *Creativity tests and artistic talent.* Paper presented at the Esther Katz Rosen Symposium on the Psychological Development of Gifted Children, Lawrence, KS. (ERIC Document Reproduction Service No. ED 355 697)

Walberg, H., & Redding, S. (1989). Strengthening family ties. *Momentum, 20*(3), 65–67.

Walters, J., & Gardner, H. (1986). The crystallizing experience: Discovering an intellectual gift. In R. Sternberg & J. Davidson (Eds.), *Conceptions of giftedness* (pp. 306–331). Cambridge, MA: Cambridge University Press.

Weisberg, R. (1986). *Creativity: Genius and other myths.* New York: W. H. Freeman.

Zuckerman, H. (1977). Scientific elite. New York: Free Press.

Study Questions ~

1. What is creativity? Why is there so much interest in this construct?

2. How would you describe the relationship between creativity and giftedness? Between creativity and psychopathology? Between creativity and insight? Between creativity and adversity?

3. What internal factors have been correlated with creativity? What external factors?

4. Are creativity tests useful for the identification of disadvantaged gifted youngsters? Why or why not?

5. What strategies appear particularly effective for schools to focus on in enhancing creativity in gifted students? What strategies have relevance for all students?

6. Why is reinforcement in the home environment seen as particularly important in relation to this construct? What activities can parents be advised to undertake to support creative development in their gifted children?

22

Thinking Skills for the Gifted

John F. Feldhusen

Gifted students, and in fact *all* students, should be taught how to think or to think more effectively (Treffinger, Callahan, & Vaughn, 1991). Although few baseline data exist on proficiency in thinking among the gifted or among children in general, many teachers and educational researchers believe that children are weak or woefully deficient in thinking ability and that these skills, whatever they are, could be measurably improved. Some research reviewed by Feldhusen and Clinkenbeard (1986) confirms the teachability of cognitive skills (Feuerstein, Miller, Hoffman, Mintzker, & Jensen, 1981; Savell, Twohig, & Rachford, 1986; Sternberg, 1985b). We have no evidence, however, that instruction in thinking skills is particularly needed by the gifted, and some evidence even indicates that they are superior in thinking ability at the point of their first identification as gifted (Anderson, 1986; Devall, 1982; Shore, Cornell, Robinson, & Ward, 1991; Spitz, 1982; Ward, 1979). However, their advanced level of ability in thinking skills clearly calls for high-level instruction if need is determined by readiness and if it is a general rule that all children should be enabled to proceed to the highest levels of achievement commensurate with their current levels of ability.

A sense that the gifted should be capable of achievements in thinking at advanced levels leads to the special concern for the development of their thinking skills. It also may be true that because many of the gifted are likely to be future leaders in the professions, business, and the arts, we want them to be highly effective thinkers, creators, and problem solvers so that they will provide optimum leadership for our society. Thus, we endeavor to build strength in thinking in students who show promise of high-level cognitive attainment, and we assume that strength in thinking will transfer to a wide variety of problem situations. Furthermore, our goal in teaching thinking skills to the gifted is to carry such instruction to much higher and more complex levels than we can for children of average ability and to introduce the higher level thinking skills earlier in the educational programs.

Several movements from psychological and educational research are converging and reporting results that have also heightened our interest in thinking skills. One is the field of metacognition research and theory development (Bruning, Schraw, & Ronning, 1995; Ormrod, 1995; Sternberg, 1985a). Another is the shift in psychology from behaviorism to cognitive science (Bruer, 1993; Gardner, 1985). Still another is the active subfield of research and theory development focusing explicitly on thinking skills (Armstrong, 1994; Nickerson, Perkins, & Smith, 1985). Studies of cognitive style (Dunn, Dunn, & Treffinger, 1992; Witkins, 1976), and to some extent learning or productivity styles (Dunn & Price, 1980), also have generated new interest in the domain of thinking skills. Finally, popular training packages, such as deBono's (1984) *CoRT* program, the Purdue Creative Thinking Program (Feldhusen, 1983), and Taylor's (1983) Talents Unlimited, generated optimism about the need for and value of thinking skills in the general curriculum and in the gifted curriculum in particular.

Closely related to the movement for the teaching of thinking skills is the renewed emphasis on higher level content in curriculum in general, but particularly in curriculum for gifted youth (VanTassel-Baska, 1994). From Bruner's (1960) publication entitled *The Process of Education*, a major movement came to American schools to develop conceptually oriented curricula. After a decade the movement waned, but it left a legacy of concern for the teaching of major concepts. Phenix (1964), in *Realms of Meaning*, and Ward (1961), in *Educating the Gifted*, both echoed this critical need for a curriculum based on major concepts, themes, or issues, especially in instruction for the gifted. Nevertheless, Sizer (1985) pointed out in his study of American high schools, *Horace's Compromise*, that in a majority of American secondary classrooms, transmission of information remains the major goal of instructors.

Great concern also exists for the knowledge base in relation to the development of thinking skills (Feldhusen, 1993, 1994; Glaser, 1984) and for the nature of thinking skills in various disciplines (Nickerson et al., 1985; Raths, Wasserman, Jonas, & Rothstein, 1986). Emerging research evidence suggests that the nature of thinking may differ from discipline to discipline and that the nature of thinking differs depending on the thinker's level of expertise (Glaser, 1984; VanTassel-Baska, 1994).

This review of methods for teaching thinking skills emphasizes general systems as well as specific applications of those systems in separate disciplines. We focus particularly on practical systems that have potential for application in K–12 programs for the gifted and talented. Thus, the major domains of thinking discussed here are critical thinking, creative thinking, the cognitive operations of the Bloom taxonomy (1956), inquiry, problem solving, and metacognitive processes.

Creative Thinking ~

Interest in teaching creative thinking dates from the early work of Guilford (1959), Taylor (1964), and Torrance and Myers (1970), as well as from the work of Osborn (1963) and Parnes (1977). These researchers paved the way for the development of creativity instructional materials and techniques that now are widely used in general school programs and that are stressed in enrichment activities for the gifted (Feldhusen & Goh, 1995; Feldhusen & Treffinger, 1985). Osborne's "brainstorming" and Parnes's creative problem-solving models now are well known in school programs, as are the familiar concepts of fluency, flexibility, originality, and elaboration, either in verbal or in nonverbal forms. Definitions of these terms follow.

Fluency

Fluency refers to the modes of thinking through which ideas are generated or recalled without regard to producing specific answers or solutions. The typical fluency activity in the classroom asks children to produce as many ideas as possible within a relatively broad framework:

> What are all the ways you can think of to remove the skin from an orange?
> What are all the alternatives the United States might have considered when faced by the U-boat (submarine) threat to shipping in World War II?
> List as many character traits as you can think of for a story character.
> What are practical uses of the dye properties of certain chemicals?

All of these tasks can be done individually or in groups. Students are typically urged to strive for quantity of ideas, avoid self- or group criticism, and feel free to build upon or extend their own ideas or those contributed by others.

Flexibility

Flexibility refers to the capacity to generate solutions or ideas that break away from or are alternative to conventional ideas. Classroom discussion can set the stage for flexible thinking by calling for alternatives to the conventional:

> Rewrite this equation to include two equal signs and no parentheses.
> How would our lives be different today if the South had won the Civil War?
> How could medical science carry on research if animals could not be used?
> Develop an alternative orthographic system.

In all efforts to evoke and develop flexible thinking, we can structure the task to call for approaches that look from different viewpoints. We hope also that rigidity or inflexibility can be overcome. One of the major programs designed to facilitate thinking in alternative ways is the *synectics approach* (Gordon, 1961; Gordon & Poze, 1980). In synectics, metaphors are used to tease out alternative ways of looking at problems (Davis, 1991). The following is an example of a classroom activity in synectics: Faced with the problem of creating a new type of society, students are to draw analogies from ant colonies. By observing ant behavior in colonies, students can be led to see ways of developing leadership and worker roles in a new society.

Originality

Originality of response implies that an idea is unusual or unique in addition to being valuable or practical. Originality often is thought to be the essence of creative thinking (Torrance, 1987). The link between fluency, flexibility, and originality also should be noted. As stated earlier, fluency means producing ideas without fear of evaluation, flexibility means looking for new or alternative connections or associations, and originality means seeking the unique or unusual. Originality obviously calls for an evaluative function in that the original thinker must be able to judge an idea or response as fitting the stimulus demand and yet as being new, novel, or unusual. Originality in creative thinking is evident in a child's proposal that curiosity be studied by observing the parallels between cats' and infants' exploratory behavior.

Elaboration

The fourth creative mode of thinking, elaboration, is the process of taking the new idea, which has been recognized as unique and potentially valuable, and developing it into something useful or practical. For example: A new idea is to create a television show that is highly entertaining for adolescents and promotes love of learning. Determining the situation, developing characters, outlining plots, and writing dialogue are all parts of the process of elaboration. A student who can take an idea and add details, integrate various correlated elements, and produce a good story or essay is an effective elaborator.

Creative Problem Solving ～

All of these skills of fluency, flexibility, originality, and elaboration should be called into play in the more complex form of creative activity called *creative problem solving*. The many models of creative problem solving (Parnes, 1981; Torrance & Myers, 1970; Treffinger, 1982, 1993) offer excellent opportunities for the gifted to learn how to combine a number of aspects of creative thinking into a sequence of problem-solving steps. Several models of problem solving will be discussed in depth later in this chapter.

The field of creative thinking is replete with packaged training programs. Feldhusen and Clinkenbeard (1986) and Feldhusen and Goh (1995) reviewed the training programs and methods, including those for creative problem solving, and found positive evidence for the teachability of creative thinking. Good training programs of the future, however, probably will move from relatively abstracted forms of training in artificial contexts to applications of principles and methods in realistic contexts and in disciplines such as science, mathematics, literature, and social studies. Training for the gifted in creative thinking should begin at the kindergarten level and continue through high school, when it should be applied in all academic disciplines. Treffinger et al. (1993) concluded, from a comprehensive and in-depth review of a large number of creative and productive thinking programs, that there are many good sets of instructional material, for K–12, for developing students' thinking skills. In their report they presented descriptions and evaluations of each program reviewed.

Creative thinking and production are both cognitive and affective processes, and thus the environment in which people try to think and solve problems can have a major impact on the activity. Amabile (1990) conducted a series of studies that showed quite clearly that a facilitative and supportive environment and intrinsic, self-generated motivation lead to enhanced and superior creative activity. Teachers must address both areas when they lead children in creative thinking activities.

Critical Thinking

Ennis (1985) defined critical thinking as "reflective and reasonable thinking that is focused on deciding what to believe or do" (p. 45). The activities covered by this definition include formulating hypotheses, questions, alternatives, and plans for experiments. Ennis (1962) published one of the early guides to the teaching of critical thinking, and Harnadek (1980) authored a widely used set of instructional materials for teaching critical thinking skills.

Ennis (1985) and Norris and Ennis (1989) delineated a structure of critical thinking skills, dividing them into the following three major categories:

1. Define and clarify:
   • Identify central issues and problems.
   • Identify conclusions.
   • Identify reasons.
   • Identify appropriate questions to ask, given a situation.
   • Identify assumptions.
2. Judge information:
   • Determine credibility of sources and observations.
   • Determine relevance.
   • Recognize consistency.
3. Infer—solve problems and draw reasonable conclusions:
   • Infer and judge inductive conclusions.
   • Deduce and judge deductive validity.
   • Predict probable consequences.

Ennis (1985) further identified a set of 13 dispositions that facilitate critical thinking:

1. Be open-minded.
2. Take a position (and change a position) when the evidence and reasons are sufficient to do so.
3. Take into account the total situation.
4. Try to be well informed.
5. Seek as much precision as the subject permits.
6. Deal in an orderly manner with the parts of a complex whole.

7. Look for alternatives.
8. Seek reasons.
9. Seek a clear statement of the issue.
10. Keep in mind the original or basic concern.
11. Use credible sources and mention them.
12. Remain relevant to the main point.
13. Be sensitive to the feelings, level of knowledge, and degree of sophistication of others.

There is an abundance of good instructional material for teaching critical thinking. For example, the books in the series entitled *Critical Thinking Handbooks*, by Paul, Benker, Martin, and Adamson (1989), provide excellent guidelines and instructional material for gifted classes. Likewise, Beyer's (1991) *Teaching Thinking Skills* covers the areas of thinking skills and the integration of those skills into the curriculum.

The teaching of critical thinking skills probably can be addressed best in gifted programs in the upper elementary grades, middle school, and high school, and predominantly in the context of subject matter or the disciplines (Paul, 1990). Although some aspects of critical thinking, particularly those related to logic, can be taught in abstracted formats (e.g., if all A are X, does it follow that all X are A?), it seems likely that early generalization of the skills to meaningful contexts will best assure the transfer of the critical thinking skills to real settings. Here is an example of a problem in critical thinking:

> The city council discussed calling for bids for a new trash truck. Alderman Henry Alexson argued that our city was the only one in the area still using the old Mack model. The mayor countered by arguing that the cost would probably be prohibitive. Alderman John Ordevay suggested that they were not identifying the central issue or problems. What do you think are the basic issues or problems?
>
> After deciding on the basic issues or problems, identify which of Ennis's 13 dispositions might be appropriate behaviors for the mayor and aldermen as they discuss the trash truck problem.

Here is another illustration of a situation that could be presented to help students develop their critical thinking skills:

> Mayor Smith urged the local TV station not to run spot commercials on AIDS prevention because they would offend the religious views of many citizens. An attorney urged that they be run during breaks in the station's airing of "soaps." Mayor Smith then argued that the attorney's solution would not be acceptable. Can you detect any contradictions or inconsistencies in the arguments?

All gifted youth should develop strength in the skills of critical thinking, and the skills should be practiced and made useful in all of the major academic areas of the curriculum. Some critics have argued that thinking skills are subject-specific—that is, that there are no general critical thinking skills that can be used in thinking in different subject matters. Ennis (1989) argued that while research is needed to clarify these issues, it seems more plausible to assume that there are some general critical thinking skills that are teachable and usable in diverse disciplines and domains of knowledge.

Cognitive Skills Represented in the Bloom Taxonomy ⌐

In a publication in 1956, *Taxonomy of Educational Objectives: Cognitive Domain*, a committee of the College Board chaired by Benjamin Bloom sought to delineate levels of cognitive functioning that could be used to classify the intellectual demands of standardized test items or teaching objectives (Bloom, 1956). Since that time, the taxonomy has come to be used widely in teaching as a system for conceptualizing levels of thinking skills or abilities. The taxonomy was presented as a teaching model for gifted students by Maker and Nielson (1995). They are undoubtedly correct in their assertion that it is one of the most widely used systems to guide the teaching of thinking skills in gifted education.

Acquisition and Transmission

At the basic end of the taxonomy are teaching and learning activities that stress the *acquisition* of knowledge or the *transmission* of information:

> Students will be able to identify all the bones of the foot.
> Students will be able to specify the major characters in Shakespeare's plays.
> Students will be able to describe the order of the Milky Way.

Maker (1982) described the student role as being a passive receiver and the teacher's role as being the provider of information.

Comprehension

At the second level, *comprehension,* instruction focuses on producing understanding. The learning process now becomes interactive and strives for meaning. Appropriate objectives at this level are:

> Students can explain the meaning of all passages in Lincoln's Gettysburg Address.
> Students can explain the metaphors in a poem.

Maker (1982) described the student role at this level as being an active participant and the teacher as questioner, organizer, and evaluator.

Application

The next level is *application.* At this level, the student learns how to use rules, principles, methods, or formulas in new situations. For example:

> The student will be able to use the methods of solving simultaneous equations to solve complex story problems.
> Given a series of complex political problems, students will be able to select the best methods to solve them.

Clearly, the application level involves students and teachers in the practical use of theoretical concepts and principles.

Analysis

The fourth level of the taxonomy, *analysis,* is a cognitive process of taking ideas or phenomena apart to identify the parts and delineate relationships among them. Analysis is also the process of detecting patterns, ascertaining the structure, or clarifying underlying principles. Here are some illustrative objectives:

> Students will be able to identify and show the relationship among the elements of a complex chemical compound.
>
> Students will be able to identify the main elements of character, mood, and setting in a spy novel and show how they interact in development of the plot.

The analysis level of thinking calls for the teacher's close monitoring of student actions to provide feedback concerning the students' accuracy in specifying parts and their interrelationships.

Synthesis

The next higher, and more complex, level of thinking to be learned by students is called *synthesis.* This is the creative process of integrating ideas, information, and theories to create a new or unique whole. This might mean learning to write a play, planning a new political system, creating a new compound, or proposing a new theory. Some illustrative objectives are:

> Students will be able to design a new form of city government.
>
> Students will write original essays on the relationship between social trends and economics.

The synthesis level requires students to use creative thinking along with all of the types of thinking represented in the preceding levels of the taxonomy. It is also likely that critical and evaluative thinking are involved in creating a synthesis of ideas.

Evaluation

The final level of thinking, *evaluation,* is a process of making judgments, selecting criteria for making judgments, and applying criteria in decision making. Several of the types of thinking in the lower levels of the taxonomy are involved in the evaluation process. A knowledge base and analytical skill are essential in evaluation. Here are some illustrative objectives:

> Use a set of 10 criteria to select employees for a new civic enterprise.
>
> Debate the justifiability of U.S. involvement in the war in the Persian Gulf.

The case study is one form of instruction for the evaluation level of thinking and learning. Making decisions concerning best courses of action or judgments about a process in a realistic case setting reflects evaluation in action.

The Bloom taxonomy is useful in conceptualizing cognitive or thinking activities involved in solving problems. The tasks or problems afford students an opportunity to learn the thinking process or algorithm involved. The teacher may structure the problems for students or help them discover problems to be solved. During the thinking activities, the teacher monitors the process, provides feedback, and often models the effective thinker in action. Students must experience successes in the thinking tasks to provide reinforcement of the skills to be learned. They often work in small groups, thinking together and reinforcing one another as they move through a task.

These thinking skills, particularly those in the higher levels of the taxonomy, are the appropriate domain for much instruction of the gifted. Gifted students have the potential to achieve much higher levels of thinking ability even though they begin new lessons with advanced levels of thinking skill as compared to children of average or low ability. The teachers' task, then, is to challenge these students to the limits of their ability, to model the thinking process, to guide them in acquiring appropriate knowledge bases in disciplines, and to provide accurate feedback as they practice thinking skills with structured problems. For the gifted, this means much time spent exploring ideas, testing the applicability of theories, synthesizing ideas into new inventions or solutions, and judging the quality of solutions.

Problem Solving ~

Perhaps all teaching of thinking skills can be viewed as teaching students to solve problems. Thinking is always an adaptive process in which the thinker must be able to utilize his or her current knowledge base to deal with new and novel situations that call for some decision or action. Some research also suggests that our task is not simply to teach students how to solve problems but also to help them become sensitive to problems that should be solved, to understand disciplines or domains of knowledge well enough to develop an awareness of the gaps or the unexplained, and to formulate hypotheses that can, in turn, lead to problem-solving activities (Getzels & Csikszentmihalyi, 1975).

Getzels and Csikszentmihalyi (1975) investigated the process of "problem finding" and presented a continuum of eight levels of initial problem confrontation ranging from the fully presented problem to the discovered problem situation. Problem finding focuses particularly on the discovered problem situation. The authors claimed that problem finding may be a more creative function than solving problems that already have been formulated. In their observations of art students who were formulating the problem of a drawing, they found that artists who considered more problem elements, explored those elements more thoroughly, and selected the most uncommon ones to use in a picture were the most creative problem finders. They concluded that the processes involved in problem finding are crucial in determining the creativity of solutions and that problem finding is central in the problem-solving process.

Related Behaviors

After reviewing the problem-solving research literature, Feldhusen, Houtz, and Ringenbach (1972) concluded that 12 cognitive components or problem solving ability or behaviors related to it had been identified through the research:

1. Sensing that a problem exists
2. Asking questions about the problem
3. Noticing relevant or critical details of the problem situation
4. Defining the problem specifically
5. Guessing or speculating about causes
6. Clarifying solution goals
7. Judging whether sufficient information is available to solve the problem or whether more information is needed
8. Redefining common objects to serve as solution elements
9. Foreseeing consequences or implications of alternative courses of action
10. Seeing a way to test or verify a possible solution
11. Selecting a correct solution when only one solution is possible
12. Selecting the best or most creative solution when several are possible

Feldhusen et al. (1972) also developed a comprehensive measure of problem-solving ability in children and found their measure to be positively correlated with other tests of logical thinking, concept formation ability, language skills, perceptual acuity, reading ability, intelligence, and general school achievement. Thus, problem solving possibly involves a complex set of cognitive operations that are basic components of several types of thinking skills. In a review of the research literature on gifted or superior problem solvers, Hoover (1988) concluded that the following were components or characteristics of their problem-solving ability:

1. Able to reason at an abstract conceptual level
2. Able to identify the specific problem to be solved
3. Effective in monitoring their own problem-solving behavior and in verifying solutions
4. Have a number of effective strategies to use in problem solving
5. Spend more time on initial planning
6. Can synthesize information in solving a problem

Creative Problem Solving Model

A number of researchers have attempted to develop training sequences to assist students in the development of problem-solving ability. The most widely used model in the United States is the creative problem solving (CPS) model pioneered by Osborn (1963), Parnes (1981), Torrance and Myers (1970), Treffinger and Huber (1975), and Isaksen, Dorval, and Treffinger (1991). Feldhusen and Treffinger (1985) summarized the creative problem solving model as follows:

Mess-Finding involves considering your goals and concerns and your own personal orientation or "style" of dealing with problems in order to determine the most important or immediate starting point for your problem solving efforts. In Mess-Finding, your major concern is to determine a broad goal or area of concern towards which your CPS efforts will be directed.

Data-Finding involves examining all of the information and impressions available about the "Mess." In this stage, you will be "sifting through" all of the data surrounding your Mess—the facts, the feelings, the questions, and the hunches and concerns that you feel—to help you understand the "Mess" better. In Data-Finding, you are attempting to clarify the most important directions you should follow during the subsequent CPS steps.

Problem-Finding. In this stage, your major task is to take the most important information that you located in the previous stage, and begin to formulate specific problem statements; you are defining the problem. In any Mess on which you're working, there may be many different problems that might be solved; in Problem-Finding, we are trying to state as many different problems or sub-problems as possible, so we can better select an appropriate problem on which to work.

Idea-Finding. Once you have formulated an appropriate and workable problem statement, the next step is to generate as many ideas as possible. You are trying to generate or produce as many possible solutions as you can for the problem. During this stage, you may use many different techniques or strategies for producing new and unusual ideas. The principle of deferred judgment (Osborn, 1963) is very important to remember. Since you are attempting to find as many solution ideas as possible, evaluating too soon or too much may inhibit your thinking and cause you to overlook very unusual or promising ideas. It is much easier to go back later and evaluate your ideas than it is to try to retrieve one really imaginative idea that was lost or held back by evaluation.

Solution-Finding. After a list of ideas has been developed, you will want to determine which ones are the most promising solutions for the problem. Solution-Finding helps you to do this. In this stage, you will first generate possible criteria to use in evaluating the ideas on your list; then you will use those criteria to conduct a detailed and systematic evaluation of the ideas. You are not simply trying to select one idea and eliminate all the rest, nor are you looking only for "perfect" ideas. You are attempting to locate, from among all the ideas you have generated, the ones that you believe have the greatest potential for solving the problem.

Acceptance-Finding. A good idea is not worth much unless it is put to use. In Acceptance-Finding, you will take the promising ideas that you identified in Solution-Finding, and decide how they can best be implemented. What help will you need? What obstacles might need to be overcome? What specific steps will need to occur? Acceptance-Finding is primarily concerned with helping good ideas become useful ideas. (pp. 66–68)

Treffinger and Huber (1975) suggested the following seven objectives for creative problem solving:

1. Be sensitive to problems.
   Given a "mess," the student should be able to:
   • describe many specific problems that could be appropriately attacked
   • describe many elements of a situation
   • employ a checklist to extend analysis of possible problems

2. Be able to define problems.
   Given a perplexing situation, the student should be able to:
   • recognize the "hidden" or "real" problem that may underlie the stated question
   • broaden the problem, or redefine it by asking "why"

    • redefine or clarify the problem by changing verbs
    • identify several possible subproblems

3. Be able to break away from habit-bound thinking.
   Given a description of a common situation, the student should be able to:
   • describe habitual ways of responding
   • evaluate the effectiveness of those responses
   • select promising alternatives
   • develop and implement a plan for using new responses

4. Be able to defer judgment.
   In viewing a perplexing situation, the student should be able to:
   • produce many responses
   • give responses without imposing evaluations
   • refrain from evaluating others' responses

5. Be able to see new relationships.
   Given perplexing situations or stimuli, the student should be able to:
   • identify similarities among objects or experiences
   • identify differences among objects or experiences
   • list ideas for relating or comparing objects/experiences

6. Be able to evaluate the consequences of one's actions.
   Given a situation calling for decisions, the student should be able to:
   • identify a variety of criteria for evaluation
   • develop many possible criteria for a problem
   • demonstrate deferred judgment with respect to criteria

7. Be able to plan for the implementation of ideas. Given a problem and a proposed solution, the student should be able to:
   • identify specific difficulties in implementation
   • demonstrate the use of implementation checklists
   • specify a plan for facilitating implementation and acceptance

Excellent guidelines for training in creative problem solving are presented in *The Creative Problem Solver's Guidebook* (Treffinger, 1995) and in *Practice Problems for Creative Problem Solving* (Treffinger, 1994). Teachers at all grade levels, K–12, can incorporate creative problem solving activities in all school subjects to help students become more effective problem solvers.

Psychological Processes

Feldhusen (in Feldhusen & Treffinger, 1985) presented a model of the problem-solving process. This model attempts to show the underlying psychological processes at each stage of problem solving. It stresses a strong role for problem generation by the problem solver and a strong role for creative syntheses of ideas generated in an idea-finding stage. The model is presented in Table 22.1.

Problem solving consists of a complex set of skills that probably are carried out in varying sequences according to the styles and habits of the individual problem

Table 22.1 ～
Model of Problem-Solving Process

Process	Problem-Solving Stages
	I. Problem Generation
Fluency	A. What are some problems our country faces as a result of the
Flexibility	energy crisis? Brainstorm problem identification.
Originality	
Deferred judgment	
Evaluation	B. What are the most critical and general problems?
	II. Problem Clarification
Analysis	A. What are illustrations of the problem?
Evaluation	B. What are things that cause the problem?
	C. What are further problems caused by the problem?
	D. What are attributes, characteristics, or dimensions of the problem?
	III. Problem Identification
Synthesis	State the problem, in light of stage II discussion, as precisely as possible.
	IV. Idea Finding
Fluency	Brainstorm for solutions.
Flexibility	A. What could we do?
Analysis	B. What could be changed?
Originality	
Deferred judgment	
	V. Synthesis of a Solution
Synthesis	A. Pick out the best elements from stage IV.
Elaboration	B. Develop an integrated solution.
Evaluation	C. Does it fit the problem statement?
	VI. Implementation
Synthesis	A. Who will do what?
Evaluation	B. How will it be done?
Originality	C. What temporal sequence will be followed?
Flexibility	D. What precautions and obstacles must be watched for?
	E. How can we overcome obstacles?

solver or the group of solvers (Hoover & Feldhusen, 1990). Grouping gifted children into clusters of four to seven for problem-solving instruction is now quite common (H. Feldhusen, 1993), as in the quality circle mode of problem solving (Harshman, 1982). The component skills of problem solving probably can be taught by first sensitizing students to the components and helping them to gain control of each component. Initial training can be in relatively abstract conditions with artificial problems or puzzles, but training should move toward application of the component skills and automatic use of a sequence of skills with applied problems in practical situations or in the disciplines. As noted earlier, students will show some unique problem-solving talents within particular disciplines, and these can be discovered and developed only through the acquisition of knowledge and experience in these disciplines.

Problem solving is a "generative" experience (Brooks & Brooks, 1993; Wittrock, 1977) through which gifted students can develop their own understandings of phenomena in disciplines or in real-world settings. Students can become more effective problem solvers through awareness and mastery of the cognitive components of problem solving.

Metacognitive Skills ～

Metacognition is a process of becoming aware of one's own thinking processes and gaining control over or skill in using orienting processes to think more effectively. Metacognition means cognitive awareness of one's own cognition or knowledge of one's own knowledge production processes. According to Flavell (1985), metacognition is "any knowledge or cognitive activity that takes as its object, or regulates, any aspect of any cognitive enterprise. It is called *meta*cognition because its core meaning is cognition about cognition" (p. 104). Flavell went on to suggest that metacognitive knowledge is knowledge about persons, tasks, and strategies. The person category refers to *beliefs* about humans as cognitive processors. The task category has to do with beliefs about the nature of the content, material, or discipline with which one must deal cognitively. Strategies are beliefs or skills one has learned in achieving cognitive goals.

There is a set of skills or cognitive orienting functions that can be brought under one's control or that can be taught. Shore and Kanevsky (1993), from a review of the research on metacognition, concluded that students who acquire metacognitive skills can do a better job of controlling their thinking, problem solving, conceptualizing, reasoning, remembering, synthesizing, and analyzing and show gains in both creative and critical thinking. Teachers have long been aware that children who know the Bloom taxonomy well, who know the processes of creative thinking, and who are aware of the elements of critical thinking can do a much better job of thinking or reasoning within cognitive frameworks.

Sternberg (1981) proposed six higher order cognitive control or orienting processes:

1. Decision as to just what the problems are that have to be solved

2. Selection of lower order components of problem solving
3. Selection of strategies for solving problems
4. Selection of representations for information
5. Decisions regarding allocation of componential resources in problem solving
6. Solution monitoring in problem solving

The use of these processes is illustrated in the following example: The students in an American history course are trying to specify the problems faced by the South prior to the Civil War (process 1). They decide to focus on lower order problems faced by some southern states (process 2). They move on to select some strategies for solving the problems that southerners might have used (process 3). They decide to represent the problems with charts (process 4). They divide up into groups to work on solutions to different subproblems (process 5). Then they appoint a committee to evaluate emerging solutions (process 6). Gifted individuals are likely to excel in becoming aware of, mastering, and controlling these processes of thinking or cognition.

Sternberg (1981) also described six metacognitive performance components:

1. *Inference* is detecting relations between objects.
2. *Mapping* is relating aspects of one area of study to another.
3. *Application* is making predictions on the basis of perceived patterns or maps.
4. *Comparison* involves the examination of a prediction in relation to alternative predictions.
5. *Justification* is a process of verifying options.
6. *Response* is communicating a solution.

The following example illustrates these six metacognitive components: Sixth graders may examine the relationship between atoms and molecules (1); search for relationships between the world of atoms, molecules, and the solar system (2); predict the response when two chemicals are combined (3); compare the prediction to alternative hypotheses or predictions that could be formulated (4); argue or justify the case for the alternative (5); and communicate the resulting chemical reaction to an audience of peers (6).

Sternberg (1986a) asserted that gifted students can develop these metacognitive skills to high levels of cognitive efficiency. All are skills that can be learned, and all are skills that can be exercised more effectively when students are aware of their efficacy and have gained control over their operations.

Feuerstein and Jensen (1980) developed a training method called instrumental conditioning that was designed to help students develop a set of metacognitive skills. The framework of those skills is presented in Table 22.2. A review of the research on Feuerstein's instrumental enrichment cognitive training programs by Savell et al. (1986) indicated that the program is teachable and that students make substantial gains in the cognitive operations after exposure to the training program. Metacognitive skills play important roles in all areas of human learning. Gifted chil-

Table 22.2 ～
Instrumental Conditioning Framework

I. Gathering all the information we need (input)

1. Using our senses (listening, seeing, smelling, tasting, touching, feeling) to gather clear and complete information (clear perception)
2. Using a system or plan so that we do not skip or miss something important or repeat ourselves (systematic exploration)
3. Giving the thing we gather through our senses and our experience a name so that we can remember it more clearly and talk about it (labeling)
4. Describing things and events in terms of where and when they occur (temporal and spatial referents)
5. Deciding which characteristics of a thing or event that always stay the same, even when changes take place (conservation, constancy, and object permanence)
6. Organizing the information we gather by considering more than one thing at a time (using two sources of information)
7. Being precise and accurate when it matters (need for precision)

II. Using the information we have gathered (elaboration)

1. Defining what the problem is, what we are being asked to do, and what we must figure out (analyzing disequilibrium)
2. Using only the part of the information we have gathered that applies to the prolem and ignoring the rest (relevance)
3. Having a good picture in our mind of what we are looking for or what we must do (interiorization)
4. Making a plan that will include the steps we need to take to reach our goal (planing behavior)
5. Remembering and keeping in mind the various pieces of information we need (broadening our mental field)
6. Looking for the relationship by which separate objects, events, and experiences can be tied together (projecting relationships)
7. Comparing objects and experiences to others to see what is similar and what is different (comparative behavior)
8. Finding the class or set to which the new object or experience belongs (categorization)
9. Thinking about different possibilities and figuring out what would happen if we were to choose one or another (hypothetical thinking)
10. Using logic to prove things and to defend our opinion (logical evidence)

(continued)

Table 22.2 continued

III. Expressing the solution to a problem (output)

1. Being clear and precise in our language to be sure that there is no question as to what the answer is; putting ourselves into the "shoes" of the listener to be sure that our answers will be understood (overcoming egocentric communication)
2. Thinking things through before we answer instead of immediately trying to answer and making a mistake, and then trying again (overcoming trial and error)
3. Counting to 10 (at least) so that we do not say or do something we will be sorry for later (restraining impulsive behavior)
4. Not fretting or panicking if for some reason we cannot answer a question even though we "know" the answer; leaving the question for a little while and then, when we return to it, using a strategy to help us find the answer (overcoming blocking)

dren can learn complex metacognitive processing skills that can be used in all areas of thinking or cognitive functioning.

From a review of the literature on metacognition, Ormrod (1995) concluded that there are six fundamental skills that can be learned to enhance metacognitive activity:

1. Being aware of one's own learning and memory capabilities and of what learning tasks can be accomplished
2. Knowing which learning strategies are effective and which are not
3. Planning an approach to a learning task that is likely to be effective
4. Using effective learning strategies
5. Monitoring one's present knowledge state
6. Knowing effective strategies for retrieval of previously stored information

These are all self-regulating behaviors. Schunk and Zimmerman (1994) presented clear evidence that such skills are teachable and that they lead to higher levels of students' sense of self-efficacy. Teachers can help children increase both their motivation and their achievements in school through the development of metacognitive learning skills.

Summary ∼

Through teaching the cognitive processes of creative thinking, critical thinking, the Bloom taxonomy, problem solving, and metacognition, the thinking skills of gifted students can be developed to help them become highly effective information processors. These thinking skills can best be developed when gifted children know or understand the thinking processes they are using, when they are guided by teachers who are themselves effective and knowledgeable thinkers, and when they are given ample time to practice the skills and receive feedback in artificial, realistic, and discipline-based contexts. Gifted children can learn the subject matter of all the disciplines most effectively through dynamic, generative, cognitive interaction with subject matter or content.

References ~

Amabile, T. M. (1990). Within you, without you: The social psychology of creativity and beyond. In M. A. Runco & R. S. Albert (Eds.), *Theories of creativity* (pp. 61–91). Newbury Park, CA: Sage.

Anderson, M. A. (1986). Protocol analysis: A methodology for exploring the information processing of gifted students. *Gifted Child Quarterly, 30*(1), 28–32.

Armstrong, T. (1994). *Multiple intelligences in the classroom.* Alexandria, VA: Association for Supervision and Curriculum Development.

Beyer, B. K. (1991). *Teaching thinking skills: A handbook for secondary teachers.* Boston: Allyn & Bacon.

Bloom, B. S. (1956). *Taxonomy of educational objectives: Cognitive domain* (Handbook 1). New York: David McKay.

Brooks, J. G., & Brooks, M. G. (1993). *In search of understanding: The case for constructivist classrooms.* Alexandria, VA: Association for Supervision and Curriculum Development.

Bruer, J. T. (1993). *Schools for thought.* Cambridge, MA: MIT Press.

Bruner, J. S. (1960). *The process of education.* Cambridge, MA: Harvard University Press.

Bruning, R. H., Schraw, G. J., & Ronning, R. R. (1995). *Cognitive psychology and instruction.* Englewood Cliffs, NJ: Prentice-Hall.

Davis, G. A. (1991). Teaching creative thinking. In N. Colangelo & G. A. Davis (Eds.), *Handbook of gifted education* (pp. 236–244). Boston: Allyn & Bacon.

deBono, E. (1984). Critical thinking is not enough. *Educational Leadership, 42*(1), 16–17.

Devall, Y. L. (1982). Some cognitive and creative characteristics and their relationships to reading comprehension in gifted and non-gifted fifth graders. *Journal for the Education of the Gifted, 5*(4), 259–273.

Dunn, R., Dunn, K., & Treffinger, D. J. (1992). *Bringing out the giftedness in your child.* New York: Wiley.

Dunn, R., & Price, G. E. (1980). The learning style characteristics of gifted students. *Gifted Child Quarterly, 24*(1), 33–36.

Ennis, R. H. (1962). A concept of critical thinking. *Harvard Educational Review, 32*(1), 81–111.

Ennis, R. H. (1985). Logical thinking. *Educational Leadership, 43*(2), 44–48.

Ennis, R. H. (1989). Critical thinking and subject specificity: Clarification and needed research. *Educational Researcher, 19,* 4–10.

Feldhusen, H. J. (1993). Individualized teaching of the gifted in regular classrooms. In C. J. Maker (Ed.), *Critical issues in gifted education* (Vol. 3, pp. 263-273). Austin, TX: Pro-Ed.

Feldhusen, J. F. (1983). The Purdue creative thinking program. In I. S. Sato (Ed.), *Creativity research and educational planning* (pp. 41–46). Los Angeles: Leadership Training Institute for the Gifted and Talented.

Feldhusen, J. F. (1993). A conception of creative thinking and creativity training. In S. G. Isaksen, M. C. Murdock, R. L. Firestein, & D. J. Treffinger (Eds.), *Nurturing and developing creativity: The emergence of a discipline* (pp. 31–50). Norwood, NJ: Ablex.

Feldhusen, J. F. (1994). Creativity, teaching and testing for. In *International Encyclopedia of Education* (T. Husen and T. Neville, Eds.). (pp. 1178-1183). New York: Pergamon.

Feldhusen, J. F., & Clinkenbeard, P. M. (1986). Creativity instructional material: A review of research. *Journal of Creative Behavior, 20*(3), 153–182.

Feldhusen, J. F., & Goh, B. E. (1995). Assessing and accessing creativity: An integrative review of theory, research, and development. *Creativity Research Journal, 8*(3), 231–247.

Feldhusen, J. F., Houtz, J. C., & Ringenbach, S. (1972). The Purdue elementary problem solving inventory. *Psychological Reports, 31,* 891–901.

Thinking Skills for the Gifted *417*

Feldhusen, J. F., & Treffinger, D. J. (1985). *Creative thinking and problem solving in gifted education.* Dubuque, IA: Kendall/Hunt.

Feuerstein, R., & Jensen, M. R. (1980). Instrumental enrichment: Theoretical basis, goals, and instruments. *Educational Forum, 44,* 401–423.

Feuerstein, R., Miller, R., Hoffman, M. B., Mintzker, Y., & Jensen, M. R. (1981). Cognitive modifiability in adolescence: Cognitive structure and the effects of intervention. *Journal of Special Education, 15,* 269–287.

Flavell, J. H. (1985). *Cognitive development.* Englewood Cliffs, NJ: Prentice-Hall.

Gardner, H. (1985). *The mind's new science: A history of the cognitive revolution.* New York: Basic Books.

Getzels, S. W., & Csikszentmihalyi, M. (1975). From problem solving to problem finding. In I. A. Taylor & J. W. Getzels (Eds.), *Perspectives in creativity* (pp. 90–116). Chicago: Aldine.

Glaser, R. (1984). Education and thinking: The role of knowledge. *American Psychologist, 29*(2), 93–104.

Gordon, W. J. J. (1961). *Synectics.* New York: Harper & Row.

Gordon, W. J. J., & Poze, T. (1980). SES: Synectics and gifted education today. *Gifted Child Quarterly, 24*(4), 147–151.

Guilford, J. P. (1959). Three faces of intellect. *American Psychologist, 14*(8), 469–479.

Harnadek, A. (1980). *Critical thinking.* Pacific Grove, CA: Midwest.

Harshman, C. L. (1982). *Quality circles: Implications for training.* Columbus, OH: Clearinghouse on Adult, Career, and Vocational Education.

Hoover, S. M. (1988). *An exploratory study of high ability students' problem solving ability.* Unpublished doctoral dissertation, Purdue University, West Lafayette, IN.

Hoover, S. M., & Feldhusen, J. F. (1990). The scientific hypothesis formulation ability of gifted ninth-grade students. *Journal of Educational Psychology, 82*(4), 838–848.

Isaksen, S. G., Dorval, K. B., & Treffinger, D. J. (1991). *Creative approaches to problem solving.* Dubuque, IA: Kendall/Hunt.

Maker, C. J. (1982). *Teaching models in education of the gifted.* Rockville, MD: Aspen Publications.

Maker, C. J., & Nielson, A. B. (1995). *Teaching models in education of the gifted.* Austin, TX: Pro-Ed.

Nickerson, R. S., Perkins, D. N., & Smith, E. E. (1985). *The teaching of thinking.* Hillsdale, NJ: Erlbaum.

Norris, S. P., & Ennis, R. H. (1989). *Evaluating critical thinking.* Pacific Grove, CA: Midwest.

Ormrod, J. E. (1995). *Human learning.* Columbus, OH: Charles E. Merrill.

Osborn, A. (1963). *Applied imagination.* New York: Scribner's.

Parnes, S. (1977). Guiding creative action. *Gifted Child Quarterly, 21,* 460–476.

Parnes, S. (1981). *The magic of your mind.* Buffalo, NY: Bearly.

Paul, R. (1990). *Critical thinking.* Rohnert Park, CA: Center for Critical Thinking.

Paul, R., Binker, A. J. A., Martin, D., & Adamson, K. (1989). *Critical thinking handbooks.* Rohnert Park, CA: Center for Critical Thinking.

Phenix, P. H. (1964). *Realms of meaning.* New York: McGraw-Hill.

Raths, L. E., Wasserman, S., Jonas, A., & Rothstein, A. (1986). *Teaching for thinking.* New York: Teachers College Press.

Savell, J. M., Twohig, P. T., & Rachford, D. L. (1986). Empirical status of Feuerstein's "instrumental enrichment" (FIE) as a method of teaching thinking skills. *Review of Educational Research, 56*(4), 381–410.

Schunk, D. H., & Zimmerman, B. J. (1994). *Self regulation of learning and performance.* Hillsdale, NJ: Erlbaum.

Shore, B. M., Cornell, D. G., Robinson, A., & Ward, V. S. (1991). *Recommended practices in gifted education.* New York: Teachers College Press.

Shore, B. M., & Kanevsky, L. S. (1993). Thinking processes: Being and becoming gifted. In K. A. Heller, F. J. Monks, & A. H. Passow (Eds.), *International handbook of research and development of giftedness and talent* (pp. 133–147). New York: Pergamon.

Sizer, T. R. (1985). *Horace's compromise: The dilemma of the American high school.* Boston: Houghton Mifflin.

Spitz, H. H. (1982). Intellectual extremes, mental age and the nature of human intelligence. *Merrill-Palmer Quarterly, 28,* 167–192.

Sternberg, R. J. (1981). A componential theory of intellectual giftedness. *Gifted Child Quarterly, 25*(2), 86–93.

Sternberg, R. J. (1985a). *Beyond IQ: A triarchic theory of human intelligence*. New York: Cambridge University Press.

Sternberg, R. J. (1985b). *Intelligence applied*. New York: Harcourt Brace Jovanovich.

Sternberg, R. J. (1986). A triarchic theory of intellectual giftedness. In R. J. Sternberg & J. E. Davidson (Eds.), *Conceptions of giftedness* (pp. 223–243). New York: Cambridge University Press.

Taylor, C. W. (Ed.). (1964). *Creativity: Progress and potential*. New York: McGraw-Hill.

Torrance, E. P. (1987). Teaching for creativity. In S. G. Isaksen (Ed.), *Frontiers of creativity research: Beyond the basics* (pp. 189–215). Buffalo, NY: Bearly.

Torrance, E. P., & Myers, R. E. (1970). *Creative learning and teaching*. New York: Dodd, Mead.

Treffinger, D. J. (1982). *Encouraging creative learning for the gifted and talented*. Ventura, CA: Office of the County Superintendent of Schools/LTI Publications.

Treffinger, D. J. (1993). Stimulating creativity: Issues and future directions. In S. G. Isaksen, M. C. Murdock, R. L. Firestein, & D. J. Treffinger (Eds.), *Nurturing and developing creativity: The emergence of a discipline* (pp. 8–27). Norwood, NJ: Ablex.

Treffinger, D. J. (1994). *Practice problems for creative problem solving* (3rd ed.). Sarasota, FL: Center for Creative Learning.

Treffinger, D. J. (1995). *The creative problem solver's guidebook* (2nd ed.). Sarasota, FL: Center for Creative Learning.

Treffinger, D. J., Callahan, C. M., & Vaughn, V. L. (1991). Research on enrichment efforts in gifted education. In M. C. Wang, M. C. Reynolds, & H. J. Walberg (Eds.), *Handbook of special education, research and practice: Vol. 4. Emerging programs* (pp. 37-55). New York: Pergamon .

Treffinger, D. J., Cross, J. A., Jr., Feldhusen, J. F., Isaksen, S. G., Remle, R. C., & Sortore, M. R. (1993). *Productive thinking handbook: Vol. 1. Rationale criteria and reviews*. Sarasota, FL: Center for Creative Learning.

Treffinger, D. J., & Huber, J. R. (1975). Designing instruction in creative problem solving. *Journal of Creative Behavior, 9*, 260–266.

VanTassel-Baska, J. (1994). Development and assessment of integrated curriculum: A worthy challenge. *Quest, 5*(2), 1–6.

Ward, M. G. (1979). Differences in the ability levels and growth gains in three higher cognitive processes among gifted and non-gifted students. *Dissertation Abstracts International, 39*, 3960A.

Ward, V. (1961). *Educating the gifted: An axiomatic approach*. Columbus, OH: Charles E. Merrill.

Witkins, H. A. (1976). Cognitive style in academic performance and in teacher-student relations. In S. Messick (Ed.), *Individuality in learning*. San Francisco: Jossey-Bass.

Wittrock, M. C. (1977). Learning as a generative process (p. 661). In. M. C. Wittrock (Ed.), *Learning and instruction* (pp. 621–631). Berkeley, CA: McCutchan.

Study Questions ~

1. Why is it important for children to learn how to think?
2. What special needs do gifted students have in learning to think?
3. What is creative thinking?
4. What is critical thinking? In what subjects is it best taught?
5. At what levels of the Bloom taxonomy should we concentrate instruction for the gifted?
6. Can problem solving be taught in all subjects? Explain.
7. What is metacognition? How can we teach it?
8. What are impediments to teaching thinking skills, and how can we overcome them?

23

Mathematics and Science for Talented Learners

Joyce VanTassel-Baska

The general concerns about mathematics and science curriculum in our schools are felt even more deeply by educators of the gifted. Since the barrage of national reports on education in the 1980s and 1990s, deficiencies in these content areas have been widely recognized, reported, and discussed. Problems center on three key areas:

1. A teaching force unable to provide appropriate-level content in math and science areas
2. Use of textbooks that are not up to date in respect to new technological and scientific discoveries; in mathematics, for example, textbooks that primarily stress computation at the elementary level
3. Little science education at the lower elementary levels; mathematics work at these levels focused on drill and practice and dominated by worksheets

Consequently, one of the first issues we must address in mathematics and science curriculum for the gifted is how to combat these generic problems and infuse the curriculum with appropriate content and methodology. Three strategies are crucial in this regard: first, identifying teachers, particularly at the elementary level, who can teach math and science to the gifted; second, developing a differentiated staffing model that will allow the teachers to work with the gifted in these areas; and third, adapting existing materials and developing others that are appropriate for these learners.

The idea of linking the mathematics and science curriculum for the gifted may be appropriate from several vantage points. First, students who are gifted in one of these areas tend to be very able in the other and have strong interests in both areas. Second, gifted students tend to enjoy mathematics and science classes more than other subject areas, especially by the time they reach junior high school, where they overwhelmingly select such courses as top choices. Third, the nature of mathematics as an applied area allows for much natural interdisciplinary overlap: Most science study requires a fundamental knowledge of mathematical topics; furthermore, scientific research is aided considerably by student understanding of probability and statistics—which are important mathematical topics for the gifted. Thus, the discussion of mathematics and science curriculum for the gifted that follows interweaves these two critical areas of intervention for gifted learners.

Ideas for integrating math and science programs for the gifted abound. The following list is meant to be suggestive of successful approaches to such a merger:

1. Team teaching among math and science teachers
2. Organization of curriculum according to themes or issues to accommodate both curriculum areas (e.g., conservation, ecology, space travel)
3. Block scheduling of math and science options for the gifted
4. Use of special projects that have a math and a science component
5. Organization of seminars on careers in math and science using biographies of eminent scientists and mathematicians as the basis for the curriculum study
6. Development of units of study on the philosophy and history of mathematics and science for the purpose of analyzing relationships between the two areas
7. Teaching of the "doing" of science and math as art forms to enhance students' appreciation of these areas

Even when mathematics and science are addressed as separate domains of inquiry, the natural ties between the two are still obvious. Educators of the gifted may wish to find ways to offer appropriate curriculum in each area to gifted learners as well as to accommodate a more integrated learning context that blurs some of the distinctions between the two domains.

Mathematics for the Gifted ⌒

Given the state of mathematics education in the United States, it is essential that special provisions be made for gifted students. Their needs cannot be met within the scope of the general mathematics curriculum. During the 1980s, we were bombarded by national reports decrying the level of mathematical competency in U.S. schools, especially when compared to other countries (Wirsup, 1986), and in the 1990s test scores in mathematics still indicate that only 6% of high-school graduating seniors are able to solve multistep problems and understand algebraic concepts (Darling-Hammond, 1990).

A mathematics curriculum for gifted students should be fast-paced, emphasize concepts rather than procedures, encourage individuals to construct ideas for themselves, and make full use of technology. Five broad goals of school mathematics identified by the National Council of Teachers of Mathematics (1989) are:

1. Becoming a mathematical problem solver
2. Learning to communicate mathematically
3. Learning to reason mathematically
4. Learning to value mathematics
5. Becoming confident in one's own ability

Clearly these goals are important for the gifted learner.

Views of teaching and learning mathematics encapsulated in the National Council of Teachers of Mathematics (NCTM) content standards (1989) also stressed the importance of early and sustained exposure to key elements, or strands, in a mathematics curriculum. These include the following:

1. Counting, calculation, and approximation
2. Likelihood and chance (probability theory)
3. Algebraic manipulation techniques
4. Spatial awareness and geometric considerations
5. Logic, reasoning, and inferential systems (statistics)
6. Algebraic structures and analysis
7. Modeling and problem solving

Special emphasis for the gifted within these strands should be on early access, in-depth opportunities for real-world applications, and the use of mathematical concepts in other domains of inquiry and as a tool in conducting research. Some specific approaches for modifying the NCTM content standards for the gifted include the following (VanTassel-Baska & Johnson, 1994):

1. Conduct a careful diagnosis of the instructional level of students in each mathematics strand
2. Select resources in each strand that allow students to move to the next level at a self-paced rate
3. Ensure that problem sets are challenging
4. Cluster gifted students together for math instruction
5. Assess students at frequent intervals for mastery of key standards within and across strands.

Sheffield (1994) analyzed appropriate interventions for the gifted based on the NCTM content standards, the professional standards for teachers, and assessment standards. Much of the intervention emphasis suggested by these standards is on project enrichment approaches already advocated for the gifted by the NCTM.

Early Access Issues

The Study of Mathematically Precocious Youth (SMPY), developed by Stanley, Keating, and Fox (1974) and implemented at multiple sites over the past 20 years (Stanley, 1997), embodies the important aspects of allowing the gifted learner early access to significant mathematics topics. This model has the following characteristics:

1. Identifying gifted students with an off-grade-level, high-powered mathematical aptitude test (the Scholastic Aptitude Test)
2. Using a diagnostic-prescriptive approach to mathematics instruction that allows students to move at a fast pace (e.g., completion of 2 years of high-school mathematics in 6 weeks) and not be subject to instruction in skills already learned
3. Utilization of existing precalculus curriculum and text materials to move students through the school-accepted scope and sequence in mathematics
4. Employing teachers who are adept at setting appropriately high learning expectations and then allowing students to meet those expectations in an individualized manner

Such an approach, which has been used extensively in Talent Search programs around the country (Mills, Ablard, & Gustin, 1994; Sawyer, 1985; Stanley, 1981; VanTassel-Baska, 1985), uses the learner's readiness for advanced mathematics as the turnkey variable for determining the level of the intervention. This method has been very successful with highly precocious youth. It also puts a premium on the completion of Advanced Placement calculus, often before the senior year of high school, and on college entrance with advanced standing. This method implies that gifted students should study a concept-rich elementary school mathematics curriculum and begin college preparatory courses as early as possible. Such radical acceleration offers the gifted student the possibility of making significant contributions in the field at an early age, typically while the individual is still in his or her 20s.

More recent research has found that much younger students than seventh graders can advance in mathematics at very rapid rates when learning prealgebra topics. In 1 year, students from grades 3-6 enrolled in a flexibly paced mathematics program gained as much as 46 percentile points from pre- to posttesting and were found to have possessed a wide range of mathematical knowledge before they began the program (Mills et al., 1994). Obviously, restricting such learners to age-grade instruction in mathematics is inappropriate, and it can even do damage in respect to motivation and future achievement. Moreover, this study and others point out the importance of identifying students for instructional advancement based on domain-specific achievement and aptitude tests rather than general ability measures and grouping them for advanced math instruction rather than for general purposes. Such identification, instruction, and grouping practices have been well supported in the literature (Kulik & Kulik, 1992; Mathews & Keating, 1995).

In a 2-year longitudinal study on the development of abilities in young math-talented children, Robinson, Abbott, Berninger, and Busse (1996) found the following:

1. That parents are good identifiers of math-precocious children in preschool and kindergarten
2. That gender differences were apparent early in quantification tasks although not in verbal or visual-spatial tasks
3. That math-precocious young children were also advanced in verbal and visual spatial reasoning, although not to the same degree

4. That math precocity remains stable or increases over time
5. That gender differences remain and increase in some ways over time

Studies such as these continue to build the evidential case for early identification and intervention for precocious children, especially in the key areas of learning where schools can deliver appropriate instruction.

Studies of early math accelerates (Kolitch & Brody, 1992) have shown positive achievement and interest effects over time, even over a period of 20 years. Moreover, they have pointed out that the problem in acceleration lies not with the learner but with the system that limits the opportunity for students to take postcalculus classes while still in high school. They have also stressed the necessity of making available outside math-related activities to sustain interest in math. In a 10-year longitudinal study of students exposed to fast-paced math acceleration, participants outperformed controls in their overall undergraduate record of accomplishment (Swiatek & Benbow, 1991).

The early access opportunity is an important modification for gifted learners from kindergarten on because many of these students have grasped mathematical concepts well before the time the concepts are usually presented in the curriculum. Studies of mathematics textbooks have revealed that more than half of such basal materials consist of review of previously taught material (Flanders, 1987). Without opportunities for fast-paced study of school mathematics, a major disservice is done to the gifted. A review of research on mathematics programs for the gifted (Sowell, 1993) found that acceleration coupled with grouping mathematically gifted learners together was the most salient aspect of effective programming.

Identification of Mathematical Precocity

Whereas the process of using the Scholastic Aptitude Test (SAT) to find math-precocious students is a highly successful strategy at middle-school levels, other assessment approaches must be employed to find such children at earlier ages. The two-step screening and identification approach has been tested with populations down to third grade, using on-grade standardized achievement tests to find students operating above 95% and then administering off-grade-level instrumentation such as the School College and Ability Test (SCAT) and the Secondary School Admissions Test (SSAT) (Lupkowski-Shoplik & Assouline, 1993; Mills, Ablard, & Stumpf, 1993). More recent research with young children has documented success in identifying math precocity through the more traditional approaches of individual intelligence and achievement tests (Robinson, 1996).

Conceptual Emphasis Linked with In-Depth Opportunities

Simply rushing gifted students through chapters in mathematics textbooks does not guarantee that they will meet all of the important goals in learning mathematics. Students should have the opportunity to construct powerful ways of thinking. Problem-centered learning using the topics recommended by the NCTM allows gifted students to conceptualize at a high level not dictated by fixed-paced courses. Conventional textbooks do not provide the integrated and relational treatment of mathematics that gifted learners need, and thus alternative sources of instructional materials must be sought. Topics not adequately addressed by current procedurally oriented texts are:

1. Problem solving
2. Estimation and mental arithmetic
3. Statistics and probability
4. Discrete mathematics
5. Mathematical structure
6. Mathematical connections
7. Use of technology

The mathematics envisioned by the NCTM is organized conceptually. For example, in algebra, although an appropriate level of skill proficiency remains a goal, the NCTM suggests a move away from a tight focus on manipulative facility to a greater emphasis on conceptual understanding, with algebra viewed more as a means of representation. Algebra should include the study of matrices and be viewed as a problem-solving tool. Similar shifts must be made in geometry, trigonometry, and calculus. Programs for gifted learners at all grade levels should include attention to the foregoing topics in a setting that challenges students to rise to the high level of thought of which they are capable.

Problem Solving

Another approach is an intensive focus on problem-solving techniques that allows the gifted to experiment freely in areas of mathematical interest and desired competence. Infusing the curriculum for the gifted with small-group or cooperative learning experiences that use a set of problem-solving strategies, such as the following, as an organizer for student work would seem most advisable:

1. Look for a pattern.
2. Make a list.
3. Guess and test.
4. Search randomly.
5. Set up an equation.
6. Work backward.

Garofalo (1993) found that gifted learners approach problems more as units of meaning and search for complexity than for easy solutions, in contrast to other learners. Thus, gifted learners need more exposure to challenging problems, relaxed grading procedures, and more time to work on such problems without penalty.

Another problem-solving approach that has gained acceptance is the mathematics competition, which provides challenging nonroutine problems. Programs such as Talent Search, Math Counts, Math-Letes, and Mathematics Olympiad are becoming increasingly popular and serve to focus attention on excellence in mathematics. Participation requires students to have a well-developed conceptual base and an excellent problem-solving ability.

Use of Technology

Computers and scientific calculators have a significant place in mathematics programs for gifted students. They facilitate problem solving by freeing students to focus on heuristics rather than on computational procedures. Technology also aids in conceptualization. Equations for conic sections, for example, can be explored and related to the geometric representation using graphic programs available on computers (and now on some inexpensive calculators). Programs such as MuMath, Maple, and Macsyma, which perform algebraic operations, solve equations, differentiate, and integrate, are changing the very face of mathematics instruction. By using technology, gifted students can build powerful mathematical schema and rise above the routine of laborious paper-and-pencil computations.

Yet research on the effectiveness of programs that use computer technology with the gifted is scanty (Sowell, 1993). One recent study (Ziegler & Terry, 1992) found that computer education was superior to creative problem solving and traditional gifted curriculum approaches for teaching problem solving to gifted students, suggesting a powerful use of computer technology in gifted education. Several promising programs, such as the following, are currently in use.

The Education Program for Gifted Youth (EPGY) at Stanford University provides computer-based accelerated instruction to gifted students in mathematics and physics, beginning with standard secondary course options and proceeding to advanced courses in college. Recent data covering 3 years of Advanced Placement courses offered through the program document low attrition and high achievement among middle- and high-school gifted students enrolled (Ravaglia, Suppes, Stillinger, & Alper, 1995).

EPGY students run the multimedia courseware at home or in school on standard IBM-compatible personal computers. This software, unlike that in traditional computer-based educational programs, is intended to stand alone, not merely to supplement a general education class. The computer presents lectures, using digitized sound and graphics, in essentially the same way that a human instructor would. These lectures are followed by on-line exercises that gauge the student's understanding as would a teacher in front of a classroom, but in greater detail. Students maintain direct telephone contact with centrally located project staff.

Many of the specialized high schools across the country offer gifted students advanced technology in many forms (Green, 1993; McBride & Lewis, 1993; Morgan, 1993). Telecommunications is widely employed by these schools to offer advanced content courses to gifted students in rural areas. New technologies, such as lasers, are available for study and limited use by students in these schools, working collaboratively with scientists in national research laboratories. Moreover, computer technology has been successfully infused into the schools' overall instructional environment.

Relationship of Mathematics to Other Fields

It is important that gifted students learn to construct relationships between mathematical topics. The 14th standard of the NCTM proposal (NCTM, 1989), called Mathematical Connections, suggests the following topics:

Relations and functions
Systems of equations and matrices
Function equations in standardized form and transformations
Complex numbers as a + bi or r(cos + sine) and ordered pairs (a,b) in the complex plane
Right-triangle ratios, trigonometric functions, and circular functions
Circular functions and series
Rectangular coordinates and polar coordinates
Explicit and parametric representations of equations
Function and its inverse, such as the logarithmic and exponential functions
Statistical procedures and their requisite probability concepts
Finite graphs and matrices
Recursive and closed-form definitions of the same sequence

By building the relationships among these topics, which are traditionally learned separately, gifted students will gain greater mathematical proficiency as well as be able to apply mathematics in other disciplines, especially physics.

Interdisciplinary skills that are essential for linking mathematical concepts to other domains include the following:

1. Graphing
2. Measurement techniques
3. Computing of descriptive statistics
4. Interpretation of graphic material
5. Pictorial displays of data
6. Preparation of written descriptions of data tables and results
7. Decisions about statistical tests and graphs, depending upon type of data
8. Use of the scientific process

These literacy skills are highly transferable to project work in other curricular areas of interest and are important interdisciplinary connectors.

Nevertheless, mathematics is a powerful field of inquiry in its own right, with linkages to other domains, primarily at the abstract level of overarching themes. VanTassel-Baska and Feldhusen (1981) used four ideas from the *Syntopicon* to organize an elementary curriculum for gifted learners. Within that curriculum, mathematics was linked to science, social studies, and language arts via the concepts of change, signs and symbols, reasoning, and problem solving. These themes had relevance both within and across each of the curricular areas cited.

More recently, Johnson and Sher (1996) developed a problem-based learning unit that links the skills of mathematics, science, and technology using the national standards as a baseline for development. This unit focuses on the problem of deer proliferation in neighborhoods.

Mathematics materials such as MEGES (formerly titled CEMREL math) and Unified Math take yet another direction in mathematics programming for the gifted. These programs, organized by mathematicians, focus on the structure of mathematics. Students are exposed to real mathematics introduced as a logical system rather than put together in the traditionally determined sequence. Such programs have worked well with gifted students but frequently have collided with the conventional ironclad precalculus sequence in schools; in such cases, the approach has usually had a short half-life.

A last area of focus for mathematics programs for the gifted has been on practical applications, on providing linkages for gifted students to the functional world of mathematics through mentorships and internships with adults who use mathematics in a significant way in their professional lives. Having an understanding of the relevance of mathematics learning in diverse career areas motivates gifted learners to take and stay with advanced coursework well into college.

Other integrative topics also appear to be important considerations in developing a powerful mathematics curriculum for the gifted. VanTassel-Baska, Olszewski, and Landau (1985) recommended the development of scope and sequence in mathematics instruction, infusing the history of mathematics, modeling, power, economy, and limits into the curriculum. In that way, gifted students might learn to appreciate mathematics as a field of study with integral ties to science, technology, and the social sciences.

Table 23.1 delineates the major advantages and disadvantages of various approaches to mathematics instruction for the gifted as they would affect school district planners. Inclusion of all these models may best address the comprehensive needs of the mathematically talented in our schools.

Science for the Gifted 〜

The science curriculum for the gifted is, in a sense, the foundation of their learning if they are to become knowledge producers rather than knowledge consumers. Fundamental internalization of scientific skills, such as observation, experimentation, and measurement, as well as adoption of an attitudinal mind-set that views the world through the lens of a scientist, provides a framework necessary for productive research in any field of inquiry. Consequently, ensuring that gifted learners have access to the following key components in a science curriculum from kindergarten through high school is essential:

1. Opportunities for laboratory experimentation and original research work
2. High-level content-based curriculum
3. Opportunities for interactions with practicing scientists
4. A strong emphasis on inquiry processes

Table 23.1 ~
A Synopsis of Advantages and Disadvantages of Implementing Key Mathematics Models for the Gifted

Acceleration of Content
Example: Study of Mathematically Precocious Youth (SMPY) (Stanley, Keating, & Fox, 1974)

Advantages	*Disadvantages*
Embodies a mastery-level learning and continual progress model	Ignores the potential in constructing a conceptually based curriculum that is richer than what exists in the schools
Uses the current school curriculum and existing textbooks	Promotes an attitude of valuing *fast* over *deep*
Employs a diagnostic/prescriptive teaching strategy	Does not allow a diversified mathematics curriculum that develops appreciation
Creates advanced learning opportunities for younger students	Can promote the "more problems" syndrome

Conceptual Organization of Mathematics Content to Promote High Level of Understanding and Appreciation
Example: The CEMREL (now termed MEGES) Program for Gifted Students in Grades 7–12

Advantages	*Disadvantages*
Developed by mathematicians who know and understand the important mathematical ideas that should be taught	Difficult to implement because of level of expertise in math required of teachers; district commitment needed to establish new framework from grades 7 to 12
Organized around a unified approach to mathematical systems rather than traditional school subjects	Does not mesh well with existing math curriculum at earlier levels
Presents a holistic program that has scope-and-sequence, materials, and training components	The whole package has to be adopted; not flexible for partial usage

Focus on Problem Solving and Heuristics
Example: Cumberland Mathematics Project (Hersberger & Wheatley, 1980; Wheatley, 1984)

Advantages	*Disadvantages*
Focuses on important process skill development within a content area	Does not value highly the intellectual content of mathematics curriculum
Allows for individual and small-group learning rate to be flexibly determined	Focuses on one learning strategy (to the exclusion of others constructing knowledge for oneself)
Represents a current trend in general mathematics teaching	Deemphasizes formal mathematics learning according to scope-and-sequence continuum
Focuses on applications of mathematics through computer and calculator activities	Creates articulation problems across all levels

(continued)

Table 23.1 continued

Integrated Perspective on Teaching Mathematics
Example: University High School Mathematics Curriculum Project University of Illinois (Davis, 1984)

Advantages	*Disadvantages*
Considers all the characteristics of mathematically able students in its design	Requires high-level teacher talent to implement effectively
Considers and incorporates new trends in mathematics teaching but does not embrace any one approach	Requires systematic access from grade 7 to grade 12 to high-level, mathematically talented students
Developed with a K–12 planning model in mind	Requires a team approach and "consistent vision" around program goals
Developed, field-tested, and researched during an 8-year period in a controlled setting	
Uses a "content expert" model for development and implementation	

5. Inclusion of science topics that focus on technological applications of science in the context of human decision making and social policy (VanTassel-Baska, Gallagher, Bailey, & Sher, 1993; VanTassel-Baska & Kulieke, 1987).

The National Science Education Standards (National Research Council, 1996) and the *Benchmarks for Science Literacy* (Project 2061, 1993) both emphasize the teaching of specific science concepts and topics, the scientific research process, and the habits of mind associated with doing science. Curriculum units that have been developed for gifted elementary students based on these standards have been found effective in enhancing the students' understanding of integrated science process skills (VanTassel-Baska, Bass, Ries, & Poland, in press).

What are some elements of exemplary science programs for the gifted that differ from a generally excellent science program for all learners? Although one might make the usual observations that such programs take students further in science and expose them to more in-depth work, it may be useful to delineate some other factors that differentiate such programs.

Science as Process

In the world of science, discoveries are made slowly and painfully (Bruner, 1983). This principle must be simulated in experiments in gifted science programs. Some of the best secondary programs in science, such as the Bronx High School of Science, Stuyvesant High School, and the Illinois Math and Science Academy, work with students to help them thoroughly understand scientific endeavor as an ongoing process whose goal is to make incremental progress in a well-defined area

(Gallagher, Barr, Barron, Marshall, & Smith, 1991). The track record of such schools in producing Westinghouse scholars is highly indicative of the attention the schools pay to the personalized aspect of learning science (Berger, 1994).

One way to exemplify the principle of science as process is to engage students in original research—an approach used in many laboratory-linked programs for the gifted. Through the preparation of research proposals as well as follow-up long-term projects, students can begin to internalize the act of doing science rather than merely simulating such activity through canned experiments. Use of a scientific paradigm such as the following may be helpful in encouraging gifted students to develop scientific investigation skills at early ages:

1. Define the problem.
2. Conduct a literature search.
3. Make hypotheses.
4. Collect data to test hypotheses.
5. Analyze data.
6. Interpret data.
7. Make conclusions.
8. Draw implications.

Through structuring activities that use such a process paradigm, gifted students may engage in and practice the process skills of a scientist: observation, experimentation, and communication.

Teachers can also enhance an understanding of scientific process by asking many open-ended questions about what students see, such as: What do you observe? How might you classify what you observe? What inferences can be made about this? These questions, and others like them, provide the chance for students to think through what they see and respond to stimuli creatively. DeVito and Krockover (1976) suggested the following way for teachers to improve their questioning techniques in science classrooms:

- Limit yourself to one question in a 15-minute period.
- Never answer your own questions.
- Eliminate "yes-or-no" response questions.
- Do not ask questions that invite aimless or guessing responses.
- Ask each child in your class at least one meaningful question a day.
- Ask narrow- and broad-response questions.
- Limit memory questions to one per hour.
- Let the students ask questions.
- Mix up your questions (thought-provoking questions, what-if questions, evaluation questions, so on).

Science as Content

Opportunities for early access to advanced science content also need to be available to gifted students. From a survey of gifted high-school students, Cross and Coleman (1992) found that the students' major complaint about general science instruction was frustration over being held back by the pace and content of the courses. In a 6-year study of middle-school-age gifted learners taking biology, chemistry, or physics in a 3-week summer program, Lynch (1992) found that these younger learners outperformed high-school students who took the courses for a full academic year. Follow-up studies documented continued success in science for these students, suggesting a need for students to start high school science level courses earlier and be able to master them in less time. Evidence also suggests that advanced study in instructionally grouped settings promotes more learning for all students (Hacker & Rowe, 1993).

Science as Collaboration

Given the nature of the knowledge explosion, probably no single person since Leibniz has been capable of correlating all content knowledge for purposes of generating new knowledge. Consequently, an important model of science for the gifted learner to understand is that of collaboration. In the world of scientific research today, real breakthroughs are made by scientific teams made up of individuals with specialized backgrounds but with a scheme for working together on current scientific problems that requires the input of combinational knowledge from several areas. Work in biochemistry provides a good example. Even the trend in awarding the prestigious Nobel Prize in the sciences has been toward a joint award to a team that has made a major contribution. Indeed, several books chronicle the importance of teams of people working arduously toward scientific discovery (Goodfield, 1981).

Ways in which collaborative work in science might be enhanced include the following approaches:

1. Structuring of small-group investigations rather than individual ones
2. Use of cooperative learning principles
3. Use of creative problem solving strategy in groups
4. Peer tutoring
5. Establishment of science mentorships
6. Organization of science centers in the classroom

Data from several summer Governor's School programs in science have demonstrated the positive impact of such programs on students' continuing with the scientific enterprise in college (Enersen, 1994). The major impacts from the experience appeared to center on the collaborative opportunities to work with talented faculty and a highly able peer group. Such reports point to a continued need to provide and structure collaborative opportunities for gifted learners.

Science as Interdisciplinary Concepts

One of the most powerful ideas that emerged out of a study by Shane (1981) of 120 scholars was that students must understand the important role of human beings in the scientific process. Leading scientists in geology, physics, chemistry, and the natural sciences who took part in the study cited the following ideas as the most powerful organizers for a science curriculum for the year 2000:

Doctrine of limits	Evolution
Interdependence	Unity of nature
Entropy-conservation	Humans as change agents
Population explosion	Unpredictability of humans
Nature of the scientific method	Plate tectonic theory

In 1990, Rutherford and Ahlgren produced the following updated list of the major scientific concepts to be studied in our schools, based on the work of the American Association for the Advancement of Science (AAAS):

- Systems
- Models
- Constancy
- Patterns of change
- Evolution
- Scale

Firmly embedded within both lists is a concern for the relationship of science and people, an important area of exploration in science programs for the gifted. The teaching of ecology, for example, as a fundamentally interactive process of humans in nature that can be viewed from the perspective of a scientist as well as the perspective of a social scientist illustrates this interdisciplinary connection.

Science as Problem Finding

Clearly, the work of Getzels and Csikszentmihalyi (1977) did much to raise our awareness of the critical role of problem finding in making original contributions in the world of art. It is also an important skill in the research paradigm of objective science. Hitting upon the right topic and asking the right questions about it are central to meaningful research. Helping gifted learners form such questions is a critical part of their science education. One way to do this is to cite a scientific event and then have students come up with a question that might begin to focus on the event. Teaching research design techniques early on also can help the gifted focus better on this specific skill. Moreover, teaching creative problem solving, especially the stage of problem generation and definition, is a useful way to get students to consider a problem more intently. For example, students might be given the following instructions: After brainstorming several ideas, choosing three, then choosing one, illustrate the problem—provide specific examples of it; elaborate on the problem—cite other problems that occur as a result; state the problem in many ways—very specifically, very generally—and develop "what-if" scenarios to describe various manifestations of it; then restate the problem as a single question. By following such techniques in a small group, students learn to discuss a problem in greater depth and rework it based on peer discussion.

Recent work in using problem-based learning in teaching science suggests the efficacy of the approach in enhancing student and teacher motivation (VanTassel-Baska et al., in press), in improving problem-finding abilities (Gallagher, Stepien, & Rosenthal, 1992), and in promoting intra- and interdisciplinary learning (Stepien, Gallagher, & Workman, 1993).

Science as Experimentation

Everyone has heard of the unusual ways in which scientists have hit upon key discoveries—by accident or while looking for something else. What has not been sufficiently explained is the nature of the great experiments that have influenced our view of the world. What were the variables under investigation, and how did scientists proceed with their ideas? Gifted learners can benefit from a close look at the history of scientific discoveries and the people who made the breakthroughs. From such study, eminent scientists and their science become real. One excellent resource for this purpose is *Great Scientific Experiments* by Rom Harre (1981). In this book, Harre treated 20 key experiments as case histories of scientists who used their creativity to understand nature. Among the experiments described are Aristotle's study of the embryology of the chick, Pasteur's preparation of artificial vaccines, and Jacob and Wollman's discoveries about genetics.

Science in Relation to Morality and Ethics

In recent decades, we have come to recognize the awesome connection between scientific discovery, technological development, and direct impact on society. Perhaps the development of the atom bomb marked the first time this connection was truly etched on our collective consciousness. Since that time, however, the connections have been repeated over and over again. Consequently, to teach science as a totally objective set of processes is to misrepresent the role of science in today's world. Gifted students need to be exposed to the social issues surrounding the scientific enterprise and to develop a philosophy of science and a code of ethics that include concerns for the moral and ethical dimensions of doing science. Thus, topics such as pollution, ecology, and conservation of natural resources deserve special attention in the context of science programs for the gifted.

Supplementary resources that use such topics as organizers are available (VanTassel-Baska, 1987). One unit uses Jean Dorst's (1970) book *Before Nature Dies* as a major reference.

> This is a comprehensive and detailed book which treats the entire earth as a single unit. Dorst explores the unforeseen ramifications of men's actions throughout nature—for example, the historical process of soil degradation, through bad agricultural practices and accelerated erosion, and the uncontrollable ravages of animals. He brilliantly illuminates the side effects of the Industrial Revolution—the progressive poisoning of the earth's seas, rivers, and atmosphere by vast quantities of industrial waste—and of the Scientific Revolution—the disruption of delicate biological balances caused by the indiscriminate use of pesticides.
>
> In many ways man's understanding of his fragile environment remains as rudimentary as that of an early nomad, and yet his technological advances have made it possible for him to have a far greater effect on his environment. He may deplore the wanton slaughter of the huge herds of buffalo of the American West in the last century, but at the same time he continues to poison the world with chemicals and industrial effluents.
>
> The preservation of wildlife is only one of the most obvious aspects of man's need to protect the world's dwindling natural resources from man's stupidity. The population explosion makes the continuation of man's present pattern of behavior suicidal. Nature

preserves and national parks are not enough. Man must develop an international poli-cy of restraint and a program of land management and environmental control. This book suggests ways in which man can learn to live in harmony with nature, before nature dies. (p. 89)

The purpose of the unit using Dorst's book is to help students gain an awareness of the problems and issues in conservation and how advances in technology have cre-ated, and continue to create, imbalances in the earth's ecosystems that permanently change them. Students also should become aware of the ways in which modem tech-nology can be used to help correct the imbalances that already have occurred. Students should understand that with the new capacity we have to change the earth, we must now assume a responsible role of stewardship over the planet's resources, before we destroy the planet's very ability to sustain us.

Science as a Set of Powerful Ideas

In his wonderful book *Search for Solutions*, Judson (1974) listed eight major ideas that he believes will influence science for the next 500 years: change, modeling, pre-diction, patterns, feedback, chance, theory, and evidence. His explication of these ideas illustrates well how they permeate present as well as past scientific and social thought. A content outline of Judson's treatment of the idea of prediction follows to illustrate the connectedness of the concept across time, culture, and area of inquiry.

    A. Ancient methods of prediction
        patterns of smoke, patterns in tortoise shells, palm reading, handwriting, tea leaves, astrology
    B. Predictions in Physics and Astronomy
        Halley's comet, eclipses, prediction of existence of the planet Neptune
    C. Predictions in Geology
        prediction of earthquakes
    D. Predictions in Medicine
        prediction of existence of blood vessels
        modern-day prediction—for example, the effect of radiation on canceous tumors, effects of drugs
    E. Predictions in Economics
        prediction of economic growth
        prediction of future supply and demand
    F. Predictions in Social Science
        prediction of achievement or adjustment

    Common concepts: measurement, theory, inference, technology

Science and Technology

Statements from the National Science Teachers Association (1985) iterated the importance of integrating science study with technology. Further, many developers of recent science materials have attempted to infuse technology into the required stu-dent text (Bank Street College Project, 1989; Biological Sciences Curriculum Study Group, 1988). These events clearly demonstrate the importance that has been attached to this linkage. Gifted students are capable of appreciating the applications of basic science to the current and proposed technology and can profit from having technological applications embedded early in their curriculum experiences in science. One resource that sets the stage for understanding the relationship of science to technology is the book and television series titled *Connections* (Burke, 1978). This opus traced tools of technology common today back to their original roots in science and illustrated well the nature of the relationship as it has evolved in different ways.

Another idea for infusing technology into a science curriculum for the gifted is through special units of study. A unit outline on space travel, presented in Table 23.2, was developed for use with gifted students of junior-high age (VanTassel-Baska, 1987).

Summary ~

Gifted learners have the capacity to do original work in science that can have a beneficial impact on society as a whole. Consequently, it is crucial for them to receive an enriched, high-powered set of learning experiences. Understanding what science is and how it works in the real world is essential to that education. Such science education, however, must be balanced with a healthy concern for the implications of scientific discovery in an ethical context.

Table 23.2 ～
Outline for Special Unit on Space Travel

I. History of Our Conception of the Cosmos
   — Ancient Greek and Babylonian perceptions
   — Stonehenge
   — Medieval astrology
   — Invention of the telescope
   — Galileo and the Copernican revolution
   — Growth of modem astronomy through bigger and better telescopes and space probes

II. The Human Dream to Fly
   — Early myths: Daedalus, Bellerophon; Skidbladnir, the magic ship of the Norse god Grey that could sail over land or sea
   — Jules Verne's visions of flying and space travel
   — Hermann Oberth's The Rocket into Interplanetary Space
   — Invention and early uses of the airplane

III. Time and Distances in Space
   — Measuring distances in space (experiment)
   — The question of destinations: Calculate how long it will take to go to the moon at presently attainable speeds. The planets? The closest star? How fast would a spaceship have to travel to reach the closest star within the lifetime of a human being?

IV. Rocketry
   — History: From Chinese rockets to Goddard and Von Braun
   — Streamlining and rocket design (experiment)
   — Powering a spaceship
   To escape Earth's gravitational pull
   In space
   The problem of fuel weight

V. The Problems of Living In Space
   — Cosmic rays, meteors
   — Temperature control (experiment: how color changes an object's ability to absorb or reflect heat)
   — Pressure in space (experiment: differences between internal and external pressure)
   — Gravity (experiment: using centrifugal force to simulate gravitational force)
   — Problems of vertigo due to weightlessness
   — Sources of food and water
   — Mental strain of spending long periods in cramped quarters

(continued)

Table 23.2 continued

VI. Unmanned Space Probes
   — Above the Earth's atmosphere
   — To the Moon
   — To Venus and Mars
   — Voyager II's close encounters with Jupiter and Saturn
   — Prospects for the future

VII. Manned Space Missions
   — Orbiting the Earth
   — Landing on the Moon
   — The space shuttle
   — Skylab
   — Future space travel

VIII. Space-Age Technology
   — Monitoring space probes from Earth
   — Controlling space probes from Earth
   — Calculating speed, direction, and power: Everything is relative
   — Back-up systems
   — Troubleshooting when things go wrong
   — Earth-bound uses for space technology

IX. Do Sentient Extraterrestrial Creatures Exist?
   — Conditions necessary for intelligent life
   — Probabilities for these conditions being met
   — Our attempts to contact and communicate with extraterrestrials

References ⌐∼

Bank Street College Project in Science and Mathematics. (1989). *The second voyage of the Mimi*. Scotts Valley, CA: Wings for Learning.

Berger, J. (1994). *The young scientists: America's future and the winning of the Westinghouse*. Reading, MA: Addison-Wesley.

Biological Sciences Curriculum Study Group. (1988). *Science for life and living: Integrating science, technology, and health*. Washington, DC: National Science Foundation.

Bruner, J. (1983). *In search of mind*. New York: Harper & Row.

Burke, J. (1978). *Connections*. Boston: Little, Brown.

Cross, T. L., & Coleman, L. J. (1992). Gifted high school students' advice to science teachers. *Gifted Child Today, 15*(5), 25–26.

Darling-Hammond, L. (1990). Achieving our goals: Superficial or structural reforms. *Phi Delta Kappan, 72*, 286–295.

Davis, R. (1984). Presentation to class at Northwestern University, Evanston, IL.

DeVito, A., & Krockover, G. (1976). *Creative sciencing*. Boston: Little, Brown.

Dorst, J. (1970). *Before natures dies*. (Trans. C. D. Sherman). Boston: Houghton Mifflin.

Enersen, D. L. (1994). Where are the scientists? Talent development in summer programs. *Journal of Secondary Gifted Education, 5*(2), 23–26.

Flanders, J. R. (1987). How much of the content in mathematics textbooks is new? *Arithmetic Teacher, 35*(1), 18–23.

Gallagher, S., Barr, D., Barron, M., Marshall, S. P., & Smith, L. (1991). A community of scholars dedicated to exploration and discovery: The Illinois Mathematics and Science Academy. *Gifted Child Today, 14*(6), 16–21.

Gallagher, S. A., Stepien, W. J., & Rosenthal, H. (1992). The effects of problem-based learning on problem solving. *Gifted Child Quarterly, 36*(4), 195–200.

Garofalo, J. (1993). Mathematical problem preferences of meaning-oriented and number-oriented problem solvers. *Journal for the Education of the Gifted, 17*(1), 26–40.

Getzels, J., & Csikszentmihalyi, M. (1977). *The creative vision.* Chicago: University of Chicago Press.

Goodfield, J. (1981). *An imagined world: A story of scientific discovery.* New York: Harper & Row.

Green, J. (1993). *A multidimensional curriculum for academically gifted students: Educating the whole person at the Indiana Academy.* Muncie, IN: Indiana Academy. (ERIC Document Reproduction Service No. ED 365 010).

Hacker, R. G., & Rowe, M. J. (1993). A study of the effects of an organization change from streamed to mixed-ability classes upon science classroom instruction. *Journal of Research in Science Teaching, 30*(3), 223–231.

Harre, R. (1981). *Great scientific experiments.* New York: Oxford University Press.

Hersberger, J., & Wheatley, G. (1980). A proposed model for the mathematics education of gifted elementary school pupils. *Gifted Child Quarterly, 24,* 37–40.

Johnson, D. T., & Sher, B. T. (1996). *Models: A study of populations.* Washington, DC: U. S. Department of Education.

Judson, H. (1974). *Search for solutions.* Bartlesville, OK: Phillips Petroleum.

Kolitch, E. R., & Brody, L. E. (1992). Mathematics acceleration of highly talented students: An evaluation. *Gifted Child Quarterly, 36*(2), 78–86.

Kulik, J. A., & Kulik, C. C. (1992). Meta-analytic findings on grouping programs. *Gifted Child Quarterly, 36*(2), 73–77.

Lupkowski-Shoplik, A. E., & Assouline, S. G. (1993). Identifying mathematically talented elementary students: Using the lower level of the SSAT. *Gifted Child Quarterly, 37*(3), 118–123.

Lynch, S. J. (1992). Fast-paced high school science for the academically talented: A six-year perspective. *Gifted Child Quarterly, 36*(3), 147–154.

Mathews, D. J., & Keating, D. P. (1995). Domain specificity and habits of mind: An investigation of patterns of high-level development. *Journal of Early Adolescence, 15,* 319–343.

McBride, R. O., & Lewis, G. (1993). Sharing the resources: Electronic outreach programs. *Journal for the Education of the Gifted, 16*(4), 372–386.

Mills, C. J., Ablard, K. E., & Gustin, W. C. (1994). Academically talented students' achievement in a flexibly paced mathematics program. *Journal for Research in Mathematics Education, 25*(5), 495–511.

Mills, C. J., Ablard, K. E., & Stumpf, H. (1993). Gender differences in academically talented young students' mathematical reasoning: Patterns across age and subskills. *Journal of Educational Psychology, 85*(2), 340–346.

Morgan, T. D. (1993). Technology: An essential tool for gifted and talented education. *Journal for the Education of the Gifted, 16*(4), 358–371.

National Council of Teachers of Mathematics. (1989). *Curriculum and evaluation standards for school mathematics.* Reston, VA: Author.

National Research Council. (1996). *National science education standards.* Washington, DC: National Academy Press.

National Science Teachers Association. (1985). *Science-technology-society: Science education for the 1980s.* Washington, DC: Author.

Project 2061, American Association for the Advancement of Science. (1993). *Benchmarks for science literacy.* New York: Oxford University Press.

Ravaglia, R., Suppes, P., Stillinger, C., & Alper, T. (1995). Computer-based mathematics and physics for gifted students. *Gifted Child Quarterly, 39*(1), 7–13.

Robinson, N. (1996, April). *Development of abilities in young, math-talented children: A two-year longitudinal study.* Paper presented at the annual meeting of the American Educational Research Association, New York City.

Robinson, N. M., Abbott, R. D., Berninger, V. W., & Busse, J. (1996). The structure of abilities in math-precocious young children: Gender similarities and differences. *Journal of Educational Psychology, 88,* 341–352.

Rutherford, J., & Ahlgren, A. (1990). *Science for all Americans.* New York: Oxford University Press.

Sawyer, R. (1985). The early identification and education of brilliant students: The Duke model. *College Board Review, 135,* 13–17, 31.

Shane, H. (1981). *A study of curriculum content for the future.* New York: College Entrance Examination Board.

Sheffield, L. J. (1994). *The development of gifted and talented mathematics students and the National Council of Teachers of Mathematics Standards.* Storrs, CT: National Research Center on the Gifted and Talented.

Sowell, E. J. (1993). Programs for mathematically gifted students: A review of empirical research. *Gifted Child Quarterly, 37*(3), 124–132.

Stanley, J. C., & Benbow, C. P. (1981). Using the SAT to find intellectually talented seventh graders. *College Board Review, 122,* 2–7, 26–27.

Stanley, J. (1997). Varieties of intellectual talent. *Journal of Creative Behavior, 31,* 93–119.

Stanley, J., Keating, D., & Fox, L. (1974). *Mathematical talent.* Baltimore, MD: Johns Hopkins University Press.

Stepien, W. J., Gallagher, S. A., & Workman, D. (1993). Problem-based learning for traditional and inter-disciplinary classrooms. *Journal for the Education of the Gifted, 16*(4), 338–357.

Swiatek, M. A., & Benbow, C. P. (1991). A 10-year longitudinal follow-up of participants in a fast-paced mathematics course. *Journal for Research in Mathematics Education, 22*(2), 138–150.

Van-Tassel-Baska, J. (1985). The talent search model: Implications for secondary school reform. *NASSP Bulletin, 69*(482), 39–47.

VanTassel-Baska, J., (ed.). (1987). *A curriculum guide to applications of science to technology for able learners.* Evanston, IL: Northwestern University Center for Talent Development. (ERIC Document Reproduction Service No. ED 289747).

VanTassel-Baska, J., Bass, G., Ries, R., & Poland, D. (in press). A national pilot study of science curriculum effectiveness for high ability students. *Gifted Child Quarterly.*

VanTassel-Baska, J., & Feldhusen, J. (1981). *Concept curriculum for the gifted.* Matteson, IL: Matteson School District #162.

VanTassel-Baska, J., Gallagher, S., Bailey, J., & Sher, B. (1993). Scientific experimentation. *Gifted Child Today, 16*(5), 42–46.

VanTassel-Baska, J., & Johnson, D. T. (1994, November). *Are standards enough?* Presentation at meeting of National Association of Gifted Children, Salt Lake City, UT.

VanTassel-Baska, J., & Kulieke, M. (1987). The role of the community in developing scientific talent. *Gifted Child Quarterly, 31*(3), 115–119.

VanTassel-Baska, J., Olszewski, P., & Landau, M. (1985). Toward developing an appropriate mathematics and science curriculum for gifted learners. *Journal for the Education of the Gifted, 8*(4), 257–272.

Wheatley, G. (1984). Instruction for the gifted. In J. Feldhusen (Ed.), *Toward excellence in gifted education* (pp. 31–44). Denver, CO: Love.

Wirsup, I. (1986). The current crises in math and science education: A climate for change. In J. VanTassel-Baska (Ed.), *Proceedings from the 9th Annual Research Symposium.* Evanston, IL: Phi Delta Kappan.

Ziegler, E. W., & Terry, M. S. (1992). Instructional methodology, computer literacy, and problem solving among gifted and talented students. *International Journal of Instructional Media, 19*(1), 45–51.

Study Questions ~

1. What should be the goals of appropriate mathematics and science programs for the gifted? Can the areas share some common goals?
2. What teaching strategies do you feel would be most effective for working with the gifted in math and science, and why?
3. How might problem-based learning be incorporated into all math/science classrooms for the gifted?
4. What might be the role of computers and other technologies in enhancing the inter-relationships between math and science?
5. What arguments would you give to support the contention that the gifted learner needs differentiated curriculum and instruction in math? In science?
6. How can the curriculum ideas presented in this chapter become a part of school programs?

24
Social Studies and Language Arts for Talented Learners

Joyce VanTassel-Baska

Verbally gifted youth have a special need for enriched and accelerated learning experiences in social studies and in the language arts. Gifted students are concerned about political and social problems, values, and moral issues. Social studies and language arts offer unusual opportunities for these students to experience intellectual activity of a high order in dealing with issues, problems, and momentous events in our times and culture. Of course, students need historical, political, psychological, and philosophical perspectives as well as the aesthetic view derived from literature. This chapter presents an overview of these two areas of the curriculum and shows the opportunities for truly challenging learning experiences for the gifted and talented in social studies and the language arts.

Social studies and English often are linked in school programs as a core curriculum or in programs of American studies. These programs provide excellent opportunities for the gifted to experience interdisciplinary study of major themes and concepts cutting across disciplines and to engage in in-depth independent research activities. Higher level courses of this nature often are offered as electives for high-ability students who are capable of intensive discussions and of making presentations to peers of the results of such projects.

Underlying the acquisition of each of these disciplines is linguistic capacity, in respect to reading, writing, speaking, and listening. Thus, a common foundation of communication skills binds the two subjects together.

Based on studies of advanced development (Bloom, 1985; Howe, 1990), verbal or linguistic giftedness develops where it is systematically encouraged and nurtured.

Where language use is valued in the home and community, and where academic experiences are provided with adequate time and attention to progress, linguistic competence may be viewed as predictable. Thus, a curriculum to nurture this ability must emphasize opportunities that reflect the level of the learner and the existing mastery of relevant skills.

Cramond (1993) noted the importance of speaking and listening skills in a verbally based curriculum, emphasizing the inclusion of foreign language, forensics, debate, creative dramatics, guided imagery, interviewing, and sociodrama in the teaching of the language arts to gifted students. She argued that such activities foster the development of speaking and listening skills at the level of communication necessary for their effective use in future careers. Each of the skills she delineated are also useful to develop in social studies classrooms.

Beck and McKeown (1996) presented important ideas for enhancing the teaching of thinking through using discourse to promote student understanding in a deliberate way. They analyzed the importance of several teacher actions or discussion strategies that appear to be necessary to provide direction toward a learning goal in the classroom. These strategies are:

- Marking (focusing)
- Revoicing (repeating student ideas)
- Turning back (textual or student-based)
- Recapping (synthesizing)
- Modeling (thinking aloud)
- Annotating (providing information)

Such an emphasis enhances teaching in both the language arts and social studies by extending inquiry-based models into a new dimension.

Social Studies for the Gifted ~

Social studies programs for the gifted at the elementary level may be embedded in full-time special classes, in a pullout/resource room model, or in a cluster grouping approach in an otherwise heterogeneous classroom. Social studies activities also may be presented in special after-school or Saturday classes for the gifted. Wherever and whatever the program setting, curricular activities are apt to focus on broad themes, issues, problems, or concepts; on substantial involvement of the students in research and independent study; on goals that stress the learning of thinking skills; and on highly interactive classroom sessions involving discussions, problem solving, simulations, and student presentations of their own work.

At the secondary level, special opportunities for the gifted in social studies may be provided through special seminars (Kolloff & Feldhusen, 1986), honors classes, acceleration in which gifted students take advanced social studies courses ahead of schedule, concurrent enrollment in college-level social studies courses while in high school or through Advanced Placement (College Board, 1983) classes. Advanced Placement courses in social studies currently are offered in American history,

European history, American government and politics, comparative government and politics, and macro- and microeconomics.

All of these arrangements are, or should be, associated with a differentiated curriculum that focuses on higher level concepts and themes, stresses the development of critical thinking skills, involves students in research and writing, includes much discussion and active interaction in class, and provides opportunities for students to present the results of their research to fellow students and to real-world audiences beyond the school setting. In all of these special class formats, the emphasis shifts from learning basics to experiencing much higher level cognitive growth. The College Board (1983) suggested that students should have the following basic knowledge and skills in social sciences by the time they leave high school:

- The ability to understand basic information developed by the social sciences, including statistical data and other materials
- Familiarity with the basic method of the social sciences—that is, with the framing and empirical testing of hypotheses
- A basic understanding of at least one of the social sciences and of how its practitioners define and solve problems
- Familiarity with how to explore a social problem or social institution by means of ideas drawn from several social sciences

The new social studies-related content standards in history (National Center for History in the Schools, 1993), geography (National Council for Geographic Education, 1994), and civics (Center for Civic Education, 1994) suggest ample opportunities for educators of the gifted to plan more advanced programs. Table 24.1 contains an excerpt from these documents pertaining to the middle elementary levels. Given the limited time allotted to social studies in the elementary-school curriculum and the limited emphasis the area receives in most gifted programs, these standards call for more depth and intensity in teaching this subject to all learners. The standards may be a good representation of what gifted learners might attain if the curriculum directly supported such mastery.

To develop a realistic program that will prepare the gifted for the real world in which the social studies become operative, Schug (1981) recommended that the whole community serve as a laboratory for social studies learning experiences. For the study of history, he recommended the following activities:

- Arrange field trips to local museums, historical societies, or historical sites.
- Develop oral history collections by tape-recording interviews with senior citizens.
- Do volunteer work at local museums or historical societies.
- Write local histories based upon written records, photographs, and interviews with resource people.
- Find and analyze historical artifacts such as weapons, tools, kitchen utensils, arrowheads, toys, clothing, letters, diaries, books, catalogs, or photographs. (Junkyards, garages, junk shops, and attics are often valuable sources of historical artifacts.)

Table 24.1 ~
A Comparison of National Standards in Three Areas
of the Social Studies

Geography *(Grade 5–8 Standards)*	*Government* *(Grade 5–8 Standards)*	*History* *(Grade 5–12 Standards)*
Environment and Society **Standard 14.** How human actions modify the physical environment The student knows and understands: • The consequences of human modification of the physical environment • How human modifications of the physical environment in one place often lead to changes in other places • The role of technology in the human modification of the physical environment **Standard 15**. How physical systems affect human systems The student knows and understands: • Human responses to variations in physical systems • How the characteristics of different physical environments provide opportunities for or place constraints on human activities • How natural hazards affect human activities **Standard 16.** The changes that occur in the meaning, use, distribution, and importance of resources The student knows and understands: • The worldwide distribution and use of resources • Why people have different viewpoints regarding resource use • How technology affects the definitions of, access to, and use of resources • The fundamental role of energy resources in society	**What are the roles of the citizen in American democracy?** *What is citizenship?* **Standard 1.** The meaning of citizenship. Students should be able to explain the meaning of American citizenship. **Standard 2.** Becoming a citizen. Students should be able to explain how one becomes a citizen of the United States. *What are the rights of citizens?* **Standard 1.** Personal rights. Students should be able to evaluate, take, and defend positions on issues involving personal rights. **Standard 2.** Political rights. Students should be able to evaluate, take, and defend positions on issues involving political rights. **Standard 3**. Economic rights. Students should be able to evaluate, take, and defend positions on issues involving economic rights. **Standard 4.** Scope and limits of rights. Students should be able to evaluate, take, and defend positions on issues regarding the proper scope and limits of rights. *What are the responsibilities of citizens?* **Standard 1.** Personal responsibilities. Students should be able to evaluate, take, and defend positions on the importance of personal responsibilities to the individual and to society. **Standard 2.** Civic responsibilities. Students should be able to evaluate, take, and defend positions on the importance of civic responsibilities to the individual and society.	**The Development of the Industrial United States (1870–1900)** **Standard 1.** Students should understand how the rise of big business, heavy industry, and mechanized farming transformed the American peoples. Students should be able to: • Demonstrate understanding of the connections between industrialization, the rise of big business, and the advent of the modern corporation • Demonstrate understanding of how rapid industrialization affected urban politics, living standards, and opportunity at different social levels • Demonstrate understanding of how agriculture, mining, and ranching were transformed • Demonstrate understanding of how industrialism, urbanization, large-scale agriculture, and mining affected the ecosystem and initiated an environmental movement **Standard 2.** Students should understand massive immigration after 1870 and how new social patterns, conflicts, and ideas of national unity developed amid growing cultural diversity. Students should be able to: • Demonstrate understanding of the sources and experiences of the new immigrants • Demonstrate understanding of Social Darwinism, race relations, and the struggle for equal rights and opportunities • Demonstrate understanding of how new cultural movements at different social levels affected American life *(continued)*

Table 24.1 continued

What dispositions or traits of character are important to the preservation and improvement of American constitutional democracy?

Standard 1. Dispositions that enhance citizen effectiveness and promote the healthy functioning of American constitutional democracy. Students should be able to evaluate, take, and defend positions on the importance of certain dispositions or traits of character to themselves and American constitutional democracy.

How can citizens take part in civic life?

Standard 1. Participation in civic and political life and the attainment of individual and public goals. Students should be able to explain the relationship between participating in civic and political life and the attainment of individual and public goals.

Standard 2. The difference between political and social participation. Students should be able to explain the difference between political and social participation.

Standard 3. Forms of political participation. Students should be able to describe the means by which Americans can monitor and influence politics and government.

Standard 4. Political leadership and public service. Students should be able to explain the importance of political leadership and public service in a constitutional democracy.

Standard 5. Knowledge and participation. Students should be able to explain the importance of knowledge to competent and responsible participation in American democracy.

Standard 3. Students should understand the rise of the American labor movement and how political issues reflected social and economic changes.

Students should be able to:

- Demonstrate how the "second industrial revolution" changed the nature and conditions of work
- Demonstrate understanding of the rise of national labor unions and the role of state and federal governments in labor conflicts
- Demonstrate understanding of how Americans grappled with the social, economic, and political problems of the late 19th century

Standard 4. Students should understand federal Indian policy and United States foreign policy after the Civil War.

Students should be able to:

- Demonstrate understanding of various perspectives on federal Indian policy, westward expansion, and the resulting struggles
- Demonstrate understanding of the roots and development of American expansionism and the causes and outcomes of the Spanish-American War

Note: Adapted from Struggling for Standards. *Education Week* Special Report, April 1995.

- Arrange a field trip to an old cemetery, where students can record dates of births and deaths and make inferences about past life spans, epidemics, and health care.
- Videotape interviews with senior citizens talking about life in the past.

Schug also proposed that a community advisory committee be organized, including representatives from business, agriculture, labor, the professions, the arts, and the political parties, to help define real issues and problems to be studied and suggest ways to involve community agencies, organizations, and groups in developing community-based activities for the gifted.

Example Programs

Social studies programs for the gifted can begin at the early childhood or primary level. Gifted children at the primary level can be engaged in discussion of basic concepts and participate in independent project activities that they plan and carry out themselves with teacher guidance. Flachner and Hirst (1976) developed one such program in New York City for the Astor Program for primary-level gifted children. Titled "200 Years, A Study of Democracy," the program uses quotations from great literature, such as Walt Whitman's *I Hear America Singing,* as vehicles for discussions.

Pioneering work in the development of social studies curricula for the gifted at the upper-elementary, middle-school, and high-school levels has been carried out at Ball State University's Burris Laboratory School by Professors Carl Keener, Penny Kolloff, and others (Keener, undated). Their work utilizes the seminar as a classroom delivery model to engage gifted youth in high-level discussions, project and research activity, presentations to real audiences, and learning of higher level thinking skills. The curriculum guides they have developed stress a global and futures orientation. The following, for example, are some of the concepts dealt with in one of the courses:

Systems	Populations
Interdependence	Scarcity/Allocations
Culture	Energy
Lifestyle	Habitat
Dignity of humans	Institution
Conflict	Sovereignty

Some of the activities or investigations proposed for youth in this program are:

- Individual or small-group investigation of an alternative global future
- Delineation of the global futures investigation
- Report on research on global futures and individualized research projects/products
- Simplification of a demographic abstraction
- Nuclear holocaust survival skills
- Appropriate technologies for developing economies—role-playing

Problem-Based Learning Applied to the Social Studies

Recently, attempts have been made to translate problem-based learning to the K–12 classroom (Gallagher, Sher, Stepien, & Workman, 1995; Stepien, Gallagher, & Workman, 1993) and to test its effectiveness. Evidence that problem-based learning is an effective tool to enhance student learning in the social studies has been reported in recent literature, which has shown the positive effects of the approach in comparison to other methods (Gallagher & Stepien, 1996).

Inquiry Approach

In developing social studies programs for the gifted, the major direction of activity is often the inquiry approach. This seems particularly appropriate for the gifted because inquiry implies the achievement of deep understanding through active search and investigation and the use of techniques of critical thinking. Taba was a principal advocate of the inquiry method, especially in the teaching of social studies. Her thoughts about teaching for thinking were presented in the volume *Curriculum Development* (Taba, 1962). Her later work toward a specific inquiry-oriented teaching model was presented in a number of publications and summarized by Maker (1982) in *Teaching Models in Education of the Gifted.* Maker suggested that four fundamental strategies characterize the Taba inquiry model:

1. *Concept development.* In this strategy students engage in the acquisition and organization of information and the development and naming of key concepts in an area of study. In a sense, this is the content acquisition stage, but Taba stressed that it must not be simply a transmission of predigested content from teacher to student but, rather, a generatively acquired grasp or understanding of content as key concepts through student interaction with basic information or data in the field of inquiry.
2. *Interpretation of data.* This strategy involves students in a number of higher level thinking activities through which they achieve a still higher level of disciplined understanding in a field. In a first approach to interpretation, students engage in listing relevant and irrelevant information and otherwise organizing the available information. At a second stage, they are led to infer causes and effects within the phenomenon under study. In a third stage, they infer prior causes and subsequent effects. The fourth step provides experiences in drawing sound conclusions based on data. Finally, students engage in generalizing and transferring their knowledge to new situations.
3. *Application of generalizations.* In this strategy students are guided to apply facts, concepts, and principles in new and real-life situations through the activities of predicting, inferring, concluding, and examining generalizations.
4. *Resolution of conflicts.* In this strategy students deal with the affective experiences of attitudes, feelings, and values in conflict situations. Students learn

how to deal with the feelings, attitudes, and values that underlie the documents or content under study.

These inquiry strategies, often based on the research and theory of Bruner (1960), provide high-level and challenging cognitive experiences for gifted youth. They demand a range of teaching skills quite unlike the usual presentation-and-lecture approach that characterizes much teaching. The payoff in cognitive growth for the gifted, however, can be substantial.

Applications of the Taba approach may be seen in science and language arts units developed by the College of William and Mary (Center for Gifted Education, 1995).

Questioning Skills

Productive learning in the social studies through inquiry, discovery, concept induction, and deductive reasoning calls for effective questioning skills on the part of both teacher and students. Through a mutual questioning process, they can clarify the accuracy of information, understand concepts better, delineate the true issue or problem, analyze complex situations, and better understand values involved in a complex situation. Torrance and Myers (1970, pp. 149–221) offered a comprehensive framework for conceptualizing teachers' and students' questions that can be used to facilitate inquiry:

1. Interpretation (What is meant by "conspicuous consumption"?)
2. Comparison-analysis (How are lakes and oceans different?)
3. Synthesis (How could you combine...?)
4. Redefinition (What is a clock other than a timepiece?)
5. Open-ended questions (Suppose that....)
6. Evaluation (Did the United States reveal moral bankruptcy in Cambodia?)
7. Sensitivity to problems (What are the United Nations' problems?)
8. Clarification of problems (What problem does OPEC pose for Western nations?)
9. Provocative questions (What if all violence were barred from TV?)
10. Hypothetical questions (What if Cortés had been killed by Montezuma?)
11. Questions to stimulate thoughtful reading (Why was Mozart called the "boy wonder"?)
12. Questions to stimulate thoughtful listening (Why does the speaker dwell on political confrontation?)

A number of writers (e.g., Hunkins, 1985; Sanders, 1960) have used the Bloom (1956) taxonomy as a theoretical model to guide students and teachers in formulating questions for inquiry. Based on the taxonomy, a pattern of questioning might be as follows:

1. Knowledge
   Teacher: Can you describe the land formation patterns along the river?
   Student: How far inland from the river should we go?

2. Comprehension
   Teacher: What are the authors really trying to tell us in this passage?
   Student: Are you saying that you want us to go beyond the literal message?
3. Application
   Teacher: Can you solve this problem using the concepts of simultaneous equations?
   Student: Does this problem have a single solution?
4. Analysis
   Teacher: How are estuaries and bays alike, and how are they different?
   Student: Must a bay always run off from a large body of water?
5. Synthesis
   Teacher: Using the concepts of geography that we have learned, can you design a new method of mapping?
   Student: Can such a map have live or animate components?
6. Evaluation
   Teacher: Which of the countries of southern Africa has the greatest potential for economic growth because of its geography?
   Student: Should we use historical factors as a part of our decision-making process?

This pattern of questioning by teachers and students illustrates an interactive inquiry situation in which students engage in higher level thinking activities and deal with significant, real-world issues and problems, a feature of thoughtful social studies classrooms (Newmann, 1990). Other excellent models for adaptation in the social studies area are the Paul model of reasoning (1995) and adaptations of Guilford's question tree of cognition, convergence, divergence, and evaluation (VanTassel-Baska, 1992).

Law Study as Social Studies in Action

Law-related curricula have been developed in several sites across the United States as a special program in the social studies. Gold, Lindquist, and Armancas-Fisher (1993) reported on one such curriculum developed and implemented through the University of Puget Sound School of Law for elementary and secondary students. Based on the multiple intelligences model of Gardner (1993), the curriculum guide emphasizes legal issues related to:

- Old-growth forests
- Internment of Japanese Americans
- The Salmon Summit
- The automobile industry
- Freedom of speech
- Search and seizure in Washington state
- Immunization
- Animal rights

The use of case studies, role playing, and interpreting polling data are predominant strategies.

A second law-centered curriculum has been developed at the Center for Research and Development in Law-Related Education (CRADLE) in Winston-Salem, North Carolina. Teacher-developed lessons are used to teach civics to gifted students—specifically the origins and evolution of the system of government, how and why the legal system operates as it does, and the rules of politicians, lawyers, judges, and citizens in using responsible government. A special feature of the program is the involvement of local attorneys in the classroom (Center for Research and Development in Law-Related Education [CRADLE], 1994). Other law-related programs and curricula have been available on a sporadic basis in many other areas of the country.

Language Arts for the Gifted ~

Descriptions of the gifted often stress their verbal abilities. Early word recognition and reading, rapid and easy learning, large vocabulary, ability to deal with complex and abstract concepts, verbal expressiveness, voracious reading, and precocious reading comprehension frequently are listed as characteristics of gifted children. At the same time, programs for the gifted have been criticized for overemphasizing language arts activities and neglecting mathematics and science. The field of gifted education appears to be oriented to verbally gifted youth.

Nevertheless, how to provide for verbally gifted youth remains a big challenge. Despite their evident precocity and the resultant need for instructional activities at a high, abstract, complex, and challenging level, programs, especially pullout-resource room-type programs, stress enrichment projects and activities that often are not presented at a high or fast-paced level. The term *enrichment* often is used to characterize programs in which there may even be purposeful avoidance of higher level content because of complaints from teachers at higher grade levels that they will have nothing left to teach if advanced content and skills are introduced earlier.

The ideal language arts program for the gifted will have to overcome such problems and offer curricular experiences that are enriching and accelerated. The best interpretation of enrichment is that which offers instruction that extends beyond normal offerings to accommodate the wider and more diverse interests of the gifted and that which does so at a higher level of abstraction and complexity to fit the precocity of the gifted child's capacity to learn rapidly. An exemplary program in the language arts at William and Mary addresses these key issues through the Interdisciplinary Curriculum Model cited in Chapter 19.

Just as national content standards work has influenced curriculum development in math, science, and social studies, so too has the work of two national groups, the International Reading Association (IRA) and the National Council of Teachers of English (NCTE), influenced important emphases in general language arts curriculum. Adaptations from these frameworks have been developed in the William and

Mary curriculum units for high-ability learners. Table 24.2 presents a comparison of the IRA/NCTE standards and the William and Mary adaptations. A content analysis reveals a stronger emphasis in the William and Mary language arts units on (1) analytical and interpretive critical reading skills, (2) persuasive writing, (3) oral communication, and (4) the formal teaching of grammar. Moreover, the William and Mary units employ a performance-based and portfolio approach to assessment, in keeping with recommendations from the language arts community (Purves, 1993).

Reading and the Study of Literature

The gifted child's major contact with the world of ideas is through literature. Books stimulate thought and provide the knowledge base required for creative thinking and problem solving. Intellectual growth in gifted children depends on their access to and regular involvement in the reading process. From the time of their earliest ability to read, they need access to a rich variety of fiction and nonfiction literature and opportunities to respond actively and creatively to what they are reading. They should have abundant opportunities, with parents and teachers, to discuss, analyze, and share the joy of what is read and, above all, to be guided by adults who model the processes of analyzing, discussing, and experiencing joy in reading.

Few research studies have focused on effective reading practices with the gifted. One study on precocious readers (Henderson, Jackson, & Mukamal, 1993) found that such readers need to be assessed carefully concerning specific areas of strength within the language arts area, lest assumptions be made about skills in which they may not be advanced or about connections between skill areas, such as reading and writing or oral language and reading, that may not be present. In another study, fifth and sixth graders who participated in a literary analysis class once a week showed significant gains over a control group on both reading comprehension and vocabulary when they were assessed with an off-grade-level standardized achievement measure (Aldrich & Mills, 1989).

Reasonable consensus exists that a reading program for the gifted should be specialized and focus on critical and creative reading behaviors (Collins & Alex, 1995), implying the need for various forms of instructional grouping. Yet whole-language advocates have recently sought to dismantle all forms of reading groups by instructional level. In a descriptive study of gifted students in general education classrooms, Matthews (1992) found that teachers who were most effective at whole language were also most effective at differentiating for the gifted and that both sets of strategies were positive experiences for the gifted.

Several authors have provided excellent guidance concerning good literature for the gifted and how to teach it to optimize learning and love of literature. In *Books for the Gifted Child*, Baskin and Harris (1980) suggested the following criteria for finding the right books for the gifted:

1. The language used in books for the gifted should be rich, varied, precise, complex, and exciting, for language is the instrument for the reception and expression of thought.

Table 24.2 ~
Alignment of the IRA/NCTE Standards for the English Language Arts to the William and Mary Language Arts Units

Standards for the English Language Arts	William and Mary Language Arts Units
1. Students read a wide range of print and nonprint texts to build an understanding of texts, of themselves, and of the cultures of the United States and the world; to acquire new information; to respond to the needs and demands of society and the workplace; and for personal fulfillment.	Emphasis on multicultural and global literature and broad-based reading.
2. Students read a wide range of literature from many periods in many genres to build an understanding of the many dimensions (e.g., philosophical, ethical, aesthetic) of human experience.	Broad-based reading in poetry, short story, biography, essay, and novel forms.
3. Students apply a wide range of strategies to comprehend, interpret, evaluate, and appreciate texts.	Major goal of analysis and interpretation of literature. (Goal #1)
4. Students adjust their use of spoken, written, and visual language to communicate effectively with a variety of audiences and for different purposes.	Sensitivity to audience built into writing and research activities.
5. Students employ a wide range of strategies as they write and use different writing process elements appropriately.	Major outcome related to effective use of all stages of the writing process. (Goal #2)
6. Students apply knowledge of language structure, language conventions, media techniques, figurative language, and genre to create, critique, and discuss print and nonprint texts.	Major goal of developing linguistic competency. (Goal #3)
7. Students conduct research on issues and interests by generating ideas and questions, and by posing problems. They gather, evaluate, and synthesize data from a variety of sources to communicate their discoveries in ways that suit their purpose and audience.	Research project that focuses on these skills based on issue identification is a feature of each unit; the use of the reasoning model underlies the teaching of all language arts strands. (Goal #5)

(continued)

Table 24.2 continued

8. Students use a wide variety of technological and informational resources to gather and synthesize information and to create and communicate knowledge.	Incorporated in research model and writing task demands.
9. Students develop an understanding of and respect for diversity in language use, patterns, and dialects across cultures, ethnic groups, geographic regions, and social roles.	Applicable to the context of selected literature.
10. Students whose first language is not English make use of their first language to develop competency in the English language arts and to develop understanding of content across the curriculum.	N/A
11. Students participate as knowledgeable, reflective, creative, and critical members of a variety of literacy communities.	Contact with authors, use of peer review, major discussions of literary works.
12. Students use spoken, written, and visual language to accomplish their own purposes.	Integrated throughout the units.

2. Books should be chosen with an eye to their open-endedness, their capacity to inspire contemplative behavior, such as through techniques of judging time sequences, shifting narrators, and unusual speech patterns of characters.

3. Books for the gifted should be complex enough to allow interpretative and evaluation behaviors to be elicited from readers.

4. Books for the gifted should help them build problem-solving skills and develop methods of productive thinking.

5. Books should provide characters as role models for emulation.

6. Books should be broad-based in form, from picture books to folktale and myths to non-fiction to biography to poetry to fiction. (p. 46)

Polette (1982) and Polette and Hamlin (1980) also offered a wealth of ideas for structuring and conducting literature programs for the gifted. Polette and Hamlin suggested the following guidelines for teachers of literature for the gifted:

There are many times when the gifted child will be alone in an opinion or belief. Encourage the child to support or deny the concepts held through the use of a wide variety of materials. At the same time, work patiently with the child in helping him or her cope with differing opinions.

Gifted children often want to explore areas that society says are not within normal expectations because of age or because of sex. Such exploration should not be discouraged if resources are available or can be found.

Encourage creative thought. The great minds of the ages are those that would not accept the idea that a thing could not be done. Science fiction of fifty years ago is science fact today. Do not dismiss an idea simply because it does not seem possible given the limits of our present knowledge.

Allow these children, within the limits of safety, to experience the consequences of their behavior, both acceptable and unacceptable behavior. Help children to examine consequences before behavior choices are made.

Let children test their ideas without threat of evaluation. Assign grades only when absolutely necessary. Parent/child/teacher conferences are far more valuable than a letter grade. Encourage the child to read, read, read! As author Scott Corbett says, "Reading gives one an entire second life and two lives are certainly better than one." (pp. 22–23)

They went on to delineate the following guidelines for the teacher of the gifted:

> The major requirements of the teacher of the gifted in a literature program include knowledge, creativity, a love of books and of reading, a respect for children and their ideas, and a high risk taking potential. The teacher must know both the positive characteristics and the prevailing negative attitudes of the students with whom he or she will work, being able to capitalize on the positive and deal effectively with the negative. Finally, the teacher must know precisely the teaching strategies that are more suited to gifted students than to the average or below average student. (p. 23)

The majority of their book is devoted to topics such as character and plot development, setting and mood, themes and values, fairy tales, folk tales, fantasy, and gifted authors.

One of the most effective literature programs available for gifted learners is the Junior Great Books Program. It is the only program that was highly rated by Aldrich and McKim (1992) in their review of programs and materials purported to be effective with the gifted. Moreover, it offers a strong inquiry-based training program for teachers, and the program has been found to be most effective at improving students' quality of discourse and enhancing their interest in literature (Nichols, 1992, 1993).

Literature programs at middle- and high-school levels should involve gifted students in reading high-quality adult literature and should help them develop skill and enthusiasm in the intellectual and aesthetic experience of literature (Mallea, 1992). Some sentiment exists for the use of good young-adult literature as well (Rakow, 1991).

In 1978, the California State Department of Education published a guide titled *Teaching Gifted Students Literature and Language in Grades Nine Through Twelve*. It offered the following suggestions for secondary literature programs for the gifted:

> Gifted students read more widely and more perceptively than do the nongifted, and they enter high school having been exposed to a variety of literary types; for example, stories, myths, tall tales, and fantasy. Their response has been primarily emotional and

superficial, their feelings deriving from vicarious or personal experience. They have given little heed to design or structure. It follows, then, that the task of the English teacher of gifted high school students is to open other literary doors. The teacher must broaden the scope and increase the depth of the students' reading by examining in specific selections the philosophies encountered and the techniques of the artist's craft. In short, the teacher must try to effect a total engagement of the learners with mature literary experience.

No single organization of literary study will accomplish the objective of total engagement. Each type of organization can, however, make a significant educational contribution, and the adoption of one type as a frame should not exclude the use of other types. The four basic organizational approaches that are most prevalent are (1) history and chronology; (2) genre; (3) textual analysis; and (4) theme or idea. (p. 6)

The use of the seminar approach to teach literature to secondary gifted students has been strongly advocated because of its context for stimulating discussion and interaction (Dixon, 1993; Taylor, 1996). Its effectiveness as a strategy has rarely been challenged.

Writing and Composition

Writing programs for the gifted should begin as soon as the students enter school and should provide an abundance of opportunities to write. Writing is a thinking process, and through writing experiences the gifted child can develop excellence in capacity to think as well as to write. Moreover, evidence exists that journal writing provides an important avenue for self-expression in the gifted, allowing opportunities for better understanding of themselves and others (Bailey, Boyce, & VanTassel-Baska, 1990; Hall, 1990).

Very young children who may lack the motor coordination to write may still be engaged in writing-related activities through the following teaching techniques (VanTassel-Baska, 1993):

1. Have the child compose a story and transcribe it for him or her as it is being developed. Read it back for editing changes or additions and elaborations. Share stories in class.
2. Encourage parents to transcribe stories at home and have the children bring them back to school for sharing.
3. Have students draw pictures to illustrate their stories and then develop titles for them.
4. Use tape recorders to record children's stories and then transcribe them later.
5. Have students compose stories at the computer or typewriter if they have mastered the device adequately enough.
6. Encourage free story building; provide students with a set of givens (characters, plot pieces, a setting).
7. Have students respond in writing to a piece of music, a picture, or a poem presented in class.
8. Allow young students the freedom to write without requiring accurate spelling and grammar.

Other emphases supported in the literature include the use of guided imagery to enhance creative writing (Jampole, Mathews, & Konopak, 1994) and the use of parents as partners with their children in the writing process (Reif, 1995).

By the time gifted students reach the intermediate grades, they should begin to master the basic skills of language and writing. Collins (1985) suggested some strategies for acclimating gifted students to writing and composition:

1. Provide opportunities for students to discuss and clarify writing assignments before they begin writing
2. Provide opportunities for students to obtain more information about a topic before they begin writing.
3. Provide specific information about the criteria you will use to correct each assignment.
4. Provide opportunities for students to review and revise written work completed earlier in the year.
5. Encourage students to edit one anothers' papers before they are handed in.
6. Provide opportunities for students to read written work aloud to individuals or to small groups of students.

Schunk and Swartz (1992) found that the teaching of a writing model through a deliberate strategy coupled with feedback on progress enhanced the achievement of gifted learners as well as their sense of self-efficacy. Even teaching the strategy without providing feedback was found to be beneficial. The strategy goal approach exposed students to the following task demands: (1) write down ideas, (2) pick a main idea, (3) plan a paragraph, (4) write topic sentence, and (5) write other sentences. Thus, the study provides additional evidence that strategy instruction facilitates gifted students' achievement and transfer learning (Scruggs, Mastropieri, Jorgensen, & Monson, 1986) and that self-efficacy is positively related to performance (Schack, 1989). Moreover, it substantiates earlier research on the superior performance of gifted students over other types of learners in monitoring their learning progress and generating their own strategies (Rogers, 1986; Scruggs & Mastropieri, 1985).

In a more recent study, gifted learners in grades 4–6 showed significant improvement in persuasive writing when provided with a visual model, specific strategies for replicating it in written form, and extensive peer and teacher feedback (VanTassel-Baska, Johnson, Hughes, & Boyce, 1996). Another recent study found that teachers who participated with their students in writing enhanced the overall fluency of writing in the classroom (Armstrong, 1994), suggesting that the role of the teacher, as well as strategy employment, enhances the writing behavior of gifted learners.

Foreign Language Study

Gifted children can benefit a great deal from the study of a second language, for such study can enhance their grasp of the structure and semantics of their own language. Foreign language study should begin as early as kindergarten or first grade and be continual throughout high school and into college. Mastery of a second (and third) language gives the gifted student a comprehensive understanding of the comparative structure of languages and their related cultures.

Thompson and Thompson (1996) stressed the importance of second language learning as a cultural, social, and linguistic experience, thus rendering it one of the most interdisciplinary experiences possible in schools. VanTassel-Baska (1987) suggested that gifted students ideally should learn Latin as well as another language because:

1. Sixty percent of English words are derived from Latin; thus, the study of this language greatly heightens vocabulary power in English.
2. Syntactic understanding, a major goal in the learning of Latin, enhances linguistic competence in English and in other languages.
3. The complexity of the language and its logical consistency make it a challenge to gifted students who enjoy learning new symbol systems, analyzing, and using deductive logic in solving problems.
4. The cultural heritage of the Western world is based on Greco-Roman traditions in art, music, and literature, as well as language. Thus, to study Latin is to gain invaluable insight into the Western cultural system.
5. Modern language tends to stress oral/aural skills with a focus on language fluency. Latin learning, conversely, stresses logical reasoning and analysis through an emphasis on translation and study of form changes at increasing levels of difficulty. In that respect, Latin is a verbal analog to the teaching of mathematics as a cumulatively organized subject area that is amenable to fast-paced instruction. Thus, Latin is an easy subject to modify for precocious students.
6. Unlike most languages, Latin has few irregularities.

She concluded that the major goals of a foreign language program for the gifted should be to develop proficiency in reading, speaking, and writing in two languages; to learn the culture and traditions that shape language; to be challenged by the interrelationships across languages in respect to form and meaning; and to appreciate and understand language systems. Wielkoszewski (1992) added the rationale of training future leaders in critical international and intercultural skills as another reason for teaching foreign languages to the gifted.

The English Language

The language arts program for the gifted should offer opportunities to study the English language. VanTassel-Baska (1993) suggested that the goals for an English language program should be to understand the syntactic structure of English (grammar) and its concomitant uses (usage); to promote vocabulary development; to foster an understanding of word relationships (analogies) and origins (etymology); and to develop an appreciation for semantics, linguistics, and the history of language. The programs of study for the English language will be augmented immensely by a concurrent foreign language study program.

Because gifted children have extreme individual differences in their mastery of the language skills of grammar, usage, and vocabulary, these segments of a program for the gifted must be highly individualized. Pretesting of skills and vocabulary always should be carried out, and instructional activities and materials should be determined diagnostically on the basis of pretest results. Gifted youth find particularly onerous instruction that covers material they already know or that is adjusted to the pace of the slowest student in a class.

Although spelling is frequently not treated as a major part of gifted programs, current studies suggest that focusing on visual memory strategies, word meanings, and etymologies and using words in speech and writing all characterize strategies used by spelling bee finalists (Olson, Logan, & Lindsey, 1989; Richards & Gipe, 1993). For some gifted students, spelling may be an area of real interest.

Oral Language Arts

Oral mastery and use of language are critical parts of the language arts program. The thinking processes involved in experiencing literature and in writing are linked intimately to, and can be enhanced by, oral language experience. Through planned experiences in discussion, debate, oral reading and interpretation, oral reports, dramatics, and panel presentations, gifted youth can learn to think effectively in and through the language, and they can learn to write more effectively.

At the primary and elementary levels, gifted children can learn to read aloud from storybooks with expressiveness, can learn to verbalize ideas through creative dramatics, and can begin to give oral reports and presentations. Beginning at the fourth or fifth grade level, they can engage in the more cognitively demanding activities of debate, acting, and research reporting. Middle-school and high-school classroom discussions can become strongly analytical, theoretical, and abstract and can deal with values and judgment. Improvisation and extemporaneous presentations, as well as formal debate, can provide high-level oral language experiences for the gifted.

Programs and curricula for the gifted should be planned carefully to incorporate these oral language experiences in the total language arts program. Teachers of the gifted also should make a continuing effort to help gifted students see the linkages among the language arts experiences of literature, writing, language, foreign language, and oral language. In all language arts program experiences, gifted youth should have access to higher level content presented at a fast pace (acceleration), much dynamic cognitive interaction with content, and a wider variety of language arts experience than characterizes the general school language arts program (enrichment). All of their language arts experiences should be linked to thematic and conceptual content and should stress the use and learning of higher level thinking skills. Through modeling by parents, teachers, and peers of their enthusiasm for language arts experiences, gifted children should develop a true love of literature, writing, and symbolic language experiences.

Summary ⌒

Experiences in social studies and language arts are essential in all programs for the gifted and talented. In these two domains, the gifted and talented can experience high-level challenges to think and grow intellectually through in-depth research, group projects, and classroom discussions. The social studies and language arts programs should be differentiated for the gifted from K to 12. Cultural literacy is essential to full actualization of the gifted and talented, and experiences in these two domains provide the base of knowledge to achieve it.

References ⌒

Aldrich, P., & McKim, G. (1992). *The consumer's guide to English-language arts curriculum.* New York: Saratoga-Warren Board of Cooperative Educational Services.

Aldrich, P., & Mills, C. J. (1989). A special program for highly able rural youth in grades five and six. *Gifted Child Quarterly, 33*(1), 11–14.

Armstrong, D. C. (1994). A gifted child's education requires real dialogue: The use of interactive writing for collaborative education. *Gifted Child Quarterly, 38*(3), 136–145.

Bailey, J. M., Boyce, L. N., & VanTassel-Baska, J. (1990). Writing, reading, and counseling connection: A framework for serving the gifted. In J. VanTassel-Baska (Ed.), *A practical guide to counseling the gifted in a school setting* (pp. 172–189). Reston, VA: Council for Exceptional Children.

Baskin, B. H., & Harris, K. H. (1980). *Books for the gifted child.* New York: Bowker.

Beck, I., & McKeown, M. (1996, April). *Building students' understanding of text ideas through discussion.* Presentation at the American Educational Research Association meeting, New York City.

Bloom, B. (1956). *Taxonomy of educational objectives: Cognitive domain.* New York: Longmans, Green.

Bloom, B. (1985). *Developing talent in young people.* New York: Ballantine.

Bruner, J. S. (1960). *The process of education.* Cambridge, MA: Harvard University Press.

California State Department of Education. (1978). *Teaching gifted students literature and language in grades nine through twelve.* Sacramento, CA: Author.

Center for Civic Education. (1994). *National standards for civics and government.* Calabasas, CA: Center for Civic Education.

Center for Gifted Education. (1995). *Autobiographies: Personal odysseys of change.* Williamsburg, VA: Author.

Center for Research and Development in Law-Related Education. (1994). *Legacy: Linking educators and the gifted with attorneys for civics: Yes! Challenging lessons for the classroom and beyond.* Winston-Salem, NC: Author.

College Board. (1983). *Academic preparation for college.* New York: Author.

Collins, J. (1985). *The effective writing teacher: 18 strategies.* Andover, MA: Newwork.

Collins, N. D., & Alex, N. K. (1995). *Gifted readers and reading instruction.* Bloomington, IN: ERIC Clearinghouse on Reading, English, and Communication. (ERIC Document Reproduction Service No. ED 379 637)

Cramond, B. (1993). Speaking and listening: Key components of a complete language arts program for the gifted. *Roeper Review, 16*(1), 44–48.

Dixon, F. A. (1993). Literature seminars for gifted and talented students. *Gifted Child Today, 16*(4), 15–19.

Education Week. (1995). Special report: Struggling for standards. Washington, DC: Author.

Flachner, J., & Hirst, B. (1976). *200 years, a study of democracy.* New York: Astor Program (Available from The Asian Foundation. 490 Hudson Street, New York, NY 10014)

Gallagher, S. A., Sher, B. T., Stepien, W. J., & Workman, D. (1995). Implementing problem-based learning in science classrooms. *School Science and Mathematics, 95*(3), 136–146.

Gallagher, S. A., & Stepien, W. J. (1996). Content acquisition in problem-based learning: Depth versus breadth in American Studies. *Journal for the Education of the Gifted, 19*(3), 257–275.

Gardner, H. (1993). *Frames of mind: The theory of multiple intelligences* (2nd ed.). London: Fontana.

Gold, J. A., Lindquist, T. L., & Armancas-Fisher, M. (1993). *Challenging students with the law: An interdisciplinary curriculum for gifted and talented students at the upper elementary and middle school levels.* Tacoma, WA: University of Puget Sound. (ERIC Document Reproduction Service No. ED 388 536)

Hall, E. G. (1990). Strategies for using journal writing in counseling gifted students. *Gifted Child Today, 13*(4), 2–6.

Henderson, S. J., Jackson, N. E., & Mukamal, R. A. (1993). Early development of language and literacy skills of an extremely precocious reader. *Gifted Child Quarterly, 37*(2), 78–83.

Howe, M. J. A. (1990). *The origins of exceptional abilities.* Oxford: Basil Blackwell.

Hunkins, F. P. (1972). *Questioning strategies and techniques.* Boston: Allyn & Bacon.

Hunkins, F. P. (1985). Helping students ask their own questions. *Social Education, 49*, 292–296.

Jampole, E. S., Mathews, F. N., & Konopak, B. C. (1994). Academically gifted students' use of imagery for creative writing. *Journal of Creative Behavior, 28*(1), 1–15.

Keener, C. (Undated). *A curricular approach for global studies.* Muncie, IN: Ball State University (Available from Curriculum Director Burris-Ball State School Corporation, 2000 University Avenue, Muncie, IN 47306)

Kolloff, P. B., & Feldhusen, J. F. (1986). Seminar: Instructional approach for gifted students. *Gifted Child Today, 9*(5), 2–7.

Maker, C. J. (1982). *Teaching models in education of the gifted.* Rockville, MD: Aspen Systems.

Mallea, K. (1992). A novel approach for the gifted reader. *Middle School Journal, 24*(1), 37–38.

Matthews, M. K. (1992, April). *Gifted students and whole language: A descriptive study of four classrooms.* Paper presented at the annual meeting of American Educational Research Association, San Francisco, CA.

National Center for History in the Schools. (1993). *National history standards project.* National Center for Hisotry in the Schools: Los Angeles, CA.

National Council for Geographic Education. (1994). *The national geography standards.* National Council for Geographic Education: Washington, DC.

Newmann, F. (1990). Qualities of thoughtful social studies classes: An empirical profile. *Journal of Curriculum Studies, 22*(3), 253–275.

Nichols, T. M. (1992). A program for teachers and students: The Junior Great Books Program. *Gifted Child Today, 15*(5), 50–51.

Nichols, T. M. (1993). *A study to determine the effects of the Junior Great Books Program on the interpretive reading skills development of gifted/able learner children.* Paper presented at the annual meeting of the Mid-South Education Research Association, Knoxville, TN.

Olson, M. W., Logan, J., & Lindsey, T. (1989). Early and current reading and spelling practices of gifted spellers. *Reading-Psychology, 10*(2), 189–201.

Paul, R. (1995). *Critical thinking.* Santa Rosa, CA: Critical Thinking Foundation.

Polette, N. (1982). *3 R's for the gifted: Reading, writing and research.* Littleton, CO: Libraries Unlimited.

Polette, N., & Hamlin, M. (1980). *Exploring books with gifted children.* Littleton, CO: Libraries Unlimited.

Purves, A. C. (1993). Setting standards in the language arts and literature classroom and the implications for portfolio assessment. *Educational Assessment, 1*(3), 175–199.

Rakow, S. R. (1991). Young adult literature for honors students? *English Journal, 80*(1), 48–51.

Reif, M. (1995). Encouraging kids to write using a variety of creative ideas can influence children to become prolific writers. *Gifted Child Today, 18*(6), 12–15.

Richards, J. C., & Gipe, J. P. (1993). Spelling lessons for gifted language arts students. *Teaching Exceptional Children, 25*(2), 12–15.

Rogers, K. B. (1986). Do the gifted think and learn differently? A review of recent research and its implications for instruction. *Journal for the Education of the Gifted, 10*, 17–39.

Sanders, N. M. (1960). *Classroom questions: What kinds?* New York: Harper & Row.

Schack, G. D. (1989). Self-efficacy as a mediator in the creative productivity of gifted children. *Journal for the Education of the Gifted, 12*, 231–249.

Schug, M. C. (1981). Using the local community to improve citizenship education for the gifted. *Roeper Review, 4*(2), 22–23.

Schunk, D., & Swartz, C. (1992, April). *Goal and feedback during writing strategy instruction with gifted students.* Presentation at the annual meeting of the American Educational Research Association, San Francisco, CA.

Scruggs, T. E., & Mastropieri, M. A. (1985). Spontaneous verbal elaboration in gifted and nongifted youths. *Journal for the Education of the Gifted, 9*, 1–10.

Scruggs, T. E., Mastropieri, M. A., Jorgensen, C., & Monson, J. (1986). Effective mnemonic strategies for gifted learners. *Journal for the Education of the Gifted, 9*, 105–121.

Stepien, W. J., Gallagher, S. A., & Workman, D. (1993). Problem-based learning for traditional and interdisciplinary classrooms. *Journal for the Education of the Gifted, 16*(4), 338–357.

Taba, H. (1962). *Curriculum development, theory and practice.* New York: Harcourt, Brace & World.

Taylor, B. (1996). The study of literature: Insights into human understanding. In J. VanTassel-Baska, D. T. Johnson, & L. N. Boyce (Eds.), *Developing verbal talent* (pp. 75–94). Boston: Allyn & Bacon.

Thompson, M. C., & Thompson, M. B. (1996). Reflections on foreign language study for high able learners. In J. VanTassel-Baska, D. T. Johnson, & L. N. Boyce (Eds.), *Developing verbal talent* (pp. 174–188). Boston: Allyn & Bacon.

Torrance, E. P., & Myers, R. E. (1970). *Creative learning and teaching.* New York: Dodd, Mead.

VanTassel-Baska, J. (1987). The case for teaching Latin to the verbally talented. *Roeper Review, 9*(3), 159–161

VanTassel-Baska, J. (1992). *Planning effective curriculum for the gifted.* Denver, CO: Love.

VanTassel-Baska, J. (1993). *Comprehensive curriculum for gifted learners.* Boston: Allyn & Bacon.

VanTassel-Baska, J., Johnson, D. T., Hughes, C., & Boyce, L. N. (1996). A study of language arts curriculum effectiveness with gifted learners. *Journal for the Education of the Gifted, 19*, 461–480.

Wielkoszewski, G. H. (1992). Why foreign language for the gifted? *Gifted Child Today, 15*(6), 28–30.

Study Questions ⁓

1. What are some major current social studies issues and problems that could be related to historical events?
2. What are major ways of organizing a classroom to facilitate discussion of social studies topics?
3. How might seminars contribute to the development of verbal talent?
4. What is the essence of inquiry activity in the social studies?
5. What are some activities you could use in teaching literature to gifted youth?
6. How could you involve gifted youth in writing to build their motivation for reading and writing?
7. Why should gifted youth study a foreign language?
8. What are some good oral language arts activities?

25

Arts and Humanities for Talented Learners

Joyce VanTassel-Baska

The approach often used in developing curriculum for the gifted is to extend and expand from the core content areas. But the arts and humanities present a unique challenge because they are not so well developed as the curriculum for the core content areas in most schools. Indeed, the curriculum areas of arts and humanities often are given short shrift. Content areas within the arts and humanities are taught as separate disciplines in most school curricula. For example, students are taught history as if it were unrelated to philosophy, language, geography, anthropology, and political science. However, a humanities approach necessarily implies integration among the social sciences, literature, and foreign languages.

The same is true for the arts. Although visual art, writing, speech, and music often are organized as credit courses, rarely is any attempt made to integrate these courses except as extracurricular projects, such as school plays or musicals. Frequently absent from the curricula are dance, sculpture, music composition, and aesthetics.

Given the weak base of arts and humanities in the regular curriculum, we have to develop new curricula for gifted learners that ultimately could be adapted into the core curriculum. This chapter focuses on the need for this curriculum development, on a philosophy to guide its development, on integration of the arts through collaboration, and on humanities approaches.

Why Arts and Humanities for the Gifted? ~

The arts and humanities offer gifted learners a unique opportunity to subject the knowledge, experience, and values they derive from all of their studies to the most rigorous scrutiny in order to develop an individual world view. To achieve this goal, education must provide the following three elements:

1. Learning should be *interpretive or integrative* of the students' knowledge and experience.
2. Learning also should be *universal;* it should move the students toward an understanding of the common culture and the students' own position relative to that culture through the study of art history, aesthetics, and philosophy.
3. Learning should develop *critical thinking* by strengthening the students' ability to question, confront, deliberate, judge, and create alternatives.

The arts often are thought to be of value only for students who have exceptional talent in the fine or performing arts. Nevertheless, exposure to the arts is important for all gifted students. They have greater sensitivities and depths of emotion than do more typical students (Clark, 1990; Hagen, 1980; Hurwitz, 1983) and therefore need corresponding experiences. The arts provide an excellent medium to address these needs. Albert Einstein (1954) eloquently described the importance of an arts and humanities role in development:

> It is not enough to teach man a specialty. Through it he may become a kind of useful machine but not a harmoniously developed personality. It is essential that the student acquire an understanding of and a lively feeling for values. He must acquire a vivid sense of the beautiful and of the morally good. Otherwise he—with his specialized knowledge—more closely resembles a well trained dog than a harmoniously developed person. (p. 172)

The arts and humanities may also be an important avenue to inner peace for gifted students. In answering the life-defining questions of "Who am I?" and "Why do I exist?" students come to see the universality of their struggle in unique ways. Piechowski (1993) noted the role of personal expression in enhancing inner growth and transformation, a role superbly filled by the arts applied to psychology. Moreover, just as the arts contribute to self-growth, they also contribute to the growth of civilizations and global understanding (Williams, 1991) in important ways.

The humanities are important, particularly for gifted learners, because they are by nature integrative, interdisciplinary, paradoxical, and cultural, as a humanities approach to curriculum and instruction for gifted learners must be. The humanities offer an epistemological view of information, which in its highest form can offer gifted learners opportunities to generate new theories. According to Piaget (1981), the epistemological point of view acknowledges:

> how the construction of a new theory is far from being reducible to the accumulation of data, but necessitates an extremely complex structuring of interpretive ideas which

are linked to the facts and which enrich them by framing them in a context. But as the ideas which have guided even the discovery of the observables, every alteration at one point gives rise to a modification of the system as a whole. This process maintains both the coherence of the system and at the same time the adequacy of its fit to the data of experience and observation. (p. viii)

In its simplest form, epistemology is the study of the structure of knowledge. By using a humanities approach to teaching the gifted, we expose them to a holistic view of knowledge that focuses on the interpretation of ideas, issues, and problems in the respective disciplines (VanTassel-Baska, 1993).

How Do We Differentiate an Arts Curriculum? ~

The term *arts* refers to the major fine and performing arts, including music, visual art, creative writing, dance, and theater. Public-school offerings in the arts are widely disparate. Secondary schools usually have more highly developed courses of study in these disciplines than do elementary schools. Typically, larger school districts have more arts instruction in the core curriculum than smaller districts have.

In 1994, the national content standards in the arts were released to the public. They represent an important collaborative effort across arts areas of national organizations and practicing artists to bring together the key knowledge base, skills, and attitudes that are important for fostering in American schools (*Education Week,* 1995). A sample of these standards for the middle elementary level in the areas of visual art and music is presented in Table 25.1. The unexcerpted standards encompass dance and dramatic expression as well.

The emphasis of the arts standards is on the equal importance of appreciating and performing in each of the areas. They also clearly stress the importance of treating the arts as intellectual disciplines, a role they typically have not been assigned in schools. For gifted programs, these standards represent a major step forward in the primacy of the arts in effective learning. Significant program efforts can be developed for gifted students in the interrelated arts as well as in individual domains, using the standards as a base. With such efforts, the artistically talented as well as the intellectually gifted could move on the continuum of arts learning from novice to expert (Clark & Zimmerman, 1987).

In any event, teachers of gifted students are not expected to teach all of these disciplines. Rather, the expansion and enrichment of existing offerings from the core curriculum can best be achieved when teachers act in a facilitating role. This usually occurs when a combination of the following approaches is used:

1. Organize field trips to arts facilities for all gifted students, using whatever community resource people are available to provide the expertise.
2. Arrange for artistically talented students from the elementary level to attend secondary arts classes.

Table 25.1 ~
Sample of Standards in Visual Arts and Music, Grades 5–8

Visual Arts	Music
Standard 1. Understanding and applying media, techniques, and processes	**Standard 1.** Singing, alone and with others, a varied repertoire of music
Standard 2. Using knowledge of structures and functions	**Standard 2.** Performing on instruments, alone and with others, a varied repertoire of music
Standard 3. Choosing and evaluating a range of subject matter, symbols, and ideas	**Standard 3.** Improvising melodies, variations, and accompaniments
Standard 4. Understanding the visual arts in relation to history and cultures	**Standard 4.** Composing and arranging music within specified guidelines
Standard 5. Reflecting upon and assessing the characteristics and merits of their work and the work of others	**Standard 5.** Reading and notating music
Standard 6. Making connections between visual arts and other disciplines	

Note: From Struggling for Standards, *Education Week* Special Report, April 1995.

---

3. Have artistically talented students hold seminars or group discussions with other gifted students to share products or performances as well as their approaches, thoughts, and feelings in the creative process.
4. Arrange for mentorships in the arts that provide ongoing relationships between gifted students and artists in the community.
5. Cluster-group artistically talented students by discipline, and arrange for master classes, magnet schools, and individual instruction.
6. Generate outlets for the students' work or performances through contacts with commercial galleries, dance companies, and music or theatrical groups; submit creative writing for publication.

In addition to the facilitator role, teachers of the gifted can make a unique curriculum contribution by promoting the idea of collaboration. Other means of integration are possible through study in such areas as art appreciation, art history, and aesthetics.

What Is Collaboration in the Arts? ~

Collaboration implies a search for a common ground, a common vocabulary, a place or framework where different artistic disciplines intersect. Once this dialogue has begun, the artists proceed to create a work that goes beyond a mere layering of disciplines to an interweaving that produces a whole greater than the sum of its parts. In the process, each discipline retains a quality and an integrity of its own.

The steps to create collaboration begin with cross-disciplinary study. This typically is limited to the study of two, or a maximum of three, artistic disciplines. Specifically, curriculum facilitators strive to:

1. Develop a common vocabulary that applies across the disciplines (e.g., space, light, tone, rhythm, improvisation, centering).
2. Encourage experimentation, exploration, and risk taking in each of the disciplines for all of the students.
3. Develop the idea that the students are the source of their art, through self-expression and self-discovery, as they experiment and explore the disciplines (differentiate between the external environment and the internal environment).
4. Introduce the concept of critique through a focus on performances or products with suggestions for improvement.
5. Develop a clear understanding of the importance of revision after critique. First performances of products are merely "rough drafts" from which artists work together to critique and revise their collaborative work.

To meet the criteria for a collaborative effort as opposed to a layering of disciplines, the following questions should be posed as the work is in progress and in its final form:

1. *Does the collaboration find common elements in each discipline?* A successful collaboration somehow identifies an idea, a theme, a word, or a concept about which each discipline has something to contribute.
2. *Can the separate elements from each discipline stand on their own?* A successful collaboration is made of parts from each artistic discipline that have their own integrity and quality.
3. *Are the separate elements of each discipline even better for being a part of the collaboration as a whole?* The collaboration should be greater than the sum of its parts.

The collaboration itself will take on a life of its own and will carry the students along with the momentum of its creative energy. The final product will not likely look much like the teacher's ideas, but a substantial amount of teacher guidance is necessary throughout its creation. The students will believe that they can claim a great deal of ownership of the collaboration, for they have been swept along in the excitement and satisfaction of developing the idea to fruition. A model program of this nature has operated in Denver for several years (Clayton Foundation, 1991).

How Is a Humanities Approach Developed? ~

The first step in developing a humanities program for gifted students is to mobilize the human resources around the philosophy and goals of the integration of knowledge and epistemology. Although teachers often view the integration of subject areas as overwhelming, beginning with two disciplines can be exciting and satisfying for teachers and students alike. Involving the students as partners with teachers in planning a humanities program is an excellent way to develop in all involved a sense of ownership.

Gifted students feel empowered by their own use of knowledge and experience. This empowerment affirms that the arts and humanities are an intrinsic component of their intellectual and emotional development and, as such, must be a part of any well-rounded education (Piirto, 1992). Many gifted students apply their knowledge situations in unique ways. This may be the essence of "creativity," which can serve as a broad-based theme for study. Through biographical examination of famous creative people, students can understand and experiment with their own creative ideas. They can see the influences of personal interest, knowledge, emotion, and intellect interacting in the lives of major contributors to a field of study. A good resource is *Mathematical People* (Albers & Alexanderson, 1985). This book presents interviews with 25 of the most famous living mathematicians in the world and gives personal vignettes that provide insights into the lives of these creative thinkers. Gifted students can use this book as a model to interview teachers, community members, or one another.

Teachers of the gifted again can act in the facilitator or convener role by bringing subject-area teachers together to begin planning interdisciplinary activities. Interdisciplinary seminars for gifted students can be organized around themes. Such seminars usually require administrative support for scheduling and arranging credit at the secondary level. At the elementary level, teachers usually have more flexibility in scheduling and implementing interdisciplinary studies. Some programs for the verbally gifted are based on a humanities model using seminars and independent study.

Smith (1992) presented an important model for understanding the conjunctive role played by the humanities in learning. He organized the roles of communication, creation, continuity, and criticism as the umbrella emphasis in an arts and humanities curriculum (see Figure 25.1). He also suggested that a set of fundamental questions be posed in relationship to studying a particular work in the arts and humanities, questions that lead us to think about these subjects in distinctly integrative ways. These questions are:

1. Who made it?
2. How was it made?
3. When was it made?
4. For whom was it made?
5. What is its message or meaning, if any?
6. What is its style?
7. What is the quality of experience it affords?
8. What was its place in the culture in which it was made?
9. What is its place in the culture or society of today?
10. What peculiar problems does it present to understanding and appreciation?

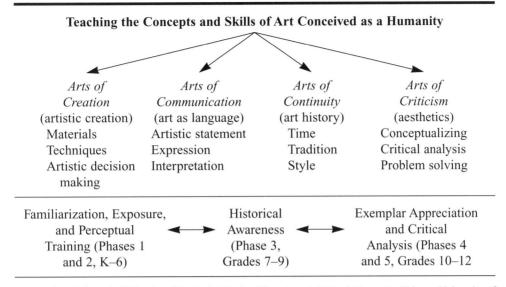

Teaching the Concepts and Skills of Art Conceived as a Humanity

Arts of Creation (artistic creation)	*Arts of Communication* (art as language)	*Arts of Continuity* (art history)	*Arts of Criticism* (aesthetics)
Materials	Artistic statement	Time	Conceptualizing
Techniques	Expression	Tradition	Critical analysis
Artistic decision making	Interpretation	Style	Problem solving

Familiarization, Exposure, and Perceptual Training (Phases 1 and 2, K–6)	Historical Awareness (Phase 3, Grades 7–9)	Exemplar Appreciation and Critical Analysis (Phases 4 and 5, Grades 10–12

Note: Adapted from A. W. Levi and R. A. Smith, *Art Education: A Critical Necessity* (Urbana: University of Illinois Press, 1991. Slightly edited.)

Figure 25.1 ～
A Percipience Curriculum (K–12)

Teachers of the gifted can engage their students in such inquiry on a regular basis because the subjects of the arts and humanities are all of the products of humankind, and thus such inquiry has relevance to any particular area of study.

Summary ～

The approaches to arts and humanities that were presented in this chapter are intended to be starting points for planning programs for gifted students. Such approaches are liberating to students, who too often are exposed to right-answer learning, and provide for individual growth through an understanding of the interrelatedness of different disciplines.

References ～

Albers, D. J., & Alexanderson, G. L. (Eds.). (1985). *Mathematical people: Profiles and interviews.* Cambridge, MA: Birkhauser Boston.

Clark, B. (1990). *Growing up gifted.* Columbus, OH: Charles E. Merrill.

Clark, G., & Zimmerman, E. (1987). *Resources for educating artistically talented students.* Syracuse, NY: Syracuse University Press.

Clayton Foundation. (1991). *Collaborative arts program*. Denver, CO: Author.

Education Week. (1995). Special report: Struggling for standards. Washington, DC: Author.

Einstein, A. (1954). *Ideas and opinions*. New York: Crown.

Hagen, E. (1980). *Identification of the gifted*. New York: Teachers College Press.

Hurwitz, A. (1983). *The gifted and talented in art*. Worcester, MA: Davis Publications.

Piaget, J. (1981). In H. Gruber, *Darwin on man* (2nd ed., p. viii). Chicago: University of Chicago Press.

Piechowski, M. (1993). Is inner transformation a creative process? *Creativity Research Journal, 6*(1 & 2), 89–98.

Piirto, J. (1992). *Understanding those who create*. Columbus, OH: Ohio Psychology Press.

Smith, R. (1992). Toward percipience: A humanities curriculum for arts and education. In B. Reimer & R. Smith (Eds.), *The arts, education, and aesthetic knowing* (pp. 51–69). Chicago: University of Chicago Press.

VanTassel-Baska, J. (1993). *Comprehensive curriculum for gifted learners* (2nd ed., p. viii). Boston: Allyn & Bacon.

Williams, H. (1991). *The language of civilization: The vital role of arts in education*. New York: President's Committee on Arts and Humanities.

Study Questions ⌇

1. How might you use a broad-based theme to emphasize the arts in a program for the gifted?

2. What is the role of arts specialists in programs for the gifted?

3. Using two common arts areas, such as visual art and music, how might a teacher of the gifted work with the music and art teachers to develop a collaborative project?

4. How does epistemology relate to the teaching of higher level thinking skills?

5. How could you use professors from a nearby college and local artists to support the infusion of the arts and humanities into programs for the gifted?

6. How might you use a humanities approach to have gifted students critique their own experience with education in the schools?

Introduction to Part Four

Helping the Gifted and Talented Achieve Excellence

The final section of this book focuses on the personalized services necessary to help gifted students develop their talents well over the course of their years of formal schooling. It portrays the roles of various facilitators of the talent development process—teachers, mentors, parents, and others—as critical to the actualization of ability and talent. The types of support needed from these individuals is explored in some depth.

When education is understood in the expanded context of perpetual self-discovery and lifelong learning, the opportunities for impacting the gifted student extend far beyond the classroom. The Seeley chapter on facilitation (Chapter 26) discusses the concept of facilitators for the gifted—individuals in the child's home, school, or community who can participate in partnerships to foster full attainment of the child's potential. Individual teachers and parents are linchpins in such a network.

Although political support and advocacy for gifted education are sporadic in the United States, there has been increasing emphasis on the certification of teachers of the gifted. Specialized courses in gifted education at the graduate level and advanced degrees with an emphasis in gifted education have improved teacher preparation for working with talented youngsters. Among the most common traits cited for teachers of the gifted are having a high degree of intelligence and knowledge about the subject matter and emotional maturity. These characteristics clearly contribute to serving as role models for gifted children.

Research demonstrates that parents who are actively involved in their child's learning positively influence the child's success (Hoover-Dempsey & Sandler, 1995). In supporting talent development, a parent or relative will be particularly helpful if he or she has a personal interest in the talent area, shows that the talent is valued, rewards development of the talent through home activities, and assumes that the child wishes to learn the talent emphasized. Parents who approach schools in helping ways and schools that value the contribution of parents to the educational process offer the best framework for an effective collaboration.

Other individuals who can play significant roles in the facilitation process are school psychologists, counselors, and mentors. Both personal and professional mentors have been shown to be highly effective in guiding gifted children toward productive and fulfilling career goals.

An updated chapter on counseling gifted students, Chapter 27, is also contained in this section. In this chapter, VanTassel-Baska reviews the recent literature on the social-emotional, academic, and career counseling issues of gifted learners and provides specific strategies for addressing special concerns about self-concept as well as the other core issues. The chapter stresses the importance of having someone in the school context assume the role of counselor for the gifted so that their affective needs and issues are given every consideration.

The final chapter of the book, Chapter 28, also by VanTassel-Baska, highlights common and uncommon views of excellence as it is understood in our society. The author discusses how difficult it is for American schools to focus scarce resources on a segment of the population that appears to be achieving excellence, and she also presents a final case for encouraging exemplary performance and achievement from those students capable of such performance. Exemplary performance should be encouraged not as an example for others to model but, rather, as a symbol of what human beings are capable of doing and being.

References ∿

Hoover-Dempsey, K. V., & Sandler, H. M. (1995). Parental involvement in children's education: Why does it make a difference? *Teachers College Record, 97*(2), 310–331.

26

Facilitators for Talented Students

Ken Seeley

Jerome and Grant are two brothers who grew up in the same family. They are only a year apart in age. As youth, they lived at home with their mother and another brother in a low-income inner-city neighborhood. Grant was the oldest of the children and he was always in trouble. He joined the neighborhood gang when he was 12 and had a history of four arrests for drug dealing and violence by the time he was 16. He rarely went to school, and when he did, he did not do well. Jerome, although only a year younger, liked school and was able to achieve in advanced classes in math. He loved chess, was president of the school chess club in middle school, and went to chess competitions all over the city. He managed to avoid the gangs and drugs in his neighborhood. How is it that Jerome did so much better even though both boys had the same parents and lived in the same home in the same neighborhood? The answer is that there were facilitators in Jerome's life who saw his assets and helped develop them. This made him more resilient to the negative pressures around him. Unfortunately, Grant did not have adults investing in him except to recruit him into gang life and crime. The role of facilitators in the life of talented youth can be pivotal in their long-term outcomes.

During the course of childhood, many significant persons impact on a child's development. In the case of gifted children, this array of significant people and the roles they play can have a great effect on the realization of the children's potential. The significant people involved in educating gifted children transcend formal education. In his landmark work, *Excellence,* Gardner (1961) stated:

> Education in the formal sense is only a part of the society's larger task of abetting the individual's intellectual, emotional and moral growth. What we must reach for is a conception of perpetual self-discovery, perpetual reshaping to realize one's best self, to be the person one could be. (p. 162)

In examining the role of significant persons in a gifted child's environment, this chapter addresses the facilitators of learning. The discussion is limited to certain major groups, even though others not included might have a significant role. It is possible that Einstein would never have reached his potential had he not had an uncle who played mathematics games with him as a child. Or the nontraditional teachers influenced by Pestalozzi who taught Einstein in a special school might have stimulated his success. Rarely does only one facilitator make the difference in the realization of potential. Rather, a network of individuals influences a child's learning both positively and negatively, as do a good deal of chance factors.

The discussion in this chapter examines the roles of teachers, parents, mentors, and support personnel. Selection of the term *facilitators* is based on Gardner's premise of "perpetual self-discovery," which can be facilitated but not created. The ultimate responsibility for learning must rest with the child. The facilitators, however, must be sensitive to learning. As Piaget (1970) stated, "Remember also that each time one prematurely teaches a child something he could have discovered for himself, that child is kept from inventing it, and consequently from understanding it completely" (p. 271).

Teachers as Facilitators ~

What Are the Roots of Teacher Preparation for Instructing Gifted Learners?

The preparation of teachers in our country began with little awareness of the problems of special students. Modeled after the European pattern, preparation for teaching in upper-level schools focused on gaining knowledge of subject matter and the criteria for mastery of content. Teachers were academic specialists, and educational settings were highly competitive in nature (Wilson, 1958). This educational philosophy dominated the early years of the United States and was, as stated by Wilson (1958):

> only slightly affected either by the movement for the training of teachers that developed during the nineteenth century or by the anxiety of public schoolmen over the differences in learning ability among the children to be taught in the established system of free universal education. (p. 365)

While this emphasis was developing, the special needs of bright and able children were also surfacing. Pressures were mounting for their academic accomplishment. Gallagher (1960) later described this growing concern:

> The present nation-wide concern about the education of gifted children apparently stems from three main sources. First, there is the American educational tradition of being concerned with individual differences of all types and adapting to them. Second, there is the undeniable impact of world crises that helped us to become aware that the country's future is related to the educational future of these children. Third, there are the needs of a complex society for a vast reservoir of highly educated and intelligent leaders in the arts and sciences. (p. 1)

Tannenbaum (1979) postulated that the half-decade following Sputnik in 1957 and the last half of the 1970s might be viewed as peak periods of interest in gifted education. Between these peaks were only occasional bright spots for gifted and talented students and their potential teachers. Teacher preparation institutions for the most part reflected society's interest in low-functioning, poorly motivated, and socially handicapped children.

This alternating or cyclical interest in the gifted was aptly described by Gardner (1961): "The critical lines of tension in our society are between emphasis on individual performance and restraints on individual performance" (p. 33). The conflict was rooted in society's dual commitment to excellence and equality in education. To foster excellence meant encouraging the gifted to work up to their potential ability, but if such efforts necessitated special educational services or teachers, they were under fire for being elitist. Conversely, support for egalitarianism, while providing increased attention to lower status students, threatened to deprive gifted students of full academic advantage to develop their own potentialities. Tannenbaum (1979) hypothesized: "Perhaps because we cannot live exclusively with excellence or egalitarianism for any length of time and tend to counterpose rather than reconcile them, we seem fated to drift from one to the other indefinitely" (p. 6).

Teacher education institutions reflected this fleeting interest in gifted education over 4 decades ago. A 1951 survey of all teacher education institutions, conducted by Wilson (1953), attempted to determine the availability of gifted education courses. Of the 400 replies, 2% indicated that they offered "required" or "elective" special courses on gifted education at the undergraduate level, and 5% reported offering courses in graduate programs. A little more than half of the responding universities stated that material dealing with the gifted was included in discussion of individual differences in courses such as education and child psychology, principles of education, and methods. Several universities utilized special summer session programs, particularly at the graduate level, to provide practicing teachers with courses in gifted education.

Davis (1954), Wilson (1958), and Snider (1960) found very few institutions offering a specific sequence of courses related to teaching the gifted. The programs at Kent State University, Hunter College, and Pennsylvania State University were exceptional at that time in that they included sequential coursework, advanced study, practica, and graduate degree offerings in this area.

What Are Teachers' Attitudes Toward the Gifted?

Researchers found that teachers with no special preparation or background in gifted education were uninterested in or even hostile toward gifted students (Wiener, 1960) and that teachers with experience working in special programs for, or doing in-service presentations about, the gifted tended to be more enthusiastic about them (Justman, 1951; Wiener, 1960). Thomas (1973) found that general education classroom teachers' attitudes were frequently negative and filled with misconceptions concerning giftedness. They further implied that these biased attitudes were forcing gifted students to modify their classroom behavior, hide their real talents, and imitate the "less bright, more normal" child.

What Are Characteristics of Teachers of the Gifted?

Authorities generally agree that successful teachers of the gifted have the following personality characteristics:

- Maturity and experience; self-confidence
- High intelligence
- Avocational interests that are intellectual in nature
- High achievement needs; desire for intellectual growth
- Favorable attitude toward gifted children
- Systematic, imaginative, flexible, and creative in attitudes and responses
- Sense of humor
- Willingness to be a "facilitator" rather than a "director" of learning
- Capacity for hard work; willingness to devote extra time and effort to teaching
- Wide background of general knowledge; specific areas of expertise (especially secondary teachers)
- Belief in and understanding of individual differences

(Abraham, 1958; Bishop, 1968; Davis, 1954; Gear, 1979; Gold, 1976; Gowan & Demos, 1964; Maker, 1975; Marland, 1971; Mirman, 1964; Newland, 1976; Torrance, 1963; Ward, 1961).

Even though these traits are seen as desirable for all teachers, they repeatedly are listed as *essential* for teachers of the gifted. Maker (1975), in an attempt to narrow the list, identified two absolute necessities for a successful teacher of the gifted: (1) a high degree of intelligence and knowledge about the subject matter being taught, and (2) emotional maturity coupled with a strong self-concept. In his review, Gold (1976) identified the same two prerequisite characteristics (high-level ability and ego strength) and pointed out the direct relationship between them.

Much has been written concerning the skills and qualifications of good teachers of gifted learners. Seeley (1979) conducted a national survey of teacher competencies needed for education of the gifted. In this study a questionnaire was sent to universities, principals, and teachers involved in gifted education. Of 21 choices, respondents placed the following five competencies as highest in importance:

1. Higher cognitive teaching and questioning
2. Curriculum modification strategies
3. Special curriculum development strategies
4. Diagnostic-prescriptive teaching skills
5. Student counseling strategies

Seeley also found agreement among the respondents that teachers of the gifted should have a master's degree in the field, experience in the general education classroom, and a variety of special competencies for teaching gifted children.

What Is the Nature of Training for Teachers of the Gifted?

According to Hershey (1979), "Students enrolled in gifted child education coursework need assurance that their training will be as qualitatively differentiated as the methodologies they are taught to use with gifted children" (p. 13). Literature indicates that preparation programs for teachers of the gifted should expect not only the mastery of concepts but also application to real situations and analysis, synthesis, and evaluation of current philosophical approaches (Feldhusen, 1973; Hershey, 1979; Newland, 1962; Rice, 1970; Waskin, 1979). In his description of teacher training programs, Schnur (1977) stated that the programs should "reflect some features of prescription and some flexibility...some of pedagogy and some of content. Perhaps the real quest is to train the teacher of the gifted to become a true master teacher" (p. 9).

Preservice training options include both undergraduate and graduate-level university-based education programs for teachers preparing for direct service with gifted children. Periodically, surveys have been conducted to determine which colleges and universities offer courses or degree programs in gifted education (Guy, 1979; Laird & Kowalski, 1972; Seeley, 1979). Results have shown constant change, with a steady increase of opportunities available for teachers both in numbers of courses offered and in number of institutions offering training (Maker, 1975). The trend has been to offer graduate rather than undergraduate degree programs, with some emphasis placed on knowledge of gifted children for all certified teachers (Maker, 1975; Seeley, 1979). This practice has ensured that teachers receive a solid background of liberal arts education before being offering specialization.

During 1981, Seeley and Hultgren (1982) conducted a study of teacher competencies and training. The primary purpose of this research was to determine the competencies or skill areas essential for teachers of gifted children. The secondary purpose was to determine to what extent university course offerings and pre- and in-service training programs have prepared practitioners, currently active in the field of gifted education, in the recognized competency areas. Higher education programs for teachers/administrators of gifted programs existed in at least 140 colleges and universities in more than 40 states. The types of program option varied from one or two courses through entire degree programs at the master's, specialist, and doctoral levels. Most common was the master's program. Many responding universities indicated that their offerings presently were being expanded to include degree programs to meet certification standards. The number and types of professional programs in gifted education appeared to be on the increase at the time of this study.

In the Seeley and Hultgren study, a large sample of practitioners (N = 528) representing 48 states also provided information. Teachers of the gifted, administrators in gifted programs, and a variety of instructional, curriculum, and support personnel were represented. The most common training options for teachers were in-service and staff development classes and summer or workshop courses. Half of the sample practitioner group (primarily the administrators and support personnel) held graduate degrees in education with emphasis on the gifted. On the whole, the group was experienced, primarily coming from the general education or special education classroom, and seemed to be adequately prepared to teach in gifted programs. The practitioners rated competencies for teachers of the gifted as follows:

1. Knowledge of nature and needs of the gifted
2. Skill in promoting higher cognitive thinking abilities and questioning techniques
3. Ability to develop methods and materials for the gifted
4. Knowledge of affective/psychological needs of the gifted
5. Skill in facilitating independent research and study skills
6. Ability to develop creative problem solving
7. Skill in individualizing teaching techniques
8. Knowledge of approaches to extension and enrichment of subject areas
9. Supervised practical experience in teaching a group of gifted students

Effective in-service training of teachers is an important activity for raising the skill levels of professionals so that they can provide appropriate education for gifted children. Stedman (1987), following his review of the effective schools research of the mid-1980s, formulated some guidelines based on successful practice. He stated that:

> most effective schools used practical, on the job training...tailored to the specific needs of staff members and students. Effective schools gave demonstration lessons to inexperienced teachers; provided extra preparation periods for novices during which the novices often observed experienced teachers; videotaped teachers' performances to help improve instruction and evaluations; and helped teachers (select) materials and teaching techniques. (p. 220)

These suggestions have strong implications for changing the typical in-service presentations and for training high-level gifted educators who can provide these types of training experiences for teachers.

What Training Should Be Required of All Teachers?

The Seeley and Hultgren (1982) research indicated that more than three fourths of university program directors and practitioners in gifted education believed all professionally trained and certified teachers should have exposure to education of the gifted. Respondents preferred a separate semester or quarter course addressing topics in gifted education for all teachers rather than a shorter unit within general education coursework, as is currently the more common practice. Hesitation on the part of some universities might reflect problems involved in adopting new curriculum requirements for existing programs or perhaps the desire to isolate gifted education as a separate program or graduate-level concentration.

With the current attention to gifted education, an introductory course addressing the major competency areas would seem desirable for all teachers. Practitioners were highly in favor of this concept, perhaps because a majority had first been classroom teachers themselves. Practitioners realized that when full-time special programs do not exist for gifted students, general education classroom teachers must assume a great responsibility for the affective and cognitive needs of gifted students. Even when such programs do exist, teachers outside the gifted classroom greatly benefit from increased understanding of identification procedures and special strategies for gifted students.

What Changes Are Needed in Training?

Institutions of higher education should offer a variety of quality program options to prepare teachers of the gifted. These programs should be taught by qualified faculty members and should address as many of the recognized competency areas as possible. Graduate degree programs covering a variety of delivery systems are most appropriate. For institutions with established programs, new areas should be emphasized, including counseling, leadership training, cultural differences, current research, underachievers, parent/community relations, and educational technological developments. Universities must design programs for teachers of the gifted that are competency-based and sensitive to the changing needs of the profession.

To ensure quality programs and professional security, practitioners working in gifted education should seek and demand high-level training. They should have available to them credit courses, degree programs, or in-service options based on relevant needs and competencies. Practitioners should continue to express concern about areas of training they deem important that have not been covered adequately in education programs. Program administrators should expect that new personnel will be of high caliber, will most likely be experienced teachers, and certainly should be especially trained to work with gifted students.

The competencies listed in the literature should be recognized as a minimal level of skill or knowledge to be required of teachers of gifted students. These lists of competencies, in addition to personal characteristics and experiences, might be used to evaluate prospective teachers according to specific program needs.

Further, national standards formulated by the National Association for Gifted Children (reported in Feldhusen & Bruch, 1985) should be helpful to universities in planning training programs and to state departments of education for certification. Close coordination among schools, higher education, and state government is necessary to implement these standards effectively.

Parents as Facilitators ~

Recently, there has been a resurgence of interest in parent involvement in education that has been driven by parents' interests in choices regarding their children's education (U.S. Dept. of Education, 1994). This has extended to a large expansion of the home school movement. There is clear indication that parents who are actively involved in their children's education augment the children's success in learning.

What Are the Characteristics of Parents of the Gifted?

Goertzel and Goertzel (1962) reported a number of characteristics of parents of eminent people they studied. Their retrospective study revealed the following characteristics of the families:

- Tended to be small families
- Usually had high socioeconomic status

- Were Caucasian and lived in an urban area
- Parents were professional
- Family roots were English, German, Jewish, and Oriental
- Were often troubled homes with interpersonal conflicts

The parents of the eminent people:

- Placed high value on education and learning (not necessarily schooling)
- Fostered an enjoyment of learning
- Provided recognition and respect for their child's ability
- Held strong opinions on social issues
- Had little tolerance for rebellion in their child
- Were dominating (mother or father)
- Held negative attitudes toward school and teachers

However, these characteristics must be viewed with some caution. The subjects of these studies were a small representation of gifted persons. The vast majority of gifted children we see in schools will never achieve the same level of national or international eminence as those reported by the Goertzels. These cautions are not intended to diminish their potential contributions to society but, rather, to indicate the limited generalizability of family characteristics of eminent persons.

General themes concerning parents as reported elsewhere in the literature tend to both support and contradict the Goertzels' work. Some of the common themes were (1) high degree of respect for the fathers who were professionals, (2) parents' sincere love of learning, and (3) stability of marriages (Roe, 1952; Terman, 1954).

In research by Bloom and Sosniak (1981), parents were found to have a great influence on the talent development of young eminent persons. Bloom and Sosniak studied 120 persons who had distinguished themselves in three general areas: artistic talent, psychomotor talent, and cognitive talent. The groups included pianists and sculptors, Olympic swimmers and tennis players, and research mathematicians and research neurologists. The authors reported common findings for the home and parenting styles of the majority of their subjects. These findings were that (1) a parent or relative had a personal interest in the child's talent area, (2) parents provided a model in valuing the talent, (3) parents encouraged and rewarded development of the talent through home activities, and (4) parents "assumed that the children would wish to learn the talent emphasized by the parents" (pp. 87–88). These results tend to support the previously cited research of parents of eminent people. No aversive or negative influences, however, were reported in the research.

Research by Cornell and Grossberg (1987) used a family environment scale to determine family characteristics that differentiate gifted children from other children. These authors found a causal relationship between environment and the gifted child's personality adjustment. Specifically, they found that family members who interacted cooperatively with minimum conflict and maximum freedom for personal expression were the most important dynamics in the environment. Furthermore, they found that neither the degree of structure imposed nor the subject of the family activities was as important to personality development as the cooperative interaction component. They stated, "We are led to the conclusion...that it is not what parents do with their children, but how they do it which is the most important to the child's personality adjustment" (p. 64).

The inaccurate stereotype of the parent of the gifted child as the "involved" parent as seen by the school must also be addressed. Factors such as parents' education, income, marital status, and family status are often seen as predictive of parent advocates or "pushy" parents (Hoover-Dempsey & Sandler, 1995). The implied corollary is that the uninvolved, disinterested parents are those with low education level who are from lower income groups and single-parent families. Hoover-Dempsey and Sandler asserted that although these factors tell part of the story, they "do not explain parents' decisions to become involved, their choice of involvement forms, or the effects of the involvement on student outcomes" (pp. 312–313). These authors pointed out that parents' decisions are driven by a mix of their understanding of their parental role, their sense of the importance of helping their children achieve success in school, and their perceptions of their children's learning needs and the school's invitations for involvement. These factors are essential to consider in understanding all parents and particularly parents of gifted learners, who often challenge both the school and the parent in determining their learning needs.

How Should Parents Relate to Schooling?

One of the greatest myths in education is that all parents think their children are gifted. Parents are often so intimidated by this myth that they feel compelled to amass large amounts of evidence of precocity before beginning any discussion of schooling for their child. Some parents seek private formal psychoeducational testing before confronting schools with requests for appropriate programming. Others provide information from home activities to demonstrate high abilities. The 6-year-old child's routine completion of *New York Times* crossword puzzles and the 10-year-old's design of a laser machine to produce holographs are but two examples of children's home activities that parents have reported.

Schooling is often a frustrating experience for parents and their gifted children. Parents expect schools to provide "talent development," but their children usually get "schooling." Bloom and Sosniak (1981) nicely differentiated "schooling" from "talent development," describing schooling as

> highly formalized, even in the early grades. There are written guidelines for what is to be learned and when it is to be learned.... Each individual is instructed as a member of a group with some notion that all are to get as nearly equal treatment as the teacher and the instructional material can supply. (p. 89)

Talent development, however, is instruction that is usually on a one-to-one basis with the instructor, who individually sets standards and timelines for mastery. According to Bloom and Sosniak, "In talent development, each child was seen as unique...and there was continual adjustment to the child learning the talent" (p. 89).

Some schools come closer than others in individualizing instruction. Some have special programs for the gifted. But rarely do we find intense instruction in talent development when we look to schools. With varying degrees of success, parents have advocated and must continue to advocate accommodations for their children. Public schools have the best resources to do the job. Mobilizing these resources is the greatest challenge we face in educating the gifted.

What Should Schools Be Doing with Parents?

Parents can be either a formidable threat to teachers and administrators or productive partners in the evolution of schools. Schools should educate parents and should also be open to learning from parents. This two-way education must provide a process for change that is evolutionary, not revolutionary. Schools can enlist parents' support through active involvement rather than passive paternalism. Parents can approach schools in a helping, rather than demanding, way. Parents need to use developmentally appropriate involvement strategies with their children around school tasks. Schools can be helpful in informing parents of the impact of advanced development on children's learning to promote an understanding of the often uneven developmental needs of gifted children. Also there needs to be a good fit between parents' involvement and school expectations for parents. If school expectations are minimal or defensive toward parents' overtures to be involved, there is often a breakdown in parent support for education. This can translate to the child who observes negative attitudes toward school from the parent and can result in an unfortunate cycle of poor relations between home and school for all involved.

Support Personnel as Facilitators ~

What Is the Role of Psychologists?

Psychologists can play a key role in identifying gifted children and in counseling them and their parents. Unfortunately, many psychologists receive little, if any, training related to the gifted. Psychologists usually are exposed to the medical model of looking for deficits through testing. Often they learn about gifted children on the job, and many become quite adept at examining children for strengths and special abilities. The deficit orientation of psychologists has to be overcome through training and experience. The emergence of more school programs for the gifted has necessitated new assignments and new approaches for psychologists. We now are seeing some changes that may be adopted for preservice and in-service training of psychologists.

Psychologists have good skills in intellectual assessment for their professional activity. Their expertise in this area is important in the testing and identification of giftedness. The intellectual assessment, coupled with good individual achievement testing, should culminate in a clear direction for parents and educators. This direction is usually a series of recommendations based on identified strengths and needs.

Psychologists also can serve an important role in counseling parents and gifted children. The psychologists' knowledge of development, learning theory, and interpersonal dynamics can assist in fostering understanding of the intellectual and personality characteristics of gifted children. Precocious behaviors on one hand and normal developmental growth on the other constitute a delicate balance. Psychologists should inform parents, educators, and children about coping with this balance in the most productive ways.

As we learn more through research and experience with gifted learners, psychologists must be involved not only in generating information for this knowledge base but also in translating it into improved assessment and programming. Understanding the uniqueness of gifted children as well as the implications of their giftedness for their normal development is an important role for psychologists.

What Is the Role of School Counselors?

Alexander and Muia (1982) described the special role of school counselors by stating, "Exceptionally bright learners, plagued at times by concomitant problems associated with their giftedness, require the warmth, support, and understanding of competent, caring persons—a job description suited to the school's guidance and counseling personnel" (p. 173). Counselors can provide a unique service in facilitating the growth of gifted students in the school context. Counselors are usually familiar with the academic programming and resources of the school. They can work closely with other support personnel in carrying out the psychologist's recommendations in planning for the gifted child's academic and social life.

To become "environmental engineers," counselors must be sensitive to the unique needs of the gifted. Scheduling appropriate classes, matching student needs with teacher styles, and counseling parents are just a few key services counselors provide in creating a growth environment. They also must be aware of the long-term implications of educational and career planning. This is indeed a complex task for these busy professionals. Counselors often are burdened with heavy caseloads, which necessitates employing special approaches to organizing services for special populations of learners such as the gifted.

Realizing the limitations of time, counselors must marshal all the help they can get from a variety of resources. Some approaches counselors use to extend their services include:

1. Setting up a teacher-adviser program for gifted students, in which a key teacher the student likes, who teaches in an area of interest of the student, serves as the adviser in planning courses, activities, and perhaps mentorships
2. Organizing groups for the gifted, wherein these students come together periodically to discuss problems and share experiences concerning the academic and social life of the school
3. Establishing a career education resource center so that gifted students can explore careers through guided reading and can identify appropriate community mentors for visitations
4. Providing a special information file for the gifted to explain programs such as Advanced Placement, CLEP (College Level Examination Program) exams, National Merit Scholarships, universities' honors programs, and so on
5. Organizing gifted students to create a "survival package" for new gifted students entering the school that gives insights into "good" teachers, special access to labs and computers, special clubs and extracurricular activities, and names and phone numbers of other gifted students available as personal resources

All of these strategies can help counselors extend their services through self-directed, peer-directed, and teacher-directed activities. Organizing the processes will take time, but once the processes are in place, the investment should pay off.

Buescher (1987) presented an excellent model for a counseling process for the gifted. The model includes curriculum considerations as well as group and individual counseling. By focusing on the critical issues in adolescence, the model gives the counselor or teacher intervention strategies for all students as well as for the gifted learner.

Silverman (1993) provided an excellent model of counseling as developmental and preventive. She pointed out that individual counseling is not usually practicable and stated, "Preventive counseling groups can be set up by the school counselor or gifted education specialist.... Counseling needs to be seen as a positive support system for healthy self-development." (p. 74).

Unfortunately, the services of counselors usually are restricted to the secondary level. Those schools that have elementary counselors are in a good position to utilize vertical planning for gifted students. For all schools, the counselor's role is an important one to utilize in programming for the gifted. The challenge lies in mobilizing these resources productively.

Mentors as Facilitators ⌇

Who Are Mentors for the Gifted?

Anyone can be a mentor to the gifted child given a careful match of interests and style. Teachers and parents are constantly surprised at whom children identify as mentors. In a general sense, a mentor is a person the child admires who provides a role model in some area of human endeavor and who stimulates and respects the child. The role varies from hero to colleague but always implies admiration and respect. Pleiss and Feldhusen (1995) pointed out the distinction between mentor, role model, and hero. The hero is admired from afar with rarely any contact. Heroes can be a source of inspiration or awakening interests for the gifted child. A role model is someone known to the gifted child and with whom the child has contact. Finally, a mentor is someone who has an intense and personal relationship with the child that can influence the child on a sustained basis.

From the school's standpoint, mentors for gifted children usually are identified by teachers who wish to extend classroom instruction using key individuals in the community. This assignment of child to community resource person assumes a mentor relationship. If we keep the preceding definition in mind, however, this assignment does not always meet the child's standards for a mentor. The term is used loosely in gifted education. We should think of two dimensions of the term. In the jargon of gifted education, a mentor is a resource person, usually from the community, who can provide supplemental educational experiences in some area of expertise. This person may be a computer analyst, an artist, or an urban geographer. Whether the child perceives this person as a mentor is subject to individual interpretation, but rarely does a community resource person become a true mentor for a child.

We in gifted education must explain the full range of mentor relationships to gifted children. They should understand that a community resource person may be called a mentor for program purposes but that the child has other significant, personal mentors—parent, relative, neighbor, teacher, or other.

The role of mentors in the development of eminent persons has been significant. Research on adult development also stresses the importance of mentors in personal and career success (Feldman, 1991; Goertzel & Goertzel, 1962; Levinson, Darrow, Klein, Levinson, & McKee, 1978; Prilliman & Richardson, 1989).

What Are the Roles of Mentors?

The role of mentor as discussed here follows the reasoning already set forth. The *personal mentor* could be anyone the gifted student identifies as having a major influence on him or her. The *resource person* is someone a school program might identify to work with a gifted student.

The Personal Mentor   Levinson et al. (1978) provided excellent insights into the role of the personal mentor. The mentor may be a *teacher* who enhances the student's skills and intellectual development. A mentor may be a *sponsor* who uses his or her influence to facilitate the child's advancement. A mentor may be a *host and guide* into a new world, acquainting the student with values, customs, and resources. According to Levinson et al., "Through his own virtues, achievements, and way of living, the mentor may be an *exemplar* that the protégé can admire and seek to emulate. He may provide counsel and moral support in time of stress" (p. 98).

Levinson et al. also discussed the outcomes of the mentor relationship, stating that the student

> may take the admired qualities of the mentor more fully into himself. He may become better able to learn from himself, to listen to the voices from within. His personality is enriched as he makes the mentor a more intrinsic part of himself. The internalization of significant figures is a major source of development in adulthood. (p. 101)

From his longitudinal research on creative achievers, Torrance (1984) found that the relationship of the mentor changed to peer level as the protégé got older. In some instances personal mentor relationships became competitive over time, but they remained friendly and respectful.

The Resource Mentor   School programs may assign mentors to supplement gifted children's education. These mentors are usually volunteers from the community who invite gifted children to visit their places of work. Boston (1975) defined this role as "the anchoring of the pupil's learning in experience and the mentor's use of the pupil's predilection" (p. 2). Boston (1978) later noted the importance of matching not only the interest of the child to the expertise of the mentor but also the teaching style to the learning style. He described the important characteristics of the mentor as follows:

1. Is usually but not always an adult
2. Has a special skill, interest, or activity that engages the learner's interest
3. Is able to guide the learner toward personally rewarding experiences

4. Is flexible, helping the learner review and revise activities
5. Is often a role model for the learner; can impart an understanding of lifestyle and attitudes different from those the student might ordinarily meet
6. Is above all interested in the student as a learner and as an individual

These characteristics and roles must be addressed when finding appropriate community mentors for the gifted. Mentorships, both personal and school-based, are essential to fully developing talent and abilities in gifted children. Pleiss and Feldhusen (1995) stated, "The effective mentor engages the child in planned activities that are carefully timed to meet his or her developmental needs, and provides opportunities for the protégé to reflect on and assimilate the experiences" (p. 160).

Another good source of resource mentors for schools is a university or college. A highly developed model was created at Purdue University as the Purdue Mentor Program (Ellington, Haeger, & Feldhusen, 1986). The students, called "protégés," are selected from a pool of gifted children with the goal of matching their needs with specific mentors from the university community. A ratio of two to four protégés per mentor is maintained to form a mentoring group. When mentors are selected, they go through a training program to promote a consistent and high-quality relationship that will make the mentor sensitive to the needs of the gifted protégés. The program is supervised by graduate assistants who provide evaluation and feedback to correct any problems that may arise.

This model has had excellent results, as evidenced by the comprehensive evaluation reports. The authors concluded:

> The mentoring process gives youth an opportunity to learn about occupations and helps them make career decisions. Mentoring also motivates youth to pursue interest and activities in fields which fit their talents. It serves an instructional function in that protégés learn valuable information about a field from the mentor. It is also clear that mentors gain valuable understanding and insights about youth through the mentoring experience. (p. 5)

Summary ~

Teachers, parents, support personnel, and mentors are all critical in the development of the whole child. Utilization of this talent pool is essential to the future of our society. We must continue to educate and expand the cadre of facilitators for gifted children if we are to realize the contributions of these talented young people.

This chapter has by no means offered an exhaustive review of facilitators who might impact the life of a gifted child. As indicated at the outset of the chapter, the possibilities of significant people are many, including but not limited to those discussed here. Grandparents, siblings, friends, and school principals are just a few others who might be important facilitators.

The roles and relationships of facilitators to gifted children must be seen as a collective network that changes over time. In educating gifted children, we must recognize and utilize this network in fulfilling our mission.

References ⌒

Abraham, W. (1958). *Common sense about gifted children*. New York: Harper & Bros.

Alexander, P., & Muia, J. (1982). *Gifted education*. Rockville, MD: Aspen Systems.

Bishop, W. E. (1968). Successful teachers of the gifted. *Exceptional Children, 34*, 317–325.

Bloom, B. S., & Sosniak, L. (1981). Talent development versus schooling. *Educational Leadership, 39*, 85–94.

Boston, B. O. (1975). *The sorcerer's apprentice*. Reston, VA: ERIC Clearinghouse on Handicapped and Gifted Children.

Boston, B. O. (1978). *Developing a community based mentorship program for gifted and talented*. Washington, DC: U.S. Department of Health, Education and Welfare, Office of Gifted and Talented.

Buescher, T. M. (1987). Counseling gifted adolescents. *Gifted Child Quarterly, 31*(2), 90–94.

Cornell, D. G., & Grossberg, I. N. (1987). Family environment and personality adjustment in gifted program children. *Gifted Child Quarterly, 31*(2), 59-64.

Davis N. (1954). Teachers of the gifted. *Journal of Teacher Education, 5*, 221–224.

Ellington, M. K., Haeger, W. W., & Feldhusen, J. F. (1986). The Purdue Mentor Program: A university-based mentorship experience for gifted children. *G/C/T, 9*, 2–5

Feldhusen, J. (1973). Practicum activities for students and gifted children in a university course. *Gifted Child Quarterly, 17*, 124–129.

Feldhusen, J. F., & Bruch, C. (1985). *Professional training committee reports*, 1984. St. Paul, MN: National Association for Gifted Children.

Feldman, D. H. (1991). Why children can't be creative. *Exceptionality Education Canada, 1*(1), 43–51.

Gallagher, J. (1960). *Analysis of research on the education of gifted children*. Springfield, IL: Office of Superintendent of Public Instruction.

Gardner, J. (1961). *Excellence: Can we be equal and excellent too?* New York: Harper & Row.

Gear, G. (1979). Teachers of the gifted: A student's perspective. *Roeper Review, 1*, 18–20.

Goertzel, V., & Goertzel, M. (1962). *Cradles of eminence*. Boston: Little, Brown.

Gold, M. (1976). Preparation of teachers for gifted and talented youngsters. *Talents & Gifts, 19*, 22–23.

Gowan, J., & Demos, G. D. (1964). *The education of the ablest*. Springfield, IL: Charles C Thomas.

Guy, M. E. (1979, July). *Introductory education for teachers of gifted children in the United States*. Paper presented to Third International Conference on Gifted/Talented Children, Jerusalem.

Hershey, M. (1979). Toward a theory of teacher education for the gifted and talented. *Roeper Review, 1*, 12–14.

Hoover-Dempsey, K. V., & Sandler, H. M. (1995). Parental involvement in children's education: Why does it make a difference? *Teachers College Record, 97*(2), 310–331.

Justman, J. (1951). Obstacles to the improvement of teaching in classes for the gifted. *Exceptional Children, 18*, 41–45.

Laird, A. W., & Kowalski, C. J. (1972). Survey of 1,564 colleges and universities on courses offered in the education of the gifted—Teacher training. *Gifted Child Quarterly, 16*, 93–111.

Levinson, D., Darrow, C. N., Klein, E. B., Levinson, M. H., & McKee, B. (1978). *Seasons of a man's life*. New York: Alfred A. Knopf.

Maker, C. J. (1975). *Training teachers for the gifted and talented: A comparison of models*. Reston, VA: Council for Exceptional Children.

Marland, S. P. (1971). *Education of the gifted and talented* (Vol. 2). Washington, DC: U.S. Office of Education.

Mirman, N. (1964). Teacher qualifications for educating the gifted. *Gifted Child Quarterly, 8*, 123–126.

Newland, T. E. (1962). Some observations on essential qualifications of teachers of the mentally superior. *Exceptional Children, 29*, 111–114.

Newland, T. E. (1976). *The gifted in socio-educational perspective*. Englewood Cliffs, NJ: Prentice-Hall.

Piaget, J. (1970). Piaget's Theory. In P. H. Mussen (Ed.), *Carmichael's manual for child psychology* (3rd ed.) (2 vols.). New York: Wiley.

Pleiss, M. K., & Feldhusen, J. F. (1995). Mentors, role models, and heroes in the lives of gifted children. *Educational Psychologist, 30*(3), 159–169.

Prillaman, D., & Richardson. (1989). *Leadership education: Developing skills for youth* (2d ed.). Monroe, NY: Trillium Press.

Rice, J. (1970). *The gifted: Developing total talent.* Springfield, IL: Charles C Thomas.

Roe, A. (1952). *The making of a scientists.* New York: Dodd, Mead.

Schnur, J. (1977, October). *Description of a teacher training program for the education of the gifted.* Paper presented at the Fifth Annual Conference on Gifted and Talented Education, Ames, IA.

Seeley, K. R. (1979). Competencies for teachers of gifted and talented children. *Journal for the Education of the Gifted, 3,* 7–13.

Seeley, K. R., & Hultgren, H. (1982). *Training teachers of the gifted* (Research monograph). Denver: University of Denver.

Silverman, L. (1993). *Counseling the gifted and talented.* Denver, CO: Love.

Snider, G. (1960). Preservice and inservice education for teachers of the gifted. In B. Shertzer (Ed.), *Working with superior students* (pp. 269–278). Chicago: Science Research Associates.

Stedman, L. C. (1987). It's time we changed the effective schools formula. *Phi Delta Kappan, 69,* 215–224.

Tannenbaum, A. (1979). Pre-Sputnik to post-Watergate concern about the gifted. In A. H. Passow (Ed.), *The gifted and talented: Their education and development* (78th yearbook of the National Society for the Study of Education, Part 1). Chicago: University of Chicago Press.

Terman, L. M. (1954). The discovery and encouragement of exceptional talent. *American Psychologist, 9,* 221–230.

Thomas, S. B. (1973). Neglecting the gifted causes them to hide their talents. *Gifted Child Quarterly, 17,* 193–197.

Torrance, E. P. (1963). *Guiding creative talent.* Englewood Cliffs, NJ: Prentice-Hall.

Torrance, E. P. (1984). The role of creativity in identification of the gifted and talented. *Gifted Child Quarterly, 28,* 153–156.

United States Department of Education, Office of Educational Research and Improvement. (1994). *National excellence: A case for developing America's talent.* Washington, DC: Author.

Ward, V. (1961). *Educating the gifted: An axiomatic approach.* Columbus, OH: Charles E. Merrill.

Waskin, Y. (1979). Filling the gap. *Roeper Review, 1,* 9–11.

Wiener, J. (1960). A study of the relationship between selected variables and attitudes of teachers toward gifted children (Doctoral dissertation, University of California at Los Angeles, 1960). *American Doctoral Dissertations, 54.*

Wilson, F. T. (1953). Preparation for teachers of gifted children. *Exceptional Children, 20,* 78–80.

Wilson, F. T. (1958). The preparation of teachers for the education of gifted children. In R. Havighurst (Ed.), *Education for the gifted* (57th yearbook of the National Society for the Study of Education, Part 2). Chicago: University of Chicago Press.

Study Questions ⌇

1. Does one need to be gifted to teach gifted children?
2. How could we improve teachers' attitudes toward gifted children?
3. How might parents and schools work together more productively to enhance the education of gifted children?
4. How could gifted children serve as facilitators to other gifted learners?
5. Why is the mentor relationship so important to gifted learners' development?

27

Counseling Talented Learners

Joyce VanTassel-Baska

The need of gifted learners for counseling is best understood in the context of their differential characteristics in the affective realm. Chapter 10 enumerated several of these characteristics, including heightened sensitivity, idealism, unusual drive to excel, and strong sense of justice. Such characteristics, although positive at face value, breed problems for the gifted in many arenas. Silverman (1993b) documented several of these problems:

- Confusion about the meaning of giftedness
- Feelings of difference
- Feelings of inadequacy
- Relentless self-criticism
- Increased levels of inner conflict
- Lack of understanding from others
- Unrealistic expectations of others
- Hostility of others toward the gifted child's abilities

Taken together, these affective characteristics and concomitant problems of the gifted represent an important basis for a strong counseling intervention as part of their program in schools. Yet in most schools counseling remains the needed provision rather than the realized one in programs for the gifted.

The history of counseling gifted learners is relatively recent with new developments each decade. Some of the developments have been consonant with general counseling trends, such as the use of nondirective approaches in the 1950s, counseling in the schools in the 1960s, and diversity issues in counseling in the 1980s and 1990s (St. Clair, 1989). Yet some developments have been unique to the field of gifted education, including specific program development begun in the 1970s.

Affective Issues and the Gifted ~

In recent years, some studies have attempted to dispel myths associated with affective issues of the gifted. Oram, Cornell, and Rutemiller (1995) studied the supposed curvilinear relationship between giftedness and social adjustment and found little relationship between the two constructs, thus helping to dispel the myth that giftedness is associated with poor social adjustment. A recent European study found similar results, concluding that the gifted are at least as well adjusted socially and emotionally as average learners (Rost & Czeschlik, 1994). Cross, Cook, and Dixon (1996) studied gifted adolescent suicide through psychological autopsies and found that underlying persistent patterns of behavior, characterized in the antecedent life context of these students, were comparable to those of nongifted students, thus helping to dispel the notion that suicide and giftedness forge an important relationship.

Another persistent myth is that the superior cognitive functioning of gifted children is totally separate from their affective functioning, an argument frequently used to hold gifted students in place with their age-mates. Luthar, Zigler, and Goldstein (1992) found that intellectually gifted adolescents were more comparable to older adolescents with similar cognitive skills and psychological adjustment than they were to their age-mates, suggesting advanced levels of affective functioning. Achter, Lubinski, and Benbow (1996) documented the advanced readiness of the gifted to show career preferences as well, based on interest and value considerations. In another study, gifted high-school seniors scored at the adult level on identity development (Howard-Hamilton & Franks, 1995), reinforcing the likelihood that gifted students are advanced in areas of affective development as well as cognitive ones.

The affective trait of resilience has been studied in relationship to the gifted, with researchers noting that there are common characteristics of both resilience and giftedness, such as reflectiveness, ability to dream, maturity, desire to learn, risk-taking, and self-understanding (Bland, Sowa, & Callahan, 1994). Sensitivity as an affective trait of giftedness has also been studied, with the research suggesting a strong relationship between cognitive awareness and the display of sensitivity in social contexts (Mendaglio, 1995). The model of sensitivity used covered four dimensions: self-awareness, perspective-taking, empathy, and emotional experience. The University of Kansas (1995) conducted a symposium that focused exclusively on the affective costs of excellence, evidence of the importance of affective issues in optimal development.

Self-Concept Issues ~

The valuing of self is fundamental to human functioning. A healthy sense of self can positively affect relationships with others, provide the basis for appropriate life and educational choices, and frame useful perspectives on a career. If the self-esteem of gifted individuals is impaired in some way, that impairment can severely inhibit their capacity to unleash their potential in the most productive channels. It does a person little good to be extremely gifted and yet be too emotionally impaired to harness the ability toward a positive personal or social end.

In a comprehensive review of the literature on the social-emotional development of the gifted, Janos and Robinson (1985) found that research has demonstrated three important aspects of self-esteem in the gifted: (1) the gifted exhibit greater psychosocial maturity than nonidentified groups as seen by their play interests, choice of older children as friends, perspective-taking, and social knowledge; (2) the gifted demonstrate average or superior psychosocial adjustment at preadolescent ages compared to nongifted groups as seen by studies that document such diverse qualities as trustworthiness under stress, sociability, reduced antisocial tendencies, fewer aggressive and withdrawal tendencies, and higher ratings on courtesy, cooperation, and self-assurance; and (3) the gifted generally exhibit higher self-esteem than other groups on self-report inventories.

In a more recent review of the literature on self-concept and the gifted, Hoge and Renzulli (1991) summarized their findings as follows:

1. Gifted students as a group show no major deficits in self-esteem.
2. Labeling a child as gifted may have a positive impact on self-esteem.
3. Movement to a highly gifted learning group from an average group may have a negative impact on self-concept.

Other studies, however, have concluded that the effect of special programming on the self-concept of the gifted was minor (Kulik & Kulik, 1982; Olszewski, Kulieke, & Willis, 1987). Yet there is evidence that self-perceived intellectual competence declines with age, as a result of more competitive social comparison groups and more rigorous expectations for performance (Stipek & MacIver, 1989).

Overall, the literature continues to suggest that gifted students, in general, have strong self-concepts in both academic and social areas as measured by self-concept inventories, although there is some evidence that highly gifted learners and gifted girls may have less positive self-esteem than other gifted students. There also appears to be some temporary reduction in self-esteem for students who relate most often with peers of equal or superior ability in special programs. Yet an overall diminished effect of program participation on self-esteem has not been demonstrated. While the assumption of positive self-concept may generally be accurate, the relationship is complex. Some factors to be considered are:

1. How to determine different aspects of self-concept—Some gifted students may be high in academic self-concept yet lower in social self-concept (VanTassel-Baska, Olszewski-Kubilius, & Kulieke, 1994) or, as was found with gifted middle-school girls, lower in their perception of physical appearance (VanTassel-Baska & Olszewski-Kubilius, 1989).
2. The way in which self-esteem and performance are related—For example, does high performance guarantee a high self-perception of competence?
3. The way in which school programs affect self-concept and self-esteem
4. The most effective type of guidance to provide to students to foster both self-esteem and performance

VanTassel-Baska (1993) offered the following ideas for promoting healthy self-concept in and among gifted students. They constitute working ideas for counselors, teachers, parents, and others who influence the lives of these students on a regular basis.

Developing Self-Knowledge

The gifted student tends to adopt a highly analytical approach to life that results in earlier self-analysis, which in turn feeds a tendency toward perfectionism in self and the expectation of perfectionism in others. An overlay of inappropriate adult expectations, such as being number one in the class or winning specialized competitions, can further affect, in a negative manner, the opportunity for such students to develop healthy identity formation. Thus, assisting gifted students with an understanding of the difference between perfection and the pursuit of excellence, for example, may be a first step in helping them mediate their world.

A gifted student must appreciate the role of competition in breeding excellence, for raising one's own personal standard in a given area is often based on the performance of others. Olympic figure skaters, for example, now must perform intricate triple toe loops not required 10 years ago in competition because the world-class standard has been raised through a single performance of excellence by one skater. This standard has thus become the basis for the "pursuit of excellence" in figure skating at world-class levels. In more general terms, competition that focuses on individual improvement and goal attainment is healthy, whereas competition in which the total focus is on winning, with performance taking precedence over learning and self-growth, is not.

There is an unfortunate perception by many gifted adolescents that the more able one is, the less effort one should have to invest in attaining goals or earning grades. In the adolescent culture it becomes important not to be a "nerd" or "bookworm" but, rather, to be the person to whom academic attainment seems effortless. Although some bright adolescents view giftedness not as a trait but as a "performance" requiring sustained effort (Kerr, Colangelo, & Gaeth, 1988), other bright students view ability as an entity that translates into turning away from challenging opportunities such as honors or Advanced Placement classes in favor of those requiring minimal effort (Stipek, 1988). These adolescent perceptions underscore the importance of learning more about the relationship between self-knowledge, perceptions of self, and selected achievement patterns.

Developing Self-Acceptance

Gifted students tend to exhibit intense sensitivity and internal responsiveness to the actions of others, which can lead to feelings of alienation or rejection when none was intended. By the same token, however, this characteristic can lead to peer ridicule and social rejection because of overreactions to trivial incidents, leaving the gifted feeling unaccepted by peers. This condition can adversely affect self-esteem (Janos & Robinson, 1985). Providing gifted students, through role-playing, scenarios, and bibliotherapy, with concrete examples of behavioral incidents that illustrate how these perceptions of difference are formed may help ameliorate such occurrences and assist with self-acceptance.

Developing Relationships

The characteristics of popular children, such as friendliness, peer dependency, and conformity to peer rules and routines (Coleman, 1980), are not typical among the gifted. The gifted frequently have fewer opportunities for positive recognition from peers and fewer friendships, and their friendship patterns more frequently involve older children and adults. In a study of concerns of gifted middle-school students (VanTassel-Baska & Olszewski-Kubilius, 1989), developing relationships was the most cited concern of the students. Thus, providing gifted students with strategies for developing new peer relationships and improving existing ones is an important way to assist their self-concept development.

Developing Appropriate Expectations of Self

Since gifted students have a propensity for expecting more of themselves than is warranted given a particular set of circumstances, they are often more critical of self than others would ever be and many times feel a conflict between internal drives for excellence and external pushes for performance that results in stress, impatience, and a lowered tolerance for ambiguity (Delisle, 1985). Helping these students negotiate a healthy balance between inner and outer expectations, as well as helping them develop reasonable expectations for performance based on ability, interest, and personality factors, is critical to the development of self.

Developing Risk-Taking Behaviors in Intellectual Contexts

Sometimes gifted students exhibit behaviors that are antithetical to intellectual risk-taking. They insist on finding the one right answer, they refuse to take on new challenges unless they are assured of the outcome reward (a grade, credit, or recognition of some kind), and they abhor being wrong. However, risk-taking behaviors are critical in the development of the intellectual inquiry process, for students will encounter serious challenges to their ideas, may find intellectual work demanding in some contexts, and may discover that authentic learning can occur from making mistakes. Thus, if students do not develop these traits as a normal part of their earlier education, the assault on their self-concept at a later time can be devastating. Creating task demands for the gifted that require intellectual risk-taking is crucial to their affective, as well as cognitive, development.

Developing Self-Concept and Self-Esteem

The guidelines set forth in the previous sections should serve as a starting point in thinking through ways to enhance self-concept and self-esteem among those gifted students who particularly need it. In addition, following these guidelines for all gifted students as a preventive measure may prove useful, as there is sufficient evidence to suggest the malleability of self-concept based on a given stage of development and situational context (Briggs, 1975). Thus, working on self-concept development with gifted students throughout the school years is a worthy program goal.

Misinterpretations about gifted students can impair their evolving sense of self. School personnel must be sensitive to individual differences among gifted students. The more gifted the student, the fewer generalizations may apply about a healthy self-concept. Personality patterns in many highly gifted students may run counter to the norm. Such students may suffer from others' perceptions that they have an "inflated" self-concept because of a preference to work alone, which appears as aloofness. This behavior, however, may be more indicative of strong self-direction, nonconformity, and a concentrated personal intent and effort. Feeling different can create a dissonance in the gifted that impairs self-esteem. Being too gifted or too creative can be internalized as detrimental, depending on the peer group. Sometimes a student's own behavior exacerbates the problem, such as when students appear too critical of themselves and others or when they hide their talents just to get along in a social setting. School problems can also affect self-concept. Poor study habits, difficulty with accepting criticism, refusal to do routine tasks, and resistance to authority constitute behaviors that would alienate teachers and peers, leading to negative appraisals of student work and potentially instilling a sense of incompetence.

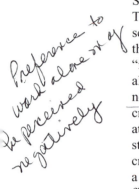

Finally, the importance of a gifted student's connection to another student cannot be overstated. Many problems of self-concept for these students are rooted in their sense of separation from peers and alienation from social worlds in which they feel unwelcome. Empathic adults cannot control social worlds, but they can facilitate the discovery of positive peer relationships with at least one other person in the student's environment. Again, as with other programs, the importance of an optimal match between the aptitude and interest of the students should be a foremost consideration.

The context for focusing on these broad approaches to self-concept development in the gifted may be the counselor's office, the home, or the classroom itself. Within the context of the classroom, several specific strategies used with individual students have been shown to be helpful when augmented with outside support. These school-based strategies include a consideration for changing the student's school program to respond better to his or her individual needs. Labeled "academic therapy" (Baska, 1990), this approach is grounded in the conception that self-concept problems can arise from the mismatch between a student and the social context in which he or she is asked to function. These problems can be ameliorated by adjusting the nature and level of classroom work, changing teachers, providing a more appropriate peer group, or offering curricular experiences to the student that provide an optimal match between learning potential and interests.

Because the education of the gifted has focused on differential characteristics and needs of the population as a point of departure for any intervention, affective differences can become the focal point for creating special counseling interventions. These interventions may be viewed as critical in three specific areas: psychosocial, academic, and career/life planning. Table 27.1 depicts the relationship between characteristics of a gifted population and the generic counseling approaches necessary to

Table 27.1 ～ Linkage of Characteristics of the Gifted to Counseling Approaches	
Characteristics	**Counseling Provision**
Cluster #1: ability to manipulate abstract symbol systems high retention rate quickness to learn and master the environment	Academic program planning that matches learner cognitive needs
Cluster #2: ability to do many things well (multipotentiality) varied and diverse interests internal locus of control (independence)	Life/career planning that presents atypical models
Cluster #3: heightened sensitivity sense of justice perfectionism	Psychosocial counseling that focuses on the preservation of affective differences

address them. A gifted child who manifests these characteristics to an intense degree is likely to suffer in various ways without appropriate counseling intervention. The nature of such suffering may manifest itself in social isolation, either self-imposed or brought about by peer ostracism; social accommodation, through reversal or homogenization of the gifted characteristics; or social acceptance seeking, through denial that the giftedness exists and by finding ways to channel intellectual energy that meet the expectations of the social norm. Any of these conditions can result in a deleterious situation for a gifted child with respect to understanding and developing talent. Thus, the nature of giftedness indicates a set of special counseling needs that extend well beyond those required for a more typical learner and individual.

Strategies for Addressing Psychosocial Needs of the Gifted ～

The literature on successful counseling interventions is rather sparse, except for that on clinical models (Ogburn-Colangelo, 1979) and applied teacher techniques such as bibliotherapy (Bailey, Boyce, & VanTassel-Baska, 1990; Frasier & McCannon, 1981). However, most educators of the gifted advocate grouping opportunities that create a nurturing, supportive environment for gifted learners as an underpinning of their social-emotional development (Gowan & Demos, 1964; Silverman, 1993). In addition there is a strong emphasis in the field on the importance of preserving affective differences and strengthening students' awareness of their inner lives so as to enhance their development potential in diverse areas (Dabrowski & Piechowski, 1977; Mendaglio & Tillier, 1992; Piechowski, 1989).

The psychosocial needs of the gifted are best addressed through clear recognition and understanding of how the population differs from the norm in the affective area. These differences then can become the basis for systematic intervention. Although many socioemotional needs exist for the gifted, focusing on a few will provide a good basis for understanding the concept of optimal match between characteristic and intervention technique. Table 27.2 presents a synthesis of seven key social-emotional needs of the gifted that phenomenologically differ from the needs of more typical students. A strategy for addressing each of these seven needs also is included; educators and parents are urged to consider these strategies for implementation in a counseling setting.

The setting in which these strategies may be used will vary depending on several circumstances, not the least of which is who the provider of the counseling service will be. For many of the suggested interventions, a small-group setting using a discussion format will work quite well. Other interventions imply establishing a climate in the home and the classroom that encourages certain kinds of behavior in the individual child. Still others call for clinical intervention or at least one-to-one, individual assistance.

Who provides assistance to the gifted child in psychosocial counseling is an open issue. If we think of this type of counseling as a part of the curriculum for the gifted, teachers certainly can be central providers. If we think of these areas of need as primarily clinical, we can turn to school and private counselors for assistance. If we think of these needs as normal developmental issues in rearing gifted children, we see parents as the appropriate providers. Because of the variety of perspectives that exists around the issue of counseling, frequently no one individual role takes responsibility for these needs. Clearly, a partnership model is needed, involving teachers, counselors, and parents integrally in the process. A more complete discussion of this issue is presented at the end of this chapter.

As mentioned earlier, there is some evidence for the effectiveness of bibliotherapy in working with gifted students. An early reference is Bailey, VanTassel-Baska, and Boyce (1990); however, more recent publications have continued to advocate its use with the gifted as a strategy for socioemotional development, one step removed from the counseling mode of self-examination (Schlichter & Burke, 1994). By allowing gifted students to read about problems and issues of giftedness and then discuss them in the context of literature allows analogies to personal situations to emerge naturally.

Special counseling of the gifted has to honor the value system, cultural and otherwise, of the student (Brown, 1993; Evans, 1993; Ford & Harris, 1995), or the expe-

Table 27.2 ～
Linkage of Counseling Needs of the Gifted to Strategies for Intervention

Social-Emotional Needs of the Gifted	Strategies to Address the Needs
To understand the ways in which they are different from other children and the ways in which they are the same	Use bibliotherapy techniques Establish group discussion seminars Hold individual dialogue sessions
To appreciate and treasure their own individuality and the individual differences of others	Promote study of biography Honor diverse talents through awards, performance sessions, special seminars, and symposia Encourage contest and competitive entry
To understand and develop social skills that allow them to cope adequately within relationships	Teach creative problem solving in dyads and small groups Create role-playing scenarios Devise appropriate simulation activities
To develop an appreciation for their high-level sensitivity that may manifest itself in humor, artistic endeavors, and intensified emotional experiences	Encourage positive and expressive outlets for sensitivity, such as tutoring, volunteer work, art, music, and drama Promote journal writing that captures feelings about key experiences
To gain a realistic assessment of their ability and talents and how they can be nurtured	Provide for regular testing and assessment procedures Provide for grouping opportunities with others of similar abilities and interests
To develop an understanding of the distinction between "pursuit of excellence" and "pursuit of perfection"	Create a "safe" environment to experiment with failure Promote risk-taking behavior
To learn the art and science of compromise	Provide "cooperation games" Work on goal setting Encourage the development of a philosophy of life

rience risks being rendered ineffective. This issue clearly calls for the use of divergent counseling alternatives based on individual differences among the gifted. Evans (1993), for example, has suggested that racism and the deficit model negatively impact on gifted minority students, creating a need for specialized counseling. She also noted several problems associated with engaging gifted students in effective multicultural counseling:

1. Lack of awareness of self as a racial being
2. Interaction with members of other cultures
3. Breakdown of former knowledge regarding racial matters and conflict
4. Pro-minority stance
5. Pro-white, anti-minority stance
6. Internalization

In one recent study of middle-school gifted students (Elmore & Zenus, 1994), those who were lower achieving appeared to benefit the most academically from the emphasis on social-emotional development and support in their classrooms. At later ages and into college such support also has proven helpful for disadvantaged students (Olszewski-Kubilius & Scott, 1992).

Strategies for Addressing Academic Counseling Needs of the Gifted ⌇

Another critical area of counseling need is providing academic planning assistance to gifted learners no later than sixth grade and consistently throughout the secondary school years. What aspects of academic planning are important to consider for these students? Again, we need to be clear about their needs in this area. Major needs include understanding academic strengths and weaknesses; understanding real-life applications of academic subjects; developing metacognitive strategies; and understanding and evaluating competing choices and opportunities. The following interventions typify a responsive school environment for these learners in respect to the stated needs.

Testing and Assessment Information

Although gifted learners usually score well on standardized tests, they frequently do not have a good understanding of what their scores mean. This is particularly true of students who take the Scholastic Aptitude Test (SAT) in junior high. Helping students understand how their score results might be interpreted for academic planning purposes is a useful service that a counseling program might provide. VanTassel-Baska (1985) developed recommendations to guide counselors in helping secondary students with academic planning (see Table 27.3).

In addition to providing students with ideas about program options based on test scores, counselors might also work with gifted students on an assessment of their strengths, weaknesses, interests, and aspirations so that they can set realistic goals for themselves in school and beyond. It is useful to consider having gifted

Table 27.3~
Ranges of Performance on the SAT and Program Options

LOW ————————————————————————→ HIGH

200–390 on SATV or SATM	400–520 on SATV or SATM	530–650 on SATM or SATV	600–800 on SATV or SATM
Program Options:	Program Options:	Program Options:	Program Options:
Honors-level work in the content area of qualification (math/verbal) Enrichment seminars Academic counseling	Fast-paced, advanced coursework during academic year in area of strength (algebra or Latin) Academic counseling University summer program	Individualized program of study Diagnostic Prescriptive (DP) approach in area of strength University programs that employ fast-paced model Academic counseling Early access to Advanced Placement (AP) Grade acceleration	Individualized program of study DP approach in area of strength University programs that employ fast-paced model Academic counseling Early access to AP Grade acceleration Advanced standing at college entrance Early admissions Mentorships Career counseling

students develop a plan of study every 2–3 years that can be monitored and updated annually.

Applied Academics

Opportunities to experience real-life extensions of academic subjects make the academic planning process more meaningful for gifted learners. Such experiences also provide insight for students into future career possibilities. In addition, at earlier stages of development such as during junior high and early high school, these opportunities provide rich experiences for students who seek to make prudent decisions on course-taking directions.

Gifted students in a number of schools are involved in community service, either as part of their course requirements or as volunteer work after school. All of the 10th- and 11th-grade students at the High School of Mathematics and Science in Durham, North Carolina, for example, participate in community service, while the 12th graders have internships and mentorships. Students in the Program for the

Exceptionally Gifted of Mary Balwin College, a 5-year combined high school/college program for exceptionally gifted girls, construct and implement a plan for community involvement at a variety of sites, including hospitals, libraries, schools, and community agencies.

Internships

Many high-school students do internships in the community through the Executive Internship Program. This program has established sites throughout the country to accommodate gifted high-school seniors for a semester. Many of these placements are in state government, providing students with the opportunity to work with legislators and staff people who are responsible for programs and budgets. Students in Illinois, for example, spend one semester in Springfield, working at the Capitol and attending a seminar 1 day a week at the local high school. In Alexandria, Virginia, the experience is more diversified; students may spend their semester working in the federal government or with other agencies such as hospitals, research labs, and corporations. In an internship, the student works as an apprentice in a professional setting. The student receives high-school credit for the experience and gains rich insights into a facet of professional life that may be a potential future career.

Mentorships

A mentorship is a type of program experience in which the student works directly with an individual on a one-to-one basis (see Chapter 26). Mentors may be adults in the community or other students with similar interests and abilities. The mentor model can serve academic planning purposes as well as psychosocial ones, for the mentor also provides an important role model to a young gifted learner. The student can see in the mentor an idealized self and in that sense realize the possibility for future accomplishments. The mentor also can serve as a guide to making good decisions about academic direction and career path.

Thus, the mentor functions as a tutor or counselor, helping to advance the student's knowledge of a given field; the mentor also provides help and encouragement in considering various challenges and opportunities. The mentor has been found to be a very important factor in a gifted person's life with respect to choices made (Haeger & Feldhusen, 1987; Pleiss & Feldhusen, 1995; Seeley, 1985). Through setting up mentorships for gifted learners, we can provide them with important access to adult models worthy of emulation.

Organization and Management Skills

For many gifted learners, access to ideas and tips on how to study, how to organize time, and how to take tests can be very useful, especially as they begin the secondary school experience. Because elementary school is typically very easy for the gifted, they never really engage in the study process during that time. When school becomes more difficult and more structured, they are ill prepared to deal with it. Their academic counseling should include attention to these areas. A list of helpful tips on effective study approaches follows:

1. Set up a study schedule that includes long- and short-term deadlines. Prepare such a schedule on a monthly calendar, monitor it weekly, and make a daily study list of what is to be done for homework, long-term projects, and so on. Work backward from deadlines to determine what has to be done on certain days.

2. Set up a study area at home—a place to go regularly to accomplish the schedule. This place should be comfortable, have necessary study tools (reference books, paper, pens), and have appropriate lighting. It could be a corner of your room or the kitchen table area or a family room niche. Just be sure it is your area.

3. Set up a study group or find one other student with whom you share interests to study with at least once per week. Quiz each other and review major areas to be learned. This kind of "peer tutoring" is helpful in building study skills that continue over time.

4. Ask for assistance in areas you do not understand. Many times, gifted learners do need help "deciphering" an assignment or a problem or a special project assignment. Be practical and ask for assistance.

5. Try to study or work on projects a little bit every day. Gifted students get into trouble when they procrastinate, letting everything go until the last minute. Frequently, secondary school assignments are too extensive for last-minute work to be sufficient. Thus, daily application is important in building the self-discipline necessary for successful study habits.

6. When alternatives are available, select outside projects that interest you, and try to be creative in your choice of media to prepare them.

Providing Information About Programs and Course Options

Another essential facet of academic counseling is helping students and families make informed choices about the selection of appropriate programs. Issues of taking Advanced Placement (AP) coursework, for example, should be discussed early so that students and parents can plan accordingly. Because AP work is available to secondary students at any age and even exclusive of a specific AP class, this option is important to consider for independent study as well as for a specific curricular offering. The College Board offers 27 courses for students in most academic areas. Major advantages of the program include:

- Taking a college-level course while still in high school
- Learning good study habits and how to best use time
- Preparing for competitive colleges
- Taking more advanced coursework in a given field
- Saving college tuition costs

At a more general level, gifted students are in need of courses that will challenge them and adequately prepare them for high-quality college work.

In a memo from prestigious colleges to secondary school principals, parents, and students (Consortium on Higher Education, 1985), the colleges expressed several areas of concern regarding lack of preparation by bright students for college. These areas include:

- Reading at an analytical and interpretative level
- The writing of essays
- Solid "discipline study"
- Essay exam opportunities
- Critical thought and inquiry

More recently expressed concerns have focused on students' lack of ability to write well in the expository mode (Kennedy, 1996).

Schools can focus on these areas of concern through careful structuring of curriculum opportunities for gifted students. Ensuring that these kinds of experiences are a major part of course options for the gifted is an important function of an academic counselors.

Academic advising also implies knowing what preparation colleges are expecting for high-ability students. Background in a foreign language, for example, is a key ingredient in a talented student's profile, and yet many counselors ignore its importance in building programs for talented learners. The following basic program constitutes strong academic preparation for high-ability learners, according to the Consortium on Higher Education (1985):

- English (3 years)
- Mathematics (3 years)
- History (2 years)
- Science (1+ years of laboratory science)
- Foreign Language (3 years of one language)
- The Arts (study of art/music)

Some key areas, then, in which academic counselors planning can assist gifted learners include:

- Encouraging them to take 3 or 4 years of a foreign language
- Encouraging gifted girls to take advanced mathematics and science courses
- Helping them to balance worthwhile academic courses with specific talent and interest areas such as music or art
- Helping them to make decisions about taking outside work during the school year
- Taking advantage of available contests and competitions
- Preparing them to seek scholarship assistance for college
- Helping them to access appropriate summer and academic year program opportunities outside of school

Much of this counseling clearly comes under the purview of the school counselor; yet teachers in academic areas also can counsel students and parents effectively on many of these issues.

Strategies for Addressing Career Counseling Needs of the Gifted~

A key resource for students and parents on college planning was developed by Berger (1990). The guide lays out step-by-step processes for making decisions about college choices and encourages beginning to explore the process as early as sixth grade. The guide notes the importance of student self-understanding as a cornerstone to making effective decisions and encourages visitation to college campuses as a prelude to analyzing and evaluating other information resources. Another useful handbook, developed by Kerr (1991) and geared toward counselors and other school personnel, addresses the various facets of working with gifted students in a counseling setting. Particularly useful are the author's insights on the psychological needs and processes attributed to the gifted. Indeed, the efficacy of addressing the career counseling needs of gifted adolescents is suggested by the results of a career counseling study conducted by Kerr and Erb (1991), which found that college students gained significantly in the development of identity as a result of specific career counseling intervention.

Exposure to atypical career models is another area of need for the gifted. Silverman (1993b) generated some key prototypes that are worthy of discussion in the classroom:

- Delayed decision making
- Serial or concurrent careers
- Interests as avocations
- Multiple options
- Synthesizing interests from many fields
- Real-life experiences for exploration
- Creation of new or unusual careers
- Exploration of life themes for career choice

One example from this list, delayed decision making, is important for gifted students to practice. The fact that many important individuals in various fields did not make career decisions until the end of their undergraduate experience can be meaningful information to students struggling to make a career decision early. The following activities might help students grapple with the issues involved in making a career decision:

1. Read biographies of five important people in fields that interest you. Trace the development of their careers.
2. Interview adult family members about the career path they chose. What were important variables in their decision?
3. "Shadow" a professional in a field of interest. What aspects of the job are most interesting and why? Keep a log of your observations.
4. Survey a group of recent high-school and college graduates from your geographical area about their career pursuits.

Each of the other career prototype issues for the gifted can be similarly explored by teachers' structuring key activities for the gifted.

VanTassel-Baska (1981) outlined a series of six strands, or elements, on which teachers and counselors can focus in career planning for gifted students. These strands, which come into play sequentially from kindergarten to Grade 12, highlight the following areas:

- Biography reading and discussion
- Small-group counseling on special issues and concerns (group dynamics, life planning, coping)
- Mentor models and independent study
- Individual assessment of abilities, interests, and personality attributes
- Academic preparation for high school and college career exploration
- Internship opportunities

This scope and sequence of key elements in a gifted and talented career counseling program emphasizes the psychosocial needs of the gifted and their need for planning and decision making at each successive stage of development.

Another career counseling need of gifted learners is in the area of life planning. Because the potential for accomplishing many things in various areas is clearly a typical profile for many gifted learners, these students have a real need to understand how they might best make decisions at various stages of development. Most adolescents have difficulty "seeing the future" much beyond the termination of the schooling process, so it is important for them to examine alternative life models, try them on, and see how they fit. Gifted girls should consider what alternatives exist around having a career and a family and in what order. Specific ideas that could be implemented in a school setting in regard to this issue include:

1. Have students develop a "philosophy of life" paper. What beliefs and values do they espouse about living? How might these beliefs and values relate to setting goals for adulthood?
2. Have students develop five goals they might address during the next 4 years. Have them work out an action plan for implementing them.
3. Use creative problem solving techniques to help students work through sample dilemmas in life planning (How might Linda decide whether to get married at 19 or finish college and begin a career first? How might Fred decide between engineering school and medicine?).
4. Have students study the lives of eminent individuals who were deliberate in their life plans, such as Thomas Jefferson. What factors influenced them at various stages of development?
5. Have students identify individuals they admire, structure a questionnaire that examines their lives at critical stages, and then interview those individuals. What events do they consider the most important in their lives? Why?

Through such focused activities and follow-up discussions, gifted learners can begin to appreciate the need for considering career and life paths at a more global level.

Who Should Counsel the Gifted? ~

The issue of who should provide counseling for the gifted frequently arises in discussions about providing these types of services. The model that works best is a confluent one in which many individuals take responsibility for various key roles in the process. Trained counselors, parents, and teachers all must assume a partnership role in order to provide sufficiently for this population.

The Role of Counselors

Certainly, individuals trained in counseling procedures constitute an important group to provide services to the gifted in the counseling area. Both school and private counselors may be helpful to this population. Many school districts designate one individual as a counselor of the gifted. These individuals usually provide academic planning assistance, some career/college planning help, and occasional individual counseling in the psychosocial area. Because their caseload typically includes many students in addition to the gifted, most of their interventions tend to be group-oriented, except for special cases. Types of intervention frequently conducted by school counselors include group seminars on selective topics; career nights; college visitations; internships in selected career areas; planning of annual courses of study; and clinical counseling on problem areas.

Private counselors can also provide assistance to gifted students. These individuals frequently are used in more serious cases or for more specialized concerns. For example, private counselors may specialize in testing, underachievement cases, or college counseling. Eliciting the services of a private counselor may be judicious if needed services of a specialized nature are not readily available in the school setting. Many times, school counselors refer families to a private counselor if the case warrants it.

The Role of Parents

Many educators view counseling the gifted as mainly the responsibility of the parents. This responsibility, however, may be difficult to undertake. Nevertheless, parents can provide important assistance to their gifted offspring in several key ways. One important role of parents is to listen to the problems, concerns, and frustrations of their gifted children. Spending quality time with gifted children cannot be overrated as an important function for a parent. Beyond listening, a parent can discuss with a child ways of coping with problems, even having a child "pretend" how to act in a given situation. Parents can ask questions about how personal and social adjustments are proceeding for their child. Monitoring progress is an important aspect of ensuring that gifted students receive appropriate options throughout school. In these ways, parents can contribute effectively to the counseling process for their children and seek outside assistance when they believe their child needs it.

Moreover, parents can provide a family context that is likely to promote intrinsic motivation in their gifted children rather than set up an environment of reward and punishment in relation to school achievement. Csikszentmihalyi (1991) cited the following as the family life issues that best foster intrinsic motivation.

- Choice and control of activities
- Clarity of rules and feedback
- Centering on intrinsic process and rewards
- Commitment, involvement, security, trust
- Challenging environment with various opportunities for action

The Role of Teachers

Another source of assistance for counseling the gifted is the teacher of the gifted, the individual who sees the behavior of the gifted child on an ongoing basis. Frequently, this individual also is skilled in the nature and needs, both cognitive and affective, of gifted children. Such a person is invaluable in the counseling process; he or she might undertake all facets of guidance, except clinical intervention. For example, classroom teachers have used techniques such as bibliotherapy very successfully with gifted learners. With this technique, students read books in which the protagonist is a gifted child with a problem of some kind. Discussion of the protagonist and his or her problem provides an instructive but safely removed context for a gifted child to identify and work on a problem area. Secondary teachers also can help with academic counseling and career counseling by including aspects of both in a year's course of study. Teachers can make use of guest speakers who represent key career areas to help a subject become more meaningful for students. Also, being available to consult on the next level courses in a given area is helpful.

Summary ～

The needs of gifted students for counseling intervention appear great in the key areas of psychosocial development, academic planning, and career education. We must find workable approaches to address these needs that accommodate the current structure of schools and recognize the nature of the constraints within that structure. Thus, parents, teachers, and counselors might cooperatively structure opportunities for affective growth in the gifted, secure in the fact that such interventions are clearly needed and can be implemented in the context of most school settings.

References ～

Achter, J., Lubinski, D., & Benbow, C. P. (1996). Multipotentiality among the intellectually gifted: "It was never there in the first place, and already it's vanishing." *Journal of Counseling Psychology, 43*(1), 65–76.

Bailey, J. M., Boyce, L. N., & VanTassel-Baska, J. (1990). Writing, reading, and counseling connection: A framework for serving the gifted. In J. VanTassel-Baska (Ed.), *A practical guide to counseling the gifted in a school setting* (pp. 172–189). Reston, VA: Council for Exceptional Children.

Baska, L. K. (1990). Education therapy for the gifted: The Chicago approach. In J. VanTassel-Baska (Ed.), *A practical guide to counseling the gifted* (2nd ed., pp. 47–52). Reston, VA: Council for Exceptional Children.

Berger, S. L. (1990). *College planning for gifted and talented youth*. Reston, VA: Council for Exceptional Children. ERIC Digest #E490. (ERIC Document Reproduction Service No. ED 321 495)

Bland, L. C., Sowa, C. J., & Callahan, C. M. (1994). An overview of resilience in gifted children. Special issue: Affective dimensions of being gifted. *Roeper Review, 17*(2), 77–80.

Briggs, D. (1975). *Your child's self-esteem*. Garden City, NY: Doubleday.

Brown, L. L. (1993). Special considerations in counseling gifted students. *School Counselor, 40*(3), 184–190.

Coleman, J. (1980). Friendship and the peer group in adolescence. In J. Adelson (Ed.), *Handbook of adolescent psychology* (pp. 408–431). New York: Wiley.

Consortium on Higher Education. (1985). *A memo to secondary school principals, parents, and students*. Boston: Author.

Cross, T. L., Cook, R. S., & Dixon, D. N. (1996). Psychological autopsies of three academically talented adolescents who committed suicide. *Journal of Secondary Gifted Education, 8*(3), 403–409.

Csikszentmihalyi, M. (1991). *Flow*. New York: Basic Books.

Dabrowski, K., & Piechowski, M. (1977). *Theory of levels of emotional development* (2 vols.). Oceanside, NY: Dabor Science.

Delisle, J. (1985). Vocational problems. In J. Freeman (Ed.), *The psychology of gifted children* (pp. 367–378). London: Wiley.

Elmore, R. F., & Zenus, V. (1994). Enhancing social-emotional development of middle school gifted students. *Roeper Review, 16*(3), 182–185.

Evans, K. (1993). Multicultural counseling. In L. Silverman (Ed.), *Counseling the gifted and talented* (pp. 277-290). Denver, CO: Love.

Ford, D. Y., & Harris, J. J., III. (1995). Underachievement among gifted African-American students: Implications for school counselors. *School Counselor, 42*(3), 196–203.

Frasier, M. M., & McCannon, C. (1981). Using bibliotherapy with gifted children. *Gifted Child Quarterly, 25*, 81–85.

Gowan, J., & Demos, G. (1964). *The education and guidance of the ablest*. Springfield, IL: Charles C Thomas.

Haeger, W., & Feldhusen, J. (1987). *Developing a mentor program*. East Aurora, NY: DOK Publishers.

Hoge, R. D., & Renzulli, J. S. (1991). *Self concept and the gifted child*. Research-based decision making series, No. 9104. Storrs, CT: National Research Center on the Gifted and Talented. (ERIC Document Reproduction Service No. ED 358 661)

Howard-Hamilton, M., & Franks, B. A. (1995). Gifted adolescents: Psychological behaviors, values, and developmental implications. *Roeper Review, 17*(3), 186–191.

Janos, P., & Robinson, N. (1985). Psychological development in intellectually gifted children. In F. Horowitz & M. O'Brien (Eds.), *The gifted and talented: Developmental perspectives* (pp. 180–187). Washington, DC: American Psychological Association.

Kennedy, C. (1996). Teaching discourse through writing. In J. VanTassel-Baska, D. Johnson, & L. Boyce (Eds.), *Developing verbal talent* (pp. 133–148). Boston: Allyn & Bacon.

Kerr, B. (1991). *A handbook for counseling the gifted and talented*. Alexandria, VA: American Association for Counseling and Development.

Kerr, B., Colangelo, N., & Gaeth, J. (1988). Gifted adolescents' attitudes toward their giftedness. *Gifted Child Quarterly, 32*(2), 245–247.

Kerr, B., & Erb, C. (1991). Career counseling with academically talented students: Effects of a value-based intervention. *Journal of Counseling Psychology, 38*(3), 309–314.

Kulik, C. C., & Kulik, J. A. (1982). Effects of ability grouping on secondary school students: A meta-analysis of evaluation findings. *American Education Research Journal, 19*, 415–428.

Luthar, S. S., Zigler, E., & Goldstein, D. (1992). Psychosocial adjustment among intellectually gifted adolescents: The role of cognitive-developmental and experiential factors. *Journal of Child Psychology and Psychiatry and Allied Disciplines, 33*(2), 361–373.

Mendaglio, S. (1995). Sensitivity among gifted persons: A multi-faceted perspective. *Roeper Review, 17*(3), 169–172.

Mendaglio, S., & Tillier, W. (1992). *Feeling bad can be good: Using Dabrowski's theory to reframe gifted children's adjustment difficulties.* Presentation at the Annual Society for the Advancement of Gifted Education Conference, Calgary, Alberta, Canada.

Ogburn-Colangelo, M. K. (1979). Giftedness as multi-level potential: A clinical example. In N. Colangelo & R. Zaffrann (Eds.), *New voices in counseling the gifted* (pp. 165–187). Dubuque, IA: Kendall/Hunt.

Olszewski, P., Kulieke, M., & Willis, G. (1987). Changes in the self-perceptions of gifted students who participate in rigorous academic programs. *Journal for the Education of the Gifted, 10*(4), 287-303.

Olszewski-Kubilius, P. M., & Scott, J. M. (1992). An investigation of the college and career counseling needs of economically disadvantaged minority gifted students. *Roeper Review, 14*(3), 141–148.

Oram, G. D., Cornell, D. G., & Rutemiller, L. A. (1995). Relations between academic aptitude and psychosocial adjustment in gifted program students. *Gifted Child Quarterly, 39*(4), 236–244.

Piechowski, M. (1989). Developmental potential and the growth of the self. In J. VanTassel-Baska & P. Olszewski-Kubilius (Eds.), *Patterns of influence: The home, the self, and the school* (pp. 87–101). New York: Teachers College Press.

Pleiss, M., & Feldhusen, J. (1995). Mentors, role models, and heroes in the lives of gifted children. *Educational Psychologist, 30*(3), 159–169.

Rost, D. H., & Czeschlik, T. (1994). The psycho-social adjustment of gifted children in middle childhood. *European Journal of Psychology of Education, 9*(1), 15–25.

Schlichter, C. L., & Burke, M. (1994). Using books to nurture the social and emotional development of gifted students. *Roeper Review, 16*(4), 280–283.

Seeley, K. (1985). Facilitators for gifted learners. In J. Feldhusen (Ed.), *Toward excellence in gifted education* (pp. 105–134). Denver, CO: Love.

Silverman, L. (1993a). Affective curriculum for the gifted. In J. VanTassel-Baska (Ed.), *Comprehensive curriculum for the gifted learner* (pp. 335-355). Boston: Allyn & Bacon.

Silverman, L. (1993b). *Counseling the gifted and talented.* Denver, CO: Love.

St. Clair, K. L. (1989). Counseling gifted students: A historical review. *Roeper Review, 12*(2), 98–102.

Stipek, D. (1988). *Motivation to learn: From theory to practice.* Englewood Cliffs, NJ: Prentice-Hall.

Stipek, D., & MacIver, D. (1989). Developmental change in children's assessment of intellectual competence. *Child Development, 60*, 521–538.

University of Kansas. (1995). *The emotional price of excellence.* Abstracts of selected papers from the Annual Esther Katz Symposium on Psychological Development of Gifted Children. Lawrence, KS: Author.

VanTassel-Baska, J. (1981). A comprehensive model of career education for the gifted and talented. *Journal of Career Education, 1*, 325–331.

VanTassel-Baska, J. (1985). The talent search model: Implications for secondary school reform. *National Association of Secondary School Principals Journal, 69*(482), 39–47.

VanTassel-Baska, J. (1993). Developing self concept in gifted individuals. In G. McEachron-Hirsch (Ed.), *Student self esteem: Integrating the self* (pp. 311–344). Lancaster, PA: Technomic.

VanTassel-Baska, J., & Olszewski-Kubilius, P. (Eds.). (1989). *Patterns of influence on gifted learners.* New York: Teachers College Press.

VanTassel-Baska, J., Olszewski-Kubilius, P., & Kulieke, M. (1994). A study of self-concept and social support in advantaged and disadvantaged seventh and eighth grade gifted students. *Roeper Review, 16*(3), 186–191.

Study Questions ~

1. Why are affective needs of the gifted as important to attend to as cognitive needs?

2. What are some specific situations that you can name of a gifted child in need of socioemotional support? What happened to the child in such situations in the short term? In the long term?

3. What if you had a child, age 8, who exhibited many of the gifted affective characteristics listed in this chapter? What interventions would you as a parent like the school to provide?
4. How appropriate is it to consider counseling interventions as part of the curriculum?
5. What aspects of the overall counseling and guidance process might best be undertaken by teachers? What would be the rationale?
6. How might a guidance program for the gifted be implemented at the elementary level? At the secondary level?

28

Excellence as a Standard for All Education: A Conclusion and a Beginning

Joyce VanTassel-Baska

What is excellence and how do we measure it? Gross (1989) equated the excellence motive with the need to achieve, the success drive, and motivation to learn at high levels. Gardner (1961) defined excellence as striving for quality in all areas of a society. Roeper (1996) viewed excellence as a standard for gifted students to achieve in psychic terms, learning to develop as ethical and moral human beings. Silverman (1993) maintained that excellence cannot be defined as "success" because our culture refuses to recognize the contributions of many disenfranchised groups, particularly women, who attain excellence in areas like homemaking and childrearing. Thus, excellence may be conceived of as a synonym for success, achievement, or psychic growth, depending on one's definitional structure.

In this final chapter, excellence is examined from the viewpoint of individual habits of mind that foster it, the role of the culture in promoting it, the relationship to technical mastery versus world-class performance, and the sometimes controversial relationship to equity. A brief commentary is included on promoting excellence in community, school, and home settings.

Excellence as Habit of Mind

My father-in-law, who was a preeminent furnace man, often was known to quip, "If a job's worth doing, then it is worth doing right." His view of work is highly consonant with the concept of excellence as a habit of mind. Excellence requires hard work, disciplined application, and above all an attitudinal disposition that implies one will put forth sufficient effort to do any work at the highest level of which one is capable at a given time.

What are the intellectual habits of mind that need to be applied to an excellence orientation? Paul (1992) captured them well in his model of thinking—intellectual honesty, integrity, and humility coupled with curiosity and intellectual independence born of an inquiring mind. Students whose thinking is held to standards such as clarity, accuracy, logical consistency, and fairness learn to improve their thinking in various ways. Passow (1988) sagely noted that educators many times enhance gifted students' knowledge without helping them think through the morality of that knowledge. Developing habits of mind constitutes an important way to pursue excellence in intellectual endeavors. When we engage in thinking and reasoning, we need to be mindful of these attitudes and standards lest arrogance and the art of manipulation become the model for achieving our ends.

Working with gifted students to help them achieve excellence requires that we abandon the Hollingworth adage of helping them learn to suffer fools gladly and get them to recognize the seriousness of the intellectual enterprise and the process of thinking that supports it. To learn humility is to approach all situations as a learner, with an attitude that other people have something to contribute to the full understanding of an idea or problem. Such humility also predisposes one to be open to experience, not bounded by an absolutist approach to learning. Clearly such understanding comes only with maturity, but it needs to be instilled early on if it is to develop at all.

Thinking about excellence as a set of attitudes to be developed and practiced over a lifetime ultimately yields an important way of understanding the concept. It also affords a basis for modeling and teaching to excellence as a standard for all gifted students.

Excellence in the Culture ⁓

What are the elements necessary in a culture to promote excellence among its citizens? Two important values that must be present are (1) the value of education and learning, and (2) the value of hard work. Those cultures that have embodied these values over history have emerged on the world stage as achieving civilizations. Currently, both Asian and European cultures have a better understanding of these principles than we do in the United States, even though we excel in productivity. International studies continue to demonstrate that our students are ill prepared for the rigors of subject matter learning in comparison to students in other first world countries. It is difficult to interpret the data in any way that does not indict the culture, since evidence suggests that students in Japan and Korea, for example, start out at comparable ability levels to American students in first grade yet diverge after that point in respect to achievement (Stevenson & Stigler, 1992). If ability does not vary, what accounts for these differences in achievement? Clearly, cultural differences in respect to values are at work.

In American society, we are somewhat ambivalent about education. We enjoy the "idea" of an educated citizen that engages vigorously in the process of democracy, yet some of us reject the notion that an education must be worked at, requiring effort and commitment over time. Thus, education comes to be viewed as a commodity, a credential to be exchanged in the marketplace, as opposed to an attitude toward learning and living. This narrow interpretation renders the process of learning as irrelevant, since it emphasizes a terminal point, not an ongoing dynamic process.

American society, then, may not be a hotbed of nurturance for excellence, with its poor understanding of the role of learning in everyday life as well as the need for the application of learning to specific areas at maximal levels. A culture that holds sports heroes, rock stars, and a cartoon mouse as cultural icons may not be able to support a deep appreciation for learning in multiple talent areas. Yet, other aspects of our society support the development of talent: the freedom and openness, the diversity of ideas and peoples, the emphasis on individualism—all are societal indicators that a climate for excellence exists. They also help explain how individuals in our society have made significant contributions in a variety of fields in spite of the absence of a strong overall value orientation toward intellectual attainment. For those who do value education in this country, access is available to the most powerful education at the university level of any society.

Technical Mastery Versus Excellence

Misconception often exists about what promotes excellence in an endeavor. Excellence is often perceived as achieving technical mastery in some area, where there is evidence that high-level skills have become automatic. Yet excellence implies "pushing the envelope" of technical mastery to another level, of finding ways to improve on past performance as opposed to merely replicating it. The child who receives a perfect score on a paper and equates that with excellence, even though the work was very easy, has a misplaced conception of excellence. The high-school student who learns the skills of argumentation at a sufficient level to engage in a debate still has much to learn about reaching a degree of excellence in the enterprise. The teacher who masters the repertoire of inquiry strategies, so effective in working with the gifted, still can improve on the last teaching moment in which they were used with students. The scientist who goes about her research in a highly competent manner still has a need to extend herself to work on new questions or to probe existing questions more deeply. All of these examples illustrate the difference between competency and the ethic of excellence.

Excellence demands that one constantly strive to go beyond one's personal best, to try to exceed one's past record, and to make a contribution of worth to a given endeavor. The process of striving for excellence may be best summed up by Browning's oft-quoted phrase: "Ah, but a man's reach should exceed his grasp or what's a heaven for?"

Excellence as World-Class Performance ∼

When we speak of excellence in the international arena, we have used the term "world-class" standards of performance. Our own national standards in the content areas have articulated levels of performance for K–12 learners at world-class levels. But what does "world-class" really mean? Perhaps our best examples can be found in sports. When Kristi Yamaguchi performed triple toe loops to win the gold medal in the winter Olympics in Norway, she set a new world-class standard for women's figure skating. All future skaters would need to demonstrate that feat to be considered world-class even though no skaters had been required to perform the maneuver before Yamaguchi. Thus, a standard was set for women's figure skating for years to come.

Similar standards are manifest in academics. The International Mathematics Olympiad recognizes "world-class" teams who compete for individual and group honors. Physics also sponsors a worldwide competition. Thus, in several areas of talent we can see the display of maximum competency where the goal is to exceed what has been done before. These are ultimate examples of moving a field forward (Feldman, 1983), as in the case of Yamaguchi, or of performing beyond expectations for one's stage of development, as in the academic Olympiad competitions (Stanley, 1990).

Yet not all individuals talented in specific fields can equal these kinds of feats. Does that imply that they are not excellent? It does speak to the extent that such standard-setting, by its very definition, would leave most people out of the loop. However, the standard-setting also works to establish a higher frame of reference for functioning within a given domain and makes clearer the path toward greater accomplishments for those who follow the individual making the breakthrough. New limits have been established to determine excellence in a field.

For most talented and gifted individuals, the pursuit of excellence is the goal, not the realization of a significant breakthrough. There remains a sense of satisfaction in doing one's best and through it making progress toward the goal. My Latin classics professor frequently commented on his joy of "laboring in the vineyards of the classics." I'm sure he did not expect to create a new blend of grape for conversion to wine, but his was a simple pleasure in serving the higher goal. And while he was not an innovator in his field, he did make substantive contributions to it in many arenas. Such an individual is necessary to advance a field through applications of new ideas and the in-depth study surrounding them.

To what extent can we claim that our current standards in academic areas are at world-class levels? While our students perform poorly on national exams that have clear and high standards, they do not excel on international comparisons either (Darling-Hammond, 1991). The argument for national standards is to infuse excellence into our schools through setting high standards for performance. Not since the curriculum projects of the 1960s have we seen such emphasis on what needs to be taught at what levels in American schools. The fact, however, that work of this nature has lain fallow for 30 years calls into question the capacity of schools to implement these standards effectively even when the standards are clearly defined: All of the standards imply that teachers are capable of translating both the content and the related pedagogy that will enhance learning (Shulman, 1987), a daunting task that remains untested to date. Moreover, they imply that all students are capable of learning at high levels, a claim that also has yet to be substantiated (Bracey, 1996). In fact, Bracey (1996) noted that no state has evidence that all students have even reached eighth-grade proficiency levels, let alone the anticipated levels of performance required in the new standards.

The difficulties with the national standards movement, of course, are manifold. Some critics argue that the standards take away local control; others argue that the standards are biased toward particular perspectives in a subject domain, as has been the case of the debate over the history standards; and still others, many in gifted education, argue that the implementation of standards is more harmful than helpful for gifted students, since interpreting the standard at the appropriate level is a teacher-driven task. Yet, for all the criticism, if the national content standards became the core curriculum tomorrow, assuming appropriate implementation, a higher uniform standard of excellence would be in place for the education of the gifted. Unfortunately, the standards movement is proceeding more slowly than may be desirable, with each state developing its own "translations" of the standards through curriculum frameworks that in time get modified further at local levels. This process has a watering down effect on the expectations for both learners and teachers. Thus, the power inherent in the national standards for promoting excellence in each subject domain has already been compromised.

Meanwhile, other countries continue to exceed our standards with larger percentages of the population, and fewer of our students perform at even modest levels. Fewer than 1% of our eligible school population takes Advanced Placement (AP) work in more than two subjects. Moreover, approximately only 10% of students taking AP exams score at the level of an AP scholar (namely, a 3, 4, or 5). Given both the cost-effectiveness and the standards of excellence employed in this program, it is telling that so few students have access to or choose not to access (since it is also elective) AP at the high-school level. A similar situation exists with the International Baccalaureate program in respect to underutilization by school districts of a rigorous precollegiate experience.

If academic excellence is to flourish in this country, then efforts like national standards and Advanced Placement coursework must succeed. Their limited impact speaks to schools preoccupied with social-political issues and problems to the detriment of learning and teaching the pursuit of excellence.

Excellence Versus Equity ⟿

John Gardner, in his classic 1961 book on excellence, posed the now famous question, "Can we be equal and excellent too?" In the current stages of school reform in this country, this issue could not be more relevant. Never have we been in greater need for a balance between these two principles in education. Equity issues are powerful in their own right. When we have millions of children attending schools in sub-standard physical conditions, with ill-trained teachers, and without up-to-date textbooks, we are brought face-to-face with the realities of inequality among schools (Kozol, 1991). Yet, are the solutions to these problems the same as those that may address the deep malaise of underachievement that plagues even our very affluent schools and districts, where curriculum is rigid instead of rigorous and age grade lockstep is the norm? I think not. For, although equity and excellence must both be addressed, the nature of the problem and the ways it manifests itself are very different. The focus for addressing equity concerns must come from outside in the form of resources for building improvement, staff development, and purchasing power for materials. An excellence emphasis, conversely, must originate within a school system with a staff making a commitment to school improvement and positive change. These internal forces can be quite powerful, even without substantial new resources, in affecting a climate of excellence.

Ironically, however, as has been the case in earlier decades of American education, we have swung very far in the direction of equity at the expense of excellence (Henry, 1994). In the process, arguments have arisen against the legitimacy of the quest for excellence itself, with the accusation that gifted education disrupts the community (Sapon-Shevin, 1995) and that the concept of giftedness has been "constructed" by self-interested groups (Margolin, 1993). To dismantle an infrastructure like gifted education on the altar of equity is to render the education of our best students inequitably at risk in the process. Excellence for all, if it means the same standards, the same curriculum, the same instructional emphases, becomes basically inequitable for all since it fails to recognize individual differences. Excellence cannot be perceived as a group norm; rather, it is an individual quest for higher learning.

True equity cannot disallow the opportunity to pursue excellence at a level and in areas most efficacious for the individual learner. To level the playing field, a phrase often used in support of equitable practices, provides no real benefit to anyone. For those who are handicapped by it, through being held back or asked to tutor others, as in the case of the gifted, this practice is not educational; it is remedial. For those who enter the game at lower levels of proficiency, it does not guarantee an enhancement of skill and ability, only a "fair" game where no one can move ahead of others because of the rules. For the referee in this "level" game, the job changes from a focus on arbitrating progress toward individual learning goals based on readiness to a focus on obliterating differences among players. So who benefits or even wants to play the game? Authentic learning and the pursuit of excellence are abandoned for an artificial appearance of equity. Bringing the top down does not bring the bottom up; it only lowers the level of play.

We would be farther ahead if we were to acknowledge a few fundamental truths about the relationship of excellence and equity:

1. All students enter the learning enterprise at different levels, based on prior experiences and developed skills and competencies.

2. To offer the same curriculum and instruction to all students is to deny that individual differences exist or matter in the enterprise of learning.

3. Excellence should be promoted in all learning endeavors, but at different levels based on personal mastery (my "excellent" essay may be merely "mediocre" for you).

4. Equity is present when all students have equal access to potential opportunities, based on reasonable standards of competence. High-school students all have access to calculus if (a) the school offers it, (b) the student has taken the prerequisite courses, and (c) the student is motivated to take advantage of the opportunity. Any of these three conditions not being met renders the educational door to access less open.

5. Lack of equity is directly linked to limitations in resources and the will to equalize them or at least establish some parity. Schools are not "equitable" contexts for the gifted when the resource share for gifted programs is less than one half of 1% of federal and many state budgets.

6. To embrace excellence in an educational sense means that schools are willing to promote talent development in all areas of the school and provide appropriate challenges for all learners in that context. Knowing what precocious learners are capable of doing at given stages of development provides an important basis for raising the excellence standards for other learners as well. To be concerned with excellence means having a willingness to strive for the highest levels of achievement for all students. Thus, maximum, not minimum, competence becomes the performance goal.

7. Excellence and equity are treated as extremes on a continuum of philosophical perspectives on the purpose of schooling, swinging from side to side like a metronome. Just as force and resistance to force in tandem can create sound in music and just as the resistance to the force of electricity creates heat in wire, so too excellence and equity must be perceived as necessary opposites to create effective schools. Only when both are held in creative tension as important values is schooling likely to improve.

Promoting Excellence in the Community ⁓

Communities, by the nature of the resources they make available, can do much to encourage educational excellence. Ready access to powerful technological resources is one example of such an effort. In communities around the country such as Blacksburg, Virginia, computers are available for use in all public places, as common as the telephone. Access to information is further enhanced by community librarians who provide expertise on information resources to all comers.

Another powerful community support to promote excellence is a university that serves as a learning and communication resource for all age-groups as well as for networks of individual communities. Access to the arts in a community is another major public avenue for promoting excellence. Community-based arts and humanities programs provide educational and aesthetic opportunities that enrich all who are interested and motivated to access new modes of experience and learning.

Thus, communities can be powerful catalysts for promoting excellence for all individuals. Obviously, however, members of communities need to be made aware of the benefits that accrue for them and their children from such community involvement.

Promoting Excellence in Schooling ~

The best way for schooling to promote excellence is through a commitment to growth and development via specific improvement mechanisms. There are many indicators of excellence that schools can use as yardsticks for purposes of self-improvement. A few of these indicators follow:

- Does the school have a stated mission, philosophy, and goals?
- Does the curriculum use materials and resources that support optimal student learning, based on the school's goals?
- Do the teachers employ inquiry-oriented techniques?
- Do the teachers use metacognitive strategies?
- Do the teachers individualize their approaches through diagnostic assessment and adaptation of curriculum based on student needs?
- Is assessment used to enhance instruction?
- Are school leadership approaches consistent with positive change efforts?

There exists a real need for schools to internalize such indicators as important benchmarks to gauge improvement for all learners.

Promoting Excellence in Parenting ~

Parenting processes can help students acquire the habits of mind associated with the pursuit of excellence in learning contexts (Hoover-Dempsey & Sandler, 1995). We know from studies of gifted families that certain practices can yield powerful positive outcomes for students. Csikszentmihalyi (1993) found that the homes of achieving adolescents were characterized by:

1. Clarity of rules and feedback
2. Consistency of standards
3. Family time for challenging activities
4. A high degree of trust and a sense of security and commitment
5. Constructive use of leisure time

Bloom (1985) also found that the values of parents of children who would achieve at high levels in adulthood coalesced around the importance of education and hard work. He noted that monitoring children's learning is a powerful part of the parenting role. Hoover-Dempsey and Sandler (1995) cited the importance of parent involvement and parent instruction as powerful mediators of student learning in specific areas. Parents clearly have a powerful role in promoting excellence. Their influence is far greater than any other resource available to young learners.

Summary ～

Although this text has concluded with a general commentary on excellence, it also presages a beginning or a redoubling of efforts to promote excellence in our schools, our homes, and our communities. If any group of educators is passionately committed to excellence, it should be those of us in gifted education. Excellence should be the goal on which we base the future work of our field, a goal for all learners and essential for those who are precocious in their development. Finding ways to nurture such learners in the ethos of excellence is a lifetime challenge for all of us.

References ～

Bloom, B. S. (1985). *Developing talent in young people.* New York: Ballantine.

Bracey, G. (1996). *Final exam: A study of the perpetual scrutiny of American education.* Washington, DC: Agency for Instructional Technology.

Csikszentmihalyi, M. (1993). *Talented teenagers: The roots of success and failure.* Cambridge, MA: Cambridge University Press.

Darling-Hammond, L. (1991). The implications of testing policy for quality and equality. *Phi Delta Kappan, 73*, 220–225.

Feldman, D. (Ed.). (1983). *Developmental conceptions of giftedness.* San Francisco: Jossey-Bass.

Gardner, J. (1961). *Excellence: Can we be equal and excellent too?* New York: Harper.

Gross, M. U. M. (1989). The pursuit of excellence or the search for intimacy? The forced-choice dilemma of gifted youth. *Roeper Review, 11*(4), 189–194.

Henry, W. A. (1994). *In defense of elitism.* New York: Doubleday.

Hoover-Dempsey, K. V., & Sandler, H. M. (1995). Parental involvement in children's education: Why does it make a difference? *Teachers College Record, 97*(2), 310–331.

Kozol, J. (1991). *Savage inequalities: Children in America's schools.* New York: Crown.

Margolin, L. (1993). A pedagogy of privilege. *Journal for the Education of the Gifted, 19*(2), 164–180.

Passow, A. H. (1988). Educating gifted persons who are caring and concerned. *Roeper Review, 11*(1), 13–15.

Paul, R. (1992). *Critical thinking: What every person needs to survive in a rapidly changing world.* Sonoma, CA: Critical Thinking Foundation.

Roeper, A. (1996). A personal statement of philosophy of George & Annemarie Roeper. *Roeper Review, 19*(1), 18–19.

Sapon-Shevin, M. (1995). Why gifted students belong in inclusive schools. *Educational Leadership, 52*(4), 64–68, 70.

Shulman, L. S. (1987). Knowledge and teaching: Foundations of the new reform. *Harvard Educational Review, 57*(1), 1–22.

Silverman, L. (1993). *Counseling the gifted and talented.* Denver, CO: Love.

Stanley, J. (1990). *My many years of working with the gifted: An academic approach.* Lecture given at the College of William and Mary, Williamsburg, VA, November 12.

Stevenson, H. W., & Stigler, J. (1992). *The learning gap: Why our schools are failing and what we can learn from Japanese and Chinese education.* New York: Simon & Schuster.

Author Index

A

Abbott, R. D., 422
Ablard, K. E., 98, 132, 318, 422, 423
Abraham, W., 476
Achter, D., 245
Achter, J., 194, 490
Ackerman, C. M., 35, 36
Ackerman, P. L., 265
Adamson, G., 131
Adamson, K., 404
Adcock, R. N., 74
Ahlgren, A., 247, 432
Albers, D. J., 468
Albert, R., 145, 220, 387, 388, 390
Aldrich, P., 451, 454
Alex, N. K., 451
Alexander, P., 483
Alexander, W., 228
Alexanderson, G. L., 368
Allan, S., 266, 267
Allen, L. Q., 220, 235
Alper, T., 425
Alvino, J., 155, 156, 159, 193, 201
Amabile, T., 251, 382, 387, 388, 403
American Association of University Women, 131, 154, 156
Ammirato, S. P., 35
Anderson, M. A., 399
Anick, C. M., 105
Apfel, N. H., 103
Apple, M. W., 255
Archambault, F., 14, 15, 263, 376
Argys, L. M., 266, 267
Arieti, S., 386, 387
Armancas-Fisher, M., 449
Armstrong, D. C., 456
Armstrong, T., 400
Arnold, K., 4, 129, 132, 133, 145
Asher, J. W., 193
ASSETS, 195
Assouline, S., 318, 423
Austin, G. A., 56
Avery, L., 309

B

Baer, J., 391
Bailey, J., 252, 429, 455, 496
Bain, S. K., 119
Baldwin, A. Y., 196
Bank Street College Project, 434
Bamburger, J., 70
Bancroft, B. A., 103, 104
Bandura, A., 219, 367, 369, 383
Bandura, M., 131
Banet, F., 74, 75, 77
Barbe, W. B., 49, 71
Barbee, A., 136
Barbour, N. B., 74
Barr, D., 430
Barron, F., 383, 385, 387
Barron, M., 430
Bartkovich, E. G., 285
Bartkovich, K. G., 271
Baska, L., 98, 102, 206, 317, 494
Baskin, B. H., 451
Bass, G., 343, 392, 429
Bates, M., 40
Bathurst, K., 30, 146
Baugher, E., 96
Bayley, N., 69, 265
Bearvais, K., 139
Beasley, W. A., 375
Beck, I., 442
Becker, B. J., 132
Becker, W. C., 104
Behan, P., 50
Belcastro, F. P., 217
Belin, D. W., 265
Bell, L. A., 154, 157
Benbow, C., 41, 50, 125, 130, 146, 148, 154, 158, 160, 173, 194, 233, 245, 262, 263, 264, 265, 266, 267, 268, 270, 271, 272, 280, 281, 282, 283, 285, 286, 288, 289, 291, 423, 490
Benker, A. J. A., 404
Berché Cruz, X., 146
Bereiter, C., 340
Berends, M., 267
Berger, J., 430
Berger, S. L., 199, 309, 503
Berliner, D. C., 262, 263
Bernal, E., 97, 100, 392
Berninger, V. W., 422
Berry, C., 382
Betts, G., 212, 213, 220, 236, 242
Beyer, B. K., 404
Biddle, B. J., 262, 263
Biological Sciences Curriculum Study Group, 434
Bireley, M., 41, 43, 46
Birch, H. G., 30
Bish, C. E., 8
Bishop, J. H., 263
Bishop, W. E., 476
Black, J. D., 38, 39
Black, K. N., 215, 282
Blackburn, A. C., 148
Bland, L., 102, 490

Bloom, B., 145, 149, 194, 235, 251, 352, 390, 400, 405, 441, 448, 480, 481, 518
Boatman, T. A., 281
Bogen, J. E., 49
Boissier, M., 263
Boix-Mansilla, V., 340
Boring, E. G., 49
Borland, J., 98, 202, 309, 320, 354, 392
Boston, B., 181, 217, 242, 309, 485
Bouchard, T. J., 19, 265
Bowles, S., 227
Boyce, L. N., 319, 343, 455, 456, 496
Boyd, L. N., 312
Bracey, G., 515
Bradway, K., 41
Brandt, R. S., 347
Brandwein, P. R., 193
Braswell, L., 106
Breard, N. S., 35
Brewer, D. J., 266, 267
Bricklin, B., 84
Bricklin, P., 84
Briggs, D., 493
Brimelow, P., 265
Brody, L. E., 98, 233, 280, 283, 284, 318, 423
Bronowski, J., 343
Brooks, J. G., 371, 374, 412
Brooks, M. G., 371, 374, 412
Brooks-Gunn, J., 69, 148
Brophy, J. E., 137
Brown, B. B., 233, 375
Brown, L. L., 496
Bruch, C. B., 97, 102, 479
Bruer, J. T., 400
Bruner, J., 56, 400, 429, 448
Bruning, R. H., 400
Brush, L. R., 131
Buerschen, T., 35
Buescher, T. M., 157, 158, 484
Burke, J., 343, 435
Burke, M., 496
Burks, B., 68
Bushnell, M., 72
Busse, J., 422
Butler-Por, N., 85, 86

C

Caldwell, M. S., 296, 322
Calic, S., 35
California State Department of Education, 454
Callahan, C., 99, 129,

132, 133, 173, 205, 295, 296, 309, 310, 318, 322, 399, 490
Campbell, D. T., 388
Canter, A., 119
Card, C. N. W., 42
Carew, J., 71
Carlson, N. R., 52
Carpenter, T. P., 105
Carroll, J. B., 1, 2, 24, 265, 266, 391
Carson, R., 235
Casserly, P. L., 157
Cattell, J. M., 71
Cattell, R. B., 21, 22, 51, 52
Center for Civic Education, 443
Center for Gifted Education, 173, 179, 448
Center for Research and Development in Law-Related Educaiton, 450
Chauncey, H., 265
Chauvin, J. C., 236
Chepko-Sade, D., 96
Chepko-Sade, S., 13
Chess, S., 30
Chitwood, D. G., 147, 148
Clark, B., 155, 350, 464
Clark, G., 219, 234, 465
Clark, K., 343
Clasen, D. R., 233, 375
Clasen, R. E., 107
Clayton Foundation, 467
Clinkenbeard, P., 219, 251, 340, 392, 399, 402
Cobb, J., 96
Cobb, S. J., 234
Cohn, S. J., 265
Colangelo, N., 35, 36, 38, 106, 244, 251, 492
Coleman, J., 493
Coleman, L. J., 430
Coleman, M., 101, 228, 252, 325
College Board, 207, 368, 442, 443
College Entrance Examination Board, 117
Collins, J., 451
Collins, N. D., 456
Colman, C., 156
Conoley, J. C., 197
Consortium on Higher Education, 502
Cook, L., 15
Cook, R. S., 490
Cooley, W. W., 105
Cornell, D., 102, 132, 199, 216, 399, 480, 490
Cowen, E. L., 106
Cox, C. M., 350, 352

521

Subject Index ~